Y0-BUP-100

ISSUES IN THE SOCIOLOGY OF RELIGION

GARLAND BIBLIOGRAPHIES IN SOCIOLOGY
General Editor Dan A. Chekki
(Vol. 8)

GARLAND REFERENCE LIBRARY
OF SOCIAL SCIENCE
(Vol. 340)

GARLAND BIBLIOGRAPHIES IN SOCIOLOGY

General Editor: Dan A. Chekki

1. *Conflict and Conflict Resolution: A Historical Bibliography*
   by Jack Nusan Porter

2. *Sociology of Sciences: An Annotated Bibliography of Invisible Colleges, 1972–1981*
   by Daryl E. Chubin

3. *Race and Ethnic Relations: An Annotated Bibliography*
   by Graham C. Kinloch

4. *Friendship: A Selected, Annotated Bibliography*
   by J.L. Barkas

5. *The Sociology of Aging: An Annotated Bibliography and Sourcebook*
   by Diana K. Harris

6. *Medical Sociology: An Annotated Bibliography, 1972–1982*
   by John G. Bruhn, Billy U. Philips, and Paula L. Levine

7. *The Clinical Sociology Handbook*
   by Jan M. Fritz

8. *Issues in the Sociology of Religion: A Bibliography*
   by Anthony J. Blasi and Michael W. Cuneo

ISSUES IN THE SOCIOLOGY OF RELIGION
A Bibliography

Anthony J. Blasi
Michael W. Cuneo

GARLAND PUBLISHING, INC. • NEW YORK & LONDON
1986

Library of Congress Cataloging-in-Publication Data

Blasi, Anthony J.
Issues in the sociology of religion.

(Garland bibliographies in sociology ; vol. 8)
(Garland reference library of social science ; vol. 340)
Includes indexes.
1. Religion and sociology—Bibliography. I. Cuneo, Michael W. II. Title. III. Series: Garland bibliographies in sociology ; v. 8. IV. Series: Garland reference library of social science ; v. 340.
Z7831.B55 1986 [BL60] 016.306′6 86-1292
ISBN 0-8240-8585-X (alk. paper)

Printed on acid-free, 250-year-life paper
Manufactured in the United States of America

CONTENTS

Preface of the General Editor xi
Preface: The Bibliography xv
Introduction: The Sociology of Religion xix
List of Abbreviations xxiv
Chapter One: Structures 1
Section A: Social Psychology and Attitudes 1
Alienation 1
Altruism 2
Anomie 3
Asceticism 4
Charisma 6
Comfort 8
Conservative 9
Deprivation 12
Everyday life 13
Fatalism 14
Identity 14
Morality 15
Morality (general) 15
Abortion 17
Abortion attitudes 17
Abortion attitudes and denomination 19
Abortion attitudes and orthodoxy 20
Abortion practice 20
Birth control 21
Capital punishment 22
Euthanasia 22
Homosexuality 22
Peace and war 23
Pornography 25
Sexual attitudes 25
Sexual conduct 26
Situation ethics 28

Social justice 29
Sterilization and vasectomy 29
Pluralism 29
Pluralism (general) 29
Accommodation 32
Assimilation and related phenomena 32
Syncretism 33
Tolerance 34
Prejudice 35
Prejudice (general) 35
Sexism 40
Reference group 40
Salience 40
Value 41
Well-being 43
Section B: Roles 44
Life cycle 44
Religious roles 44
Apprentice 44
Campus ministry 45
Clergy 45
Clergy (general) 45
Clergy image 65
Clergy mobility 66
Clergy role: content and role conflict 67
Clergy wives 73
Discipleship 74
Founder 74
Leadership 74
Membership 75
Mendicancy 79
Military chaplain 79
Missionary 79
Prophet 79
Saint 80
Seeker 80
Seminarian 80
Shaman 84
Sister/nun 84
Witch 86

Worker priests 87
Youth ministry 87
Sex roles 88
Sex roles (general) 88
Women 88
Section C: Organization 92
Organization (general) 92
Ashram 98
Associational 98
Authority 98
Base communities 100
Bureaucracy 101
Communality 101
Commune 102
Denomination 104
Diocese 107
Hierocracy 108
Monasticism 108
Orders/congregations 109
Papacy 115
Parish/local congregation 115
Power 123
Synagogue 124
Underground church 124
Section D: Politics and Religion 125
Politics (general) 125
Activism 144
Section E: Stratification (social inequality) 147
Stratification (general) 147
Caste 160
Class 161
Elite 162
Mobility (vertical) 163
Chapter Two: Processes 167
Section A: Conversion and Conversion Maintenance 167
Section B: Role Entry and Role Exit 175
Apostasy 175
Ex-clergy 176
Ex-nuns 177
Vocations 178

Section C: Deviance and Legitimation 183
Deviance 183
Legitimation 185
Plausibility structures 186
Social control 186
Section D: Organizational Change and Process 188
Institutionalization 188
Inter-religious conflict 188
Merger and ecumenism 189
Schism 192
Section E: Social Movements 193
Social movements (general) 193
Anti-cult movement 197
Civil rights 198
Messianism and millenarianism 201
New religions 206
Temperance movement 211
Section F: Secularization 212
Secularization (general) 212
Disenchantment 223
Privatization 223
Section G: Protestant Ethic 224
Section H: Evolution (societal) 234
Chapter Three: Disciplinary Conceptualizations 237
Section A: Definition of Religion 237
Section B: Religiosity 240
Religiosity (general) 240
Belief 242
Atheism 246
Death of God 248
Fundamentalism 249
God, image of 251
Heresy 252
Literalism 252
Orthodoxy (doctrinal) 252
Commitment 254
Dimensions of religiosity 257
Cognitive 261
Consequential 261
Devotionalism 262

Experiental dimension 262
Popular religion 266
Section C: Practices and Ritual 271
Practices 271
Almsgiving 271
Baptism 271
Confession 271
Contributions 272
Cursillo 272
Fasting 273
Glossolalia 273
Healing 274
Meditation 275
Pilgrimage 275
Possession 275
Prayer 276
Preaching 276
Proselytizing 276
Revivalism 277
Testimony 278
Ritual 278
Section D: Typology 283
Sectarianism 283
Types 284
Church 288
Cult 288
Denomination (type) 291
Mysticism 292
Sect 293
Section E: Theories and Problematics 300
Theories and problematics (general) 300
Civil religion 301
Conflict theory 305
Critical theory 305
Functionalism 306
Integration (social) 308
Interpretive and hermeneutic sociology 310
Levels of inclusiveness 310
Levels of inclusiveness (general) 310
Localism 311

Marxism 312
Phenomenology 316
Positivism 317
Positivism (general) 317
Reductionism 317
Science and religion 317
Sociolinguistics 319
Sociology of knowledge 319
Structuralism 319
Surrogates for religion 320
Symbolic interactionism 321
Symbolic realism 322
Systems theory 322
Transcendence 323
Author Index 325
Subject Index 361

PREFACE OF THE GENERAL EDITOR

The increasing rate of change in recent years poses some bewildering and complex problems for modern societies. Issues such as abortion, euthanasia, inequality and injustice, poverty, discrimination, human rights, and nuclear armaments and war have undercurrents of religious controversy. Community leaders and legislators are frequently confronted with public debates and controversies on a wide spectrum of social problems that have some relevance to religion and morals. Among young people and among members of small religious and quasi-religious movements, the winds of change are blowing.

Religious beliefs and practices have been a universal feature of all societies. According to Emile Durkheim every society needs a religion. Religion takes many forms and plays different roles. It can be a solid foundation for social cohesiveness of a society or it can be a powerful source of tension and conflict between groups. Religion as a set of symbolic forms relates humans to the ultimate conditions of their existence. The experiences of misfortune, suffering, and death give rise to profound questions about the meaning of it all. Religious symbols provide a context of meaning where these experiences can be dealt with when other forms of explanation and problem solution have failed.

The study of religion as it relates to other institutions of society is central to the sociology of religion. Sociologists are interested in studying how religion is organized and how it affects our behavior in family life, economic achievement, and political and cultural activities. Sociologists also examine the belief systems developed by people in different circumstances and how religious beliefs change over time as circumstances change. Sociologists of religion have asked important questions such as: What are the social functions of religion? Is today's world becoming less religious? Can organized religion influence large-scale social action and societal change? Sociologists have long been fascinated with the way belief systems seem to change the course of history and influence the character and development of nations.

A common assumption today is that religion is becoming less and less important in modern industrial societies. However, not all sociologists share this view. Despite widespread secularization in modern societies, there is evidence that people continue to express a belief in some supernatural reality that is beyond the forces of nature and physical laws. Recent public opinion polls in the United States suggest a rising tide of religious interest. Nevertheless, there are inconsistencies and contradictions: levels of morality and ethics tend to remain low; hunger is a reality for the poor; and levels of self-esteem are low for many persons.

In the 1980's there has been a renewed interest in religion and its role in public life. Religious cultures and themes tend to mold the nature of collective life and serve as a basis for public moral dialogue. Changes since the 1960's have significantly altered long established relations between religion and culture. Traditional distinctions between the religious and secular are being blurred. The changing character of religious pluralism in America includes, among others, a decline of the liberal establishment and a resurgence of conservative religious and moral interests. For some observers, Moral Majority, prolife groups, charismatic renewal, new quasi-religious cults and sects, antinuclear coalitions—all are embodied in American religion. American democratic ideals and especially the general pattern of changing roles for women have also, it appears, changed the ideological and social structure of American religion.

There seems to be a common belief that science and religion are incompatible. Increasing emphasis on materialism, the growth of science, and the secularization process are not considered to be conducive to religiosity. However, the lack of adequate understanding of religion by many seems to be the root cause of several intergroup conflicts. There is a need to maintain a balance between the religious and scientific view of life, for as Albert Einstein remarked, "Science without religion is lame, religion without science is blind."

This reference volume includes important and representative works on issues in the sociology of religion. Furthermore, it focuses on religious structures, processes, concepts, theories, and problematics. It is well organized, inclusive, and up to date. This wide-ranging guide to a large and growing field, by Anthony J. Blasi and Michael W. Cuneo, Centre for Religious Studies, University of Toronto, will, I hope, stimulate further research.

Dan A. Chekki
University of Winnipeg

PREFACE
The Bibliography

The sociology of religion can be understood in a wide sense as the non-theological study of religious phenomena, or, in a narrow sense, as the study of religion in the academic discipline of sociology. The authors have limited this bibliographic compilation to the narrow sense; entries represent endeavors to study religion in the academic discipline of sociology and in allied disciplines, such as anthropology and political science, when they employ sociological methods and pursue typically sociological problematics.

The bibliography organizes the entries by the issues that are treated and discussed in the sociology of religion, rather than by the names of religious organizations or personalities. Its purpose is to give sociologists, students, and religionists convenient access to the literature on the sociological questions that are relevant to the study of religion. Hence the title to the work is *Issues in the Sociology of Religion: A Bibliography*.

Chapter One focuses on religious structures, beginning at the individual level of social psychological states and attitudes, proceeding next to religious roles and types of religious organization, and concluding with the interrelationship at the societal level between religion and politics, and between religion and social stratification. Chapter Two focuses on social processes, again beginning at the individual level with the study of conversion, then proceeding to the study of role entry and role exit, deviance and legitimation, and concluding with the broader issues of organizational change, social movements, secularization, the Protestant Ethic, and societal evolution. Chapter Three focuses on the formal theoretical conceptualizations that have emerged in the sociology of religion. Topics include the definition of religion, the study of religiosity, the related study of religious practice and ritual, types of religion, and identifiable theoretical schools and approaches in the field.

The subsections within each chapter provide the basic organization of the entries. The user is advised to first consult the subject index, then the Table of Contents. If interested, for example, in studies of the clergy, the user can find the term in the Subject Index. Alternatively, one can look at the Table of Contents and locate Section B, Roles, in the first chapter. Here a number of roles—apprentice, campus minister, etc.—are listed in alphabetical order. Clergy studies follow, and the various entries are listed in the text by the alphabetical order of the authors' surnames. Where one author has several studies under the same heading, they appear in chronological order by date of publication. Where an entry appears under more than one heading, notations direct the user to a specific numbered entry for full bibliographic information. Each entry is numbered according to its order of appearance in the text. Users who are interested in the works of a particular author should consult the Author Index.

Several kinds of entry are included: books, journal articles, articles which appear in anthologies or collections, Ph.D. dissertations, and M.A. theses. Well-known classics which were first published in languages other than English are cited only in the English translation. Other non-English works are cited in the language of first publication as well as any English translation. There are many entries of French, German, Italian, Portuguese, and Spanish works as well as English ones. Generally, dissertations and theses are included if they have been cited in the literature. The bibliography is relatively inclusive, within space limitations. It covers the literature up to and including 1984, excluding most Ph.D. dissertations and M.A. theses that have never been cited, unpublished meeting papers, convention proceedings, and textbooks.

Annotations are given for the chapter, section, or subsection headings rather than for individual entries. Thus the user might consult the headings for any annotative information before seeking out the individual entries. The annotations are of an introductory nature and are provided primarily for the benefit of users who are not familiar with the field.

The research method has been relatively straightforward. Entries have been taken from the principal journals in the field—*Sociological Analysis* and *Social Compass*. Additional entries have been selected from two major interdisciplinary journals—the *Journal for the Scientific Study of Religion* and the *Review of Religious Research*. A knowledge of monographs in the field and an examination of book reviews in the journals led to more entries. In addition, an unsystematic exposure to general sociological journals resulted in the inclusion of additional articles and books. The footnotes and lists of references in each of the articles and books that the authors of this bibliography could obtain further increased the number of entries. Finally, previously published bibliographic essays were consulted; these often defined the field broadly, necessitating a cautious selectiveness. These bibliographic works include the annual update that appears in *Social Compass* (Belgium); *Social Scientific Study of Religion: A Bibliography* by Morris I. Berkowitz and J.E. Johnson (Pittsburgh: University of Pittsburgh Press, 1967); *Sociologie du Christianisme: Bibliographie Internationale (1900–1961)* by Hervé Carrier and Emile Pin (Rome: Presses de l'Université Grégorienne, 1964); *Sociología de la Religión y Teología, Estudio Bibliográfico*, by the Instituto Fe y Secularidad (Madrid: Ed. Cuadernos para el Dialogo, 1975, 1978); and *La Religion au Canada: bibliographie annotée des travaux en sciences humaines des religions, 1945–1970/Religion in Canada: Annotated Inventory of Scientific Studies of Religion, 1945–1972*, by Stewart Crysdale and Jean-Paul Montminy (Québec: Presses de l'Université Laval, 1974).

INTRODUCTION
The Sociology of Religion

The sociology of religion began with the beginning of sociology itself. Auguste Comte conceived of his new "science of society" as a functional substitute, predicated upon social scientific principles, for supernaturalist religion. Karl Marx, whose basic philosophic insights have been foundational for many sociological conceptualizations, started his intellectual quest with a critique of religion. With these two thinkers, a criticism of theistic religion was integral to the science of society. But Comte and Marx were not concerned simply to argue about theological issues. Comte, for his part, flatly equated theism with error and sought to replace it with "positive" knowledge. Marx, however, regarded religion as a product of society and saw the proper scientific task to be the criticism of society, not primarily of religion. Indeed, Marx, though an atheist himself, directed his nost strident invective against professional atheists who criticized what they deemed to be illusions rather than improving a world which, according to Marx, made illusions necessary.

Neither Comte nor Marx succeeded in organizing sociology as a scholarly discipline. Comte was marginal to the intellectual world, though he has his allies in philosophy, and Marx dedicated his efforts toward the political issues of the day and toward an extended critique of capitalist economics. Despite the pervasive influence of these two figures, it was primarily Max Weber and Emile Durkheim who drew the disciplinary boundaries and defined the subject matter for sociology. Significantly, extensive analyses of religion were decisive to the scholarly enterprises of both thinkers.

Durkheim, who won acceptance for sociology in the French academic world, viewed the power of religious symbols as evidence for the constraint of society on its individual members. He compared the social power of religious symbols found in so-called simple or primitive societies to the collective representations which are found in complex ones. This kind of comparative approach meant that both the study of tribal societies and of industrial ones, which would be designated in the English-speaking world respectively as "anthropology" and "sociology," were included in Durkheim's *sociologie*. The second generation of Durkheim's school, the *Année sociologique* tradition, was less interested in the relevance of religion to the modern world. For this reason present-day sociologists of religion refer to Durkheim's writings more often than to more recent ones written in his tradition. Durkheim is still looked to for basic theoretical formulations, even though much of his work is dated and, from a contemporary perspective, lacking in methodological and conceptual refinement. Parallels to the *Année sociologique* school are to be found in such British anthropologists as Edward B. Tylor and A.R. Radcliffe-Brown, and in the writings of Herbert Spencer.

Max Weber was the towering figure in early twentieth-century German social science. His interpretive problematic, which united the comparative and historical approaches, was articulated in methodological essays that are still relevant, and poses issues which are still debated in the discipline. His comparative investigations of world civilizations were assiduously sensitive to the scope and meaning of broad historical processes; his insights were crystalized in a series of studies on what are commonly designated today as the "world religions." Above all others, Weber bequeathed an extraordinarily rich legacy to contemporary sociologists of religion.

Meanwhile, the sociology of religion experienced a quite different but parallel development within institutional religion. Church historians began to make more or less systematic analyses of the quantitative data that were drawn from archival sources. Promoted in France by Gabriel Le Bras, this genre of work was in time applied to contemporary religious phenomena and used for church planning purposes. It is often referred to in the literature as *sociologie religieuse*. A similar kind of research prospectus developed concurrently in the United States through the efforts of H. Paul Douglas. Thus by mid-century there was a modest polypraxis of sociologies of religion—a critical sociology of religious ideation, directly inspired or indirectly influenced by Marx; a comparative sociology of religious cultures, at points awkardly straddling the distinctive traditions of Durkheim and Weber; and a quantitative sociology of church membership and participation.

It would be reasonable to think that the collective influence of Comte, Marx, Durkheim, and Weber would have accorded the sociology of religion a respected, if not privileged, status within the wider discipline. It might also be assumed that the exemplary studies by such diverse scholars as Georg Simmel, Bronislaw Malinowski, and H. Richard Niebuhr would be representative of a vibrant and theoretically coherent subdiscipline. And one would expect that the empirical work in the subdiscipline done by W.E.B. DuBois before the turn of the century, the *sociologie religieuse* tradition in Europe, and the pastoral planners in the United States would have served as research paradigms for students. It was not to be. The world of the mid-century was secular enough, at least in academia, to convince sociologists that religious phenomena were of little interest. With a few bright exceptions, the sociology of religion was largely confined to the analysis of one or two questionnaire items appended to studies of extra-religious phenomena. And this was so despite evidence of a religious revival in parts of the western world.

When, in the 1960's, the sociology of religion organized itself, it did so more or less independently and not as a centerpiece of general sociology. The *sociologie religieuse* school was already represented by the journal *Social Compass*, which over the years would become less quantitative in focus and more theoretical and comparative. Other journals emerged in Europe, and the Conférence Internationale de la Sociologie Religieuse (later Conférence Internationale de la Sociologie des Religions) began to meet on a regular basis. The applied quantitative tradition in the United States was represented in the Religious Research Association and its journal, *Review of Religious Research*. The interdisciplinary Society for the Scientific Study of Religion included from the outset many sociologists, and a good number of sociological works have continued to appear in its *Journal for the Scientific Study of Religion*. And the American Catholic Sociological Association, originally founded in the 1930's by Catholic sociologists who felt peripheral to the American sociological associations, subsequently entered the academic mainstream and changed its name and purpose; hence the Association for the Sociology of Religion, which now has a subdisciplinary rather than a denominational identity and membership, has emerged as an international English-language professional society of sociologists of religion, and the *American Catholic Sociological Review* has become *Sociological Analysis. A Journal in the Sociology of Religion*. All four of these journals—two interdisciplinary and two sociological—serve the field today.

The importance of religion as an aspect of social reality was heightened in the 1970's and 1980's; there were provocative sect and cult phenomena among youth, a politicization of religion in both industrial and developing countries, and a paradoxical diminution of middle-class participation in religion on the one hand accompanied by a growth of religious enthusiasm among particular middle-class people on the other. Participant observation and sophisticated quantitative analyses of these developments have comprised a growth industry that is reflected by the contents of the field's journals today.

With a fair amount of excitement in the field, the undergraduate course in the sociology of religion has become standard fare. Indeed, it is now a course title that is duly expected among a sociology department's offerings rather than a departmental concession to the predilection of an individual faculty member. Moreover, the sociology of religion is now a specialty in graduate-level sociological study, with an array of classical and contemporary theories and its own specialized quantitative and qualitative know-how. Meanwhile, a parallel specialization in the sociology of religion is developing in religious studies programs; it remains to be seen what form of relationship will evolve between sociology and religious studies programs as a consequence of this.

As part of the development of the field over its first century, there is an extensive scientific literature on many of the field's topics and central concepts. Today the researcher need not begin *de novo*, and indeed would be remiss to proceed without having read up on the specific subject at hand. The student can and should read the works in the field firsthand rather than rely upon summary textbook accounts. This bibliography is designed to make the copious literature in the subdiscipline more accessible to the student and to the professional researcher.

ABBREVIATIONS

The use of abbreviations is being kept to a minimum in order to enhance the ease with which the bibliography can be used. Thus only the four principal English-language journals of the field are abbreviated:

JSSR	*Journal for the Scientific Study of Religion*
RRR	*Review of Religious Research*
SA	*Sociological Analysis. A Journal in the Sociology of Religion*
SC	*Social Compass* (English and French)

Issues in the Sociology of Religion

CHAPTER ONE: STRUCTURES

These entries concern entities or relatively static objects. They differ from those in Chapter Two, which are processes, and they differ from the entries in Chapter Three, which are theoretical frameworks of the discipline.

SECTION A: SOCIAL PSYCHOLOGY AND ATTITUDES

An important aspect of social reality is the relationship between the individual and society. In this relationship, socio-cultural phenomena, such as religions, influence and are influenced by psychological states and personal attitudes.

Alienation

There are two important meanings to this term in the literature. On the one hand, the Marxian usage refers to a human creation, such as an idea, becoming separated from individuals and even having power over them. On the other hand, there is the more psychological usage, referring to people feeling a distance from their own activity and regretting what they feel compelled to do on a regular basis.

1. Büntig, Aldo-J. RELIGION -- ENAJENACION EN UNA SOCIEDAD DEPENDIENTE. Buenos Aires: Editorial Guadalupe, 1973.

2. Crane, William H. "Alienation in the New African Society." SC 12 (1965): 367-377.

3. Maduro, Otto. "Trabajo y religión segun Karl Marx." CONCILIUM 151 (Spanish Series, 1980): 19-29.
   "Travail et religion selon Karl Marx." CONCILIUM 151 (French Series, 1980): 21-29.

4. Maranell, Gary M. "Religiosity and Alienation." Ch. 12 in RESPONSES TO RELIGION. STUDIES IN THE SOCIAL PSYCHOLOGY OF RELIGIOUS BELIEF. Lawrence: University of Kansas Press, 1974.

5. O'Dea, Thomas F. ALIENATION, ATHEISM AND THE RELIGIOUS CRISIS. New York: Sheed and Ward, 1969.

6. Photiadis, John D., and John F. Schnabel. "Religion: A Persistent Institution in a Changing Appalachia." RRR 19,1 (1977): 32-42.

7. Pin, Emile Jean. "En guise d'introduction: comment se sauver de l'anomie et de l'aliénation. Jesus People et Catholiques Pentecostaux." SC 21,3 (1974): 227-239.

8. Quinney, Richard. "Political Conservatism, Alienation, and Fatalism: Contingencies of Social Status and Religious Fundamentalism." SOCIOMETRY 27,3 (1964): 314-320.

9. Spenner, Kenneth. RELIGION AND ALIENATION. Unpublished M.A. thesis, University of Notre Dame, 1973.

10. Tygart, Clarence E. "Work Alienation and Politics among Clergy." JOURNAL OF VOCATIONAL BEHAVIOR 5,1 (1974): 103-114.

Altruism

11. Blaikie, Norman W.H. "Altruism in the Professions: The Case of the Clergy." AUSTRALIAN AND NEW ZEALAND JOURNAL OF SOCIOLOGY 10,2 (1974): 84-89.

12. Christenson, James A. "Religious Involvement, Values, and Social Compassion." SA 37,3 (1976): 218-227.

13. Harris, Mary B., Sheldon M. Benson, and Carroll L. Hall. "The Effects of Confession on Altruism." JOURNAL OF SOCIAL PSYCHOLOGY 96 (1975): 187-192.

14. Langford, Barbara J., and Charles C. Langford. "Review of the Polls: Church Attendance and Self Perceived Altruism." JSSR 13,2 (1974): 221-222.

15. Neal, Marie Augusta. "Commitment to Altruism in Sociological Analysis." SA 43,1 (1982): 1-22.

16. Nelson, L.D., and Russell R. Dynes. "The Impact of Devotionalism and Attendance on Ordinary and Emergency Helping Behavior." JSSR 15,1 (1976): 47-59.

17. Sorokin, Pitirim A. THE WAYS AND POWER OF LOVE: TYPES, FACTORS, AND TECHNIQUES OF MORAL TRANSFORMATION. Boston: Beacon Press, 1954.

18. Spilka, Bernard. "Religious Values and Social Cmpassion: A Problem in Theory and Measurement." RRR 11 (1970): 149-150.

19. Terian, Sara M.K. THE OTHER SIDE OF GOOD SAMARITANISM: THE HELPING ETHIC IN JUDEO-CHRISTIAN IDEOLOGY AND PRACTICE. Unpublished Ph.D. dissertation, University of Notre Dame, 1984.

20. Thiessen, Victor. WHO GIVES A DAMN? A STUDY OF CHARITABLE CONTRIBUTIONS. Unpublished Ph.D. dissertation, University of Wisconsin, 1968.

Anomie

Most contemporary sociologists understand anomie to be a lack of rule in one's life, a state of normlessness in which acceptable and unacceptable lines of conduct are not clearly distinct. The term was used in sociology first by Emile Durkheim, as a secular word for a state of being sinful, a state of not being in an ordered relationship with a basic sense of the sacred values of a society.

21. Carr, Leslie G., and William J. Hauser. "Anomie and Religiosity: An Empirical Re-examination." JSSR 15,1 (1976): 69-74.

22. Dean, Dwight C. "Anomie, Powerlessness, and Religious Participation." JSSR 7 (1968): 252-254.

23. Dean, Dwight C., and Jon A. Reeves. "Anomie: A Comparison of a Catholic and a Protestant Sample." SOCIOMETRY 25 (1962): 209-212.

24. Fahey, Frank J., and Djuro J. Vrga. "The Anomic Character of a Schism." RRR 12,3 (1971): 177-185.

25. Fay, Leo F. "Differential Anomic Responses in a Religious Community." SA 39,1 (1978): 62-76

26. Hong, Lawrence K. "Anomia and Religiosity: Some Evidence for Reconceptualization." RRR 22,3 (1981): 233-244.

27. Juarez Rubens Brandão Lopes. DESENVOLVIMENTO E MUNDANÇA SOCIAL: FORMAÇAO DA SOCIEDADE URBANO-INDUSTRIAL NO BRASIL. São Paulo: Companhia Editora Nacional, 1968.

28. Keedy, T.C. "Anomie and Religious Orthodoxy." SOCIOLOGY AND SOCIAL RESEARCH 43 (1958): 34-37.

29. Lee, Gary R., and Robert W. Clyde. "Religion, Socioeconomic Status, and Anomie." JSSR 13 (1974): 35-47.

30. Liu, William T. A STUDY OF THE SOCIAL INTEGRATION OF CATHOLIC MIGRANTS IN A SOUTHERN COMMUNITY. Unpublished Ph.D. dissertation, Florida State University, 1958.

31. Liu, William T. "The Marginal Catholics in the South. A Revision of Concepts." AMERICAN JOURNAL OF SOCIOLOGY 65 (1960): 383-390.

32. Martin, Jack, and Steven Stack. "The Effect of Religiosity on Alienation: A Multivariate Analysis of Normlessness." SOCIOLOGICAL FOCUS 16,1 (1983): 65-76.

33. McCloskey, David D. "Whatever Happened to Anomie? A Comment on Lee and Clyde's 'Religion and Anomie.'" JSSR 13,4 (1974): 497-502.

34. Nelsen, Hart M. "Sectarianism, World View, and Anomie." SOCIAL FORCES 51 (1972): 226-233.

* Pin, Emile Jean. "En guise d'introduction: comment se sauver de l'anomie et de l'aliénation. Jesus People et Catholiques Pentecostaux." Cited above as item 7.

35. Poblete, Renato, and Thomas F. O'Dea. "Anomie and the 'Quest for Community': The Formation of Sects among the Puerto Ricans of New York." AMERICAN CATHOLIC SOCIOLOGICAL REVIEW 21,1 (1960): 18-36. Reprinted in T. O'Dea, SOCIOLOGY AND THE STUDY OF RELIGION. THEORY, RESEARCH, INTERPRETATION. New York: Basic, 1970, pp. 180-198.

36. Potvin, Raymond H. "Role Uncertainty and Commitment among Seminary Faculty." SA 37,1 (1976): 45-52.

37. Putney, Snell, and Russell Middleton. "Ethical Relativism and Anomia." AMERICAN JOURNAL OF SOCIOLOGY 67,4 (1962): 430-435.

38. Svenson, Eric. RELIGIOUS LIFE IN TRANSITION: A STUDY OF THE EFFECTS OF DE-REGULARIZATION ON RELIGIOUS COMMITMENT. Unpublished Ph.D. dissertation, New School for Social Research, 1978.

39. Wassef, W.Y. "The Influence of Religion, Socio-Economic Status and Education on Anomie." SOCIOLOGICAL QUARTERLY 18,2 (1967): 233-238.

Asceticism

40. Caillat, Colette. "L'ascétisme chez les Jaina." ARCHIVES DE SOCIOLOGIE DES RELIGIONS 18 (1964): 45-53.

41 Ghurye, G.S. "Ascetic Origins." SOCIOLOGICAL BULLETIN 1,2 (1952): 162-184.

42. Honigsheim, P. "Formen der Askese und ihr kultursoziologischer Hintergrund." In J. Matthes (ed.), RELIGIÖSER PLURALISMUS UND GESELLSCHAFTSSTRUKTER / RELIGIOUS PLURALISM AND SOCIAL STRUCTURE, INTERNATIONALES JAHRBUCH FÜR RELIGIONSSOZIOLOGIE 1. Köln, Opladen: Westdeutscher Verlag, 1965, pp. 15-23.

43. Johnson, Benton. "Ascetic Protestantism and Political Preference." PUBLIC OPINION QUARTERLY 26 (1962): 35-46.

44. Johnson, Benton. "Ascetic Protestantism and Political Preference in the Deep South." AMERICAN JOURNAL OF SOCIOLOGY 69 (1964): 359-366.

45. Largement, R. "L'ascétisme dans la civilisation suméro-sémitique." ARCHIVES DE SOCIOLOGIE DES RELIGIONS 18 (1964): 27-34.

46. LeBras, Gabriel. "Place de l'ascétisme dans la sociologie des religions." ARCHIVES DE SOCIOLOGIE DES RELIGIONS 18 (1964): 21-26.

47. Moberg, David O. "Theological Self-Classification and Ascetic Views of Students." RRR 10 (1969): 100-107.

48. Mueller, Gert H. "Asceticism and Mysticism. A Contribution towards the Sociology of Faith." In G. Dux, T. Luckmann and J. Matthes (eds.), ZUR THEORIE DER RELIGION. RELIGION UND SPRACHE/SOCIOLOGICAL THEORIES OF RELIGION. RELIGION AND LANGUAGE. INTERNATIONALES JAHRBUCH FÜR RELIGIONSSOZIOLOGIE/INTERNATIONAL YEARBOOK FOR THE SOCIOLOGY OF RELIGION, Bd. 8, Opladen: Westdeutscher Verlag, 1973, pp. 68-132.

49. Robbins, James M. "Religious Involvement, Asceticism and Abortion among Low Income Black Women." SA 41,1 (1981): 365-374.

50. Séguy, Jean. "L'ascèse dans les sectes d'origine protestante." ARCHIVES DE SOCIOLOGIE DES RELIGIONS 18 (1964): 55-70.

51 Swatos, William H., Jr. "Church-Sect and Cult: Bringing Mysticism Back In." SA 42,1 (1981): 17-26.

52. Tamney, Joseph B. "Fasting and Modernization." JSSR 19,2 (1980): 129-137.

53. Thorner, Isidor. CHRISTIAN SCIENCE AND ASCETIC PROTESTANTISM: A STUDY IN THE SOCIOLOGY OF RELIGION, PERSONALITY TYPE AND SOCIAL STRUCTURE. Cambridge: Harvard University Press, 1951.

54. Thorner, Isidor. "Ascetic Protestantism, Gambling and the One-Price System." AMERICAN JOURNAL OF ECONOMICS AND SOCIOLOGY 15,2 (1956): 161-172.

55. Vajda, Georges. "Le rôle et la signification de l'ascétisme dans la religion juive." ARCHIVES DE SOCIOLOGIE DES RELIGIONS 18 (1964): 35-43.

56. Weber, Max. "Religious Rejections of the World and their Directions." In H.H. Gerth and C.Wright Mills (eds.), FROM MAX WEBER: ESSAYS IN SOCIOLOGY. New York: Oxford University Press, 1946, pp. 323-359.

57. Weber, Max, "Die protestantischen Sekten und der Geist des Kapitalismus." GESAMMELTE AUFSATZE ZUR RELIGIONS-SOZIOLOGIE, Bd. I. Tübingen: J.C.B. Mohr (Paul Siebeck), 1920, 1963-66, pp. 207-236.
"The Protestant Sects and the Spirit of Capitalism." In H.H. Gerth and C.W.Mills (eds.), FROM MAX WEBER: ESSAYS IN SOCIOLOGY. New York: Oxford University Press, 1946, pp. 302-322.

58. Weber, Max. "Asceticism: World-Rejecting and Inner-Worldly." In M. Weber, ECONOMY AND SOCIETY. AN OUTLINE OF INTERPRETIVE SOCIOLOGY, Vol. I, ed. by Guenther Roth and Claus Wittich. Berkeley: University of California Press, 1978, pp. 541-544.

Charisma

Charisma is social power that pertains to a person by virtue of a special status attributed to that person by others.

59. Agodi, Maria Carmela. "Il carisma dopo Weber." SOCIOLOGIA 3 (1980): 123-163.

60. Barnes, Douglas F. "Charisma and Religious Leadership: An Historical Analysis." JSSR 17,1 (1978): 1-18.

61. Baubérot, Jean. "Nathan Söderblom: un réformateur religieux?" SC 29,1 (1982): 59-73.

62. Berger, Alan L. "Hasidism and Moonism: Charisma in the Counter-culture." SA 41,4 (1981): 375-390.

63. Berger, Peter L. "Charisma and Religious Innovation: The Social Location of Israelite Prophecy." AMERICAN SOCIOLOGICAL REVIEW 28,6 (1963): 940-950.

64. Bird, Frederick. "Charisma and Ritual in New Religious Movements." In J. Needleman and G. Baker (eds.), UNDERSTANDING THE NEW RELIGIONS. New York: Seabury, 1978, pp. 173-189.

65. Bosk, Charles L. "The Routinization of Charisma: The Case of the Zaddik." In Harry M. Johnson (ed.), RELIGIOUS CHANGE AND CONTINUITY. SOCIOLOGICAL PERSPECTIVES. San Francisco: Jossey-Bass, 1979, pp. 150-167.

66. Burke, Kathryn L., and Merlin B. Brinkerhoff. "Capturing Charisma: Notes on an Elusive Concept." JSSR 20,3 (1981): 274-284.

67. Fauré, Guy-Olivier. "Charisme et réforme sociale en Inde." SC 29,1 (1982): 75-92.

68. Freund, Julien. "Le charisme selon Max Weber." SC 23,4 (1976): 383-396.

69. Friendland, William H. "For a Sociological Concept of Charisma." SOCIAL FORCES 43,1 (1964): 18-26.

70. Hammond, Phillip E., Luis Salinas, and Douglas Sloane. "Types of Clergy Authority: Their Measurement, Location, and Effects." JSSR 17,3 (1978): 241-253.

71 Johnson, Doyle Paul. "Dilemmas of Charismatic Leadership: The Case of the People's Temple." SA 40,4 (1979): 315-323.

72. Léger, Danièle. "Charisma, Utopia and Communal Life. The Case of Neorural Apocalyptic Communes in France." SC 29,1 (1982): 41-58.

73. Malina, Bruce J. "Jesus as Charismatic Leader?" BIBLICAL THEOLOGY BULLETIN 14 (1984): 55-62.

74. Piepe, Anthony. "Charisma and the Sacred. A Reevaluation." PACIFIC SOCIOLOGICAL REVIEW 14,2 (1971): 147-162.

75. Ross, Jack C. TRADITIONALISM AND CHARISMA IN A RELIGIOUS GROUP: MEMBERSHIP CAREERS AND ROLE CONTINGENCIES OF QUAKERS. Unpublished Ph.D. dissertation, University of Minnesota, 1964.

76. Roucek, Joseph S. "The Changing Concepts of Charismatic Leadership." In J. Matthes (ed.), THEORETISCHE ASPEKTE DER RELIGIONS-SOZIOLOGIE II/SOCIOLOGY OF RELIGION: THEORETICAL PERSPECTIVES II. INTERNATIONALES JAHRBUCH FÜR RELIGIONSSOZIOLOGIE 3. Köln and Opladen: Westdeutscher Verlag, 1967, pp. 87-100.

77. Séguy, Jean. "Charisme, sacerdoce, fondation: autour de L.M. Grignion de Montfort." SC 29,1 (1982): 5-24.

78. Sharot, Stephen. "Hasidism and the Routinization of Charisma." JSSR 19,4 (1980): 325-336.

79. Shils, Edward. "Charisma, Order, Status." AMERICAN SOCIOLOGICAL REVIEW 30,2 (1965): 199-213.

80. Shokeid, Moshe. "From Personal Endowment to Bureaucratic Appointment: The Transition in Israel of the Communal Religious Leaders of Moroccan Jews." JSSR 19,2 (1980): 105-113.

81. Stark, Rodney, and Lynne Roberts. "The Arithmetic of Social Movements: Theoretical Implications." SA 43,1 (1982): 53-68.

82. Stark, Werner. "The Routinization of Charisma: A Consideration of Catholicism." SA 26,4 (1965): 203-211.

83. Stark, Werner. THE SOCIOLOGY OF RELIGION, Vol. IV. New York: Fordham University Press, 1970.

84. Swatos, William H., Jr. "The Disenchantment of Charisma: A Weberian Assessment of Revolution in a Rationalized World." SA 42,2 (1981): 119-136.

85. Swatos, William H., Jr. "Revolution and Charisma in a Rationalized World: Weber Revisited and Extended." In Ronald M. Glassman and Vatro Murvar (eds.), MAX WEBER'S POLITICAL SOCIOLOGY. A PESSIMISTIC VISION OF A RATIONALIZED WORLD. Westport, Ct.: Greenwood, 1984, pp. 201-215.

86. Theobald, Robin. "The Role of Charisma in the Development of Social Movements." ARCHIVES DE SCIENCES SOCIALES DES RELIGIONS 25,49 (1980): 83-100.

87. Toth, Michael A. THE THEORY OF THE TWO CHARISMAS. Washington: University Press of America, 1971.

88. Wallis, Roy. "The Social Construction of Charisma." SC 29,1 (1982): 25-39.

89. Wallis, Roy (ed.) MILLENNIALISM AND CHARISMA. Belfast: Queen's University of Belfast, 1982. Contains items 90, 2038, 2393.

90. Wallis, Roy. "Charisma, Commitment and Control in a New Religious Movement." In Roy Wallis (ed.), MILLENNIALISM AND CHARISMA. (item 89), pp. 73-140.

* Weber, Max. "Charismatic Authority," and "The Routinization of Charisma." In Weber, ECONOMY AND SOCIETY. AN OUTLINE OF INTERPRETIVE SOCIOLOGY (volume cited above in item 58), pp. 241-254.

91. Wilson, Bryan R. THE NOBLE SAVAGES: THE PRIMITIVE ORIGINS OF CHARISMA AND ITS CONTEMPORARY SURVIVAL. Berkeley: University of California Press, 1975.

Comfort

92. Glock, Charles Y., et al. TO COMFORT AND TO CHALLENGE. Berkeley: University of California Press, 1967.

93. Hobart, Charles W. "Church Involvement and the Comfort Thesis in Alberta." JSSR 13,4 (1974): 463-470.

94. Johnson, Benton. "A Sociological Perspective on the New Religions." In Thomas Robbins and Dick Anthony (eds.), IN GODS WE TRUST (item 367), pp. 51-66.

95. Perkins, H. Wesley. "Organized Religion as Opiate or Prophetic Stimulant: A Study of American and English Assessments of Social Justice in Two Urban Settings." RRR 24,3 (1983): 206-224.

* Photiadis, John D., and John F. Schnabel. "Religion: A Persistent Institution in a Changing Appalachia." Cited above as item 6.

Conservative

96. Bibby, Reginald W., and Merlin B. Brinkerhoff. "The Circulation of the Saints: A Study of People Who Join Conservative Churches." JSSR 12,3 (1973): 273-283. Also in S. Crysdale and L. Wheatcroft (eds.), RELIGION IN CANADIAN SOCIETY. Toronto: Macmillan of Canada, 1976, pp. 346-358.

97. Bibby, Reginald W., and Merlin B. Brinkerhoff. "Circulation of the Saints Revisited: A Longitudinal Look at Conservative Church Growth." JSSR 22,3 (1983): 253-262.

98. Bouma, Gary D. "The Real Reason One Conservative Church Grew." RRR 20,2 (1979): 127-137.

99. Bouma, Gary D. HOW THE SAINTS PERSEVERE: SOCIAL FACTORS IN THE VITALITY OF THE CHRISTIAN REFORMED CHURCH. Clayton, Victoria, Australia: Monash University, Department of Anthropology and Sociology, 1984.

100. Bromley, David G., and Anson Shupe (eds.) NEW CHRISTIAN POLITICS. Macon, Georgia: Mercer University Press, 1984. Contains items 638, 757.

101. Bruce, Steve. ONE NATION UNDER GOD? Belfast, Northern Ireland: The Queen's University, Department of Social Studies, 1983.

102. Bruce, Steve. "Research Note: Identifying Conservative Protestantism." SA 44,1 (1983): 65-70.

103. Bruce, Steve. "The Persistence of Religion: Conservative Protestantism in the United Kingdom." SOCIOLOGICAL REVIEW 31,3 (1983): 453-470.

104. DeJong, Gordon F., and Joseph E. Faulkner. "The Church, Individual Religiosity, and Social Justice." SA 28 (1967): 34-43.

105. Ebaugh, Helen Rose Fuchs, and C. Allen Haney. "Church Attendance and Attitudes toward Abortion: Differentials in Liberal and Conservative Churches." JSSR 17,4 (1978): 407-413.

106. Ezcurra, Ana Maria. "Neoconservative and Ideological Struggle toward Central-America in the U.S.A." SC 30,2-3 (1983): 349-362.

107. Fleming, J.J., and G.W. Marks. "Mobilizing for Jesus: Evangelicals and the 1980 Election in the United States." LA REVUE TOCQUEVILLE 3,1 (1980): 195-208.

108. Gannon, Thomas M. "The New Christian Right in America as a Social and Political Force." ARCHIVES DE SCIENCES SOCIALES DES RELIGIONS 52 (1981): 68-82.

109. Hadaway, Christopher Kirk. "Conservatism and Social Strength in a Liberal Denomination." RRR 21,3 (1980): 302-314.

110. Hadden, Jeffrey K. "Televangelism and the New Christian Right." In Hadden and Theodore E. Long (eds.), RELIGION AND RELIGIOSITY IN AMERICA. STUDIES IN HONOR OF JOSEPH H. FICHTER. New York: Crossroad, 1983, pp. 114-127. Contains item 120.

111. Hadden, Jeffrey K. "Televangelism and the Mobilization of a New Christian Right Family Policy." In William V. D'Antonio and Joan Aldous (eds.), FAMILIES AND RELIGIONS. CONFLICT AND CHANGE IN MODERN SOCIETY. Beverly Hills, California: Sage, 1983, pp. 247-266.

112. Hammond, Phillip E. "In Search of a Protestant Twentieth Century: American Religion and Power since 1900." RRR 24,4 (1983); 281-294.

113. Harper, Charles L., and Kevin Leicht. "Religious Awakenings and Status Politics: Sources of Support for the New Religious Right." SA 45,4 (1984): 339-353.

114. Hill, Samuel S. "NRPR: The New Religious-Political Right in America." In E. Barker (ed.), OF GODS AND MEN (item 2396), pp. 109-126.

115. Hunter, James Davison. AMERICAN EVANGELICALISM. CONSERVATIVE RELIGION AND THE QUANDARY OF MODERNITY. New Brunswick: Rutgers University Press, 1983.

116. Kelley, Dean M. WHY CONSERVATIVE CHURCHES ARE GROWING. A STUDY IN THE SOCIOLOGY OF RELIGION. New York: Harper and Row, 1972. Revised edition, San Francisco: Harper and Row, 1977.

117. Kelley, Dean M. "Why Conservative Churches are Still Growing." JSSR 17,2 (1978): 165-172. Also in P.H. McNamara (ed.), RELIGION: NORTH AMERICAN STYLE. Belmont, California: Wadsworth, 1984, pp.88-94.

118. Kitay, Philip M. RADICALISM AND CONSERVATISM TOWARD CONVENTIONAL RELIGION. Teachers College, Publication No. 919. New York: Columbia University Press, 1947.

119. Liebman, Robert C., and Robert Wuthnow (eds.) THE NEW CHRISTIAN RIGHT. Hawthorne, New York: Aldine, 1983. Contains item 2255.

120. Lorentzen, Louise J. "Evangelical Life Style Concerns Expressed in Political Action." SA 41,2 (1980): 144-154. Also in J. Hadden and T. Long (eds.), RELIGION AND RELIGIOSITY IN AMERICA (item 110), pp. 99-113. Also in P.H. McNamara (ed.), RELIGION: NORTH AMERICAN STYLE (volume cited in item 117), pp. 225-235.

* Maranell, Gary M. RESPONSES TO RELIGION. STUDIES IN THE SOCIAL PSYCHOLOGY OF RELIGIOUS BELIEF. Cited above as item 4.

121 Schindeler, Fred, and David Hoffman. "Theological and Political Conservatism: Variations in Attitudes among Clergymen of One Denomination." CANADIAN JOURNAL OF POLITICAL SCIENCE 1 (1968): 429-441.

122. Schoenfeld, Eugen. "Image of Man: The Effect of Religion on Trust. A Research note." RRR 20,1 (1978): 61-67.

123. Schwartz, Paul Anthony, and James McBride. "The Moral Majority in the U.S.A. as a New Religious Movement." In Eileen Barker (ed.), OF GODS AND MEN (item 2396), pp. 127-146.

124. Smidt, Corwin, and James M. Penning. "Religious Commitment, Political Conservatism, and Political and Social Tolerance in the United States: A Longitudinal Analysis." SA 43,3 (1982): 231-246.

125. Stacey, William A., and Anson Shupe. "Religious Values and Religiosity in the Textbook Adoption Controversy in Texas, 1981." RRR 25,4 (1984): 321-333.

126. Symington, Thomas A. RELIGIOUS LIBERALS AND CONSERVATIVES. TEACHERS COLLEGE CONTRIBUTIONS TO EDUCATION, No. 64. Teachers College, Columbia University, 1935.

127. Weima, J. "Authoritarianism, Religious Conservatism and Sociocentric Attitudes in Roman Catholic Groups." HUMAN RELATIONS 18,3 (1965): 231-240.

128. Wiley, Norbert. "Religious and Political Liberalism among Catholics." SA 28 (1967): 142-148.

129. Wuthnow, Robert. "Religious Commitment and Conservatism: In Search of an Elusive Relationship." In Charles Y. Glock (ed.), RELIGION IN SOCIOLOGICAL PERSPECTIVE: ESSAYS IN THE EMPIRICAL STUDY OF RELIGION. Belmont, Calif.: Wadsworth, 1973, pp. 117-132.

130. Zimmerman, Franklin K. "Religion as Conservative Force." JOURNAL OF ABNORMAL AND SOCIAL PSYCHOLOGY 28,4 (1934): 473-474.

Deprivation

131. Aberle, David F. "A Note on Relative Deprivation Theory as Applied to Millenarian and Other Cult Movements." In S. Thrupp (ed.), MILLENNIAL DREAMS IN ACTION: COMPARATIVE STUDIES IN SOCIETY AND HISTORY, SUPPLEMENT II. The Hague: Mouton, 1962. Also in W.A. Lessa and E.Z. Vogt (eds.), READER IN COMPARATIVE RELIGION. New York: Harper and Row, 1965.

132. Baer, Hans A. "A Field Perspective of Religious Conversion: The Levites of Utah." RRR 19,3 (1978): 279-294.

133. Boisen, Anton T. "Economic Distress and Religious Experience." PSYCHIATRY 2 (1939): 185-194.

134. Boisen, Anton T. "Religion and Hard Times." SOCIAL ACTION 5 (1939): 8-35.

135. Bradfield, Cecil David. AN INVESTIGATION OF NEO-PENTECOSTALISM. Unpublished Ph.D. dissertation, American University, 1975.

136. Bradfield, Cecil David. NEO-PENTECOSTALISM: A SOCIOLOGICAL ASSESSMENT. Washington: University Press of America, 1979.

137. Christopher, Stefan, John Fearon, John McCoy, and Charles Nobbe. "Social Deprivation and Religiosity." JSSR 10,4 (1971): 385-393.

138. Dittes, James E. "Conceptual Deprivation and Statistical Rigor: Comments on 'Social Deprivation and Religiosity.'" JSSR 10,4 (1971): 393-395.

139. Emmons, Charles F., and Jeff Sobal. "Paranormal Beliefs: Testing the Marginality Hypothesis." SOCIOLOGICAL FOCUS 14,1 (1981): 49-56.

140. Garrison, Vivian. "Sectarianism and Psychosocial Adjustment: A Controlled Comparison of Puerto Rican Pentecostals and Catholics." In Irving I. Zaretsky and Mark P. Leone (eds.), RELIGIOUS MOVEMENTS IN CONTEMPORARY AMERICA. Princeton: Princeton University Press, 1974, pp. 298-329.

141. Glock, Charles Y. "The Role of Deprivation in the Origin and Evolution of Religious Groups." In Robert Lee and Martin E. Marty (eds.), RELIGION AND SOCIAL CONFLICT. New York: Oxford University Press, 1964. Also Ch. 13 of Glock and Rodney Stark, RELIGION AND SOCIETY IN TENSION. Chicago: Rand McNally, 1965. Reprinted in Charles Y. Glock (ed.), RELIGION IN SOCIOLOGICAL PERSPECTIVE: ESSAYS IN THE EMPIRICAL STUDY OF RELIGION. Belmont, Calif.: Wadsworth, 1973, pp. 207-220.

142. Hashimoto, Hideo, and William McPherson. "Rise and Decline of Sokagakkai: Japan and the United States." RRR 17,2 (1976): 82-92.

143. Hill, Clifford. "Immigrant Sect Development in Britain: A Case of Status Deprivation?" SC 18,2 (1971): 231-236.

144. Hine, Virginia. "The Deprivation and Disorganization Theories of Social Movements." In I.I. Zaretsky and M.P. Leone (eds.), RELIGIOUS MOVEMENTS IN CONTEMPORARY AMERICA (volume cited in item 140), pp. 646-661.

145. Hoge, Dean R., and Jackson W. Carroll. "Determinants of Commitment and Participation in Suburban Protestant Churches." JSSR 17,2 (1978): 107-127.

146. Hoge, Dean R., and David T. Polk. "A Test of Theories of Protestant Church Participation and Commitment." RRR 21,3 (1980): 315-329.

147. Holt, A.E. "Case Records as Data for Studying the Condition of Religious Experience by Social Factors." AMERICAN JOURNAL OF SOCIOLOGY 32 (1926): 227-236.

148. Johnson, C. Lincoln, and Andrew J. Weigert. "An Emerging Faith-Style: A Research Note on the Catholic Charismatic Renewal." SA 39,2 (1978): 165-172.

149. McNamara, Patrick H., and Arthur St.George. "Blessed are the Downtrodden? An Empirical Test." SA 39,4 (1978): 303-320.

150. Nelson, Geoffrey K. "Dépossession et besoins à l'origine des groupes religieux." SC 18,2 (1971): 237-246.

151. Schwartz, Gary. SECT IDEOLOGIES AND SOCIAL STATUS. Chicago: University of Chicago Press, 1970.

152. Simmonds, Robert B., James T. Richardson, and Mary W. Harder. "A Jesus Movement Group: An Adjective Check List Assessment." JSSR 15,4 (1976): 323-337.

153. Wallis, Roy, and Steve Bruce. "The Stark-Bainbridge Theory of Religion: A Critical Analysis and Counter Proposals." SA 45,1 (1984): 11-28.

154. Wright, Stuart A., and William V. D'Antonio. "The Substructure of Religion: A Further Study." JSSR 19,3 (1980): 292-298.

Everyday life

155. Bondolfi, Alberto. "Lecture épistémologique et éthique des sociologies du quotidien." SC 28,4 (1981): 429-440.

156. Isambert, François André. "Vie quotidienne, éthique et religion." SC 28,4 (1981): 441-445.

157. Lalive d'Epinay, Christian. "By Way of Introduction: The Flow of Everyday Life, the Reflow of History/En guise d'introduction: flux du quotidien, reflux de l'histoire." SC 28,4 (1981): 333-339.

158. Lalive d'Epinay, Christian, et al. "Popular Culture, Religion and Everyday Life." SC 28,4 (1981): 405-427.

159. Remy, Jean. "Sacredness and Everyday Life. Foreword/Sacralité et vie quotidienne. Avant-propos." SC 29,4 (1982): 263-265.

160. Remy, Jean. "Vie quotidienne, production de valeurs et religion." SC 29,4 (1982): 267-281.

161. Voyé, Liliane. "Religion, Values and Everyday Life." SC 28,4 (1981): 447-452.

Fatalism

162. Souffrant, Claude. "Un catholicisme de résignation en Haïti. Sociologie d'un recueil de cantiques religieux." SC 17,3 (1970): 425-438.

Identity

163. Collins, Randall. SOCIOLOGICAL INSIGHT. AN INTRODUCTION TO NON-OBVIOUS SOCIOLOGY. New York: Oxford University Press, 1982, pp. 30-59.

164. Dashefsky, Arnold. "And the Search Goes on: The Meaning of Religio-Ethnic Identity and Identification." SA 33,4 (1972): 239-245.

165. Gordon, David. "The Jesus People: An Identity Synthesis Interpretation." URBAN LIFE AND CULTURE 3,2 (1974): 159-179.

166. Lazerwitz, Bernard. "Contrasting the Effects of Generation, Class, Sex, and Age on Group Identification in the Jewish and Protestant Communities." SOCIAL FORCES 49,1 (1970): 50-59.

167. Lazerwitz, Bernard. "Religious Identification and its Ethnic Correlates: A Multivariate Model." SOCIAL FORCES 52 (1973): 204-222.

168. Maurer, H.H. "The Consciousness of Kind of a Fundamentalist Group." AMERICAN JOURNAL OF SOCIOLOGY 31 (1926): 485-506.

169. Mol, Johannes J. (Hans). IDENTITY AND THE SACRED. A SKETCH FOR A NEW SOCIAL-SCIENTIFIC THEORY OF RELIGION. Oxford: Blackwell, 1976; New York: Free Press, 1977.

170. Mol, Johannes J. (Hans) (ed.) IDENTITY AND RELIGION: INTERNATIONAL, CROSS-CULTURAL APPROACHES. Beverly Hills: Sage, 1978. Contains items 374, 1985, 2902, 3408.

171. Moles, Abraham A., and Tamar Grunewald. "Altérité et identité vues par le psycho-sociologue. Une étude trans-culturelle du Judaïsme." SC 18,3 (1971): 357-373.

172. Morland, J. Kenneth. "Religion and Identity in the South." In Harold F. Kaufman, J. Kenneth Morland, and Herbert H. Fockler (eds.), GROUP IDENTITY IN THE SOUTH: DIALOGUE BETWEEN THE TECHNOLOGICAL AND THE HUMANISTIC. Starkville: Mississippi State University, Department of Sociology, 1975, pp. 107-124.

173. Salisbury, W. Seward. "Religious Identification, Mixed Marriages and Conversion." JSSR 8,1 (1969): 125-129.

174. Snook, John B. RELIGIOUS IDENTIFICATION. Unpublished doctoral dissertation, Columbia University, 1967.

175. Wick, J.A. "Identity and Commitment of Young Sisters in a Religious Community." REVIEW FOR RELIGIOUS 30,1 (1971): 19-40.

176. Zerubavel, Eviatar. "Easter and Passover: On Calendars and Group Identity." AMERICAN SOCIOLOGICAL REVIEW 47,2 (1982): 284-289.

Morality

Morality (general)

177. Angell, R.C. "Preferences for Moral Norms in Three Problem Areas." AMERICAN JOURNAL OF SOCIOLOGY 67 (1962): 650-660.

178. Ansart, Pierre, Jean Cazeneuve, and Paul H. Maucorps. "Enquête sur les attitudes morales des groupements." CAHIERS INTERNATIONAUX DE SOCIOLOGIE 37 (1964): 149-160.

179. Barnsley, John H. THE SOCIAL REALITY OF ETHICS. THE COMPARATIVE ANALYSIS OF MORAL CODES. London: Routledge and Kegan Paul, 1972.

180. Bird, Frederick. "The Pursuit of Innocence: New Religious Movements and Moral Accountability." SA 40,4 (1979): 335-346. Also in J.K. Hadden and T.E. Long (eds.), RELIGION AND RELIGIOSITY IN AMERICA (volume cited in item 110), pp. 54-69.

181 Cazeneuve, Jean. "Les cadres sociaux de la morale stoïcienne dans l'Empire romain." CAHIERS INTERNATIONAUX DE SOCIOLOGIE 34 (1963): 13-26.

182. Faulkner, Joseph E., and Gordon F. DeJong. "A Note on Religiosity and Moral Behavior of a Sample of College Students." SC 15,1 (1968): 37-44

183. Houtart, François. "Religion et éthique: une approche marxiste." SC 31,2-3 (1984): 233-245.

184. Jones, Larry A. CHRISTIAN MORALISM: A SOCIOLOGICAL ANALYSIS. Unpublished Ph.D. dissertation, University of Chicago, 1975.

185. Jones, Larry A. "Empirical Evidence on Moral Contextualism." RRR 19,3 (1978): 246-252.

186. Kunz, Phillip R., and Eric M. Jaehne. A SOCIOLOGICAL APPROACH TO MORALITY. Lanham, Maryland: University Press of America, 1983.

187. Leites, Edmund. "Autonomy and the Rationalization of Moral Discourse." SA 35,2 (1974): 95-101.

188. Luhmann, Niklas. "Soziologie der Moral." In N. Luhmann and Stephan H. Pfürtner, THEORIETECHNIK UND MORAL. Frankfurt: Suhrkamp, 1978.

189. MacIntyre, Alasdair. SECULARIZATION AND MORAL CHANGE. London: Oxford University Press, 1967.

* Mol, Johannes J. (Hans). IDENTITY AND THE SACRED. Cited above as item 169.

190. Morgan, S. Philip. "A Research Note on Religion and Morality: Are Religious People Nice People?" SOCIAL FORCES 61 (1983): 683-692.
King, Morton B., and Richard A. Hunt. "Measuring Religion: A Comment on Morgan." SOCIAL FORCES 62,4 (1984): 1087-1088.
Morgan, S. Philip. "Reply to King and Hunt." SOCIAL FORCES 62,4 (1984): 1089-1090.

191. Philibert, Paul J. "Moral Maturity and Education beyond Conventional Morality." RRR 23,3 (1982): 286-296.

192. Schöfthäler, Traugott. "The Social Foundations of Morality: Durkheimian Problems and the Vicissitudes of Niklas Luhmann's Systems Theories of Religion, Morality and Personality." SC 31,2-3 (1984): 185-197.

193. Sixel, Friedrich W. "Beyond Good and Evil? A Study of Luhmann's Sociology of Morals." THEORY, CULTURE AND SOCIETY 2,1 (1983): 35-47.

194. Stark, Werner. THE SOCIAL BOND. AN INVESTIGATION INTO THE BASES OF LAW-ABIDINGNESS. VOLUME FOUR: ETHOS AND RELIGION. New York: Fordham University Press, 1983.

195. Tipton, Steven. GETTING SAVED FROM THE SIXTIES. Unpublished Ph.D. dissertation, Harvard University, 1977.

196. Tipton, Steven M. GETTING SAVED FROM THE SIXTIES. MORAL MEANING IN CONVERSION AND CULTURAL CHANGE. Berkeley: University of California Press, 1982.

Abortion

197. Compton, Paul A., Lorna Goldstrom, and J.M. Goldstrom. "Religion and Legal Abortion in Northern Ireland." JOURNAL OF BIOSOCIAL SCIENCE 6,4 (1974): 493-500.

198. Davis, N.J. "Clergy Abortion Brokers: A Transactional Analysis of Social Movement Development." SOCIOLOGICAL FOCUS 6,4 (1973): 87-109.

199. Daynes, Byron W., and Raymond Tatalovich. "Religious Influence and Congressonal Voting on Abortion." JSSR 23,2 (1984): 197-200.

200. Ladrière, Paul. "Religion, morale et politque: le débat sur l'avortement." SC 20,3 (1973): 417-454.

201. Mormont, Marc, Catherine Mougenot, and Danielle Ruquoy. "Univers mental et stratégie des évêques. La déclaration des évêques de Belgique sur l'avortement." SC 20,3 (1973): 475-496.

202. Pett, Mark E. RELIGION AND THE ABORTION PATIENT: A STUDY OF ANXIETY AS A FUNCTION OF RELIGIOUS BELIEF AND PARTICIPATION AND THE DECISION-MAKING PROCESS. Unpublished Ph.D. dissertation, University of Iowa, 1975.

* Robbins, James M. "Religious Involvement, Asceticism and Abortion among Low Income Black Women." Cited above as item 49.

203. Williams, Dorie Giles. "Religion, Beliefs about Human Life, and the Abortion Decision." RRR 24,1 (1982): 40-48.

Abortion attitudes

204. Baker, Ross K., Laurily K. Epstein, and Rodney D. Forth. "Matters of Life and Death: Social, Political, and Religious Correlates of Attitudes on Abortion." AMERICAN POLITICS QUARTERLY 9 (1981): 89-102.

205. Bardis, Panos. "Abortion Attitudes Among Catholic College Students." ADOLESCENCE 10 (1975): 433-441.

206. Blake, Judith. "Abortion and Public Opinion: The 1960-1970 Decade." SCIENCE 171 (1971): 540-549.

207. Blake, Judith. "The Abortion Decisions: Judicial Review and Public Opinion." In Edward Manier et al. (eds.) ABORTION: NEW DIRECTIONS FOR PUBLIC POLICY. Notre Dame: University of Notre Dame Press,1977, pp. 51-81.

208. Blasi, Anthony J., Peter MacNeil, and Robert O'Neill. "The Relationship between Abortion Attitudes and Catholic Religiosity." SOCIAL SCIENCE 50,1 (1975): 34-39.

209. Brinkerhoff, Merlin B., and Marlene M. MacKie. "Religious Denominations' Impact upon Gender Attitudes: Some Methodological Implications." RRR 25,4 (1984): 365-378.

210. Clayton, Richard R., and William L. Tolone. "Religiosity and Attitudes toward Induced Abortion: An Elaboration of the Relationship." SA 34,1 (1973): 26-39.

211. D'Antonio, William V., and Steven Stack. "Religion, Ideal Family Size, and Abortion: Extending Renzi's Hypothesis." JSSR 19,4 (1980): 397-408.

212. Finner, Stephen L., and Jerome D. Gamache. "The Relationship between Religious Commitment and Attitudes toward Induced Abortion." SA 30,1 (1969): 1-12.

213. Heimer, David D. "Abortion Attitudes among Catholic University Students: A Comparative Research Note." SA 37,3 (1976): 255-260.

214. Hertel, Bradley, Gerry E. Hendershot, and James W. Grimm. "Religion and Attitudes towards Abortion: A Study of Nurses and Social Workers." JSSR 13 (1974): 23-34.

215. Jelen, Ted. G. "Respect for Life, Sexual Morality, and Opposition to Abortion." RRR 25,3 (1984): 220-231.

216. Liu, William. "Abortion and the Social System." In Edward Manier et al. (eds.), ABORTION: NEW DIRECTIONS FOR PUBLIC POLICY (volume cited in item 207), pp. 138-157.

217. Malak, Sharon Jo. "A Study of Catholic College Students' Attitudes toward Abortion." SOCIAL SCIENCE 47 (1972): 229-230.

218. McCormick, E. Patricia. ATTITUDES TOWARD ABORTION. EXPERIENCES OF SELECTED BLACK AND WHITE WOMEN. Lexington, Massachusetts: Lexington Books (Heath), 1975.

219. McIntosh, William Alex, Letitia T. Alston, and Jon P. Alston. "The Differential Impact of Religious Preference and Church Attendance on Attitudes toward Abortion." RRR 20,2 (1979): 195-213.

220. Neitz, Mary Jo. "Family, State, and God: Ideologies of the Right-to-Life Movement." SA 42,3 (1981): 265-276.

221. Petersen, Larry R. RELIGION AND THE RIGHT TO LIFE. RELIGIOUS AND SOCIAL DETERMINANTS OF ATTITUDES TOWARD ABORTION AND CAPITAL PUNISHMENT. Unpublished M.A. thesis, Washington State University, 1974.

222. Petersen, Larry R., and Armand L. Mauss. "Religion and the 'Right to Life': Correlates of Opposition to Abortion." SA 37,3 (1976): 243-254.

223. Price-Bonham, Sharon, Barbara Santes, and John M. Bonham. "An Analysis of Clergymen's Attitudes toward Abortion." RRR 17 (1975): 15-27.

224. Renzi, Mario. "Ideal Family Size as an Intervening Variable between Religion and Attitudes toward Abortion." JSSR 14 (1975): 23-27.

225. Richardson, James T., and Sandie Fox. "Religion and Voting on Abortion Reform: A Follow-up Study." JSSR 14 (1975): 159-164.

226. Tedrow, Lucky M., and E.R. Mahoney. "Trends in Attitudes toward Abortion: 1972-1976." PUBLIC OPINION QUARTERLY 43 (1979): 181-189.

227. Traina, Frank J. "Catholic Clergy on Abortion: Preliminary Findings on a New York State Survey." FAMILY PLANNING PERSPECTIVES 6 (1974): 151-156.

Abortion attitudes and denomination

228. Balakrishnan, T.R, Shan Ross, John Allingham, and John F. Kanter. Attitudes toward Abortion of Married Women in Metropolitan Toronto." SOCIAL BIOLOGY 19 (1972): 35-42.

229. Blake, Judith. "Elective Abortion and our Reluctant Citizenry: Research on Public Opinion in the United States." In H.J. Osofsky and J.D. Osofsky (eds.), THE ABORTION EXPERIENCE: PSYCHOLOGICAL AND MEDICAL IMPACT. Hagarstown, Md.: Harper and Row, Medical Dept., 1973, pp. 447-467.

* Ebaugh, Helen Rose Fuchs, and C. Allen Haney. "Church Attendance and Attitudes toward Abortion: Differentials in Liberal and Conservative Churches." Cited above as item 105.

230. Harter, C.L., and J.D. Beasley. "A Survey Concerning Induced Abortions in New Orleans." AMERICAN JOURNAL OF PUBLIC HEALTH 57 (1967): 1937-47.

231. Lipson, Gerald, and Dianne Wolman. "Polling Americans on Birth Control and Population." FAMILY PLANNING PERSPECTIVES 4 (1972): 39-42.

232. McIntosh, William Alex, and Jon P. Alston. "Review of the Polls: Acceptance of Abortion among White Catholics and Protestants, 1962 and 1975." JSSR 16,3 (1977): 295-303.

233. Peyton, F.W., A.R. Starry, and T.R. Leidy. "Women's Attitudes Concerning Abortion." OBSTETRICS AND GYNECOLOGY 34 (1969): 182-88.

234. Rao, S.L.N., and Leon F. Bouvier. "Socioeconomic Correlates of Attitudes toward Abortion in Rhode Island: 1971." AMERICAN JOURNAL OF PUBLIC HEALTH 64 (1974): 765-774.

235. Richardson, James T., and Sandie Wightman Fox. "Religious Affiliation as a Predictor of Voting Behavior in Abortion Reform Legislation." JSSR 11 (1972): 347-359.

* Richardson, James T., and Sandie Wightman Fox. "Religion and Voting on Abortion Reform: A Follow-up Study." Cited above as item 225.

236. Ryder, Norman B., and Charles F. Westoff. REPRODUCTION IN THE UNITED STATES, 1965. Princeton: Princeton University Press, 1971, pp. 279-280.

Abortion attitudes and orthodoxy

237. Wagenaar, Theodore C., and Patricia E. Bartos. "Orthodoxy and Attitudes of Clergymen toward Homosexuality and Abortion." RRR 18,2 (1977): 114-125.

Abortion practice

238. Bachi, Roberto, and Judah Matras. "Contraception and Induced Abortions among Jewish Maternity Cases in Israel." MILBANK MEMORIAL FUND QUARTERLY 40 (1962): 207-229.

239. Bogen, Iver. "Attitudes of Women who have had Abortions." JOURNAL OF SEX RESEARCH 10 (1974): 97-109.

240. Cobb, J.C. "Abortion in Colorado 1967-1969: Changing Attitudes and Practices since the New Law." ADVANCES IN PLANNED PARENTHOOD 5 (1970): 186-189.

241. Jones, Gavin, and Dorothy Nortman. "Roman Catholic Fertility and Family Planning: A Comparative Review of the Literature." STUDIES IN FAMILY PLANNING 24 (1968): 1-27.

242. Leon, Joseph J., and Patricia G. Steinhoff. "Catholics' Use of Abortion." SA 36,2 (1975): 125-136.

243. Pion, R.J., et al. "Abortion Request and Post-Operative Response: A Washington Community Survey." NORTHWEST MEDICINE 69 (1970): 693-698.

244. Requena, Mariano. "Social and Economic Correlates of Induced Abortions in Santiago, Chile." DEMOGRAPHY 2 (1965): 33-49.

245. Steinhoff, Patricia G. "Background Characteristics of Abortion Patients." In H. Osofsky and J. Osofsky (eds.), THE ABORTION EXPERIENCE (volume cited in item 229), pp. 206-231.

246. Treffers, P.E. "Abortion in Amsterdam." POPULATION STUDIES 20 (1967): 295-309.

Birth control

* Bachi, Roberto, and Judah Matras. "Contraception and Induced Abortions among Jewish Maternity Cases in Israel." Cited above as item 238.

247. Elifson, Kirk W., and Joseph Irwin. "Black Ministers' Attitudes toward Population Size and Birth Control." SA 38,3 (1977): 252-257.

248. Groat, H. Theodore, Arthur G. Neal, and Evelyn C. Knisely. "Contraceptive Nonconformity among Catholics." JSSR 14,4 (1975): 367-377.

249. Heaton, Tim B., and Sandra Calkins. "Family Size and Contraceptive Use among Mormons: 1965-1975." RRR 25,2 (1983): 102-113.

250. Hutjes, J.M. "Dutch Catholics on Birth Control and Sexuality." SOCIOLOGIA NEERLANDICA 11,2 (1975): 144-158.

251. Jackson, Audrey R. "A Model for Determining Information Diffusion in a Family Planning Program." JOURNAL OF MARRIAGE AND THE FAMILY 34 (1972): 503-513.

* Lipson, Gerald, and Dianne Wolman. "Polling Americans on Birth Control and Population." Cited above as item 231.

252. Moore, Maurice J. DEATH OF A DOGMA? THE AMERICAN CATHOLIC CLERGY'S VIEWS OF CONTRACEPTION. Chicago: Community and Family Study Center, 1973.

253. O'Connell, Brian J. "Dimensions of Religiosity among Catholics." RRR 16 (1975): 198-207.

254. Perez Ramirez, Gustavo. "Les attentes vis-à-vis de la déclaration pontificale sur la régulation des naissances en Amérique latine en 1967." SC 15 (1968): 443-452.

255. Potvin, Raymond H., Charles F. Westoff, and Norman B. Ryder. "Factors Affecting Catholic Wives' Conformity to their Church Magisterium's Position on Birth Control." JOURNAL OF MARRIAGE AND FAMILY 30 (1968): 263-272.

256. Schreuder, Osmund, and Jan Hutjes. PRIESTER ZUR GEBURTENREGELUNG. EINE EMPIRISCHE ERHEBUNG. München: Kaiser Verlag, and Mainz: Matthias Grünewald Verlag, 1972.

257. Thomlinson, Ralph. "Prevented Births, Naturalness and Roman Catholic Doctrine." POPULATION REVIEW 14,1-2 (1970): 17-35.

258. Westoff, Charles F., and Larry L. Bumpass. "The Revolution in Birth Control Practices of U.S. Roman Catholics." SCIENCE 179 (1973): 41-44.

259. Westoff, Charles F., and Elise F. Jones. "The Secularization of U.S. Catholic Birth Control Practices." FAMILY PLANNING PERSPECTIVES 9,5 (1977): 203-207.

Capital Punishment

* Petersen, Larry R. RELIGION AND THE RIGHT TO LIFE. RELIGIOUS AND SOCIAL DETERMINANTS OF ATTITUDES TOWARD ABORTION AND CAPITAL PUNISHMENT. Cited above as item 221.

Euthanasia

260. Alston, Jon P. "Review of the Polls: Three Current Religious Issues: Marriage of Priests, Intermarriage and Euthanasia." JSSR 15,1 (1976): 75-78.

261. Hilhorst, Henri W.A. "Religion and Euthanasia in the Netherlands. Exploring a Diffuse Relationship." SC 30,4 (1983): 491-502.

262. Lazerine, Neil G. PROFESSIONAL PERSPECTIVES ON EUTHANASIA: A COMPARATIVE STUDY OF NURSES AND CLERGYMEN. Unpublished Ph.D. dissertation, Bowling Green, 1977.

263. Nagi, Mostafa, M.D. Pugh, and Neil G. Lazerine. "Attitudes of Catholic and Protestant Clergy toward Euthanasia." OMEGA 8,2 (1977-78): 153-164.

Homosexuality

264. Alston, John P. "Review of the Polls: Attitudes toward Extra-marital and Homosexual Relations." JSSR 13,4 (1974): 479-481.

265. Enroth, Ronald M. "The Homosexual Church: An Ecclesiastical Extension of a Subculture." SC 21,3 (1974): 355-360.

266. Greenberg, David F., and Marcia H. Bystryn. "Christian Intolerance of Homosexuality." AMERICAN JOURNAL OF SOCIOLOGY 88,3 (1982): 515-548.

* Wagenaar, Theodore C., and Patricia E. Bartos. "Orthodoxy and Attitudes of Clergymen toward Homosexuality and Abortion." Cited above as item 237.

Peace and war

267. Baron, Salo W. "Impact of Wars on Religion." POLITICAL SCIENCE QUARTERLY 67 (1952): 534-572.

268. Bastenier, Albert. "Paul VI et la paix. Analyse de sept discours pontificaux." SC 21,4 (1974): 489-502.

269. Beemsterboer, Kees. "La 'Semaine pour la Paix' aux Pays-Bas. Action et évaluation." SC 21,4 (1974): 473-488.

270. Campbell, Keith. RELIGIOSITY AND ATTITUDES TOWARD SELECTED WARS: A CORRELATIONAL STUDY. Unpublished Ph.D. dissertation, University of Missouri-Columbia, 1977.

271. Campbell, Keith, and Donald Granberg. "Religiosity and Attitude toward the Vietnam War: A Research Note Using National Samples." SA 40,3 (1979): 254-256.

272. Chanteloup, Robert E. "Hawks and Doves: An Analysis of a Catholic Attitude toward Nuclear War." SA 31,1 (1970): 23-35.

273. Connors, John F., III, Richard C. Leonard, and Kenneth E. Burnham. "Religion and Opposition to War among College Students." SA 29,4 (1968): 211-219.

274. Dahlke, H.D. "Values and Group Behavior in Two Camps for Conscientious Objectors." AMERICAN JOURNAL OF SOCIOLOGY 51,1 (1945): 22-33.

275. Droba, D.D. "Churches and War Attitudes." SOCIOLOGY AND SOCIAL RESEARCH 16 (1932): 547-552.

276. Easthope, Gary. "Religious War in Northern Ireland." SOCIOLOGY 10,3 (1976): 427-450.

277. Eckhardt, William. "Religious Beliefs and Practices in Relation to Peace and Justice." SC 21,4 (1974): 463-472.

278. Freund, Julien. "La paix selon la foi et selon l'Eglise." SC 21,4 (1974): 433-449.

279. Fuse, Toyomasa. "Religion, War and the Institutional Dilemma: A Sociological Interpretation." JOURNAL OF PEACE RESEARCH 2 (1968): 196-210. Also in SC 15,4 (1968): 367-382.

280. Granberg, Donald, and Keith E. Campbell. "Certain Aspects of Religiosity and Orientations toward the Vietnam War among Missouri Undergraduates." SA 34,1 (1973): 40-49.

281. Hamilton, R.F. "A Research Note on the Mass Support for 'Tough' Military Initiatives." AMERICAN SOCIOLOGICAL REVIEW 33 (1968): 439-445.

282. Houtart, François. "Les églises européennes et la paix. Réflexions sociologiques sur leur engagement et leur pensée." SC 21,4 (1974): 451-462.

283. Kelly, James R. "Catholicism and Modern Memory: Some Sociological Reflections on the Symbolic Foundations of the Rhetorical Force of the Pastoral Letter, 'The Challenge of Peace.'" SA 45,2 (1984): 131-144.

284. Kimwra, Y. "Religious Affiliations of War Brides in Hawaii and their Marital Adjustment." SOCIAL PROCESS 26 (1963): 88-95.

285. Lewis, Robert A. "A Contemporary Religious Enigma: Churches and War." JOURNAL OF POLITICAL AND MILITARY SOCIOLOGY 3,1 (1975): 57-70.

286. Martin, David. "The Peace Sentiment: Old and New." In Eileen Barker (ed.), NEW RELIGIOUS MOVEMENTS: A PERSPECTIVE FOR UNDERSTANDING SOCIETY. New York: Mellen, 1982, pp. 107-122.

287. Quinley, Harold E. "Hawks and Doves among the Clergy: Protestant Reactions to the War in Vietnam." MINISTRY STUDIES 3 (1969): 5-20.

288. Quinley, Harold E. "The Protestant Clergy and the War in Vietnam." PUBLIC OPINION QUARTERLY 34,4 (1970): 43-52.

289. Quinley, Harold E. THE PROPHETIC CLERGY. SOCIAL ACTIVISM AMONG PROTESTANT MINISTERS. New York: Wiley, 1974.

290. Simmons, Jimmie R. SOURCES OF POLITICAL SOCIALIZATION TO INTERNATIONAL CONFLICT: INFLUENCE OF THE MASS MEDIA, FAMILY, PEER GROUP, SCHOOL AND RELIGION ON ADOLESCENTS' ORIENTATIONS TOWARDS WAR AND PEACE. Unpublished Ph.D. dissertation. University of Washington, Seattle, 1974.

291. Starr, Jerold M. "Religious Preference, Religiosity, and Opposition to War." SA 36,4 (1975): 323-334.

292. Sundback, Susan. "The Church, Crisis and War." ACTA SOCIOLOGICA 25,4 (1982): 443-454.

293. Tygart, Clarence E. "Religiosity and University Student Anti-Vietnam War Attitudes: A Negative or Curvilinear Relationship?" SA 32,2 (1971): 120-129.

294. Tygart, Clarence E. "Social Movement Participation: Clergy and the Anti-Vietnam War Movement." SA 34,3 (1973): 202-211.

295. Walker, Paul R. THE INFLUENCE OF THE CHRISTIAN CHURCH IN AMERICA ON PEACE AND WAR, 1914-1935. Unpublished M.A. thesis, Clark University, 1936.

296. Yinger, J. Milton. RELIGION IN THE STRUGGLE FOR POWER: A STUDY IN THE SOCIOLOGY OF RELIGION. Durham, North Carolina, 1946. Reprinted in New York: Arno Press, 1980.

297. Zahn, Gordon C. GERMAN CATHOLICS AND HITLER'S WARS. New York: Sheed and Ward, 1962.

298. Zahn, Gordon C. "War and Religion in a Sociolgoical Perspective." SC 21,4 (1974): 421-431.

Pornography

299. Wood, Michael, and Michael Hughes. "The Moral Basis of Moral Reform: Status Discontent vs. Culture and Socialization as Explanations of Anti-Pornography Social Movement Adherence." AMERICAN SOCIOLOGICAL REVIEW 49,1 (1984): 86-99.

300. Zurcher, Louis A., Jr., et al. "The Anti-Pornography Campaign: A Symbolic Crusade." SOCIAL PROBLEMS 19 (1971): 217-238.

Sexual attitudes

301. Acock, Alan C., and Vern L. Bengtson. "On the Relative Influence of Mothers and Fathers: A Covariance Analysis of Political and Religious Socialization." JOURNAL OF MARRIAGE AND THE FAMILY 40 (1978): 519-530.

302. Alston, Jon P. "Review of the Polls: Attitudes of White Protestants and Catholics towards Nonmarital Sex." JSSR 13,1 (1974): 73-74.

* Alston, Jon P. "Review of the Polls: Attitudes towards Extramarital and Homosexual Relations." Cited above as item 264.

303. De Neuter, Patrick. "Amour, sexualité et religion. Enquête par questionnaire et par images d'aperception auprès d'un groupe de collégiens." SC 19,3 (1972): 365-387.

304. Greeley, Andrew M. "The Sexual Revolution among Catholic Clergy." RRR 14 (1973): 91-100.

305. Greeley, Andrew M. THE RELIGIOUS IMAGINATION. Los Angeles: Sadlier, 1981.

306. Hampe, Gary D. "Interfaith Dating: Religion, Social Class and Premarital Sexual Attitudes." SA 32,2 (1971): 97-106.

307. Hornick, Joseph P. "Premarital Sexual Attitudes and Behavior." SOCIOLOGICAL QUARTERLY 19,4 (1978): 534-544.

* Hutjes, J.M. "Dutch Catholics on Birth Control and Sexuality." Cited above as item 250.

308. King, K., T. Abernathy, Ira E. Robinson, and J. Balswick. "Religiosity and Sexual Attitudes and Behavior among College Students." ADOLESCENCE 11 (1976): 535-539.

309. Libby, Roger W., Louis Gray, and Mervin White. "A Test and Reformulation of Reference Group and Role Correlates of Premarital Sexual Permissiveness Theory." JOURNAL OF MARRIAGE AND THE FAMILY 40 (1978): 79-90.

310. Neal, Marie Augusta. "Perspectiva sociológica de los planteamientos morales de la sexualidad hoy." CONCILIUM 100 (1974): 450-462.

* O'Connell, Brian J. "Dimensions of Religiosity among Catholics." Cited above as item 253.

311. Wulf, Jean, David Prentice, Donna Hansum, Archie Ferrar, and Bernard Spilka. "Religiosity and Sexual Attitudes and Behavior among Evangelical Christian Singles." RRR 26,2 (1984): 110-131.

Sexual conduct

312. Bell, Robert R., and Jay B. Chaskes. "Premarital Sexual Experience among Coeds, 1958 and 1968." JOURNAL OF MARRIAGE AND THE FAMILY 32 (1970): 81-84.

313. Cardwell, Jerry D. "The Relationship between Religious Commitment and Premarital Sexual Permissiveness: A Five Dimensional Analysis." SA 30 (1969): 72-80.

314. Carns, Donald E. RELIGIOSITY, PREMARITAL SEXUALITY AND THE AMERICAN COLLEGE STUDENT: AN EMPIRICAL STUDY. Unpublished Ph.D. dissertation, Indiana University, 1969.

315. Clayton, Richard R. "Religious Orthodoxy and Premarital Sex." SOCIAL FORCES 47 (1969): 469-474.

316. Clayton, Richard R. "Religiosity and Premarital Sexual Permissiveness: Elaboration of the Relationship and Debate." SA 32,2 (1971): 81-96.

317. Clayton, Richard R. "Premarital Sexual Intercourse: Substantive Test of the Contingent Consistency Model." JOURNAL OF MARRIAGE AND THE FAMILY 34 (1972): 273-281.

318. Clayton, Richard R., and Harwin L. Voss. "Shacking Up: Cohabitation in the 1970's." JOURNAL OF MARRIAGE AND THE FAMILY 39 (1977): 273-292.

319. Davidson, J. Kenneth, Sr., and Gerald R. Leslie. "Premarital Sexual Intercourse: An Application of Axiomatic Theory Construction." JOURNAL OF MARRIAGE AND THE FAMILY 39 (1977): 15-25.

* De Neuter, Patrick. "Amour, sexualité et religion. Enquête par questionnaire et par images d'aperception auprès d'un groupe de collégiens." Cited above as item 303.

320. Glass, J. Conrad, Jr. "Premarital Sexual Standards among Church Youth Leaders: An Exploratory Study." JSSR 11 (1972): 361-367.

321. Groat, H. Theodore, Arthur G. Neal, and Evelyn C. Knisely. "Contraceptive Nonconformity among Catholics." JSSR 14 (1975): 367-377.

322. Harrison, Danny E., Walter H. Bennett, and Gerald Globetti. "Attitudes of Rural Youth toward Premarital Sexual Permissiveness." JOURNAL OF MARRIAGE AND THE FAMILY 31 (1969): 783-787.

323. Heltsley, Mary E., and Carlfred B. Broderick. "Religiosity and Premarital Sexual Permissiveness. Re-examination of Reiss's Traditionalism Proposition." JOURNAL OF MARRIAGE AND THE FAMILY 31,3 (1969): 441-443. Followed by Ira L. Reiss's response, pp. 444-445.

324. Henze, Lura F., and John W. Hudson. "Personal and Family Characteristics of Cohabitating and Noncohabitating College Students." JOURNAL OF MARRIAGE AND THE FAMILY 36 (1974): 722-727.

325. Hobart, Charles W. "Sexual Permissiveness in Young English and French Canadians." JOURNAL OF MARRIAGE AND THE FAMILY 34 (1972): 292-303.

* King, K., T. Abernathy, I. Robinson, and J. Balswick. "Religiosity and Sexual Attitudes and Behavior among College Students." Cited above as item 308.

326. Lyness, Judith L., Milton E. Lipetz, and Keith E. Davis. "Living Together: An Alternative to Marriage." JOURNAL OF MARRIAGE AND THE FAMILY 34 (1972): 305-314.

327. Mahoney, E.R. "Religiosity and Sexual Behavior among Heterosexual College Students." JOURNAL OF SEX RESEARCH 16 (1980): 97-113.

328. Maranell, Gary M., Richard A. Dodder, and David F. Mitchell. "Social Class and Premarital Sexual Permissiveness: A Subsequent Test." JOURNAL OF MARRIAGE AND THE FAMILY 32 (1970): 85-88.

329. Middendorp, C.P., W. Brinkman, and W. Koomen. "Determinants of Premarital Sexual Permissiveness: A Secondary Analysis." JOURNAL OF MARRIAGE AND THE FAMILY 32 (1970): 369-379.

330. Peterman, Dan J., Carl A. Ridley, and Scott M. Anderson. "A Comparison of Cohabiting and Noncohabiting College Students." JOURNAL OF MARRIAGE AND THE FAMILY 36 (1974); 344-354.

331. Ruppel, Howard J., Jr. "Religiosity and Premarital Permissiveness: A Methodological Note." SA 30,3 (1969): 176-188.

332. Ruppel, Howard J., Jr. "Religiosity and Premarital Sexual Permissiveness: A Response to the Reiss-Heltsley and Brockerick Debate." JOURNAL OF MARRIAGE AND THE FAMILY 32 (1970): 647-655.

333. Schulz, Barbara, George W. Bohrnstedt, Edgar F. Borgatta, and Robert R. Evans. "Explaining Premarital Sexual Intercourse among College Students: A Causal Model." SOCIAL FORCES 56,1 (1977): 148-165.

334. Stack, Steven, and Mary Jeanne Kanavy. "The Effect of Religion on Forcible Rape: A Structural Analysis." JSSR 22,1 (1983): 67-74.

335. Strong, Leslie D. "Alternative Marital and Family Forms: Their Relative Attractiveness to College Students and Correlates of Willingness to Participate in Nontraditional Forms." JOURNAL OF MARRIAGE AND THE FAMILY 40 (1978): 495-503.

336. Verner, Arthur M., and Cyrus S. Stewart. "Adolescent Sexual Behavior in Middle America Revisited: 1970-1973." JOURNAL OF MARRIAGE AND THE FAMILY 36 (1974): 728-735.

* Wulf, Jean, David Prentice, Donna Hansum, Archie Ferrar, and Bernard Spilka. "Religiosity and Sexual Attitudes and Behavior among Evangelical Christian Singles." Cited above as item 311.

337. Wuthnow, Robert, and Charles Y. Glock. "Religious Loyalty, Defection, and Experimentation among College Youth." JSSR 12 (1973) 157-180.

Situation ethics

* Jones, Larry A. CHRISTIAN MORALISM: A SOCIOLOGICAL ANALYSIS. Cited above as item 184.

* Jones, Larry A. "Empirical Evidence on Moral Contexualism." Cited above as item 185.

Social justice

* DeJong, Gordon F., and Joseph E. Faulkner. "The Church, Individual Religiosity, and Social Justice." Cited above as item 104.

338. Hoge, Dean R., Esther Heffernan, Eugene F. Hemrick, Hart M. Nelsen, James P. O'Connor, Paul J. Philibert, and Andrew D. Thompson. "Desired Outcomes of Religious Education and Youth Ministry in Six Denominations." RRR 23,3 (1982): 230-254.

339. Neal, Marie Augusta. "How Prophecy Lives." SA 33,3 (1972): 125-141.

* Perkins, H. Wesley. "Organized Religion as Opiate or Prophetic Stimulant: A Study of American and English Assessments of Social Justice in Two Urban Settings." Cited above as item 95.

Sterilization and vasectomy

340. Eckhardt, Kenneth W., and Gerry E. Hendershot. "Religious Preference, Religious Participation, and Sterilization Decisions: Findings from the National Survey of Family Growth, Cycle II." RRR 25,3 (1984): 232-246.

341. Grindstaff, Carl F., and G. Edward Ebanks. "Protestant and Catholic Couples who Have Chosen Vasectomy." SA 36,1 (1975): 29-42.

Pluralism

The co-existence of different religions as well as non-religious world views has received attention in the discipline. After the entries which focus on pluralism in general, studies of related phenomena are grouped under five other headings.

Pluralism (general)

342. Berger, Peter L. "Secularization and Pluralism." INTERNATIONAL YEARBOOK FOR THE SOCIOLOGY OF RELIGION 2 (1966): 73-84.

343. Berger, Peter L. "Aspects sociologiques du pluralisme." ARCHIVES DE SOCIOLOGIE DES RELIGIONS 23 (1967): 117-127.

344. Berk, Marc. "Pluralist Theory and Church Policy Positions on Racial and Sexual Equality." SA 39,4 (1978): 338-350.

345. Bourdillon, M.F.C. "Pluralism and Problems of Belief." ARCHIVES DE SCIENCES SOCIALES DES RELIGIONS 54,1 (1982): 21-42.

346. Bourg, Carroll J. "Politics and Religion." SA 41,4 (1981): 297-316.

347. Cole, William A., and Phillip E. Hammond. "Religious Pluralism, Legal Development, and Societal Complexity: Rudimentary Forms of Civil Religion." JSSR 13,2 (1974): 177-189.

348. Corm, G.G. CONTRIBUTION A L'ETUDE DES SOCIETES MULTICONFESSION-NELLES. EFFECTS SOCIO-JURIDIQUES ET POLITIQUES DU PLURALISME RELIGIEUX. Paris: Libraire generale de Droit et de Jurisprudence, 1971.

349. Dykstra, J.W. "Problems of a Religiously Pluralistic Society." SOCIOLOGY AND SOCIAL RESEARCH 45,4 (1961): 401-406.

350. Fitzpatrick, Joseph. "Cultural Pluralism and Religious Identification: A Review." SA 25,2 (1964): 129-134.

351. Goddijn, Walter. "Pluralisme religieux et chrétienté." SC 10:1 (1963): 53-74.

352. Hambye, Francis, and Jean Remy. "Pluralisme culturel et symbolique de l'environnement. Applications au phénomène religieux." SC 16,3 (1969): 343-354.

353. Hammond, Phillip. "Religious Pluralism and Durkheim's Integration Thesis." In Allan W. Eister (ed.), CHANGING PERSPECTIVES IN THE SCIENTIFIC STUDY OF RELIGION. New York: Wiley, 1974, pp. 115-142.

354. Herberg, Will. "Protestant-Catholic Tensions in Pluralistic America." YALE DIVINITY NEWS (1960): 3-11.

355. Herberg, Will. "The 1961 Harlan Paul Douglass Lectures. Religion in a Secularized Society: Some Aspects of America's Three-Religion Pluralism. Lecture II." RRR 4 (1962): 33-45.

356. Kruijt, J.P., and W. Goddijn. "Cloisonnement et décloisonnement culturels comme processus sociologiques." SC 9 (1962): 63-107.

357. Lemert, Charles C. "Cultural Multiplexity and Religious Polytheism." SC 21,3 (1974): 241-253.

358. Lenski, Gerhard. "Religious Pluralism in Theoretical Perspective." In J. Matthes (ed.), INTERNATIONALES JAHRBUCH FÜR RELIGIONSSOZIOLOGIE I. Köln and Opladen: Westdeutscher Verlag, 1965, pp. 25-41.

359. Mariante, Benjamin R. PLURALIST SOCIETY, PLURALIST CHURCH. Washington: University Press of America, 1981.

360. Matthes, Joachim. "Le pluralisme vertical en Allemagne." SC 9,1-2 (1962) 21-38.

361. Matthijssen, A.J.M. "Catholic Intellectual Emancipation in the Western Countries of Mixed Religion." SC 6,3 (1959): 91-113.

362. Moreux, Colette. "Quelques aspects du pluralisme religieux au Québec." RELATIONS 378 (1973): 10-11.

363. Mörth, Ingo. "Vom pluralismus zum Integrismus. Aspekte religiösen Alltagsbewußtseins." SCHWEIZERISCHE ZEITSCHRIFT FÜR SOZIOLOGIE 9 (1983): 559-578.

364. Parsons, Talcott. "Religion in a Modern Pluralistic Society." RRR 7,3 (1966): 125-146.

365. Poblete Barth, Renato. "El pluralismo en la Iglesia: el caso de Chile." PRO MUNDI VITA 45 (1973): 19-22.

366. Remy, J. "La religion dans une société pluraliste. Jalons pour observation du phénomène." SC 31,5-6 (1966): 379-390.

367. Robbins, Thomas, and Dick Anthony (eds.) IN GODS WE TRUST. New Brunswick, N.J.: Transaction, 1981. Contains items 94, 1249, 1723, 1977, 2019, 2058, 2389, 3117, 3385.

368. Stauffer, Robert E. "Church Members' Ignorance of Doctrinal Pluralism: A Probable Source of Church Cohesion." JSSR 12,3 (1973): 345-348.

369. Steeman, Theodore M. RELIGIOUS PLURALISM AND NATIONAL INTEGRATION. Unpublished Ph.D. dissertation, Harvard University, 1973.

370. Tamney, Joseph B., and John G. Condran. "The Decline of Religious Homogeneity: The Indonesian Situation." JSSR 19,3 (1980): 267-280.

371. Thomas, John L. "Family Values in a Pluralistic Society." AMERICAN CATHOLIC SOCIOLOGICAL REVIEW 23 (1962): 30-40.

372. Thung, Mady A. "From Pillarization to New Religious Pluralism." SC 30,4 (1983): 503-524.

373. Thurlings, Jan M.G. "The Case of Dutch Catholicism: A Contribution to the Theory of the Pluralistic Society." SOCIOLOGIA NEERLANDICA 7 (1971): 118-136.

374. Thurlings, Jan. M.G. "Identity and Pluralism. A Case-Study." In Hans Mol (ed.), IDENTITY AND RELIGION (item 170), pp. 169-177.

375. Yinger, J. Milton. "Religion and Social Change: Problems of Integration and Pluralism among the Privileged." RRR 4,3 (1963): 129-148. Also in R.D. Knudten (ed.), THE SOCIOLOGY OF RELIGION. AN ANTHOLOGY. New York: Appleton-Century-Crofts, 1967, pp. 496-512.

376. Yinger, J. Milton. "Pluralism, Religion, and Secularism." JSSR 6 (1967): 17-28.

Accommodation

377. Snow, David A. "A Dramaturgical Analysis of Movement Accommodation: Building Idiosyncrasy Credit as a Movement Mobilization Strategy." SYMBOLIC INTERACTION 2 (1979): 23-44.

378. White, O. Kendall. "Mormonism in America and Canada: Accommodation to the Nation-State." CANADIAN JOURNAL OF SOCIOLOGY 3 (1978): 161-181.

379. White, O. Kendall. "Mormon Resistance and Accommodation: From Communitarian Socialism to Corporate Capitalism." In Scott B. Cummings (ed.), SELF-HELP IN URBAN AMERICA: PATTERNS OF MINORITY ECONOMIC DEVELOPMENT. Port Washington, N.Y.: Kennikat, 1980, pp. 89-112, 219-221.

Assimilation and related phenomena

380. Alba, R.D. ASSIMILATION AMONG AMERICAN CATHOLICS. Unpublished Ph.D. dissertation, Columbia University, 1974.

381. Cain, Leonard D., Jr. "Japanese-American Protestants: Acculturation and Assimilation." RRR 3 (1962): 113-121.

382. Gordon, Milton. ASSIMILATION IN AMERICAN LIFE: THE ROLE OF RACE, RELIGION, AND NATIONAL ORIGINS. New York: Oxford University Press, 1964.

383. Groenenberg, Adrian Laurens. THE SOCIAL GEOGRAPHY OF THE NETHERLANDERS IN SOUTH-WESTERN ONTARIO WITH SPECIAL REFERENCE TO THE ROLE OF THE CHURCHES IN THE INTEGRATION OF THE IMMIGRANTS. Unpublished M.A. thesis, University of Western Ontario, 1966.

384. Herberg, Will. "Integration of the Jew into America's Three-Religion Society." JOURNAL OF CHURCH AND STATE 5 (1963): 28-40.

385. Kayal, Philip M., and Joseph M. Kayal. THE SYRIAN-LEBANESE IN AMERICA: A STUDY IN RELIGION AND ASSIMILATION. Boston: Twayne, 1975.

386. Lampe, Philip E. "Assimilation and the School System." SA 37,3 (1976) 228-242.

387. Lampe, Philip E. "Religion and the Assimiliation of Mexican Americans." RRR 18,3 (1977): 243-253.

388. Lebra, Takie S. "Religious Conversion as a Breakthrough for Transculturation: A Japanese Sect in Hawaii." JSSR 9 (1970): 181-196.

389. McNamara, Patrick H. "Catholicism, Assimilation and the Chicano Movement: Los Angeles as a Case Study." In R. de la Garza et al.(eds.), CHICANOS AND NATIVE AMERICANS. Englewood Cliffs, N.J.: Prentice-Hall, 1973, pp. 124-130.

390. Porter, Judith R., and Alexa A. Albert. "Subculture or Assimilation? A Cross-Cultural analysis of Religion and Women's Role." JSSR 16,4 (1977): 345-359.

391. Saloutos, T. "The Greek Orthodox Church in the United States and Assimilation." INTERNATIONAL MIGRATION REVIEW 7,4 (1973): 395-407.

392. Shanabruch, Charles. THE CHICAGO CATHOLIC CHURCH'S ROLE AS AN AMERICANIZER, 1893-1928. Unpublished Ph.D. dissertation, University of Chicago, 1975.

393. Sharot, Stephen. "Minority Situation and Religious Acculturation: A Comparative Analysis of Jewish Communities." COMPARATIVE STUDIES IN SOCIETY AND HISTORY 16,3 (1974): 329-354.

394. Sharot, Stephen. "Native Jewry and the Religious Anglicization of Immigrants in London: 1870-1905." JEWISH JOURNAL OF SOCIOLOGY 16,1 (1974): 39-56.

395. Woodrum, Eric, Colbert Rhodes, and Joe R. Feagin. "Japanese American Behavior: Its Types, Determinants, and Consequences." SOCIAL FORCES 58,4 (1980): 1235-1254.

Syncretism

Juxtaposition of religious elements from diverse traditions.

396. Bastide, Roger. "Contribuição ao estudo do sincretismo catolico fetichista." SOCIOLOGIA 1 (1946): 11-43.

397. Bastide, Roger. LES RELIGIONS AFRO-BRESILIENNES: CONTRIBUTION A UNE SOCIOLOGIE DES INTERPENETRATIONS DE CIVILISATIONS. Paris: Presses Universitaires de France, 1960.
THE AFRICAN RELIGIONS OF BRAZIL. TOWARD A SOCIOLOGY OF THE INTERPENETRATION OF CIVILIZATIONS, translated by Helen Sebba. Baltimore: Johns Hopkins University Press, 1978.

398. Bastide, Roger. "Une secte dahoméenne à Porto-Novo: le yehovisme." In MELANGES D'HISTOIRE DES RELIGIONS OFFERTS A H.-C. PUECH. Paris: Presses Universitaires de France, 1974, pp. 585-589.

399. Cela, Jorge. "Sincretimso afro-americano: introducción a un estudio comparativo." ESTUDIOS SOCIALES (Dominican Republic) 6 (1973): 159-172.

400. Fernandes, G. "O sincretismo gêge-nago-catolico como expresão dinamica dum sentimento de inferiordade." MEMOIRS DE L'INSTITUT FRANÇAIS d'AFRIQUE NOIRE 27 (1953): 125-126.

401. Lanternari, Vittorio. "Syncrétismes, messianismes, néo-traditionalismes. Postface à une étude des mouvements religieux de l'Afrique Noire." ARCHIVES DE SOCIOLOGIE DES RELIGIONS 19 (1965): 99-116.

402. Ortiz, Renato. "Du syncrétisme à la synthèse: Umbanda, une religion Brésilienne/From Syncretism to Synthesis: Umbanda, a Brazilian Religion." ARCHIVES DE SCIENCES SOCIALES DES RELIGIONS 20,40 (1975): 89-97.

403. Rodrigues, José Honorio. BRAZIL AND AFRICA. Berkeley: University of California Press, 1965.

404. Smith, T. Lynn. "Three Specimens of Religious Syncretism in Latin America." INTERNATIONAL REVIEW OF MODERN SOCIOLOGY 4,1 (1974): 1-18.

405. Valente, Walderman. SINCRETISMO RELIGIOSO AFRO-BRAZILEIRO. São Paulo: Cia. Editora Nacional, 1955.

Tolerance

406. Burkman, Thomas W. "The Urakami Incidents and the Struggle for Religious Toleration in Early Meiji Japan." JAPANESE JOURNAL OF RELIGIOUS STUDIES 1,2-3 (1974): 143-216.

407. Filsinger, Erik E. "Tolerance of Non-Believers: A Cross-Tabular and Log Linear Analysis of Some Religious Correlates." RRR 17,3 (1976): 232-240.

408. Mensching, Gustav. TOLERANZ UND INTOLERANZ IN DER RELIGIONSWELT. Auscklis: Societas Theologorum Universitatis Latviensis, 1953.

409. Mensching, Gustav. TOLERANZ UND WAHRHEIT IN DER RELIGION. Heidelberg: Quelle und Meyer, 1955.
TOLERANCE AND TRUTH IN RELIGION, translated and augmented in collaboration with the author by H.-J. Klimkeit. University, Alabama: University of Alabama Press, 1971.

* Smidt, Corwin, and James M. Penning. "Religious Commitment, Political Conservatism, and Political and Social Tolerance in the United States: A Longitudinal Analysis." Cited above as item 124.

410. Steiber, Steven R. "The Influence of the Religious Factor on Civil and Sacred Tolerance, 1958-71." SOCIAL FORCES 58,3 (1980): 811-832.

411. Whitt, Hugh P., and Hart M. Nelsen. "Residence, Moral Traditionalism, and Tolerance of Atheists." SOCIAL FORCES 54 (1975): 328-340.

Prejudice

Prejudice (general)

412. Allen, Russell O. RELIGION AND PREJUDICE: AN ATTEMPT TO CLARIFY THE PATTERNS OF RELATIONSHIP. Unpublished Ph.D. dissertation, University of Denver, 1965.

413. Allen, Russell O., and Bernard Spilka. "Committed and Consensual Religion: A Specification of Religion-Prejudice Relationships." JSSR 6 (1967): 191-206.

414. Allport, Gordon W. "The Religious Context of Prejudice." JSSR 5 (1966): 447-457.

415. Allport, Gordon W., James A. Gillespie, and Jacquelin Yount. "The Religious Context of Prejudice." In William A. Sadler (ed.), PERSONALITY AND RELIGION. New York: Harper and Row, 1970.

416. Allport, Gordon W., and J.M. Ross. "Personal Religious Orientation and Prejudice." JOURNAL OF PERSONALITY AND SOCIAL PSYCHOLOGY 5 (1967): 432-443.

417. Amerson, Philip A. RACISM AND SUBURBAN CONGREGATIONS. Unpublished Ph.D. dissertation, Emory University, 1976.

418. Amerson, Philip A., and Jackson W. Carroll. "The Suburban Church and Racism: Is Change Possible?" RRR 20,3 (1979): 335-349.

419. Andrewski, Stanislas. "An Economic Interpretation of Antisemitism in Eastern Europe." JEWISH JOURNAL OF SOCIOLOGY 5,2 (1963): 201-213.

420. Armatas, Phillip J. A FACTOR ANALYTIC STUDY OF PATTERNS OF RELIGIOUS BELIEF IN RELATION TO PREJUDICE. Unpublished Ph.D. dissertation, University of Denver, 1962.

421. Batson, C. Daniel. "Religion as Prosocial: Agent or Double Agent?" JSSR 15 (1976): 29-45.

422. Batson, C. Daniel, Stephen J. Naifeh, and Suzanne Pate. "Social Desirability, Religious Orientation, and Racial Prejudice." JSSR 17,1 (1978): 31-41.

423. Blum, Barbara Sandra, and John H. Mann. "The Effect of Religious Membership on Religious Prejudice." JOURNAL OF SOCIAL PSYCHOLOGY 52 (1960): 97-101.

424. Burnham, Kenneth E., John F. Connors, III, and Richard C. Leonard. "Religious Affiliation, Church Attendance, Religious Education and Student Attitudes toward Race." SA 30,4 (1969): 235-244.

425. Chalfant, H. Paul, and Charles W. Peek. "Religious Affiliation, Religiosity and Racial Prejudice: A New Look at Old Relationships." RRR 25,2 (1983): 155-161.

426. Cody, Wilson. "Extreme Religious Values and Prejudice." JOURNAL OF ABNORMAL AND SOCIAL PSYCHOLOGY 70 (1960): 312-316.

427. Crespi, F. "Impegno religioso e pregiudizio." RIVISTA DI SOCIOLOGIA 24 (1972): 109-140.

428. Cross, J.L. "The American Protective Association: A Sociological Analysis of the Periodic Literature of the Period, 1890-1900." AMERICAN CATHOLIC SOCIOLOGICAL REVIEW 10 (1949): 172-187.

429. Cygnar, Thomas E., Cardell K. Jacobson, and Donald L. Noel. "Religiosity and Prejudice: An Interdimensional Analysis." JSSR 16,2 (1977): 183-191.

430. Dever, John Preston. PREJUDICE AND RELIGIOUS TYPES: A FOCUSED STUDY OF SOUTHERN BAPTISTS (A REPLICATION). Unpublished M.A. thesis, University of Louisville, 1969.

431. Erskine, H.G. "The Polls: Religious Prejudice, Part I." PUBLIC OPINION QUARTERLY 29,3 (1965): 486-496.

432. Feagin, Joseph R. "Prejudice and Religious Types: A Focused Study of Southern Fundamentalists." JSSR 4 (1964): 3-13.

433. Feagin, Joseph R. "Prejudice, Orthodoxy, and the Social Situation." SOCIAL FORCES 44 (1965): 46-56.

434. Filippone, Vincenzo. "Riflessioni su pregiudizio e religione." RIVISTA DI SOCIOLOGIA 4 (1966): 41-52.

* Filsinger, Erik. "Tolerance of Non-Believers: A Cross-Tabular and Log Linear Analysis of Some Religious Correlates." Cited above as item 407.

435. Ford, Charles E., and Gregory Schinert. "The Relation of Ethnocentric Attitudes to Intensity of Religious Practice." JOURNAL OF EDUCATIONAL SOCIOLOGY 32 (1958): 157-162.

436. Friedrichs, Robert W. "Christians and Residential Exclusion: An Empirical Study of a Northern Dilemma." JOURNAL OF SOCIAL ISSUES 15 (1959): 14-23.

437. Friedrichs, Robert W. "Decline in Prejudice among Church-Goers Following Clergy-Led Open Housing Campaigns." JSSR 10 (1971): 152-156.

438. Glock, Charles Y., and Rodney Stark. CHRISTIAN BELIEFS AND ANTI-SEMITISM. New York: Harper, 1969.

439. Gorsuch, Richard L., and Daniel Aleshiere. "Christian Faith and Ethnic Prejudice: Review of Research." JSSR 13,3 (1974): 281-307.

440. Gregory, W. Edgar. "The Orthodoxy of the Authoritarian Personality." JOURNAL OF SOCIAL PSYCHOLOGY 45 (1957): 217-232.

441. Harris, Rosemary. PREJUDICE AND TOLERANCE IN ULSTER: A STUDY OF NEIGHBOURS AND "STRANGERS" IN A BORDER COMMUNITY. Manchester: Manchester University Press, 1972.

442. Hoge, Dean R., and Jackson Carroll. "Religiosity and Prejudice in Northern and Southern Cities." JSSR 12 (1973): 181-197.

443. Johnson, Doyle P. "Religious Commitment, Social Distance, and Authoritarianism." RRR 18,2 (1977): 99-113.

444. Klineberg, O., T. Tentori, F. Crespi, and V. Filippone-Thaulero. RELIGIONE E PREGIUDIZIO. Bologna: Cappelli, 1968.

445. Lamanna, Richard A., and J.B. Stephenson. "Religious Prejudice and Intended Voting Behavior." SA 25 (1964): 121-125.

446. Lipset, Seymour Martin. "Some Statistics on Bigotry in Voting." COMMENTARY 30 (October 1960): 286-290.

447. Liu, William T. "The Community Reference System, Religiosity, and Race Attitudes." SOCIAL FORCES 39 (1961): 324-328.

448. Loomis, Charles P., and Julian Samora. "Prejudice and Religious Activity in Mexico and the United States: A Note." SA 26 (1965): 212-216.

449. Lotz, Roy. "Another Look at the Orthodoxy-anti-Semitism Nexus." RRR 18,2 (1977): 126-133.

450. Maranell, Gary M. "An Examination of Some Religious and Political Attitude Correlates of Bigotry." SOCIAL FORCES 45 (1967): 356-362.

* Maranell, Gary M. RESPONSES TO RELIGION. STUDIES IN THE SOCIAL PSYCHOLOGY OF RELIGIOUS BELIEF. Cited above as item 4.

451. Martin, J.G., and F.W.Westie. "The Tolerant Personality." AMERICAN SOCIOLOGICAL REVIEW 24 (1959): 521-528.

452. Mauss, Armand L. MORMONISM AND MINORITIES. Unpublished Ph.D. dissertation, University of California at Berkeley, 1970.

453. Mauss, Armand L. MORMONS AND MINORITIES. Richmond, Calif.: University of California Press, 1974.

454. O'Reilly, Charles T., and Edward J. O'Reilly. "Religious Beliefs of Catholic College Students and their Attitudes toward Minorities." JOURNAL OF ABNORMAL AND SOCIAL PSYCHOLOGY 49 (1954): 378-380.

455. Petersen, Larry R., and K. Peter Takayama. "Religious Commitment and Conservatism: Toward Understanding an Elusive Relationship." SA 45,4 (1984): 354-371.

456. Petropoulos, Nicholas P. "Religion and Prejudice among Greek Americans." JSSR 18,1 (1979): 68-77.

457. Photiadis, John D., and Jeanne Biggar. "Religiosity, Education and Ethnic Distance." AMERICAN JOURNAL OF SOCIOLOGY 67,4 (1962): 127-134.

458. Prothro, E.T., and M.O. King. "A Comparison of Ethnic Attitudes of College Students and Middle Class Adults from the Same State." JOURNAL OF SOCIAL PSYCHOLOGY 36 (1952): 53-58.

459. Ray, John J., and Dianne Doratis. "Religiocentrism and Ethnocentrism: Catholic and Protestant in Australian Schools." SA 32,3 (1971): 170-179.

460. Roof, Wade Clark. "Religious Orthodoxy and Minority Prejudice: Causal Relationship or Reflection of Localistic World View?" AMERICAN JOURNAL OF SOCIOLOGY 80,3 (1974): 643-664.

461. Rosenblum, A.L. "Ethnic Prejudice as Related to Social Class and Religiosity." SOCIOLOGY AND SOCIAL RESEARCH 43 (1958): 272-275.

462. Roy, Ralph Lord. APOSTLES OF DISCORD: A STUDY OF ORGANIZED BIGOTRY AND DISRUPTION ON THE FRINGES OF PROTESTANTISM. Boston: Beacon, 1953.

463. Rymph, Raymond C., and Jeffrey K.Hadden. "The Persistence of Regionalism in Racial Attitudes of Methodist Clergy." SOCIAL FORCES 49 (1970): 41-50.

464. Sartain, James A. ATTITUDES OF PARENTS AND CHILDREN TOWARDS DESEGREGATION. Unpublished Ph.D. dissertation, Vanderbilt University, 1966.

465. Shinert, Gregory, and Charles E. Ford. "The Relation between Ethnocentric Attitudes and Intensity of Religious Practice." JOURNAL OF EDUCATIONAL SOCIOLOGY 32 (1958): 159-162.

466. Spilka, Bernard, and James F. Reynolds. "Religion and Prejudice: A Factor-Analytic Study." RRR 6,3 (1965): 163-168.

467. Spoerl, D.T. "Some Aspects of Prejudice as Affected by Religion and Education." JOURNAL OF SOCIAL PSYCHOLOGY 33 (1951): 69-76.

468. Stark, Rodney. "Through a Stained Glass Darkly: Reciprocal Protestant-Catholic Images in America." SA 25,3 (1964): 159-166.

469. Stark, Rodney. "Rokeach, Religion and Reviewers: Keeping an Open Mind." RRR 11,2 (1970): 151-155.

470. Stark, Rodney, and Charles Y. Glock. "Prejudice and the Churches." In C. Glock and Ellen Siegelman (eds.), PREJUDICE U.S.A. New York: Praeger, 1969, pp. 80-86. Also in C.Y. Glock (ed.), RELIGION IN SOCIOLOGICAL PERSPECTIVE (volume cited in item 141), pp. 88-101.

471. Stark, Rodney, Charles Y. Glock, and Harold E. Quinley. WAYWARD SHEPHERDS: PREJUDICE AND THE PROTESTANT CLERGY. New York: Harper and Row, 1971.

472. Strickland, Bonnie R., and Sallie Cone Weddell. "Religious Orientation, Racial Prejudice, and Dogmatism: A Study of Baptists and Unitarians." JSSR 11,4 (1972): 395-399.

473. Strommen, Merton P. "Religious Education and the Problem of Prejudice." RELIGIOUS EDUCATION 62 (1967): 52-59.

474. Struening, E.L. "Antidemocratic Attitudes in a Midwest University." In H.H. Remmers (ed.), ANTI-DEMOCRATIC ATTITUDES IN AMERICAN SCHOOLS. Evanston: Northwestern University Press, 1963.

475. Thompson, Robert C., Jerry B. Michel, and T. John Alexander. "Christian Orthodoxy, Authoritarianism and Prejudice." ROCKY MOUNTAIN SOCIAL SCIENCE JOURNAL 7 (1970): 117-123.

476. Vanecko, James J. "Religious Behavior and Prejudice: Some Dimensions and Specifications of the Relationship." RRR 8 (1966): 27-37.

477. Vanecko, James J. "Types of Religious Behavior and Levels of Prejudice." SA 28 (1967): 119-120.

478. Whitman, Frederick L. "Subdimensions of Religiosity and Race Prejudice." RRR 3 (1962): 166-174.

479. Wilson, W. Cody. "Extrinsic Religious Values and Prejudice." JOURNAL OF ABNORMAL AND SOCIAL PSYCHOLOGY 60 (1960): 286-288.

Sexism

480. Barrish, Gerald, and Michael R. Welch. "Student Religiosity and Discriminatory Attitudes toward Women." SA 41,1 (1980): 66-73.

* Berk, Marc. "Pluralist Theory and Church Policy Positions on Racial and Sexual Equality." Cited above as item 344.

481. Peek, Charles W. "Deficient Methods or Different Data?" SOCIAL FORCES 60,4 (1982): 1159-1167.

482. Peek, Charles W., and Sharon Brown. "Sex Prejudice among White Protestants: Like or Unlike Ethnic Prejudice?" SOCIAL FORCES 59,1 (1980): 169-185.

483. Powell, Brian, and Lala Carr Steelman. "Fundamentalism and Sexism: A Reanalysis of Peek and Brown." SOCIAL FORCES 60,4 (1982): 1154-1158.

484. Wallace, Ruth A. "Bringing Women in: Marginality in the Churches." SA 36,4 (1975): 291-303.

Reference group

A reference group is not necessarily an actual social entity; rather, it is the social category with which one compares oneself or toward which one looks for a general orientation toward the social world. Religious labels or groups can serve as a person's reference group.

485. Brooks, Mary Louise. "Religious Denominations as Reference Groups among a College Population." JSSR 7,1 (1968): 108.

486. Carrier, Hervé. "Le rôle des groupes référence dans l'intégration des attitudes religieuses." SC 8,2 (1960): 139-160. "The Role of Reference Groups in the Integration of Religious Attitudes." In Joan Brothers (ed.), READINGS IN THE SOCIOLOGY OF RELIGION. London: Pergamon, 1967.

487. Garrett, William R. "Reference Groups and Role Strains Related to Spiritual Well-Being." SA 40,1 (1979): 43-58.

Salience

Salience is a matter of how important religion is in one's everyday life.

488. Bahr, Howard M., Lois Franz Bartel, and Bruce A. Chadwick. "Orthodoxy, Activism, and the Salience of Religion." JSSR 10 (1971): 69-75.

489. Bainbridge, William Sims, and Rodney Stark. "Friendship, Religion, and the Occult: A Network Study." RRR 22,4 (1981): 313-327.

490. Currie, Raymond, Leo F. Klug, and Charles R. McCombs. "Intimacy and Saliency: Dimensions for Ordering Religious Experiences." RRR 24,1 (1982): 19-32.

491. Gibbs, David R., Samuel A. Mueller, and James R. Wood. "Doctrinal Orthodoxy, Salience, and the Consequential Dimension." JSSR 12 (1973): 33-52.

492. Hadaway, Christopher K., and Wade Clark Roof. "Religious Commitment and the Quality of Life in American Society." RRR 19,3 (1978): 295-307.

* Maranell, Gary M. "A Comparison with Other Religious Attitude Scales." Ch. 11 in RESPONSES TO RELIGION. STUDIES IN THE SOCIAL PSYCHOLOGY OF RELIGIOUS BELIEF. Volume cited above as item 4.

493. Moberg, David O. "The Salience of Religion in Everyday Life: Selected Evidence from Survey Research in Sweden and America." SA 43,3 (1982): 205-217.

494. Perkins, Richard B. TRADITIONAL RELIGIOSITY AND THE CONSEQUENTIAL DIMENSION: THE INFLUENCE OF SALIENCE AS AN ORIENTATIONAL STYLE. Unpublished Ph.D. dissertation, University of Massachusetts, 1977.

* Petersen, Larry R., and K. Peter Takayama. "Religious Commitment and Conservatism: Toward Understanding an Elusive Relationship." Cited above as item 455.

495. Putney, Snell, and Russell Middleton. "Dimensions and Correlates of Religious Ideologies." SOCIAL FORCES 39,4 (1961): 285-290.

496. Roof, Wade Clark, and Richard B. Perkins. "On Conceptualizing Salience in Religious Commitment." JSSR 14 (1975): 111-128.

497. Stark, Rodney, and Charles Y. Glock. AMERICAN PIETY: THE NATURE OF RELIGIOUS COMMITMENT. Berkeley: University of California Press, 1968.

498. Willaime, Jean-Paul. "La relégation superstructurelle des références culturelles. Essai sur le champ religieux dans les sociétés capitalistes post-industrielles." SC 24,4 (1977): 323-338.

Value

499. Adler, Franz. "The Value Concept in Sociology." AMERICAN JOURNAL OF SOCIOLOGY 62,3 (1956): 272-279.

500. Becker, Howard. "Supreme Values and the Sociologist." AMERICAN SOCIOLOGICAL REVIEW 6 (1941): 155-172.

501. Benoit, André. "Valeurs sociales transmises par l'enseignement secondaire des églises et de l'état en Colombie." SC 16,1 (1969): 29-49.

502. Brown, Sheila. "De l'adhésion à un nouveau système religieux à la transformation d'un système de valeurs: étude d'une communauté rurale africaine." SC 19,1 (1972): 83-91.

503. Del Grande, Mary Vera. A STUDY OF THE VALUES OF CATHOLIC HIGH SCHOOL STUDENTS OF DIFFERING SOCIO-ECONOMIC BACKGROUNDS AND THE RELATIONSHIP OF THESE VALUES TO THOSE OF THEIR PARENTS. Unpublished Ph.D. Dissertation, St. Louis University, 1960.

504. Faase, Thomas P. MAKING THE JESUITS MORE MODERN. Unpublished Ph.D. dissertation, Cornell University, 1977.

505. Faase, Thomas P. MAKING THE JESUITS MORE MODERN. Washington: University Press of America, 1981.

506. Faase, Thomas P. "Making Jesuits More Modern: Changing Values in a Changing Religious Order." SOCIAL ACTION 32 (1982). 65-86.

507. Faase, Thomas P. "International Differences in Value Ranking and Religious Style among Jesuits." RRR 24,1 (1982): 3-18.

508. Fitzpatrick, Joseph P. "Catholic Sociology Revisited: The Challenge of Alvin Gouldner." THOUGHT 53,209 (1978): 123-132.

509. Furfey, Paul Hanley. THE SCOPE AND METHOD OF SOCIOLOGY. New York: Harper and Row, 1953.

510. Hutcheon, Pat Duffy. "Value Theory: Towards Conceptual Clarification." BRITISH JOURNAL OF SOCIOLOGY 23,2 (1972): 172-187.

511. Johnson, Benton. "Do Holiness Sects Socialize in Dominant Values?" SOCIAL FORCES 39,4 (1961): 309-316.

512. Kluckhohn, Clyde, et al. "Values and Value Orientations in the Theory of Action." In Talcott Parsons and Edward A. Shils (eds.), TOWARD A GENERAL THEORY OF ACTION. Cambridge: Harvard University Press, 1951, pp. 388-433.

513. Kolb, William L. "Values, Positivism and the Functional Theory of Religion." SOCIAL FORCES 31 (1953): 305-311. Also in J.M. Yinger (ed.), RELIGION, SOCIETY AND THE INDIVIDUAL. New York: Macmillan, 1957, pp. 599-609.

514. Lapointe, Gérard. STRUCTURES SOCIALES ET ATTITUDES RELIGIEUSES DU DIOCESE DE SAINT-ANNE DE LA POCATIERE. Université Laval, Centre de Recherches en Sociologie Religeuse, 1967.

515. Parenti, Michael. "Political Values and Religious Cultures. Jews, Catholics and Protestants." JSSR 6,2 (1967): 259-269.

516. Parsons, Talcott. "Religious and Economic Symbolism in the Western World." In Harry M. Johnson (ed.), RELIGIOUS CHANGE AND CONTINUITY. SOCIOLOGICAL PERSPECTIVES. San Francisco: Jossey-Bass, 1979, pp. 1-48.

517. Rettig, Salomon, and Benjamin Pasamanick. "Invariance in Factor Structure of Moral Value Judgments from American and Korean College Students." SOCIOMETRY 25,1 (1962): 73-84.

518. Scheler, Max. "The Thomist Ethic and the Spirit of Capitalism." SA 25 (1964): 4-19.

519. Simey, Lord. "The Reshaping of Social Values in Developing Societies." SC 13,1 (1966): 53-68.

* Spilka, Bernard. "Religious Values and Social Compassion: A Problem in Theory and Measurement." Cited above as item 18.

520. Weima, J. "Authoritarian Personality, Anti-Catholicism and the Experience of Religious Values." SC 11,2 (1964): 13-25.

Well-being

Religious or spiritual well-being refers to the religious aspect of the quality of life.

521. Duke, James T., and Barry L. Johnson. "Spiritual Well-Being and the Consequential Dimension of Religiosity." RRR 26,1 (1984): 59-72.

* Garrett, William R. "Reference Groups and Role Strains Related to Spiritual Well-Being." Cited above as item 487.

522. Moberg, David O. (ed.) SPIRITUAL WELL-BEING. Washington: University Press of America, 1979. Contains item 617.

523. Moberg, David O. "Subjective Measures of Spiritual Well-Being." RRR 25,4 (1984): 351-364.

524. Moberg, David O., and Patricia M. Brusek. "Spiritual Well-Being: A Neglected Subject in Quality of Life Research." SOCIAL INDICATORS RESEARCH 5 (1978): 303-323.

525. St. George, Arthur, and Patrick H. McNamara. "Religion, Race and Psychological Well-Being." JSSR 23,4 (1984): 351-363.

526. Steinitz, Lucy Y. "Religiosity, Well-Being, and Weltanschauung among the Elderly." JSSR 19,1 (1980): 60-67.

527. Thorson, James A., and Thomas C. Cook, Jr. (eds.) SPIRITUAL WELL-BEING OF THE ELDERLY. Springfield, Ill.: Charles C. Thomas, 1980.

528. Wuthnow, Robert, Kevin Christiano, and John Kuzlowski. "Religion and Bereavement: A Conceptual Framework." JSSR 19,4 (1980): 408-422.

SECTION B: ROLES

A social role is a regularized or routinized complex of lines of conduct. The sociological conceptualization of roles has been embodied in what is loosely identified as "role theory." Relatively little formal role theory has been formulated in the sociology of religion; most of the entries below therefore appear under headings which identify particular religious roles: the apprentice, the bishop, etc.

Life cycle

529. Bell, Bill D. "Church Participation and the Family Life Cycle." RRR 13 (1971): 57-64.

530. Fee, Joan L., Andrew M. Greeley, William C. McCready, and Theresa A. Sullivan. YOUNG CATHOLICS. A REPORT TO THE KNIGHTS OF COLUMBUS. Los Angeles: Sadlier, 1981.

531. Fichter, Joseph H. "The Profile of Catholic Religious Life." AMERICAN JOURNAL OF SOCIOLOGY 58,2 (1952): 145-149.

532. Finner, Stephen L. "New Methods for the Sociology of Religion." SA 31,4 (1970): 197-202.

* Greeley, Andrew M. THE RELIGIOUS IMAGINATION. Cited above as item 305.

533. Nelson, Erland. "Patterns of Religious Attitude Shifts from College to Fourteen Years Later." PSYCHOLOGICAL MONOGRAPHS 70,17 (1956): 1-15.

534. Schroeder, Widick. "Age Cohorts, the Family Life Cycle, and Participation in the Voluntary Church in America: Implications for Membership Patterns, 1950-2000." THE CHICAGO THEOLOGICAL SEMINARY REGISTER 65 (1975): 13-28.

Religious roles

Apprentice

* Bird, Frederick "The Pursuit of Innocence: New Religious Movements and Moral Accountability." Cited above as item 180.

Campus ministry

535. Ennis, Joseph Guyon. THE ROLE EXPECTATION OF ROMAN CATHOLIC CAMPUS CHAPLAINS AND ROMAN CATHOLIC UNDERGRADUATES FOR THE ROMAN CATHOLIC CAMPUS CHAPLAIN. Unpublished Ph.D. dissertation, St. John's University, 1975.

536. Hammond, Phillip E. "The Campus Ministry and Academic Values. An Interpretation of Some Findings in a Questionnaire Survey." JOURNAL OF HIGHER EDUCATION 36,5 (1965): 274-278.

537. Hammond, Phillip E. THE CAMPUS CLERGYMAN. New York: Basic Books, 1966.

538. Hammond, Phillip E., and Robert E. Mitchell. "The Segmentation of Radicalism: The Case of the Protestant Campus Minister." AMERICAN JOURNAL OF SOCIOLOGY 71 (1965): 133-143.

539. Hargrove, Barbara. "Church Student Ministries and the New Consciousness." In C.Y. Glock and R.N. Bellah (eds.), THE NEW RELIGIOUS CONSCIOUSNESS (item 2407), pp. 205-226.

540. Thomas, Michael Cager. ORGANIZED RELIGION AT A STATE UNIVERSITY: A SOCIOLOGICAL ANALYSIS. Unpublished M.A. thesis, University of Alabama, 1966.

Clergy

Clergy (general)

541. Alston, Jon P., and Larry A. Platt. "Religious Humor: A Longitudinal Content Analysis of Cartoons." SA 30,4 (1969): 217-222.

542. Ammerman, Nancy Tatom. LOCALISM, SOUTHERN CULTURE, AND THE ROLE OF CLERGYMEN IN THE CIVIL RIGHTS MOVEMENT IN A SOUTHERN COMMUNITY. Unpublished M.A. thesis, University of Louisville, 1977.

543. Ammerman, Nancy T. "The Civil Rights Movement and the Clergy in a Southern Community." SA 41,4 (1981): 339-350.

544. Balswick, Jack O. "Theology and Political Attitudes among Clegymen." SOCIOLOGICAL QUARTERLY 11 (1970): 396-404.

545. Balswick, Jack O., and Gary L. Faulkner. "Identification of Ministerial Cliques. A Sociometric Approach." JSSR 9,4 (1970): 303-310.

546. Basaure Avila, Luz. "Analyse de l'attitude sociale du clergé en Amérique Latine et opinions des étudiants." SC 12,1-2 (1965): 114-120.

547. Berenson, William, Kirk W. Elifson, and Tandy Tollerson, III. "Preachers in Politics: A Study of Political Activism among the Black Ministry." JOURNAL OF BLACK STUDIES 6 (1976): 373-392.

548. Betts, George Herbert. THE BELIEFS OF 700 MINISTERS. New York: Abingdon Press, 1929.

549. Betts, George H. "Comparison of the Theological Beliefs of Ministers and Theological Students." In Leo Rosten (ed.), RELIGIONS IN AMERICA. New York: Simon and Schuster, 1955.

550. Birrell, W.D., J.E. Greer, and D.J.D. Roche. "The Political Role and Influence of the Clergy in Northern Ireland." SOCIOLOGICAL REVIEW 27,3 (1979): 491-512.

* Blaikie, Norman W.H. "Altruism in the Professions: The Case of the Clergy." Cited above as item 11.

551. Blaikie, Norman W.H. "The Use of 'Denomination' in Sociological Explanation: The Case of the Position of Clergy on Social Issues." JSSR 15 (1976): 79-86.

552. Blaikie, Norman W.H. THE PLIGHT OF THE AUSTRALIAN CLERGY: TO CONVERT, CARE OR CHALLENGE? St. Lucia: University of Queensland Press, 1979.

553. Blanchard, Dallas A. SOME SOCIAL AND ORIENTATIVE CORRELATES OF CAREER CHANGE AND CONTINUITY AS REVEALED AMONG UNITED METHODIST PASTORS OF THE ALABAMA-WEST FLORIDA CONFERENCE, 1960-1970. Unpublished Ph.D. dissertation, Boston University, 1972.

554. Blanchard, Dallas A. "Seminary Effects on Professional Role Orientations." RRR 22,4 (1981): 346-361.

555. Blizzard, Samuel W. "The Minister's Dilemma." THE CHRISTIAN CENTURY 73 (April 25, 1956): 508-510.

556. Bock, E. Wilbur. "The Female Clergy: A Case of Professional Marginality." AMERICAN JOURNAL OF SOCIOLOGY 72 (1967): 531-539.

557. Bock, E. Wilbur. "The Decline of the Negro Clergy." PHYLON 29 (1968): 48-64.

558. Bogan, R.V. THE LIFE WORLDS OF PRIESTS. A STUDY OF RECENTLY ORDAINED ROMAN CATHOLIC PRIESTS. M. Phil. thesis, University of Surrey, 1976.

559. Bonifield, William C. "The Minister in the Labor Market." In Phillip E. Hammond and Benton Johnson (eds.), AMERICAN MOSAIC. SOCIAL PATTERNS OF RELIGION IN THE UNITED STATES. New York: Random House, 1970, pp. 209-220.

560. Bonifield, William C., and Edgar W. Mills. "The Clergy Labor Markets and Wage Determination." JSSR 19,2 (1980): 146-158.

561. Bonn, Robert L., and Ruth T. Doyle. "Secularly Employed Clergy." JSSR 13,3 (1974): 325-343.

562. Boulard, Fernand. ESSOR OU DECLIN DU CLERGE FRANÇAIS. Paris: du Cerf, 1947.

563. Bradfield, Cecil D., and R. Ann Myers. "Clergy and Funeral Directors: An Exploration in Role Conflict." RRR 21,3 (1980): 343-350.

564. Braude, L. "The Rabbi: Some Notes on Identity Clash." JEWISH SOCIAL STUDIES 22,1 (1960): 43-52.

565. Broughton, Walter, and Edgar W. Mills,Jr. "Resource Inequality and Accumulative Advantage: Stratification in the Ministry." SOCIAL FORCES 58,4 (1980): 1289-1301.

566. Brown, R.E., and Joseph H. Fichter. "The Changing Face of the Priesthood." AMERICA 10 (1972): 531-534..

567. Bunnik, R.J. "The Ecclesiastical Minister and Marriage: An Attempt at Clarification." SC 12,1-2 (1965): 53-100.

568. Burch, Genevieve. CAREER CHANGE OF CLERGY TO SECULAR OCCUPATIONS: DEVELOPMENT OF A THEORETICAL FRAMEWORK. Unpublished M.A. thesis, University of Maryland, 1969.

569. Burgalassi, Silvano. PRETI IN CRISI? TENDENZE SOCIOLOGICHE DEL CLERO ITALIANO. Fossano: Esperienze, 1970.

570. Burgalassi, Silvano. "Situazione e problemi del clero rurale italiano." PRESENZA PASTORALE 10-11 (1974): 875-880.

571. Campbell, Ernest Q., and Thomas F. Pettigrew. "Racial and Moral Crisis: The Role of Little Rock Ministers." AMERICAN JOURNAL OF SOCIOLOGY 64 (1959): 509-516.

572. Campbell, Ernest Q., and Thomas F. Pettigrew. CHRISTIANS IN RACIAL CRISIS: A STUDY OF LITTLE ROCK'S MINISTRY. Washington: Public Affairs Press, 1959.

573. Campos, G.G. "La révolte du clergé en Amérique Latine." HOMME ET SOCIETE 17 (1970): 183-208.

574. Carey, Raymond G. DETERMINANTS OF MORALE OF THE ROMAN CATHOLIC DIOCESAN PRIESTS OF THE ARCHDIOCESE OF CHICAGO. Unpublished Ph.D. dissertation, Loyola University of Chicago, 1971.

575. Carlin, Jerome E., and Saul H. Mendlovitz. "The American Rabbi: A Religious Specialist Responds to Loss of Authority." In M. Sklare (ed.), THE JEWS: SOCIAL PATTERNS OF AN AMERICAN GROUP. Glencoe, Ill.: Free Press, 1958, 1960.

576. Carroll, Jackson W. "Structural Effects of Professional Schools on Professional Socialization: The Case of Protestant Clergymen." SOCIAL FORCES 50 (1971): 61-74.

577. Carroll, Jackson W., and Robert L. Wilson. "Clergy Supply and Demand: Research in Progress." THEOLOGICAL EDUCATION 13,2 (1977): 107-117.

578. Carroll, Jackson W., and Robert L. Wilson. TOO MANY PASTORS? New York: Pilgrim, 1980.

579. Carron, Juan. "El cambio social y el clero en el Paraguay." REVISTA PARAGUAYA DE SOCIOLOGIA 4 (1967): 129-132.

580. Carsh, Henry. DIMENSIONS OF MEANING AND VALUE IN A SAMPLE OF FAIRY TALES. Unpublished doctoral dissertation, Princeton University, 1965.

581. Carsh, Henry. "The Role of the Clergy in a Sample of Fairy Tales." SC 13 (1966): 431-438.

582. Clarke, P.B. "The Imam of Ismailis." In Michael Hill (ed.), A SOCIOLOGICAL YEARBOOK OF RELIGION IN BRITAIN 8. London: SCM, 1975, pp. 123-318.

583. Coates, Charles H., and Robert C. Kistler. "Protestant Clergymen in a Metropolitan Community." RRR 6 (1965): 147-152.

584. Comfort, R.O. "Survey of Activities and Training of Selected Rural Ministers in the U.S." RURAL SOCIOLOGY 12,4 (1947): 375-387.

585. Cooper, Charles W., Jr. "United Church of Christ Pastors: A Demographic and Psychographic Description" RRR 13 (1972): 212-218.

586. Costa, Ricardo. RECUPERATION DU POUVOIR ET PRODUCTION DE CONNAISSANCE DANS LE CLERGE D'AMERIQUE LATINE (1966-1970). Paris: Centre Lebret, 1972.

587. Costa, Ricardo. "Le problème des 'médiations' en sociologie de la connaissance. A propos des documents du clergé latino-américain (1966-1970)." ARCHIVES DE SCIENCES SOCIALES DES RELIGIONS 37 (1974): 43-77.

588. Costa, Ricardo. FRONTIERES DU SENS, FRONTIERES DU POUVOIR. LE DISCOURS DU CLERGE D'AMERIQUE LATINE, 1966-1970. Paris: Centre Lebret, 1974.

589. Cryns, Arthur G. "Dogmatism of Catholic Clergy and Ex-Clergy: A Study of Ministerial Role Perseverance and Open-Mindedness." JSSR 9,3 (1970): 239-244.

590. Cusack, Andrew. JOB SATISFACTION AND PERSONALITY CHARACTERISTICS OF THE DIOCESAN PRIESTHOOD OF THE STATE OF CONNECTICUT. Unpublished Ph.D. dissertation, St. John's University, New York, 1973.

591. Dahm, Karl-Wilhelm. PFARRER UND POLITIK. SOZIALE POSITION UND POLITISCHE MENTALITAT DES DEUTSCHEN EVANGELISCHEN PFARRERSTANDES ZWISCHEN 1918 UND 1933. Band 29 der DORTMUNDER SCHRIFTEN ZUR SOZIALFORSCHUNG. Köln and Opladen: Westdeutscher Verlag, 1965.

592. Daniel, M. "Catholic, Evangelical and Liberal in the Anglican Priesthood." In D.A. Martin (ed.), A SOCIOLOGICAL YEARBOOK OF RELIGION IN BRITAIN 1. London: SCM, 1968, pp. 115-123.

* Davis, N.J. "Clergy Abortion Brokers: A Transactional Analysis of Social Movement Development." Cited above as item 198.

593. Dellepoort, J., N. Greinacher, and W. Menges. DIE DEUTSCHE PRIESTERFRAGE. EINE SOZIOLOGISCHE UNTERSUCHUNG UBER KLERUS UND PRIESTERNACHWUCHS IN DEUTSCHLAND. Mainz: Matthias Grünwald, 1961.

594. Dellepoort, J., N. Greinacher, and W. Menges. "Le problème sacerdotal en Europe occidentale." SC 8,5 (1961): 425-445.

595. Dempsey, K. "Secularization and the Protestant Clergy." AUSTRALIAN AND NEW ZEALAND JOURNAL OF SOCIOLOGY 9,3 (1973): 46-50.

596. Dewey, Gerald J. INCONGRUITY AND CONFLICT IN THE PASTORAL ROLE OF THE CATHOLIC PRIEST: AN INVESTIGATION OF SOCIAL CHANGE. Unpublished doctoral dissertation, University of Notre Dame, 1967.

597. Dittes, James E. "Research on Clergymen: Factors Influencing Decisions for Religious Service and Effectiveness in the Vocation." RELIGIOUS EDUCATION 57,4 (1962): 141-165.

598. Donovan, John D. THE CATHOLIC PRIEST. Unpublished Ph.D. dissertation, Harvard University, 1951.

599. Donovan, John D. "The American Catholic Hierarchy: A Social Profile." AMERICAN CATHOLIC SOCIOLOGICAL REVIEW 19 (1958): 98-122.

600. Dowdy, Edwin, and Gillian Lupton. "The Clergy and Organised Religion." In P. Boreham et al. (eds.), THE PROFESSIONS IN AUSTRALIA. St. Lucia: University of Queensland Press, 1976.

601. Driedger, Leo, and William H. Form. "Religious Typology and the Social Ideology of the Clergy." INTERNATIONAL JOURNAL OF COMPARATIVE SOCIOLOGY 17,1-2 (1976): 1-18.

602. Dubach, Alfred T. "Entre la résistence et l'adaptation: situation professionnelle du prêtre en Suisse." SC 12,2 (1972): 291-299.

603. Dudley, Roger L., and Des Cummings, Jr. "Factors Related to Pastoral Morale in the Seventh-Day Adventist Church." RRR 24,2 (1982): 127-137.

604. Duncan, H.G. "Reactions of Ex-Ministers toward the Ministry." JOURNAL OF RELIGION 12 (1932): 100-115.

605. Eisenstadt, Shmuel N. "The Axial Age: The Emergence of Transcendental Visions and the Rise of Clerics." ARCHIVES EUROPEENNES DE SOCIOLOGIE 23,2 (1982): 294-314.

* Elifson, Kirk W., and Joseph Irwin. "Black Ministers' Attitudes toward Population Size and Birth Control." Cited above as item 247.

606. Evans, R.H. "Parish Priests, Political Power and Decision-Making: An Italian Case." AMERICAN BEHAVIORAL SCIENTIST 17,6 (1974): 813-826.

607. Evjen, Rudolph. A STUDY OF THE ATTITUDE OF CLERGYMEN OF ALL DENOMINATIONS TOWARD SOCIAL WORK IN GENERAL AND THE COMMUNITY CHEST IN PARTICULAR IN COLUMBUS. Unpublished M.A. thesis, Ohio State University, 1936.

608. Ference, Thomas P., Fred H. Goldner, and Richard R. Ritti. "Priests and Church: The Professionalization of an Organization." AMERICAN BEHAVIORAL SCIENTIST 14 (1971): 507-524.

609. Fichter, Joseph H. "The Religious Professional." RRR 1,3-4 (1960): 89-101, 150-170.

610. Fichter, Joseph H. RELIGION AS AN OCCUPATION. Notre Dame: University of Notre Dame Press, 1961.

611. Fichter, Joseph H. "A Comparative View of the Parish Priest." ARCHIVES DE SOCIOLOGIE DES RELIGIONS 16 (1963): 44-48.

612. Fichter, Joseph H. PRIEST AND PEOPLE. New York: Sheed and Ward, 1965.

613. Fichter, Joseph H. AMERICA'S FORGOTTEN PRIESTS. New York: Harper and Row, 1968.

614. Fichter, Joseph H. "The Myth of the Hyphenated Clergy." THE CRITIC 27,3 (Dec. 1968 - Jan. 1969): 16-24.

615. Fichter, Joseph H. "Catholic Church Professionals." THE ANNALS 387 (1970): 77-85.

616. Fichter, Joseph H. ORGANIZATION MAN IN THE CHURCH. Cambridge, Massachusetts: Schenckman, 1974.

617. Fichter, Joseph H. "Super-Saints and Mini-Saints." In David O. Moberg (ed.), SPIRITUAL WELL-BEING. SOCIOLOGICAL PERSPECTIVES (item 522), pp. 255-263.

618. Fichter, Joseph H. THE REHABILITATION OF CLERGY ALCOHOLICS. ARDENT SPIRITS SUBDUED. New York: Human Sciences Press, 1982.

619. Fichter, Joseph H. "The Myth of Clergy Burnout." SA 45,4 (1984): 373-382.

620. Fukuyama, Yoshio. THE MINISTRY IN TRANSITION: A CASE STUDY OF THEOLOGICAL EDUCATION. University Park, Pa.: The Pennsylvania State University Press, 1972.

621. Gannon, Thomas M. THE INTERNAL SOCIAL ORGANIZATION AND BELIEF SYSTEM OF AMERICAN PRIESTS. Unpublished Ph.D. dissertation, University of Chicago, 1972.

622. Gannon, Thomas M. "The Impact of Structural Differences on the Catholic Clergy." JSSR 18,4 (1979): 350-362.

623. Gannon, Thomas M. "Catholic Religious Orders in Sociological Perspective." In Ross P. Scherer (ed.), AMERICAN DENOMINATIONAL ORGANIZATION. A SOCIOLOGICAL VIEW (item 1172), pp. 159-193.

624. Gaudet, R. "Canadian Priest in Profile." AMERICA 126,10 (1972): 258-260.

625. Germain-Brodeur, Elisabeth. LE CLERGE CATHOLIQUE DU CANADA, 1969-1971. Québec: Centre de Recherches en Sociologie Religieuse, 1973.

626. Gessner, John Conrad. PRIESTLY PERSISTERS AND RESIGNERS: TESTING A FRAMEWORK OF OCCUPATIONAL CHOICE. Unpublished M.A. thesis, University of Notre Dame, 1973.

627. Glock, Charles Y., and Benjamin Ringer. "Church Policy and the Attitudes of Ministers on Social Issues." AMERICAN SOCIOLOGICAL REVIEW 21 (1956): 148-156. Reprinted as Ch. 12 in Charles Y. Glock and Rodney Stark, RELIGION AND SOCIETY IN TENSION (volume cited in item 141).

628. Goldner, Fred H., Thomas P. Ference, and Richard R. Ritti. "Priests and Laity: A Profession in Transition." SOCIOLOGICAL REVIEW. Monograph 20 (1973): 119-137.

629. Goldner, Fred H., Richard R. Ritti, and Thomas P. Ference. "The Production of Cynical Knowledge in Organizations." AMERICAN SOCIOLOGICAL REVIEW 42,4 (1977): 539-551.

630. Goussidis, Alexandre. "Analyse statistique et sociographique des ordinations dans l'Eglise de Grèce entre 1950 et 1969." SC 22,1 (1975): 107-148.

631. Greeley, Andrew M. "Priest, Church and the Future from a Sociological Viewpoint." CHICAGO STUDIES (1971): 115-129.

632. Greeley, Andrew M. THE CATHOLIC PRIEST IN THE UNITED STATES: SOCIOLOGICAL INVESTIGATIONS. Washington: U.S. Catholic Conference, 1971.

633. Greeley, Andrew M. PRIESTS IN THE UNITED STATES: REFLECTIONS ON A SURVEY. New York: Doubleday, 1972.

* Greeley, Andrew M. "The Sexual Revolution among Catholic Clergy." Cited above as item 304.

634. Greeley, Andrew M. THE AMERICAN CATHOLIC. A SOCIAL PORTRAIT. New York: Basic Books, 1977.

635. Griffin, James. AN INVESTIGATION OF THE WORK SATISFACTION OF PRIESTS OF THE ARCHDIOCESE OF BOSTON. Unpublished Ph.D. dissertation, Boston College, 1970.

636. Gustafson, James M. "The Clergy in the United States." DAEDALUS 92 (1963): 724-743. Also in SC 12,1 (1965): 35-52; and in Kenneth S. Lynn (ed.), THE PROFESSIONS IN AMERICA. Boston: Houghton-Mifflin, 1965, pp. 70-90.

637. Guth, James L. "Southern Baptist Clergy: Vanguard of the Christian Right?" In Robert C. Liebman and Robert Wuthnow (eds.), THE NEW CHRISTIAN RIGHT. Hawthorne, New York: Aldine, 1983, pp. 117-130.

638. Guth, James L. "The Politics of Preachers: Southern Baptist Ministers and Christian Right Activism." In David G. Bromley and Anson Shupe (eds.), NEW CHRISTIAN POLITICS (item 100), pp. 235-249.

639. Hadden, Jeffrey K. "A Study of the Protestant Ministry in America." JSSR 5,1 (1965): 10-23.

640. Hadden, Jeffrey K. THE GATHERING STORM IN THE CHURCHES: THE WIDENING GAP BETWEEN CLERGY AND LAYMEN. Garden City: Doubleday, 1969.

641. Haimes, Peter, and Mavis Hetherington. "Attitudes of the Clergy toward Behavior Problems of Children." JOURNAL OF SOCIAL PSYCHOLOGY 62 (1964): 329-334.

642. Hall, Douglas T., and Benjamin Schneider. ORGANIZATIONAL CLIMATES AND CAREERS. THE WORK LIVES OF PRIESTS. New York: Seminar Press, 1973.

643. Hamelin, Louis-Edmond. "Evolution numérique séculaire du clergé catholique dans le Québec." RECHERCHES SOCIOGRAPHIQUES 2,2 (1961): 189-241.

* Hammond, Phillip E. "The Campus Ministry and Academic Values. An Interpretation of Some Findings in a Questionnaire Survey." Cited above as item 536.

* Hammond, Phillip E. THE CAMPUS CLERGYMAN. Cited above as item 537.

644. Hargrove, Barbara. "Ministers at the Margin." In C.Y. Glock and R. Bellah (eds.), THE NEW RELIGIOUS CONSCIOUSNESS (volume cited in item 539).

645. Hassinger, Edward W., J. Kenneth Benson, James H. Dorsett, and John S. Holik. "Ministers in Rural Churches of Missouri." In John D. Photiadis (ed.), RELIGION IN APPALACHIA. Morgantown, West Virginia: Center for Extension and Continuing Education, Division of Social and Economic Development, Office of Research and Development, West Virginia University, 1978, pp. 359-393.

646. Henriot, Peter J. "The Coincidence of Political and Religious Attitudes." RRR 8 (1966): 50-58.

647. Hesser, Gary W. "Organizational Dilemmas of Religious Professionals (or, 'I Never Promised You A Rose Garden')." In Ross P. Scherer (ed.), AMERICAN DENOMINATIONAL ORGANIZATION. A SOCIOLOGICAL VIEW. Pasadena, California: William Carey Library, 1980, pp. 262-290.

648. Hicks, Thomas H. "A Study of the Background, Level of Job Satisfaction, Maturity, and Morale of 'Delayed Vocation' Catholic Priests." RRR 22,4 (1981): 328-345.

649. Higgins, Edward. "Les rôles religieux dans le contexte multi-racial sud-african: le profil du ministère dans le calvinisme et le catholicisme." SC 19,1 (1972): 29-47.

650. Hirikoshi, Hiroko. "Islamic Scholasticism, Social Conflicts and Political Power." SC 31,1 (1984): 75-89.

651. Hoge, Dean R., and John E. Dyble. "The Influence of Assimilation on American Protestant Ministers' Beliefs, 1928-1978." JSSR 20,1 (1981): 64-77.

652. Hoge, Dean R., John E. Dyble, and David T. Polk. "Organizational and Situational Influences on Vocational Commitment of Protestant Ministers." RRR 23,2 (1981): 133-149.

653. Holland, J.B., and Charles P. Loomis. "Goals of Rural Ministers." SOCIOMETRY 11,3 (1948): 217-229.

654. Hoonaert, Eduardo. "O padre Católico, visto, pelos indigenas do Brasil e do Maranhão." REVISTA ECLESIASTICA BRASILEIRA 36,142 (1976): 347-364.

655. Houtart, François. "The City and the Priests." SOCIAL ORDER 5,4 (1955): 169-174.

656. Humphreys, Claire. "Structural Inconsistency and Vocation-Related Tension." RRR 16,1 (1974): 31-40.

657. Jeffries, Vincent, and Clarence E. Tygart. "More on Clergy and Social Issues." JSSR 13,3 (1974): 309-324.

658. Jiminez Cadeña, Gustavo. THE ROLE OF THE RURAL PARISH PRIEST AS AN AGENT OF SOCIAL CHANGE IN CENTRAL COLOMBIA. Unpublished Ph.D. dissertation, University of Wisconsin, 1965.
SACERDOTE Y CAMBIO SOCIAL. ESTUDIO SOCIOLOGO EN LOS ANDES COLOMBIANOS. Bogotá: Ediciones Tercer Mundo, 1967.

659. Johnson, Benton. "Theology and Party Preference among Protestant Clergymen." AMERICAN SOCIOLOGICAL REVIEW 31 (1966): 200-208.

660. Johnson, Benton. "Theology and the Position of Pastors on Public Issues." AMERICAN SOCIOLOGICAL REVIEW 32 (1967): 433-442.

661. Johnstone, Ronald L. "Negro Preachers Take Sides." RRR 11 (1969): 81-89.

662. Jud, Gerald J., Edgar W. Mills, Jr., and Genevieve Walters Burch. EX-PASTORS: WHY MEN LEAVE THE PARISH MINISTRY. Philadelphia: Pilgrim Press, 1970.

663. Kaiser, Marvin Anthony. A STUDY OF ROMAN CATHOLIC DIOCESAN PRIESTS: A SOCIOLOGICAL ANALYSIS. Unpublished Ph.D. dissertation, University of Nebraska, Lincoln, 1979.

664. Kauffmann, Michel. "Regard statistique sur les prêtres qui quittent le ministère." SC 17,4 (1970): 495-502.

665. Keller, H.E. DIE SOZIOLOGISCHE HERKUNFT DER KATHOLISCHEN PFARRER IN DER DIOZESE WÜRZBURG DER GEGENWART. Würzburg, 1939.

666. Kelly, H.E. "Role Satisfaction of the Catholic Priest." SOCIAL FORCES 50 (1971): 75-84.

667. Kelly, James R. "The Spirit of Ecumenism: How Wide, How Deep, How Mindful of Truth?" RRR 20,2 (1978): 180-194.

668. Kerkhofs, J. "Demography of the Priesthood." PERSPECTIVES 5 (1960): 30-31.

669. Kiernan, James. FRAGMENTED PRIEST. Durban: Unity Publications, 1970.

670. King, H., and J.C. Baylor. "Mortality among Lutheran Clergymen." MILBANK MEMORIAL FUND QUARTERLY 3 (1968): 155-163.

671. King, H., and J.C. Baylor. "The Health of the Clergy. A Review of Demographic Literature." DEMOGRAPHY 1 (1969): 27-43.

672. Kirsten, Lawrence K. THE LUTHERAN ETHIC: THE IMPACT OF RELIGION ON LAYMEN AND CLERGY. Detroit: Wayne State University Press, 1970.

673. Koller, Norman B., and Joseph D. Retzer. "The Sounds of Silence Revisited." SA 41,2 (1980): 155-161. Also in Jeffrey K. Hadden and Theodore E. Long (eds.), RELIGION AND RELIGIOSITY IN AMERICA (volume cited in item 110), pp. 89-98.

674. Koval, John, and Robert Bell. A STUDY OF PRIESTLY CELIBACY. Chicago: National Federation of Priests' Councils, 1970.

675. Larson, Richard F. "Psychiatric Orientations of a Selected Sample of New England Clergy." MENTAL HYGIENE 49,3 (1965): 341-346.

676. Larson, Richard F. "Social and Cultural Characteristics of a Selected Sample of New England Clergymen." RRR 6 (1965): 131-137.

677. Larson, Richard F. "Clergymen's Subjective Feelings of Competence when Dealing with Emotionally Disturbed People." RRR 10,3 (1969): 140-150.

678. Lauer, Robert H. "Organizational Punishment: Punitive Relations in a Voluntary Association." HUMAN RELATIONS 26,2 (1973): 189-202.

* Lazerine, Neil G. PROFESSIONAL PERSPECTIVES ON EUTHANASIA: A COMPARATIVE STUDY OF NURSES AND CLERGYMEN. Cited above as item 262.

679. Leat, Diana. "Putting God Over: The Faithful Counselors." SOCIOLOGICAL REVIEW 21,4 (1973): 561-572.

680. Lehman, Edward C., Jr. PROJECT SWIM: A STUDY OF WOMEN IN MINISTRY. Valley Forge, Pennsylvania: The Ministers Council, American Baptist Churches, 1979.

681. Lehman, Edward C., Jr. "Patterns of Lay Resistance to Women in Ministry." SA 41,4 (1981): 317-338.

682. Lehman, Edward C., Jr. "Organizational Resistance to Women in Ministry." SA 42,2 (1981): 101-118.

683. Lennon, James, et al. "Survey of Catholic Clergy and Religious Personnel." SOCIAL STUDIES 1,2 (1972): 137-143.

684. Lennon, James, et al. "Survey of Diocesan Clergy." SOCIAL STUDIES 1,2 (1972): 144-158.

685. Linblade, Zondra Gale. PATTERN-MAINTENANCE AND INTEGRATION WITHIN A NORMATIVE ORGANIZATION: THE ROMAN CATHOLIC PRIESTHOOD IN THE UNITED STATES. Unpublished Ph.D. dissertation, Loyola University of Chicago, 1976.

686. Longino, Charles F., Jr., and Jeffrey K. Hadden. "Dimensionality of Belief among Mainstream Protestant Clergy." SOCIAL FORCES 55,1 (1976): 30-42.

687. Longino, Charles F., Jr., and Gay C. Kitson. "Parish Clergy and the Aged: Examining Stereotypes." JOURNAL OF GERONTOLOGY 31,3 (1976): 333-339.

688. Madden, James. AN EXPLORATORY STUDY OF THE JOB SATISFACTION OF DIOCESAN PRIESTS. Unpublished Ph.D. dissertation, University of Notre Dame, 1973.

* Maranell, Gary M. RESPONSES TO RELIGION. STUDIES IN THE SOCIAL PSYCHOLOGY OF RELIGIOUS BELIEF. Cited above as item 4.

689. Martin, David. A GENERAL THEORY OF SECULARIZATION. New York: Harper, 1978, pp. 278-308.

690. McNamara, Patrick H. "Social Action Priests in the Mexican American Community." SA 29,4 (1968): 177-185.

691. Mills, Edgar W. "Career Change in the Protestant Ministry." MINISTRY STUDIES 3 (1969): 5-21.

692. Mills, Edgar, and Garry Hesser. "A Contemporary Portrait of Clergymen." In G. Bucher and P. Hill (eds.), CONFUSION AND HOPE. Philadelphia: Fortress, 1974.

693. Mills, Edgar W., and John P. Koval. STRESS IN THE MINISTRY. Washington: Ministry Studies Board, 1971.

694. Mitchell, Robert Edward. MINISTER-PARISHIONER RELATIONS. Unpublished Ph.D. dissertation, Columbia University, 1962.

695. Mitchell, Robert Edward. "When Ministers and their Parishioners have Different Social Class Position." RRR 7 (1965): 28-41.

696. Mitchell, Robert E. "Age and the Ministry. Consequences for Minister-Parishioner and Minister-Minister Relations." RRR 8,3 (1967): 166-175.

697. Montezemolo, M.E. "Una ricerca pilota sui vescovi italiani." CRITICA SOCIOLOGICA 20 (1971): 61-81.

698. Moore, E.H., and C. Mammer. "Ministers in Retirement." SOCIOLOGY AND SOCIAL RESEARCH 32 (1948): 920-927.

699. Moore, John. "The Catholic Priesthood." In M. Hill (ed.), A SOCIOLOGICAL YEARBOOK OF RELIGION IN BRITAIN 8. London: SCM, 1975, pp. 30-60.

* Moore, Maurice J. DEATH OF A DOGMA? THE AMERICAN CATHOLIC CLERGY'S VIEWS OF CONTRACEPTION. Cited above as item 252.

700. Moran, Robert E. "Liturgy, Authority and Tradition. Priestly Attitudes and the Age Factor." RRR 10,1 (1969): 73-80.

701. Morgan, D.H.J. "The Social and Educational Background of Anglican Bishops." BRITISH JOURNAL OF SOCIOLOGY 20 (1969): 295-310.

702. Naegele, K.D. "Clergymen, Teachers and Psychiatrists: A Study in Roles and Socialization." CANADIAN JOURNAL OF ECONOMICS AND POLITICAL SCIENCE 22 (1956): 46-62.

* Nagi, Mostafa, M.D. Pugh, and Neil G. Lazerine. "Attitudes of Catholic and Protestant Clergy toward Euthanasia." Cited above as item 263.

703. Nauss, Allen H., and Harry G. Coiner. "The First Parish Placement: Stayers and Movers." RRR 12 (1971): 95-101.

704. Neal, Marie Augusta. VALUES AND INTERESTS IN SOCIAL CHANGE. Englewood Cliffs: Prentice-Hall, 1965.

705. Neal, Marie Augusta, and M. Clasby. "Priests' Attitudes toward Women." In W.C. Bier (ed.), WOMEN IN MODERN LIFE. New York: Fordham University Press, 1968.

706. Nelsen, Hart M. "Why do Pastors Preach on Social Issues?" THEOLOGY TODAY 32 (1975): 56-73.

707. Nelsen, Hart M., and Robert F. Everett. "Impact of Church Size on Clergy Role and Career." RRR 18,1 (1976): 62-73.

708. Nelsen, Hart M., and Mary Ann Maguire. "The Two Worlds of Clergy and Congregation: Dilemmas for Mainline Denominations." SA 41,1 (1980): 74-80.

709. Newman, Jeremiah. "The Priests of Ireland: A Socio-Religious Survey. 1: Numbers and Distribution. 2: Patterns of Vocations." IRISH ECCLESIASTICAL RECORD 98,1 (1962): 1-27; 98,2 (1962): 65-91.

710. Nieves, Alvar. CORRELATES OF CLERGY COMMITMENT: THE SALVATION ARMY OFFICERS, AN ILLUSTRATIVE CASE STUDY. Unpublished Ph.D. dissertation, Virginia Polytechnic Institute and State University, 1977.

711. O'Donovan, Thomas R., and Arthur X. Deegan. "Some Career Determinants of Church Executives." SOCIOLOGY AND SOCIAL RESEARCH 48 (1963): 58-68.

712. O'Donovan, T.R., and A.X. Deegan. "A Comparative Study of the Orientations of a Selected Group of Church Executives." SOCIOLOGY AND SOCIAL RESEARCH 48 (1964): 330-339.

713. Peachey, Paul. "Radicalization of the Religious Idiom and the Social Dislocation of the Clergy." ANGLICAN THEOLOGICAL REVIEW 55,3 (1973): 277-289.

714. Perez Ramirez, Gustavo, and Yván Labelle. EL PROBLEMA SACERDOTAL EN AMERICA LATINA. ESTUDIOS SOCIO-RELIGIOSOS LATINO-AMERICANOS 16. Fribourg and Bogotá: FERES, 1964.

715. Perez Ramirez, Gustavo, and Isaac Wust. LA IGLESIA EN COLOMBIA. Freiburg: FERES, 1961.

716. Peterson, Robert W. STATUS ATTAINMENT PROCESSES IN RELIGIOUS ORGANIZATIONS. Unpublished Ph.D. dissertation, University of Wisconsin-Madison, 1976.

717. Peterson, Robert W., and Richard A. Schoenherr. "Organizational Status Attainment of Religious Professionals." SOCIAL FORCES 56,3 (1978): 794-822.

718. Pickering, W.S.F., and J.L. Blanchard. TAKEN FOR GRANTED: A SURVEY OF THE PARISH CLERGY OF THE ANGLICAN CHURCH OF CANADA. Toronto: The General Synod of the Anglican Church of Canada, 1967.

719. Pin, Emile. "The Priestly Function in Crisis," translated by John Drury. In Karl Rahner (ed.), THE IDENTITY OF THE PRIEST. New York: Paulist Press, 1969, 45-58.

720. Poblete Barth, Renato. CRISIS SACERDOTAL. Santiago de Chile: Ed. del Pacifico, 1965.

721. Poblete Barth, Renato. EL SACERDOTE CHILEÑO. ESTUDIO SOCIOLOGICO. Santiago: Centro Belarmino, Departamento de Investigaciones Socioculturales, 1971.

722. Poeisz, J.J. "The Priests of the Dutch Church Province. Number and Functions." SC 14 (1967): 233-253.

723. Ponce Garcia, J., and O. Uzin Fernandes. EL CLERO EN BOLIVIA, 1968. Cuernavaca, México: Centro Intercultural de Documentación, 1970.

724. Potel, Julien. LE CLERGE FRANÇAIS. Paris: Ed. du Centurion, 1967.

* Potvin, Raymond H. "Role Uncertainty and Commitment among Seminary Faculty." Cited above as item 36.

* Price-Bonham, Sharon, Barbara Santes, and John M. Bonham. "An Analysis of Clergymen's Attitudes toward Abortion." Cited above as item 223.

* Quinley, Harold E. "Hawks and Doves among the Clergy: Protestant Reaction to the War in Vietnam." Cited above as item 287.

* Quinley, Harold E. "The Protestant Clergy and the War in Vietnam." Cited above as item 288.

* Quinley, Harold E. THE PROPHETIC CLERGY. SOCIAL ACTIVISM AMONG PROTESTANT MINISTERS. Cited above as item 289.

725. Ranson, Stewart, Alan Bryman, and Bob (C.R.) Hinings. CLERGY, MINISTERS, AND PRIESTS. Boston: Routledge and Kegan Paul, 1977.

726. Reidy, M.T.V., and L.C. White. "The Measurement of Traditionalism among Roman Catholic Priests: An Exploratory Study." BRITISH JOURNAL OF SOCIOLOGY 28,2 (1977): 226-241.

727. Remond, R. "L'évolution du comportement des prêtres en matière politique." In R. Metz and J. Schlick (eds.), POLITIQUE ET FOI. Strasbourg: Cerdic, 1972, pp. 80-100.

728. Rendtorff, Trutz. DER PFARRER IN DER MODERNEN GESELLSCHAFT. Hamburg: Furche Verlag, 1960.

729. Ritti, Richard R., Thomas P. Ference, and Fred H. Goldner. "Professions and their Plausibility: Priests, Work, and Belief Systems." SOCIOLOGY OF WORK AND OCCUPATIONS 1,1 (1974): 24-51.

730. Roberts, H.W. "The Rural Negro Minister: His work and Salary." RURAL SOCIOLOGY 12 (1947): 285-295.

731. Roberts, H.W. "The Rural Negro Minister: His Personal and Social Characteristics." SOCIAL FORCES 27,3 (1949): 291-300.

732. Roche, D.J.D., W.D. Birrell, and J.E. Greer. "A Socio-Political Opinion Profile of Clergymen in Northern Ireland." SOCIAL STUDIES. IRISH JOURNAL OF SOCIOLOGY 4,2 (1975): 143-151.

733. Roche de Coppens, P. "The Worker-Priest Movement: An Essay on the Emergence, Growth and Waning of the Worker-Priests in France and of the Sociocultural Factors that Lay behind it." REVISTA INTERNACIONAL DE SOCIOLOGIA 31,5-6 (1973): 215-238.

734. Rochte, Frederick C. DEPARTURE FROM THE PASTORATE: A STUDY OF SOUTHERN BAPTIST MINISTERS. Unpublished M.A. thesis, Wake Forest University, 1967.

735. Rodehaver, M.W. "Ministers on the Move: A Study of Mobility in Church Leadership." RURAL SOCIOLOGY 13,4 (1948): 400-410.

736. Rodehaver, M.W., and Luke M. Smith. "Migration and Occupational Structure: The Clergy." SOCIAL FORCES 29,4 (1951): 416-421.

737. Rousseau, André. "Le jeune clergé des années 70." ACTES DES RECHERCHES EN SCIENCES SOCIALES 44-45 (1982): 70-71.

738. Royle, Marjorie H. "Women Pastors. What Happens after Placement?" RRR 24,4 (1982): 116-127.

739. Ruark, Katherine. CLERGY DIVORCE AND ITS IMPACT UPON CLERGY MOBILITY WITHIN THE CHURCH SYSTEM. Unpublished Ph.D. dissertation, Florida State University, 1977.

740. Rueth, Thomas W. VOCATIONAL SATISFACTION AMONG ROMAN CATHOLIC PRIESTS. Unpublished Ph.D. dissertation, Loyola University of Chicago, 1973.

741. Ruiz Olabuenaga, J.I. "Ex-prêtres en Espagne." SC 17,4 (1970): 503-516.

742. Ryan, M. Desmond. THE CHURCH-SOCIETY RELATIONSHIP: A SURVEY OF THE OPINIONS OF INDIANA CATHOLIC CLERGY. Indianapolis, Indiana: Indiana Catholic Conference, 1977.

743. Rye, Gary Charles. HISPANICS AND THE ROMAN CATHOLIC CLERGY: A CASE STUDY OF CONFLICT. Unpublished Ph.D. dissertation, United States International University, 1977.

* Rymph, Raymond C., and Jeffrey K. Hadden. "The Persistence of Regionalism in Racial Attitudes of Methodist Clergy." Cited above as item 463.

744. Savramis, Demosthenes. DIE SOZIALE STELLUNG DER PRIESTER IN GRIECHENLAND. Leiden: Brill, 1968.

745. Schallert, Eugene J., and Jacqueline M. Kelley. "Some Factors Associated with Voluntary Withdrawal from the Catholic Priesthood." LUMEN VITAE 25 (1970): 425-460.
"Some Factors Associated with Voluntary Withdrawal from the Catholic Priesthood." THE HOMILETIC AND PASTORAL REVIEW 81 (1970-71): 95-106, 177-183, 254-267.

* Schindeler, Fred, and David Hoffman. "Theological and Political Conservatism: Variations in Attitudes among Clergymen of One Denomination." Cited above as item 121.

746. Schnabel, John F. VALIDATION OF CONSTRUCTS FOR PREDICTING OCCUPATIONAL ADAPTATIONS. Unpublished Ph.D. dissertation, University of Notre Dame, 1973.

747. Schneider, Louis, and Louis A. Zurcher. "Toward Understanding the Catholic Crisis: Observations on Dissident Priests in Texas." JSSR 9 (1970): 197-209.

748. Schoenherr, Richard A., and Andrew M. Greeley. "Role Commitment Processes and the American Catholic Priesthood." AMERICAN SOCIOLOGICAL REVIEW 39 (1974): 407-426.

749. Schoenherr, Richard A., and Annemette Sorensen. "Social Change in Religious Organizations: Consequences of Clergy Decline in the U.S. Catholic Church." SA 43,1 (1982): 23-52.

* Schreuder, Osmund, and Jan Hutjes. PRIESTER ZUR GEBURTENREGELUNG. EINE EMPIRISCHE ERHEBUNG. Cited above as item 256.

750. Schwartz, David F. BELIEF AS ASSUMPTIVE SYSTEM: CHANGING CONCEPTION OF CREED, CODE AND CULT AMONG CONTEMPORARY AMERICAN CATHOLIC PRIESTS. Unpublished Ph.D. dissertation, Loyola University (Chicago), 1978.

751. Seidler, John. REBELLION AND RETREATISM AMONG AMERICAN CATHOLIC CLERGY. Unpublished Ph.D. dissertation, University of North Carolina, Chapel Hill, 1972.

752. Seidler, John. "Priest Protest in the Human Catholic Church." NATIONAL CATHOLIC REPORTER 10 (May 3, 1974): 7, 14.

753. Seidler, John. "Priest Resignations, Relocations, and Passivity." NATIONAL CATHOLIC REPORTER 10 (May 10, 1974): 7, 14.

754. Seidler, John. "Priest Resignations in a Lazy Monopoly." AMERICAN SOCIOLOGICAL REVIEW 44,5 (1979): 763-783.

755. Shand, J.A. RELIGIOUS BELIEFS OF CHICAGO CLERGY. Unpublished Ph.D. dissertation, University of Chicago, 1953.

756. Sharot, Stephen. "Religious Change in Native Orthodoxy in London, 1870-1914: Rabbinate and Clergy." JEWISH JOURNAL OF SOCIOLOGY 15,2 (1973): 167-187.

757. Shupe, Anson, and William A. Stacey. "Public and Clergy Sentiments toward the Moral Majority: Evidence from the Dallas-Fort Worth Metroplex." In David G. Bromley and Anson Shupe (eds.), NEW CHRISTIAN POLITICS (item 100), pp. 91-100.

758. Shupe, Anson D. Jr., and James R. Wood. "Sources of Leadership Ideology in Dissident Clergy." SA 34,3 (1973): 185-201.

759. Siefer, G. (ed.) STERBEN DIE PRIESTER AUS?: SOZIOLOGISCHE UBERLEGUNGEN ZUR FUNKTIONSWANDEN EINES BERUFSSTANDES. Essen: Driewer, 1973.

760, Silverman, David. "Clerical Ideologies: A Research Note." BRITISH JOURNAL OF SOCIOLOGY 19,3 (1968): 326-333.

761. Smith, James O., and Gideon Sjoberg. "Origins and Career Patterns of Leading Protestant Clergymen." SOCIAL FORCES 39,4 (1961): 290-296

762. Smith, Thomas R. THE PASTOR-HUSBAND AND WIFE: CORRELATES OF THEOLOGICAL PERSPECTIVES, MARITAL ADJUSTMENT, JOB SATISFACTION AND WIFE'S PARTICIPATION IN THE CHURCH. Unpublished Ph.D. dissertation, Florida State, 1977.

763. Snook, John B. "The Protestant Clergyman in America. The Problem in Analyzing his Career." SC 16,4 (1969): 485-492.

764. Sorensen, Andrew A. THE DEVELOPMENT OF ALCOHOLISM AMONG ROMAN CATHOLIC AND PROTESTANT EPISCOPAL CLERGYMEN. Unpublished Ph.D. dissertation, Yale University, 1972.

765. Sorensen, Andrew A. "Need for Power among Alcoholic and Non-Alcoholic Clergy."JSSR 13,1 (1973): 101-108.

766. Sorensen, Andrew A. ALCOHOLIC PRIESTS: A SOCIOLOGICAL STUDY. New York: Seabury, 1977.

* Stark, Rodney, Charles Y. Glock, and Harold E. Quinley. WAYWARD SHEPHERDS. Cited above as item 471.

767. Stewart, James H. A CAREER MODEL OF A PROFESSIONAL ORGANIZATION. A STUDY OF ORGANIZATIONAL EFFECTIVENESS. Unpublished M.A. thesis, University of Notre Dame, 1970.

768. Stewart, James H. "Values, Interests, and Organizational Change: The National Federation of Priests' Councils." SA 34,4 (1973): 281-295.

769. Stewart, James H. AMERICAN CATHOLIC LEADERSHIP. A DECADE OF TURMOIL 1966-1976. The Hague: Mouton, 1978.

770. Stewart, James H. "When Priests Began to Bargain." RRR 20,2 (1979): 168-179.

771. Stone, David R. A STUDY OF ROLE PERCEPTIONS AS INDICES OF SOCIAL DISTANCE BETWEEN UNITED CHURCH OF CANADA CLERGYMEN AND UNITED CHURCH UNDERGRADUATES. Unpublished M.A. thesis, Wayne State University, 1968.

772. Strommen, Merton P., Milo L. Brekke, Ralph C. Underwager, and Arthur L. Johnson. A STUDY OF GENERATIONS. Minneapolis: Augsburgh Publishing, 1972.

773. Struzzo, John A. "Professionalism and the Resolution of Authority Conflicts among the Catholic Clergy." SA 31,2 (1970): 92-106.

774. Stryckman, Paul. "Note de recherche: le clergé séculier du Québec." RECHERCHES SOCIOLOGIQUES 10,1 (1969): 116-122.

775. Stryckman, Paul. LES PRETRES DU QUEBEC D'AUJOURD'HUI. Québec: Université de Laval, Centre de Recherches en Sociologie Religieuse, 1970.

776. Stryckman, Paul. LES PRETRES DU QUEBEC, AUJOURD'HUI, VOL. II. Québec: Université de Laval, Centre de Recherches en Sociologie Religieuse, 1973.

777. Stryckman, Paul, and Robert Gaudet. PRIESTS IN CANADA, 1971: A REPORT ON ENGLISH-SPEAKING CLERGY. Québec: Centre de Recherches en Sociologie Religieuse, Faculté de Théologie, Université Laval, 1971.

778. Stryckman, Paul, and Robert Gaudet. "Priests under Stress." In Stewart Crysdale and Les Wheatcroft (eds.), RELIGION IN CANADIAN SOCIETY. Toronto: Macmillan of Canada, 1976, pp. 336-345.

779. Subramaniam, K. BRAHMIN PRIEST OF TAMIL NADU. New York: Halsted, 1975.

780. Szafran, Robert F. "The Distribution of Influence in Religious Organizations." JSSR 15,4 (1976): 339-349.

781. Szafran, Robert F., Robert W. Peterson, and Richard A. Schoenherr. "Ethnicity and Status Attainment: The Case of the Roman Catholic Clergy." SOCIOLOGICAL QUARTERLY 21 (1980): 41-51.

782. Thompson, Robert C. PROFESSIONALIZATION AMONG THE CLERGY. Unpublished Ph.D. dissertation, Washington State University, 1977.

783. Towler, Robert. "The Changing Status of the Ministry." CRUCIBLE (May 1968): 73-78. Reproduced with changes as "The Social Status of the Anglican Minister." In Roland Robertson (ed.), SOCIOLOGY OF RELIGION. Baltimore: Penguin, 1970, pp. 443-450.

784. Towler, Robert, and Anthony P.M. Coxon. THE FATE OF THE ANGLICAN CLERGY. A SOCIOLOGICAL STUDY. London: Macmillan, 1979.

* Traina, Frank J. "Catholic Clergy on Abortion: Preliminary Findings on a New York State Survey." Cited above as item 227.

785. Tygart, Clarence E. A STUDY OF CLERGYMEN: WORK, IDEAS AND POLITICS. Unpublished Ph.D. dissertation, University of California at Los Angeles, 1969.

* Tygart, Clarence E. "Social Movement Participation: Clergy and the Anti-Vietnam War Movement." Cited above as item 294.

* Tygart, Clarence E. "Work Alienation and Politics among Clergy." Cited above as item 10.

786. Tygart, Clarence E. "The Clergy." In Phyllis L. Stewart and Muriel G. Cantor (eds.), VARIETIES OF WORK EXPERIENCE. Cambridge, Massachusetts: Schenkman, 1974, pp. 80-96.

787. Tygart, Clarence E. "The Role of Theology among Other 'Belief' Variables for Clergy Civil Rights Activism." RRR 18,3 (1977): 271-278.

788. Valenzano, Paolo M., and Benevenuto Castellani. "L'evoluzione del clero italiano: una propostadi riflessione." BOLLETINO DI STATISTICA E SOCIOLOGIA RELIGIOSA 4 (1974): 65-74.

789. Vassallo, M. MEN IN BLACK. A REPORT ON MALTA'S DIOCESAN CLERGY. Malta: P.R.S. Publication, 1973.

790. Vera, Hernan. PROFESSIONALIZATION AND PROFESSIONALISM OF CATHOLIC PRIESTS. Gainesville: University Presses of Florida, 1982.

791. Verryn, Trevor David. "Anglican and Roman Catholic Priests in South Africa: Some Questionnaire Responses." SC 19,1 (1972): 93-99.

792. Verscheure, J. "Recherches sur le prêtre: problèmes méthodologiques." SC 16,4 (1969): 453-469.

* Wagenaar, Theodore C., and Patricia E. Bartos. "Orthodoxy and Attitudes of Clergymen toward Homosexuality and Abortion." Cited above as item 237.

793. Wade, A.L., and J.V. Berreman. "Are Ministers Qualified for Marriage Counselling?" SOCIOLOGY AND SOCIAL RESEARCH 35,2 (1950): 106-112.

794. Wagner, A. DIE SCHWEIZERISCHE PRIESTERFRAGE. UNTERSUCHUNG ZUM PROBLEM DES PRIESTERNACHWUCHSES. St. Gallen: Schweizerisches Pastoralsoziologisches Institut, 1968.

795. Waltz, A.K., and R.L. Wilson. "Ministers' Attitudes toward Integration." PHYLON 19,2 (1958): 195-199.

796. Ward, Conor K. PRIESTS AND PEOPLE: A STUDY IN THE SOCIOLOGY OF RELIGION. Liverpool: Liverpool University Press, 1961.

797. Webb, Sam C., and Dayton D. Hultgren. "Differentiation of Clergy Subgroups on the Basis of Vocational Interests." JSSR 12,3 (1973): 311-324.

798. Wilson, Bryan R. "The Pentecostal Minister." In B.R Wilson (ed.), PATTERNS OF SECTARIANISM (item 3213), pp. 138-157.

799. Winter, J. Alan. "The Attitudes of Societally-Oriented and Parish-Oriented Clergy: An Empirical Comparison." JSSR 9 (1970): 59-66.

800. Wurzbacher, Gerard, et al. DER PFARRER IN DER MODERNEN GESELLSCHAFT. SOZIOLOGISCHE STUDIEN ZUR BERUFSSITUATION DES EVANGELISCHEN PFARRERS. Hamburg: Furche Verlag, 1960.

801. Zeegers, G.H.L. "Osterreich im Rahmen der weltweiten Priesterfrage." SC 4,3-4 (1956): 101-107.

802. Zulehner, Paul M., and S.R. Graupe. WIE PRIESTER HEUTE LEBEN. ERGEBNISSE DER WIENER PRIESTERUNTERSUCHUNG 1967. Wien: Herder, 1970.

Clergy image

803. Rabin, Pierre. "Ce que le jeunes pensent du prêtre et de la vie religieuse. Résultats d'une enquête en collèges secondaires libres (France)." LUMEN VITAE 8 (1953): 667-681.

804. Busian, Callistus. "Priests and the Rising Generation of Priests in the Opinion of Brazilians." SC 8,4 (1961): 317-326.

805. Doherty, John F. "The Image of the Priest: A Study in Stereotyping." PHILIPPINE SOCIOLOGICAL REVIEW 12,1-2 (1964): 70-76.

806. Glock, Charles Y., and Philip Ross. "Parishioners' Views of How Ministers Spend their Time." RRR 2,4 (1961): 170-175. Reprinted as Ch. 7 in Charles Y. Glock and Rodney Stark, RELIGION AND SOCIETY IN TENSION (volume cited in item 141).

807. Gustafsson, Berndt. "People's View of the Minister and the Lack of Ministers in Sweden." ARCHIVES DE SOCIOLOGIE DES RELIGIONS 22 (1966): 135-144.

808. Johnstone, Ronald L. "The Public Image of Lutheran Pastors." LUTHERAN QUARTERLY 24 (1972): 397-409.

809. Johnstone, Ronald L. "Public Images of Protestant Ministers and Catholic Priests: An Empirical Study of Anti-Clericalism in the U.S." SA 33,1 (1972): 34-49.

810. Le Bras, Gabriel. "L'image du clerc." ARCHIVES DE SOCIOLOGIE DES RELIGIONS 23 (1967): 23-36.

811. Markert, David DeSales. OPINIONS ABOUT THE PRIESTHOOD IN CATHOLIC HIGH SCHOOL BOYS AND MINOR SEMINARIANS. Unpublished doctoral dissertation, Loyola University (Chicago), 1963.

812. Piwowarski, Wladyslaw. "The Image of the Priest in the Eyes of Parishioners in Three Rural Parishes." SC 15,3-4 (1968): 235-249.

813. Reny, Paul, and Jean-Paul Rouleau. LE FRERE ET LA RELIGIEUSE VUS PAR LES ETUDIANTS DU NIVEAU COLLEGIAL. Québec: Centre de Recherches en Sociologie Religieuse, Université Laval, 1975.

814. Rosato, N. EXPECTATIVAS SOCIALES Y SACERDOCIO. INVESTIGACION SOCIOLOGICA DE LA IMAGEN DEL SACERDOTE EN BUENOS AIRES. Buenos Aires: Ecoisyr, 1971.

815. Rouleau, Jean-Paul. LE PRETRE, LE FRERE ET LA RELIGIEUSE VUS PAR DES ETUDIANTS DE COLLEGES. Québec: Université Laval, Centre de Recherches en Sociologie Religieuse, 1971.

816. Schreuder, Osmond. "The Parish Priest as a Subject of Criticism." SC 8,2 (1961): 111-120.

Clergy mobility

817. Mitchell, Robert E. "Polity, Church Attractiveness, and Ministers' Careers: An Eight Denominational Study of Interchurch Mobility." JSSR 5,2 (1966): 241-258.

818. Nauss, Allen. "The Relation of Pastoral Mobility to Effectiveness." RRR 15,2 (1974): 80-86.

819. Smith, Luke M. "The Clergy: Authority Structure, Ideology, and Migration." AMERICAN SOCIOLOGICAL REVIEW 18 (1953): 242-248.

Clergy role: content and role conflict

820. Abbott, Andrew. "Religion, Psychiatry, and Problems of Everyday Life." In Jeffrey K. Hadden and Theodore E. Long (eds.), RELIGION AND RELIGIOSITY IN AMERICA (volume cited in item 110), pp. 133-143.

821. Beech, Lawrence A. "Denominational Affiliation and Styles of Authority in Pastoral Counselling." JSSR 9 (1970): 245-246.

822. Bentz, W. Kenneth. "Consensus between Role Expectations and Role Behavior among Ministers." COMMUNITY MENTAL HEALTH 4,4 (1968): 301-306.

823. Bentz, W. Kenneth. "The Influence of the Community on the Mental Health Role of Ministers." RRR 14 (1972): 37-40.

824. Blaikie, Norman W.H. "Styles of Ministry: Some Aspects of the Relationship between 'the Church' and 'the World.'" In Allan Black and Peter Glasner (eds.), PRACTICE AND BELIEF. STUDIES IN THE SOCIOLOGY OF AUSTRALIAN RELIGION. Sydney: Allen and Unwin, 1983, pp. 43-61.

825. Blass, Jerome H. "Role Preferences among Jewish Seminarians." SA 38,1 (1977): 59-64.

826. Blizzard, Samuel W. "The Roles of the Rural Parish Minister, the Protestant Seminaries, and the Sciences of Social Behavior." RELIGIOUS EDUCATION 50,6 (1955): 383-392.

827. Blizzard, Samuel W. "Role Conflicts of the Urban Minister." CITY CHURCH 7,4 (1956): 13-15.

828. Blizzard, Samuel W. "The Protestant Parish Minister's Integrating Roles." RELIGIOUS EDUCATION 53 (1958): 374-380. Also in Wayne E. Oates (ed.), THE MINISTER'S OWN MENTAL HEALTH. Great Neck, N.Y.: Channel Press, 1961.

829. Blizzard, Samuel W. "The Parish Minister's Self-Image of his Master Role." PASTORAL PSYCHOLOGY 9 (1958): 25-32. Also in Wayne E. Oates (ed.), THE MINISTER'S OWN MENTAL HEALTH (volume cited in item 828.)

830. Blizzard, Samuel W. "The Parish Minister's Self-Image and Variability in Community Culture." PASTORAL PSYCHOLOGY 10 (1959): 27-36.

831. Bocock, Robert J. "The Role of the Anglican Clergyman." SC 17,4 (1970): 533-544.

832. Bormann, Günther. "Studien zu Berufsbild und Berufswirklichkeit evangelischer Pfarrer in Württemberg. Die Herkunft der Pfarrer. Ein geschichtlich-statistischer Überblick von 1700-1956." SC 13,2 (1966): 95-137.

833. Bormann, Günther. "Studien zu Berufsbild und Berufswirklichkeit evangelischer Pfarrer in Württemberg: Tendenzen der Berufseinstellung und des Berufsverhaltens." In J. Matthes (ed.), BEITRAGE ZUR RELIGIONS-SOZIOLOGISCHEN FORSCHUNG/ESSAYS ON RESEARCH IN THE SOCIOLOGY OF RELIGION. INTERNATIONALES JAHRBUCH FÜR RELIGIONS-SOZIOLOGIE 4. Köln and Opladen: Westdeutscher Verlag, 1968, pp. 158-209.

834. Brothers, Joan. "Social Change and the Role of the Priest." SC 10,6 (1963): 447-489.

835. Brothers, Joan. "The Priest's Role." NEW SOCIETY 105 (1964): 137-142.

836. Campiche, Roland J., and Claude Bovay. "Prêtres, pasteurs, rabbins: changement de rôle? Bibliographie thématique." ARCHIVES DE SCIENCES SOCIALES DES RELIGIONS 48,1 (1979): 133-183.

837. Carroll, Jackson W. "Some Issues in Clergy Authority." RRR 23,2 (1981): 99-117.

838. Chapman, S.H. "The Contemporary Pastorate." AMERICAN SOCIOLOGICAL REVIEW 9 (1944): 595-602.

839. Chapman, S.H. "The Minister: Professional Man of the Church." SOCIAL FORCES 23,2 (1944): 202-206.

840. Coates, Charles H., and Robert C. Kistler. "Role Dilemmas of Protestant Clergymen in a Metropolitan Community." RRR 6 (1965): 147-152.

841. Cummings, Elaine, and Charles Cummings. "Clergymen as Counselor." AMERICAN JOURNAL OF SOCIOLOGY 69 (1963): 234-243.

842. Deschwanden, Leo von. "Die Rolle des Gemeindepriesters zwischen Kirche und Gesellschaft." In J. Wössner (ed.), RELIGION IM UMBRUCH: SOZIOLOGISCHE BEITRAGE ZUR SITUATION VON RELIGION UND KIRCHE IN DER GEGENWARTIGEN GESELLSCHAFT. Stuttgart: Ferdinand Enke Verlag, 1972, pp. 395-409.

843. Dewey, Gerald. "The Resolution of Role Conflict among Clergymen." SA 32,1 (1971): 21-30.

* Ennis, Joseph Guyon. THE ROLE EXPECTATION OF ROMAN CATHOLIC CAMPUS CHAPLAINS AND ROMAN CATHOLIC UNDERGRADUATES FOR THE ROMAN CATHOLIC CAMPUS CHAPLAIN. Cited above as item 535.

844. Evans, Theodore Q. "The Brethren Pastor: Differential Conceptions of an Emerging Role." JSSR 3,1 (1963): 43-51.

845. Fasola-Bologna, Alfredo. "Il ruolo del sacerdote nelle aspettative della popolazione di una parrocchia romana." RIVISTA DI SOCIOLOGIA 6,15 (1968): 69-88.

846. Fulton, Robert L. "The Clergyman and the Funeral Director: A Study in Role Conflict." SOCIAL FORCES 39 (1961): 317-323.

847. Gannon, Thomas M. "Priest/Minister. Profession or Non-profession?" RRR 12,2 (1971): 66-79.

848. Gannon, Thomas M. "The Effect of Segmentation in the Religious Clergy." SA 40,3 (1979): 183-196.

849. Glasner, A.M. AN ANALYSIS OF THE RELATIONSHIP BETWEEN DIFFERENT ORGANISATIONAL SITUATIONS AND THE STRUCTURE AND LATENT CONFLICTS OF THE ROLE OF THE CLERIC: A CRITICAL REVIEW OF THE LITERATURE. Unpublished M.Sc. thesis, University of London, 1970.

850. Glass, J. Conrad, Jr. "Ministerial Job Satisfaction Scale." RRR 17,2 (1976): 153-157.

851. Goddijn, Walter. "Le rôle du prêtre dans l'église et la société." SC 12,1-2 (1965): 21-33.

852. Goddijn, Walter. "Rollen-Konflikte des Priesters." LEBENDIGE SEELSORGE 17 (1966): 136-138.

853. Goldstein, Sidney I. "The Role of an American Rabbi." SOCIOLOGY AND SOCIAL RESEARCH 38 (1953): 32-37.

854. Gustafson, James M. "Analysis of the Problem of the Role of the Minister." JOURNAL OF RELIGION 34 (1954): 187-191.

855. Hadden, Jeffrey K. "Role Conflict and the Crisis in the Churches." MINISTRY STUDIES 2 (1968): 16-29.

856. Hagstrom, Warren O. "The Protestant Clergy as a Profession: Status and Prospects." BERKELEY PUBLICATIONS IN SOCIETY AND INSTITUTIONS 3 (1957): 1-12.

857. Hammond, Phillip E., A. Gedricks, E. Lawler, and L. Turner. "Clergy Authority and Friendship with Parishioners." PACIFIC SOCIOLOGICAL REVIEW 15 (1972): 185-201.

* Hammond, Phillip E., Luis Salinas, and Douglas Sloane. "Types of Clergy Authority: Their Measurement, Location, and Effects." Cited above as item 70.

858. Hicks, Frederick. "Politics, Power and the Role of the Village Priest in Paraguay." JOURNAL OF INTER-AMERICAN STUDIES 9,2 (1967): 273-282.

859. Hoge, Dean R., John E. Dyble, and David T. Polk. "Influence of Role Preference and Role Clarity on Vocational Commitment of Protestant Ministers." SA 42,1 (1981): 1-16.

860. Ingram, Larry C. "Notes on Pastoral Power in the Congregational Tradition." JSSR 19,1 (1980): 40-48.

861. Ingram, Larry C. "Leadership, Democracy, and Religion: Role Ambiguity among Pastors in Southern Baptist Churches." JSSR 20,2 (1981): 119-129.

862. Jammes, Jean-Marie. "The Social Role of the Priest." AMERICAN CATHOLIC SOCIOLOGICAL REVIEW 16 (1955): 94-103.

863. Jarvis, Peter. "The Parish Ministry as a Semi-Profession." SOCIOLOGICAL REVIEW 23,4 (1975): 911-922.

864. Jarvis, Peter. "Profession in Process: A Theoretical Model for the Ministry." SOCIOLOGICAL REVIEW 24,2 (1976): 351-364.

865. Johnson, Jeff G. AN ANALYSIS AND DESCRIPTION OF ROLE EXPECTATIONS FOR MINISTERS OF THE SOUTHERN CALIFORNIA DISTRICT OF THE LUTHERAN CHURCH-MISSOURI SYNOD. Unpublished doctoral dissertation, University of Southern California, 1961.

866. Jolson, Alfred J. "The Role of the Priest in a Diaspora Church. A Study of the Role of the Priest in St. Olav's Parish, Oslo, Norway." SC 17,4 (1970): 553-568.

867. Kerkhofs, J. "Aspects sociologiques du sacerdoce." NOUVELLE REVUE THEOLOGIQUE 82,3 (1960): 289-299.

868. Larson, Richard F. "Clerical and Psychiatric Conception of the Clergyman's Role in the Therapeutic Setting." SOCIAL PROBLEMS 11 (1964): 419-427.

869. Leiffer, Murray H. "Changing Expectations and Ethics in the Professional Ministry." RRR 11,3 (1970): 219.

870. Macdonald, Allan Francis. A SOCIOLOGICAL STUDY OF TEAM MINISTRY IN THE ROMAN CATHOLIC ARCHDIOCESE OF HARTFORD, CONNECTICUT. Unpublished Ph.D. dissertation, Catholic University of America, 1978.

871. Madigan, Francis C. "Role Satisfactions and Length of Life in a Closed Population." AMERICAN JOURNAL OF SOCIOLOGY 67,6 (1962): 640-649.

872. Magrauer, B. "Variations in Pastoral Role in France." AMERICAN CATHOLIC SOCIOLOGICAL REVIEW 9,1 (1950): 15-24.

873. McSweeney, Bill. "The Priesthood in Sociological Theory." SC 21,1 (1974): 5-23.

874. Mills, Edgar W. "Types of Role Conflict among Clergymen." MINISTRY STUDIES 2 (1968): 13-15.

875. Moore, John. "Some Aspects of the Sociology of Priesthood." SOCIAL STUDIES 3,2 (1974): 118-136.

876. Moore, M. "Demonstrating the Rationality of an Occupation: The Depiction of their Occupation by 'Progressive Clergymen.'" SOCIOLOGY 8,1 (1974): 111-123.

877. Morrow, William Robert, and Ahmed Thomas James Matthews. "Role-Definitions of Mental-Hospital Chaplains." JSSR 5 (1966): 421-434.

878. Nauss, Allen. "Problems in Measuring Ministerial Effectiveness." JSSR 11,2 (1972): 141-151.

* Nauss, Allen. "The Relation of Pastoral Mobility to Effectiveness." Cited above as item 818.

879. Pickering, W.S.F. "A Search for New Approaches to the Sociological Study of the Priesthood." In N. Lash and J. Rhymer (eds.), THE CHRISTIAN PRIESTHOOD. NINTH DOWNSIDE SYMPOSIUM. London: Longmann and Todd, 1970, pp. 189-211.

880. Pin, Emile. "The Advantages and Disadvantages of the Professionalisation of the Priesthood." IDOC 68,2 (1968): 1-10; 68,3 (1968): 1-14.

881. Pin, Emile. "The Priestly Function in Crisis." CONCILIUM 43 (1969): 45-58.

882. Plyler, Henry E. VARIATION OF MINISTERIAL ROLES BY SIZE AND LOCATION OF CHURCH. Unpublished doctoral dissertation, University of Missouri, 1961.

883. Reilly, Mary Ellen. "Perceptions of the Priest Role." SA 36,4 (1975): 347-356.

884. Reilly, Mary Ellen. "A Case Study of Role Conflict: Roman Catholic Priests." HUMAN RELATIONS 31 (1978): 77-90.

885. Richard, Yann. "Le rôle du clergé: tendances contradictoires du charisme iranien contemporain." ARCHIVES DE SCIENCES SOCIALES DES RELIGIONS 55,1 (1983): 5-28.

886. Roux, R.R. de. "Reflexiones sociológicas sobre el actual ejercicio del ministerio sacerdota." THEOLOGICA XAVERIANA (Bogotá) 25,1 (1975): 41-48.

887. Ruesink, D.C. A STUDY OF THE SEMINARY STUDENT'S PERCEPTION OF PRACTITIONER ROLES TO BE PERFORMED BY THE MINISTER. Unpublished doctoral dissertation, North Carolina State University, 1967.

888. Scanzoni, John. RESOLUTION OF ROLE INCOMPATIBILITY IN CHURCH AND SECT CLERGY MARRIAGE. Unpublished Ph.D. dissertation, University of Oregon, 1964.

889. Scanzoni, John. "Resolution of Occupational-Conjugal Role Conflict in Clergy Marriages." JOURNAL OF MARRIAGE AND THE FAMILY 27,3 (1965): 396-402.

890. Schreuder, Osmund. "Le caractère professionnel du sacerdoce." SC 12,1-2 (1965): 5-19.

891. Schroeder, Widick. "Lay Expectations of the Ministerial Role: An Exploration of Protestant-Catholic Differentials." JSSR 2 (1963): 217-227.

892. Schuller, David S., Merton P. Strommen, and Milo Brekke (eds.) MINISTRY IN AMERICA. San Francisco: Harper and Row, 1980.

893. Sharot, Stephen. "The British and American Rabbinate: A Comparison of Authority Structures, Role Definitions and Role Conflicts." In M. Hill (ed.), A SOCIOLOGICAL YEARBOOK OF RELIGION IN BRITAIN 8. London: SCM, 1975, pp. 139-158.

894. Shimada, K. "Social Role and Role Conflicts of the Protestant Parish Minister: Focused on S.W. Blizzard's Study." JAPANESE SOCIOLOGICAL REVIEW 10 (1960): 29-50.

895. Smith, Donald P. CLERGY IN THE CROSS FIRE. COPING WITH ROLE CONFLICTS IN THE MINISTRY. Philadelphia: Westminister, 1973.

896. Smith, R., C. Black, B. Hoffman, and S. Burkett Milner. SOCIOLOGICAL STUDIES OF AN OCCUPATION: THE MINISTRY. Evanston, Illinois: Murray and Dorothy Leifer Bureau of Social and Religious Research, 1974.

897. Somerfeld, Richard E. ROLE CONCEPTIONS OF LUTHERAN MINISTERS IN THE ST. LOUIS AREA. Unpublished doctoral dissertation, Wasington University, 1957.

* Stark, Werner. THE SOCIOLOGY OF RELIGION, Vol. 4. Cited above as item 83.

898. Stewart, James H. "The Changing Role of the Catholic Priest in his Ministry in an Inner City Context: A Study in Role Change." SA 30,2 (1969): 81-90.

899. Stryckman, Paul. "La pratique du ministère paroissial. Une étude sociologique." COMMUNAUTE CHRETIENNE 9 (1970): 269-286.

900. Stryckman, Paul. "Validation empirique d'une typologie des pratiques du prêtre pasteur." CAHIERS DU CENTRE DE RECHERCHES EN SOCIOLOGIE RELIGIEUSE 2 (1978): 57-89.

901. Stryckman, Paul. "Les défis occupationnels du clergé." RECHERCHES SOCIOGRAPHIQUES 19,2 (1979): 223-250.

902. Stuhr, Walter M., Jr. "The Public Style of Ministry: Methodological Considerations in a Study of Church and Community." RRR 9 (1968): 97-104.

903. Taylor, Mary G., and Shirley Foster Hartley. "The Two-Person Career: A Classic Example." SOCIOLOGY OF WORK AND OCCUPATIONS 2 (1975): 354-372.

904. Tonna, B. "The Allocation of Time among Clerical Activities: A Study in a Brussels Parish." SC 10,1 (1963): 93-106

905. Towler, Robert. "The Role of the Clergy." In N. Lash and J. Rhymer (eds.), THE CHRISTIAN PRIESTHOOD. NINTH DOWNSIDE SYMPOSIUM (volume cited in item 879), pp. 165-186.

906. Verryn, T.D. THE VANISHING CLERGYMAN. A SOCIOLOGICAL STUDY OF THE PRIESTLY ROLE IN SOUTH AFRICA. Braamfonteyn: The South African Council of Churches, 1971.

907. Whipple, Charles. THE TEACHING MINISTRY OF THE PRIEST IN THE EPISCOPAL CHURCH. Unpublished Ph.D. dissertation, New York University, 1959.

908. Wilson, Bryan R. "Role Conflicts and Status Contradictions of the Pentecostal Minister." AMERICAN JOURNAL OF SOCIOLOGY 64,5 (1959): 494-504.

909. Wimberley, Ronald C. "Mobility in Ministerial Career Patterns: Exploration." JSSR 10,3 (1971): 249-253.

910. Zishka, Ronald L. THE CONSENSUS OF CLERGY ROLE TASK EXPECTATIONS AND CONGREGATIONAL VIABILITY. Unpublished doctoral dissertation, Ohio State University, 1973.

Clergy wives

911. Finch, Janet. "Devising Conventional Performances: The Case of Clergymen's Wives." SOCIOLOGICAL REVIEW 28,4 (1980): 851-870.

912. Hartley, Shirley Foster. "Marital Satisfaction among Clergy Wives." RRR 19,2 (1978): 178-191.

913. Hartley, Shirley F., and Mary G. Taylor. "Religious Beliefs of Clergy Wives." RRR 19,1 (1977): 63-72.

* Scanzoni, John. RESOLUTION OF ROLE INCOMPATIBILITY IN CHURCH AND SECT CLERGY MARRIAGE. Cited above as item 888.

* Scanzoni, John. "Resolution of Occupational-Conjugal Role Conflict in Clergy Marriages." Cited above as item 889.

914. Smith, Herman W. "Urbanization, Secularization, and Roles of the Professional's Wife." RRR 13 (1972): 134-139.

* Taylor, Mary G., and Shirley Foster Hartley. "The Two-Person Career: A Classic Example." Cited above as item 903.

Discipleship

Disciples are the first generation of followers of a founder or great religious figure.

915. Glick, Steven. AN ANALYSIS OF THE CHANGE PROCESS IN THE GURU-DISCIPLE RELATIONSHIP. Unpublished doctoral dissertation, Temple University, 1982.

916. Wach, Joachim. MEISTER UND JUNGER. ZWEI RELIGIONSSOZIOLOGISCHE BETRACHTUNGEN. Tübingen: J.C.B. Mohr (Paul Siebeck), 1925.

917. Wach, Joachim. "Master and Disciple: Two Religio-Sociological Studies." JOURNAL OF RELIGION 42,1 (1962): 1-21.

Founder

* Barnes, Douglas F. "Charisma and Religious Leadership: An Historical Analysis." Cited above as item 60.

* Stark, Werner. THE SOCIOLOGY OF RELIGION, Vol. IV. Cited above as item 83.

Leadership

918. Garcia de Cortazar, Fernando. "Análisis sociológico del episcopado español de la Restauración." REVUE INTERNATIONALE DE SOCIOLOGIE 18-20 (1976): 63-90.

919. Harrison, Paul. "Religious Leadership in America." In Donald R. Cutler (ed.), THE RELIGIOUS SITUATION: 1969. Boston: Beacon, 1969, pp. 957-979.

920. Hayashida, Cullen T. "The Isolation of Leadership: A Case-Study of a Precarious Religious Organization." RRR 17,2 (1976): 141-152.

921. Imse, Thomas P. "Spiritual Leadership and Organizational Leadership. The Dilemma of Being Pope." SC 16,2 (1969): 275-280.

922. Kohn, Rachael L.E. "Praising the Lord and Penetrating the Community: Transition and Dual Leadership Functions in a Contemporary Hebrew Christian Group." SA 45,1 (1984): 29-40.

* Morgan, D.H.J. "The Social and Educational Background of Anglican Bishops." Cited above as item 701.

* Shokeid, Moshe. "From Personal Endowment to Bureaucratic Appointment: The Transition in Israel of the Communal Religious Leaders of Moroccan Jews." Cited above as item 80.

923. Smith, James A., Jr."Methodist Episcopacy: From the General to the Specific." RRR 7 (1966): 163-167.

924. Wood, James R. "Leaders, Values, and Societal Change." SA 45,1 (1984): 1-10.

Membership

* Bibby, Reginald W., and Merlin B. Brinkerhoff. "Circulation of the Saints Revisited: A Longitudinal Look at Conservative Church Growth." Cited above as item 97.

925. Boisen, Anton T. "Factors Which Have to do with the Decline of the Country Church." AMERICAN JOURNAL OF SOCIOLOGY 22 (1916): 177-192.

926. Boling, T. Edwin. FACTORS RELATED TO THE CONGRUENCE AND INCONGRUENCE OF MEMBERSHIP IN WHITE PROTESTANT RELIGIOUS ORGANIZATIONS. Unpublished Ph.D. dissertation, Ohio State University, 1968.

927. Bouma, Gary D. "Keeping the Faithful: Patterns of Membership Retention in the Christian Reformed Church." SA 41,3 (1980): 259-264.

928. Bouma, Gary D. "Australian Religiosity: Some Trends since 1966." In Alan Black and Peter Glasner (eds.), PRACTICE AND BELIEF. STUDIES IN THE SOCIOLOGY OF AUSTRALIAN RELIGION. Sydney: Allen and Unwin, 1983, pp. 15-24.

929. Bultena, Louis. "Church Membership and Church Attendance in Madison, Wisconsin." AMERICAN SOCIOLOGICAL REVIEW 14 (1949): 384-389.

930. Burger, Annemarie. RELIGIONSZUGEHORIGKEIT UND SOZIALES VERHALTEN. UNTERSUCHUNGEN UND STATISTIKEN DER NEUEREN ZEIT IN DEUTSCHLAND. - KIRCHE UND KONFESSION,4. Göttingen: Vandenhoeck und Ruprecht, 1964.

931. Campbell, Colin, and Robert W. Coles. "Religiosity, Religious Affiliation and Religious Belief." RRR 14,3 (1973): 151-158.

932. Campbell, Thomas C., and Yoshio Fukuyama. THE FRAGMENTED LAYMAN. Pilgrim Press, 1970.

933. Carrier, Hervé. PSYCHO-SOCIOLOGIE DE L'APPARTENANCE RELIGIEUSE. Rome: Presses de l'Université Grégorienne, 1960. SOCIOLOGY OF RELIGIOUS BELONGING. New York: Herder and Herder, 1965.

934. Cuber,John F. "Marginal Church Participants." SOCIOLOGY AND SOCIAL RESEARCH 25 (1940): 57-62.

935. Currie, Raymond F. "Belonging, Commitment and Early Socialization in a Western City." In S. Crysdale and L. Wheatcroft (eds.), RELIGION IN CANADIAN SOCIETY (volume cited in item 778).

936. Dann, Graham M.S. "Religious Belonging in a Changing Catholic Church." SA 37,4 (1976): 283-297.

937. Davis, Winston. "Japanese Religious Affiliations: Motives and Obligations." SA 44,2 (1983): 131-146.

938. Deconchy, Jean-Pierre. "Cohérence du corpus orthodoxe et réglage de l'appartenance au groupe-Eglise." ARCHIVES DE SCIENCES SOCIALES DES RELIGIONS 36 (1973): 103-118.

939. Dhooghe, Jos. "Organizational Problems Regarding Different Types of Membership in the Church." SC 15,2 (1968): 93-99.

940. Dobbelaere, Karel. "Une typologie de l'intégration à l'Eglise." SC 15,2 (1968): 117-141.

941. Estruch, Juan. "Catholics and the Institutional Church: Obedience vs. Critical Distance." SC 17,3 (1970): 379-401.

942. Feige, Andreas. "Comments on the Relationship between Church Membership and Piety." SC 29,2-3 (1982): 187-208.

943. Fichter, Joseph H. "The Marginal Catholic. An Institutional Approach." SOCIAL FORCES 32 (1953): 167-173. Also in J.M. Yinger (ed.), RELIGION, SOCIETY AND THE INDIVIDUAL. New York: Macmillan, 1957, pp. 423-433.

944. Finner, Stephen L. "Religious Membership and Religious Preference: Equal Indicators of Religiosity?" JSSR 9 (1970): 273-279.

945. Fukuyama, Yoshio. THE MAJOR DIMENSIONS OF CHURCH MEMBERSHIP. Unpublished Ph.D. dissertation, University of Chicago, 1960.

946. Fukuyama, Yoshio. "The Major Dimensions of Church Membership." RRR 2 (1961): 154-161.

947. Hadaway, Christopher Kirk. SOURCES OF DENOMINATIONAL GROWTH IN AMERICAN PROTESTANTISM. Unpublished Ph.D. dissertation, University of Massachusetts, 1978.

948. Hadaway, Christopher Kirk. "The Demographic Environment and Church Membership Change." JSSR 20,1 (1981): 77-89.

949. Hill, Reuben. "L'appartenance religieuse chez les Mormons." SC 12,3 (1965): 171-176.

950. Hoge, Dean R., and David A. Roozen (eds.) UNDERSTANDING CHURCH GROWTH AND DECLINE 1950-1978. New York: Pilgrim Press, 1979. Contains item 1273.

* Kelley, Dean M. WHY CONSERVATIVE CHURCHES ARE GROWING. Cited above as item 116.

951. Kunz, Phillip R., and Merlin B. Brinkerhoff. "Growth in Religious Organizations: A Comparative Study." SOCIAL SCIENCE 45 (1970): 215-222.

952. Landis, Benson Y. "Trends in Church Membership in the United States." THE ANNALS 332 (1960): 1-9.

953. Lazerwitz, Bernard. "Past and Future Trends in the Size of American Jewish Denominations." JOURNAL OF REFORM JUDAISM 26 (1979): 77-82.

954. Lazerwitz, Bernard, and Michael I. Harrison. "A Comparison of Denominational Identification and Membership." JSSR 19,4 (1980): 361-367.

955. Le Bras, Gabriel. "Mesures des appartenances religieuses en France. Premier bilan méthodologique." ARCHIVES DE SOCIOLOGIE DES RELIGIONS 2 (1956): 17-21.

956. Lizcano, Manuel. "Typologie et modes d'appartenance et de dissidence chrétiennes dans une société de tradition catholique, telle la société espagnole." SC 12,2 (1965): 245-251.

957. Maryo, Joann S. FACTORS RELATED TO SIMILARITY, REJECTION AND RELIGIOUS AFFILIATION. Unpublished M.A. thesis, Michigan State University, 1958.

958. McKinney, William, and Dean R. Hoge. "Community and Congregational Factors in the Growth and Decline of Protestant Churches." JSSR 22,1 (1983): 51-66.

959. Perry, Everett L., and Dean R. Hoge. "Faith Priorities of Pastor and Laity as a Factor in the Growth and Decline of Presbyterian Congregations." RRR 22,3 (1981): 221-232. Also in P.H. McNamara (ed.), RELIGION: NORTH AMERICAN STYLE (volume cited in item 117), pp. 95-104.

960. Remy, Jean, and F. Hambye. "L'Appartenance religieuse comme expression de structures culturelles latentes: problème de méthode." SC 16,3 (1969): 327-342.

961. Rodd, L.S. "Church Affiliation and Denominational Values." SOCIOLOGY 2,1 (1968): 79-90.

* Ross, Jack C. TRADITIONALISM AND CHARISMA IN A RELIGIOUS GROUP: MEMBERSHIP CAREERS AND ROLE CONTINGENCIES OF QUAKERS. Unpublished Ph.D. dissertaion, University of Minnesota, 1964. Cited above as item 75.

962. Scarpati, Rosario. "Il problema dell'appartenenza religiosa durante il passagio da una civilizzazione pre-tecnica ad una civilizzazione tecnica: il caso del Messogiorno d'Italia." SOCIOLOGIA RELIGIOSA 7,9-10 (1963): 32-51.

963. Sissons, Peter L. "Concepts of Church Membership." In Michael Hill (ed.), SOCIOLOGICAL YEARBOOK OF RELIGION IN BRITAIN 4. London: SCM, 1971, pp. 62-83.

964. Stark, Rodney. ESTIMATING CHURCH MEMBERSHIP RATES FOR ECOLOGICAL AREAS. Washington: United States Government Printing Office, 1980. 1980.

965. Stark, Rodney, Williams Sims Bainbridge, and Lori Kent. "Cult Membership in the Roaring Twenties: Assessing Local Receptivity." SA 42,2 (1981): 137-162.

966. Vaillancourt, Jean-Guy. PAPAL POWER. A STUDY OF VATICAN CONTROL OVER LAY CATHOLIC ELITES. Berkeley: University of California Press, 1980.

967. Vallier, Ivan, and Jean-Guy Vaillancourt. "Catholicism, Laity, and Industrial Society: A Cross National Study of Religious Change." ARCHIVES DE SOCIOLOGIE DES RELIGIONS 23 (1967): 99-102.

968. Warner, R. Stephen. "Visits to a Growing Evangelical and a Declining Liberal Church in 1978." SA 44,3 (1983): 243-254.

969. Westhues, Kenneth. "The Church in Opposition." SA 37,4 (1976): 299-314. Also in P.H. McNamara (ed.), RELIGION: NORTH AMERICAN STYLE (volume cited in item 17), pp. 215-225.

Mendicancy

970. Walter, Eugene Victor. "Pauperism and Illth: An Archaeology of Social Policy." SA 34,4 (1973): 239-254.

Military chaplain

971. Abercrombie, Clarence L.,III. THE MILITARY CHAPLAIN. Beverley Hills, Calif.: Sage Library of Social Research, Vol. 37, 1977.

972. Aronis, Alexander B. A COMPARATIVE STUDY OF THE OPINIONS OF NAVY CHAPLAINS AND THEIR COMMANDING OFFICERS ON THE ROLE EXPECTATIONS, DEFICIENCIES, AND PREFERRED IN-SERVICE EDUCATION FOR NAVY CHAPLAINS. Unpublished Ph.D. dissertation, American University, 1971.

973. Burchard, Waldo W. THE ROLE OF THE MILITARY CHAPLAIN. Unpublished Ph.D. dissertation, University of California, Berkeley, 1953.

974. Burchard, Waldo W. "Role Conflicts of Military Chaplains." AMERICAN SOCIOLOGICAL REVIEW 19 (1954): 528-535. Also in J.M. Yinger (ed.), RELIGION, SOCIETY AND THE INDIVIDUAL (volume cited in item 943), pp. 586-599.

975. Zahn, Gordon C. THE MILITARY CHAPLAINCY: A STUDY OF ROLE TENSION IN THE ROYAL AIR FORCE. Toronto: University of Toronto Press, 1969.

Missionary

976. Potter, Sarah. "The Making of Missionaries in the Nineteenth Century: Conversion and Convention." In M. Hill (ed.), A SOCIOLOGICAL YEARBOOK OF RELIGION IN BRITAIN 8. London: SCM, 1975, pp. 103-124.

Prophet

977. Fabian, Johannes. "Tod dem Prophet. Ein Dokument zu einer prophetischen Situation." SOCIOLOGUS 17 (1967): 131-146.

978. Halsey, J.J. "The Genesis of a Modern Prophet." AMERICAN JOURNAL OF SOCIOLOGY 9,3 (1906): 310-328.

979. Kincheloe, Samuel C. "The Prophet as a Leader." SOCIOLOGY AND SOCIAL RESEARCH 12,5 (1928): 461-468.

980. Lourie, Richard. "The Prophet and the Marrano: Two Ways of Religious Being in the Soviet Union." SOCIAL RESEARCH 41,2 (1974): 328-339.

981. Martindale, Don. "Priests and Prophets in Palestine." In Martindale, SOCIAL LIFE AND CULTURAL CHANGE. Princeton: Van Nostrand, 1962, pp. 239-307.

Saint

982. Delooz, Pierre. "Pour une étude sociologique de la sainteté canonisée dans l'Eglise catholique." ARCHIVES DE SOCIOLOGIE DES RELIGIONS 13 (1962): 17-43.
"Towards a Sociological Study of Canonized Sainthood in the Catholic Church." In Stephen Wilson (ed.), SAINTS AND THEIR CULTS (item 986), pp. 189-216.

983. Delooz, Pierre. SOCIOLOGIE ET CANONISATIONS. Liège, 1969.

984. Desroche, Henri, Andre Vauchez, and Jacques Maitre. "Sociologie de la sainteté canonisée." ARCHIVES DE SOCIOLOGIE DES RELIGIONS 30 (1970): 109-115.

985. Wilson, Stephen. "Cults of Saints in the Churches of Central Paris." COMPARATIVE STUDIES IN SOCIETY AND HISTORY 22 (1980): 548-575.

986. Wilson, Stephen (ed.) SAINTS AND THEIR CULTS. STUDIES IN RELIGIOUS SOCIOLOGY, FOLKLORE AND HISTORY. Cambridge: Cambridge University Press, 1983.

Seeker

987. Lofland, John. DOOMSDAY CULT: A STUDY OF CONVERSION, PROSELYTIZATION AND MAINTENANCE OF FAITH. Englewood Cliffs, N.J.: Prentice-Hall, 1966.

988. Straus, Roger. "Changing Oneself: Seekers and the Creative Transformation of Experience." In John Lofland (ed.), DOING SOCIAL LIFE. New York: Wiley, 1976, pp. 252-272.

Seminarian

989. Allen, James E. "Family Planning Attitudes of Seminary Students." RRR 9 (1967): 52-55.

990. Berg, Philip L. "Professionalism and Lutheran Seminarians." LUTHERAN QUARTERLY 4 (1968): 406-441.

991. Berg, Philip L. "Socialization into the Ministry: A Comparative Analysis." SA 30,2 (1969): 59-71.

992. Berg, Phillip L. "Self-Identified Fundamentalism among Protestant Seminarians: A Study of Persistence and Change in Value-Orientations." RRR 12 (1971): 88-94.

* Betts, George H. "Comparison of the Theological Beliefs of Ministers and Theological Students." In Leo Rosten (ed.), RELIGIONS IN AMERICA. Cited above as item 549.

* Blass, Jerome H. "Role Preferences among Jewish Seminarians." Cited above as item 825.

993. Boulard, Fernand. "Qui êtes-vous, jeunes ou adultes des centres ou groupes de formation? Quelques résultats d'une enquête nationale auprès des séminaristes." VOCATION 273 (1976): 38-82.

994. Bowdern, Thomas Stephen. A STUDY OF VOCATIONS: AN INVESTIGATION INTO THE ENVIRONMENTAL FACTORS OF VOCATION TO THE PRIESTHOOD AND THE RELIGIOUS LIFE IN THE UNITED STATES FROM 1919 TO 1929. Unpublished doctoral dissertation, Saint Louis University, 1936.

995. Bowman, Jerome Francis. A STUDY OF SELECTED SOCIAL AND ECONOMIC FACTORS IN THE FORMATION OF A RELIGIOUS VOCATION. Unpublished M.A. thesis, Loyola University (Chicago), 1958.

996. Brooks, Robert M. THE FORMER MAJOR SEMINARIAN: A STUDY OF CHANGE IN STATUS. Unpublished doctoral dissertation, University of Notre Dame, 1960.

997. Carroll, Jackson W. SEMINARIES AND SEMINARIANS. A STUDY OF THE PROFESSIONAL SOCIALIZATION OF PROTESTANT CLERGYMEN. Unpublished Ph.D. dissertation, Princeton Theological Seminary, 1970.

998. Dougherty, Denis. "The Rate of Perseverance to Ordination of Minor Seminary Graduates." SA 29,1 (1968): 35-38.

999. Dougherty, John. "Do Priests Encourage Vocations? A Fact Study of 275 Seminarians." THE ECCLESISASTICAL REVIEW 81 (1929): 561-573.

1000. Flatt, Bill. "Predicting Academic Success of Graduate Students in Religion." RRR 14,2 (1973): 110-111.

* Fukuyama, Yoshio. THE MINISTRY IN TRANSITION. A CASE STUDY OF THEOLOGICAL EDUCATION. Cited above as item 620.

1001. Gilbert, James D. "What Makes Boys Seminarians?" THE PRIEST 14 (1958): 1034-1038; "Who Inspires Vocations?" THE CATHOLIC EDUCATOR 29 (1959): 308-309.

1002. Gustavus, William T. "The Ministerial Student: A Study in the Contradictions of a Marginal Role." RRR 14,3 (1973): 187-193.

1003. Hall, J.O. "Note on the Relationship between Attitudes toward the Scientific Method and the Background of Seminarians." SOCIAL FORCES 39,1 (1960): 49-52.

1004. Hartley, Loyde H., and David S. Schuller. "Theological Schools." In Ross P. Scherer (ed.), AMERICAN DENOMINATIONAL ORGANIZATION (item 1172), pp. 225-244.

1005. Jamison, William G. "Predicting Academic Achievement of Seminary Students." RRR 6 (1965): 90-96.

1006. Jończyk, Jósef. "Los motivos de ingreso en los seminarios en Polonia." VIDA CATOLICA EN POLONIA 8-9,114 (1975): 50-54.

1007. Kleinman, Sherryl. "Making Professionals into 'Persons': Discrepancies in Traditional and Humanistic Expectations of Professional Identity." SOCIOLOGY OF WORK AND OCCUPATIONS 8,1 (1981): 61-87.

1008. Kleinman, Sherryl. EQUALS BEFORE GOD. SEMINARIANS AS HUMANISTIC PROFESSIONALS. Chicago: University of Chicago Press, 1984.

1009. Kleinman, Sherryl, and Gary Alan Fine. "Rhetorics and Action in Moral Organizations: Social Control of Little Leaguers and Ministry Students." URBAN LIFE 8,3 (1979): 275-294.

1010. Labelle, Yvan, and Gustavo Pérez Ramirez. EL PROBLEMA SACERDOTAL EN AMERICA LATINA. Bogota and Friburgo: FERES-CIS, 1964.

1011. Lindskoog, Donald, and Roger E. Kirk. "Some Life-History and Attitudinal Correlates of Self-Actualization among Evangelical Seminary Students." JSSR 14 (1975): 51-55.

1012. Lonsway, Francis A. SEMINARIANS IN THEOLOGY: A STUDY OF BACKGROUNDS AND PERSONALITIES. Washington: Center for Applied Research in the Apostolate, 1968.

1013. Lonsway, Francis A. "Characteristics of Persisters and Withdrawals among Seminarians." THEOLOGICAL EDUCATION 8,3 (1972): 198-205.

1014. MacGreil, Michael. "Irish Theologians' Views on Proposed Seminary Changes." SOCIAL STUDIES 2,4 (1973): 415-422.

1015. Magni, Klas G. "Reactions to Death Stimuli among Theology Students." JSSR 9 (1970): 247-248.

1016. Maloney, Daniel J. AGE DIFFERENCES IN THE PERCEIVED INFLUENCE OF PERSONAL FACTORS ON VOCATION CHOICE. Unpublished M.A. thesis, Catholic University of America, 1963.

* Markert, David DeSales. OPINIONS ABOUT THE PRIESTHOOD IN CATHOLIC HIGH SCHOOL BOYS AND MINOR SEMINARIANS. Cited above as item 811.

1017. McNamara, Robert J. "Intellectual Values: Campus and Seminary." SA 25 (1964): 200-211.

1018. Mills, Bobby Eugene. CAREER CHOICE AMONG THEOLOGICAL STUDENTS. Unpublished Ph.D. dissertation, Syracuse University, 1977.

1019. Nauss, Allen. "Personality Changes among Students in a Conservative Seminary." JSSR 11,4 (1972): 377-388.

1020. Newman, William M. "Role Conflict in the Ministry and the Role of the Seminary: A Pilot Study." SA 32,4 (1971): 238-248.

1021. Potvin, Raymond, and Antanas Suziedelis. SEMINARIANS OF THE SIXTIES: A NATIONAL SURVEY. Washington: Center for Applied Research in the Apostolate, 1969.

1022. Roscoe, John T., and Paul A. Girling. "A Survey of Values of American Theological Students." RRR 11,3 (1970): 210-218.

1023. Routhier, François, and Paul Stryckman. LES ETUDIANTS DES GRANDS SEMINAIRES DE LA VIE SACERDOTALE. Partially published by Routhier as "Les séminaristes d'aujourd'hui seront-ils les prêtres de demain?" in LE PRETRE, HIER, AUJOURD'HUI, DEMAIN. Montréal: Editions Fides, 1970, pp. 322-333.

1024. Routhier, François, and Grégoire Tremblay. LE PROFIL SOCIOLOGIQUE DU SEMINARISTE QUEBECOIS. Université Laval, Centre de Recherches en Sociologie Religieuse, 1968.

* Ruesink, D.C. A STUDY OF THE SEMINARY STUDENT'S PERCEPTION OF PRACTITIONER ROLES TO BE PERFORMED BY THE MINISTER. Cited above as item 887.

1025. Sans Vila, J. CIENTO TRES VOCACIONES TARDIAS HOY EN EL SEMINARIO MAJOR DE BARCELONA. DATOS DE UN ENCUESTA. Barcelona: Seminario Conciliar, 1955.

1026. Stenger, Hermann. "Aptitudes mentales comparées et orientation intellectuelle des étudiants en théologie de langue allemande." SC 8,4 (1961): 305-316.

1027. Van Nostrand, Michael E. THE CALL TO THE MINISTRY FROM ANOTHER CAREER: PERCEPTIONS OF CHRISTIAN VOCATION HELD BY CATHOLIC AND PROTESTANT SEMINARIANS. Unpublished Ph.D. dissertation, Catholic University of America, 1970.

1028. Ventimiglia, Joseph C. "Career Commitment among Continuing and Exiting Seminary Students." SA 38,1 (1977): 49-58.

1029. Ventimiglia, Joseph C. "Significant Others in the Professional Socialization of Catholic Seminarians." JSSR 17,1 (1978): 43-52.

1030. Wuthnow, Robert. "New Forms of Religion in the Seminary." RRR 12,2 (1971): 80-87. Reprinted in Charles Y. Glock (ed.), RELIGION IN SOCIOLOGICAL PERSPECTIVE (volume cited in item 141), pp. 187-203.

Shaman

1031. Grim, John A. SHAMAN: PATTERNS OF SIBERIAN AND OJIBWAY HEALING. Norman: University of Oklahoma Press, 1983.

Sister/nun

1032. Aquina, Mary. "A Sociological Study of a Religious Congregation of African Sisters in Rhodesia." SC 14,1 (1967): 3-32.

1033. Bennett, Frederick A. "What Makes a Happy (or Unhappy) Nun?" REVIEW FOR RELIGIOUS 29 (1970): 380-390.

1034. Bluth, Elizabeth Jean. A CONVENT WITHOUT WALLS: A CASE STUDY IN SOCIOLOGICAL INNOVATION. Unpublished Ph.D. dissertation, University of California, 1969.

1035. Campbell-Jones, Suzanne. IN HABIT: A STUDY OF WORKING NUNS. New York: Pantheon, 1978.

1036. Casey, Catherine Elizabeth. A DESCRIPTIVE STUDY OF THE ISOLATE SISTER-TEACHER AND THE QUALITY OF COMMUNITY LIFE AMONG ROMAN CATHOLIC TEACHING SISTERS. Unpublished Ph.D. dissertation, University of Texas, 1976.

1037. Ebaugh, Helen Rose Fuchs. OUT OF THE CLOISTER. A STUDY OF ORGANIZATIONAL DILEMMAS. Austin: University of Texas Press, 1977.

1038. Ebaugh, Helen Rose Fuchs, and Paul Ritterband. "Education and the Exodus from Convents." SA 39,3 (1978): 257-264.

1039. Eisikovits, Rivka A. THE SISTERS OF OUR LADY OF CHARITY OF THE GOOD SHEPHERD 1835-1977 - A STUDY IN CULTURAL ADAPTATION. Unpublished Ph.D. dissertation, University of Minnesota, 1978.

* Fay, Leo F. "Differential Anomic Responses in a Religious Community." Cited above as item 25.

1040. Fichter, Joseph H. "Sisters and Nurses." REVIEW FOR RELIGIOUS 38,6 (1979): 839-845.

1041. Gilfeather, Katherine Anne. RELIGIOSAS EN APOSTOLADOS MARGINALES. Santiago, Chile: Centro Bellarmino, 1978.

1042. Gilfeather, Katherine Anne. "Women Religious, the Poor, and the Institutional Church in Chile." JOURNAL OF INTERAMERICAN STUDIES AND WORLD AFFAIRS 21 (1979): 129-155. Also in D.H. Levine (ed.), CHURCHES AND POLITICS IN LATIN AMERICA. Beverly Hills, Calif.: Sage, 1979, pp. 198-224.

1043. Hammersmith, Sue Kiefer. BECOMING A NUN: SOCIAL ORDER AND CHANGE IN A RADICAL COMMUNITY. Unpublished Ph.D. dissertation, Indiana University, 1976.

1044. Hill, Blake. WOMEN AND RELIGION: A STUDY OF SOCIALIZATION IN A COMMUNITY OF CATHOLIC SISTERS. Unpublished doctoral dissertation, University of Kentucky, 1967.

1045. Hillery, George A. "The Convent: Community, Prison, or Task Force?" JSSR 8 (1969): 140-151.

1046. McAuley, Ethel Ann Nancy. VOWS. COMMITMENT AND ROMAN CATHOLIC SISTERS: A DESCRIPTIVE STUDY OF A CONGREGATION. Unpublished Ph.D. dissertation, United States International University, 1975.

1047. Melamed, Audrey R., Manual S. Silverman, and Gloria J. Lewis. "Three Year Follow-up of Women Religious on the 16 Personality Factor Questionnaire." RRR 15 (1974): 64-70.

1048. Molitor, M. Margaret Anne. A COMPARATIVE STUDY OF DROPOUTS AND NON-DROPOUTS IN A RELIGIOUS COMMUNITY. Unpublished Ph.D. dissertation, Catholic University of America, 1967.

1049. Moran, Robert E. DEATH AND REBIRTH: A CASE STUDY OF REFORM EFFORTS OF A ROMAN CATHOLIC SISTERHOOD. Unpublished Ph.D. dissertation, University of California, 1972.

1050. Murphy, Roseanne. "Organizational Change and the Individual: A Case of the Religious Community." SA 25,2 (1964): 91-98.

1051. Murphy, Roseanne. A COMPARATIVE STUDY OF ORGANIZATIONAL CHANGE IN THREE RELIGIOUS COMMUNITIES. Unpublished Ph.D. dissertation, University of Notre Dame, 1966.

1052. Murphy, Roseanne. "Factors Influencing the Developmental Pace of Religious Communities." SA 27 (1966): 157-169.

1053. Murphy, Roseanne, and William T. Liu. "Organizational Stances and Change: A Comparative Study of Three Religious Communities." RRR 8 (1966): 37-50.

1054. Neal, Marie Augusta. "The Relation between Religious Belief and Structural Change in Religious Orders: Developing an Effective Measuring Instrument." RRR 12 (1970): 2-16.

1055. Neal, Marie Augusta. "The Relation between Religious Belief and Structural Change in Religious Orders: Some Evidence." RRR 13 (1971): 153-164.

1056. Neal, Marie Augusta. "A Theoretical Analysis of Renewal in Religious Orders in the U.S.A." SC 18,1 (1971): 7-26.

1057. Norr, James L., and Jeanne Schweickert. "Organizational Change and Social Participation: Results of Renewal in a Women's Religious Order." RRR 17,2 (1976): 120-133.

1058. Oliss, Patricia Ann. BELIEFS, BEHAVIORAL NORMS AND COMMITMENT IN FOUR RELIGIOUS ORDERS. Unpublished M.A. thesis, Wayne State University, 1971.

1059. O'Toole, Mary George. SISTERS OF MERCY OF MAINE. A RELIGIOUS COMMUNITY AS SOCIAL SYSTEM. Unpublished doctoral dissertation, Catholic University of America, 1964.

1060. Ramold, Mary Regis. THE URSULINES OF MOUNT ST. JOSEPH: A RELIGIOUS COMMUNITY AS A SOCIAL SYSTEM. Unpublished doctoral dissertation, Catholic University of America, 1964.

1061. Rice, Mary of St. Denis. TRAINING PROGRAMS OF GOOD SHEPHERD CONVENTS. Unpublished M.A. thesis, Catholic University of America, 1936.

1062. Salazar, Regina Clare. CHANGES IN THE EDUCATION OF ROMAN CATHOLIC RELIGIOUS SISTERS IN THE UNITED STATES FROM 1952 TO 1967. Unpublished Ph.D. dissertation, University of Southern California, 1971.

1063. SanGiovanni, Lucinda F. EX-NUNS. A STUDY OF EMERGENT ROLE PASSAGE. Norwood, New Jersey: Ablex Publishing Company, 1978.

1064. Thompson, Mary. MODIFICATIONS IN IDENTITY: A STUDY OF THE SOCIALIZATION PROCESS DURING A SISTER FORMATION PROGRAM. Unpublished Ph.D. dissertation, University of Chicago, 1963.

1065. Wedge, Rosalma Blanche (Alma Maria). THE OCCUPATIONAL MILIEU OF THE CATHOLIC SISTER. Unpublished Ph.D. dissertation, St. John's University, 1966.

* Wick, J.A. "Identity and Commitment of Young Sisters in a Religious Community." Cited above as item 175.

Witch

1066. Alfred, Randall H. "The Church of Satan." In C.Y. Glock and R.N. Bellah (eds.), THE NEW RELIGIOUS CONSCIOUSNESS (item 2407), pp. 180-202.

1067. Franklyn, J. DEATH BY ENCHANTMENT. AN EXAMINATION OF ANCIENT AND MODERN WITCHCRAFT. London: Hamilton; and New York: Putnam, 1971.

1068. Mair, L. "Witchcraft. Review Article." BRITISH JOURNAL OF SOCIOLOGY 23,1 (1972): 109-116.

1069. Scott, Gini Graham. CULT AND COUNTERCULT: A STUDY OF A SPIRITUAL GROWTH GROUP AND A WITCHCRAFT ORDER. Westport, Ct.: Greenwood Press, 1980.

1070. Tiryakian, Edward A. (ed.) ON THE MARGIN OF THE VISIBLE: SOCIOLOGY, THE ESOTERIC AND THE OCCULT. New York: Wiley-Interscience, 1974.

1071. Truzzi, Marcello. "The Occult Revival as Popular Culture. Some Random Observations on the Old and Nouveau Witch." SOCIOLOGICAL QUARTERLY 13,1 (1972): 16-36.

1072. Truzzi, Marcello. "Towards a Sociology of the Occult: Notes on Modern Witchcraft." In Irving I. Zaretsky and Mark P. Leone (eds.), RELIGIOUS MOVEMENTS IN CONTEMPORARY AMERICA (volume cited in item 140), pp. 628-645.

1073. Weisman, Richard. WITCHCRAFT, MAGIC, AND RELIGION IN 17TH-CENTURY MASSACHUSETTS. Amherst: University of Massachusetts Press, 1984.

1074. Wilson, M.H. "Witch Beliefs and Social Structure." AMERICAN JOURNAL OF SOCIOLOGY 56,4 (1951): 307-313.

Worker priests

* Roche de Coppens, P. "The Worker-Priest Movement: An Essay on the Emergence, Growth and Waning of the Worker-Priests in France and of the Sociocultural Factors that Lay Behind it." Cited above as item 733.

1075. Poulat, Emile. NAISSANCE DES PRETRES OUVRIERS. Paris: Casterman, 1965.
Italian translation: I PRETI OPERAI (1943-1947). Brescia: Morcelliana, 1967.

1076. Poulat, Emile. "The Future of the Worker Priest." MODERN CHURCHMAN (June 1959): 191-199.

1077. Poulat, Emile. "Notes sur la psychologie religieuse des prêtres ouvriers." JOURNAL DE PSYCHOLOGIE NORMALE ET PATHOLOGIQUE 1 (1957): 51-66.

1078. Poulat, Emile. "Religion et politique. De l'abbé Grégoire aux prêtres-ouvriers." CRITIQUE 13,123-124 (1957): 757-770.

Youth ministry

* Hoge, Dean R., et al. "Desired Outcomes of Religious Education and Youth Ministry in Six Denominations." Cited above as item 338.

Sex Roles

Sex roles (general)

1079. Brinkerhoff, Merlin B. "Religion and Goal Orientations: Does Denomination Make a Difference?" SA 39,3 (1978): 203-218.

1080. Brogan, Donna, and Nancy G. Kutner. "Measuring Sex-Role Orientation: A Normative Approach." JOURNAL OF MARRIAGE AND THE FAMILY 38 (1976): 31-40.

1081. Harder, Mary W. "Sex Roles in the Jesus Movement." SC 21 (1974): 345-353.

1082. Lipman-Blumen, Jean. "How Ideology Shapes Women's Lives." SCIENTIFIC AMERICAN 226 (Jan. 1972): 32-42.

1083. Martin, Patricia Yancey, Marie Withers Osmond, Susan Hesselbart, and Meredith Wood. "The Significance of Gender as a Social and Demographic Correlate of Sex Role Attitudes." SOCIOLOGICAL FOCUS 13,4 (1980): 383-396.

1084. Molm, Linda D. "Sex Role Attitudes and the Employment of Married Women: The Direction of Causality." SOCIOLOGICAL QUARTERLY 19,4 (1978): 522-533.

1085. Robak, Nicholas, and Sylvia Clavan. "Perception of Masculinity among Males in Two Traditional Family Groups." SA 36,4 (1975): 335-346.

1086. Suziedelis, Antanas, and Raymond H. Potvin. "Sex Differences in Factors Affecting Religiousness among Catholic Adolescents." JSSR 20,1 (1981): 38-51.

1087. Tomeh, Aida K. "Sex-Role Orientation: An Analysis of Structural and Attitudinal Predictors." JOURNAL OF MARRIAGE AND THE FAMILY 40 (1978): 341-354.

1088. Vanfossen, Beth Ensminger. "Sexual Stratification and Sex-Role Stratification." JOURNAL OF MARRIAGE AND THE FAMILY 39 (1977): 563-574.

Women

1089. Andezian, Sossie. "Pratiques féminines de l'Islam en France." ARCHIVES DE SCIENCES SOCIALES DES RELIGIONS 55,1 (1983): 53-66.

1090. Bainbridge, William Sims, and Laurie Russell Hatch. "Women's Access to Elite Careers: In Search of a Religion Effect." JSSR 21,3 (1982): 242-255.

* Bock, E. Wilber. "The Female Clergy: A Case of Professional Marginality." Cited above as item 556.

1091. Boecken, Ch. KIRCHLICHKEIT UND RELIGIOSITAT BEI ARBEITERFRAUEN AUS DEM RUHRGEBIET. Inaugural-Dissertation zur Erlangung des Grades eines Doktors der Sozialwissenschaften bei der Wirtschafts- und Sozialwissenschaftlichen Fakultät der Universität Göttingen. Göttingen: Wirtschafts- und Sozialwissenschaftlichen Fakultät der Universität Göttingen, 1969.

* Brinkerhoff, Merlin B., and Marlene M. MacKie. "Religious Denominations' Impact upon Gender Attitudes: Some Methodological Implications." Cited above as item 209.

1092. Chambers, Patricia P., and H. Paul Chalfant. "A Changing Role or the Same Old Handmaidens: Women's Role in Today's Church." RRR 19,2 (1978): 192-197.

1093. Cote, Pauline. DE LA PROTESTATION FEMININE: LES FEMMES DANS LE RENOUVEAU CHARISMATIQUE. Unpublished thèse de Maîtrise en science politique, Université Laval, 1984.

1094. De Vaus, David A. "The Impact of Children on Sex Related Differences in Church Attendance." SA 43,2 (1982): 145-154.

1095. Dowdall, Jean A. "Women's Attitudes toward Employment and Family Roles." SA 35,4 (1974): 251-262.

1096. Dumont-Johnson, Micheline. "Les communautés religieuses et la condition féminine." RECHERCHES SOCIOGRAPHIQUES 19,1 (1978): 79-102.

* Finch, Janet. "Devising Conventional Performances: The Case of Clergymen's Wives." Cited above as item 911.

1097. Finney, John M., III. THE RELIGIOUS COMMITMENT OF AMERICAN WOMEN. Unpublished Ph.D. dissertation, University of Wisconsin, 1971.

1098. Galilea, C., Katherine Gilfeather, and J. Puga. LAS MUJERES QUE TRABAJAN EN LA IGLESIA: LA EXPERIENCIA CHILENA. Santiago, Chile: Centro Bellarmino, 1976.

1099. Gilfeather, Katherine. "The Changing Role of Women in the Catholic Church in Chile." JSSR 16,1 (1977): 39-54.

* Gilfeather, Katherine Anne. "Women Religious, The Poor, and the Institutional Church in Chile." Cited above as item 1042.

* Gilfeather, Katherine Anne. RELIGIOSAS EN APOSTOLADOS MARGINALES. Cited above as item 1041.

* Greeley, Andrew M. THE RELIGIOUS IMAGINATION. Cited above as item 305.

1100. Greeley, Andrew M., and Mary G. Durkin. ANGRY CATHOLIC WOMEN. Chicago: Thomas More Press, 1984.

1101. Hacker, Helen. "Toward a Feminist Reformation of Biblical Religion." RELIGION, THE CUTTING EDGE. NEW ENGLAND SOCIOLOGIST 5,1 (1984): 25-36.

* Hartley, Shirley F., and Mary G. Taylor. "Religious Beliefs of Clergy Wives." Cited above as item 913.

1102. Haywood, Carol Lois. "The Authority and Empowerment of Women among Spiritualist Groups." JSSR 22,2 (1983): 157-166.

1103. Jacobs, Janet. "The Economy of Love in Religious Commitment: The Deconversion of Women from Nontraditional Religious Movements." JSSR 23,2 (1984): 155-171.

1104. Kosa, J., et al. "Marriage, Career, and Religiousness among Catholic College Girls." MARRIAGE AND FAMILY LIVING 24 (1962): 376-380.

1105. Lacelle, Elisabeth (ed.) LA FEMME ET LA RELIGION AU CANADA FRANÇAIS. Montreal: Bellarmin, 1979.

1106. Lazar, Morty M. "The Role of Women in Synagogue Ritual in Canadian Conservative Congregations." JEWISH JOURNAL OF SOCIOLOGY 20,2 (1978): 165-171.

* Lehman, Edward C., Jr. PROJECT SWIM: A STUDY OF WOMEN IN MINISTRY. Cited above as item 680.

* Lehman, Edward C., Jr. "Patterns of Lay Resistance to Women in Ministry." Cited above as item 681.

* Lehman, Edward C., Jr. "Organizational Resistance to Women in Ministry." Cited above as item 682.

1107. Lenski, Gerhard E. "Social Correlates of Religious Interest." AMERICAN SOCIOLOGICAL REVIEW 18 (1953): 533-544.

1108. McMurry, Martha J. RELIGION AND WOMEN'S SEX ROLE TRADITIONALISM. Unpublished Ph.D. dissertation, Indiana University, 1975.

1109. McMurry, Martha J. "Religion and Women's Sex Role Traditionalism." SOCIOLOGICAL FOCUS 11 (1978): 81-95.

1110. Neal, Marie Augusta. "Women in Religion: A Sociological Perspective." SOCIOLOGICAL INQUIRY 45,4 (1975): 33-39.

1111. Neal, Marie Augusta. "Women in Religious Symbolism and Organization." SOCIOLOGICAL INQUIRY 49 (1979): 218-250. Also in Harry M. Johnson (ed.), RELIGIOUS CHANGE AND CONTINUITY. SOCIOLOGICAL PERSPECTIVES. San Francisco: Jossey-Bass, 1979, pp. 218-250.

1112. Neal, Marie Augusta. "Sociology and Sexuality: A Feminist Perspective." CHRISTIANITY AND CRISIS 39,8 (1979): 118-122.

* Neal, Marie Augusta, and M. Clasby. "Priests' Attitudes toward Women." Cited above as item 705.

* Porter, Judith R., and Alexa A. Albert. "Subculture or Assimilation? A Cross-Cultural Analysis of Religion and Women's Role." Cited above as item 390.

1113. Porterfield, E. Amanda. MAIDENS, MISSIONARIES, AND MOTHERS: AMERICAN WOMEN AS SUBJECTS AND OBJECTS OF RELIGIOUSNESS. Unpublished Ph.D. dissertation, Stanford University, 1975.

1114. Richardson, James T. "The 'Old Right' in Action: Mormon and Catholic Involvement in an Equal Rights Amendment Referendum." In David G. Bromley and Anson Shupe (eds.), NEW CHRISTIAN POLITICS. Macon, Georgia: Mercer University Press, 1984, pp. 213-233.

* Royle, Marjorie H. "Women Pastors. What Happens after Placement?" Cited above as item 738.

* SanGiovanni, Lucinda F. EX-NUNS. A STUDY OF EMERGENT ROLE PASSAGE. Cited above as item 1063.

1115. Shakir, Moin. "Status of Women: Islamic View." SOCIAL SCIENTIST (India) 4,7 (1976): 70-75.

* Taylor, Mary G., and Shirley Foster Hartley. "The Two-Person Career: A Classic Example." Cited above as item 903.

1116. Tedlin, Kent. "Religious Preference and Pro/Anti Activism on the Equal Rights Amendment Issue." PACIFIC SOCIOLGOICAL REVIEW 21 (1978): 55-66.

1117. Ulbrich, Holley, and Myles Wallace. "Women's Work Force Status and Church Attendance." JSSR 23,4 (1984): 341-350.

* Wallace, Ruth A. "Bringing Women in: Marginality in the Churches." Cited above as item 484.

1118. Warenski, Marilyn. PATRIARCHS AND POLITICS: THE PLIGHT OF THE MORMON WOMAN. New York: McGraw-Hill, 1978.

1119. Welch, Michael R. "Female Exclusion from Religious Roles: A Cross-Cultural Test of Competing Explanations." SOCIAL FORCES 61,1 (1982): 79-98.

1120. Welch, Susan. "Support among Women for the Issues of the Women's Movement." SOCIOLOGICAL QUARTERLY 16 (1975): 216-227.

SECTION C: ORGANIZATION

Organization is the coherent and enduring relationship of statuses and roles within social groups. Many of the entries which are indexed under the term are studies of church polity - the form of governance of various churches. The subheadings which follow these entries focus on types and aspects of religious organization.

Organization (general)

1121. Balswick, Jack O., and Norman R. Layne, Jr. "Studying Social Organization in the Local Church. A Sociometric Approach." RRR 14,2 (1973): 101-109.

1122. Beckford, James A. "Religious Organization: A Trend Report and Bibliography." CURRENT SOCIOLOGY 21,2 (1973): 64-69.

1123. Beckford, James A. "Two Contrasting Types of Sectarian Organization." In R. Wallis (ed.), SECTARIANISM (item 3212), pp. 70-85.

1124. Beckford, James A. "Structural Dependence in Religious Organizations: From 'Skid-Road' to Watch Tower." JSSR 15,2 (1976): 169-175.

1125. Benson, J. Kenneth, and James H. Dorsett. "Toward a Theory of Religious Organizations." JSSR 10 (1971): 138-151.

1126. Benson, J. Kenneth, and Edward W. Hassinger. "Organization Set and Resources as Determinants of Formalization in Religious Organizations." RRR 14 (1972): 30-36.

1127. Bormann, Günther. "L'organisation sociale de l'Eglise évangélique du Würtemberg." SC 16,2 (1969): 185-225.

1128. Bormann, Günther, and Sigrid Bormann-Heischkeil. THEORIE UND PRAXIS KIRCHLICHER ORGANISATION. EIN BEITRAGE ZUR SOZIOLOGISCHEN FORSCHUNG, 3. Opladen: Westdeutscher Verlag, 1969, 1971.

1129. Brannon, Robert C.L. "Organizational Vulnerability in Modern Religious Organizations." JSSR 10,1 (1971): 27-32.

1130. Burch, Hobart A. DENOMINATIONS AND COUNCILS OF CHURCHES: COMPETITIVE OR COMPLEMENTARY? Unpublished Ph.D. dissertation, Brandeis University, 1965.

1131. Cantrell, Randolph, James F. Krile, and George A. Donohue. "The Community Involvement of Yoked Parishes." RURAL SOCIOLOGY 47 (1982): 45-55.

1132. Cantrell, Randolph, James F. Krile, and George A. Donohue. "Parish Autonomy: Measuring Denominational Differences." JSSR 22,3 (1983): 276-287.

1133. Caporale, Rocco. DYNAMICS OF HIEROCRACY. A STUDY OF CONTINUITY-IN-CHANGE OF A RELIGIOUS SYSTEM. THE SECOND VATICAN COUNCIL OF THE ROMAN CATHOLIC CHURCH. Unpublished Ph.D. dissertation, Columbia University, 1965.

1134. Caporale, Rocco. "The Dynamics of Hierocracy: Process of Continuity-in-Change of the Roman Catholic System during Vatican II." SA 28,2 (1967): 59-68.

1135. Davis, Jerome. "A Study of Protestant Church Boards of Control." AMERICAN JOURNAL OF SOCIOLOGY 38 (1932): 418-431.

* Dhooghe, Jos. "Organizational Problems regarding Different Types of Membership in the Church." Cited above as item 939.

1136. Dowdy, Edwin, and Gillian Lupton. "Some Aspects of Organizational Efficacy in Australian Churches." In Allan Black and Peter Glasner (eds.), PRACTICE AND BELIEF. STUDIES IN THE SOCIOLOGY OF AUSTRALIAN RELIGION. Sydney: Allan and Unwin, 1983, pp. 62-73.

1137. Dumont, Fernand. "Recherches sur les groupements religieux." SC 10,2 (1963): 171-191.

1138. Evers, H.D. "Die soziale Organisation der singhalesischen Religion." KOLNER ZEITSCHRIFT FÜR SOZIOLOGIE UND SOZIAL-PSYCHOLOGIE 16,2 (1964): 314-326.

1139. Glock, Charles Y. "Origine et évolution des groupes religieux." ARCHIVES DE SOCIOLOGIE DES RELIGIONS 16 (1963): 29-38.

1140. Gustafson, Paul M. STRUCTURAL ELEMENTS AND ORGANIZATIONAL BEHAVIOR. Unpublished Ph.D. dissertation, University of Minnesota, 1953.

1141. Harrison, Paul. AUTHORITY AND POWER IN THE FREE CHURCH TRADITION: A SOCIAL CASE STUDY OF THE AMERICAN BAPTIST CONVENTION. Princeton: Princeton University Press, 1959.

1142. Hinings, C. Robin, and Alan Bryman. "Size and Administrative Component in Churches." HUMAN RELATIONS 27,5 (1974): 457-475.

1143. Hinings, C. Robin, and Bruce D. Foster. "The Organization Structure of Churches: A Preliminary Model." SOCIOLOGY 7,1 (1973): 93-105.

1144. Hoc, Joseph M.N.-H. THE SYSTEM OF CONTROLLED DECENTRALIZATION OF THE CATHOLIC CHURCH. Unpublished Ph.D. dissertation, Stanford University, 1961.

1145. Homer, D.G. "Administrative Organization of the Mormon Church." POLITICAL SCIENCE QUARTERLY 57,1 (1942): 51-71.

1146. Hougland, James G., Jr. CONTROL AND POLICY IN PROTESTANT CONGREGATIONS. Unpublished Ph.D. dissertation, Indiana University, 1976.

1147. Hougland, James G., Jr., and James R. Wood. "'Inner Circles' in Local Churches: An Application of Thompson's Theory." SA 40,3 (1979): 226-239.

1148. Hougland, James G., and James R. Wood. "Control in Organizations and the Commitment of Members." SOCIAL FORCES 59,1 (1980): 85-105.

1149. Isichei, E.A. "Organization and Power in the Society of Friends." ARCHIVES DE SOCIOLOGIE DES RELIGIONS 10,19 (1965): 31-47.

1150. Kaufman, Harold F. RELIGIOUS ORGANIZATION IN KENTUCKY. Lexington, Ky.: Agricultural Experiment Station Bulletin 524, 1948.

1151. Kaufmann, Franz-Xavier. "Religion et bureaucratie -- le problème de l'organisation religieuse." SC 21,1 (1974): 101-107.

1152. Klein, Josephine. "Structural Aspects of Church Organization." In J. Matthes (ed.), BEITRAGE ZUR RELIGIONSSOZIOLOGISCHEN FORSCHUNG / ESSAYS ON RESEARCH IN THE SOCIOLOGY OF RELIGION. INTERNATIONALES JAHRBUCH FÜR RELIGIONSSOZIOLOGIE, 5. Köln, Opladen: Westdeutscher Verlag, 1968, pp. 101-122.

1153. Kroef, Justus M.A. van der. "Religious Organization and Economic Process in Indonesia." SOUTHWESTERN SOCIAL SCIENCE QUARTERLY 39,3 (1958): 187-202.

1154. Langrod, G. "Le mécanisme institutionel de l'Eglise catholique abordé sous l'angle de la science administrative." SC 16,2 (1969): 241-254.

* Lehman, Edward C., Jr. "Organizational Resistance to Women in Ministry." Cited above as item 682.

1155. Lewins, Frank. "Continuity and Change in a Religious Organization: Some Aspects of the Australian Catholic Church." JSSR 16,4 (1977): 371-382.

1156. Makler, Harry M. "Centralization/Decentralization in Formal Organizations: A Case Study of American Protestant Denominations." RRR 5,1 (1963): 5-11.

1157. Mensching, Gustav. "Religion." In Werner Ziegenfuss (ed.), HANDBUCH DER SOZIOLOGIE. Stuttgart: Ferdinand Enke Verlag, 1956, pp. 841-874.

1158. Millett, David. "A Typology of Religious Organizations Suggested by the Canadian Census." SA 30,2 (1969): 108-119.

* Mitchell, Robert E. "Polity, Church Attractiveness, and Ministers' Careers: An Eight Denominational Study of Inter-Church Mobility." Cited above as item 817.

1159. Moberg, David O. "Theological Position and Institutional Characteristics of Protestant Congregations: An Exploratory Study." JSSR 9,1 (1970): 53-58.

1160. Moulin, Léo. "La science politique et le gouvernement des communautés religieuses." REVUE INTERNATIONALE DES SCIENCES ADMINISTRATIVES 17 (1951): 42-67.

1161. Moulin, Léo. "Le gouvernement des communautés religieuses comme type de gouvernement mixte." REVUE FRANÇAISE DE SCIENCE POLITIQUE 2 (1952): 335-355.

1162. Moulin, Léo. "Les formes de gouvernement local et provincial dans les ordres religieuses." REVUE INTERNATIONALE DES SCIENCES ADMINISTRATIVES 20,1 (1955): 101.

1163. Moulin, Léo. "Policy Making in the Religious Orders." GOVERNMENT AND OPPOSITION 1,1 (1965): 25-54.

1164. Mueller, Samuel A. "Rokeach and the Church: A Theory of Organizational Reaction Formation." RRR 8 (1967): 131-140.

* Murphy, Roseanne. A COMPARATIVE STUDY OF ORGANIZATIONAL CHANGE IN THREE RELIGIOUS COMMUNITIES. Cited above as item 1051.

* Murphy, Roseanne, and William T. Liu. "Organizational Stance and Change: A Comparative Study of Three Religious Communities." Cited above as item 1053.

1165. Ofshe, Richard. "The Social Development of the Synanon Cult: The Managerial Strategy of Organizational Transformation." SA 41,2 (1980): 109-127.

1166. Parsons, Talcott. "Some Comments on the Pattern of Religious Organization in the United States." In T. Parsons, STRUCTURE AND PROCESS IN MODERN SOCIETIES. Glencoe: Free Press, 1960.

1167. Petersen, James C. "Organizational Structure and Program Change in Protestant Denominations." ORGANIZATION AND ADMINISTRATIVE SCIENCES 6,4 (1975-76): 1-13.

1168. Poisson, Bernard. "Schéma d'analyse de l'organisation religieuse." SOCIOLOGIE ET SOCIETES 1,2 (1969): 147-167.

1169. Pratt, Henry J. "Organizational Stress and Adaptation to Changing Political Status. The Case of the National Council of Churches of Christ in the United States." AMERICAN BEHAVIORAL SCIENTIST 17,6 (1974): 865-883.

1170. Rankin, Robert Parks. RELIGIOUS IDEALS AND CHURCH ADMINISTRATION: A SOCIOLOGICAL STUDY OF METHODISM. Unpublished Ph.D. dissertation, University of California at Berkeley, 1958.

1171. Scalf, John H., Michael J. Miller, and Charles W. Thomas. "Goal Specificity, Organizational Sructure, and Participant Commitment in Churches." SA 34,3 (1973): 169-184.

1172. Scherer, Ross P. (ed.) AMERICAN DENOMINATIONAL ORGANIZATION. A SOCIOLOGICAL VIEW. Pasadena, California: William Carey Library, 1980. Contains items 623, 1004, 1460, 2198, 2231.

1173. Séguy, Jean. "Réflexions sur 'Religious Organization' par James Beckford." CURRENT SOCIOLOGY/LA SOCIOLOGIE CONTEMPORAINE 21,3 (1973): 188-203.

1174. Siebel, W. FREIHEIT UND HERRSCHAFTSTRUKTUR IN DER KIRCHE. EINE SOZIOLOGISCHE STUDIE. Berlin: Morus, 1971.

1175. Sommerfeld, Richard. "Conceptions of the Ultimate and the Social Organization of Religious Bodies." JSSR 7,2 (1968): 179-196.

1176. Szafran, Robert F. THE OCCURENCE OF STRUCTURAL INNOVATION WITHIN RELIGIOUS ORGANIZATION. Unpublished Ph.D. dissertation, University of Wisconsin-Madison, 1977.

1177. Takayama, K. Peter. "Administrative Structures and Political Processes in Protestant Denominations." PUBLIUS: THE JOURNAL OF FEDERALISM 4 (1971): 5-37.

1178. Takayama, K. Peter. PATTERNS OF RELIGIOUS BUREAUCRACY: A COMPARATIVE STUDY OF PROTESTANT DENOMINATIONS. Unpublished Ph.D. dissertation, Southern Illinois University, Carbondale, 1971.

1179. Takayama, K. Peter. "Formal Policy and Change of Structure: Denominational Assemblies." SA 36,1 (1975): 17-28.

1180. Takayama, K. Peter, and Lynn Weber Cannon. "Formal Policy and Power Distribution in American Protestant Denominations." SOCIOLOGICAL QUARTERLY 20,3 (1979): 321-332.

1181. Takayama, K. Peter, and Diane G. Sachs. "Polity and Decision Premises: The Church and the Private School." JSSR 15,3 (1976): 269-278.

1182. Turner, Donald Everett. SOME EFFECTS OF BUREAUCRACY UPON PROFESSIONALS WHO WORK IN COMPLEX ORGANIZATIONS: AUTHORITY AND EVALUATION IN THE ROMAN CATHOLIC CHURCH. Unpublished Ph.D. dissertation, Stanford University, 1971.

1183. Weber, Paul-Günter. RELIGIOSITÄT UND SOZIALE ORGANISATION-FORMEN IN SEKTEN. EINE RELIGIONSSOZIOLOGISCHE STUDIE DREIER SEKTENGRUPPEN. Köln/Wien: Böhlau Verlag, 1975.

1184. Westhues, Kenneth. "Religious Organization in Canada and the United States." INTERNATIONAL JOURNAL OF COMPARATIVE SOCIOLOGY 17 (1976): 206-225.

*Westhues, Kenneth. "The Church in Opposition." Cited above as item 969.

1185. White, O. Kendall, Jr. "Constituting Norms and the Formal Organization of American Churches." SA 33,2 (1972): 95-109.

1186. Wilson, John. "The Relation between Ideology and Organization in a Small Religious Group: The British Israelites." RRR 10,1 (1968): 51-60.

1187. Winter, Gibson. "Religious Organizations." Ch. 11 in W. Lloyd Warner (ed.), THE EMERGENT AMERICAN SOCIETY. VOLUME I: LARGE SCALE ORGANIZATIONS. New Haven: Yale University Press, 1967, pp. 408-491.

1188. Winter, Gibson. RELIGIOUS IDENTITY: A STUDY OF RELIGIOUS ORGANIZATION. New York: Macmillan, 1968.

1189. Wood, James R. "Personal Commitment and Organizational Constraint: Church Officials and Racial Integration." SA 33,3 (1972): 142-151.

1190. Wood, James R. "Legitimate Control and 'Organizational Transcendence.'" SOCIAL FORCES 54,1 (1975): 199-211.

1191. Wood, James R. LEADERSHIP IN VOLUNTARY ORGANIZATIONS: THE CONTROVERSY OVER SOCIAL ACTION IN PROTESTANT CHURCHES. New Brunswick, New Jersey: Rutgers University Press, 1981.

1192. Yeo, Stephen A. "A Contextual View of Religious Organisation." SOCIOLOGICAL YEARBOOK OF RELIGION IN BRITAIN 6 (1973): 207-234.

1193. Young, Barry, and John E. Hughes. "Organizational Theory and the Canonical Parish." SA 26,2 (1965): 57-71.

Ashram

1194. Volinn, Ernest. LEAD US FROM DARKNESS: THE ALLURE OF A RELIGIOUS SECT AND ITS CHARISMATIC LEADER. Unpublished Ph.D. dissertation, Columbia University, 1982.

Associational

In associational organization the person affiliates with the religion for a circumscribed purpose. It contrasts communal membership, in which family, friends and work associates all help comprise one's religious world.

1195. Lenski, Gerhard. THE RELIGIOUS FACTOR: A SOCIOLOGIST'S INQUIRY. Garden City: Doubleday, 1961.

1196. Nelson, Geoffrey K. "Communal and Associational Churches." RRR 12 (1971): 102-110.

Authority

1197. Azzi, Riolando. "Catholicismo popular e autoridade eclesiastica na evolucão historica do Brasil. RELIGIAO E SOCIEDADE 1 (1977): 125-149.

1198. Bartholomew, John Niles. "A Sociological View of Authority in Religious Organizations." RRR 23,2 (1981): 118-132.

* Beech, Lawrence A. "Denominational Affiliation and Styles of Authority in Pastoral Counselling." Cited above as item 821.

* Carroll, Jackson W. "Some Issues in Clergy Authority." Cited above as item 837.

1199. Dahm, Charles William. AUTHORITY AND CONFLICT IN THE ROMAN CATHOLIC CHURCH: IDEOLOGICAL AND POLITICAL CONSTRAINTS ON DEMOCRATIZATION IN AN AUTHORITARIAN INSTITUTION. Unpublished Ph.D. dissertation, University of Wisconsin, Madison, 1978.

* Hammond, Phillip E., A. Gedricks, E. Lawler, and L. Turner. "Clergy Authority and Friendship with Parishioners." Cited above as item 857.

* Hammond, Phillip E., Luis Salinas, and Douglas Sloane. "Types of Clergy Authority: Their Measurement, Location, and Effects." Cited above as item 70.

* Haywood, Carol Lois. "The Authority and Empowerment of Women among Spiritualist Groups." Cited above as item 1102.

1200. Hégy, Pierre. L'AUTORITE DANS LE CATHOLICISME CONTEMPORAIN, DU SYLLABUS A VATICAN II. Paris: Beauchesne, 1975.

1201. Hougland, James G., Jr., Jon M. Shepard, and James R. Wood. "Discrepancies in Perceived Organizational Control: Their Incidence and Importance in Local Churches." SOCIOLOGICAL QUARTERLY 20,1 (1979): 63-76.

1202. Houtart, François, "Conflicts of Authority in the Roman Catholic Church." SC 16,3 (1969): 309-325.

* Imse, Thomas P. "Spiritual Leadership and Organizational Leadership. The Dilemma of Being Pope." Cited above as item 921.

* Ingram, Larry C. "Notes on Pastoral Power in the Congregational Tradition." Cited above as item 860.

1203. Koller, Douglas B. "Belief in the Right to Question Church Teachings, 1958-71." SOCIAL FORCES 58,1 (1979): 290-304.

* Moran, Robert E. "Liturgy, Authority and Tradition. Priestly Atttitudes and the Age Factor." Cited above as item 700.

1204. O'Dea, Thomas F. "Authority and Freedom in the Church: Tension, Balance and Contradiction. An Historical-Sociological View." THE JURIST 31,1 (1971): 223-249.

* O'Donovan, Thomas R., and Arthur X. Deegan. "Some Career Determinants of Church Executives." Cited above as item 711.

* Smith, Luke M. "The Clergy: Authority Structure, Ideology, Migration." Cited above as item 819.

1205. Sprague, T. W. "Some Notable Features in the Authority Structure of a Sect." SOCIAL FORCES 21,3 (1943): 344-350.

* Stewart, James H. AMERICAN CATHOLIC LEADERSHIP: A DECADE OF TURMOIL 1966-1976. Cited above as item 769.

* Struzzo, John A. "Professionalism and the Resolution of Authority Conflicts among the Catholic Clergy." Cited above as item 773.

1206. Taylor, Mary G. AUTHORITY AND COMPLIANCE IN A NORMATIVE ORGANIZATION: A STUDY OF THE SAN FRANCISCO PRESBYTERY. Unpublished Ph.D. dissertation, University of California, Berkeley, 1969.

1207. Trotter, Donald F. A STUDY OF AUTHORITY AND POWER IN THE STRUCTURE AND DYNAMICS OF THE SOUTHERN BAPTIST CONVENTION. Unpublished D.R.E. thesis, Southern Baptist Theological Seminary, 1962.

* Vaillancourt, Jean-Guy. PAPAL POWER. A STUDY OF VATICAN CONTROL OVER LAY CATHOLIC ELITES. Cited above as item 966.

1208. Van Billoen, Etiènne. "Le modèle d'autorité dans l'Eglise." SC 20,3 (1973): 405-425.

1209. Vincent, Gilbert. "La mise en place d'un nouveau type d'autorité. Signification sociologique de la prédication et interprétation ecclésiologique de la mort du Christ dans le protestantisme." ARCHIVES DE SCIENCES SOCIALES DES RELIGIONS 20,39 (1975): 147-158.

1210. Wallis, Roy. "Ideology, Authority, and the Development of Cultic Movements." SOCIAL RESEARCH 41,2 (1974): 299-327.

1211. Warwick, Donald. "The Centralization of Ecclesiastical Authority: An Organizational Perspective." CONCILIUM 91,1 (1974): 109-118.

1212. Willems, Emilio. "Validation of Authority in Pentecostal Sects of Chile and Brazil." JSSR 4 (1967): 253-258.

1213. Wood, James R. "Authority and Controversial Policy: The Churches and Civil Rights." AMERICAN SOCIOLOGICAL REVIEW 35 (1970): 1057-69.

1214. Yeandel, Francis Arthur. SOCIAL AUTHORITY AND SOCIAL PERCEPTION. A LABORATORY STUDY OF THE EFFECT OF PRESSURE TO CONFORM PERCEPTUALLY, APPLIED BY RELIGIOUS AND MILITARY AUTHORITY SURROGATES. Unpublished Ph.D. dissertation, University of Notre Dame, 1966.

Base communities

Important in Latin America, base communities are religious groupings in which the laity apply religious perspectives to practical problems. These problems range from the specifically religious to the social and political.

1215. Bruneau, Thomas C. "Basic Christian Communities in Latin America. Their Nature and Significance (Especially in Brazil.)" In D.H. Levine (ed.), CHURCHES AND POLITICS IN LATIN AMERICA. Beverly Hills, Calif.: Sage, 1979, pp. 225-237.

1216. Büntig, Aldo-J. "Las comunidades de base en la acción política." CONCILIUM 104 (Spanish Series, 1975): 111-121.

1217. Deelen, Godfried. KIRCHE AUF DEM WEG ZUM VOLKE. SOZIOLOGISCHE BETRACHTUNGEN UBER KIRCHLISCHE BASISGEMEINDEN IN BRASILIEN. Metingen: BKV Brasilienkundverlag, 1982.

1218. Gregory, Afonso. COMUNIDADES ECLESIAIS DE BASE. UTOPIA OU REALIDADE? Rio de Janeiro: Ceris; Petrópolis: Vozes, 1973.

1219. Opazo, Andrés, and David Smith. "Decadencia populista, protesta popular y comunidades de base en Panama." ESTUDIOS SOCIALES CENTROAMERICANOS 11,33 (1982): 249-271.

1220. Rolim, Francisco C. "Communidades eclesiais de base et camadas populares." ENCONTROS COM A CIVILIZAÇAO BRASILEIRA 22 (1980): 89-114.

1221. Welz Scroeter, Cristina. "Consideraciones sociológicas para la formación de comunidades de base en los grandes centros urbanos." CATEQUESIS LATINOAMERICANA(Asunción) 5,19 (1973): 175-178.

Bureaucracy

1222. Page, Charles H. "Bureaucracy and the Liberal Church." REVIEW OF RELIGION 16 (1952): 137-150.

1223. Thompson, Kenneth A. "Bureaucracy and the Church." In D. Martin (ed.), A SOCIOLOGICAL YEARBOOK OF RELIGION IN BRITAIN 1. London: SCM, 1968, pp. 32-45.

Communality

Communality is the extent to which one's associates in non-religious aspects of life belong to the same religious group.

1224. Anderson, Charles H. "Religious Communality among White Protestants, Catholics and Mormons." SOCIAL FORCES 46,4 (1968): 501-508.

1225. Anderson, Charles H. "Religious Communality among Academics." JSSR 7,1 (1968): 87-96.

1226. Anderson, Charles H. "Denominational Differences in White Protestant Communality." RRR 10,1 (1969): 66-72.

1227. Anderson, Charles H. "Religious Communality and Party Preference." SA 30,1 (1969): 32-41.

1228. Demerath, Nicholas J., III. SOCIAL CLASS IN AMERICAN PROTESTANTISM. Chicago: Rand McNally, 1965.

1229. Dynes, Russell R. "The Consequences of Sectarianism for Social Participation." SOCIAL FORCES 35 (1957): 331-334.

1230. Flora, Cornelia Butler. "Social Dislocation and Pentecostalism: A Multivariate Analysis." SA 34,4 (1973): 296-307.

1231. Hiller, Harry H. "Communality as a Dimension of Ecumenical Negativism." RRR 12 (1971): 111-114.

* Hoge, Dean R., and Jackson W. Carroll. "Determinants of Commitment and Participation in Suburban Protestant Churches." Cited above as item 145.

1232. Ishwaran, K. "Calvinism and Social Behaviour in a Dutch-Canadian Community." In K. Ishwaran (ed.), THE CANADIAN FAMILY. Toronto: Holt, Rinehart and Winston, 1971, pp. 297-316.

* Lenski, Gerhard. THE RELIGIOUS FACTOR: A SOCIOLOGIST'S INQUIRY. Cited above as item 1195.

1233. McRae, James A. "Changes in Religious Communalism Desired by Protestants and Catholics." SOCIAL FORCES 61,3 (1983): 709-730.

* Nelson, Geoffrey K. "Communal and Associational Churches." Cited above as item 1196.

1234. Saunders, John V.D. "Organização social de uma congregação protestante no estado da Guanabara, Brasil." SOCIOLOGIA (São Paulo) 22,4 (1960): 415-450; and 23,1 (1961): 37-66.

* Stark, Rodney, and Charles Y. Glock. AMERICAN PIETY: THE NATURE OF RELIGIOUS COMMITMENT. Cited above as item 497.

Commune

A settlement embracing familial, economic, residential, and (in the case of religious communes) religious aspects of life.

1235. Aidala, Angela A. IDEOLOGICAL SYSTEMS: A LONGITUDINAL STUDY OF NORMS, VALUES, AND IDEOLOGY IN SIXTY URBAN COMMUNAL LIVING GROUPS. Unpublished Ph.D. dissertation, Columbia University, 1979.

1236. Aidala, Angela A. "Worldviews, Ideologies and Social Experimentation: Clarification and Replication of 'The Consciousness Reformation.'" JSSR 23,1 (1984): 44-59.

1237. Baer, Hans A. THE LEVITES OF UTAH: THE DEVELOPMENT OF AND CONVERSION TO A SMALL MILLENARIAN SECT. Unpublished Ph.D. dissertation, University of Utah, 1976.

1238. Barthel, Diane L. AMANA: FROM PIETIST SECT TO AMERICAN COMMUNITY. Lincoln: University of Nebraska Press, 1984.

1239. Boldt, Edward D. ACQUIESCENCE AND CONVENTIONALITY IN A COMMUNAL SOCIETY. Unpublished Ph.D. dissertation, University of Alberta, 1968.

1240. Borowski, Karol. ATTEMPTING AN ALTERNATIVE SOCIETY. A SOCIOLOGICAL STUDY OF A SELECTED COMMUNAL-REVITALIZATION MOVEMENT IN THE UNITED STATES. Norwood, Pennsylvania: Norwood Editions, 1984.

1241. Chesebro, Scott E. THE MENNONITE URBAN COMMUNE: A HERMENEUTIC-DIALECTICAL UNDERSTANDING OF ITS ANABAPTIST IDEOLOGY AND PRACTICE. Unpublished Ph.D. dissertation, University of Notre Dame, 1982.

1242. Cuneo, Michael W. THE SHAKERS: A CASE STUDY IN THE DYNAMICS OF AN ESTABLISHED SECT. Unpublished M.A. thesis, University of St. Michael's College, 1982.

1243. Desroche, Henri. "'Heavens on earth.' Micromiliénarismes et communnautarisme utopique en Amérique du Nord de XVIIe au XIXe siècle." ARCHIVES DE SOCIOLOGIE DES RELIGIONS 4 (1957): 57-92.

1244. Gabovitch, B. "Les kibboutsim d'inspiration religieuse." ARCHIVES DE SOCIOLOGIE DES RELIGIONS 2 (1956): 98-101.

1245. Gollin, Gillian Lindt. MORAVIANS IN TWO WORLDS. A STUDY OF CHANGING COMMUNITIES. New York: Columbia University Press, 1967.

1246. Gollin, Gillian Lindt. "Religious Communitarianism in America. A Review of Recent Research." ARCHIVES INTERNATIONALES DE SOCIOLOGIE DE LA COOPERATION ET DU DEVELOPPEMENT 28 (1970): 125-155.

1247. Hall, John R. THE WAYS OUT: UTOPIAN COMMUNAL GROUPS IN AN AGE OF BABYLON. London: Routledge and Kegan Paul, 1978.

1248. Harder, Mary W. THE CHILDREN OF CHRIST COMMUNE: A STUDY OF A FUNDAMENTALIST COMMUNAL SECT. Unpublished Ph.D. dissertation, University of Nevada, Reno, 1972.

1249. Hillery, George A. "Freedom, Love, and Community: An Outline of a Theory." In Thomas Robbins and Dick Anthony (eds.), IN GODS WE TRUST (item 367), pp. 303-325.

1250. Hillery, George A., and Paula C. Morrow. "The Monastery as a Commune." INTERNATIONAL REVIEW OF MODERN SOCIOLOGY 6 (1976): 139-154.

1251. Kanter, Rosabeth Moss. COMMITMENT AND COMMUNITY. Cambridge, Mass.: Harvard University Press, 1972.

1252. Mandelker, Ira L. RELIGION, SOCIETY, AND UTOPIA IN NINETEENTH-CENTURY AMERICA. Amherst: University of Massachusetts Press, 1984.

1253. Mikkelsen, Michael A. THE BISHOP HILL COLONY. A RELIGIOUS COMMUNIST SETTLEMENT IN HENRY COUNTY, ILLINOIS. Baltimore: Johns Hopkins Press, 1892.

1254. Morelli, Anne. "Faut-il poser le phénomène communautaire en termes de religion ou de pouvoir?" RECHERCHES SOCIOGRAPHIQUES 10,1 (1979): 91-98.

1255. Nordquist, Ted. ANANDA COOPERATIVE VILLAGE: A STUDY OF THE VALUES AND ATTITUDES OF A NEW AGE RELIGIOUS COMMUNITY. Monograph series, no. 16. The religionshistoriske institut. Uppsala University, Uppsala, Sweden, 1978.

1256. Pilarzyk, Thomas J., and Cardell K. Jacobson. "Christians in the Youth Culture: The Life History of an Urban Commune." WISCONSIN SOCIOLOGIST 14 (1977): 136-151.

1257. Richardson, James T., Mary W. Stewart, and Robert Simmonds. ORGANIZED MIRACLES. A STUDY OF A CONTEMPORARY, YOUTH COMMUNAL, FUNDAMENTALIST ORGANIZATION. New Brunswick, N.J.: Transaction, 1979.

1258. Rigby, Andrew, and Bryan S. Turner. "Communes, hippies et religion sécularisées. Quelques aspects sociologiques de formes actuelles de religiosité." SC 20,1 (1973): 5-18.

1259. Simmonds, Robert B. THE PEOPLE OF THE JESUS MOVEMENT: A PERSONALITY ASSESSMENT OF MEMBERS OF A FUNDAMENTALIST RELIGIOUS COMMUNITY. Unpublished Ph.D. dissertation, University of Nevada, Reno, 1977.

1260. Simmonds, Robert, James T. Richardson, and Mary W. Harder. "Organizational Aspects of a Jesus Movement Community." SC 21 (1974): 269-281.

* Simmonds, Robert B., James T. Richardson, and Mary W. Harder. "A Jesus Movement Group: An Adjective Check List Assessment." Cited above as item 152.

1261. Stephan, Karen H. "Religion and the Survival of Utopian Communities." JSSR 12,1 (1973): 89-100.

1262. Treece, James William, Jr. "Theories on Religious Communal Development." SC 18,1 (1971): 85-100.

1263. Voisin, Michel. "Communautés utopiques et structures sociales: le cas de la Belgique Françophone." REVUE FRANÇAISE DE SOCIOLOGIE 18,2 (1977): 271-300.

1264. Whitworth, John McKelvie. GOD'S BLUEPRINTS: A SOCIOLOGICAL STUDY OF THREE UTOPIAN SECTS. London: Routledge and Kegan Paul, 1975.

1265. Whitworth, John McKelvie. "Communitarian Groups and the World." In Roy Wallis (ed.), SECTARIANISM (item 3212), pp. 117-137.

1266. Zablocki, Benjamin D. THE JOYFUL COMMUNITY. Baltimore: Penguin, 1971. Chicago: University of Chicago Press, 1980.

Denomination - also see Typology in Chapter Three

The entries which follow focus on denominational identity as a variable, usually to discover whether people's denominational affiliation varies with some other attribute. In Chapter Three, the term denomination is used differently; there it represents a type of religious orientation to the social world.

1267. Allinsmith, Wesley, and Beverly Allinsmith. "Religious Affiliation and Political-Economic Atttitude: A Study of Eight Major U.S. Religious Groups." PUBLIC OPINION QUARTERLY 12 (1948): 377-389.

* Anderson, Charles H. "Denominational Differences in White Protestant Communality." Cited above as item 1226.

1268. Bahr, Howard M. "Shifts in the Denominational Demography of Middletown, 1924-1977." JSSR 21,2 (1982): 99-114.

1269. Bell, Wendell, and Maryanne T. Force. "Religious Preference, Familism and the Class Structure." MIDWEST SOCIOLOGIST 19 (1957): 79-86.

* Berk, Marc. "Pluralist Theory and Church Policy Positions on Racial and Sexual Equality." Cited above as item 344.

* Blaikie, Norman W.H. "The Use of 'Denomination' in Sociological Explanation: The Case of the Position of Clergy on Social Issues." Cited above as item 551.

* Brinkerhoff, Merlin B., and Marlene M. MacKie. "Religious Denominations' Impact upon Gender Attitudes: Some Methodological Implications." Cited above as item 209.

1270. Burchard, Waldo W. "Denominational Correlates of Changing Religious Beliefs in College." SA 31,1 (1970): 36-45.

1271. Davidson, James D. "Patterns of Belief at the Denominational and Congregational Levels." RRR 13 (1972): 197-205.

1272. DeJong, Gordon F., and Thomas R. Ford. "Religious Fundamentalism and Denominational Preference in the Southern Appalachian Region." JSSR 5,1 (1965): 24-33.

1273. Doyle, Ruth T., and Sheila M. Kelly. "Comparison of Trends in Ten Denominations, 1950-75." In Dean R. Hoge and David A. Roozen (eds.), UNDERSTANDING CHURCH GROWTH AND DECLINE 1950-78 (item 950), pp. 144-159.

* Ebaugh, Helen Rose Fuchs, and C. Allen Haney. "Church Attendance and Attitudes toward Abortion: Differentials in Liberal and Conservative Churches." Cited above as item 105.

1274. Ethridge, F. Maurice, and Joe R. Feagin. "Varieties of 'Fundamentalism': A Conceptual and Empirical Analysis of Two Protestant Denominations." SOCIOLOGICAL QUARTERLY 20,1 (1979): 37-48.

* Finner, Stephen L. "Religious Membership and Religious Preference: Equal Indicators of Religiosity?" Cited above as item 944.

1275. Glasner, Peter E. "Religion and Divisiveness in Australia." In I. Pilowsky (ed.), CULTURES IN COLLISION. Adelaide: Australian National Association for Mental Health, 1975.

1276. Goldstein, Sidney. "Socioeconomic Differentials among Religious Groups in the United States." AMERICAN JOURNAL OF SOCIOLOGY 74 (1969): 612-631.

1277. Greeley, Andrew M. ETHNICITY, DENOMINATION, AND INEQUALITY. Beverly Hills, California: Sage, 1976.

1278. Harrison, Michael I., and Bernard Lazerwitz. "Do Denominations Matter?" AMERICAN JOURNAL OF SOCIOLOGY 88,2 (1982): 356-377.

* Hartley, Shirley F., and Mary G. Taylor. "Religious Beliefs of Clergy Wives." Cited above as item 913.

1279. Hessels, A. "L'Appartenance religieuse et l'utilisation des loisirs du dimanche." SC 11,2 (1964): 27-39.

* Hoge, Dean R., et al. "Desired Outcomes of Religious Education and Youth Ministry of Six Denominations." Cited above as item 338.

1280. Klemmack, David L., and Jerry D. Cardwell. "Interfaith Comparison of Multidimensional Measures of Religiosity." PACIFIC SOCIOLOGICAL REVIEW 16,4 (1973): 495-507.

1281. Kruijt, J.P. "The Influence of Denominationalism on Social Life and Organizational Patterns." ARCHIVES DE SOCIOLOGIE DES RELIGIONS 8 (1959): 105-112.

* Lazerwitz, Bernard. "Past and Future Trends in the Size of American Jewish Denominations." Cited above as item 953.

1282. Lazerwitz, Bernard, and Michael I. Harrison. "American Jewish Denominations: A Social and Religious Profile." AMERICAN SOCIOLOGICAL REVIEW 44,4 (1979): 656-666. Also in P.H. McNamara (ed.), RELIGION: NORTH AMERICAN STYLE (volume cited in item 117), pp. 184-195.

* Lenski, Gerhard E. "Social Correlates of Religious Interest." Cited above as item 1107.

1283. McCallister, Ian. "Religious Commitment and Social Attitudes in Ireland." RRR 25,1 (1983): 3-20.

* McMurry, Martha J. RELIGION AND WOMEN'S SEX ROLE TRADITIONALISM. Cited above as item 1108.

* McMurry, Martha J. "Religion and Women's Sex Role Traditionalism." Cited above as item 1109.

1284. Nelsen, Hart M. "Religious Conformity in an Age of Disbelief: Contextual Effects of Time, Denomination, and Family Processes upon Church Decline and Apostasy." AMERICAN SOCIOLOGICAL REVIEW 46,5 (1981): 632-640.

1285. Nelsen, Hart M. "The Influence of Social and Theological Factors upon the Goals of Religious Education." RRR 23,3 (1982): 255-263.

1286. Nosanchuk, T.A. "Dimensions of Canadian Religions: A Preliminary Study." JSSR 7,1 (1968): 109-110.

1287. Philibert, Paul J., and Dean R. Hoge. "Teachers, Pedagogy and the Process of Religious Education." RRR 23,3 (1982): 264-285.

1288. Poit, Carl H. "A Study Concerning Religious Belief and Denominational Affiliation." RELIGIOUS EDUCATION 57,3 (1962): 214-216.

1289. Richey, Russell E. (ed.) DENOMINATIONALISM. Nashville: Abingdon, 1977.

* Rodd, L.S. "Church Affiliation and Denominational Values." Cited above as item 961.

1290. Schmidtchen, G. PROTESTANTEN UND KATHOLIKEN: SOZIOLOGISCHE ANALYSE KONFESSIONELLER KULTUR. Bern: A. Francke, 1973.

1291. Stark, Rodney, and Charles Y. Glock. "The New Denominationalism." RRR 7 (1965): 8-17.
Reprinted as Ch.5 in Charles Y. Glock and Rodney Stark, RELIGION AND SOCIETY IN TENSION (volume cited in item 141).

1292. Tabory, Ephraim, and Bernard Lazerwitz. "Americans in the Israeli Reform and Conservative Denominations: Religiosity under an Ethnic Shield?" RRR 24,3 (1983): 177-187.

1293. Warren, Bruce L. THE RELATIONSHIPS BETWEEN RELIGIOUS PREFERENCE AND SOCIO-ECONOMIC ACHIEVEMENT OF AMERICAN MEN. Unpublished Ph.D. dissertation, University of Michigan, 1970.

1294. Warren, Bruce L. "Socioeconomic Achievement and Religion: The American Case." SOCIOLOGICAL INQUIRY 40 (1970): 130-155. Also in E.O. Laumann (ed.), SOCIAL STRATIFICATION. Indianapolis: Bobbs-Merrill, 1970, pp. 130-155.

1295. Wimberley, Ronald C., and James A. Christenson. "Civil Religion and Other Religious Identitites." SA 42,2 (1981): 91-100.

Diocese

1296. Cuadrench, J. "La diócesis. Ensayo para un análisis sociológico." REVISTA DEL INSTITUTO DE CIENCIAS SOCIALES 18 (1971): 415-452.

* Perez, Gustavo, and Isaac Wust. LA IGLESIA EN COLOMBIA. Cited above as item 715.

* Poisson, Bernard. "Schéma d'analyse de l'organisation religieuse." Cited above as item 1168.

1297. Vallier, Ivan. "Comparative Studies of Roman Catholicism. Dioceses as Strategic Units." SC 16,2 (1969): 147-184.

Hierocracy

1298. Murvar, Vatro. "Max Weber's Concept of Hierocracy: A Study in the Typology of Church-State Relationships." SA 28 (1967): 69-84.

1299. Murvar, Vatro. "Integrative and Revolutionary Capabilities of Religion." In Harry M. Johnson (ed.), RELIGIOUS CHANGE AND CONTINUITY (volume cited in item 516), pp. 74-86.

Monasticism

1300. Blazowich, A. SOZIOLOGIE DES MÖNCHTUMS UND DER BENEDIKTINERREGEL. Wien: Herder, 1954.

1301. Della Fave, L. Richard, and George A. Hillery, Jr. "Status Inequality in a Religious Community: The Case of a Trappist Monastery." SOCIAL FORCES 59,1 (1980): 62-84.

1302. Dudley, Charles J., and George A. Hillery, Jr. "Freedom and Monastery Life." JSSR 18,1 (1979): 18-28.

1303. Goddijn, H.P.M. "The Monastic Community Life in our Times." SC 12,1-2 (1965): 101-113.

* Hillery, George A. "Freedom, Love, and Community: An Outline of a Theory." Cited above as item 1249.

1304. Hillery, George A. "Triangulation in Religious Research: A Sociological Approach to the Study of Monasteries." RRR 23,1 (1981): 22-38.

1305. Hillery, George A., Jr., Charles J. Dudley, and Paula C. Morrow. "Toward a Sociology of Freedom." SOCIAL FORCES 55,3 (1977): 685-700.

* Hillery, George A., and Paula C. Morrow. "The Monastery as a Commune." Cited above as item 1250.

1306. Mantzaridis, Georges. "New Statistical Data Concerning the Monks of Mount Athos." SC 22,1 (1975): 97-106.

1307. Marliere, M. ETUDE D'UN GROUPE DE TROIS MONASTERES BOUDDHIQUES SIS A THONBURI (THAILANDE). ESSAI DE SOCIOGRAPHIE BOUDDHIQUE. Geneva: Droz, 1977.

1308. Mendelson, E. Michael. SANGHA AND STATE IN BURMA: A STUDY OF MONASTIC SECTARIANISM AND LEADERSHIP. Ithaca, N.Y.: Cornell University Press, 1975.

1309. Savramis, Demosthenes. ZUR SOZIOLOGIE DES BYZANTINISCHEN MÖNCHTUMS. Leiden: Brill, 1962.

1310. Séguy, Jean. "Les sociétés imaginées: monachisme et utopie." ANNALES 2 (1971): 328-354.

Orders/congregations

There is a technical distinction between religious orders and congregations based on the type of vows the members take. In sociological terms, however, the two types of organizations are the same. They are voluntary associations of celibates which share their properties communally, maintain an internal authority structure, and engage in some common religious observance or mission.

See also Sisters above, items 1032-1065, for most studies of women's orders and congregations.

1311. Ammentorp, William, and Brian Fitch. THE COMMITTED: A SOCIOLOGICAL STUDY OF THE BROTHERS OF CHRISTIAN SCHOOLS. Winona, Minn.: St. Mary's College Press, 1968.

1312. Baan, M.A. "Structural and Cultural Changes in the Dutch Franciscan Province." SC 13,3 (1966): 245-256.

1313. Baan, M.A., and L. Grond. "Inventaire statistique de l'Ordre des Freres Mineurs dans le Nord-Ouest de l'Europe." SC 13,3 (1966): 257-275.

1314. Bergeron, Cécile. COMMUNAUTES RELIGIEUSES ET EDUCATION. Unpublished M.A. thesis, Université de Sherbrooke, 1970-71.

1315. Bohr, Ronald H. "Dogmatism and Age of Vocational Choice in Two Religious Orders." JSSR 7,2 (1968): 282-283.

1316. Bonte, W. de. "The Components of the Novitiate. Introduction to an Inquiry." SC 13,5-6 (1966): 401-414.

* Bowman, Jerome Francis. A STUDY OF SELECTED SOCIAL AND ECONOMIC FACTORS IN THE FORMATION OF A RELIGIOUS VOCATION. Cited above as item 995.

1317. Brodrick, James. THE ECONOMIC MORALS OF THE JESUITS: AN ANSWER TO DR. H. M. ROBERTSON. London: Oxford University Press, 1934.

1318. Browne, J.P. FACTORS CONTRIBUTING TO A PREFERENCE FOR CHANGE IN DEFINITION OF THE SOCIETY OF ST. SULPICE. Unpublished Ph.D. dissertation, Catholic University of America, 1974.

1319. Brunetta, Giuseppe. "Una ricerca socioreligiosa sui Cappuccini." AGGIORNAMENTI SOCIALI (Italy) 9-10 (1974): 617-632.

1320. Burgalassi, Silvano. "La vita conventuale nelle aspettative del sociologo." STUDI FRANCESE 4 (1970): 451-460.

1321. Burns, M. Sheila. A COMPARATIVE STUDY OF SOCIAL FACTORS IN RELIGIOUS VOCATIONS TO THREE TYPES OF WOMEN'S COMMUNITIES: ABSTRACT OF A DISSERTATION. Washington: Catholic University of America Press, 1957.

1322. Calabro, William Vincent. SOME ORGANIZATIONAL DETERMINANTS OF ORIENTATION TO CHANGE: A CASE STUDY OF THE ATTITUDES OF WOMEN RELIGIOUS TO THE CALL FOR "AGGIORNAMENTO" IN THE CATHOLIC CHURCH. Unpublished doctoral dissertation, New York University, 1976.

1323. Carli, R., F. Crespi, and G. Pavan. ANALISI DELL'ORDINE DEI FRATI MINORI CAPPUCCINI. Milan, Etas Kompass, 1974. ANALISI DELL'ORDINE DEI FRATI MINORI CAPPUCCINI. METODOLOGIA E DOCUMENTAZIONE. Rome: Laurentianum, 1974.

1324. Coser, Lewis. "The Militant Collective: Jesuits and Lenninists." SOCIAL RESEARCH 40 (1973): 110-128.

1325. Culligan, Martin J. FACTORS THAT INFLUENCE VOCATIONS TO THE VINCENTIAN FATHERS. Unpublished M.A. thesis, De Paul University, 1964.

1326. Dallaire, Micheline. "Origine sociale des religieuses de l'Hôpital-Général de Québec." REVUE D'HISTOIRE DE L'AMERIQUE FRANÇAISE 23,4 (1969-70): 559-581.

1327. Denault, Bernard. SOCIOGRAPHIE GENERALE DES COMMUNAUTES RELIGIEUSES AU QUEBEC (1837-1969): ELEMENTS DE PROBLEMATIQUE. Thèse, Faculté de théologie, Université de Sherbrooke, 1972.

1328. Denault, Bernard, and Benoît Lévesque. ELEMENTS POUR UNE SOCIOLOGIE DES COMMUNAUTES RELIGIEUSES AU QUEBEC. Sherbrooke: Université de Sherbrooke, and Montréal: Les Presses de l'Université de Montréal, 1975.

1329. De Rosa, Gabriele. "I Fratelli Cavanis e la società religiosa Veneziana nel Clima della Restaurazione." RIVISTA DI SOCIOLOGIA 11,1-3 (1973): 43-62.

* Dumont-Johnson, Micheline. "Les communautés religieuses et la condition féminine." Cited above as item 1096.

* Faase, Thomas Philip. MAKING THE JESUITS MORE MODERN. Cited above as item 504.

1330. Faase, Thomas P. "Bulwark-Catholics and Conciliar-Humanists in the Society of Jesus." SOCIOLOGICAL QUARTERLY 21,4 (1980): 511-527.

* Faase, Thomas P. MAKING THE JESUITS MORE MODERN. Cited above as item 505.

* Faase, Thomas P. "Making Jesuits More Modern: Changing Values in a Changing Religious Order." Cited above as item 506.

* Faase, Thomas P. "International Differences in Value Ranking and Religious Style among Jesuits." Cited above as item 507.

1331. Fecher, Con J. LIFE-STYLE AND DEMOGRAPHY OF CATHOLIC RELIGIOUS SISTERHOODS AND HEALTH OF OTHER RELIGIOUS GROUPS. Dayton, Ohio: University of Dayton Press, 1975.

* Fichter, Joseph H. RELIGION AS AN OCCUPATION. Cited above as item 610.

1332. Francis, E.K. "Toward a Typology of Religious Orders." AMERICAN JOURNAL OF SOCIOLOGY 55 (1950): 437-449.

* Gannon, Thomas M. "The Effect of Segmentation in the Religious Clergy." Cited above as item 848.

* Gannon, Thomas M. "Catholic Religious Orders in Sociological Perspective." Cited above as item 623.

1333. Gannon, Thomas M. "Problem-Solving Versus Problem-Setting: The Case of the Jesuit General Survey." RRR 23,4 (1982): 337-353. Followed by a commentary by Carroll J. Bourg, pp. 353-356.

1334. Goddijn, H.P.M. "The Sociology of Religious Orders and Congregations." SC 7,5-6 (1960): 431-448.

1335. Gundlach, G. ZUR SOZIOLOGIE DER KATHOLISCHEN IDEENWELT UND DES JESUITENORDENS. Freiburg, 1927.

1336. Hill, Michael. THE RELIGIOUS ORDER IN A SOCIOLOGICAL CONTEXT: A STUDY OF VIRTUOSO RELIGION AND ITS LEGITIMATION IN THE NINETEENTH CENTURY CHURCH OF ENGLAND. Unpublished Ph.D. thesis, University of London, 1971.

1337. Hill, Michael. "Typologie sociologique de l'ordre religieux." SC 18,1 (1971): 45-64.

1338. Hill, Michael. THE RELIGIOUS ORDER. London: Heinemann, 1973.

1339. Hostie, Raymond. "Vie et mort des instituts religieux." SC 18,1 (1971): 145-147.

1340. Hostie, Raymond. VIE ET MORT DES ORDRES RELIGIEUX. APPROCHES PSYCHOSOCIOLOGIQUES. Paris: Desclée de Brouwer, 1972. VIDA Y MUERTE DE LAS ORDENES RELIGIOSAS: ESTUDIO PSICOSOCIOLOGICO. Bilbao: Desclée, 1973.

* Humphreys, Claire. "Structural Inconsistency and Vocation-Related Tension." Cited above as item 656.

1341. Jioultsis, Basil. "Religious Brotherhoods -- a Sociological View." SC 22,1 (1975): 67-84.

1342. Laloux, Joseph. "Une enquête sur une congrégation religieuse." SC 18,1 (1971): 142-144.

1343. Le Bras, Gabriel. "Les confréries chrétiennes, problèmes et propositions." REVUE HISTORIQUE DU DROIT FRANÇAIS ET ETRANGER 19-20 (1940-41): 320-363.

1344. Légaré, Jacques. "Les religieuses du Canada: leur évolution numérique entre 1965 et 1980." RECHERCHES SOCIOGRAPHIQUES 10,1 (1969): 7-21.

1345. Lennon, James, et al. "A Survey of Male Religious Orders." SOCIAL STUDIES 1,2 (1972): 159-180.

1346. Lennon, James, et al. "Survey of Orders of Sisters." SOCIAL STUDIES 1,2 (1972): 181-200.

1347. Lennon, James, et al. "Survey of Brothers." SOCIAL STUDIES 1,2 (1972): 201-223.

1348. Lessard, Marc-André, and Jean-Paul Montminy. "Le recensement des religieuses du Canada." DONUM DEI 11 (1966): 259-386; and RECHERCHES SOCIOGRAPHIQUES 8,1 (1967): 15-47.

1349. Lévesque, Benoît. SOCIOLOGIE D'UNE GENESE: D'UN PROJET PRIMITIVEMENT UTOPIQUE A UNE CONGREGATION RELIGIEUSE. Unpublished Ph.D. dissertation, Sorbonne, 1975.

1350. Lévesque, Benoît. "L'ordre religieux comme projet rêvé: utopie et/ou Secte? Etude comparative d'un cas." ARCHIVES DE SCIENCES SOCIALES DES RELIGIONS 41 (1976): 77-108.

1351. Madigan, Francis C. "Are Sex Mortality Differentials Biologically Caused?" MILBANK MEMORIAL FUND QUARTERLY 35 (1957): 202-223.

* Madigan, Francis C. "Role Satisfactions and Length of Life in a Closed Population." Cited above as item 871.

1352. Mehok, William J. "What Do Jesuits Do?" SC 8,6 (1961): 567-574.

1353. Mehok, William J. "Jesuit Trends." RRR 10 (1969): 177-180.

1354. Menges, Walter. DIE ORDENSMÄNNER IN DER BUNDESREPUBLIK DEUTSCHLAND. EINE EMPIRISCHE UNTERSUCHUNG. Köln: Wienland, 1969.

* Moulin, Léo. "La science politique et le gouvernement des communautés religieuses." Cited above as item 1160.

* Moulin, Léo. "Le gouvernement des communautés religieuses comme type de gouvernement mixte." Cited above as item 1161.

* Moulin, Léo. "Les formes de gouvernement local et provincial dans les ordres religieuses." Cited above as item 1162.

1355. Moulin, Léo. "Pour une sociologie des ordres religieux." SC 10,2 (1963): 145-170.

* Moulin, Léo. "Policy Making in the Religious Orders." Cited above as item 1163.

1356. Munick, Jeanette. UNFORESEEN RETIREMENT: A COMMUNITY OF NUNS IN TRANSITION. Unpublished Ph.D. dissertation, University of Southern California, 1977.

* Neal, Marie Augusta. "A Theoretical Analysis of Renewal in Religious Orders in the U.S.A." Cited above as item 1056.

1357. O'Connell, John J. "The Integration and Alienation of Religious to Religious Orders." SC 18,1 (1971): 65-84.

1358. Petersen, Larry R., and K. Peter Takayama. "Local/Cosmopolitan Theory and Religiosity among Catholic Nuns and Brothers." JSSR 22,4 (1983): 303-315.

1359. Pin, Emile. "Les instituts religieux apostoliques et le changement socio-culturel." NOUVELLE REVUE THEOLOGIQUE 87,4 (1965): 395-411. Also in Herve Carrier and Emile Pin (eds.), ESSAIS DE SOCIOLOGIE RELIGIEUSE. Paris: Spes, 1967.

1360. Rouleau, Jean-Paul. "Mouvement et ordres religieux aujourd'hui." LES MOUVEMENTS RELIGIEUX AUJOURD'HUI. THEORIES ET PRATIQUES. LES CAHIERS DE RECHERCHES EN SCIENCES DE LA RELIGION 5 (1984): 175-205.

1361. Sacks, Howard L. "The Effect of Spiritual Exercises on the Integration of Self-System." JSSR 18,1 (1979): 46-50.

1362. Sampson, Samuel Franklin. A NOVITIATE IN A PERIOD OF CHANGE: AN EXPERIMENTAL CASE STUDY IN SOCIAL RELATIONSHIPS. Unpublished doctoral dissertation, Cornell University, 1968.

1363. Sampson, Samuel F. CRISIS IN THE CLOISTER. A SOCIOLOGICAL ANALYSIS OF SOCIAL RELATIONSHIPS AND CHANGE IN A NOVITIATE. Norwood, New Jersey: Ablex, 1978.

1364. Santy, H. "The Problems of Female Religious Congregations: Some Force-Lines for Sociological Research." SC 16,2 (1969): 255-264.

1365. Scarvagliere, Giuseppe. L'INSTITUTO RELIGIOSO COME FATTO SOCIALE. Padova: Ed. Laurenziane, 1973.

* Séguy, Jean. "Charisme, sacerdoce, fondation: autour de L. M. Grignion de Montfort." Cited above as item 77.

1366. Servais, Emile, and Francis Hambye. "Structure et signification: problème de méthode en sociologie des organisations claustrales." SC 18,1 (1971): 27-44.

1367. Sharma, Arvind. "How and Why did Women in Ancient India Become Buddhist Nuns?" SA 38,3 (1977): 239-251.

1368. Stoop, W. "Quartre enquêtes sur la signification de la vie religieuse parmi quatre groupes différents de religieux aux Pays-Bas." SC 18,1 (1971): 117-122.

1369. Vazquez, Jesús Maria. LOS RELIGIOSOS ESPANOLES, HOY (ESTUDIO SOCIOLOGICO). Madrid: Organizacion Sala Ed., 1973.

1370. Vazquez, Jesús Maria. "Los religiosos españoles, hoy (Sintesis de Conclusiones)." CUADERNOS DE REALIDADES SOCIALES 4 (1974): 133-159.

1371. Verdonk, A.L.T. "Réorientation ou désintégration? Une enquête sociologique sur une congrégation religieuse masculine aux Pays-Bas." SC 18,1 (1971): 123-141.

1372. Vollmer, Howard M. "Member Commitment and Organizational Competence in Religious Orders." BERKELEY PUBLICATIONS IN SOCIETY AND INSTITUTIONS 3,1 (1957): 13-26.

1373. Weigert, Andrew J. "An Emerging Intellectual Group within a Religious Organization: An Exploratory Study of Change." SC 18,1 (1971): 101-115.

1374. Whitley, Cuthbert M. THE REVITALIZATION PROCESS IN RELIGIOUS LIFE: A STUDY OF A BENEDICTINE CONGREGATION. Unpublished Ph.D. dissertation, Catholic University of America, 1977.

Papacy

* Imse, Thomas. "Spiritual Leadership and Organizational Leadership. The Dilemma of Being Pope." Cited above as item 921.

* Vaillancourt, Jean-Guy. PAPAL POWER. A STUDY OF VATICAN CONTROL OVER LAY CATHOLIC ELITES. Cited above as item 966.

Parish/local congregation

1375. Abbott, M. Martina. A CITY PARISH GROWS AND CHANGES. Washington: Catholic University of America Press, 1953.

1376. Anderson, Susan. SEX DIFFERENTIALS IN PROTESTANT LOCAL CHURCH LEADERSHIP AND PARTICIPATION. Unpublished Ph.D. dissertation, Indiana Unviersity, 1977.

1377. Anfossi, A. "Funzione della parrocchia e partizipazione di parrocchiani alla vita religiosa in comuni agricoli della Sardegna." QUADERNI DI SOCIOLOGIA 16,2 (1967): 190-216.

1378. Apostal, Robert A., and James R. Ditzler. "Research Note: Dogmatism and Attitudes toward Religious Change." SA 32,3 (1971): 180-183.

1379. Belanger, Paul. LES ASSOCIATIONS PAROISSIALES ET LA CONCEPTION DE LA PAROISSE A SAINT-JEROME-DE-L'AUVERGNE. Unpublished M.A. thesis, l'Université Laval, 1963.

1380. Bergman, Richard D. "Group Standards in a Protestant Congregation." RRR 4,2 (1963): 96-104.

1381. Boulard, Fernand. NELLE PARROCCHIE DI CAMPAGNA. Brescia: Morcelliana, 1948.

1382. Braga, G. "Tipologia delle sottostructure della parrocchie siciliana." SOCIOLOGIA RELIGIOSA 1 (1957): 119-138.

1383. Bressan, V. "La participation sociale dans la vie d'une paroisse urbaine." SC 9,3 (1962): 243-257.

1384. Brewer, Earl D.C., et al. PROTESTANT PARISH. A CASE STUDY OF RURAL AND URBAN PARISH PATTERNS. Atlanta: Communicative Arts Press, 1967.

1385. Brothers, Joan B. "Two Views of the Parish." THE FURROW 16 (1965): 471-478.

1386. Bussi, N. "Sociologia della comunità parrocchiale." ORIENTAMENTI PASTORALI 1 (1950): 96-108.

1387. Christy, Richard D. HIDDEN FACTORS IN RELIGIOUS CONFLICT: A SOCIOLOGICAL ANALYSIS. Unpublished M.A. thesis, University of Waterloo, 1969.

1388. Cieslak, Michael J. "Parish Responsiveness and Parishioner Commitment." RRR 26,2 (1984): 132-147.

1389. Ciesluk, Joseph E. NATIONAL PARISHES IN THE UNITED STATES. Washington: Catholic University of America Press, 1944.

1390. Clark, D.B. "The Sociological Study of the Parish." EXPOSITORY TIMES 82,10 (1971): 296-300.

1391. Clarke, Thomas. PARISH SOCIETIES. Washington: The Catholic University of America Press, 1943.

1392. Clarke, Thomas. PARISH SOCIOLOGY. Washington: The Catholic University of America Press, 1945.

1393. Contigualia, C. "Una Tipica Parrocchia Siciliana, Totorici." STUDI SOCIALI 5 (1964): 414-428.

1394. Curtis, J.H., F. Avesing, and I. Klosek. "Urban Parishes as Social Areas." AMERICAN CATHOLIC SOCIOLOGICAL REVIEW 18,4 (1957): 319-325.

* Davidson, James D. "Patterns of Belief at the Denominational and Congregational Levels." Cited above as item 1271.

1395. Delacroix, S. "Parish Inquiries in France." AMERICAN CATHOLIC SOCIOLOGICAL REVIEW 13,3 (1952): 169-173.

1396. Di Valenza, Alberto C. "La realtà parrocchiale: riflessioni metodologiche." SOCIOLOGIA RELIGIOSA 17-18 (1968): 133-142.

1397. Donovan, John D. "The Sociologist Looks at the Parish." AMERICAN CATHOLIC SOCIOLOGICAL REVIEW 11,2 (1950): 66-73.

1398. Donus, Robert B. "Greek-Americans in a Pan-Orthodox Parish: A Sociologist's View." ST. VLADIMIR THEOLOGICAL QUARTERLY (1974): 44-52.

1399. Duocastella, Rogelio. COMO ESTUDIAR UNA PARROQUIA. Barcelona: ISPA, Nova Terra, 1967.

1400. Egberink, L. "La paroisse, quelques aspects des recherches." SC 6,2 (1958-1959): 56-68.

1401. Falardeau, Jean-Charles. "The Parish as an Institutional Type." CANADIAN JOURNAL OF ECONOMICS AND POLITICAL SCIENCE 15,3 (1949): 365-371.

1402. Favreau, Bernard. MONOGRAPHIE DE LA PAROISSE DE SAINT-HYACINTHE. ETUDE DE LA NATALITE, DE LA NUPTIALITE ET DE LA MORTALITE A PARTIR DES REGISTRES DE LA PAROISSE ET DE LA DESSERTE, ET INTERPRETATION SOCIOLOGIQUE DES CHANGEMENTS SURVENUS. Unpublished M.A. thesis, Université de Montréal, 1965.

1403. Fichter, Joseph H. "Institutional Environment and Religious Life." LUMEN VITAE 6,1-2 (1951): 165-172.

1404. Fichter, Joseph H. SOUTHERN PARISH: DYNAMICS OF A CITY CHURCH, Vol.I. Chicago: University of Chicago Press, 1951.

1405. Fichter, Joseph H. "Conceptualizations of the Urban Parish." SOCIAL FORCES 31 (1952): 43-46.

1406. Fichter, Joseph H. "Structure of Parish Societies." AMERICAN ECCLESIASTICAL REVIEW 107 (1952): 351-359.

1407. Fichter, Joseph H. "Major Issues of Parish Sociology." AMERICAN ECCLESIASTICAL REVIEW 128,5 (1953): 369-383.

1408. Fichter, Joseph H. SOCIAL RELATIONS IN THE URBAN PARISH. Chicago: University of Chicago Press, 1954.

1409. Fichter, Joseph H. SOZIOLOGIE DER PFARRGRUPPEN. Muenster: Aschendorf, 1958.

1410. Fichter, Joseph H. "The Parish and Social Integration." SC, 7,1 (1960): 39-48.

1411. Fichter, Joseph H. "The Urban Parish as a Social Group." In J. Brothers (ed.), READINGS IN THE SOCIOLOGY OF RELIGION (volume cited in item 486).

1412. Fortin, G. "Les changements socio-culturels dans une paroisse agricole." RECHERCHES SOCIOGRAPHIQUES 2 (1961): 151-170.

1413. Fosselman, David Harold. TRANSITION IN THE DEVELOPMENT OF A DOWNTOWN PARISH. Washington: Catholic University of America Press, 1952.

1414. Froyen, Virginia. SOCIAL LIFE IN A RURAL PARISH IN WESTERN IRELAND - GLENCOLUMBCILLE. Unpublished M.A. thesis, University of Minnesota, 1967.

1415. Fürstenberg, Friedrich. "The Future Scope of the Sociology of the Parish." SC 13,4 (1966): 305-308.

1416. Glock, Charles Y., and Rodney Stark. "Dilemmas of the Parish Church." Ch. 6 in RELIGION AND SOCIETY IN TENSION (volume cited in item 141), pp. 123-143.

1417. Goldschmidt, D., F. Greiner, and H. Schelsky (eds.) SOZIOLOGIE DER KIRCHENGEMEINDE. Stuttgart: Ferdinand Enke Verlag, 1960.

1418. Goldstein, Reine. "Types de comportement religieux et cadres sociaux dans deux paroisses anglaises." REVUE FRANÇAIS DE SOCIOLOGIE 6,1 (1965): 58-67.

1419. Greeley, Andrew M. "Suburban Parish." COMMONWEAL (1959): 537-539.

1420. Greeley, Andrew M. "The Urban Parish under a Microscope." SOCIAL ORDER 9,7 (1959): 335-339.

1421. Greeley, Andrew M. "Some Aspects of Interaction between Religious Groups in an Upper Middle Class Roman Catholic parish." SC 9,1-2 (1962): 39-61.

* Greeley, Andrew M. THE RELIGIOUS IMAGINATION. Cited above as item 305.

1422. Greinacher, Norbert von. SOZIOLOGIE DER PFARREI. WEGE ZUR UNTERSUCHUNG. Colmar, Freiburg: Alsatia Verlag, 1955.

1423. Greytag, J. DIE KIRCHENGEMEINDE IN SOZIOLOGISCHER SICHT. ZIEL UND WEG EMPIRISCHER FORSCHUNGEN. Hambourg: Furche-Verlag, 1959.

1424. Grichting, Wolfgang Leo. ORGANIZATIONAL STRUCTURE AND CLIMATE: THE CASE OF THE ROMAN CATHOLIC PARISH. Unpublished Ph.D. dissertation, University of Michigan, 1968.

1425. Grichting, Wolfgang Leo. PARISH STRUCTURE AND CLIMATE IN AN ERA OF CHANGE. A SOCIOLOGIST'S INQUIRY. Washington: C.A.R.A., 1969.

1426. Grumelli, Antonio. "Spunti di sociologia parrocchiale." AGGIORNAMENTI SOCIALI 14 (1963): 699-710.

1427. Gundlach, G. "Zur Soziologie der Pfarrgemeinde." DAS WORTH IN DER ZEIT 1 (1933): 12-20.

1428. Herman, Nancy J. "Conflict in the Church: A Social Network Analysis of an Anglican Congregation." JSSR 23,1 (1984): 60-74.

* Hougland, James G., Jr. CONTROL AND POLICY IN PROTESTANT CONGREGATIONS. Cited above as item 1146.

* Hougland, James G., Jr., and James R. Wood. "'Inner Circles' in Local Churches: An Application of Thompson's Theory." Cited above as item 1147.

* Houtart, François. "The City and the Priest: Social Relations of the Urban Parish." Cited above as item 655.

1429. Houtart, François. "La paroisse urbaine americaine." EVANGELISER 9 (1955): 55-66.

1430. Houtart, François. "Les paroisses de Chicago." CHRONIQUE SOCIALE DE FRANCE 63,1 (1955): 77-84.

1431. Houtart, François. "Dimensions nouvelles de la paroisse urbaine." NOUVELLE REVUE THEOLOGIQUE 80,4 (1958): 384-394.

1432. Houtart, François. "Sociologie de la paroisse comme assemblée eucharistique." SC 10,1 (1963): 75-91.

1433. Houtart, François. "La paroisse dans la ville." INFORMATIONS CATHOLIQUES INTERNATIONALES 243 (1965): 19-29.

* Ingram, Larry C. "Notes on Pastoral Power in the Congregational Tradition." Cited above as item 860.

1434. Karcher, Barbara C., Ira E. Robinson, and Jack O. Balswick. "Fichter's Typology and Changing Meanings in the Catholic Church." SA 33,3 (1972): 166-176.

1435. Kincheloe, Samuel C. "The Behavior Sequence of a Dying Church." RELIGIOUS EDUCATION 24 (1929): 329-345.

1436. Köster, R. DIE KIRCHENTREUEN. ERFAHRUNGEN UND ERGEBNISSE EINER SOZIOLOGISCHEN UNTERSUCHUNG IN EINER GROSSTADTISCHEN EVANGELISCHEN KIRCHENGEMEINDE. Stuttgart: Ferdinand Enke Verlag, 1959.

1437. Larson, Donald E. SOME SOCIOLOGICAL ASPECTS OF CHURCH RELOCATION: A STUDY OF A MIDDLE CLASS PARISH. Unpublished M.A. thesis, Indiana University, Bloomington, 1959.

1438. Layne, Norman R., Jr., and Jack O. Balswick. ASCENSION AT THE CROSSROADS: A CASE STUDY OF A CHURCH CAUGHT IN THE TURBULENCE OF RAPID SOCIAL CHANGE. Athens, Georgia: Institute of Community and Area Development and the Department of Sociology, 1973.

1439. Layne, Norman R., Jr., and Jack O. Balswick. "Church Generation: A Neglected Research Issue." SA 38,3 (1977): 258-265.

1440. Le Bras, Gabriel. "Pour l'étude de la paroisse rurale." REVUE D'HISTOIRE DE L'EGLISE DE FRANCE 23 (1937): 486-502.

1441. Leent, J.A.A. van. "The Sociology of Parish and Congregation." SC 8,6 (1961): 535-558.

1442. Littlejohn, J. WESTRIGG: THE SOCIOLOGY OF A CHEVIOT PARISH. New York: Humanities, 1963.

1443. Lizza, G. PARROCCHIA SUBURBANA. INDAGINE SOCIO-RELIGIOSA. Pescara: Tipographia Quaglietta, 1975.

1444. Luckmann, Thomas. "Four Protestant Parishes in Germany: A Study in the Sociology of Religion." SOCIAL RESEARCH 26,4 (1959): 423-448.

1445. Matthes, Joachim. "Struktur und Funktion der Kirchengemeinde." In EINFUHRUNG IN DIE RELIGIONSSOZIOLOGIE. II. KIRCHE UND GESELLSCHAFT. Hamburg: Rowolt, 1968, pp. 93-101.

1446. McGaw, Douglas B. CONGREGATION AND RELIGIOUS COMMITMENT: A COMPARATIVE STUDY OF RELIGIOUS MEANING AND BELONGING. Unpublished Ph.D. dissertation, University of Massachusetts, Amherst, 1977.

1447. McGaw, Douglas B. "Commitment and Religious Community: A Comparison of a Charismatic and a Mainline Congregation." JSSR 18,2 (1979): 146-163.

1448. McGaw, Douglas B. "Meaning and Belonging in a Charismatic Congregation: An Investigation into Sources of Neo-Pentecostal Success." RRR 21,3 (1980): 284-301.

1449. McGaw, Douglas B., and Elliott Wright. A TALE OF TWO CONGREGATIONS. COMMITMENT AND SOCIAL STRUCTURE IN A CHARISMATIC AND MAINLINE CONGREGATION. Hartford, Hartford Seminary Foundation, 1981.

1450. Miner, H. SAINT-DENIS, A FRENCH-CANADIAN PARISH. Chicago: University of Chicago Press, 1939.

* Mitchell, Robert Edward. MINISTER-PARISHIONER RELATIONS. Cited above as item 694.

1451. Monzel, N. "Soziologie der Pfarrei." LEBENDIGE SEELSORGE 3 (1952): 156-160.

1452. Moreux, Colette. FIN D'UNE RELIGION? MONOGRAPHIE D'UNE PAROISSE CANADIENNE-FRANÇAISE. Montréal: Presses de l'Université de Montréal, 1969.

1453. Nelson, John J., and Harry H. Hiller. "Norms of Verbalization and the Decision Making Process in Religious Organizations." JSSR 20,2 (1981): 173-180.

1454. Nesti, Arnaldo. "Per una analisi della parocchia cattolica in Italia." IDOC INTERNAZIONALE 4,19 (1973): 29-44.

1455. Nuesse, C. Joseph. "The Relation of Financial Assessments to Status in a Rural Parish." AMERICAN CATHOLIC SOCIOLOGICAL REVIEW 9,1 (1948): 26-38.

1456. Nuesse, C. Joseph. "American Research Bearing upon the Sociology of the Parish." LUMEN VITAE 6,1-2 (1951): 157-159.

1457. Nuesse, C. Joseph. "Membership Trends in a Rural Catholic Parish." RURAL SOCIOLOGY 22 (1957): 123-130.

1458. Nuesse, C. Joseph, and T. Harte (eds.) THE SOCIOLOGY OF THE PARISH: AN INTRODUCTORY SYMPOSIUM. Milwaukee: Bruce, 1951.

1459. Oppen, D. von. "Strukturfragen der christlichen Gemeinde." ZEITSCHRIFT FÜR EVANGELISCHE ETHIK 5 (1961): 293-306.

1460. Perry, Everett L. "Congregational Models for Missions -- Factors in Adaptation and Goal Attainment." In Ross P. Scherer (ed.), AMERICAN DENOMINATIONAL ORGANIZATION (item 1172), pp. 245-261.

1461. Pickering, W.S.F. "The Church in a Changing Society." In BULLETIN OF THE COUNCIL FOR SOCIAL SERVICE, Anglican Church of Canada, No. 187 (September 1963).

1462. Pickering, W.S.F., and J.E. Winston Jackson. "A Brief Sociological Examination of Local United and Anglican churches." CANADIAN JOURNAL OF THEOLOGY 14,4 (1968): 249-261.

1463. Pin, Emile. INTRODUCTION A L'ETUDE SOCIOLOGIQUE DES PAROISSES CATHOLIQUES. CRITERES DE CLASSIFICATION ET TYPOLOGIE. Paris: Action Populaire, 1956.

1464. Pin, Emile. PRATIQUE RELIGIEUSE ET CLASSES SOCIALES DANS UNE PAROISSE URBAINE. SAINT-POTHIN A LYON. Paris: Editions Spes, 1956.

1465. Pin, Emile. "Can the Urban Parish be a Community? GREGORIANUM 41,3 (1960): 393-423. Also in SC 8,6 (1961): 503-534.

1466. Pin, Emile. "La sociologie de la paroisse." PAROISSE ET MISSION 17 (1962): 16-29.

1467. Pin, Emile. LA PAROISSE CATHOLIQUE. LES FORMES VARIABLES D'UN SYSTEME SOCIAL. Presses Universitaires Grégorienne, Rome, 1963.

1468. Pinto, Leonard J., and Kenneth E. Crow. "The Effects of Size on Other Structural Attributes of Congregations within the Same Denomination." JSSR 21,4 (1982): 304-316.

1469. Remy, Jean, Jean-Pierre Hiernaux, and Emile Servais. "Le phénomène paroissial aujourd'hui: éléments pour une interrogation sociologique." LUMIERE ET VIE 25,123 (1975): 25-36.

1470. Rendtorff, Trutz. "Kirchengemeinde und Kerngemeinde, kirchensoziologische Bemerkungen zur Gestalt der Ortsgemeinde." KIRCHE IN DER ZEIT 13,4 (1958): 109-113. Also in F. Fürstenberg (ed.), RELIGIONSSOZIOLOGIE. SOZIOLOGISCHE TEXTE, 19. Berlin: Luchterhand, 1964, 1970, pp. 235-247.

1471. Rendtorff, Trutz. "Pfarrsoziologie." In K. Galling (ed.), DIE RELIGION IN GESCHICHTE UND GEGENWART. Tübingen, 1961, pp. 305-306.

1472. Rich, Mark. THE LARGER PARISHES OF TOMPKINS COUNTY. Unpublished Ph.D. dissertation, Cornell, 1936.

1473. Rigali, Lucius J. RELIGIOUS COMMITMENT AND SOCIAL INVOLVEMENT IN SELECTED FRANCISCAN PARISHES. Unpublished Ph.D. dissertation, Boston University Graduate School, 1974.

1474. Schasching, J. "Soziologie der Pfarre." In H. Rahner (ed.), PFARRE. Freiburg: 1956, pp. 97-124.

1475. Scheuer, Joseph F. "Church Parish Population Profiles." AMERICAN CATHOLIC SOCIOLOGICAL REVIEW 12 (1956): 131-142.

1476. Scheuer, Joseph F., Joseph B. Schuyler, and Frank A. Santopolo. "Parish Sociology." THOUGHT 30,117 (1955): 243-259.

1477. Schnepp, Gerald. LEAKAGE FROM A CATHOLIC PARISH. Unpublished Ph.D. dissertation, Catholic University of America, 1938.

1478. Schreuder, Osmund. "Ein soziologischer Richtungsbegriff der Pfarrei." SC 6,6 (1959): 177-203.

1479. Schreuder, Osmund. KIRCHE IM VORORT. SOZIOLOGISCHE ERKUNDUNG EINER PFARREI. Freiburg: Herder, 1962.

1480. Schuyler, Joseph B. "The Parish Studied as a Social System." AMERICAN CATHOLIC SOCIOLOGICAL REVIEW 17,4 (1956): 320-337.

1481. Schuyler, Joseph B. "Potential Elements of Organization and Disorganization in the Parish: As Seen in Northern Parish." AMERICAN CATHOLIC SOCIOLOGICAL REVIEW 18,2 (1957): 98-117.

1482. Schuyler, Joseph B. NORTHERN PARISH: A SOCIOLOGICAL AND PASTORAL STUDY. Chicago: Loyola University Press, 1960.

1483. Settle, Lester M. THE FUNCTIONAL COMMUNITY AND PARISH ORGANIZATION, WEST COLCHESTER RESEARCH PROJECT. Th.M. thesis, Pine Hill Divinity Hall, Dalhousie University, 1970. Toronto: Division of Outreach, United Church of Canada, 1971.

1484. Sokolski, A. "Méthode de planning paroissial urbain." SC 7,4 (1960): 313-324.

1485. Sullivan, T. "The Application of Shevky-Bell Indices to Parish Analysis." AMERICAN CATHOLIC SOCIOLOGICAL REVIEW 22,2 (1961): 168-171.

1486. Sweetser, Thomas. THE CATHOLIC PARISH: SHIFTING MEMBERSHIP IN A CHANGING CHURCH. Chicago: Center for the Scientific Study of Religion, 1974.

1487. Van Hemert, Martien. "La pratique dans le cadre des modèles pastoraux." SC 30,4 (1983): 457-475.

1488. Vrijhof, P.H. "Some Remarks Concerning the Parish as a Social Problem and as a Topic for Social Research in the Netherlands after 1945." ARCHIVES DE SOCIOLOGIE DES RELIGIONS 8 (1959): 121-123.

1489. Wall, David F. PARISH COUNCILS IN THE CATHOLIC CHURCH: PARTICIPATION AND SATISFACTION OF MEMBERS. Unpublished Ph.D. dissertation, Catholic University of America, 1979.

1490. Ward, C.K. "Some Aspects of the Social Structure of a Roman Catholic Parish." SOCIOLOGICAL REVIEW 6,1 (1958): 75-93.

1491. Wilson, Charles Lee. "A Social Picture of a Congregation." AMERICAN SOCIOLOGICAL REVIEW 10 (1945): 418-422.

1492. Wolfe, James. "Three Congregations." In C.Y. Glock and R.N. Bellah (eds.), THE NEW RELIGIOUS CONSCIOUSNESS (item 2407), pp. 227-244.

1493. Wrobel, Paul. OUR WAY. FAMILY, PARISH, AND NEIGHBORHOOD IN A POLISH-AMERICAN COMMUNITY. Notre Dame: University of Notre Dame Press, 1979.

Power

1494. Beckford, James A. "The Restoration of 'Power' to the Sociology of Religion." SA 44,1 (1983): 11-32.

* Hougland, James G., Jr., Jon M. Shepard, and James R. Wood. "Discrepancies in Perceived Organizational Control: Their Incidence and Importance in Local Churches." Cited above as item 1201.

1495. Hougland, James G., Jr., and James R. Wood. "Determinants of Organizational Control in Local Churches." JSSR 18,2 (1979): 132-145.

1496. Luidens, Donald A. "Bureaucratic Control in a Protestant Denomination." JSSR 21,2 (1982): 163-175.

1497. McGuire, Meredith B. "Discovering Religious Power." SA 44,1 (1983): 1-10.

1498. Moreux, Colette. "Idéologies religieuses et pouvoir: l'exemple du catholicisme québécois." CAHIERS INTERNATIONAUX DE SOCIOLOGIE 64 (1978): 35-62.

1499. Redekop, Calvin. "Decision-Making in a Sect." RRR 2,2 (1960): 79-86.

1500. Scott, Gini Graham. THE MAGICIANS. A STUDY OF THE USE OF POWER IN A BLACK MAGIC GROUP. New York: Irvington, 1982.

* Szafran, Robert F. "The Distribution of Influence in Religious Organizations." Cited above as item 780.

1501. Wilson, John, and Harvey K. Clow. "Themes of Power and Control in a Pentecostal Assembly." JSSR 20,3 (1981): 241-250. Also in P.H. McNamara (ed.), RELIGION: NORTH AMERICAN STYLE (volume cited in item 117), pp. 132-140.

* Yinger, J. Milton. RELIGION IN THE STRUGGLE FOR POWER. Cited above as item 296.

Synagogue

1502. Brownstein, Henry H. CHANGE IN THE FUNCTION OF SOCIAL INSTITUTIONS: THE CASE OF THE SYNAGOGUE. Unpublished Ph.D. dissertation, Temple University, 1977.

1503. Engelman, V.Z. "The Jewish Synagogue in the United States." AMERICAN JOURNAL OF SOCIOLOGY 41(1935): 44-51.

1504. Glazer, Nathan. AMERICAN JUDAISM. Chicago: University of Chicago Press, 1957.

1505. Lipman, V.D. "Synagogal Organization in Anglo-Jewry." JEWISH JOURNAL OF SOCIOLOGY 1,1 (1959): 80-93.

Underground church

The underground church is a form of collective dissidence within a religious organization. Some of the organization's members form a social structure, usually informally, which parallels the official organizational structure.

1506. Houtart, François. "Les groupes spontanés dans l'Eglise contemporaine: Réflexions sociologiques." COMMUNION 1 (1970): 60-73. Also in VERBUM CARO 93 (1970): 43-60.

1507. McGuire, Meredith B. "Toward a Sociological Interpretation of the 'Underground Church' Movement." RRR 14,1 (1972): 41-47.

1508. McGuire, Meredith B. "An Interpretive Comparison of Elements of the Pentecostal and Underground Church Movements in American Catholicism." SA 35,1 (1974): 57-65.

1509. Steeman, Theodore M. "The Underground Church." In Donald R. Cutler (ed.), THE RELIGIOUS SITUATION: 1969. Boston: Beacon, 1969, pp. 713-748.

SECTION D: POLITICS AND RELIGION

Politics (general)

1510. Akhavi, Shahrough. RELIGION AND POLITICS IN CONTEMPORARY IRAN: CLERGY-STATE RELATIONS IN THE PAHLAVI PERIOD. Albany: State University of New York Press, 1980.

1511. Alexander, Robert J. "New Social and Political Trends in the Roman Catholic Church." JOURNAL OF INTERNATIONAL AFFAIRS 12,2 (1958): 144-149.

1512. Alford, Robert R. "Religion and Class Voting." In R. Alford, PARTY AND SOCIETY. Chicago: Rand McNally, 1963, pp. 272-278.

1513. Alford, Robert R. "The Social Bases of Political Cleavage in 1962." In John Meisel (ed.), PAPERS ON THE 1962 ELECTION. Toronto: University of Toronto Press, 1964, pp. 203-234.

* Allinsmith, Wesley, and Beverly Allinsmith. "Religious Affiliation and Politico-Economic Attitude: A Study of Eight Major U.S. Religious Groups." Cited above as item 1267.

1514. Alston, Jon P., Charles W. Peek, and C. Ray Wingrove. "Religiosity and Black Militancy: A Reappraisal." JSSR 11 (1971): 252-261.

1515. Amir Arjomand, Said. "Religion, Political Action and Legitimate Domination in Shi'ite Iran: Fourteenth to Eighteenth Centuries A.D." ARCHIVES EUROPEENNES DE SOCIOLOGIE 20,1 (1979): 59-109.

* Anderson, Charles H. "Religious Communality and Party Preference." Cited above as item 1227.

1516. Anderson, Donald N. "Ascetic Protestantism and Political Preference." RRR 7 (1966): 167-171.

1517. Anderson, Grace M. THE RELATIONSHIP BETWEEN RELIGIOUS AFFILIATION AND SECULAR ATTITUDES AND BEHAVIOR. Unpublished M.A. thesis, McMaster University, 1964.

1518. Anderson, Grace M. "Voting Behaviour and the Ethnic Religious Variable: A Study of a Federal Election in Hamilton, Ontario." CANADIAN JOURNAL OF ECONOMICS AND POLITICAL SCIENCE 32,1 (1966): 27-37.

1519. Aver, E., C. Hames, Jacques Maitre, and Guy Michelat. "Pratique religieuse et comportement electoral à travers les sondages d'opinion." ARCHIVES DE SOCIOLOGIE DES RELIGIONS 29 (1970): 27-52.

1520. Avila, Raphaël. RELIGION Y SOCIEDAD POLITICA - EL CASO DE NICARAGUA. Dissertation doctorale en sociologie, l'Université Catholique de Louvain, 1982.

1521. Avila, Raphaël. "Religion et société politique au Nicaragua après la révolution sandiniste." SC 30,2-3 (1983): 233-259.

* Balswick, Jack O. "Theology and Political Attitudes among Clergymen." Cited above as item 544.

1522. Bastian, Jean-Pierre. "Protestantismo y politica in Mexico." REVISTA MEXICANA DE SOCIOLOGIA 43,4 (1981): 1947-1966.

1523. Bauer, Julien. "Israël et ses significations pour le Judaïsme religieux." LES CAHIERS DU CENTRE DE RECHERCHES EN SOCIOLOGIE RELIGIEUSE 3 (1980): 83-104.

1524. Bayart, Jean-François. "La fonction politique des églises au Cameroun." REVUE FRANÇAISE DE SCIENCE POLITIQUE 23,3 (1973): 513-536.

1525. Beach, Stephen W. "Religion and Political Change in Northern Ireland." SA 38,1 (1977): 37-48.

1526. Bedouelle, G. L'EGLISE D'ANGLETERRE ET LA SOCIETE POLITIQUE CONTEMPORAINE. Paris: Pichon et Durand-Auzias, 1968.

1527. Behrman, L.G. "Patterns of Religious and Political Attitudes and Activities during Modernization: Santiago, Chile." SOCIAL SCIENCE QUARTERLY 53 (1972): 520-533.

1528. Bergesen, Albert. "Political Witch-Hunts: The Sacred and the Subversive in Cross-National Perspective." AMERICAN SOCIOLOGICAL REVIEW 42 (1977): 220-233.

1529. Bergesen, Albert. "A Durkheimian Theory of Political Witch-Hunts with the Chinese Cultural Revolution of 1966-1969 as an Example." JSSR 17 (1978): 19-29.

1530. Bergesen, Albert. THE SACRED AND THE SUBVERSIVE: POLITICAL WITCH-HUNTS AS NATIONAL RITUALS. Storrs, Connecticut: Society for the Scientific Study of Religion, 1984.

* Birrell, W.D., J.E. Greer, and D.J.D. Roche. "The Political Role and Influence of the Clergy in Northern Ireland." Cited above as item 550.

1531 Bonnet, Serge. "Politique et religion dans l'oeuvre d'Emile Poulat." REVUE FRANÇAISE DE SCIENCE POLITIQUE 30,3 (1980): 599-607.

1532. Bourdieu, Pierre, and Monique de Saint Martin. "La sainte famille. L'épiscopat français dans le champ du pouvoir." ACTES DE LA RECHERCHE EN SCIENCES SOCIALES 44-45 (1982): 2-53.

* Bourg, Carroll J. "Politics and Religion." Cited above as item 346.

1533. Bourg, Carroll J. "The Politics of Religious Movements." In E. Barker (ed.), OF GODS AND MEN (item 2396), pp. 45-64.

1534. Braswell, George W., Jr. A MOSAIC OF MULLAHS AND MOSQUES: RELIGION AND POLITICS IN IRANIAN SHI'AH ISLAM. Unpublished Ph.D. dissertation, University of North Carolina, 1975.

1535. Brechon, Pierre, and Bernard Denni. "L'univers politique des catholiques pratiquants. Une enquête par questionnaire dans huit assemblées dominicales grenobloises." REVUE FRANÇAIS DE SOCIOLOGIE 24,3 (1983): 505-534.

* Bromley, David G., and Anson Shupe (eds.) NEW CHRISTIAN POLITICS. Cited above as item 100.

* Bruce, Steve. ONE NATION UNDER GOD? Cited above as item 101.

1536. Bruneau, Thomas C. THE POLITICAL TRANSFORMATION OF THE BRAZILIAN CATHOLIC CHURCH. New York: Cambridge University Press, 1974.

1537. Budd, Susan. "Religion and Protest." RELIGION. JOURNAL OF RELIGION AND RELIGIONS 4,2 (1974): 156-159.

* Buntig, Aldo-J. "Las comunidades de base en la acción política." Cited above as item 1216.

1538. Caceres Prendes, Jorge. "Radicalización politica y pastoral popular en El Savlador: 1969-1979." ESTUDIOS SOCIALES CENTRO-AMERICANOS 11,33 (1982): 93-153.

1539. Calvo, Roberto (pseudonym). "The Church and the Doctrine of National Security." JOURNAL OF INTERAMERICAN STUDIES AND WORLD AFFAIRS 21 (1979): 69-88. Also in Daniel H. Levine (ed.), CHURCHES AND POLITICS IN LATIN AMERICA. Beverly Hills: Sage, 1979, pp. 135-154.

1540. Campbell, Douglas F. RELIGION AND VALUES AMONG NOVA SCOTIA COLLEGE STUDENTS. Unpublished Ph.D. dissertation, The Catholic University of America, 1964.

1541. Campbell, Douglas F. "Religion and Values among Nova Scotian College Students." SA 27,2 (1966): 80-93.

1542. Campiche, Roland, and G. de Rham. "Hypothèses sur religion et politique en Suisse." REVUE SUISSE DE SOCIOLOGIE 3 (1977): 83-89.

1543. Capelo, Manuel. "La doctrina social de la Iglesia como fuente de inspiración de las decisions de política económica." REVISTA DE ESTUDIOS SOCIALES 7 (1973): 101-124.

1544. Carlton, F.T. "Technological Advance, Government and Religion." SOCIOLOGY AND SOCIAL RESEARCH 41,2 (1956): 115-120.

1545. Cayrac-Blanchard, Françoise. "Evolution politique de l'Islam en Indonésie." PROJET 140 (1979): 1281-1286.

1546. Chartain, François. L'EGLISE ET LES PARTIES DANS LA VIE POLITIQUE DU PARAGUAY DEPUIS L'INDEPENDENCE. Unpublished Ph.D. dissertation, University of Paris, 1972.

1547. Cheal, David J. RELIGIOUS AND POLITICAL PARTICIPATION. Unpublished Ph.D. dissertation, Birmingham (England) University, 1971.

1548. Cheal, David J. "Political Radicalism and Religion: Competitors for Commitment." SC 22,2 (1975): 245-260.

1549. Christie, A. "The Political Use of Imported Religion: An Historical Example from Java." ARCHIVES DE SOCIOLOGIE DES RELIGIONS 9/17 (1964): 53-62.

1550. Cipriani, Roberto. "La religiosité populaire en Italie: deux recherches sur la magie et la politique dans le sud du pays." SC 23, 2-3 (1976): 221-231.

1551. Cipriani, Roberto. "Simbolismo, politica e religione." SOCIOLOGIA 13,1 (1979): 25-50.

1552. Clark, S.D. "The Religious Sect in Canadian Politics." AMERICAN JOURNAL OF SOCIOLOGY 51,3 (1945): 207-216. Reprinted in S.D. Clark, THE DEVELOPING CANADIAN COMMUNITY. Toronto: University of Toronto Press, 1962. Reprinted, in B.R. Blishen, F.E. Jones, K.D. Naegele, and J. Porter (eds.), CANADIAN SOCIETY. SOCIOLOGICAL PERSPECTIVES. 3rd edition. Toronto: Macmillan, 1971, pp. 324-335.

1553. Cohen, Steven Martin, and Robert E. Kapsis. "Religion, Ethnicity, and Party Affiliation in the U.S.: Evidence from Pooled Electoral Surveys, 1968-72." SOCIAL FORCES 56,2 (1977): 637-653.

1554. Converse, P.E. "Religion and Politics: The 1960 Election." In Angus Campbell, Philip E. Converse, Warren E. Miller, and Donald E. Stokes (eds.), ELECTIONS AND THE POLITICAL ORDER. New York: Wiley, 1966.

* Dahm, Karl-Wilhelm. PFARRER UND POLITIK. SOZIALE POSITION UND POLITISCHE MENTALITÄT DES DEUTSCHEN EVANGELISCHEN PFARRERSTANDES ZWISCHEN 1918 UND 1933. Cited above as item 591.

1555. Dahm, Karl, Niklas Luhmann, and D. Stoodt. RELIGION - SYSTEM UND SOZIALISATION. BAND II, REIHE THEOLOGIE UND POLITIK. Darmstat, Neuwied: Luchterhand, 1972.

1556. Dann, Norman K. CONCURRENT SOCIAL MOVEMENTS: A STUDY OF THE INTERRELATIONSHIPS BETWEEN POPULIST POLITICS AND HOLINESS RELIGION. Unpublished Ph.D. dissertation, Syracuse University, 1974.

1557. Dembinsky, Ludwik. "Les choix politiques des structures confessionnelles en Pologne." REVUE FRANÇAISE DE SCIENCE POLITIQUE 23,3 (1973): 537-549.

1558. Desai, A.R. "National Integration and Religion." SOCIOLOGICAL BULLETIN 12,1 (1963): 53-65.

1559. Dijck, Cees van. "Islam and Socio-Political Conflicts in Indonesian History." SC 31,1 (1984): 5-25.

1560. Dodson, Michael. "The Christian Left in Latin American Politics." In Daniel H. Levine (ed.), CHURCHES AND POLITICS IN LATIN AMERICA. Beverly Hills: Sage, 1979, pp. 111-134. Also in JOURNAL OF INTERAMERICAN STUDIES AND WORLD AFFAIRS 21 (1979): 45-68.

1561. Dujardin, D., Freddy Raphaël, and Henri Rosenfeld. "Influence du facteur religieux sur la vie économique, politique et familiale à Strasbourg. Travail et religion." REVUE DES SCIENCES SOCIALES DE LA FRANCE DE L'EST 5 (1976): 17-50.

1562. Eberts, Paul R. "Changes in Political Attitudes by Socio-Religious Groupings." SOCIOLOGICAL FOCUS 1,3 (1968): 31-54.

1563. Eckstein, Susana. "La ley férrea de la oligarquia y las relationes interorganizacionales: las nexos entra la Iglesia y el Estado en Mexico." REVISTA MEXICANA DE SOCIOLOGIA 37,2 (1975): 327-348.

1564. Elinson, Howard. "The Implications of Pentecostal Religion for Intellectualism, Politics, and Race Relations." AMERICAN JOURNAL OF SOCIOLOGY 70 (1965): 403-415.

* Evans, Robert H. "Parish Priests, Political Power, and Decision-Making. An Italian Case." Cited above as item 606.

* Ezcurra, Ana Maria. "Neoconservative and Ideological Struggle toward Central-America in the U.S.A." Cited above as item 106.

1565. Faouzi, Adel. "Islam, réformisme et nationalisme dans la résistance à la colonisation française en Algérie (1830-1930)." SC 25,3-4 (1978): 419-432.

1566. Fathi, Asghar. "The Islamic Pulpit as a Medium of Political Communication." JSSR 20,2 (1981): 163-172.

1567. Fee, Joan L. "Party Identification among American Catholics, 1972, 1973." ETHNICITY 3 (1976): 53-69.

* Fee, Joan L., Andrew M. Greeley, William C. McCready, and Theresa A. Sullivan. YOUNG CATHOLICS. Cited above as item 530.

* Fleming, J.J., and G.W. Marks. "Mobilizing for Jesus: Evangelicals and the 1980 Election in the United States." Cited above as item 107.

1568. Fouilloux, Etiènne. "Religion et politique en Méditerranée orientale (1878-1914)." ARCHIVES DE SCIENCES SOCIALES DES RELIGIONS 50,2 (1980): 167-175.

1569. Frigolé Reinach, Joan. "Religión y politica en un pueblo murciano entre 1966-1976: la crisis del nacional catolicismo desde le perspectiva local." REVISTA ESPAÑOLA DE INVESTIGACIONES SOCIOLOGICAS 23 (1983): 77-126.

* Gannon, Thomas M. "The New Christian Right in America as a Social and Political Force." Cited above as item 108.

1570. Girod, R. "Clivages confessionnels et gouvernement de tous les partis." REVUE SUISSE DE SOCIOLOGIE 3 (1977): 93-104.

1571. Glantz, Oscar. "Protestant and Catholic Voting Behavior in a Metropolitan Area." PUBLIC OPINION QUARTERLY 23 (1959): 73-82.

1572. Glock, Charles Y., and Rodney Stark. Ch. 11 in RELIGION AND SOCIETY IN TENSION (volume cited in item 141).

1573. Gold, David. INFLUENCE OF RELIGIOUS AFFILIATION ON VOTING BEHAVIOR. Unpublished Ph.D. dissertation, University of Chicago, 1953.

1574. Golde, Günter. "Voting Patterns, Social Context, and Religious Affiliation in South West Germany." COMPARATIVE STUDIES IN SOCIETY AND HISTORY 24,1 (1982): 25-56.

1575. Grand'Maison, Jacques. NATIONALISME ET RELIGION. VOL. I: NATIONALISME ET REVOLUTION CULTURELLE. VOL. II: RELIGION ET IDEOLOGIES POLITIQUES. Montréal: Editions Beauchemin, 1970.

1576. Greeley, Andrew M., and William C. McCready. ETHNICITY IN THE UNITED STATES. A PRELIMINARY RECONNAISSANCE. New York: Wiley, 1974.

1577. Greer, Scott. "Catholic Voters and the Democratic Party." PUBLIC OPINION QUARTERLY 25 (1961): 611-625.

1578. Gregory,W. Edgar. DOCTRINE AND ATTITUDE: A STUDY OF THE RELATIONSHIP BETWEEN RELIGIOUS BELIEFS AND SOCIO-POLITICAL-ECONOMIC ATTITUDES. Unpublished Ph.D. dissertation, University of California, Berkeley, 1955.

1579. Greilsammer, Alain. "Sociologie électorale du protestantisme français." ARCHIVES DE SCIENCES SOCIALES DES RELIGIONS 49,1 (1980): 119-146.

1580. Grignon, Claude. "Sur les relations entre les transformations du champ religieux et les transformations de l'espace politique." ACTES DE LA RECHERCHE EN SCIENCES SOCIALES 16 (1977): 3-34.

1581. Grupp, Fred W., Jr., and William M. Newman. "Political Ideology and Religious Preference: The John Birch Society and Americans for Democratic Action." JSSR 12,4 (1973): 401-413.

1582. Hadden, Jeffrey K. "An Analysis of Some Factors Associated with Religion and Political Affiliation in a College Population." JSSR 2,2 (1963): 209-216.

* Hadden, Jeffrey K. "Televangelism and the New Christian Right." Cited above as item 110.

1583. Hammond, John L. "Revival Religion and Anti-Slavery Politics." AMERICAN SOCIOLOGICAL REVIEW 39,2 (1974): 175-186.

1584. Hammond, John L. THE POLITICS OF BENEVOLENCE. REVIVAL RELIGION AND AMERICAN VOTING BEHAVIOR. Norwood, New Jersey: Ablex, 1979.

1585. Hammond, Phillip E. "An Approach to the Political Meaning of Evangelicalism in Present-Day America." ANNUAL REVIEW OF THE SOCIAL SCIENCES OF RELIGION 5 (1981): 187-202.

1586. Hanf, Theodor. "The 'Political Secularization' Issue in Lebanon." ANNUAL REVIEW OF THE SOCIAL SCIENCES OF RELIGION 5 (1981): 225-253.

1587. Hanna, Mary T. CATHOLICS AND AMERICAN POLITICS. Cambridge, Massachusetts: Harvard University Press, 1979.

* Hashimoto, Hideo, and William McPherson. "Rise and Decline of Sokagakkai: Japan and the United States." Cited above as item 142.

1588. Hazelrigg, L.E. "Religious and Class Bases of Political Conflict in Italy." AMERICAN JOURNAL OF SOCIOLOGY 75 (1970): 496-511.

1589. Hendricks, John Stephen. RELIGIOUS AND POLITICAL FUNDAMENTALISM: THE LINK BETWEEN ALIENATION AND IDEOLOGY. Unpublished Ph.D. dissertation, University of Michigan, 1977.

* Henriot, Peter J. "The Coincidence of Political and Religious Attitudes." Cited above as item 646.

1590. Hermassi, Elbaki. "Politics and Culture in the Middle East." SC 25,3-4 (1978): 445-464.

1591. Hermet, Guy. "Les fonctions politiques des organisations religieuses dans les régions à pluralisme limité." REVUE FRANÇAISE DE SCIENCE POLITIQUE 23 (1973): 439-472.

1592. Hero, Alfred O. AMERICAN RELIGIOUS GROUPS VIEW FOREIGN POLICY: TREND IN RANK-AND-FILE OPINION, 1937-1969. Duke University Press, 1973.

* Hicks, Frederick. "Politics, Power and the Role of the Village Priest in Paraguay." Cited above as item 858.

* Hill, Samuel S. "NRPR: The New Religious-Political Right in America." Cited above as item 114.

1593. Honsberger, H., and J. Zisyadis. "Partis politique et Eglise évangélique réformée vaudoise." REVUE SUISSE DE SOCIOLOGIE 3 (1977): 175-191.

1594. Hopkins, Raymond F. "Christianity and Socio-Political Change in Sub-Sahara Africa." SOCIAL FORCES 44,4 (1966): 555-562.

1595. Houtart, François. "Les interrelation entre champ religieux et champ politique dans la société singhalaise." SC 20,2 (1973): 105-138.

1596. Houtart, François. "Buddhism and Politics in South East India." SOCIAL SCIENTIST (India) 5,3 (1976): 3-22; and 5,4 (1976): 30-45.

1597. Houtart, François. "Theravada Buddhism and Political Power -- Construction and Destructuration of its Ideological Function." SC 24,2-3 (1977): 207-246.

1598. Houtart, François. "Religion et champ politique: cadre théorique pour l'étude des sociétés capitalistes périphériques." SC 24,2-3 (1977): 265-272.

1599. Houtart, François. RELIGION AND IDEOLOGY IN SRI LANKA. Maryknoll, N.Y.: Orbis, 1980.

1600. Houtart, François, and Geneviève Lemercinier. "Conscience religieuse et conscience politique en Amérique Centrale." SC 30,2-3 (1983): 153-174.

1601. Hunt, C.L. "The Life Cycles of Dictatorships as Seen in Treatment of Religious Institutions." SOCIAL FORCES 27,4 (1949): 365-369.

1602. Hunter, James D. "The New Class and the Young Evangelicals." RRR 2,2 (1980): 155-169.

1603. Iqbal, S.M. "Political Thought in Islam." SOCIOLOGICAL REVIEW (1st Series) 1,3 (1908): 249-261.

1604. Irving, William P. "Explaining the Religious Basis of the Canadian Partisan Identity: Success on the Third Try." CANADIAN JOURNAL OF POLITICAL SCIENCE 7,3 (1974): 560-563.

1605. Isambert, François A. "Comportement politique et attitude religieuse." In R. Metz and J. Schlick (eds.), POLITIQUE ET FOI. Strasbourg: Cerdic, 1972, pp. 11-41.

1606. Isambert, François A. "Signification de quelques correspondances empiriques entre comportements politiques et religieux." ARCHIVES DE SOCIOLOGIE DES RELIGIONS 17,33 (1972): 49-70.

1607. Isambert, François A. "Religion et politique. Discussions internationales." ARCHIVES DE SCIENCES SOCIALES DES RELIGIONS 49,1 (1980): 77-82.

1608. Janosik, Robert J. "Religion and Political Involvement: A Study of Black African Sects." JSSR 13,2 (1974): 161-175.

* Jiminez Cadeña, Gustavo. THE ROLE OF THE RURAL PARISH PRIEST AS AN AGENT OF SOCIAL CHANGE IN CENTRAL COLOMBIA. SACERDOTE Y CAMBIO SOCIAL. ESTUDIO SOCIOLOGO EN LOS ANDES COLOMBIANOS. Cited above as item 658.

* Johnson, Benton. "Ascetic Protestantism and Political Preference." Cited above as item 43.

* Johnson, Benton. "Ascetic Protestantism and Political Preference in the Deep South." Cited above as item 44.

* Johnson, Benton. "Theology and Party Preference among Protestant Clergymen." Cited above as item 659.

* Johnson, Benton. "Theology and the Position of Pastors on Public Issues." Cited above as item 660.

1609. Johnson, Stephen D., and Joseph B. Tamney. "The Christian Right and the 1980 Presidential Election." JSSR 21,2 (1982): 123-131.

* Johnstone, Ronald L. "Negro Preachers Take Sides." Cited above as item 661.

1610. Kang, Wi Jo. "Belief and Political Behavior in Ch'ondogyo." RRR 10 (1968): 38-43.

1611. Kertzer, David I. COMRADES AND CHRISTIANS. RELIGION AND POLITICAL STRUGGLE IN COMMUNIST ITALY. Cambridge: Cambridge University Press, 1980.

1612. Kessler, C.S. "Islam, Society and Political Behaviour. Some Comparative Implications of the Malay Case." BRITISH JOURNAL OF SOCIOLOGY 23,1 (1972): 33-50.

1613. Knoke, David. "Religious Involvement and Political Behavior: A Loglinear Analysis of White Americans, 1952-1968." SOCIOLOGICAL QUARTERLY 15 (1974): 51-65.

1614. Knoke, David. "Religion, Stratification and Politics: America in the 1960's." AMERICAN JOURNAL OF POLITICAL SCIENCE 18 (1974): 331-346.

1615. Kowalewski, David. "Religious Belief in the Brezhnev Era: Renaissance, Resistance and Realpolitik." JSSR 19,3 (1980): 280-292.

1616. Lalive d'Epinay, Christian. "Elites protestantes, politique et procès du développement. Le cas de l'Argentine." REVUE FRANÇAISE DE SOCIOLOGIE 15,4 (1974): 553-569.

* Lamanna, Richard A., and J.B. Stephenson. "Religious Prejudice and Intended Voting Behavior." Cited above as item 445.

1617. Latreille, André, and André Siegfried. LES FORCES RELIGIEUSES ET LA VIE POLITIQUE. 23E CAHIER DE LA FONDATION NATIONALE DES SCIENCES POLITIQUES. Paris: A. Colin, 1951.

1618. Laumann, E., and D. Segal. "Status Inconsistency and Ethno-religious Membership as Determinants of Social Participation and Political Attitudes." AMERICAN JOURNAL OF SOCIOLOGY 77 (1971): 36-61.

1619. Levine, Daniel H. RELIGION AND POLITICS IN LATIN AMERICA: THE CATHOLIC CHURCH IN VENEZUELA AND COLUMBIA. Princeton: Princeton University Press, 1981.

1620. Lewy, Guenter. "Changing Conceptions of Political Legitimacy: Abandonment of Theocracy in the Islamic world." In David Spitz (ed.), POLITICAL THEORY AND SOCIAL CHANGE. New York: Aldine-Atherton, 1967.

1621. Liebman, Charles S. "Religion and Political Integration in Israel." JEWISH JOURNAL OF SOCIOLOGY 17,1 (1975): 17-27.

1622. Liebman, Charles S., and Eliezer Don-Yehiya. RELIGION AND POLITICS IN ISRAEL. Bloomington: Indiana University Press, 1984.

* Liebman, Robert C., and Robert Wuthnow (eds.) THE NEW CHRISTIAN RIGHT. Cited above as item 119.

1623. Liénard, Georges, and André Rousseau. "Conflit symbolique et conflit social dans le champ religieux. Propositions théoriques et analyse d'un conflit suscité par l'Action Catholique Ouvrière dans le nord de la France." SC 19,2 (1972): 263-290.

1624. Lijphart, A. "Class Voting and Religious Voting in the European Democracies: A Preliminary Report." ACTA POLITICA 6 (1971): 158-171.

1625. Linden, Ian, and Jane Linden. CHURCH AND REVOLUTION IN RWANDA. New York: Holmes and Meier, 1977.

1626. Linz, Juan J. "Religion and Politics in Spain: From Conflict to Consensus above Cleavage." SC 27,2-3 (1980): 255-277.

1627. Lipset, Seymour Martin. AGRARIAN SOCIALISM: THE COOPERATIVE COMMONWEALTH FEDERATION IN SASKATCHEWAN. Garden City: Anchor Books, 1968, 208-212 and 227-228. First published by the University of California Press, 1950.

1628. Lipset, Seymour Martin. "Religion and Politics in the American Past and Present." In R. Lee and M. Marty (eds.), RELIGION AND SOCIAL CONFLICT (volume cited in item 141).

1629. Lockard, Kathleen G. RELIGION AND POLITICAL DEVELOPMENT IN UGANDA, 1962-1972. Unpublished Ph.D. dissertation, University of Wisconsin, 1974.

* Lorentzen, Louise J. "Evangelical Life Style Concerns Expressed in Political Action." Cited above as item 120.

1630. Lovelace, Arthur Boorne. THE ROLE OF THE UNITED CHURCH IN SOCIAL POLITICS. Unpublished M.A. thesis, McGill University, 1936.

1631. Madron, Thomas W., Hart M. Nelsen, and Raytha L. Yokley. "Religion as a Determinant of Militancy and Political Participation among Black Americans." AMERICAN BEHAVIORAL SCIENTIST 17,6 (1974): 783-797.

1632. Maître, Jacques. "Processus politiques et dynamique religieuse." ARCHIVES DE SCIENCES SOCIALES DES RELIGIONS 49,1 (1980): 146-150.

1633. Mann, William E. SECT, CULT, AND CHURCH IN ALBERTA. Unpublished Ph.D. dissertation, University of Toronto, 1953. Abridged version published as SECT, CULT, AND CHURCH IN ALBERTA. Toronto: University of Toronto Press, 1955.

* Maranell, Gary M. RESPONSES TO RELIGION. Cited above as item 4.

1634. Marzal, Antonio. "La critica religiosa de la politica." PERSPECTIVA SOCIAL (1977): 105-111.

1635. Maurer, Heinrich H. "The Political Attitudes of the Lutheran Parish in America." AMERICAN JOURNAL OF SOCIOLOGY 33 (1928): 568-585.

1636. Mayeur, J.M. "Catholicisme intransigent, catholicisme social, Democratie Chrétienne." ANNALES -- ECONOMIES, SOCIETES, CIVILISATIONS 27,2 (1972): 483-499.

1637. Mayeur, J.M. "L'évolution des positions des autorités religieuses en matière politique." In R. Metz and J. Schlick (eds.), POLITIQUE ET FOI. Strasbourg, Cerdic, 1972, pp. 42-58.

1638. McClerren, Beryl F. THE SOUTHERN BAPTIST STATE NEWSPAPERS AND THE RELIGIOUS ISSUE DURING THE PRESIDENTIAL CAMPAIGNS OF 1928 AND 1960. Unpublished Ph.D. dissertation, Southern Illinois University, 1963.

1639. McDonald, Lynn. "Religion and Voting: A Study of the 1968 Canadian Federal Election in Ontario." CANADIAN REVIEW OF SOCIOLOGY AND ANTHROPOLOGY 6,3 (1969): 129-144.

1640. McGovern, Eileen M. POLITICIAL ORIENTATION AND SOCIALIZATION BACKGROUND. Unpublished Ph.D. dissertation, St. Louis University, 1969.

1641. McKinney, M.M. "Religion and Elections." PUBLIC OPINION QUARTERLY 8,1 (1944): 110-114.

1642. Meisel, John. "Religious Affiliation and Voting Behaviour." CANADIAN JOURNAL OF ECONOMICS AND POLITICAL SCIENCE 22 (1956): 481-496.

1643. Mendelson, E. Michael. "Buddhism and the Burmese Establishment." ARCHIVES DE SOCIOLOGIE DES RELIGIONS 9,17 (1964): 85-96.

* Mendelson, E. Michael. SANGHA AND STATE IN BURMA: A STUDY OF MONASTIC SECTARIANISM AND LEADERSHIP. Cited above as item 1308.

1644. Menendez, Albert J. RELIGION AT THE POLLS. Philadelphia: Westminster, 1977.

1645. Michelat, Guy, and Michel Simon. "Catholiques declarés et irreligieux communisants: vision du monde et perception du champ politique." ARCHIVES DE SOCIOLOGIE DES RELIGIONS 35 (1973): 57-112.

1646. Michelat, Guy, and Michel Simon. "Systèmes d'opinions, choix politiques, pratiques religieuses et caractéristiques socio-démographiques: Résultats d'une analyse typologique." ARCHIVES DE SCIENCES SOCIALES DES RELIGIONS 37 (1974): 87-115.

1647. Michelat, G., and M. Simon. CLASSE, RELIGION, COMPORTEMENT POLITIQUE. Paris: Editions Sociales, 1977.

1648. Milanesi, Giancarlo. "Religious Identity and Political Commitment in the 'Christians for Socialism' Movement in Italy." SC 23,2-3 (1976): 241-257.

1649. Miller, W.E., and P.C. Stouthard. "Confessional Attachment and Electoral Behavior in the Netherlands." EUROPEAN JOURNAL OF POLITICAL RESEARCH 3,3 (1975): 219-258.

1650. Miller, William L. "The Religious Revival and American Politics." CONFLUENCE 4 (1955): 44-56.

1651. Mobley, G. Melton. "The Political Influence of Television Ministers." RRR 25,4 (1984): 314-320.

1652. Mol, Johannes J. (Hans). "Religion and Political Allegiance." AUSTRALIAN JOURNAL OF POLITICS AND HISTORY 16 (1970): 320-333.

1653. Moodie, T. Dunbar. "The Dutch Reformed Churches as Vehicles of Political Legitimation in South Africa." SOCIAL DYNAMICS 1,2 (1975): 158-166.

1654. Moodie, T. Dunbar. THE RISE OF AFRIKANERDOM: POWER, APARTHEID, AND THE AFRIKANER CIVIL RELIGION. Berkeley: University of California Press, 1975.

1655. Moore, Robert. "The Political Effects of Village Methodism." SOCIOLOGICAL YEARBOOK OF RELIGION IN BRITAIN 6 (1973): 156-182.

1656. Mosca, Gaetano. "Church, Sects and Parties." SOCIAL FORCES 14,1 (1933): 53-63.

* Murvar, Vatro. "Max Weber's Concept of Hierocracy: A Study in the Typology of Church-State Relationships." Cited above as item 1298.

1657. Murvar, Vatro. "Russian Religious Structures. A Study in Persistent Church Subservience." JSSR 7,1 (1968): 1-22.

1658. Nelsen, Hart M., and Sandra Baxter. "Ministers Speak on Watergate: Effects of Clergy Role During Political Crisis." RRR 23,2 (1981): 150-166.

1659. Nicholls, D. "Politics and Religion in Haiti." CANADIAN JOURNAL OF POLITICAL SCIENCE 3 (1970): 400-414.

1660. Olaechea Labeyan, Juan B. "Incidencias políticas en la cuestión del clero indígena en Filipinas." REVISTA INTERNACIONAL DE SOCIOLOGIA 30,1-2 (1973): 153-186.

1661. Omark, Richard. "The Decline of Russian Religious Power. Church-State Relations, 1439-1503." SC 21,2 (1974): 207-214.

1662. Orum, Anthony M. "Religion and the Rise of the Radical White: The Case of Southern Wallace Support in 1968." SOCIAL SCIENCE QUARTERLY 51 (1970): 674-688.

1663. O'Toole, Roger. "Some Social-Psychological Aspects of Sectarian Social Movements: A Study in Politics and Religion." In G. Dux, T. Luckmann and J. Matthes (eds.), BEITRÄGE ZUR RELIGIONSSOZIOLOGIE/ CONTRIBUTIONS TO THE SOCIOLOGY OF RELIGION, INTERNATIONAL JAHRBUCH FÜR WISSENS UND RELIGIONSSOZIOLOGIE/INTERNATIONAL YEARBOOK FOR SOCIOLOGY OF KNOWLEDGE AND RELIGION, Bd. 9. Opladen: Westdeutscher Verlag, 1975, pp. 161-199.

1664. O'Toole, Roger. "Sectarianism in Politics: The Internationalists and the Socialist Labour Party." In Stewart Crysdale and Les Wheatcroft (eds.), RELIGION IN CANADIAN SOCIETY (volume cited in item 778), pp. 321-334.

1665. O'Toole, Roger. "Some Good Purpose: Notes on Religion and Political Culture in Canada." ANNUAL REVIEW OF THE SOCIAL SCIENCES OF RELIGION 6 (1982): 177-217.

1666. Pace, Enzo. "Charismatics and the Political Presence of Catholics." SC 25,1 (1978): 85-99.

* Parenti, Michael. "Political Values and Religious Cultures. Jews, Catholics and Protestants." Cited above as item 515.

* Peek, Charles W., and Sharon Brown. "Sex Prejudice among White Protestants: Like or Unlike Ethnic Prejudice?" Cited above as item 482.

1667. Phadnis, Urmila. RELIGION AND POLITICS IN SRI LANKA. New Delhi: Manolcar, 1976.

1668. Pomian-Srzednicki, Maciej. RELIGIOUS CHANGE IN CONTEMPORARY POLAND. London: Routledge and Kegan Paul, 1982.

* Poulat, Emile. "Religion et politique. De l'abbé Grégoire aux prêtres-ouvriers." Cited above as item 1078.

* Pratt, Henry J. "Organizational Stress and Adaptation to Changing Political Status. The Case of the National Council of Churches of Christ in the United States." Cited above as item 1169.

* Quinley, Harold E. THE PROPHETIC CLERGY. SOCIAL ACTIVISM AMONG PROTESTANT MINISTERS. Cited above as item 289.

* Quinney, Richard. "Political Conservatism, Alienation, and Fatalism: Contingencies of Social Status and Religious Fundamentalism." Cited above as item 8.

1669. Raphaël, Freddy, Jacques Demange, and Henri Rosenfeld. "Influence du facteur religieux sur la vie économique, politique et familiale à Strasbourg." REVUE DES SCIENCES SOCIALES DE LA FRANCE DE L'EST 4,4 (1975): 117-181.

1670. Reinhardt, Robert M. RELIGION AND POLITICS: THE POLITICAL BEHAVIOR OF WEST VIRGINIA PROTESTANT FUNDAMENTALIST SECTARIANS. Unpublished Ph.D. dissertation, University of West Virginia, 1974.

* Remond, R. "L'évolution du comportement des prêtres en matière politique." Cited above as item 727.

1671. Reny, Paul, and Jean Paul Rouleau. "Charismatiques et socio-politiques dans l'Eglise catholique au Québec." SC 25,1 (1978): 125-143.

1672. Riccamboni, Giancarlo. "The Italian Communist Party and the Catholic World." SC 23,2-3 (1976): 141-169.

1673. Ringer, Benjamin B., and Charles Y. Glock. "The Political Role of the Church as Defined by its Parishioners." PUBLIC OPINION QUARTERLY 18 (1954): 337-347.

1674. Rojek, Dean G. "The Protestant Ethic and Political Preference." SOCIAL FORCES 52 (1973): 168-177.

1675. Rose, Arnold M. "The Mormon Church and Utah Politics: An Abstract of a Statistical Study." AMERICAN SOCIOLOGICAL REVIEW 7 (1942): 853-854.

1676. Rosenthal, Erwin I.J. ISLAM IN THE MODERN NATIONAL STATE. London: Cambridge University Press, 1965.

1677. Rothenberg, Stuart, and Frank Newport. THE EVANGELICAL VOTER. RELIGION AND POLITICS IN AMERICA. Washington: Free Congress Foundation, 1984.

1678. Roucek, Joseph S. "Religion und Politik in den Vereinigten Staaten." ZEITSCHRIFT FÜR POLITIK 9 (1962): 172-180. "The Role of Religion in American Politics." JOURNAL OF HUMAN RELATIONS 11 (1963): 350-362.

1679. Rousseau, André. "Chrétiens pour le Socialisme et Action Catholique Ouvrière. Deux stratégies socio-religieuses en France." SC 25,1 (1978): 101-123.

1680. Rovan, J. LE CATHOLICISME POLITIQUE EN ALLEMAGNE. Paris: Editions du Seuil, 1956.

1681. Roy, Ralph Lord. "Conflict from the Communist Left and the Radical Right." In Robert Lee and Martin E. Marty (eds.), RELIGION AND SOCIAL CONFLICT (volume cited in item 141).

1682. Rulland, W.B. "Church-State Relations in America: Status and Trends." SOCIAL FORCES 28,1 (1949): 83-86.

1683. Särlvik, B. "Socioeconomic Position, Religious Behavior, and Voting in the Swedish Electorate." QUALITY AND QUANTITY 4 (1970): 95-116.

1984. Sayari, Binnaz. RELIGION AND POLITICAL DEVELOPMENT IN TURKEY. Unpublished Ph.D. dissertation, City University of New York, 1976.

1685. Schiff, Garry S. TRADITION AND POLITICS -- THE RELIGIOUS PARTIES OF ISRAEL. Detroit: Wayne State University Press, 1977.

* Schindeler, Fred, and David Hoffman. "Theological and Political Conservatism: Variations in Attitudes among Clergymen of One Denomination." Cited above as item 121.

1686. Schoenfeld, Eugen. "A Preliminary Note on Love and Justice: The Effect of Religious Values on Liberalism and Conservatism." RRR 16,1 (1974): 41-46.

1687. Schwartz, Mildred. PUBLIC OPINION AND CANADIAN IDENTITY. Berkeley: University of California Press, 1967, pp. 158-164.

* Schwartz, Paul Anthony, and James McBride. "The Moral Majority in the U.S.A. as a New Religious Movement." Cited above as item 123.

1688. Shupe, Anson D., Jr. "Conventional Religion and Political Participation in Postwar Rural Japan." SOCIAL FORCES 55,3 (1977): 613-629.

1689. Shupe, Anson, and William Stacey. BORN AGAIN POLITICS AND THE MORAL MAJORITY: WHAT SOCIAL SURVEYS REALLY SHOW. New York: Mellen, 1982.

1690. Silva, Ruth C. RUM, RELIGION AND VOTES. Pennsylvania State University Press, 1962.

1691. Silverstein, Sandford. "Occupational Class and Voting Behaviour: Electoral Support of a Left-Wing Protest Movement in a Period of Prosperity." In S.M. Lipset, AGRARIAN SOCIALISM (item 1627), pp. 435-479.

1692. Simpson, George E. "Political Cultism in West Kingston, Jamaica." SOCIAL AND ECONOMIC STUDIES 4,2 (1955): 133-149.

1693. Simpson, John H. "Moral Issues and Status Politics." In Robert Liebman and Robert Wuthnow (eds.,), THE NEW CHRISTIAN RIGHT (item 119), pp. 187-205.

1694. Simson, U. "Der Islam: ein Träger politischer Ideen?" SCHWEIZERISCHE ZEITSCHRIFT FÜR SOZIOLOGIE 9 (1983): 677-686.

1695. Sinda, M. LE MESSIANISME CONGOLAIS ET SES INCIDENCES POLITIQUES. Paris: Payot, 1972.

1696. Sironneau, Jean-Pierre. SECULARISATION ET RELIGIONS POLITIQUES. The Hague: Mouton, 1982.

1697. Skocpol, Theda. "Rentier State and Shi'a Islam in the Iranian Revolution." THEORY AND SOCIETY 11,3 (1982): 265-283.

* Smidt, Corwin, and James M. Penning. "Religious Commitment, Political Conservatism, and Political and Social Tolerance in the United States: A Longitudinal Analysis." Cited above as item 124.

1698. Smith, Brian H. THE CHURCH AND POLITICS IN CHILE. CHALLENGES TO MODERN CATHOLICISM. Princeton: Princeton University Press, 1982.

1699. Smith, Donald Eugene. RELIGION AND POLITICAL DEVELOPMENT. Boston: Little, Brown, 1970.

1700. Smith, R.W. "Religious Influence in the Background of the British Labour Party." SOUTHWESTERN SOCIAL SCIENCE QUARTERLY 37,4 (1975): 355-369.

1701. Sockeel-Richarté, P.F.-P. "L'Islam et le politique en Malaysia." PROJET 140 (1979): 1287-1293.

1702. Stange, Douglas C. "Al Smith and the Republican Party at Prayer: The Lutheran Vote -- 1928." REVIEW OF POLITICS 32,3 (1970): 347-364.

1703. Stark, Rodney. "Class, Radicalism, and Religious Involvement in Great Britain." AMERICAN SOCIOLOGICAL REVIEW 29 (1964): 698-706. Reprinted as Ch. 10 in C.Y. Glock and R. Stark, RELIGION AND SOCIETY IN TENSION (volume cited in item 141).

1704. Stellway, Richard J. "The Correspondence between Religious Orientation and Socio-Political Liberalism and Conservatism." SOCIOLOGICAL QUARTERLY 14 (1973): 430-439.

1705. Summers, Gene F., Doyle P. Johnson, Richard L. Hough, and Kathryn Veatch. "Ascetic Protestantism and Political Preference: A Re-Examination." RRR 12 (1970): 17-25.

1706. Swanson, Guy E. RELIGION AND REGIME. A SOCIOLOGICAL ACCOUNT OF THE REFORMATION. Ann Arbor, Michigan: University of Michigan Press, 1967.

1707. Tamney, Joseph B. "Church-State Relations in Christianity and Islam." RRR 15,1 (1974): 10-18.

1708. Tennekes, Johannes. "Le mouvement pentecôtiste chilien et la politique." SC 25,1 (1978): 55-80.

1709. Tibi, B. "Die gegenwärtige politische Revitalisierung des Islam: eine religionssoziologische Bedeutung." SCHWEIERISCHE ZEITSCHRIFT FÜR SOCIOLOGIE 9 (1983): 677-686.

1710. Turner, Bryan S., and Michael Hill. "Methodism and the Pietist Definition of Politics: Historical Development and Contemporary Evidence." In M. Hill (ed.), A SOCIOLOGICAL YEARBOOK OF RELIGION IN BRITAIN 8. London: SCM, 1975, pp. 159-180.

* Tygart, Clarence E. A STUDY OF CLERGYMEN: WORK, IDEAS AND POLITICS. Cited above as item 785.

* Tygart, Clarence E. "Work Alienation and Politics among Clergy." Cited above as item 10.

1711. Utrecht, Ernst. "Religion and Social Protest in Indonesia." SC 25,3-4 (1978): 395-418.

1712. Utrecht, Ernst. "The Muslim Merchant Class in the Indonesian Social and Political Struggles." SC 31,1 (1984): 27-55.

1713. Vaillancourt, Jean-Guy. "Les groupes socio-politiques progressistes dans le Catholicisme Québécois contemporain." LES MOUVEMENTS RELIGIEUX AUJOURD'HUI. THEORIES ET PRATIQUES. LES CAHIERS DE RECHERCHES EN SCIENCES DE LA RELIGION 5 (1984): 261-282.

1714. Varga, Ivan. "The Politicisation of the Transcendent: A Quasi-Sociological Postscript." In J.M. Bak and G. Benecke (eds.), RELIGION AND RURAL REVOLT. Manchester: Manchester University Press, 1984, pp. 470-481.

* Weber, Max. THE SOCIOLOGY OF RELIGION, translated by E. Fischoff. Boston: Beacon, 1963. Ch. 6 in M. Weber, ECONOMY AND SOCIETY, Vol. I. Cited above in item 58.

1715. Weissbrod, Lilly. "Gush Emunim Ideology - From Religious Doctrine to Political Action." MIDDLE EASTERN STUDIES 18 (1982): 265-275.

1716. Whyte, John. CATHOLICS IN WESTERN DEMOCRACIES: A STUDY IN POLITICAL BEHAVIOR. Dublin: Gill and Macmillan, 1981.

1717. Wichmann, A.A. "Buddhism, Economic Development and Neutralism in Burma." SOUTHWESTERN SOCIAL SCIENCE QUARTERLY 46,1 (1965): 20-27.

* Wiley, Norbert. "Religious and Political Liberalism among Catholics." Cited above as item 128.

1718. Wimberley, Ronald C. "Dimensions of Commitment: Generalizing from Religion to Politics." JSSR 17,3 (1978): 225-240.

1719. Wimberley, Ronald C. "Civil Religion and the Choice for President: Nixon in '72." SOCIAL FORCES 59,1 (1980): 44-61.

1720. Winter, J. Alan. "On the Mixing of Morality and Politics: A Test of a Weberian Hypothesis." SOCIAL FORCES 49 (1970-71): 36-41.

1721. Wright, Frank. "Protestant Ideology and Politics in Ulster." ARCHIVES EUROPEENNES DE SOCIOLOGIE 14,2 (1973): 213-280.

1722. Wuthnow, Robert. EXPERIMENTATION IN AMERICAN RELIGION. Berkeley: University of California Press, 1978.

1723. Wuthnow, Robert. "Political Aspects of the Quietistic Revival." In T. Robbins and D. Anthony (eds.), IN GODS WE TRUST (item 367), pp. 229-243.

* Yinger, J. Milton. RELIGION IN THE STRUGGLE FOR POWER. Cited above as item 296.

1724. Yinger, J. Milton, and Stephen J. Cutler. "The Moral Majority Viewed Sociologically." SOCIOLOGICAL FOCUS 15,4 (1982): 289-306.

1725. Zylberberg, Jacques. "Les catholicismes chiliens et le politique." CAHIERS DU CENTRE DE RECHERCHES EN SOCIOLOGIE RELIGIEUSE 2 (1978): 170-219.

Activism

Engaging in political and social agitation out of a religious motivation and in the name of a religious organization, especially by religious officials, is often controversial.

* Ammerman, Nancy Tatom. LOCALISM, SOUTHERN CULTURE, AND THE ROLE OF CLERGYMEN IN THE CIVIL RIGHTS MOVEMENT IN A SOUTHERN COMMUNITY. Cited above as item 542.

* Ammerman, Nancy T. "The Civil Rights Movement and the Clergy in a Southern Community." Cited above as item 543.

* Bahr, Howard M., Lois Franz Bartel, and Bruce A. Chadwick. "Orthodoxy, Activism, and the Salience of Religion." Cited above as item 488.

* Berenson, William, Kirk W. Elifson, and Tandy Tollerson, III. "Preachers in Politics: A Study of Political Activism among the Black Ministry." Cited above as item 547.

1726. Blacker, C. "Le Soka-Gakkai japonais. L'activisme politique d'une secte bouddhiste." ARCHIVES DE SOCIOLOGIE DES RELIGIONS 9,17 (1964): 63-67.

1727. Blume, N. "Clergymen and Social Action." SOCIOLOGY AND SOCIAL RESEARCH 54 (1970): 237-248.

1728. Broughton, Walter. "Religiosity and Opposition to Church Social Action: A Test of a Weberian Hypothesis." RRR 19,2 (1978): 154-166.

1729. Cantrell, Randolph, James Krile, and George Donahue. "The External Adaptation of Religious Organizations." SA 41,4 (1981): 351-364.

1730. Davis, Jerome. "The Social Action Pattern of the Protestant Religious Leader." AMERICAN SOCIOLOGICAL REVIEW 1 (1936): 105-144.

1731. DeKadt, E. CATHOLIC RADICALS IN BRAZIL. London: Oxford University Press, 1970.

1732. Demerath, Nicholas J., III, Gerald Marwell, and Michael T. Aiken. DYNAMICS OF IDEALISM. San Francisco: Jossey-Bass, 1971.

1733. Garrett, William R. "Politicized Clergy: A Sociological Interpretation of the 'New Breed.'" JSSR 12,4 (1973): 383-399.

* Greeley, Andrew M. THE RELIGIOUS IMAGINATION. Cited above as item 305.

* Guth, James L. "The Politics of Preachers: Southern Baptist Ministers and Christian Right Activism." Cited above as item 638.

1734. Hadden, Jeffrey K., and Raymond C. Rymph. "The Marching Ministers." TRANS-ACTION 3 (1966): 38-41.

1735. Hadden, Jeffrey K., and Raymond C. Rymph. "Social Structure and Civil Rights Involvement: A Case Study of Protestant Ministers." SOCIAL FORCES 45 (1966): 51-61.

* Koller, Norman B., and Joseph D. Retzer. "The Sounds of Silence Revisited." Cited above as item 673.

1736. Martin, William. CHRISTIANS IN CONFLICT. Unpublished Ph.D. dissertation, Harvard University, 1968.

1737. McConahay, John B., and Joseph C. Hough, Jr. "Love and Guilt-Oriented Dimensions of Christian Belief." JSSR 12 (1973): 132-133.

1738. McNamara, Patrick H. "Priests, Protests, and Poverty Intervention." SOCIAL SCIENCE QUARTERLY 50 (1969): 695-702.

1739. Moberg, David O. THE GREAT REVERSAL: EVANGELISM VERSUS SOCIAL CONCERN. Philadelphia: Lippincott, 1972.

1740. Nelsen, Hart M., et al. "Ministerial Roles and Social Actionist Stance: Protestant Clergy and Protest in the Sixties." AMERICAN SOCIOLOGICAL REVIEW 38 (1973): 375-386.

1741. Pangborn, Cyrus Ransom. FREE CHURCHES AND SOCIAL CHANGE. A CRITICAL STUDY OF THE COUNCIL FOR SOCIAL ACTION OF THE CONGREGATIONAL CHURCHES OF THE UNITED STATES. Unpublished Ph.D. dissertation, Columbia University, 1951.

1742. Pearson, D.G. "Race, Religiosity and Political Activism: Some Observations on West Indian Participation in Britain." BRITISH JOURNAL OF SOCIOLOGY 29,3 (1978): 340-357.

* Petersen, Larry R., and K. Peter Takayama. "Religious Commitment and Conservatism: Toward Understanding an Elusive Relationship." Cited above as item 455.

* Quinley, Harold E. THE PROPHETIC CLERGY. SOCIAL ACTIVISM AMONG PROTESTANT MINISTERS. Cited above as item 289.

1743. Quinley, Harold E. "The Dilemmas of an Activist Church: Protestant Religion in the Sixties and Seventies." JSSR 13,1 (1974): 1-21.

* Shupe, Anson D., Jr., and James R. Wood. "Sources of Leadership Ideology in Dissident Clergy." Cited above as item 758.

* Stark, Rodney, Charles Y. Glock, and Harold E. Quinley. WAYWARD SHEPHERDS. Cited above as item 471.

* Tedlin, Kent. "Religious Preference and Pro/Anti Activism on the Equal Rights Amendment Issue." Cited above as item 1116.

* Tygart, Clarence E. "The Role of Theology among Other 'Belief' Variables for Clergy Civil Rights Activism." Cited above as item 787.

1744. Varacalli, Joseph A. THE AMERICAN CATHOLIC CALL FOR LIBERTY AND JUSTICE FOR ALL: AN ANALYSIS IN THE SOCIOLOGY OF KNOWLEDGE. Unpublished Ph.D. dissertation, Rutgers University, 1980.

1745. Varacalli, Joseph A. TOWARD THE ESTABLISHMENT OF LIBERAL CATHOLICISM IN AMERICA. Washington: University Press of America, 1983.

* Winter, J. Alan. "The Attitudes of Societally-Oriented and Parish-Oriented Clergy: An Empirical Comparison." Cited above as item 799.

* Winter, J. Alan. "On the Mixing of Morality and Politics: A Test of a Weberian Hypothesis." Cited above as item 1720.

1746. Winter, J. Alan. "Clergy Reaction to Hypothetical Parish Unrest Over a Clergyman's Social Activism." SC 18,2 (1971): 293-302.

1747. Winter, J. Alan. "Political Activism among the Clergy: Sources of a Deviant Role." RRR 14,3 (1973): 178-186.

1748. Wolcott, Roger T. "The Church and Social Action: Steelworkers and Bishops in Youngstown." JSSR 21,1 (1982): 71-79.

* Wood, James R. LEADERSHIP IN VOLUNTARY ORGANIZATIONS. THE CONTROVERSY OVER SOCIAL ACTION IN PROTESTANT CHURCHES. Cited above as item 1191.

1749. Zahn, Gordon C. "Religion, Sociology and the Milieu: Formula for Activism?" SA 29,3 (1968): 115-121.

SECTION E: STRATIFICATION (social inequality).
Also see Protestant Ethic in Ch. 2 (below), and Popular Religion (below) in this chapter.

Stratification (general)

1750. Alant, C.J. "The Relevance of Socio-Economic Groups in the Analysis of the Nederduitse Gereformeerde Kerk in South Africa." SC 19,1 (1972): 21-28.

1751. Allen, Sheila. "Class, Culture and Generation." SOCIOLOGICAL REVIEW 21 (1973): 437-446.

1752. Allingham, John Douglas. RELIGIOUS AFFILIATION AND SOCIAL CLASS IN ONTARIO. Unpublished M.A. thesis, McMaster University, 1962.

1753. Alston, Jon P. "Religious Mobility and Socioeconomic Status." SA 32,3 (1971): 140-148.

1754. Alston, Jon P. "Socioeconomic Correlates of Belief." JSSR 11 (1972): 180-186.

1755. Alston, Jon P., and William Alex McIntosh. "An Assessment of the Determinants of Religious Participation." SOCIOLOGICAL QUARTERLY 20,1 (1979): 49-62.

* Bell, Wendell, and Maryanne T. Force. "Religious Preference, Familism and the Class Structure." Cited above as item 1269.

* Boisen, Anton T. "Economic Distress and Religious Experience." Cited above as item 133.

* Boisen, Anton T. "Religion and Hard Times." Cited above as item 134.

1756. Boisen, Anton T. RELIGION IN CRISIS AND CUSTOM. New York: Harper, 1945.

* Broughton, Walter, and Edgar W. Mills, Jr. "Resource Inequality and Accumulative Advantage: Stratification in the Ministry." Cited above as item 565.

1757. Brown, Diana. "Umbanda e classes sociais." RELIGIAO E SOCIEDADE 1 (1977): 31-42.

1758. Brown, James Stephen. "Social Class, Inter-Marriage, and Church Membership in a Kentucky Community." AMERICAN JOURNAL OF SOCIOLOGY 57 (1951): 232-242.

1759. Brunetta, Giuseppe. "Religiosità nel mondo operaio. Una inchiesa nel varesotto." AGGIORNAMENTI SOCIALI 11 (1978): 707-720.

* Bultena, Louis. "Church Membership and Church Attendance in Madison, Wisconsin." Cited above as item 929.

1760. Burchinal, Lee G. "Some Social Status Criteria and Church Membership and Church Attendance." JOURNAL OF SOCIAL PSYCHOLOGY 49 (1959): 53-64.

1761. Burchinal, Lee G., and L.E.Chancellor. "Social Status, Religious Affiliation, and Ages at Marriage." MARRIAGE AND FAMILY LIVING 25 (1963): 219-221.

1762. Burchinal, Lee G., and William F. Kenkel. "Religious Identification and Occupational Status of Iowa Grooms, 1953-7." AMERICAN SOCIOLOGICAL REVIEW 27 (1962): 526-532.

1763. Burgalassi, S. "Catégories sociales et accueil de la doctrine en Italie." CONCILIUM (French Series, 1978): 11-30.

1764. Burton, Lewis. "Social Class in the Local Church: A Study of Two Methodist Churches in the Midlands." SOCIOLOGICAL YEARBOOK OF RELIGION IN BRITAIN 8 (1975): 15-39.

1765. Campbell, Colin. "The Secret Religion of the Educated Classes." SA 39,2 (1978): 146-156.

1766. Cantril, Hadley. "Educational and Economic Composition of Religious Groups." AMERICAN JOURNAL OF SOCIOLOGY 48 (1943): 574-579.

1767. Carpenter, Niles, and M.E. Wagner. "The Relation of Nationality and Religion to Income." SOCIAL FORCES 5 (1926): 140-146.

1768. Centro de Estudios Cristianos. ASPECTOS RELIGIOSOS DE LA SOCIEDAD URUGUAYA. Montevideo: Centro de Estudios Cristianos, 1965.

1769. Chalfant, H. Paul. CLASSIFICATION OF THE VARIABLES OF SOCIO-ECONOMIC CLASS, ECOLOGICAL PLACE AND LEADERSHIP STYLE IN URBAN CHURCH CONGREGATIONS. Unpublished M.A. thesis, Oklahoma State University, 1967.

1770. Cipriani, Roberto. "Tendances actuelles dans les recherches sociologiques sur le thème 'religion et classe ouvrière.'" SC 27,2-3 (1980): 297-305.

1771. Clark, S.D. CHURCH AND SECT IN CANADA. Toronto: University of Toronto Press, 1948.

1772. Covello, Vincent T., and Jacqueline A. Ashby. "Inequality in a Divided Society: An Analysis of Data from Northern Ireland." SOCIOLOGICAL FOCUS 13,2 (1980): 87-98.

1773. Davidson, James D., Jr. SOCIAL CLASS AND TEN DIMENSIONS OF RELIGIOUS INVOLVEMENT. Unpublished Ph.D. dissertation, University of Notre Dame, 1969.

1774. Davidson, James D. "Socio-Economic Status and Ten Dimensions of Religious Commitment." SOCIOLOGY AND SOCIAL RESEARCH 61 (1977): 462-485.

1775. Davies, J. Kenneth. "The Mormon Church: Its Middle Class Propensities." RRR 4 (1963): 84-95.

1776. Day, Graham, and Martin Fitton. "Religion and Social Status in Rural Wales: 'Buchedd' and its Lessons for Concepts of Stratification in Community Studies." SOCIOLOGICAL REVIEW 23,4 (1975): 867-891.

1777. Decker, Carmer C. THE RELATIONSHIP OF ESCHATOLOGICAL EMPHASIS TO ECONOMIC STATUS OF TWO METHODIST CHURCHES IN BLOOMINGTON. Unpublished M.A. thesis, Indiana University, Bloomington, 1947.

1778. DeJong, Gordon F. "Religious Fundamentalism, Socio-Economic Status, and Fertility Attitudes in the Southern Appalachians." DEMOGRAPHY 2 (1965): 540-548.

* Del Grande, Mary Vera. A STUDY OF THE VALUES OF CATHOLIC HIGH SCHOOL STUDENTS OF DIFFERING SOCIO-ECONOMIC BACKGROUNDS AND THE RELATIONSHIP OF THESE VALUES TO THOSE OF THEIR PARENTS. Cited above as item 503.

1779. Demerath, Nicholas J., III. RELIGIOUS ORIENTATIONS AND SOCIAL CLASS. Unpublished M.A. thesis, University of California at Berkeley, 1961.

1780. Demerath, Nicholas J., III. "Social Stratification and Church Involvement: The Church-Sect Distinction Applied to Individual Participation." RRR 2 (1961): 146-154.

* Demerath, Nicholas J., III. SOCIAL CLASS IN AMERICAN PROTESTANTISM. Cited above as item 1228.

1781. Dillingham, Harry C. "Protestant Religion and Social Status." AMERICAN JOURNAL OF SOCIOLOGY 70 (1965): 416-422.

1782. Dillingham, Harry C. "Rejoinder to 'Social Class and Church Participation.'" AMERICAN JOURNAL OF SOCIOLOGY 73 (1967): 110-114.

1783. Dubar, Claude. "Structure confessionnelle et classes sociales au Liban." REVUE FRANÇAISE DE SOCIOLOGIE 15,3 (1974): 301-328.

1784. Du Bois, W.E.B. THE PHILADELPHIA NEGRO. A SOCIAL STUDY, chs. 31, 32, 33. New York: Schocken, 1967 (first published 1899).

1785. Duocastella Rosell, Rogelio. SOCIOLOGIA RELIGIOSA DE UNA CIUDAD INDUSTRIAL. Paris: Instituto Sociologia y Pastoral Aplicada, 1961.

1786. Dutra, Eliana Regina de Freitas. "A Igreja e as classes populares em Minas no década de vinte." REVISTA BRASILEIRA DE ESTUDIOS POLITICOS 49 (1979): 71-98.

1787. Dynes, Russell R. "The Church-Sect Typology and Socio-Economic Status." AMERICAN SOCIOLOGICAL REVIEW 20 (1955): 555-560. Also in J.M. Yinger (ed.), RELIGION, SOCIETY AND THE INDIVIDUAL (volume cited in item 943), pp. 471-480.

* Dynes, Russell R. "The Consequences of Sectarianism for Social Participation." Cited above as item 1229.

1788. Ergil, D. "Secularization as Class Conflict: The Turkish Example." ASIAN AFFAIRS 62,1 (1975): 69-80.

1789. Erskine, Hazel G. "The Polls: Church Attendance." PUBLIC OPINION QUARTERLY 28 (1964): 671-679.

1790. Erskine, Hazel G. "The Polls: Organized Religion." PUBLIC OPINION QUARTERLY 29 (1965): 326-337.

* Ethridge, F. Maurice, and Joe R. Feagin. "Varieties of 'Fundamentalism': A Conceptual and Empirical Analysis of Two Protestant Denominations." Cited above as item 1274.

1791. Featherman, David L. "The Socioeconomic Achievement of White Religio-Ethnic Subgroups: Social and Psychological Explanations." AMERICAN SOCIOLOGICAL REVIEW 36 (1971): 207-222.

* Fernandes, G. "O sincretismo gêgo-nago-catolico como expresão dinamica dum sentimento de inferiordade." Cited above as item 400.

1792. Ferreira de Camargo, P.C., and M. Berezousky Singer. "La religión de los favorecidos." REVISTA PARAGUAYA DE SOCIOLOGIA 12,33 (1975): 97-110.

1793. Finkler, K. "Dissident Sectarian Movements, the Catholic Church, and Social Class in Mexico." COMPARATIVE STUDIES IN SOCIETY AND HISTORY 25,2 (1983): 277-305.

* Finney, John M., III. THE RELIGIOUS COMMITMENT OF AMERICAN WOMEN. Cited above as item 1097.

1794. Ford, Thomas R. "Status, Residence, and Fundamentalist Beliefs in the Southern Appalachian Region." SOCIAL FORCES 39 (1960): 41-49.

1795. Ford, Thomas R. "Religious Thought and Beliefs in the Southern Appalachians as Revealed by an Attitude Survey." RRR 3,1 (1961): 2-21.

1796. Freiberg, J.W. "L'idéologie, l'état et la conflit des classes dans les 'religions' de la chine ancienne." L'HOMME ET LA SOCIETE 41-42 (1976): 197-232.

* Fukuyama, Yoshio. "The Major Dimensions of Church Membership." Cited above as item 946.

1797. Gaede, Stan. "Religious Participation, Socioeconomic Status, and Belief-Orthodoxy." JSSR 16,3 (1977): 245-253.

1798. Gallagher, Charles F. RELIGION, CLASS, AND FAMILY IN SPAIN. American Universities Field Staff VIII, No. 7, October 1973.

* Glock, Charles Y., and Rodney Stark. CHRISTIAN BELIEFS AND ANTI-SEMITISM. Cited above as item 438.

1799. Gockel, Galen L. "Income and Religious Affiliation: A Regression Analysis." AMERICAN JOURNAL OF SOCIOLOGY 74 (1969): 632-647.

1800. Goldschmidt, Walter. "Class Denominationalism in Rural California Churches." AMERICAN JOURNAL OF SOCIOLOGY 49 (1944): 348-355.

* Goldstein, Sidney. "Socioeconomic Differentials among Religious Groups in the U.S." Cited above as item 1276.

1801. Goodall, Raymond M. RELIGIOUS STYLE AND SOCIAL CLASS. Unpublished M.A. thesis, University of British Columbia, 1970.

1802. Goode, Erich. SOCIAL CLASS AND CHURCH PARTICIPATION. Doctoral dissertation, Columbia University, 1966. Published by Arno Press, New York, 1980.

1803. Goode, Erich. "Social Class and Church Participation." AMERICAN JOURNAL OF SOCIOLOGY 72 (1966): 102-111.

1804. Goode, Erich. "Class Styles of Religious Sociation." THE BRITISH JOURNAL OF SOCIOLOGY 19,1 (1968): 1-16.

* Greeley, Andrew M. ETHNICITY, DENOMINATION, AND INEQUALITY. Cited above as item 1277.

* Greeley, Andrew M. THE AMERICAN CATHOLIC. A SOCIAL PORTRAIT. Cited above as item 634.

1805. Greeley, Andrew M. "Catholics and the Upper Middle Class: A Comment on Roof." SOCIAL FORCES 59,3 (1981): 824-830.

1806. Gustafsson, Berndt. "Sozialschichtung und Kirchenleben in Schweden." SOZIALE WELT 2 (1951): 178-180.

* Hampe, Gary D. "Interfaith Dating: Religion, Social Class and Premarital Sexual Attitudes." Cited above as item 306.

1807. Hazelrigg, Lawrence E. "Occupation and Religious Practice in Italy. The Thesis of 'Working-Class Alienation.'" JSSR 11,4 (1972): 335-346.

1808. Hoben, Allan. "Traditional Amhara Society." In A. Tuden and L. Plotnicov, SOCIAL STRATIFICATION IN AFRICA. New York: Free Press, 1970.

1809. Hollingshead, August. ELMSTOWN'S YOUTH. New Haven: Yale University Press, 1949.

1810. Hollingshead, August. "Selected Characteristics of Classes in a Middle Western Community." In R. Bendix and S.M. Lipset, CLASS, STATUS, AND POWER. Glenco: Free Press, 1953.

1811. Holt, John B. "Holiness Religion: Cultural Shock and Social Reorganization." AMERICAN SOCIOLOGICAL REVIEW 5 (1940): 740-747. Abridged version in J.M. Yinger (ed.), RELIGION, SOCIETY AND THE INDIVIDUAL (volume cited in item 943), pp. 463-470.

1812. Homan, Roger. "Sunday Observance and Social Class." In D. Martin and M. Hill (eds.), A SOCIOLOGICAL YEARBOOK OF RELIGION IN BRITAIN 3. London: SCM, 1970, pp. 78-91.

1813. Houtart, François. "Religion et lutte des classes en Amérique Latine." SC 26,2-3 (1979): 195-236.

1814. Houtart, François, and Geneviève Lemercinier. "Modèles culturels socio-religieux des groupes élitiques catholiques à Sri Lanka." SC 20,2 (1973): 303-320.

1815. Hutchinson, Harry William. VILLAGE AND PLANTATION LIFE IN NORTH-EASTERN BRAZIL. Seattle: University of Washington Press, 1957.

1816. Isambert, François-André. "Classes sociales et pratique religieuse paroissiale." CAHIERS INTERNATIONAUX DE SOCIOLOGIE 14 (1953): 141-153.

* Johnson, Benton. "Do Holiness Sects Socialize in Dominant Values?" Cited above as item 511.

1817. Kaplan, Berton. "The Structure of Adaptive Sentiments in a Lower Class Religious Group in Appalachia." JOURNAL OF SOCIAL ISSUES 21 (1965): 126-141.

1818. Kaufman, Harold. "Prestige Classes in a New York Rural Community." In R. Bendix and S.M. Lipset, CLASS, STATUS AND POWER (volume cited in item 1810), pp. 190-203.

1819. Kephart, W.M. "Status after Death." AMERICAN SOCIOLOGICAL REVIEW 15 (1950): 635-643.

* Knoke, David. "Religion, Stratification and Politics: America in the 1960's." Cited above as item 1614.

1820. Krueger, E.T. "Negro Religious Expression." AMERICAN JOURNAL OF SOCIOLOGY 38 (1932): 22.

1821. Lalive d'Epinay, Christian, and Jacques Zylberberg. "Développement inégal, conscience de classe et religion. Etude de la classe ouvrière et de la petite bourgeoisie dans une région d'industrialisation désarticulée (Chili)." REVUE TUNISIENNE DES SCIENCES SOCIALES 11,36-39 (1974): 89-125.

1822. Laumann, Edward O. "The Social Structure of Religious and Ethnoreligious Groups in a Metropolitan Community." AMERICAN SOCIOLOGICAL REVIEW 34 (1969): 182-197.

1823. Lazerwitz, Bernard. "A Comparison of Major U.S. Religious Groups." JOURNAL OF THE AMERICAN STATISTICAL ASSOCIATION 56 (1961): 568-579.

1824. Lazerwitz, Bernard. "Religion and Social Structure in the United States." In L. Schneider (ed.), RELIGION, CULTURE AND SOCIETY. New York: Wiley, 1966, pp. 426-439.

* Lee, Gary R., and Robert W. Clyde. "Religion, Socioeconomic Status and Anomie." Cited above as item 29.

1825. Lee, J. Oscar. "Religion among Ethnic and Racial Minorities." THE ANNALS 332 (1960): 112-125.

1826. Lefever, Harry G. GHETTO RELIGION: A STUDY OF THE RELIGIOUS STRUCTURES AND STYLES OF A POOR WHITE COMMUNITY IN ATLANTA, GEORGIA. Unpublished Ph.D. dissertation, Emory University, 1971.

1827. Lefever, Harry G. "The Religion of the Poor: Escape or Creative Force?" JSSR 16,3 (1977): 225-236. Also in P.H. McNamara (ed.), RELIGION: NORTH AMERICAN STYLE (volume cited in item 117), pp. 246-256.

1828. Lefever, Harry G. "The Value-Orientations of the Religious Poor." SA 43,3 (1982): 219-230.

1829. Lemercinier, Geneviève. "Aspects sociologiques de la genèse de l'Islam." SC 25,3-4 (1978): 359-369.

* Lenski, Gerhard E. "Social Correlates of Religious Interest." Cited above as item 1107.

* Lenski, Gerhard E. THE RELIGIOUS FACTOR. A SOCIOLOGIST'S INQUIRY. Cited above as item 1195.

1830. Lewis, Herbert S. "Wealth among the Shoa Galla." In A. Tuden and L. Plotnicov, SOCIAL STRATIFICATION IN AFRICA (volume cited in item 1808).

1831. Loubser, Jan J. "Calvinism, Equality, and Inclusion: The Case of Afrikaner Calvinism." In S. Eisenstadt, THE PROTESTANT ETHIC AND MODERNIZATION. New York: Basic Books, 1968, pp. 367-383.

1832. Lynd, Robert, and Helen Lynd. MIDDLETOWN. New York: Harcourt and Brace, 1929.

1833. MacLaren, A. Allan. RELIGION AND SOCIAL CLASS. London: Routledge and Kegan Paul, 1974.

1834. Mamiya, Laurence H. "From Black Muslim to Bilalian: The Evolution of a Movement." JSSR 21,2 (1982): 138-152.

* Mann, William E. SECT, CULT, AND CHURCH IN ALBERTA. Cited above as item 1633.

* Maranell, Gary M. "Religiosity, Affiliation, and Social Class: Two Community Studies." Ch. 7 in Maranell, RESPONSES TO RELIGION. Cited above as item 4.

* Maranell, Gary M., Richard A. Dodder, and David F. Mitchell. "Social Class and Premarital Sexual Permissiveness: A Subsequent Test." Cited above as item 328.

1835. Maynard, Jeanine. EXPLORING THE IDEOLOGY OF NEO-PENTECOSTALS AND THEIR ATTITUDES TOWARDS CONCERN FOR SOCIAL STATUS. Unpublished M.A. thesis, University of Massachusetts, Amherst, 1974.

* McCallister, Ian. "Religious Commitment and Social Attitudes in Ireland." Cited above as item 1283.

1836. McConnell, John W. Ch. 12 in THE EVOLUTION OF SOCIAL CLASSES. Washington: American Council on Public Affairs, 1942.

1837. McKinley, Donald Gilbert. "Religious Behavior and Compensation." Ch. 9 in D.G. McKinley, SOCIAL CLASS AND FAMILY LIFE. New York: Free Press, 1964.

1838. McKinney, R.I. RELIGION IN HIGHER EDUCATION AMONG NEGROES. New Haven: Yale University Press, 1945.

1839. McLeod, Hugh. "Class, Community and Region: The Religious Geography of Nineteenth-Century England." SOCIOLOGICAL YEARBOOK OF RELIGION IN BRITAIN 6 (1973): 29-72.

1840. McLeod, Hugh. "The Dechristianisation of the Working Class in Western Europe (1850-1900)." SC 27,2-3 (1980): 191-214.

1841. McLeod, Hugh. RELIGION AND THE PEOPLE OF WESTERN EUROPE 1789-1970. New York: Oxford University Press, 1981.

1842. Menges, Walter. "Sociale Schichtung und kirchliches Verhalten in der Grossstadt." HERDER-KORRESPONDENZ 15 (1960-61): 280-286.

* Michelat, G., and M. Simon. CLASSE, RELIGION, COMPORTEMENT POLITIQUE. Cited above in item 1647.

1843. Mitchell, J.C. "Race and Status in South Central Africa." In A. Tuden and L. Plotnicov, SOCIAL STRATIFICATION IN AFRICA (volume cited in item 1808).

1844. Moberg, David O. "Does Social Class Shape the Church?" RRR 1 (1960): 110-115.

1845. Mueller, Charles W., and Weldon T. Johnson. "Socioeconomic Status and Religious Participation." AMERICAN SOCIOLOGICAL REVIEW 40 (1975): 785-800.

1846. Nelsen, Hart M., and Raymond H. Potvin. "Toward Disestablishment: New Patterns of Social Class, Denomination and Religiosity among Youth?" RRR 22,2 (1980): 137-154.

1847. Nesti, Arnaldo. "Problemi e tendenze nella religione popolare come fenomeno delle classi subalterne." In A. L'Abate et al., STUDI E RICERCHE DI SOCIOLOGIA. Pistoia: Tellini, 1973, pp. 85-116.

1848. Nesti, Arnaldo. "Religion et classe ouvrière dans les sociétés industrielles. Une hypothèse de recherche." SC 27,2-3 (1980): 169-190.

1849. Niebuhr, H. Richard. THE SOCIAL SOURCES OF DENOMINATIONALISM. New York: Holt, 1929.

* Nuesse, C. Joseph. "The Relation of Financial Assessments to Status in a Rural Parish." Cited above as item 1455.

1850. Nunn, Clyde Z. "Child-Control through a 'Coalition with God.'" CHILD DEVELOPMENT 35 (1964): 417-432.

1851. Obenhaus, Victor, W. Widick Schroeder, and C.D. England. "Church Participation Related to Social Class and Type of Center." RURAL SOCIOLOGY 23,3 (1958): 298-308.

1852. Opazo Bernales, Andrés. "La fonction de l'Eglise dans la lutte pour l'hégémonie." SC 26,2-3 (1979): 237-260.

1853. Opazo Bernales, Andrés. "Hacia una comprensión teórica de la religión de los oprimidos." ESTUDIOS SOCIALES CENTRO-AMERICANOS 11,33 (1982): 11-58.

1854. Opazo Bernales, Andrés. "Les conditions sociales du surgissement d'une Eglise populaire." SC 30,2-3 (1983): 175-209.

1855. Perlman, Melvin L. "Stratification among Ganda and Nyoro." In A. Tuden and L. Plotnicov, SOCIAL STRATIFICATION IN AFRICA (volume cited in item 1808).

1856. Perry, Everett L. "Socio-Economic Factors and American Fundamentalism." RRR 1,2 (1959): 57-61.

* Peterson, Robert W. STATUS ATTAINMENT PROCESSES IN RELIGIOUS ORGANIZATIONS. Cited above as item 716.

* Peterson, Robert W., and Richard A. Schoenherr. "Organizational Status Attainment of Religious Professionals." Cited above as item 717.

* Photiadis, John D., and John F. Schnabel. "Religion: A Persistent Institution in a Changing Appalachia." Cited above as item 6.

1857. Pillai, Mary. "The Non-Brahmin Movement and Desacralization." SC 29,4 (1982): 349-368.

1858. Pin, Emile. In F. Houtart and E. Pin, THE CHURCH AND THE LATIN AMERICAN REVOLUTION. New York: Sheed and Ward, 1965.

1859. Pope, Liston. MILLHANDS AND PREACHERS. New Haven: Yale University Press, 1942.

1860. Porter, John. THE VERTICAL MOSAIC. Toronto: University of Toronto Press, 1965, pp. 98-103, 511-519.

1861. Prandi, Carlo. "Religion et classes subalternes en Italie." ARCHIVES DE SCIENCES SOCIALES DES RELIGIONS 43,1 (1977): 93-139.

1862. Preston, Harley. RELATIONSHIP OF ESCHATOLOGICAL EMPHASIS TO ECONOMIC STATUS OF PROTESTANT CHURCHES IN BLOOMINGTON. Unpublished M.A. thesis, Indiana University, Bloomington, 1939.

* Quinney, Richard. "Political Conservatism, Alienation, and Fatalism: Contingencies of Social Status and Religious Fundamentalism." Cited above as item 8.

1863. Rama, Carlos M. LA RELIGION EN EL URUGUAY. Montevideo: Ediciones Nuestra Tiempo, 1964.

1864. Redman, Barbara J. "An Economic Analysis of Religious Choice." RRR 21,3 (1980): 330-342.

1865. Ribeiro de Oliveira, Pedro. "Religião e dominação de classe: o caso da romanização." RELIGIAO E SOCIEDADE 6 (1980): 167-187.

* Rodrigues, José Honorio. BRAZIL AND AFRICA. Cited above as item 403.

1866. Rokkan, S. "Geography, Religion, and Social Class: Crosscutting Cleavages in Norwegian Politics." In Seymour M. Lipset and Stein Rokkan (eds.), PARTY SYSTEMS AND VOTER ALIGNMENTS: CROSS-NATIONAL PERSPECTIVES. New York: Free Press, 1967.

1867. Rolim, Francesco. "Religion et pauvreté." CONCILIUM 151 (French Series, 1980): 53-61.

1868. Roof, Wade Clark. "Socioeconomic Differentials among White Socioreligious Groups in the United States." SOCIAL FORCES 58,1 (1979): 280-289.

1869. Roof, Wade Clark. "Unresolved Issues in the Study of Religion and the National Elite: Response to Greeley." SOCIAL FORCES 59,3 (1981): 831-836.

1870. Rousseau, André. "Différenciation religieuse et position de classe." ARCHIVES DE SCIENCES SOCIALES DES RELIGIONS 49,1 (1980): 7-28.

1871. Rousseau, André. "Les classes moyennes et l'aggiornamento de l'Eglise." ACTES DE LA RECHERCHE EN SCIENCES SOCIALES 44-45 (1982): 55-68.

1872. Saniel, Josefa M. "The Mobilization of Traditional Values in the Modernization of Japan." In R.N. Bellah (ed.), RELIGION AND PROGRESS IN MODERN ASIA. New York: Free Press, 1965.

1873. Sargent, Leslie W. "Occupational Status in a Religious Group." RRR 4,3 (1963): 149-155.

* Särlvik, B. "Socioeconomic Position, Religious Behavior, and Voting in the Swedish Electorate." Cited above as item 1683.

1874. Schommer, Cyril O., Leo D. Rachiele, and John Kosa. "Socio-Economic Background and Religious Knowledge of Catholic College Students." AMERICAN CATHOLIC SOCIOLOGICAL REVIEW 21 (1960): 229-237.

* Schwartz, Gary. SECT IDEOLOGIES AND SOCIAL STATUS. Cited above as item 151.

1875. Schwartz, Norman B. "Protestantism, Community Organization and Social Status: Different Responses to Missions in a Guatemala Town." CULTURES ET DEVELOPPEMENT (Louvain) 4,3 (1972): 585-600.

1876. Scoville, Warren C. "The Economic Status of Huguenots." In Scoville, THE PERSECUTION OF HUGUENOTS AND FRENCH ECONOMIC DEVELOPMENT. Berkeley: University of California Press, 1960.

1877. Simpson, John H., and John Hagan. "Conventional Religiosity, Attitudes toward Conflict Crime, and Income Stratification in the United States." RRR 23,2 (1981): 167-179.

1878. Soares, Glaucio Ary Dillon, and José Reyna. "Status socioecónomico, religiosidad y dogmatismo en México." REVISTA MEXICANA DE SOCIOLOGIA 28 (1966): 889-910.

1879. Spiegel, Yorick (ed.) KIRCHE UND KLASENBILDUNG. STUDIEN ZUR SITUATION DER KIRCHEN IN DER BUNDESREPUBLIK DEUTSCHLAND. Franckfurt/Main: Suhrkamp Verlag, 1974.

1880. Stark, Rodney. "The Economics of Piety: Religious Commitment and Social Class." In G. Thielbar and S. Feldman (eds.), ISSUES IN SOCIAL INEQUALITY. Boston: Little, Brown, 1972, pp. 483-503.

1881. Sykes, Richard E. "The Changing Class Structure of Unitarian Parishes in Massachusetts, 1780-1800." RRR 12 (1970): 26-34.

* Szafran, Robert F., Robert W. Peterson, and Richard A. Schoenherr. "Ethnicity and Status Attainment: The Case of the Roman Catholic Clergy." Cited above as item 781.

1882. Thalheimer, Fred. "Continuity and Change in Religiosity." PACIFIC SOCIOLOGICAL REVIEW 8 (1965): 101-108.

1883. Turcotte, Paul André. "Education catholique et nationalisme dans l'enseignement secondaire québécois." SC 31,4 (1984): 365-377.

* Utrecht, Ernst. "The Muslim Merchant Class in the Indonesian Social and Political Struggles." Cited above as item 1712.

1884. Vattel, E. Daniel. "Ritual and Stratification in Chicago Negro Churches." AMERICAN SOCIOLOGICAL REVIEW 7 (1942): 352-361.

1885. Von Martin, Alfred. SOCIOLOGY OF THE RENAISSANCE. New York: Harper, 1963.

1886. Vrcan, Srdjan. "Classe sociale et religion en Yougoslavie." CONCILIUM 151 (French Series, 1980): 81-91.

1887. Warburton, T. Rennie. "Religion and the Control of Native Peoples." In S. Crysdale and L. Wheatcroft (eds.), RELIGION IN CANADIAN SOCIETY (volume cited in item 778), pp. 412-422.

1888. Warner, W. Lloyd, et al. DEMOCRACY IN JONESVILLE. New York: Harper, 1949.

1889. Warner, W. Lloyd, and Paul S. Lunt. THE SOCIAL SYSTEM OF A MODERN COMMUNITY. New Haven: Yale University Press, 1941.

* Warren, Bruce L. THE RELATIONSHIPS BETWEEN RELIGIOUS PREFERENCE AND SOCIO-ECONOMIC ACHIEVEMENT OF AMERICAN MEN. Cited above as item 1293.

* Warren, Bruce L. "Socioeconomic Achievement and Religion: The American Case." Cited above in item 1294.

* Weber, Max. "Die protestantischen Sekten und der Geist des Kapitalismus."
"The Protestant Sects and the Spirit of Capitalism." Cited above as item 57.

* Weber, Max. THE SOCIOLOGY OF RELIGION, translated by Ephraim Fischoff. Boston: Beacon, 1963. Also in M. Weber, ECONOMY AND SOCIETY, Vol. 1. (volume cited above as item 58), pp. 399-634.

1890. West, James. PLAINVILLE, USA. New York: Columbia University Press, 1945.

1891. Wickham, E.R. CHURCH AND PEOPLE IN AN INDUSTRIAL CITY. London: Lutterworth, 1957.

1892. Willems, Emilio. "Protestantismus und Klassenstruktur in Chile." KÖLNER ZEITSCHRIFT FÜR SOZIOLOGIE UND SOZIALPSYCHOLOGIE 12 (1960): 652-671.

1893. Willems, Emilio. "Culture Change and the Rise of Protestantism in Brazil and Chile." In S. Eisenstadt (ed.), THE PROTESTANT ETHIC AND MODERNIZATION. New York: Basic Books, 1963.

1894. Willems, Emilio. FOLLOWERS OF THE NEW FAITH: CULTURE CHANGE AND THE RISE OF PROTESTANTISM IN BRAZIL AND CHILE. Nashville: Vanderbilt University Press, 1967.

1895. Williams, C.R "The Welsh Religious Revival, 1904-05." BRITISH JOURNAL OF SOCIOLOGY 3(1952): 242-259.

1896. Yinger, J. Milton. "Religion and Social Change: Functions and Dysfunctions of Sects and Cults among the Disprivileged." RRR 4,2 (1963): 65-84. Also in R.D. Knudten (ed.), THE SOCIOLOGY OF RELIGION, AN ANTHOLOGY (volume cited in item 375), pp. 482-495.

* Yinger, J. Milton. "Religion and Social Change: Problems of Integration and Pluralism among the Privileged." Cited above as item 375.

Caste

1897. Alexander, K.C. "Caste and Christianity in Kerela." SC 18,4 (1971): 551-560.

1898. Carstairs, G.M. THE TWICE-BORN: A STUDY OF A COMMUNITY OF HIGH-CASTE HINDUS. London: Hogarth Press, 1957.

1899. Gandhi, Raj S. "The Caste-Joint Family Axis of Hindu Social System, the Ethos of Hindu Culture and the Formation of Hindu Personality." SOCIOLOGUS 24,1 (1974): 56-64.

1900. Harper, Edward B. "Ritual Pollution as an Integrator of Caste and Religion." In E.B. Harper, RELIGION IN SOUTH ASIA. Seattle: University of Washington Press, 1964.

1901. Houtart, François, and Geneviève Lemercinier. "Religion et production des structures sociales. Catholicisme et structure des castes dans une région du sud de l'Inde." CONCILIUM 151 (French Series, 1980): 43-51.

1902. Hourtart, François, and Geneviève Lemercinier. "Religion and castes - South India. An Introduction. Religion et castes - L'Inde du Sud. En guise d'introduction." SC 28,2-3 (1981): 145-162.

1903. Jain, S.P. "Religion, Caste, Class and Education in a North Indian Community." SOCIOLOGY AND SOCIAL RESEARCH 53,4 (1969): 482-489.

1904. Jeffrey, Robin. "Religious Symbolisation of the Transition from Caste to Class: The Temple-Entry Movement in Travancore, 1860-1940." SC 28,2-3 (1981): 269-291.

1905. Kannan, C.T "Intercaste Marriage in Bombay." SOCIOLOGICAL BULLETIN 10,2 (1961): 53-68.

1906. Lemercinier, Geneviève. "Relationships between Means of Production, Caste and Religion. The Case of Kerala between the 13th and the 19th Century." SC 28,2-3 (1981): 163-199.

1907. Lemercinier, Geneviève. "The Effect of the Caste System on Conversions to Christianity in Tamilnadu." SC 28,2-3 (1981): 237-268.

1908. Ramu, G.N., and Paul D. Wiebe. "Occupational and Educational Mobility in Relation to Caste in Urban India." SOCIOLOGY AND SOCIAL RESEARCH 58,1 (1973): 84-94.

1909. Roy, Ajit. "The Nature of Power in Indian Society with Special Reference to Class-Caste Structure." RELIGION AND SOCIETY (India) 21,3 (1974): 44-54.

1910. Ryan, B. CASTE IN MODERN CEYLON: THE SINHALESE SYSTEM IN TRANSITION. New Brunswick, N.J.: Rutgers University Press, 1953.

1911. Sachchidananda. "Emergent Scheduled Caste Elite in Bihar." RELIGION AND SOCIETY (India) 21,3 (1974): 55-61.

1912. Smythe, H.H., and T. Gershuny. "Jewish Castes of Cochin India." SOCIOLOGY AND SOCIAL RESEARCH 41,2 (1956): 108-111.

1913. Srivinas, M.N. RELIGION AND SOCIETY AMONG THE COORGS OF SOUTH INDIA. New York: Asia Publishing House, 1965.

1914. Strizower, Schifra. "Jews as an Indian Caste." JEWISH JOURNAL OF SOCIOLOGY 1 (1959): 43-57. Reprinted in L. Schneider (ed.), RELIGION, CULTURE AND SOCIETY (volume cited in item 1824), pp. 220-232.

Class

* Alford, Robert R. "Religion and Class Voting." In R. Alford, PARTY AND SOCIETY. Cited above as item 1512.

1915. Dulong, Renaud. "L'Eglise de l'Ouest et les luttes de classe dans la paysannerie." LA PENSEE 175 (1974): 82-103.

1916. Fichter, Joseph H. "High School Influence on Social-Class Attitudes." SA 33,4 (1972): 246-252.

1917. Hoult, Thomas F. "Economic Class Consciousness in American Protestantism." AMERICAN SOCIOLOGICAL REVIEW 15 (1950): 97-100; and 17 (1952): 349-350.

1918. Isambert, François André. "L'abstention religieuse de la classe ouvrière." CAHIERS INTERNATIONALE DE SOCIOLOGIE 25 (1958): 116-134.

1919. Isambert, François André. CHRISTIANISME ET CLASSE OUVRIERE. Paris and Tournai: Casterman, 1961.
Pp. 43-53 are summarized as "Is the Religious Abstention of the Working Class a General Phenomenon?" in L. Schneider (ed.), RELIGION, CULTURE AND SOCIETY (volume cited in item 1824), pp. 400-402.

1920. Isambert, François André. "Les ouvriers et l'Eglise catholique." REVUE FRANÇAISE DE SOCIOLOGIE 15,4 (1974): 529-551.

1921. Kehrer, Günter. DAS RELIGIÖSE BEWUSSTSEIN DES INDUSTRIEARBEITERS. EINE EMPIRISCHE STUDIE. München: Piper, 1967.

* Lazerwitz, Bernard. "Contrasting the Effects of Generation, Class, Sex, and Age on Group Identification in the Jewish and Protestant Communities." Cited above as item 166.

* Maurer, Heinrich H. "The Political Attitudes of the Lutheran Parish in America." Cited above as item 1635.

* Mitchell, Robert E. "When Ministers and Their Parishioners Have Different Social Class Position." Cited above as item 695.

* Pin, Emile. PRATIQUE RELIGIEUSE ET CLASSES SOCIALES DANS UNE PAROISSE URBAINE. SAINT-POTHIN A LYON. Paris: Editions Spes, 1956. Cited above as item 1464. Pp. 395-408 translated by Stanley Gray in L. Schneider (ed.), RELIGION, CULTURE AND SOCIETY (volume cited in item 1824), pp. 411-420.

1922. Pope, Liston. "Religion and Class Structure." ANNALS OF THE AMERICAN ACADEMY OF POLITICAL AND SOCIAL SCIENCE 256 (1948): 84-91.

1923. Simmel, Georg. "A Contribution to the Sociology of Religion." AMERICAN JOURNAL OF SOCIOLOGY 11 (1905): 359-376.

1924. Small, Albion W. "The Church and Class Conflicts." AMERICAN JOURNAL OF SOCIOLOGY 24 (1919): 481-501.

* Stark, Rodney. "Class, Radicalism, and Religious Involvement in Great Britain." Cited above as item 1703.

1925. Turner, Bryan S. "Class Solidarity and System Integration." SA 38,4 (1977): 345-358.

Elite

1926. Breines, A.E. "An Elite as Response to Crisis in Religious Organizations." AMERICAN CATHOLIC SOCIOLOGICAL REVIEW 20 (1959): 43-52.

1927. Bryman, Alan. "Sociology of Religion and Sociology of Elites. Elite and Sous-Elite in the Church of England." ARCHIVES DE SCIENCES SOCIALES DES RELIGIONS 19/38 (1974): 109-121.

1928. Eccel, A. Chris. "The Differential Socio-Religious Impact of the Definition of Religious Elite in Christianity and Islam." SC 31,1 (1984): 105-123.

1929. Fry, C. Luther. "The Religious Affiliations of American Leaders." SCIENTIFIC MONTHLY 36 (1933): 241-249.

1930. Mandelbaum, David G. "Introduction" to E.B. Harper, RELIGION IN SOUTH ASIA (volume cited in item 1900).

1931. Plotnicov, Leonard. "Modern African Elite of Jos" (Nigerian city). In A. Tuden and L. Plotnicov (eds.), SOCIAL STRATIFICATION IN AFRICA (volume cited in item 1808).

1932. Sarachandra, Ediriweera R. "Traditional Values and the Modernization of a Buddhist Society: The Case of Ceylon." In R.N. Bellah (ed.), RELIGION AND PROGRESS IN MODERN ASIA (volume cited in item 1872).

1933. Sharot, Stephen. "Instrumental and Expressive Elites in a Religious Organization -- The United Synagogue in London." ARCHIVES DE SCIENCES SOCIALES DES RELIGIONS 43,1 (1977): 141-155.

1934. Vallier, Ivan. "Roman Catholic Elites in Latin America." In S.M. Lipset and A. Solari (eds.), ELITES IN LATIN AMERICA. New York: Oxford University Press, 1967, pp. 190-232.

* Yinger, J. Milton. "Religion and Social Change: Problems of Integration and Pluralism among the Privileged." Cited above as item 375.

Mobility (vertical)

1935. Alston, Jon P. "Occupational Placement and Mobility of Protestants and Catholics, 1953-1964." RRR 10,3 (1969): 135-140.

1936. Alston, Jon P. "Aggregate Social Mobility among Major Protestant Denominations and Major Religious Groups, 1939-1969." SA 34,3 (1973): 230-235.

1937. Bode, J.G. "Status and Mobility of Catholics Vis-a-Vis Several Protestant Denominations: More Evidence." SOCIOLOGICAL QUARTERLY 11,1 (1970): 103-111.

1938. Bopegamage, A. "Status Seekers in India." ARCHIVES EUROPEENNES DE SOCIOLOGIE 20,1 (1979): 19-39.

* Christy, Richard D. HIDDEN FACTORS IN RELIGIOUS CONFLICT: A SOCIOLOGICAL ANALYSIS. Cited above as item 1387.

1939. Curtis, Richard F. "Occupational Mobility and Church Participation." SOCIAL FORCES 38,4 (1960): 315-319.

1940. Fereira de Camargo, C.P. ASPECTOS SOCIOLOGICOS DEL ESPIRITISMO IN SAO PAULO. Bogotá and Friburgo: Oficina Internacional del Investigaciones de FERES, 1961.

1941. Gandhi, Raj S. "The Rise of Jainism and its Adoption by the Vaishyas of India: A Case Study in Sanskritisation and Status Mobility." SC 24,2-3 (1977): 247-260.

1942. Gusfield, Joseph R. "Social Structure and Moral Reform: A Study of the Woman's Christian Temperance Union." AMERICAN JOURNAL OF SOCIOLOGY 61 (1955): 221-232.

1943. Kosa, John, and John Nash. "The Social Ascending of Catholics." SOCIAL ORDER 8 (1958): 98-103.

1944. Krausy, E. "Occupation and Social Advancement in Anglo Jewry." JEWISH JOURNAL OF SOCIOLOGY 4,1 (1962): 82-90.

1945. Lauer, Robert H. "Occupational and Religious Mobility in a Small City." SOCIOLOGICAL QUARTERLY 16 (1975): 380-392.

1946. Mueller, Samuel A. "Changes in the Social Status of Lutheranism in Ninety Chicago Suburbs, 1950-1960." SA 27,3 (1966): 138-145.

1947. Nelsen, Hart M., and William E. Snizek. "Musical Pews: Rural and Urban Models of Occupational and Religious Mobility." SOCIOLOGY AND SOCIAL RESEARCH 60 (1976): 279-289.

1948. Nelson, Geoffrey K., and R.A. Clews. MOBILITY AND RELIGIOUS COMMITMENT. Birmingham: University of Birmingham, 1971.

1949. O'Kane, James. "Economic and Non-Economic Liberalism, Upward Mobility Potential and Catholic Working-Class Youth." SOCIAL FORCES 48,4 (1970): 499-506.

1950. Organic, Harold. RELIGIOUS AFFILIATION AND SOCIAL MOBILITY IN CONTEMPORARY AMERICAN SOCIETY: A NATIONAL STUDY. Unpublished Ph.D. dissertation, University of Michigan, 1963.

1951. Peñaloza, F., and E.E. McDonough. "Social Mobility in a Mexican American Community." SOCIAL FORCES 44 (1965): 498-505.

* Ramu, G.N., and Paul D. Wiebe. "Occupational and Educational Mobility in Relation to Caste in Urban India." Cited above as item 1908.

1952. Van Roy, Ralph F., Frank D. Bean, and James R. Wood. "Social Mobility and Doctrinal Orthodoxy." JSSR 12,4 (1973): 427-439.

1953. Weller, Neil J. RELIGION AND SOCIAL MOBILITY IN INDUSTRIAL SOCIETY. Unpublished Ph.D. dissertation, University of Michigan, 1960.

CHAPTER TWO: PROCESSES

The entries in this chapter focus on the social dynamics of the religious world. Section A lists studies of personal religious change. Section B, Role Entry and Role Exit, focuses on the movement of persons into and out of various aspects of religious structures. Section C, Organizational Change, includes studies of organizational mergers and schisms. Section D, Social Movements, lists studies of people mobilizing resources in religious changes. The final three sections include studies of societal-level phenomena; Section E, Secularization, Section F, Protestant Ethic, and Section G, Deviance and Legitimacy, focus on three distinct processes which occur in societies.

SECTION A: CONVERSION AND CONVERSION MAINTENANCE

Conversion usually represents a change in a person from a state of relative religious dormancy to one of relative religious activation. This can occur with or without a change of religious affiliation (horizontal mobility). Sometimes the term conversion is used in the literature to refer to simple changes in affiliation which are occasioned by inter-religious marriages or other extra-religious factors.

1954. Adams, Robert Lynn, and John Mogey. "Marriage, Membership and Mobility in Church and Sect." SA 28 (1967): 205-214.

1955. Allison, Joel. "Religious Conversion: Regression and Progression in an Adolescent Experience." JSSR 8,1 (1969): 23-38.

* Alston, Jon P. "Religious Mobility and Socioeconomic Status." Cited above as item 1753.

1956. Anzai, Shin, "Newly-Adopted Religions and Social Change on the Ryukyu Islands (Japan) (with Special Reference to Catholicism)." SC 23,1 (1976): 57-70.

1957. Austin, Roy L. "Empirical Adequacy of Lofland's Conversion Model." RRR 18,3 (1977): 282-287.

1958. Austin, Roy L. "Reply to Richardson's Comments on 'Empirical Adequacy of Lofland's Conversion Model.'" RRR 19,3 (1978): 323-324.

1959. Aviad, Janet. RETURN TO JUDAISM. RELIGIOUS RENEWAL IN JERUSALEM. Chicago: University of Chicago Press, 1983.

1960. Babchuck, Nicholas, Harry J. Crockett, and John A. Bailey. "Change in Religious Affiliation and Family Stability." SOCIAL FORCES 45 (1967): 551-555.

* Baer, Hans A. THE LEVITES OF UTAH: THE DEVELOPMENT OF AND CONVERSION TO A SMALL MILLENARIAN SECT. Cited above as item 1237.

* Baer, Hans A. "A Field Perspective of Religious Conversion: The Levites of Utah." Cited above as item 132.

1961. Balch, Robert W. "Looking Behind the Scenes in a Religious Cult: Implications for the Study of Conversion." SA 41,2 (1980): 137-143. Also in P.H. McNamara (ed.), RELIGION: NORTH AMERICAN STYLE (volume cited in item 117), pp. 309-316.

1962. Bankston, William B., Craig J. Forsyth, and H. Hugh Floyd, Jr. "Toward a General Model of the Process of Radical Conversion: An Interactionist Perspective on the Transformation of Self-Identity." QUALITATIVE SOCIOLOGY 4,4 (1981): 279-297.

1963. Barker, Eileen. THE MAKING OF A MOONIE. BRAINWASHING OR CHOICE? Oxford: Basil Blackwell, 1984.

1964. Beckford, James. "Accounting for Conversion." BRITISH JOURNAL OF SOCIOLOGY 29,2 (1978): 249-262.

* Bibby, Reginald W., and Merlin B. Brinkerhoff. "The Circulation of the Saints: A Study of People Who Join Conservative Churches." Cited above as item 96.

1965. Bibby, Reginald W., and Merlin B. Brinkerhoff. "When Proselytizing Fails: An Organizational Analysis." SA 35,3 (1974): 189-200.

1966. Billette, André. "Conversion and Consonance: A Sociology of White American Catholic Converts." RRR 8 (1967): 100-104.

1967. Billette, André. "Se raconter une histoire... Pour une analyse révisée de la conversion." SC 23,1 (1976): 47-56.

1968. Boling, T. Edwin. "Southern Baptist Migrants and Converts: A Study of Southern Religion in the Urban North." SA 33,3 (1972): 188-199.

* Bopegamage, A. "Status Seekers in India." Cited above as item 1938.

1969. Brock, Timothy C. "Implications of Conversion and Magnitude of Cognitive Dissonance." JSSR 1,2 (1961-62): 198-203.

* Brown, Sheila. "De l'adhésion à un nouveau système religieux à la transformation d'un système de valeurs: étude d'une communauté rurale africaine." Cited above as item 502.

1970. Currin, Theresa E.V. THE INDIAN IN DURBAN: AN EXPLORATORY STUDY OF THE ROMAN CATHOLIC INDIAN MINORITY, WITH SPECIAL EMPHASIS ON THE SOCIOLOGICAL ASPECTS OF CONVERSION. Unpublished M. Soc. Sc. thesis, University of Natal, 1962.

1971. Daner, Francine J. "Conversion to Krishna Consciousness: The Transformation from Hippie to Religious Ascetic." In R. Wallis (ed.), SECTARIANISM (item 3212), pp. 53-69.

1972. Demerath, Nicholas J., III. "Trends and Anti-Trends in Religion Change." In Wilbert E. Moore and Eleanor B. Sheldon (eds.), TOWARD THE MEASUREMENT OF SOCIAL CHANGE. New York: Sage, 1968, pp. 349-445.

1973. Downton, James V., Jr. SACRED JOURNEYS: THE CONVERSION OF YOUNG AMERICANS TO DIVINE LIGHT MISSION. New York: Columbia University Press, 1979.

1974. Downton, James V., Jr. "An Evolutionary Theory of Spiritual Conversion and Commitment: The Case of Divine Light Mission." JSSR 19,4 (1980): 381-396. Also in P.H. McNamara (ed.), RELIGION: NORTH AMERICAN STYLE (volume cited in item 117), pp. 296-309.

1975. Ebaugh, Helen Rose Fuchs, and Sharron Lee Vaughn. "Ideology and Recruitment in Religious Groups." RRR 26,2 (1984): 148-157.

1976. Gordon, S. "Personality and Attitude Correlates of Religious Conversion." JSSR 4 (1964): 660-663.

1977. Greeley, Andrew M. "Religious Musical Chairs." In T. Robbins and D. Anthony (eds.), IN GODS WE TRUST (item 367), pp. 101-126.

1978. Greil, Arthur L. "Previous Dispositions and Conversion to Perspectives of Social and Religious Movements." SA 38,2 (1977): 115-125.

1979. Greil, Arthur L., and David R. Rudy. "Conversion to the World View of Alcoholics Anonymous." QUALITATIVE SOCIOLOGY 6,1 (1983): 5-28.

1980. Hadaway, Christopher Kirk. "Denominational Switching and Membership Growth: In Search of a Relationship." SA 39,4 (1978): 321-337.

1981. Harms, Ernest. "Ethical and Psychological Implications of Religious Conversion." RRR 3,3 (1962): 122-131.

1982. Harrison, Michael I. "Preparation for Life in the Spirit: The Process of Initial Commitment to a Religious Movement." URBAN LIFE AND CULTURE 2 (1974): 387-414.

1983. Heirich, Max. "Change of Heart: A Test of Some Widely Held Theories about Religious Conversion." AMERICAN JOURNAL OF SOCIOLOGY 83,3 (1977): 653-680.

1984. Hoge, Dean R. CONVERTS, DROPOUTS, RETURNEES: A STUDY OF RELIGIOUS CHANGE AMONG CATHOLICS. New York: Pilgrim Press, 1981.

* Hoge, Dean R., et al. "Desired Outcomes of Religious Education and Youth Ministry in Six Denominations." Cited above as item 338.

1985. Jones, R. Kenneth. "Paradigm Shifts and Identity Theory: Alternation as a Form of Identity Management." In Hans Mol (ed.), IDENTITY AND REIGION (item 170), pp. 59-82.

1986. Jules-Rosette, Bennetta. AFRICAN APOSTLES: RITUAL AND CONVERSION IN THE CHURCH OF JOHN MARANKE. Ithaca, N.Y.: Cornell University Press, 1975.

1987. Kim, Byong-suh. "Religious Deprogramming and Subjective Reality." SA 40,3 (1979): 197-207.

1988. Kluegel, James R. "Denominational Mobility: Current Patterns and Recent Trends." JSSR 19,1 (1980): 26-39.

1989. Landa, J.F. "Conversion and the Patterning of Christian Experience in Malitbog, Central Panay, Philippines." PHILIPPINE SOCIOLOGICAL REVIEW 13,2 (1965): 96-121.

* Lauer, Robert H. "Occupational and Religious Mobility in a Small City." Cited above as item 1945.

1990. Lazerwitz, Bernard. "Intermarriage and Conversion. A Guide for Future Research." JEWISH JOURNAL OF SOCIOLOGY 13,1 (1971): 41-63.

1991. Lazerwitz, Bernard. "Jewish-Christian Marriages and Conversion." JEWISH SOCIAL STUDIES 43,1 (1981): 31-46.

1992. Lebra, Takie Sugiryama. AN INTERPRETATION OF RELIGIOUS CONVERSION: A MILLENNIAL MOVEMENT AMONG JAPANESE-AMERICANS IN HAWAII. Unpublished Ph.D. dissertation, University of Pittsburgh, 1967.

* Lebra, Takie Sugiryama. "Religious Conversion as a Breakthrough for Transculturation: A Japanese Sect in Hawaii." Cited above as item 388.

1993. Lebra, Takie Sugiryama. "Millenarian Movements and Resocialization." AMERICAN BEHAVIORAL SCIENTIST 16 (1972): 195-217.

* Lemercinier, Geneviève. "The Effect of the Caste System on Conversions to Christianity in Tamilnadu." Cited above as item 1907.

* Lofland, John. DOOMSDAY CULT: A STUDY OF CONVERSION, PROSELYTIZATION AND MAINTENANCE OF FAITH. Cited above as item 987.

1994. Lofland, John. "Becoming a World-Saver Revisited." AMERICAN BEHAVIORAL SCIENTIST 20,6 (1977): 805-819.

1995. Lofland, John. "Crowd Joys." URBAN LIFE 10 (1982): 255-381.

1996. Lofland, John, and Norman Skonovd. "Conversion Motifs." JSSR 20,4 (1981): 373-385.

1997. Lofland, John, and Norman Skonovd. "Patterns of Conversion." In E. Barker (ed.), OF GODS AND MEN (item 2396), pp. 1-24.

1998. Lofland, John, and Rodney Stark. "Becoming a World-Saver: A Theory of Conversion to a Deviant Perspective." AMERICAN SOCIOLOGICAL REVIEW 30 (1965): 862-875.

1999. Long, Theodore E., and Jeffrey K. Hadden. "Religious Conversion and the Concept of Socialization: Integrating the Brainwashing and Drift Models." JSSR 22,1 (1983): 1-14.

2000. Lopez de Ceballos, Paloma. "Conversions à Singapour. Contribution à une sociologie de la mutation socio-religieuse." SC 23,1 (1976): 23-46.

2001. Lynch, Frederick R. "Toward a Theory of Conversion and Commitment to the Occult." AMERICAN BEHAVIORAL SCIENTIST 20 (1977): 887-907.

2002. Maves, Paul B. "Conversion: A Behavioral Category." RRR 5,1 (1963): 41-48.

2003. McGee, Michael. "Meher Baba - the Sociology of Religious Conversion." THE GRADUATE JOURNAL 9,1-2 (1976) 43-71.

2004. McKeefery, W.J. A CRITICAL ANALYSIS OF QUANTITATIVE STUDIES OF RELIGIOUS AWAKENING. Unpublished Ph.D. dissertation, Union Theological Seminary and Columbia Teachers College, 1949.

2005. Mueller, Samuel A. "Dimensions of Interdenominational Mobility in the United States." JSSR 10 (1971): 76-84.

2006. Nash, Dennison J., and Peter L. Berger. "Church Commitment in an American Suburb: An Analysis of the Decision to Join." ARCHIVES DE SOCIOLOGIE DES RELIGIONS 13 (1962): 105-120.

* Nelsen, Hart M., and William E. Snizek. "Musical Pews: Rural and Urban Models of Occupational and Religious Mobility." Cited above as item 1947.

2007. Newport, Frank. "The Religious Switcher in the United States." AMERICAN SOCIOLOGICAL REVIEW 44,4 (1979): 528-552.

2008. Nguyen van Phone, Joseph. "Essai de construction et d'utilisation d'un modèle de conversion religieuse suivant l'example constantinien." REVUE FRANÇAISE DE SOCIOLOGIE 13,4 (1972): 516-549.

2009. Parrucci, Dennis J. "Religious Conversion: A Theory of Deviant Behavior." SA 29,3 (1968): 144-154.

2010. Photiadis, John, and William Schweiker. "Attitudes toward Joining Authoritarian Organizations and Sectarian Churches." JSSR 9,3 (1970): 227-235.

2011. Pilarzyk, Thomas J. "Conversion and Alternation Processes in the Youth Culture." PACIFIC SOCIOLOGICAL REVIEW 21,4 (1978): 379-405.

2012. Preston, David L. "Meditative Ritual Practice and Spiritual Conversion-Commitment: Theoretical Implications Based on the Case of Zen." SA 43,3 (1982): 257-270.

2013. Prus, Robert C. "Religious Recruitment and the Management of Dissonance: A Sociological Perspective." SOCIOLOGICAL INQUIRY 46 (1976): 127-134.

2014. Rambo, Lewis R. "Current Research on Religious Conversion." RELIGIOUS STUDIES REVIEW 8 (1982): 146-159.

2015. Richardson, James T. (ed.) CONVERSION CAREERS: IN AND OUT OF THE NEW RELIGIONS. Beverly Hills, California: Sage, 1978.

2016. Richardson, James T. "Comments on Austin's Article, 'Empirical Adequacy of Lofland's Conversion Model.'" RRR 19,3 (1978): 320-323.

2017. Richardson, James T. "Conversion, Brainwashing and Deprogramming." THE CENTER MAGAZINE 15,2 (1982): 18-24.

2018. Richardson, James T., and Mary Stewart. "Conversion Process Models and the Jesus Movement." AMERICAN BEHAVIORAL SCIENTIST 20,6 (1977): 819-838.

2019. Richardson, James T., Mary White Stewart, and Robert B. Simmonds. "Conversion to Fundamentalism." In T. Robbins and D. Anthony (eds.), IN GODS WE TRUST (item 367), pp. 127-139.

2020. Robbins, Thomas. "Constructing Cultist 'Mind Control.'" SA 45,3 (1984): 241-256.

2021. Robertson, Roland. "Conversion and Cultural Change." Ch. 6 in R. Robertson, MEANING AND CHANGE. EXPLORATIONS IN THE CULTURAL SOCIOLOGY OF MODERN SOCIETIES. New York: New York University Press, 1978, pp. 186-222.

2022. Roof, Wade Clark, and Christopher Kirk Hadaway. "Review of the Polls. Shifts in Religious Preference -- the Mid-Seventies." JSSR 16,4 (1977): 409-412.

2023. Roof, Wade Clark, and Christopher Kirk Hadaway. "Denominational Switching in the Seventies: Going beyond Stark and Glock." JSSR 18,4 (1979): 363-379.

2024. Russel, Margo. "Religion as a Social Possession - Afrikaner Reactions to the Conversion of Bushmen to Their Church." ARCHIVES DE SCIENCES SOCIALES DES RELIGIONS 44,1 (1977): 59-73.

* Salisbury, W. Seward. "Religious Identification, Mixed Marriages and Conversion." Cited above as item 173.

2025. Seggar, John F., and Reed H. Blake. "Post-Joining Nonparticipation: An Exploratory Study of Convert Inactivity." RRR 11,3 (1970): 204-210.

2026. Seggar, John F., and Phillip R. Kunz. "Conversion: Evaluation of a Step-Like Process for Problem-Solving." RRR 13,3 (1972): 178-185.

2027. Shepherd, William C. "Conversion and Adhesion." In H.M. Johnson (ed.), RELIGIOUS CHANGE AND CONTINUITY. SOCIOLOGICAL PERSPECTIVES (volume cited in item 516), pp. 251-263.

2028. Simmonds, Robert B. "Conversion or Addiction: Consequences of Joining a Jesus Movement Group." AMERICAN BEHAVIORAL SCIENTIST 20,6 (1977): 909-924.

2029. Singer, Merrill. "The Use of Folklore in Religious Conversion: The Chassidic Case." RRR 22,2 (1980): 170-185.

2030. Snow, David A., and Cynthia Phillips. "The Lofland-Stark Conversion Model: A Critical Reassessment." SOCIAL PROBLEMS 27 (1980): 430-447.

2031. Stanley, Gordon. "Personality and Attitude Correlates of Religious Conversion." JSSR 4 (1964): 60-63.

2032. Stark, Rodney, and William Bainbridge. "Networks of Faith: Interpersonal Bonds and Recruitment to Cults and Sects." AMERICAN JOURNAL OF SOCIOLOGY 85 (1980): 1376-1395.

* Stark, Rodney, and Charles Y. Glock. AMERICAN PIETY: THE NATURE OF RELIGIOUS COMMITMENT. Cited above as item 497.

* Straus, Roger A. "Changing Oneself: Seekers and the Creative Transformation of Experience." Cited above as item 988.

2033. Straus, Roger A. "Religious Conversion as a Personal and Collective Accomplishment." SA 40,2 (1979): 158-165.

2034. Suaud, Charles. "Conversions religieuses et reconversions économiques." ACTES DE LA RECHERCHE EN SCIENCES SOCIALES 44-45 (1982): 95-108.

2035. Tamney, Joseph B. AN EXPLORATORY STUDY OF RELIGIOUS CONVERSION. Unpublished Ph.D. dissertation, Cornell University, 1962.

2036. Tamney, Joseph B. "The Social Psychology of Conversion." In William T. Liu and Nathaniel Pallone (eds.), CATHOLICS, U.S.A. New York: Wiley, 1970, pp. 399-418.

2037. Taylor, Bryan. "Conversion and Cognition. An Area for Empirical Study in the Microsociology of Religious Knowledge." SC 23,1 (1976): 5-22.

2038. Taylor, David. "Becoming New People: The Recruitment of Young Americans into the Unification Church." In Roy Wallis (ed.), MILLENNIALISM AND CHARISMA (item 89), pp. 177-230.

2039. Travisano, Richard V. ALTERNATION AND CONVERSION IN JEWISH IDENTITIES. Unpublished M.A. thesis, University of Minnesota, 1967.

2040. Travisano, Richard V. "Alternation and Conversion as Qualitatively Different Transformations." In Gregory P. Stone and Harvey A. Farberman (eds.), SOCIAL PSYCHOLOGY THROUGH SYMBOLIC INTERACTION. Waltham, Massachusetts: Ginn-Blaisdell, 1970, pp. 594-606.

2041. Tremmel, William C. "The Converting Choice." JSSR 10,1 (1971): 17-26.

2042. Turner, Paul R. "Religious Conversion and Community Development." JSSR 18,3 (1979): 252-260.

2043. Wallace, Ruth. SOME SOCIAL DETERMINANTS OF CHANGE OF RELIGIOUS AFFILIATION. Unpublished Ph.D. dissertation, University of California, Berkeley, 1968.

2044. Wallace, Ruth. "A Model of Change of Religious Affiliation." JSSR 14 (1975): 345-355.

2045. Wilson, Stephen R. "Becoming a Yogi: Resocialization and Deconditioning as Conversion Processes." SA 45,4 (1984): 301-314.

2046. Wimberley, Ronald C., Thomas Hood, et al. "Conversion in a Billy Graham Crusade." In M.D. Pugh (ed.), COLLECTIVE BEHAVIOR: A SOURCE BOOK. St. Paul, Minnesota: West, 1980, pp. 278-285.

2047. Zetterberg, Hans L. "Religious Conversion as a Change of Social Roles." SOCIOLOGY AND SOCIAL RESEARCH 36 (1952): 159-166.

SECTION B: ROLE ENTRY AND ROLE EXIT

Apostasy

2048. Albrecht, Stan L., and Howard M. Bahr. "Patterns of Religious Disaffiliation: A Study of Lifelong Mormons, Mormon Converts, and Former Mormons." JSSR 22,4 (1983): 366-379.

2049. Brinkerhoff, Merlin B., and Kathryn L. Burke. "Disaffiliation: Some Notes on 'Falling from the Faith.'" SA 41,1 (1980): 41-54.

2050. Caplovitz, David, and Fred Sherrow. THE RELIGIOUS DROP-OUTS. APOSTASY AMONG COLLEGE STUDENTS. Beverly Hills: Sage, 1977 (Sage Library of Social Research, vol. 44).

2051. Dudley, Roger Louis. "Alienation from Religion in Adolescents from Fundamentalist Religious Homes." JSSR 17,4 (1978): 389-398.

2052. Greeley, Andrew M. "A Social Science Model for the Consideration of Religious Apostasy." CONCILIUM 66 (1971): 125-134.

* Greeley, Andrew M. "Religious Musical Chairs." Cited above as item 1977.

* Hoge, Dean R. CONVERTS, DROPOUTS, RETURNEES: A STUDY OF RELIGIOUS CHANGE AMONG CATHOLICS. Cited above as item 1984.

2053. Hunsberger, Bruce E. "A Reexamination of the Antecedents of Apostasy." RRR 21,2 (1980): 158-170.

2054. Hunsberger, Bruce E. "Apostasy: A Social Learning Perspective." RRR 25,1 (1983): 21-38.

2055. Hunsberger, Bruce, and L.B. Brown. "Religious Socialization, Apostasy, and the Impact of Family Background." JSSR 23,3 (1984): 239-251.

2056. Mauss, Armand L. "Dimensions of Religious Defection." RRR 10,3 (1969): 128-135.

* Nelsen, Hart M. "Religious Conformity in an Age of Disbelief: Contextual Effects of Time, Denomination, and Family Processes upon Church Decline and Apostasy." Cited above as item 1284.

2057. Peter, Karl, Edward D. Boldt, Ian Whitaker, and Lance W. Roberts. "The Dynamics of Religious Defection among Hutterites." JSSR 21,4 (1982): 327-337.

2058. Roof, Wade Clark. "Alienation and Apostasy." In T. Robbins and D. Anthony (eds.), IN GODS WE TRUST (item 367), pp. 87-99.

* Schnepp, Gerald. LEAKAGE FROM A CATHOLIC PARISH. Cited above as item 1477.

2059. Skonovd, Norman. APOSTASY: THE PROCESS OF DEFECTION FROM RELIGIOUS TOTALISM. Unpublished Ph.D. dissertation, University of California, Davis, 1981.

2060. Wright, Stuart A. A SOCIOLOGICAL STUDY OF DEFECTION FROM CONTROVERSIAL NEW RELIGIOUS MOVEMENTS. Unpublished Ph.D. dissertation, University of Connecticut, 1983.

* Wuthnow, Robert. EXPERIMENTATION IN AMERICAN RELIGION. Cited above as item 1722.

* Wuthnow, Robert, and Charles Y. Glock. "Religious Loyalty, Defection, and Experimentation among College Youth." Cited above as item 337.

2061. Zelan, Joseph. CORRELATES OF RELIGIOUS APOSTASY. Unpublished M.A. thesis, University of Chicago, 1962.

2062. Zelan, Joseph. "Religious Apostasy, Higher Education, and Occupational Choice." SOCIOLOGY OF EDUCATION 41 (1968): 370-379.

Ex-Clergy

* Cryns, Arthur G. "Dogmatism of Catholic Clergy and Ex-Clergy: A Study of Ministerial Role Perseverence and Open-Mindedness." Cited above as item 589.

2063. Dellacava, Frances A. STATUS ABROGATION: A STUDY OF THE FORMER ROMAN CATHOLIC PRIEST. Unpublished Ph.D. dissertation, Fordham University, 1973.

2064. Dellacava, Frances A. "Becoming an Ex-Priest: The Process of Leaving a High Commitment Status." SOCIOLOGICAL INQUIRY 45 (1975): 41-49.

* Duncan, H.G. "Reactions of Ex-Ministers toward the Ministry." Cited above as item 604.

* Jud, Gerald J., Edgar W. Mills, and Genevieve Walters Burch. EX-PASTORS: WHY MEN LEAVE THE PARISH MINISTRY. Cited above as item 662.

* Kauffmann, Michel. "Regard statistique sur les prêtres qui quittent le ministère." Cited above as item 664.

2065. Newson, Janice Angela. THE ROMAN CATHOLIC CLERICAL EXODUS: A STUDY OF ROLE-ADAPTATION AND ORGANIZATIONAL CHANGE. Unpublished Ph.D. dissertation, University of Toronto, 1976.

2066. Reinheimer, George Edward. A COMPARATIVE STUDY OF THE VOCATIONAL INTERESTS AND VALUES OF ROMAN CATHOLIC PRIESTS ACTIVE IN THE MINISTRY AND ROMAN CATHOLIC PRIESTS WHO HAVE LEFT THE ACTIVE MINISTRY. Unpublished Ph.D. dissertation, St. John's University, 1973.

* Ruiz Olabuenaga, José Ignatio. "Ex-prêtres en Espagna." Cited above as item 741.

2067. Ruiz Olabuenaga, José Ignatio. LOS EX-SACERDOTES Y EX-SEMINARISTAS EN ESPAÑA. Cuernavaca: Cidoc, 1971.

* Schallert, Eugene J., and Jacqueline M. Kelley. "Some Factors Associated with Voluntary Withdrawal from the Catholic Priesthood." Cited above as item 745.

* Seidler, John. "Priest Resignations in a Lazy Monopoly." Cited above as item 754.

2068. Walters Burch, Genevieve. "The Ex-Pastor's Message to the Church as an Occupational System." SC 17 (1970): 517-532.

2069. Willaime, Jean-Paul. LES EX-PASTEURS. Strasbourg: Centre de Sociologie du Protestantisme, 1979.

2070. Wilson, Robert Wayne. PERSISTENCE AND CHANGE IN THE PRIESTLY ROLE IN RELATION TO ROLE-SATISFACTION: A STUDY OF ROMAN CATHOLIC PRIESTS AND EX-PRIESTS. Unpublished Ph.D. dissertation, New York University, 1974.

Ex-nuns

* Ebaugh, Helen R.F. OUT OF THE CLOISTER. Cited above as item 1037.

* Molitor, M.M.A. A COMPARATIVE STUDY OF DROPOUTS AND NONDROPOUTS IN A RELIGIOUS COMMUNITY. Cited above as item 1048.

* SanGiovanni, Lucinda F. EX-NUNS. A STUDY OF EMERGENT ROLE PASSAGE. Cited above as item 1063.

Vocations

2071. Blasi, Anthony J. ACOLYTES' PERCEPTIONS AND CHOICE OF THE SACERDOTAL OCCUPATION: A SOCIAL STUDY OF ROLE-TAKING. Unpublished Ph.D. dissertation, University of Notre Dame, 1973.

2072. Blasi, Anthony J. "Vocations and Perceptions." SA 36 (1975): 67-72.

* Bohr, Ronald H. "Dogmatism and Age of Vocational Choice in Two Religious Orders." Cited above as item 1315.

* Bormann, Günther. "Studien zu Berufsbild und Berufswirklichkeit evangelischer Pfarrer in Württemberg: Tendenzen der Berufseinstellung und des Berufsverhaltens." Cited above as item 833.

* Bowdern, Thomas Stephen. A STUDY OF VOCATIONS: AN INVESTIGATION INTO THE ENVIRONMENTAL FACTORS OF VOCATION TO THE PRIESTHOOD AND THE RELIGIOUS LIFE IN THE UNITED STATES FROM 1919 TO 1929. Cited above as item 994.

2073. Bowdern, Thomas Stephen. "Letter to the Editor." AMERICA 65 (1941): 410.

2074. Bowdern, Thomas Stephen. "How Vocations Grow." REVIEW FOR RELIGIOUS 1 (1942): 364-375.

* Bowman, Jerome Francis. A STUDY OF SELECTED SOCIAL AND ECONOMIC FACTORS IN THE FORMATION OF A RELIGIOUS VOCATION. Cited above as item 995.

2075. Burgalassi, Silvano. "Il problema delle vocazioni religiosi e del clero secolare in una diocesi toscana." ORIENTAMENTI SOCIALI 10,14 (1954): 312-316.

2076. Burgalassi, Silvano. "La vocazione in rapporto all'ambiente socio-religioso." SOCIOLOGIA RELIGIOSA 1 (1957): 65-70.

2077. Burgalassi, Silvano. "Il problema delle vocazioni ecclesiastiche." IL MULINO 1 (1978): 87-99.

* Burns, M. Sheila. A COMPARATIVE STUDY OF SOCIAL FACTORS IN RELIGIOUS VOCATIONS TO THREE TYPES OF WOMEN'S COMMUNITIES: ABSTRACT OF A DISSERTATION. Cited above as item 1321.

2078. Carlton, E. "'The Call': The Concept of Vocation in the Free Church Ministry." In D. Martin (ed.), A SOCIOLOGICAL YEARBOOK OF RELIGION IN BRITAIN 1. London: SCM, 1968, pp. 106-114.

2079. Carrier, Hervé. LA VOCATION. DYNAMISMES PSYCHO-SOCIOLOGIQUES. Rome: Presses de l'Université Grégorienne, 1966.
LA VOCAZIONE. DINAMISMI PSICHO-SOCIOLOGICI. Torino: Elle Di Ci, 1967.

2080. Coxon, Anthony P.M. A SOCIOLOGICAL STUDY OF THE SOCIAL RECRUITMENT, SELECTION, AND PROFESSIONAL SOCIALIZATION OF ANGLICAN ORDINANDS. Unpublished Ph.D. thesis, University of Leeds, 1965.

2081. Coxon, Anthony P.M. "Patterns of Occupational Recruitment: The Anglican Ministry." SOCIOLOGY 1 (1967): 73-79.

* Culligan, Martin J. FACTORS THAT INFLUENCE VOCATIONS TO THE VINCENTIAN FATHERS. Cited above as item 1325.

2082. Curcione, Nicholas R. STRUCTURAL FACTORS AFFECTING CAREER COMMITMENT: A STUDY OF RECRUITMENT TO THE CLARETIAN PRIESTHOOD. Unpublished Ph.D. dissertation, University of California, Los Angeles, 1970.

2083. Curcione, Nicholas R. "Family Influence on Commitment to the Priesthood: A Study of Altar Boys." SA 34,4 (1973): 265-280.

2084. Dellepoort, J. "Statistiques concernant les vocations sacerdotales en Hollande." LUMEN VITAE 6,1-2 (1951): 261-262.

2085. Dellepoort, J. "Analyse sociographique et statistique des vocations sacerdotales aux Pays-Bas." In E. Collard et al. (eds.), VOCATION DE LA SOCIOLOGIE RELIGIEUSE -- SOCIOLOGIE DES VOCATIONS. Tournai: Casterman, 1958, pp. 118-131.

2086. Diaz-Mozaz, José M. "Les vocations en Espagne." SC 12,4-5 (1965): 303-311.

* Dittes, James E. "Research on Clergymen: Factors Influencing Decisions for Religious Service and Effectiveness in the Vocation." Cited above as item 597.

2087. Donovan, Paul A. BIRTH ORDER AND CATHOLIC PRIESTS. Unpublished Ph.D. dissertation, Northwestern University, 1976.

* Dougherty, Denis. "The Rate of Perseverance to Ordination of Minor Seminary Graduates." Cited above as item 998.

* Dougherty, John. "Do Priests Encourage Vocations? A Fact Study of 275 Seminarians." Cited above as item 999.

* Fee, Joan L., Andrew M. Greeley, Wiliam C. McCready, and Theresa A. Sullivan. YOUNG CATHOLICS. A REPORT TO THE KNIGHTS OF COLUMBUS. Cited above as item 530.

* Fichter, Joseph H. RELIGION AS AN OCCUPATION. Cited above as item 610.

2088. Fichter, Joseph H. CATHOLIC PARENTS AND THE CHURCH VOCATION: A STUDY OF PARENTAL ATTITUDES IN A CATHOLIC DIOCESE. Washington: Center for Applied Research in the Apostolate, 1967.

* Gilbert, James D. "What Makes Boys Seminarians?" Cited above as item 1001.

2089. Giuriati, Paolo. "Dinamica vocazionale in cifre. Il flusso delle entrate e uscite nel Seminario Maggiore di Padova dal 1950-51 al 1970-71." STUDIA PATAVINA 2 (1977): 245-310.

* Goussidis, Alexandre. "Analyse statistique et sociographique des ordinations dans l'Eglise de Grèce entre 1950 et 1969." Cited above as item 630.

2090. Hamelin, Louis-Edmond. "Contribution aux recherchers sociales au Québec par une étude des variations régionales du nombre de vocations sacerdotales." CAHIERS DE GEOGRAPHIE DE QUEBEC 2,3 (1957): 5-36.

2091. Healy, Charles C. THE RELATION OF OCCUPATIONAL CHOICE TO THE SIMILARITY BETWEEN SELF AND OCCUPATIONAL RATINGS. Unpublished Ph.D. dissertation, Columbia University, 1967.

* Hicks, Thomas H. "A Study of the Background, Level of Job Satisfaction, Maturity, and Morale of 'Delayed Vocation' Catholic Priests." Cited above as item 648.

2092. Hoge, Dean R., Raymond H. Potvin, and Kathleen M. Gerry. RESEARCH ON MEN'S VOCATIONS TO THE PRIESTHOOD AND THE RELIGIOUS LIFE. Washington: United States Catholic Conference, 1984.

2093. Horrigan, J.P. OCCUPATIONAL RECRUITMENT: PREDICTING INTELLECTUAL INTEREST IN THE ROMAN CATHOLIC PRIESTHOOD. Unpublished M.A. thesis, University of Guelph (Ontario), 1971.

2094. Horrigan, J.P., and Kenneth Westhues. "A Model for the Study of Occupational Choice of the Roman Catholic Priesthood." SA 32,4 (1971): 229-237.

2095. Houtart, François. "The Sociology of Vocation." In H. Poage and G. Lievin (eds.), TODAY'S VOCATION CRISIS. Westminster: Newman Press, 1962, pp. 21-48.

2096. Houtart, François. "La vocation au sacerdoce comme perception collective de valeurs." ARCHIVES DE SOCIOLOGIE DES RELIGIONS 16 (1963): 39-43.

2097. Jaeckels, Ronald. A STUDY OF THE SOCIAL BACKGROUND FACTORS OF SEMINARIANS OF THE WESTERN PROVINCE PREPARING FOR THE PRIESTHOOD IN THE SOCIETY OF THE DIVINE WORD. Unpublished M.A. thesis, Catholic University of America, 1959.

2098. James, William R. A COMPARATIVE STUDY OF ATTITUDES TOWARD VOCATION TO THE PRIESTHOOD OF EIGHTH-, NINTH- AND TWELFTH-GRADE BOYS. Unpublished M.A. thesis, Catholic University of America, 1961.

2099. Jolson, Alfred J. "The Role of the Priest and Obstacles to Priestly Vocations in Oslo, Norway: A Research Note." SA 31,2 (1970): 115-117.

2100. Kennedy, Robert D. A STUDY IN THE SOCIAL BACKGROUNDS OF PRIESTS AND SEMINARIANS IN THE AMERICAN PROVINCE OF THE OBLATES OF ST. FRANCIS DE SALES. Unpublished M.A. thesis, Catholic University of America, 1954.

2101. Lindenthal, Jacob Jay. THE DELAYED DECISION TO ENTER THE MINISTRY: A STUDY IN OCCUPATIONAL CHANGE. Unpublished Ph.D. dissertation, Yale University, 1967.

2102. Lindenthal, Jacob Jay. "The Delayed Decision to Enter the Ministry: Some Issues and Prospects." RRR 9 (1968): 108-114.

2103. Lindner, Traugot, Leopold Lentner, and Adolf Holl. PRIESTERBILD UND BERUFSWAHLMOTIVE. ERGEBNISSE EINER SOZIAL-PSYCHOLOGISCHEN UNTERSUCHUNG BEI DEN WIENER MITTELSCHÜLERN. Wien: Herder Verlag, 1963.

* Maloney, Daniel J. AGE DIFFERENCES IN THE PERCEIVED INFLUENCE OF PERSONAL FACTORS ON VOCATION CHOICE. Cited above as item 1016.

2104. Masson, Joseph. "Vocations to the Priesthood and Environment: An Enquiry into the Belgian Congo, Ruanda and Urundi." LUMEN VITAE 13 (1958): 120-145.

2105. Mattez, M.T. QUELQUES ASPECTS DU CONTEXTE SOCIOLOGIQUE DE LA VOCATION RELIGIEUSE. Louvain: Université Catholique, 1955.

2106. McCarrick, Theodore E. AN ANALYSIS OF THE SOCIAL FACTORS AFFECTING VOCATIONAL SUPPLY TO THE DIOCESAN PRIESTHOOD IN THE ARCHDIOCESE OF NEW YORK, 1928-1958. Unpublished M.A. thesis, Catholic University of America, 1960.

2107. McCarrick, Theodore E. THE VOCATION PARISH: AN ANALYSIS OF A GROUP OF HIGH VOCATION SUPPLYING PARISHES IN THE ARCHDIOCESE OF NEW YORK TO DETERMINE THE COMMON CHARACTERISTICS OF THE VOCATION PARISH. Unpublished Ph.D. dissertation, Catholic University of America, 1963.

* Mills, Bobby Eugene. CAREER CHOICE AMONG THEOLOGICAL STUDENTS. Cited above as item 1018.

2108. Muelder, Walter G. "Recruitment of Negroes for Theological Studies." RRR 5,3 (1964): 152-156.

2109. Musgrove, Frank. "Late-Entrants to the Anglican Ministry: A Move into Marginality." SOCIOLOGICAL REVIEW 23,4 (1975): 841-866.

2110. Nebreda, Julián. "La crisis vocacional del Instituto Marista y su futuro en Andalucia." CUADERNOS DE REALIDADES SOCIALES 6 (1974): 59-107.

2111. Nebreda, Julián. O RENACER O MORIR: UNA REFLEXION SOCIO-RELIGIOSA SOBRE LA CRISIS VOCACIONAL. Madrid: Instituto Teológico de Vida Religiosa, 1974.

* Newman, Jeremiah. "The Priests of Ireland: A Socio-Religious Survey. 2: Patterns of Vocations." Cited above as item 709.

2112. Newman, Jeremiah, Liam Ryan, and Conor K. Ward. "Attitudes of Young People towards Vocations (Part of a Study Commissioned by the Irish Hierarchy)." SOCIAL STUDIES 1,5 (1972): 531-550.

2113. Orsini, Gabriele di. "Aspetti della secolarizzazione. (Il giorno del Signore e le vocazioni in Italia con particolare attenzione all'Abruzzo-Molise)." SOCIOLOGIA. RIVISTA DI SCIENZE SOCIALI (NS) 11,2-3 (1977): 151-180.

2114. Poblete, Renato. "Vocations -- Problems and Promise." In J.J. Considine (ed.), THE RELIGIOUS DIMENSION IN THE NEW LATIN AMERICA. Notre Dame: Fides, 1966, pp. 148-158.

2115. Poeisz, J.J. "Déterminants sociaux des inscriptions dans les séminaires et des ordination de nouveaux prêtres aux Pays-Bas." SC 10,6 (1963): 491-524.

* Routhier, François, and Paul Stryckman. LES ETUDIANTS DES GRANDS SEMINAIRES DE LA VIE SACERDOTALE. Partially published by Routhier as "Les séminaristes d'aujourd'hui seront-ils prêtres de demain?" in LE PRETRE, HIER, AUJOURD'HUI, DEMAIN. Cited above as item 1023.

* Routhier, François, and Grégoire Tremblay. LE PROFIL SOCIOLOGIQUE DU SEMINARISTE QUEBECOIS. Cited above as item 1024.

2116. Ryan, Edmund J. Summary of "Some Psychological Implications of the Vocation Survey: Natural Factors Affecting Vocations to the Priesthood." NATIONAL CATHOLIC EDUCATION ASSOCIATION BULLETIN 53 (1956): 57-58.

2117. Suaud, Charles. "Contribution à une sociologie de la vocation: destin religieux et projet scolaire." REVUE FRANÇAISE DE SOCIOLOGIE 15,1 (1974): 75-112.

2118. Suaud, Charles. LA VOCATION -- CONVERSION ET RECONVERSION DES PRETRES RURAUX. Paris: Editions de Minuit, 1978.

2119. Taras, Piotr. "Conditionnements sociaux des vocations sacerdotales en Pologne." SC 17,4 (1970): 545-552.

2120. Tarleton, M. Rose Bernard. THE RELATION OF PERCEIVED ATTITUDES OF REFERENCE GROUP MEMBERS TO PERSONAL ATTITUDES TOWARD AND DECISIONS TO ENTER ROMAN CATHOLIC SISTERHOODS. Unpublished Ph.D. dissertation, Catholic University of America, 1968.

2121. Towler, Robert. "Puritan and Antipuritan. Types of Vocation to the Ordained Ministry." In D. Martin (ed.), A SOCIOLOGICAL YEARBOOK OF RELIGION IN BRITAIN 2. London: SCM, 1969, pp. 109-122.

* Van Nostrand, Michael E. THE CALL TO THE MINISTRY FROM ANOTHER CAREER: PERCEPTIONS OF CHRISTIAN VOCATION HELD BY CATHOLIC AND PROTESTANT SEMINARIANS. Cited above as item 1027.

2122. Zdaniewicz, Witold. "Le problème des vocations religieuses en Pologne." SC 15,3-4 (1968): 209-234.

SECTION C. DEVIANCE AND LEGITIMATION

Deviance

2123. Abrams, J. Keith, and L. Richard Della Fave. "Authoritarianism, Religiosity, and the Legalization of Victimless Crimes." SOCIOLOGY AND SOCIAL RESEARCH 61 (1976): 68-82.

2124. Albrecht, Stan L., Bruce A. Chadwick, and David S. Alcorn. "Religiosity and Deviance: Application of an Attitude-Behavior Contingent Consistency Model." JSSR 16,3 (1977): 263-274.

2125. Allen, D.E., and H.S. Sandhu. "A Comparative Study of Delinquents and Non-Delinquents: Family Affect, Religion, and Personal Income." SOCIAL FORCES 46 (1967): 263-269.

* Bergesen, Albert. "Political Witch-Hunts: The Sacred and the Subversive in Cross-National Perspective." Cited above as item 1528.

* Bergesen, Albert. "A Durkheimian Theory of Political Witch-Hunts with the Chinese Cultural Revolution of 1966-1969 as an Example." Cited above as item 1529.

* Bergesen, Albert. THE SACRED AND THE SUBVERSIVE: POLITICAL WITCH-HUNTS AS NATIONAL RITUALS. Cited above as item 1530.

2126. Coogan, John Edward. "Religion a Preventive of Delinquency." FEDERAL PROBATION 18 (1954): 29-35.

2127. Dominic, R.G.S. "Religion and the Juvenile Delinquent." AMERICAN CATHOLIC SOCIOLOGICAL REVIEW 15 (1954): 256-264.

2128. Elifson, Kirk W., David M. Petersen, and C. Kirk Hadaway. "Religion and Delinquency: A Contextual Analysis." CRIMINOLOGY 21 (1983): 505-527.

2129. Ellwood, Robert S., Jr. ALTERNATIVE ALTARS: UNCONVENTIONAL AND EASTERN SPIRITUALITY IN AMERICA. Chicago: University of Chicago Press, 1979.

2130. Erikson, Kai T. WAYWARD PURITANS. A STUDY IN THE SOCIOLOGY OF DEVIANCE. New York: Wiley, 1966.

2131. Falk, G. "Religion, Personal Integration, and Criminality." JOURNAL OF EDUCATIONAL SOCIOLOGY 35 (1961): 159-161.

2132. Gannon, Thomas M. "Religious Attitude and Behavior Changes of Institutional Delinquents." SA 28 (1967): 215-225.

2133. Hampshire, Annette P., and James A. Beckford. "Religious Sects and the Concept of Deviance." BRITISH JOURNAL OF SOCIOLOGY 34,2 (1983): 208-229.

2134. Hepworth, Mike, and Bryan S. Turner. CONFESSION. STUDIES IN DEVIANCE AND RELIGION. Boston: Routledge and Kegan Paul, 1982.

2135. Knudten, Richard D. "The Religion of the Indiana Baptist Prisoner." RRR 19, 1 (1977): 16-31, 42.

2136. Knudten, Richard D., and Mary S. Knudten. "Juvenile Delinquency, Crime, and Religion." RRR 12 (1971): 130-152.

2137. Middleton, Russell, and Putney Snell. "Religion, Normative Standards, and Behavior." SOCIOMETRY 25 (1962): 141-152.

2138. Middleton, Warren C., and Paul J. Fay. "Attitudes of Delinquent and Non-Delinquent Girls toward Sunday Observance, the Bible, and War." JOURNAL OF EDUCATIONAL PSYCHOLOGY 32 (1941): 555-558.

2139. Miller, M. "The Place of Religion in the Lives of Juvenile Offenders." FEDERAL PROBATION 29 (1965): 50-54.

2140. Powers, G.E. "Prevention Through Religion." In W.E. Ames and C.F. Wellford (eds.), DELINQUENCY PREVENTION: THEORY AND PRACTICE. Englewood Cliffs: Prentice-Hall, 1967.

2141. Rhodes, A., and Albert Reiss, Jr. "The 'Religious Factor' and Delinquent Behavior." JOURNAL OF RESEARCH IN CRIME AND DELINQUENCY 7 (1970): 83-98.

2142. Smith, Philip M. "Prisoners' Attitudes Toward Organized Religion." RELIGIOUS EDUCATION 51 (1956): 462-464.

* Stack, Steven, and Mary Jeanne Kanavy. "The Effect of Religion on Forcible Rape: A Structural Analysis." Cited above as item 334.

2143. Stark, Rodney, Daniel P. Doyle, and Lorie Kent. REDISCOVERING MORAL COMMUNITIES: CHURCH MEMBERSHIP AND CRIME. Seattle: Center for Law and Justice, University of Washington, 1979.

2144. Stark, Rodney, Daniel P. Doyle, and Lorie Kent. "Rediscovering Moral Communities: Church Membership and Crime." In Travis Hirschi and Michael Gott Fredson (eds.), UNDERSTANDING CRIME. Beverly Hills: Sage, 1980.

2145. Stark, Rodney, Daniel P. Doyle, and Lorie Kent. "Religion and Delinquency: The Ecology of a 'Lost' Relationship." JOURNAL OF RESEARCH IN CRIME AND DELINQUENCY 19 (1982): 4-26.

2146. Tittle, Charles R., and Michael R. Welch. "Religiosity and Deviance: Toward a Contingency Theory of Constraining Effects." SOCIAL FORCES 61,3 (1983): 653-682.

2147. Wattenberg, W. "Church Attendance and Juvenile Misconduct." SOCIOLOGY AND SOCIAL RESEARCH 34 (1950): 195-202.

Legitimation

2148. Fenn, Richard K. "Religion and the Legitimation of Social Systems." In A.W. Eister (ed.), CHANGING PERSPECTIVES IN THE SCIENTIFIC STUDY OF RELIGION (volume cited as item 353), pp. 143-161.

2149. Gellner, Ernest. LEGITIMATION OF BELIEF. London: Cambridge University Press, 1974.

* Moodie, T. Dunbar. "The Dutch Reformed Churches as Vehicles of Political Legitimation in South Africa." Cited above as item 1653.

* Skocpol, Theda. "Rentier State and Shi'a Islam in the Iranian Revolution." Cited above as item 1697.

2150. Weissbrod, Lilly. "Delegitimation and Legitimation as a Continuous Process: A Case Study of Israel." MIDDLE EAST JOURNAL 35 (1981): 527-543.

2151. Willaime, Jean-Paul. "De la fonction infrapolitique du religieux." ANNUAL REVIEW OF THE SOCIAL SCIENCES OF RELIGION 5 (1981): 167-186.

Plausibility structures

2152. Berger, Peter L. THE SACRED CANOPY. ELEMENTS OF A SOCIOLOGICAL THEORY OF RELIGION. Garden City, N.Y.: Anchor Doubleday, 1967.

2153. Hammond, Phillip E., and James Davison Hunter. "On Maintaining Plausibility: The Worldview of Evangelical College Students." JSSR 23,3 (1984): 221-238.

2154. Roof, Wade Clark. COMMUNITY AND COMMITMENT. RELIGIOUS PLAUSIBILITY IN A LIBERAL PROTESTANT CHURCH. New York: Elsevier, 1978.

2155. Simmons, J.L. "On Maintaining Deviant Belief Systems: A Case Study." SOCIAL PROBLEMS 11 (1964): 250-256.

2156. Snow, David A., and Richard Machalek. "On the Presumed Fragility of Unconventional Beliefs." JSSR 21,1 (1982): 15-26.

2157. Snow, David A., and Richard Machalek. "Second Thoughts on the Presumed Fragility of Unconventional Beliefs." In E. Barker (ed.), OF GODS AND MEN (item 2396), pp. 25-44.

Social control

2158. Burkett, Steven R., and Mervin White. "Hellfire and Delinquency: Another Look." JSSR 13 (1974): 445-462.

2159. Gannon, Thomas M. "Religious Control and Delinquent Behavior." SOCIOLOGY AND SOCIAL RESEARCH 51 (1967): 418-431.

2160. Gerharz, George P. "Secularization as Loss of Social Control: Toward a New Theory." SA 31,1 (1970): 1-11.

2161. Higgins, Paul C., and Gary L. Albrecht. "Hellfire and Delinquency Revisited." SOCIAL FORCES 55 (1977): 952-958.

2162. Hirschi, Travis, and Rodney Stark. "Hellfire and Delinquency." SOCIAL PROBLEMS 17 (1969): 202-213. Reprinted in C.Y. Glock (ed.), RELIGION IN SOCIOLOGICAL PERSPECTIVE (volume cited in item 141), pp. 75-87.

* Hougland, James G., and James R. Wood. "Control in Organizations and the Commitment of Members." Cited above as item 1148.

2163. Hunt, C.L. "Religious Ideologies as a Means of Social Control." SOCIOLOGY AND SOCIAL RESEARCH 33,3 (1949): 180-187.

2164. Jensen, Gary F., and Maynard L. Erickson. "The Religious Factor and Delinquency: Another Look at the Hellfire Hypothesis." In Robert Wuthnow (ed.), THE RELIGIOUS DIMENSION: NEW DIRECTIONS IN QUANTITATIVE RESEARCH. New York: Academic Press, 1979, 157-177.

* Kleinman, Sherryl, and Gary Alan Fine. "Rhetorics and Action in Moral Organizations: Social Control of Little Leaguers and Ministry Students." Cited above as item 1009.

2165. Kvaraceus, W.C. "Delinquent Behavior and Church Attendance." SOCIOLOGY AND SOCIAL RESEARCH 28 (1944): 284-289.

2166. Lemieux, Raymond. "Religion et socialisation de déviances. Concurrences et alternatives dans le rapports entre discours religieux et pratiques médicales." CAHIERS DE RECHERCHES EN SCIENCES DE LA RELIGION 4 (1982): 271-295.

2167. Loveless, E., and F. Lodato. "Social Control and Religious Preference." SA 28,1 (1967): 226-228.

2168. McIntosh, William Alex, Starla D. Fitch, J. Branton Wilson, and Kenneth L. Nyberg. "The Effect of Mainstream Religious Social Controls on Adolescent Drug Use in Rural Areas." RRR 23,1 (1981): 54-75.

2169. Nelson, L.D. "Functions and Dimensions of Religion." SA 35,4 (1974): 263-272.

* Nunn, Clyde Z. "Child-Control Through a 'Coalition with God.'" Cited above as item 1850.

2170. Peek, Charles W., H. Paul Chalfant, and Edward V. Wilton. "Sinners in the Hands of an Angry God: Fundamentalist Fears about Drunken Driving." JSSR 18,1 (1979): 29-39.

2171. Photiadis, John. "Overt Conformity to Church Teaching as a Function of Religious Beliefs and Group Participation." AMERICAN JOURNAL OF SOCIOLOGY 70 (1965): 423-428.

2172. Pickering, W.S.F. "Hutterites and Problems of Persistence and Social Control in Religious Communities." ARCHIVES DE SCIENCES SOCIALES DES RELIGIONS 44,1 (1977): 75-92.

2173. Richardson, John G., and Georgie A. Weatherby. "Belief in an Afterlife as Symbolic Sanction." RRR 25,2 (1983): 162-169.

2174. Ross, Edward A. "Social Control V: Religion." AMERICAN JOURNAL OF SOCIOLOGY 2 (1896): 433-445.

* Stark, Werner. THE SOCIAL BOND. AN INVESTIGATION INTO THE BASES OF LAW-ABIDINGNESS. VOLUME FOUR: ETHOS AND RELIGION. Cited above as item 194.

2175. Travers, J.F., and R.G. Davis. "A Study of Religious Motivation and Delinquency." THE JOURNAL OF EDUCATIONAL SOCIOLOGY 34 (1961): 205-220.

SECTION D: ORGANIZATIONAL CHANGE AND PROCESS

The entries in this section pertain more to the changes and processes of organizations than to the changes which may take place within them.

Institutionalization

2176. O'Dea, Thomas F. "Five Dilemmas in the Institutionalization of Religion." JSSR 1 (1961): 30-39. Reprinted in R.D. Knudten (ed.), THE SOCIOLOGY OF RELIGION (volume cited in item 375), pp. 185-194; and in L. Schneider (ed.), RELIGION, CULTURE AND SOCIETY (volume cited in item 1824), pp. 580-588.

2177. O'Dea, Thomas F. "Sociological Dilemmas: Five Paradoxes of Institutionalism." In E.A. Tiryakian (ed.), SOCIOLOGICAL THEORY, VALUES AND SOCIOCULTURAL CHANGE. New York: Free Press, 1963, pp. 71-89. Reprinted in T.F. O'Dea, SOCIOLOGY AND THE STUDY OF RELIGION. THEORY, RESEARCH, INTERPRETATION. New York: Basic Books, 1970, pp. 240-255.

Inter-religious conflict

2178. Campiche, Roland. "Religion, source de conflits ou ciment de l'unité suisse?" ARCHIVES DE SCIENCES SOCIALES DES RELIGIONS 25,49 (1980): 43-57. First published in REVUE SUISSE DE SOCIOLOGIE 3 (1978).

* Easthope, Gary. "Religious War in Northern Ireland." Cited above as item 276.

2179. Giles, H.H. "Community Conflicts Related to Religious Difference." JOURNAL OF INTERGROUP RELATIONS 2,2 (1962): 145-148.

* Herberg, Will. "Protestant-Catholic Tensions in Pluralist America." Cited above as item 354.

2180. Jenkins, R. "Religious Conflict in Northern Ireland." In David Martin (ed.), A SOCIOLOGICAL YEARBOOK OF RELIGION IN BRITAIN 2. London: SCM, 1969, pp. 103-108.

2181. Kane, John J. CATHOLIC-PROTESTANT TENSIONS IN AMERICA. Chicago: Regnery, 1955.

2182. Salisbury, W. Seward. "Las religiones en Estados Unidos de América: conflicto, acomodación y consenso." REVISTA MEXICANA DE SOCIOLOGIA 24,3 (1962): 849-866.

2183. Steiner, Jesse Frederick. "The Changing Status of Religious Conflict." In Steiner, THE AMERICAN COMMUNITY IN ACTION. CASE STUDIES OF AMERICAN COMMUNITIES. New York: Holt, 1928, pp. 264-278.

2184. Underwood, Kenneth W. PROTESTANT AND CATHOLIC. RELIGIOUS AND SOCIAL INTERACTION IN AN INDUSTRIAL COMMUNITY. Boston: Beacon Press, 1957.

* Wright, Frank. "Protestant Ideology and Politics in Ulster." Cited above as item 1721.

Merger and ecumenism

2185. Berger, Peter L. "A Market Model for the Analysis of Ecumenicity." SOCIAL RESEARCH 30,1 (1963): 77-93.

2186. Black, Allan W. "The Sociology of Ecumenism: Initial Observations on the Formation of the Uniting Church in Australia." In Allan Black and Peter Glasner (eds.), PRACTICE AND BELIEF (volume cited in item 824), pp. 86-107.

2187. Boldon, Dean A. THE ECUMENICAL MOVEMENT IN AMERICA: PROTESTANT CONCILIARISM AS INTERORGANIZATIONAL RELATIONS. Unpublished Ph.D. dissertation, Vanderbilt University, 1976.

2188. Bryman, Alan, and C. Robin Hinings. "Participation, Reform and Ecumenism: The View of Laity and Clergy." SOCIOLOGICAL YEARBOOK OF RELIGION IN BRITAIN 7 (1974): 13-25.

2189. Bryman, Alan, Stewart Ranson, and C. Robin Hinings. "Churchmanship and Ecumenism." JOURNAL OF ECUMENICAL STUDIES 11 (1974): 467-475.

2190. Call, Lon Ray. THE FEDERATION AND MERGER OF LOCAL RELIGIOUS GROUPS. Unpublished Ph.D. dissertation, Columbia University, 1936.

2191. Corbon, Jean. "Psycho-sociologie de l'oecuménisme au Proche-Orient." LUMEN VITAE 19,3 (1964): 414-430.

2192. Currie, Robert. METHODISM DIVIDED: A STUDY IN THE SOCIOLOGY OF ECUMENICALISM. London: Faber and Faber, 1968.

2193. Dornbusch, Sanford M., and Roger Irle. "The Failure of Presbyterian Union." AMERICAN JOURNAL OF SOCIOLOGY 64,4 (1959): 352-356.

2194. Douglass, H. Paul. CHURCH UNITY MOVEMENTS IN THE UNITED STATES. New York: Institute of Social and Religious Research, 1934.

2195. File, Ed. A SOCIOLOGICAL ANALYSIS OF CHURCH UNION IN CANADA: NON-THEOLOGICAL FACTORS IN INTERDENOMINATIONAL CHURCH UNION UP TO 1925. Unpublished Ph.D. dissertation, Boston University, 1961.

2196. Filippone, Vincenzo. "Analisi culturale e ecumenismo." RIVISTA DI SOCIOLOGIA 5,14 (1967): 129-136.

2197. Flynn, Robert John. CHURCH INVOLVEMENT, CHURCH GOALS, AND COMMUNITY STRUCTURAL DIFFERENTIATION: SOCIAL INFLUENCES ON ATTITUDES TOWARDS CHURCH CONSOLIDATION. Unpublished M.A. thesis, Carleton University, 1970.

2198. Garrett, William R. "Interplay and Rivalry between Denominational and Ecumenical Organization." In R.P. Scherer (ed.), AMERICAN DENOMINATIONAL ORGANIZATION (item 1172), pp. 346-362.

2199. Kail, Robert C. "Ecumenism, Clergy Influence and Liberalism: An Investigation into the Sources of Lay Support for Church Union." CANADIAN REVIEW OF SOCIOLOGY AND ANTHROPOLOGY 8,3 (1971): 142-163.

2200. Kelly, James R. "Who Favors Ecumenism? A Study of Some of the Correlates of Support for Ecumenism." SA 32,3 (1971): 158-169.

2201. Kelly, James R. "Sources of Support for Ecumenism: A Sociological Study." JOURNAL OF ECUMENICAL STUDIES 8 (1971): 1-9.

2202. Kelly, James R. "Attitudes toward Ecumenism: An Empirical Investigation." JOURNAL OF ECUMENICAL STUDIES 9,2 (1972): 341-351.

* Kelly, James R. "The Spirit of Ecumenism: How Wide, How Deep, How Mindful of Truth?" Cited above as item 667.

2203. Kelly, James R. "Roman Catholic Catechists and Their Ecumenical Attitudes." RRR 25,4 (1984): 379-386.

* Hiller, Harry H. "Communality as a Dimension of Ecumenical Negativism." Cited above as item 1231.

2204. Lalive d'Epinay, Christian. "L'esprit et le champ oecuméniques de pasteurs sud-américains." SC 14,5-6 (1967): 423-437.

2205. Lee, Robert. THE SOCIAL SOURCES OF CHURCH UNITY. Nashville: Abington, 1960.

2206. MacRae, Peter Howard. THE ANGLICAN CHURCH AND THE ECUMENICAL MOVEMENT IN NEW BRUNSWICK. Unpublished M.A. thesis, University of New Brunswick, 1969.

2207. Mann, William E. "The Canadian Church Union, 1925." In Nils Ehrenstrom and Walter Muelder (eds.), INSTITUTIONALISM AND CHURCH UNITY. New York: Association Press, 1963, pp. 171-193.

2208. Mantzaridis, Georges. "La naissance du dogme relatif à l'unité de l'Eglise." SC 22,1 (1975): 19-32.

2209. Mehl, Roger. "Modifications dans la structure et la comportement des églises protestantes de France à la suite du movement oecuménique." ARCHIVES DE SOCIOLOGIE DES RELIGIONS 22 (1966): 81-88.

2210. Mol, Johannes J. (Hans). "The Merger Attempts of the Australian Churches." ECUMENICAL REVIEW 21 (1969): 21-31.

2211. Myers, Phyllis Goudy, and James D. Davidson. "Who Participates in Ecumenical Activity?" RRR 25,3 (1984): 185-203.

2212. Newman, William M. THE UNITED CHURCH OF CHRIST MERGER: A SOCIOLOGICAL ANALYSIS OF IDEAS, ORGANIZATIONS AND SOCIAL CHANGE. Unpublished Ph.D. dissertation, New School for Social Research, 1970.

2213. Pletsch, Donald J. ECUMENICISM IN TWO PROTESTANT CHURCHES IN ONTARIO. Unpublished M.Sc. thesis, University of Guelph, 1966.

2214. Saunders, LaVell E. "The Gradient of Ecumenism and Opposition to Religious Intermarriage." RRR 17,2 (1976): 107-119.

2215. Séguy, Jean. "Les oecuménismes du XVIIe siècle et les relations internationale de l'époque." ARCHIVES DE SOCIOLOGIE DES RELIGIONS 23 (1967): 129-134.

2216. Séguy, Jean. "Thèses et hypothèses en oecuménologie." SC 15,6 (1968): 433-442.

2217. Séguy, Jean. LES CONFLITS DU DIALOGUE. Paris: Cerf, 1973.

2218. Smith, P.M. "Protestant Comity in Metropolitan Pittsburgh." AMERICAN SOCIOLOGICAL REVIEW 8 (1943): 425-432.

2219. Taggart, Morris. "Ecumenical Attitudes in the Evangelical Covenant Church of America." RRR 9 (1967): 36-44.

2220. Thomas, John L. RELIGION AND THE AMERICAN PEOPLE. Westminster, Maryland: Newman, 1963.

2221. Turner, Bryan S. "Institutional Persistence and Ecumenism in Northern Methodism." In David Martin (ed.), A SOCIOLOGICAL YEARBOOK OF RELIGION IN BRITAIN 2. London: SCM, 1969, pp. 47-57.

2222. Turner, Bryan S. "The Sociological Explanation of Ecumenicalism." EXPOSITORY TIMES 82,12 (1971): 356-361. Reprinted in C.L. Mitton (ed.), THE SOCIAL SCIENCES AND THE CHURCHES. Edinburgh: T. & T. Clark, 1972.

2223. Van Leeuwen, Bertulf. "Législation des mariages mixtes et rapports entre catholiques et protestants." SC 11,2 (1964): 1-12.

Schism

2224. Doherty, Robert W. "Religion and Society: The Hicksite Separation of 1827." AMERICAN QUARTERLY 17,1 (1965): 63-80.

2225. Doherty, Robert W. THE HICKSITE SEPARATION: A SOCIOLOGICAL ANALYSIS OF RELIGIOUS SCHISM IN EARLY NINETEENTH CENTURY AMERICA. New Brunswick, N.J.: Rutgers University Press, 1967.

* Fahey, Frank J., and Djuro Vrga. "The Anomic Character of a Schism. Differential Perception of Functions of the Serbian Orthodox Church by Two Feuding Factions." Cited above as item 24.

2226. Fanfani, Amintore. SCISMA E SPIRITO CAPITALISTICO IN INGHLITERRA. Milano: Dovida e Gadda, 1932.

2227. Guilbaud, Georges T. "Deux fois treize ou une théorie du schisme." ARCHIVES DE SCIENCES SOCIALES DES RELIGIONS 45,2 (1978): 181-187.

2228. Mitchell, Robert Cameron. "Towards the Sociology of Religious Independency." JOURNAL OF RELIGION IN AFRICA 3 (1970): 2-21.

2229. O'Dea, Thomas F. "Catholic Sectarianism: A Sociological Analysis of the So-Called Boston Heresy Case." RRR 3 (1961): 49-63. Also in T.F. O'Dea, SOCIOLOGY AND THE STUDY OF RELIGION (volume cited in item 2177), pp. 23-38.

2230. Rogerson, Alan. "Témoins de Jéhovah et Etudiants de la Bible. Qui est schismatique?" SC 24,1 (1977): 33-34.

2231. Takayama, K. Peter. "Strains, Conflicts, and Schisms in Protestant Denominations." In Ross P. Scherer (ed.), AMERICAN DENOMINATIONAL ORGANIZATION (item 1172), pp. 298-322.

2232. Tuberville, G. "Religious Schism in the Methodist Church: A Sociological Analysis of the Pine Grove Case." RURAL SOCIOLOGY 14 (1949): 29-39.

2233. Vrga, Djuro, and Frank J. Fahey. "The Relationship of Religious Practices and Beliefs to Schism." SA 31,1 (1970): 46-55.

2234. Wilson, John. "The Sociology of Schism." In M. Hill (ed.), A SOCIOLOGICAL YEARBOOK OF RELIGION IN BRITAIN, VOL. 4. London: SCM Press, 1971, pp. 1-20.

SECTION E: SOCIAL MOVEMENTS

Religious social movements involve the mobilization of resources and people around a religious cause, symbol or expectation.

Social movements (general)

* Aberle, D. "A Note on Relative Deprivation Theory as Applied to Millenarian and Other Cult Movements." Cited above as item 131.

2235. Beckford, James A. "Explaining Religious Movements." INTERNATIONAL SOCIAL SCIENCE JOURNAL 29,2 (1977): 235-239.

2236. Beckford, James A. "Interprétation des mouvements religieux." REVUE INTERNATIONALE DES SCIENCES SOCIALES 29,2 (1977): 257-271.

2237. Bernard, G., and P. Caprasse. "Religious Movements in the Congo: A Research Hypothesis." CAHIERS ECONOMIQUES ET SOCIAUX 3,1 (1965): 49-60.

* Bourg, Carroll J. "The Politics of Religious Movements." Cited above as item 1533.

2238. Bromley, David G., and Anson D. Shupe, Jr. "MOONIES" IN AMERICA. CULT, CHURCH, AND CRUSADE. Beverly Hills, California: Sage, 1979.

2239. Bromley, David G., and Anson D. Shupe, Jr. "'Just a Few Years Seem Like a Lifetime': A Role Theory Approach to Participation in Religious Movements." In Louis Kriesberg (ed.), RESEARCH IN SOCIAL MOVEMENTS, CONFLICT AND CHANGE. Greenwich, Connecticut: Jai Press, 1979.

* Dann, Norman K. CONCURRENT SOCIAL MOVEMENTS: A STUDY OF THE INTERRELATIONSHIPS BETWEEN POPULIST POLITICS AND HOLINESS RELIGION. Cited above as item 1556.

2240. De Craemer, Willy. THE JAMAA AND THE CHURCH. A BANTU CATHOLIC MOVEMENT IN ZAIRE. New York: Oxford University Press, 1977.

2241. Farquhar, J.N. MODERN RELIGIOUS MOVEMENTS OF INDIA. New York: Macmillan, 1915.

2242. Fernandez, J.W. "African Religious Movements -- Types and Dynamics." JOURNAL OF MODERN AFRICAN STUDIES 2,4 (1964): 531-549.

2243. Ferreira de Camargo, P.C. O MOVIMENTO DE NATAL. The Hague: Institute of Social Studies, 1968.

2244. Finn, James. "American Catholics and Social Movements." In Philip Gleason (ed.), CONTEMPORARY CATHOLICISM IN THE UNITED STATES. Notre Dame: University of Notre Dame Press, 1969, pp. 127-146.

2245. Fry, Peter F. "Manchester, século XIX e São Paulo século XX -- dois movimentos religiosos." RELIGIAO E SOCIEDADE 3 (1978): 25-52.

2246. Gerlach, Luther P., and Virginia H. Hine. "Five Factors Crucial to the Growth and Spread of a Modern Religious Movement." JSSR 7 (1968): 23-40.

2247. Gerlach, Luther P., and Virginia H. Hine. PEOPLE, POWER, CHANGE: MOVEMENTS OF SOCIAL TRANSFORMATION. Indianapolis: Bobbs-Merrill, 1970.

* Greil, Arthur L. "Previous Dispositions and Conversion to Perspectives of Social and Religious Movements." Cited above as item 1978.

2248. Harrison, Michael I. "Dimensions of Involvement in Social Movements." SOCIOLOGICAL FOCUS 10 (1977): 353-366.

2249. Harrison, Michael I., and John K. Maniha. "Dynamics of Dissenting Movements Within Established Organizations: Two Cases and a Theoretical Interpretation." JSSR 17,3 (1978): 207-224.

2250. Houtart, François. "Mouvements religieux du tiers-monde, formes de protestation contre l'introduction de rapports sociaux capitalistes (parties 1 et 2)." CIVILISATIONS 27,1-2 (1977): 81-98; 27,3-4 (1977): 245-258.

2251. Houtart, François, and André Rousseau. L'EGLISE ET LES MOUVEMENTS REVOLUTIONNAIRES. Brussels: Ed. Vie Ouvrière, 1972.

* Jeffrey, Robin. "Religious Symbolisation of the Transition from Caste to Class: The Temple-Entry Movement in Travancore, 1860-1940." Cited above as item 1904.

2252. Johnson, Norris R., David A. Choate, and William Bunis. "Attendance at a Billy Graham Crusade: A Resource Mobilization Approach." SA 45,4 (1984): 383-392.

2253. King, Arthur. "Religion and Rights: A Dissenting Minority as a Social Movement in Romania." SC 28,1 (1981): 113-119.

* Kohn, Rachael L.E. "Praising the Lord and Penetrating the Community: Transition and Dual Leadership Functions in a Contemporary Hebrew Christian Group." Cited above as item 922.

* Lanternari, Vittorio. "Syncrétismes, messianismes, néo-traditionalismes. Postface à une étude des mouvements religieux de l'Afrique Noire." Cited above as item 401.

2254. Leverrier, Roger. "Arrière-plan socio-politique et caractéristiques des nouvelles religions au Corée. Le cas du Tong Hak." SC 25,2 (1978): 217-237.

2255. Liebman, Robert C. "Mobilizing the Moral Majority." In R. Liebman and R. Wuthnow (eds.), THE NEW CHRISTIAN RIGHT (item 119), pp. 49-73.

2256. Lofland, John, and Michael Jamison. "Social Movement Locals: Modal Member Structures." SA 45,2 (1984): 115-129.

2257. Maiolo, John R., William V. D'Antonio, and William T. Liu. "Sources and Management of Strain in a Social Movement: Some Preliminary Observations." SA 29,2 (1968): 67-78.

2258. Mayrl, William W. "Marx' Theory of Social Movements and the Church-Sect Typology." SA 37,1 (1976): 19-31.

2259. McNall, Scott G. "The Sect Movement." PACIFIC SOCIOLOGICAL REVIEW 6 (1963): 60-64.

2260. Morgan, J. Graham. "The Development of Sociology and the Social Gospel in America." SA 30,1 (1969): 42-53.

2261. Murvar, Vatro. "Towards a Sociological Theory of Religious Movements." JSSR 141 (1975): 229-256.

2262. Nelson, Charles H. "The Eric Janssonist Movement of Pre-Industrial Sweden." SA 38,3 (1977): 209-225.

2263. Newman, William M., and William V. D'Antonio. "For Christ's Sake: A Study of Key '73 in New England." RRR 19,2 (1978): 139-153.

* O'Toole, Roger. "Some Social-Psychological Aspects of Sectarian Social Movements: A Study in Politics and Religion." Cited above as item 1663.

2264. Pfautz, Harold W. CHRISTIAN SCIENCE. THE SOCIOLOGY OF A SOCIAL MOVEMENT AND RELIGIOUS GROUP. Unpublished Ph.D. dissertation, University of Chicago, 1954.

2265. Pickering, W.S.F. "'Religious Movements' of Church Members in Two Working-Class Towns in England." ARCHIVES DE SOCIOLOGIE DES RELIGIONS 11 (1961): 129-140.

* Pillai, Mary. "The Non-Brahmin Movement and Desacralization." Cited above as item 1857.

2266. Poulat, Emile. "Contrôle et production des mouvements religieux." ARCHIVES DE SCIENCES SOCIALES DES RELIGIONS 50,1 (1980): 129-141.

2267. Rodinson, Maxime. "Mouvements sociaux et mouvements idéologiques." CAHIERS INTERNATIONAUX DE SOCIOLOGIE 53 (1972): 197-212.

* Rouleau, Jean-Paul. "Mouvement et ordres religieux aujourd'hui." Cited above as item 1360.

2268. Schrey, Henry H. "Sectes et mouvements religieux." CHRONIQUE SOCIAL DE LA FRANCE 62 (1954): 467-532.

2269. Shupe, Anson David, Jr. "Toward a Structural Perspective of Modern Religious Movements." SOCIOLOGICAL FOCUS 6 (1973): 83-99.

2270. Shupe, Anson D., and David G. Bromley. "The Moonies and the Anti-Cultists: Movement and Countermovement in Conflict." SA 40,4 (1979): 325-334. Reprinted in J.K. Hadden and T.E. Long (eds.), RELIGION AND RELIGIOSITY IN AMERICA (volume cited in item 110), pp. 70-83.

2271. Siffredi, Alejandra. "Movimenti socio-religiosi fra gli Indios del Chaco argentino." CRITICA SOCIOLOGICA 36 (1975-76): 167-204.

* Snow, David A. "A Dramaturgical Analysis of Movement Accommmo-dation: Building Idiosyncrasy Credit as a Movement Mobilization Strategy." Cited above as item 377.

2272. Stark, Rodney, and William Sims Bainbridge. "Of Churches, Sects, and Cults: Preliminary Concepts for a Theory of Religious Movements." JSSR 18,2 (1979): 117-133.

* Stark, Rodney, and Lynne Roberts. "The Arithmetic of Social Movements: Theoretical Implications." Cited above as item 81.

* Theobald, Robin. "The Role of Charisma in the Development of Social Movements." Cited above as item 86.

2273. Wallace, Anthony F.C. "Revitalization Movements." AMERICAN ANTHROPOLOGIST 58 (1956): 264-281.

2274. Wallis, Roy. SALVATION AND PROTEST: STUDIES OF SOCIAL AND RELIGIOUS MOVEMENTS. New York: St. Martin's Press, 1979.

2275. Watson, G. Llewellyn. "Social Structure and Social Movements: The Black Muslims in the U.S.A. and the Ras-Tafarians in Jamaica." BRITISH JOURNAL OF SOCIOLOGY 24,3 (1973): 188-204.

2276. Wertheim, Willem F. "Religious Reform Movements in South and South-East Asia." ARCHIVES DE SOCIOLOGIE DES RELIGIONS 12 (1961): 53-62.

2277. Willems, Emilio. "Religious Mass Movements and Social Change in Brazil." In Eric N. Baklanoff (ed.), NEW PERSPECTIVES OF BRAZIL. Nashville: Vanderbilt University Press, 1966, pp. 205-232.

* Wolcott, Roger T. "The Church and Social Action: Steelworkers and Bishops in Youngstown." Cited above as item 1748.

2278. Wuthnow, Robert. "World Order and Religious Movements." In Albert Bergesen (ed.), STUDIES OF THE MODERN WORLD SYSTEM. New York: Academic Press, 1980, pp. 57-75.

2279. Zald, Mayer N. "Theological Crucibles: Social Movements in and of Religion." RRR 23,4 (1982): 317-336.

2280. Zylberberg, Jacques. "Le dieu caché retrouvé: le mouvement vers le sacré." LES MOUVEMENTS RELIGIEUX AUJOURD'HUI. THEORIES ET PRATIQUES. LES CAHIERS DE RECHERCHES EN SCIENCES DE LA RELIGION 5 (1984): 19-51.

Anti-cult movement

2281. Beckford, James A. "Politics and the Anti-Cult Movement." ANNUAL REVIEW OF THE SOCIAL SCIENCES OF RELIGION 3 (1979): 169-190.

2282. Bromley, David G., and James T. Richardson (eds.) THE BRAIN-WASHING/DEPROGRAMMING CONTROVERSY: SOCIOLOGICAL, PSYCHOLOGICAL, LEGAL AND HISTORICAL PERSPECTIVES. Lewiston, N.Y.: Edwin Mellen Press, 1983.

* Kim, Byong-suh. "Religious Deprogramming and Subjective Reality." Cited above as item 1987.

2283. Richardson, James T., and Barend van Driel. "Public Support for Anti-Cult Legislation." JSSR 23,4 (1984): 412-418.

2284. Robbins, Thomas. "Religious Movements, the State, and the Law: Reconceptualizing 'the Cult Problem.'" REVIEW OF LAW AND SOCIAL CHANGE 9,1 (1980): 33-49.

2285. Robbins, Thomas, and Dick Anthony. "Deprogramming, Brainwashing and the Medicalization of Deviant Religious Groups." SOCIAL PROBLEMS 29,3 (1982): 283-297.

2286. Shupe, Anson D., and David G. Bromley. THE NEW VIGILANTES: DEPROGRAMMERS, ANTI-CULTISTS, AND THE NEW RELIGIONS. Beverly Hills: Sage, 1980.

2287. Shupe, Anson D., and David G. Bromley. "Apostates and Atrocity Stories: Some Parameters in the Dynamics of Deprogramming." In Bryan R. Wilson (ed.), THE SOCIAL IMPACT OF NEW RELIGIOUS MOVEMENTS. New York: Rose of Sharon Press, 1981, pp. 179-215.

2288. Shupe, Anson D., Bert L. Hardin, and David G. Bromley. "A Comparison of Anti-Cult Movements in the United States and West Germany." In E. Barker (ed.), OF GODS AND MEN (item 2396), pp. 177-194.

2289. Shupe, Anson D., Roger Spielmann, and Sam Stigall. "Deprogramming. The New Exorcism." AMERICAN BEHAVIORAL SCIENTIST 20,6 (1977): 941-956.

Civil rights

* Ammerman, Nancy Tatom. LOCALISM, SOUTHERN CULTURE, AND THE ROLE OF CLERGYMEN IN THE CIVIL RIGHTS MOVEMENT IN A SOUTHERN COMMUNITY. Cited above as item 542.

* Ammerman, Nancy T. "The Civil Rights Movement and the Clergy in a Southern Community." Cited above as item 543.

2290. Blasi, Anthony J. SEGREGATIONIST VIOLENCE AND CIVIL RIGHTS MOVEMENTS IN TUSCALOOSA. Washington: University Press of America, 1980.

2291. Bloom, J. THE NEGRO CHURCH AND THE MOVEMENT FOR EQUALITY. Unpublished M.A. thesis, University of California at Berkeley, 1966.

* Burnham, Kenneth E., John F. Connors, III, and Richard C. Leonard. "Religious Affiliation, Church Attendance, Religious Education and Student Attitudes toward Race." Cited above as item 424.

* Campbell, Ernest Q., and Thomas F. Pettigrew. CHRISTIANS IN RACIAL CRISIS: A STUDY OF LITTLE ROCK'S MINISTRY. Cited above as item 572.

* Campbell, Ernest Q., and Thomas F. Pettigrew. "Racial and Moral Crisis: The Role of Little Rock Ministers." Cited above as item 571.

* Demerath, Nicholas J., III, Gerald Marwell, and Michael T. Aiken. DYNAMICS OF IDEALISM. Cited above as item 1732.

2292. Earle, Clifford J. "How Presbyterians Think about Civil Rights." SOCIAL PROGRESS (CHURCH AND SOCIETY) 59 (1969): 5-35.

2293. Eckhardt, Kenneth W. "Religiosity and Civil Rights Militancy." RRR 11 (1970): 197-203.

2294. Fish, John, Gordon Nelson, Walter Stuhr, and Lawrence Witmer. THE EDGE OF THE GHETTO. A STUDY OF CHURCH INVOLVEMENT IN COMMUNITY ORGANIZATION. New York: Seabury, 1968.

2295. Fukuyama, Yoshio. "Parishioners' Attitudes towards Issues in the Civil Rights Movement." SA 29,2 (1968): 94-103.

* Hadden, Jeffrey K., and Raymond C. Rymph. "Social Structure and Civil Rights Involvement: A Case Study of Protestant Ministers." Cited above as item 1735.

2296. Hunt, Larry L., and Janet G. Hunt. "Black Religion as Both Opiate and Inspiration of Civil Rights Militance: Putting Marx's Data to the Test." SOCIAL FORCES 56,1 (1977): 1-14.

2297. Johnstone, Ronald L. MILITANT AND CONSERVATIVE COMMUNITY LEADERSHIP AMONG NEGRO CLERGYMEN. Unpublished Ph.D. dissertation, University of Michigan, 1963.

2298. Lamanna, Richard A., and J.J. Coakley. "The Catholic Church and the Negro." In P. Gleason (ed.), CONTEMPORARY CATHOLICISM IN THE UNITED STATES (volume cited in item 2244), pp. 147-194.

2299. Lee, Carleton. "Religious Roots of Negro Protest." In Arnold Rose (ed.), ASSURING FREEDOM TO THE FREE. Detroit: Wayne State University Press, 1964.

2300. Marx, Gary T. PROTEST AND PREJUDICE. A STUDY OF BELIEF IN THE BLACK COMMUNITY. New York: Harper and Row, 1967.

2301. Marx, Gary T. "Religion: Opiate or Inspiration of Civil Rights Militancy among Negroes?" AMERICAN SOCIOLOGICAL REVIEW 32 (1967): 64-72.

2302. McCoy, Charles S. "The Churches and Protest Movements for Racial Justice." In R. Lee and M.Marty (eds.), RELIGION AND SOCIAL CONFLICT (volume cited in item 141), pp. 37-54.

2303. Nelsen, Hart M., Thomas W. Madron, and Raytha Yokley. "Black Religion's Promethean Motif: Orthodoxy and Militancy." AMERICAN JOURNAL OF SOCIOLOGY 81 (1975): 139-146.

2304. Nelsen, Hart M., and Raytha Yokley. "Presbyterians, Civil Rights and Church Pronouncements." RRR 12,1 (1970): 43-50.

2305. Nelsen, Hart M., and Raytha Yokley. "Civil Rights Attitudes of Rural and Urban Presbyterians." RURAL SOCIOLOGY 35 (1970): 161-174.

* Quinley, Harold E. THE PROPHETIC CLERGY. SOCIAL ACTIVISM AMONG PROTESTANT MINISTERS. Cited above as item 289.

2306. Roy, Ralph Lord. "The Clergyman and the Civil Rights Movement." SOCIAL FORCES 10,6 (1963): 548-549.

* Tygart, Clarence E. "The Role of Theology among other 'Belief' Variables for Clergy Civil Rights Activism." Cited above as item 787.

2307. Wood, James R. PROTESTANT ENFORCEMENT OF RACIAL INTEGRATION POLICY: A SOCIOLOGICAL STUDY IN THE POLITICAL ECONOMY OF ORGANIZATIONS. Unpublished Ph.D. dissertation, Vanderbilt University, 1967.

* Wood, James R. "Authority and Controversial Policy: The Churches and Civil Rights." Cited above as item 1213.

2308. Wood, James R. "Unanticipated Consequences of Organizational Coalitions: Ecumenical Cooperation and Civil Rights Policy." SOCIAL FORCES 50 (1971): 512-521.

* Wood, James R. "Personal Commitment and Organizational Constraint: Church Officials and Racial Integration." Cited above as item 1189.

* Wood, James R. "Legitimate Control and 'Organizational Transcendence.'" Cited above as item 1190.

* Wood, James R. LEADERSHIP IN VOLUNTARY ORGANIZATIONS. THE CONTROVERSY OVER SOCIAL ACTION IN PROTESTANT CHURCHES. Cited above as item 1191.

2309. Wood, James R., and Mayer N. Zald. "Aspects of Racial Integration in the Methodist Church: Sources of Resistance to Organizational Policy." SOCIAL FORCES 45 (1966): 255-265.

Messianism and millenarianism

Religious movements sometimes arise from an expected coming of a messiah. This is usually coupled with a dramatic condemnation of the prevailing world order.

* Aberle, D. "A Note on Relative Deprivation Theory as Applied to Millenarian and other Cult Movements." Cited above as item 131.

2310. Allan, Graham. "A Theory of Millennialism: The Irvingite Movement as an Illustration." BRITISH JOURNAL OF SOCIOLOGY 25,3 (1974): 296-311.

* Baer, Hans A. THE LEVITES OF UTAH: THE DEVELOPMENT OF AND CONVERSION TO A SMALL MILLENARIAN SECT. Cited above as item 1237.

2311. Balandier, Georges. "Messianismes et nationalismes en Afrique noire." CAHIERS INTERNATIONAUX DE SOCIOLOGIE 14 (1953): 41-65.

2312. Balandier, Georges. "Brèves remarques sur les messianismes de l'Afrique Congolaise." ARCHIVES DE SOCIOLOGIE DES RELIGIONS 5 (1958): 91-95.

2313. Barabas, Alicia M. "Mesianismo chinauteco. Una respuesta politico-religiosa ante la crisis." REVISTA MEXICANA DE CIENCIAS POLITICAS Y SOCIALES 23,88 (1977): 53-85.

2314. Barber, Bernard. "Acculturation and Messianic Movements." AMERICAN SOCIOLOGICAL REVIEW 6 (1941): 663-669.

2315. Barkum, Michael. "Millenarianism in the Modern World." THEORY AND SOCIETY 1,2 (1974): 117-146.

2316. Bastide, Roger. "Le messianisme chez les Noirs du Brésil." MONDE NON-CRETIEN (N.S.) 3 (1950): 301-308.

2317. Bastide, Roger. "Le messianisme raté." ARCHIVES DE SOCIOLOGIE DES RELIGIONS 5 (1958): 31-37.

2318. Bastide, Roger. "Messianisme et développement économique et social." CAHIERS INTERNATIONAUX DE SOCIOLOGIE 31 (1961): 3-14.

2319. Bastide, Roger. "Le messianisme et la faim." In R. Bastide (ed.), LE PROCHAIN ET LA LOINTAIN. Paris: Cujas, 1970, pp. 259-266.

2320. Bayer, A.E. "The Man Who Died. A Narrative Account of the Dutch Fisherman, Lou, and His Group." RRR 10 (1969): 81-88.

2321. Berger, Peter L. "Motif messianique et processus social dans le Bahaisme." ARCHIVES DE SOCIOLOGIE DES RELIGIONS 4 (1957): 93-107.

2322. Birnbaum, Norman. "Luther et le millénarisme." ARCHIVES DE SOCIOLOGIE DES RELIGIONS 5 (1958): 101-102.

2323. Burridge, Kenelm. NEW HEAVEN, NEW EARTH: A STUDY OF MILLENARIAN ACTIVITIES. New York: Schocken, 1975.

2324. Busch, Lawrence. "A Tentative Guide to Constructing the Future: Self-Conscious Millenarianism." SOCIOLOGICAL PRACTICE 1,1 (1976): 27-39.

2325. Chesneaux, Jean. "Le millénarisme des Taïping." ARCHIVES DE SOCIOLOGIE DES RELIGIONS 16 (1963): 122-124.

2326. Cohn, Norman. THE PURSUIT OF THE MILLENNIUM. New York: Harper, 1957.

2327. Cohn, Norman. Réflexions sur le millénarisme." ARCHIVES DE SOCIOLOGIE DES RELIGIONS 5 (1958): 103-107.

2328. Cohn, Norman. "Medieval Millenarism: Its Bearing on the Comparative Study of Millenarian Movements." In S.L. Thrupp (ed.), MILLENNIAL DREAMS IN ACTION (volume cited in item 131), pp. 31-43. Also in L. Schneider (ed.), RELIGION, CULTURE AND SOCIETY (volume cited in item 1824), pp. 168-178.

2329. Cozin, Mark. "A Millenarian Movement in Korea and Great Britain." SOCIOLOGICAL YEARBOOK OF RELIGION IN BRITAIN 6 (1973): 100-121.

2330. Desroche, Henri. "Les messianismes et la catégorie de l'échec." CAHIERS INTERNATIONAUX DE SOCIOLOGIE N.S. 10,35 (1963): 61-84.

2331. Desroche, Henri. DIEUX D'HOMMES. DICTIONNAIRE DES MESSIANISMES ET MILLENARISMES DE L'ERE CHRETIENNE. La Haye, Paris: Mouton, 1969.

2332. Desroche, Henri. "Idéologies révolutionnaires et messianismes religieux." ECONOMIE ET HUMANISME 196 (1970): 11-32.

2333. Desroche, Henri. SOCIOLOGIE DE L'ESPERANCE. Calmann-Lévy, 1973. SOCIOLOGY OF HOPE, translated by Carol Martin-Sperry. London: Routledge and Kegan Paul, 1979.

2334. Desroche, Henri, and J. Gutwirth. "Un Messianisme juif." ARCHIVES DE SCIENCES SOCIALES DES RELIGIONS 40 (1975): 139-143.

2335. Eberhardt, J. "Messianisme en Afrique du Sud." ARCHIVES DE SOCIOLOGIE DES RELIGIONS 4 (1957): 31-56.

2336. Eichler, M. "Some Comments Concerning Murvar's 'Messianism in Russia: Religious and Revolutionary.'" JSSR 11,2 (1972): 187-191.

2337. Fuchs, Stephen. REBELLIOUS PROPHETS: A STUDY OF MESSIANIC MOVEMENTS IN INDIAN RELIGIONS. London: Asia Publishing House, 1965.

2338. Gonzalez-Estefani y Robles, J.M. MESSIANISMO Y SECULARIZACION EN LOS MOVIMIENTOS SOCIALES CONTEMPORANEOS. Madrid, 1969.

2339. Guiart, Jean. "Institutions religieuses traditionelles et messianismes moderns à Fiji." ARCHIVES DE SOCIOLOGIE DES RELIGIONS 4 (1957): 3-30.

2340. Guiart, Jean. "Naissance et avortement d'un messianisme." ARCHIVES DE SOCIOLOGIE DES RELIGIONS 7 (1959): 3-44.

2341. Guiart, Jean, and Peter Worsley. "La répartition des mouvements millénaristes en Mélanésie." ARCHIVES DE SOCIOLOGIE DES RELIGIONS 5 (1958): 38-46.

2342. Hadzimichali, Nectaire. "L'Eglise Orthodoxe grecque et le messianisme en Afrique." SC 22,1 (1975): 85-96.

2343. Haubert, M. "Indiens et Jésuites au Paraguay. Rencontre de deux messianismes." ARCHIVES DE SOCIOLOGIE DES RELIGIONS 27 (1969): 119-133.

* Juarez Rubens Brandão Lopes. DESENVOLVIMENTO E MUNDANÇA SOCIAL: FORMAÇAO DA SOCIEDADE URBANO-INDUSTRIAL NO BRASIL. Cited above as item 27.

2344. Kanter, Rosabeth Moss. "Commitment and the Internal Organization of Millennial Movements." AMERICAN BEHAVIORAL SCIENTIST 16,2 (1972): 219-243.

2345. Kaufmann, Robert. MILLENARISME ET ACCULTURATION. Bruxelles: Institut de Sociologie de l'Université Libre de Bruxelles, 1964.

2346. Kovalevsky, Pierre. "Millénarisme et parousie, messianisme et missions chrétiennes." ARCHIVES DE SOCIOLOGIE DES RELIGIONS 5 (1958): 108-110.

2347. Kovalevsky, Pierre. "Messianisme et millénarisme russes?" ARCHIVES DE SOCIOLOGIE DES RELIGIONS 5 (1958): 47-70.

2348. La Barre, Weston. "Materials for a History of Studies of Crisis Cults: A Bibliographic Essay." CURRENT ANTHROPOLOGY 12 (1971): 3-44.

2349. Lanternari, Vittorio. THE RELIGIONS OF THE OPPRESSED. A STUDY OF MODERN MESSIANIC CULTS, translated by Lisa Sergio. New York: Knopf, 1963.

* Lanternari, Vittorio. "Syncrétismes, messianismes, néo-traditionalismes. Postface à une étude des mouvements religieux de l'Afrique Noire." Cited above as item 401.

* Lebra, Takie Sugiyama. "Millenarian Movements and Resocialization." Cited above as item 1993.

2350. Lewy, Guenter. RELIGION AND REVOLUTION. New York: Oxford University Press, 1974.

2351. Mêtraux, Alfred. "Messiahs of South America." INTER-AMERICAN QUARTERLY 3,2 (1941): 53-60.

2352. Mêtraux, Alfred. "Les messies de l'Amérique du Sud." ARCHIVES DE SOCIOLOGIE DES RELIGIONS 4 (1957): 108-112.

2353. Mühlmann, Wilhelm E. (ed.) CHILIASMUS UND NATIVISMUS. STUDIEN ZUR PSYCHOLOGIE, SOZIOLOGIE UND HISTORISCHEN KASUISTIK DER UMSTURZBEWEGUNGEN. Berlin, 1961.

2354. Mühlmann, Wilhelm E. MESSIANISMES REVOLUTIONNAIRES DU TIERS MONDE, translated by J. Baudrillard. Paris: Gallimard, 1968.

2355. Murvar, Vatro. "Messianism in Russia: Religious and Revolutionary." JSSR 10 (1973): 277-338.

2356. Negrão, Lisias N. "Messianismo e espiritismo." CADERNOS (Brazil) 8 (1975): 329-357.

2357. O'Connor, Mary. "Two Kinds of Religious Movements among the Mayo Indians of Sonora, Mexico." JSSR 18,3 (1979): 260-268.

2358. Pereira de Queiroz, M. Isaura. "Messiasbewegungen in Brasilien." STADEN-JAHRBUCH 4 (1956): 133-144.

2359. Pereira de Queiroz, M. Isaura. LA GUERRE SAINTE AU BRESIL: LE MOUVEMENT MESSIANIQUE DU CONTESTADO. São Paulo, 1957.

2360. Pereira de Queiroz, M. Isaura. "Die Fanatiker des 'Contestado.'" STADEN-JAHRBUCH 5 (1957): 203-215.

2361. Pereira de Queiroz, Maria Isaura. "L'influence de milieu social interne sur les mouvements messianiques brésiliens." ARCHIVES DE SOCIOLOGIE DES RELIGIONS 5 (1958): 3-30.

2362. Pereira de Queiroz, M. Isaura. "Classifications des messianismes brésiliens." ARCHIVES DE SOCIOLOGIE DES RELIGIONS 5 (1958): 111-120.

2363. Pereira de Queiroz, Maria Isaura. "Mouvements messianiques et developpement économique au Brésil." ARCHIVES DE SOCIOLOGIE DES RELIGIONS 16 (1963): 109-121.

2364. Pereira de Queiroz, M. Isaura. "Indianische Messiasbewegungen in Brasilien." STADEN-JAHRBUCH 11,2 (1963-64): 31-44.

2365. Pereira de Queiroz, Maria Isaura. "Millénarismes et messianismes." ANNALES. ECONOMIES, SOCIETES, CIVILISATIONS 19 (1964): 330-344.

2366. Pereira de Queiroz, Maria Isaura. REFORME ET REVOLUTION DANS LES SOCIETES TRADITIONNELLES: HISTOIRE ET ETHNOLOGIE DES MOUVEMENTS MESSIANIQUES. Paris: Anthropos, 1968.

2367. Pereira de Queiroz, Maria Isaura. "Mythes et mouvements messianiques." DIOGENE 90 (1975): 90-114.

2368. Pereira de Queioroz, Maria Isaura. "Messies, thaumaturges et 'dualité catholique' au Brésil." REVUE INTERNATIONALE DES SCIENCES SOCIALES 29,2 (1977): 323-337.

2369. Queiroz, Vinhas Maurício de. MESSIANISMO E CONFLITO SOCIAL. Rio de Janeiro, 1966.

2370. Séguy, Jean. "David Lazzaretti et le secte apocalyptique des Giurisdavidici." ARCHIVES DE SOCIOLOGIE DES RELIGIONS 5 (1958): 71-87.

2371. Séguy, Jean. "Messianisme et échec social; les Témoins de Jéhovah." ARCHIVES DE SOCIOLOGIE DES RELIGIONS 21 (1966): 89-100.

2372. Séguy, Jean. "Millénarisme et 'ordres adventistes': Grignion de Montfort et les 'Apôtres des Derniers Temps.'" ARCHIVES DE SCIENCES SOCIALES DES RELIGIONS 53,1 (1982): 23-48.

2373. Sharot, Stephen. "Jewish Millenarianism: A Comparison of Medieval Communities." COMPARATIVE STUDIES IN SOCIETY AND HISTORY 22,3 (1980): 394-415.

2374. Sharot, Stephen. MESSIANISM, MYSTICISM, AND MAGIC: A SOCIOLOGICAL ANALYSIS OF JEWISH RELIGIOUS MOVEMENTS. Chapel Hill, North Carolina: University of North Carolina Press, 1982.

* Sinda, M. LE MESSIANISME CONGOLAIS ET SES INCIDENCES POLITIQUES. Cited above as item 1695.

2375. Stark, Werner. "The Psychology of Social Messianism." SOCIAL RESEARCH 25,2 (1958): 145-157.

2376. Straelen, H. van. "Un messianisme japonais contemporain." ARCHIVES DE SOCIOLOGIE DES RELIGIONS 4 (1957): 123-132.

2377. Talmon, Yonina. "Pursuit of the Millennium: The Relation between Religious and Social Change." ARCHIVES EUROPEENNES DE SOCIOLOGIE 3,1 (1962): 125-148.

2378. Talmon, Yonina. "Millenarian Movements." ARCHIVES EUROPEENNES DE SOCIOLOGIE 7,2 (1966): 159-200.

2379. Talmon, Yonina. "Conditions de développement des groupements millénaristes." ARCHIVES EUROPEENNES DE SOCIOLOGIE 7,2 (1973): 159-200.

2380. Urbano, Henrique Osvaldo. "Millénarisme et trinité chrétienne. Quelques notes sur le discours millénariste dans les Andes." LES CAHIERS DU CENTRE DE RECHERCHES EN SOCIOLOGIE RELIGIEUSE 1 (1977): 133-144.

* Wallis, Roy (ed.) MILLENNIALISM AND CHARISMA. Cited above as item 89.

2381. Wallis, Wilson D. MESSIAHS, THEIR ROLE IN CIVILIZATION. Washington: American Council on Public Affairs, 1943. Excerpts in J.M. Yinger (ed.), RELIGION, SOCIETY AND THE INDIVIDUAL (volume cited in item 943), pp. 578-586.

2382. Wallis, Wilson D. "Quelques aspects du messianisme." ARCHIVES DE SOCIOLOGIE DES RELIGIONS 5 (1958): 99-100.

2383. Werner, Ernest. "Les mouvements messianiques au Moyen Age." ARCHIVES DE SOCIOLOGIE DES RELIGIONS 16 (1963): 73-75.

2384. Wilson, Bryan R. MAGIC AND THE MILLENNIUM. New York: Harper and Row, 1973.

2385. Worsley, Peter. THE TRUMPET SHALL SOUND. A STUDY OF CARGO CULTS IN MELANESIA. London: MacGibbon and Kee, 1957.

2386. Zygmunt, Joseph F. "Prophetic Failure and Chiliastic Identity: The Case of Jehovah's Witnesses." AMERICAN JOURNAL OF SOCIOLOGY 75 (1970): 926-948.

New religions

Only works on new religions as a general socio-cultural phenomenon are included; studies of individual new religions are omitted.

2387. Acquaviva, Sabino. IL SEME RELIGIOSO DELLA RIVOLTA. Milano: Rusconi, 1979.

* Aidala, Angela A. "Worldviews, Ideologies and Social Experimentation: Clarification and Replication of 'The Consciousness Reformation.'" Cited above as item 1236.

2388. Anthony, Dick, and Thomas Robbins. "The Effect of Detente on the Growth of New Religions: Reverend Moon and the Unification Church." In J. Needleman and G. Baker (eds.), UNDERSTANDING THE NEW RELIGIONS. New York: Seabury, 1979, pp. 80-100.

2389. Anthony, Dick, and Thomas Robbins. "New Religions, Families, and 'Brainwashing.'" In T. Robbins and D. Anthony (eds.), IN GODS WE TRUST (item 367), pp. 263-274.

2390. Anthony, Dick, and Thomas Robbins. "Spiritual Innovation and the Crisis of American Civil Religion." DAEDALUS 111,1 (1982): 215-234.

2391. Anthony, Dick, Thomas Robbins, and P. Schwartz. "Contemporary Religious Movements and the Secularisation Premise." CONCILIUM 161 (1983): 1-8.

2392. Bainbridge, William Sims, and Rodney Stark. "Cult Formation: Three Compatible Models." SA 40,4 (1979): 283-295. Also in J.K. Hadden and T.E. Long (eds.), RELIGION AND RELIGIOSITY IN AMERICA (volume cited in item 110), pp. 35-53.

2393. Balch, Robert W. "Bo and Peep: A Case Study of the Origins of Messianic Leadership." In Roy Wallis (ed.), MILLENNIALISM AND CHARISMA (item 89), pp. 13-72.

2394. Barker, Eileen (ed.) NEW RELIGIOUS MOVEMENTS: A PERSPECTIVE FOR UNDERSTANDING SOCIETY. New York: Mellen, 1982. Contains item 286.

2395. Barker, Eileen. "New Religious Movements in Britain: The Context and the Membership." SC 30,1 (1983): 33-48.

2396. Barker, Eileen (ed.) OF GODS AND MEN. NEW RELIGIOUS MOVEMENTS IN THE WEST. Proceedings of the 1981 Annual Conference of the British Sociological Association, Sociology of Religion Study Group. Macon, Georgia: Mercer University Press, 1983. Contains items 114, 123, 1533, 1997, 2157, 2288, 3264.

2397. Beckford, James A. "Cults, Controversy and Control: A Comparative Analysis of the Problems Posed by New Religious Movements in the Federal Republic of Germany and France." SA 42,3 (1981): 249-264.

2398. Beckford, James A. "Young People and New Religious Movements/Les jeunes générations et les nouveaux mouvements religieux. An Introduction/Introduction." SC 30,1 (1983): 5-12.

2399. Beckford, James A. "The Public Response to New Religious Movements in Britain." SC 30,1 (1983): 49-62.

2400. Beckford, James A. "Holistic Imagery and Ethics in New Religious and Healing Movements." SC 31,2-3 (1984): 259-272.

* Bird, Frederick. "Charisma and Ritual in New Religious Movements." Cited above as item 64.

* Bird, Frederick. "The Pursuit of Innocence: New Religious Movements and Moral Accountability." Cited above as item 180.

2401. Bird, Frederick, and William Reimer. "New Religious and Para-Religious Movements in Montreal." In S. Crysdale and L. Wheatcroft (eds.), RELIGION IN CANADIAN SOCIETY (volume cited in item 778), pp. 307-320.

2402. Bird, Frederick, and William Reimer. "Participation Rates in New Religious and Para-Religious Movements." JSSR 21,1 (1982): 1-14. Also in P.H. McNamara (ed.), RELIGION: NORTH AMERICAN STYLE (volume cited in item 117), pp. 283-295.

2403. Bromley, David G., and Anson D. Shupe, Jr. "Perfect Families: Visions of the Future in a New Religious Movement." MARRIAGE AND FAMILY REVIEW 4,3-4 (1981): 119-129.

2404. Coleman, John. "The Religious Significance of New Religious Movements." CONCILIUM 161 (1983): 9-16.

2405. Ellwood, Robert S., Jr. THE EAGLE AND THE RISING SUN: AMERICANS AND THE NEW RELIGIONS OF JAPAN. Philadelphia: Westminster Press, 1974.

* Ellwood, Robert S., Jr. ALTERNATIVE ALTARS. UNCONVENTIONAL AND EASTERN SPIRITUALITY IN AMERICA. Cited above as item 2129.

2406. Foucart, Eric. "Le phénomène des sectes. Essai de synthèse." LES CAHIERS DU CENTRE DE RECHERCHES EN SOCIOLOGIE RELIGIEUSE 2 (1978): 90-132.

2407. Glock, Charles Y., and Robert N. Bellah (eds.) THE NEW RELIGIOUS CONSCIOUSNESS. Berkeley: University of California Press, 1976. Contains items 539, 1066, 1492.

2408. Hardin, Bert. "Rückzug in die Innerlichkeit? Jugendsekten als moralisches Alternativerlebnis." In Martin Furian (ed.), GEFÄHRDEDE JUGEND. Heidelberg: Quelle & Meyer, 1980.

2409. Hardin, Bert. "Quelques aspects du phénomène des nouveaux mouvements religieux en République Fédérale d'Allemagne." SC 30,1 (1983): 13-32.

2410. Hardin, Bert, and W. Kuner. "Entstehung und Entwicklung der Vereinigungskirche in der Bundesrepublik Deutschland." In Günther Kehrer (ed.), DAS ENTSTEHEN EINER NEUEN RELIGION. München: Kösel Verlag, 1981.

* Jacobs, Janet. "The Economy of Love in Religious Commitment: The Deconversion of Women from Nontraditional Religious Movements." Cited above as item 1103.

* Johnson, Benton. "A Sociological Perspective on the New Religions." Cited above as item 94.

2411. Kilbourne, Brock K. "The Conway and Siegelman Claims Against Religious Cults: An Assessment of Their Data." JSSR 22,4 (1983): 380-385.

2412. Kilbourne, Brock K., and James T. Richardson. "Cults Versus Families: A Case of Misattribution of Cause?" MARRIAGE AND FAMILY REVIEW 4,3-4 (1981): 81-100.

2413. Kilbourne, Brock, and James T. Richardson. "Psychotherapy and New Religions in a Pluralistic Society." AMERICAN PSYCHOLOGIST 39,3 (1984): 237-251.

2414. Lans, Jan M. van der, and Frans Derks. "Les nouvelles religions aux Pays-Bas. Contexte, appartenance, réactions." SC 30,1 (1983): 63-83.

* Lofland, John. DOOMSDAY CULT. Cited above as item 987.

2415. Mat-Hasquin, Michèle. LES SECTES CONTEMPORAINES. Bruxelles: Editions de l'Université de Bruxelles, 1982.

2416. Morelli, Anne. "Les sectes religieuses sont-elles en Belgique un danger montant?" CAHIERS MARXISTES 91 (1981): 7-18.

2417. Morelli, Anne. "A propos des sectes religieuses en Belgique. Les recherches à l'Université de Bruxelles." SC 30,1 (1983): 137-141.

* Nordquist, Ted. ANANDA COOPERATIVE VILLAGE: A STUDY IN THE BELIEFS, VALUES, AND ATTITUDES OF A NEW AGE RELIGIOUS COMMUNITY. Cited above as item 1255.

2418. Preston, David L. "Becoming a Zen Practitioner." SA 42,1 (1981): 47-55.

2419. Rajana, E.W. A SOCIOLOGICAL STUDY OF NEW RELIGIOUS MOVEMENTS: CHILEAN PENTECOSTALISM AND JAPANESE NEW RELIGION. Unpublished Ph.D. dissertation, London School of Economics, 1974.

2420. Richardson, James T. "From Cult to Sect: Creative Eclecticism in New Religious Movements." PACIFIC SOCIOLOGICAL REVIEW 22 (1979): 139-166.

2421. Richardson, James T. "Financing the New Religions: Comparative and Theoretical Considerations." JSSR 21,3 (1982): 255-268.

2422. Richardson, James T. "New Religious Movements in the United States: A Review." SC 30,1 (1983): 85-110.

2423. Robbins, Thomas. "Church, State and Cult." SA 42,3 (1981): 209-226.

2424. Robbins, Thomas, and Dick Anthony. "New Religious Movements and the Social System." ANNUAL REVIEW OF THE SOCIAL SCIENCES OF RELIGION 2,1 (1978): 1-28.

* Robbins, Thomas, and Dick Anthony (eds.) IN GODS WE TRUST. Cited above as item 367.

* Scott, Gini Graham. CULT AND COUNTERCULT: A STUDY OF A SPIRITUAL GROWTH GROUP AND A WITCHCRAFT ORDER. Cited above as item 1069.

2425. Shupe, Anson D. SIX PERSPECTIVES ON NEW RELIGIONS: A CASE STUDY APPROACH. New York: Edwin Mellen, 1981.

2426. Stark, Rodney (ed.) RELIGIOUS MOVEMENTS: GENESIS, EXODUS AND NUMBERS. New York: Rose of Sharon Press, 1983.

* Stark, Rodney, and Lynne Roberts. "The Arithmetic of Social Movements: Theoretical Implications." Cited above as item 81.

* Tipton, Steven M. GETTING SAVED FORM THE SIXTIES. Cited above as item 195.

2427. Tipton, Steven M. "New Religious Movements and the Problems of a Modern Ethic." SOCIOLOGICAL INQUIRY 49,2-3 (1979): 286-312.

* Tipton, Steven M. GETTING SAVED FROM THE SIXTIES. Cited above as item 196.

2428. Tipton, Steven M. "The Moral Logic of Alternative Religions." DAEDALUS 111,1 (1982): 185-213.

2429. Wallis, Roy. THE REBIRTH OF THE GODS? REFLECTIONS ON NEW RELIGIONS IN THE WEST. Belfast: The Queen's University, 1978.

* Wallis, Roy (ed.) MILLENNIALISM AND CHARISMA. Cited above as item 89.

2430. Wallis, Roy. THE ELEMENTARY FORMS OF THE NEW RELIGIOUS LIFE. London: Routledge & Kegan Paul, 1984.

2431. Westley, Frances. "'The Cult of Man': Durkheim's Predictions and New Religious Movements." SA 39,2 (1978): 135-145.

2432. Westley, Frances. THE COMPLEX FORMS OF THE RELIGIOUS LIFE: A DURKHEIMIAN VIEW OF THE NEW RELIGIOUS MOVEMENTS. Unpublished Ph.D. dissertation, McGill University, 1978.

2433. Westley, Frances. THE COMPLEX FORMS OF THE RELIGIOUS LIFE. A DURKHEIMIAN VIEW OF NEW RELIGIOUS MOVEMENTS. Chico, California: Scholars Press, 1983.

2434. Wilson, Bryan (ed.) THE SOCIAL IMPACT OF NEW RELIGIOUS MOVEMENTS. New York: Rose of Sharon, 1981. Contains item 3582.

* Wright, Stuart A. A SOCIOLOGICAL STUDY OF DEFECTION FROM CONTROVERSIAL NEW RELIGIOUS MOVEMENTS. Cited above as item 2060.

2435. Wright, Stuart A. "Post-Involvement Attitudes of Voluntary Defectors from Controversial New Religious Movements." JSSR 23,2 (1984): 172-182.

2436. Wuthnow, Robert. THE CONSCIOUSNESS REFORMATION. Berkeley: University of California Press, 1976.

* Wuthnow, Robert. EXPERIMENTATION IN AMERICAN RELIGION. Cited above as item 1722.

* Wuthnow, Robert. "Political Aspects of the Quietistic Revival." Cited above as item 1723.

Temperance movement

2437. Allen, John L. THE METHODIST BOARD OF TEMPERANCE AS AN INSTRUMENT OF CHURCH POLICY. Unpublished Ph.D. dissertation, Yale University, 1957.

* Gusfield, Joseph R. "Social Structure and Moral Reform: A Study of the Woman's Christian Temperance Union." Cited above as item 1942.

2438. Gusfield, Joseph R. SYMBOLIC CRUSADE. STATUS POLITICS AND THE AMERICAN TEMPERANCE MOVEMENT. Urbana: University of Illinois Press, 1963.

* Hammond, John L. THE POLITICS OF BENEVOLENCE. REVIVAL RELIGION AND AMERICAN VOTING BEHAVIOR. Cited above as item 1584.

2439. Hougland, James G., James R. Wood, and Samuel A. Mueller. "Organizational 'Goal Submergence': The Methodist Church and the Failure of the Temperance Movement." SOCIOLOGY AND SOCIAL RESEARCH 58,4 (1974): 408-416.

2440. Wilson, John, and Kenneth Manton. "Localism and Temperance." SOCIOLOGY AND SOCIAL RESEARCH 59 (1975): 121-135.

SECTION F: SECULARIZATION

This term has various meanings in the literature. In some cases it simply refers to the separation of religion from other institutions such as education, government, and medicine. In other cases it refers to the retreat of religion from the public forum, and in still others it refers to the disappearance of religion.

Secularization (general)

2441. Acquaviva, Sabino S. "Neopaganesimo e società industriale." IL MULINO 9,7 (1959): 275-345.

2442. Acquaviva, Sabino S. "The Psychology of Dechristianisation in the Dynamics of the Industrial Society." SC 7,3 (1960): 209-225.

2443. Acquaviva, Sabino S. L'ECLISSI DEL SACRO NELLA CIVILTA INDUSTRIALE. Milan: Ed. di Communità, 1961 (2nd enlarged ed., 1966).
THE DECLINE OF THE SACRED IN INDUSTRIAL SOCIETY, translated by Patricia Lipscomb. Oxford: Basil Blackwell, 1979.

2444. Acquaviva, Sabino S., and Gustavo Guizzardi (eds.) RELIGIONE E IRRELIGIONE NELL'ETA POST-INDUSTRIALE. Rome: A.V.E. Editrice, 1971.

2445. Acquaviva, Sabino S., and Gustavo Guizzardi. LA SECOLARIZZAZIONE. Bologna: Il Mulino, 1973.

2446. Albrecht, Stan L., and Tim B. Heaton. "Secularization, Higher Education, and Religiosity." RRR 26,1 (1984): 43-58.

2447. Alston, John P., and Richard C. Hollinger. "Correlates of Perceived Secularization." JSSR 11,4 (1972): 401-403.

* Anthony, Dick, Thomas Robbins, and P. Schwartz. "Contemporary Religious Movements and the Secularisation Premiss." Cited above as item 2391.

2448. Arellano, Estuardo. "El proceso de urbanización en América Latina y la secularización." In FE Y SECULARIZACION EN AMERICA LATINA. Bogotá and Quito: Departamento de Pastoral de CELAM, Colección IPLA, n. 12, 1972, pp. 25-34.

2449. Barclay, Harold B. "Some Aspects of the Secularization Process in the Arab Sudan." HUMAN ORGANIZATION 24 (1965): 84-90.

2450. Becker, Howard. "Säkularisierungsprozesse." KÖLNER VIERTELJAHRESHEFTE FÜR SOZIOLOGIE 10 (1932): 283-294, 450-463.

2451. Becker, Howard. "Processes of Secularization: An Ideal-Typical Analysis with Special Reference to Personality Change as Affected by Population Movement." SOCIOLOGICAL REVIEW 24 (1932): 138-154 (Part I); 226-286 (Part II).

2452. Bensimon, Doris. "Aspects de l'abandon de la pratique religieuse en milieu juif français. Résultats préliminaires d'une enquête." SC 18,3 (1971): 413-425.

* Berger, Peter L. "Secularization and Pluralism." Cited above as item 342.

2453. Berger, Peter L. "A Sociological View of the Secularization of Theology." JSSR 6 (1967): 3-16.

2454. Berger, Peter L. FACING UP TO MODERNITY. EXCURSIONS IN SOCIETY, POLITICS, AND RELIGION. New York: Basic Books, 1977, pp. 162-181.

2455. Berger, Peter L. "Zukunft der Religion. Soziologische Betrachtungen zur Säkularisierung." EVANGELISCHE KOMMENTARE 4 (1971): 317-322.

2456. Berkes, Niyazi. THE DEVELOPMENT OF SECULARISM IN TURKEY. Montreal: McGill Univ. Press, 1964.

2457. Billiet, Jaak. "Secularization and Compartmentalization in the Belgian Educational System. An Analysis of the Problems Relevant to the Revision of the School Pact." SC 20,4 (1973): 569-591.

2458. Birnbaum, Norman. "Säkularisation. Zur Soziologie der Religion in der heutigen Gesellschaft des Westens." MONATSCHRIFT FÜR PASTORALTHEOLOGIE 48,3 (1959): 68-84.

2459. Brothers, Joan. "Secularización: realidad o fantasía?" CONCILIUM 81 (Spanish Series, 1973): 45-57.

2460. Campbell, Colin. "The Cult, the Cultic Milieu and Secularization." In Michael Hill (ed.), A SOCIOLOGICAL YEARBOOK OF RELIGION IN BRITAIN 5. London: SCM Press, 1972, pp. 119-136.

2461. Caplow, Theodore. "Looking for Secularization in Middletown." In P.H. McNamara (ed.), RELIGION: NORTH AMERICAN STYLE, 2nd ed. (volume cited in item 117), pp. 104-110.

2462. Cipriani, Roberto. "Il concetto sociologico di secolarizzazione." SOCIOLOGIA. RIVISTA DI SCIENZE SOCIALI 7,2 (1973): 135-144.

2463. Cipriani, Roberto. "Sécularisation ou retour du Sacré?" ARCHIVES DE SCIENCES SOCIALES DES RELIGIONS52,2 (1982): 141-150.

2464. Corbetta, P.G., and F. Ricardo. "Analisi di alcuni aspetti del processo di secularizazione in un quartiere urbano." STUDI DI SOCIOLOGIA 10,1 (1972): 29-79.

* Dempsey, K. "Secularization and the Protestant Clergy." Cited above as item 595.

2465. De Neve, André. "Secularization in Russian Sociology of Religion." SC 20 (1973): 593-601.

2466. Deshen, Shlomo. "The Varieties of Abandonment of Religious Symbols." JSSR 11,1 (1972): 33-41.

2467. Dittes, James E. "The Concept of Secularization in Empirical Research (L. Shiner): Comments." JSSR 6,2 (1967): 190, 220, 235.

2468. Dobbelaere, Karel. SECULARIZATION: A MULTI-DIMENSIONAL CONCEPT. London: Sage, 1981.

2469. Dobbelaere, Karel. "Secularization Theories and Sociological Paradigms: Convergences and Divergences." SC 31,2-3 (1984): 199-219.

2470. Dobbelaere, Karel, and Jan Lauwers. "Definition of Religion -- a Sociological Critique." SC 20 (1973): 535-568.

2471. Dobbelaere, Karel, Jan Lauwers, and Mieke Ghesquiere-Waelkens. "Sécularisation et humanisation dans les institutions hospitalières chrétiennes." SC 20,4 (1973): 553-568.

2472. Eccel, A. Chris. RAPIDLY INCREASING SOCIETAL SCALE AND SECULARIZATION: A CENTURY OF HIGHER MUSLIM EDUCATION AND THE PROFESSIONS IN EGYPT. Unpublished Ph.D. dissertation, University of Chicago, 1978.

* Ergil, D. "Secularization as Class Conflict: The Turkish Example." Cited above as item 1788.

2473. Faia, Michael A. "Secularization and Scholarship among American Professors." SA 37,1 (1976): 63-73.

2474. Fallding, Harold. "Secularization and the Sacred and Profane." THE SOCIOLOGICAL QUARTERLY 8 (1967): 349-364.

2475. Fenn, Richard K. "Max Weber on the Secular: A Typology." RRR 10 (1969): 159-169.

2476. Fenn, Richard K. "The Secularization of Values. An Analytical Framework for the Study of Secularization." JSSR 8,1 (1969): 112-124.

2477. Fenn, Richard K. "The Process of Secularization: A Post-Parsonian View." JSSR 9,2 (1970): 117-136.

* Fenn, Richard K. "Religion and the Legitimation of Social Systems." Cited above as item 2148.

2478. Fenn, Richard K. TOWARD A THEORY OF SECULARIZATION. Storrs, Connecticut: Society for the Scientific Study of Religion, 1978.

2479. Flint, John T. "The Secularization of Norwegian Society." COMPARATIVE STUDIES IN SOCIETY AND HISTORY 6,3 (1963-64): 325-344.

2480. Forster, Peter G. "Secularization in the English Context. Some Conceptual and Empirical Problems." SOCIOLOGICAL REVIEW 20,2 (1972): 153-168.

2481. Gargarin, Iu. V. "The Abandonment of Sectarianism in the Komi USSR." SOVIET SOCIOLOGY 8,3-4 (1969-70): 358-381.

2482. Gellner, Ernest. "Sanctity, Puritanism, Secularisation and Nationalism in North Africa. A Case Study." ARCHIVES DE SCIENCES SOCIALES DES RELIGIONS 15 (1963): 71-86.

* Gerharz, George P. "Secularization as Loss of Social Control: Toward a New Theory." Cited above as item 2160.

2483. Germani, Gino. "Secularización y desarrollo económico." In CENTRO LATINO-AMERICANO DE PESQUISAS EM CIENCIAS SOCIAIS/CENTRO LATINOAMERICANO DE INVESTIGACIONES EN CIENCIAS SOCIALES, RESISTENCIAS A MUDANÇA. Rio de Janeiro, 1960, pp. 261-279.

2484. Glasner, Peter E. "'Idealization' and the Social Myth of Secularization." In M. Hill (ed.), A SOCIOLOGICAL YEARBOOK OF RELIGION IN BRITAIN 8. London: SCM Press, 1975, pp. 7-14.

2485. Glasner, Peter E. THE SOCIOLOGY OF SECULARISATION. A CRITIQUE OF A CONCEPT. Boston: Routledge and Kegan Paul, 1977.

* Gonzalez-Estefani y Robles, J.M. MESSIANISMO Y SECULARIZACION EN LOS MOVIMIENTOS SOCIALES CONTEMPORANEOS. Cited above as item 2338.

2486. Gonzalez, Santos. "Sociología del hecho religioso: el concepto de secularización." CUADERNOS DE REALIDADES SOCIALES 20-21 (1982): 199-229.

2487. Goode, Erich. "Some Sociological Implications of Religious Secularization." SC 16,2 (1969): 265-273.

2488. Goodridge, R. Martin. "Relative Secularization and Religious Practice." SA 29,3 (1968): 122-135.

2489. Greeley, Andrew M. UNSECULAR MAN. THE PERSISTENCE OF RELIGION. New York: Schocken, 1972.

2490. Greeley, Andrew M. "Religion in a Secular Society." SOCIAL RESEARCH 41,2 (1974): 226-240.

2491. Grumelli, Antonio. "Athéisme et sécularisation: La dimension sociologique." BOLLETINO D'INFORMAZIONE. SECRETARIATUS PRO NON CREDENTIBUS 3,4 (1968): 11-13.

2492. Grumelli, Antonio. "Secularization: Between Belief and Unbelief." In R. Caporale and A. Grumelli (eds.), THE CULTURE OF UNBELIEF (item 2830), pp. 77-90.

2493. Guindon, Hubert. "The Social Evolution of Quebec Reconsidered." CANADIAN JOURNAL OF ECONOMICS AND POLITICAL SCIENCE 26 (1960): 533-551.

2494. Guizzardi, Gustavo. "Secolarizzazione: anno zero." REGNO 8 (1974): 183-185.

2495. Guizzardi, Gustavo. "Aspetti del mutamento religioso: ecclissi del sacro e secolarizzazione." RIVISTA ITALIANA DI SOCIOLOGIA (1974): 3-43.

2496. Guizzardi, Gustavo. "Sécularisation et idéologie ecclésiale. Hypothèse de travail." SC 24,4 (1977): 383-405.

2497. Guizzardi, Gustavo. "Secolarizzazione e ideologia ecclesiastica." RASSEGNE ITALIANA DI SOCIOLOGIA 3 (1978): 429-457.

2498. Gupta, G.R "Secularization and Dynamics of Social Change in India." SOCIOLOGUS 21,2 (1971): 168-183.

2499. Hammond, Phillip E. "Secularization, Incorporation and Social Relations." AMERICAN JOURNAL OF SOCIOLOGY 72 (1966): 188-194.

2500 Herberg, Will. "Religion in a Secularized Society." RRR 3,4 (1962): 145-158.

2501. Hertel, Bradley R., and Hart M. Nelsen. "Are We Entering a Post-Christian Era? Religious Belief and Attendance in America, 1957-1968." JSSR 13 (1974): 409-419.

2502. Hughey, Michael W. "The Idea of Secularization in the Works of Max Weber: A Theoretical Outline." QUALITATIVE SOCIOLOGY 2,1 (1979): 85-111.

2503. Iguacen Glaria, Félix. SECULARIZACION Y MUNDO CONTEMPORANEO. PERSPECTIVAS SOCIOLOGICAS. Madrid; Publicaciones ICCE, 1974.

2504. Isambert, François André. "La sécularisation interne du christianisme." REVUE FRANÇAISE DE SOCIOLOGIE 17,4 (1976): 573-589.

2505. Jiminez, Jesús, and Juan Estruch. LA SECULARIZACION EN ESPAÑA. Bilbao: Mensajero, 1972.

2506. Krausz, Ernest. "Religion and Secularization. A Matter of Definitions." SC 18,2 (1971): 203-212.

2507. Krejci, Jaroslav. "Religion and Anti-Religion: Experience of a Transition." SA 36,2 (1975): 108-124.

2508. Labbens, Jean. "Déchristianisation ou sécularisation? Les mots et les réalités." CHRONIQUE SOCIAL DE LA FRANCE 72,8 (1964): 491-497.

2509. Laeyendecker, Leonardus. "The Sociological Approach to Secularization." CONCILIUM 47 (1969): 9-19.

2510. Larkin, Gerald. "Isolation, Integration and Secularization: A Case Study of the Netherlands." SOCIOLOGICAL REVIEW 3 (1974): 401-418.

2511. Lauwers, Jan. "Les théories sociologiques concernant la sécularisation -- Typologie et critique." SC 20,4 (1973): 523-533.

2512. Lebedev, A.A. "The Secularization of the Population of a Socialist City." SOVIET SOCIOLOGY 12,1 (1973): 77-106.

2513. Le Bras, Gabriel. "Déchristianisation: mot fallacieux." SC 10,6 (1963): 445-452.

2514. Lidz, Victor M. "Secularization, Ethical Life, and Religion in Modern Societies." In H.M. Johnson (ed.), RELIGIOUS CHANGE AND CONTINUITY. SOCIOLOGICAL PERSPECTIVES (volume cited in item 516), pp. 191-217.

2515. Luckmann, Thomas. "On Religion in Modern Society: Individual Consciousness, World View, Institution." JSSR 2,2 (1962): 147-163.

2516. Luckmann, Thomas. "Secolarizzazione, un mito contemporaneo." CULTURA E POLITICA 14 (1969): 175-182.

2517. Luft, Murray C. RELIGIOUS SECULARIZATION: A STUDY OF A CONTEMPORARY BAPTIST CHURCH. Unpublished M.A. thesis, University of Calgary, 1969.

2518. Lüschen, Günther, Zaharj Staikof, Veronica Stolte Heiskanen, and Conor Ward. "Family, Ritual and Secularization. A Cross-National Study Conducted in Bulgaria, Finland, Germany and Ireland." SC 19,4 (1972): 519-536.

2519. Maertens, Jean-Thierry. "La désacralisation et le merveilleux religieux." In Fernand Dumont, Jean-Paul Montminy, and Michel Stein (eds.), LE MERVEILLEUX. DEUXIEME COLLOQUE SUR LES RELIGIONS POPULAIRES. 1971. Québec: Les Presses de l'Université Laval, 1973, pp. 111-130.

2520. Martin, David A. "Toward Eliminating the Concept of Secularization." In Julius Gould (ed.), PENGUIN SURVEY OF THE SOCIAL SCIENCES. Harmondsworth and Baltimore: Penguin, 1965, pp. 169-182. Also in D. Martin, THE RELIGIOUS AND THE SECULAR (item 2523), pp. 9-22.

2521. Martin, David A. "Some Utopian Aspects of the Concept of Secularization." In J. Matthes (ed.), THEORETISCHE ASPEKTE DER RELIGIONSSOZIOLOGIE I / SOCIOLOGY OF RELIGION: THEORETICAL PERSPECTIVES I. INTERNATIONALES JAHRBUCH FÜR RELIGIONSSOZIOLOGIE 2. Köln and Opladen: Westdeutscher Verlag, 1966, pp. 87-97.

2522. Martin, David A. A SOCIOLOGY OF ENGLISH RELIGION. New York: Basic Books, 1967.

2523. Martin, David A. THE RELIGIOUS AND THE SECULAR: STUDIES IN SECULARIZATION. New York: Schocken; and London: Routledge and Kegan Paul, 1969.

2524. Martin, David A. "Notes for a General Theory of Secularization." ARCHIVES EUROPEENES DE SOCIOLOGIE 10,2 (1969): 192-201.

2525. Martin, David A. TRACTS AGAINST THE TIMES. London: Lutterworth Press, 1976.

2526. Martin, David A. THE DILEMMAS OF CONTEMPORARY RELIGION. New York: St. Martin's, 1978.

* Martin, David A. A GENERAL THEORY OF SECULARIZATION. Cited above as item 689.

2527. Matthes, Joachim. "Bemerkungen zur Säkularisierungsthese in der neueren Religionssoziologie." In D. Goldschmidt and J. Matthes (eds.), PROBLEME DER RELIGIONSSOZIOLOGIE. KÖLNER ZEITSCHRIFT FÜR SOZIOLOGIE UND SOZIALPSYCHOLOGIE, SONDERHEFT 6. Köln and Opladen: Westdeutscher Verlag, 1962, 1966, pp. 65-77.

2528. Moberg, David O. "Die Säkularisierung und das Wachstum der Kirchen in den Vereinigten Staaten." KÖLNER ZEITSCHRIFT FÜR SOZIOLOGIE UND SOZIALPSYCHOLOGIE 10 (1958): 430-438.

2529. Mol, Johannes J. (Hans). "Secularization and Cohesion." RRR 11,3 (1970): 183-191.

* Moreux, Colette. FIN D'UNE RELIGION? MONOGRAPHIE D'UNE PAROISSE CANADIENNE-FRANÇAISE. Cited above as item 1452.

2530\. O'Dea, Thomas F. "The Secularization of Culture." COMMONWEAL 64 (1956): 67-69.

2531\. Oppen, D. von. "Die Sükularisierung als soziologisches Problem." In C. Bourbeck and H.D. Wendland (eds.), DIAKONIE ZWISCHEN KIRCHE UND WELT. Hamburg, 1958, pp. 37-52.

* Orsini, Gabriele di. "Aspetti della secolarizzazione. (Il giorno del Signore e le vocazioni in Italia con particolare attenzione all'Abruzzo-Molise)." Cited above as item 2113.

2532\. Parisi, Arturo. "Tra ripresa ecclesiastica ed eclissi della secolarizzazione." CITTA E REGIONE 7 (1978): 32-46.

2533\. Parsons, Talcott. "Religion in Postindustrial America: The Problem of Secularization." SOCIAL RESEARCH 41,2 (1974): 193-225.

2534\. Paulson, Steven K. "Printed Advertisements as Indicators of Christian Institutional Secularization." RRR 19,1 (1977): 78-83.

2535\. Perkins, H. Wesley. "Religious Content in American, British, and Canadian Popular Publications from 1937 to 1979." SA 45,2 (1984): 159-165.

2536\. Pétursson, Pétur. CHURCH AND SOCIAL CHANGE. A STUDY OF THE SECULARIZATION PROCESS IN ICELAND 1830-1930. Helsingborg, Sweden: Plus Ultra, 1983.

2537\. Pfautz, Harold W. "The Sociology of Secularization: Religious Groups." AMERICAN JOURNAL OF SOCIOLOGY 61 (1955): 121-128.

2538\. Pfautz, Harold W. "Christian Science: A Case Study of the Social Psychological Aspect of Secularization." SOCIAL FORCES 34,4 (1956): 246-251.

2539\. Pickering, W.S.F. "The Secularized Sabbath: Formerly Sunday Now Weekend." In Michael Hill (ed.), A SOCIOLOGICAL YEARBOOK OF RELIGION IN BRITAIN 5. London: SCM, 1972, pp. 33-47.

2540\. Pinder, R. "Religious Change in the Process of Secularization." THE SOCIOLOGICAL REVIEW 19,3 (1971): 343-366.

2541\. Piwowarski, Wladyslaw. "Industrialization and Popular Religiosity in Poland." SA 37,4 (1976): 315-320.

2542\. Poblete, Renato. "Formas especificas del proceso latinoamericano de secularización." In Instituto Fe y Secularidad, FE CRISTIANA Y CAMBIO SOCIAL EN AMERICA LATINA. ENCUENTRE DE EL ESCORIAL, 1972. Salamanca: Sigueme, 1973, pp. 159-177.

* Pomian-Srzednicki, Maciej. RELIGIOUS CHANGE IN CONTEMPORARY POLAND. Cited above as item 1668.

2543. Porter, Judith R. "Secularization, Differentiation, and the Function of Religious Value Orientations." SOCIOLOGICAL INQUIRY 43,1 (1973): 67-74.

2544. Raphaël, Freddy. "Judaism and Secularization." SC 18,3 (1971): 399-412.

2545. Rendtorff, Trutz. "Zur Säkularisierungsproblematik. Über die Weiterentwicklung der Kirchensoziologie zur Religionssoziologie." In J. Matthes (ed.), THEORETISCHE ASPEKTE DER RELIGIONSSOZIOLOGIE I / SOCIOLOGY OF RELIGION: THEORETICAL PERSPECTIVES I. INTERNATIONALES JAHRBUCH FÜR RELIGIONSSOZIOLOGIE 2. Köln and Opladen: Westdeutscher Verlag, 1966, pp. 51-71.

* Rigby, Andrew, and Bryan S. Turner. "Communes, hippies et religion sécularisées -- quelques aspects sociologiques de formes actuelles de religiosité." Cited above as item 1258.

2546. Rigney, Daniel, Richard Machalek, and Jerry D. Goodman. "Is Secularization a Discontinuous Process?" JSSR 17,4 (1978): 381-387.

2547. Robertson, Roland. "Sociologists and Secularization." SOCIOLOGY 5,3 (1971): 297-312.

2548. Robertson, Roland. "Religion and Sociological Factors in the Analysis of Secularization." In A.W. Eister (ed.), CHANGING PERSPECTIVES IN THE SCIENTIFIC STUDY OF RELIGION (volume cited in item 353), pp. 41-60.

2549. Robertson, Roland. "Biases in the Analysis of Secularization." In R. Robertson, MEANING AND CHANGE (volume cited in item 2021), pp. 258-276.

2550. Rodriguez, Jaime F. EDUCACION CATOLICA Y SECULARIZATION EN COLOMBIA. Bogotá: Stella, 1970.

2551. Rodrigues, Jaime F. "Análisis critico al marco teórico de la secularización en las relaciones Religión-Sociedad." REVISTA PARAGUAYA DE SOCIOLOGIA 15,41 (1978): 35-56.

2552. Roggero, Elio. SOCIOLOGIA E SECOLARIZZAZIONE. Torino: Giappichelli, 1973.

* Roof, Wade Clark. COMMUNITY AND COMMITMENT. Cited above as item 2154.

2553. Rosanna, Enrica. SECOLARIZZAZIONE O TRANSFUNZIONALIZZAZIONE DELLA RELIGION? RAPPORTO CRITICO SU UNA DISCUSSIONE ATTUALE IN SOCIOLOGIA DELLA RELIGION. Zurich: PAS Verlag; Roma: LAS, 1973.

2554. Roth, Guenther. "Religion and Revolutionary Beliefs: Sociological and Historical Dimensions in Max Weber's Work -- in Memory of Ivan Vallier (1927-1974)." SOCIAL FORCES 55,2 (1976): 257-272.

2555. Rusconi, G.E. GIOVANI E SECOLARIZZAZIONE. Firenze: Vallecchi, 1969.

2556. Ryan, Claude. "Pouvoir religieux et sécularisation." RECHERCHES SOCIOGRAPHIQUES 7,1-2 (1966): 101-110.

2557. Salisbury, W. Seward. "Religion and Secularization." SOCIAL FORCES 36,3 (1958): 197-205.

2558. Savramis, Demosthenes. "Das Vorurteil von der Entchristlichung der Gegenwartsgesellschaft." KÖLNER ZEITSCHRIFT FÜR SOZIOLOGIE UND SOZIALPSYCHOLOGIE 19,2 (1967): 263-282.

2559. Scotford-Archer, M., and M. Vaughan. "Education, Secularization, Desecularization and Resecularization." In D.A. Martin and M. Hill (eds.), A SOCIOLOGICAL YEAROOK OF RELIGION IN BRITAIN 3. London: SCM Press, 1970.

2560. Sharot, Stephen. "Secularization, Judaism and Anglo-Jewry." In M. Hill (ed.), A SOCIOLOGICAL YEARBOOK OF RELIGION IN BRITAIN 4. London: SCM Press, 1972, pp. 121-140.

2561. Shiner, Larry. THE SECULARIZATION OF HISTORY. Nashville: Abingdon, 1966.

2562. Shiner, Larry. "The Concept of Secularization in Empirical Research." JSSR 6 (1967): 207-220.

2563. Stark, Rodney. "Age and Faith: A Changing Outlook or an Old Process?" SA 29,1 (1968): 1-10.

2564. Stark, Rodney, and William Sims Bainbridge. "Secularization, Revival and Cult Formation." ANNUAL REVIEW OF THE SOCIAL SCIENCES OF RELIGION 4 (1980): 85-119.

2565. Stark, Rodney, and William Sims Bainbridge. "Secularization and Cult Formation in the Jazz Age." JSSR 20,4 (1981): 360-373.

2566. Swatos, William H., Jr. "The Relevance of Religion: Iceland and Secularization Theory." JSSR 23,1 (1984): 32-43.

2567. Tamney, Joseph B. "Functional Religiosity and Modernization in Indonesia." SA 41,1 (1980): 55-65.

2568. Thalheimer, Fred. "Religiosity and Secularization in the Academic Professions." SOCIOLOGY OF EDUCATION 46 (1973): 183-202.

2569. Toch, Hans H., and Robert Anderson. "'Secularization' in College: An Exploratory Study." RELIGIOUS EDUCATION 59 (1964): 490-502.

2570. Tomka, Miklós. "A Balance of Secularization in Hungary." SC 28,1 (1981): 25-42.

2571. Varacalli, Joseph A. "Peter L. Berger and the Problem of Modern Religious Commitment." RELIGION, THE CUTTING EDGE. NEW ENGLAND SOCIOLOGIST 5,1 (1984): 143-151.

2572. Varga, Ivan. "Le sécularisation de la jeunesse hongroise." ARCHIVES DE SOCIOLOGIE DES RELIGIONS 23 (1967): 45-64.

2573. Watzke, James. "Paganization and Dechristianization, or the Crisis in Institutional Symbols. A Problem in Sociological Interpretation." SC 16,1 (1969): 91-99.

2574. Weigert, Andrew J., and Darwin L. Thomas. "Secularization: A Cross-National Study of Catholic Male Adolescents." SOCIAL FORCES 49 (1970): 28-36.

2575. Weigert, Andrew J., and Darwin L. Thomas. "Secularization and Religiosity: A Cross-National Study of Catholic Adolescents in Five Societies." SA 35,1 (1974): 1-23.

2576. Weissbrod, Lilly. "Religion as National Identity in a Secular Society." RRR 24,3 (1983): 188-205.

2577. Westhues, Kenneth. "An Elaboration and Test of a Secularization Hypothesis in Terms of Open-Systems Theory of Organization." SOCIAL FORCES 49,3 (1971): 460-469.

2578. Weston, D.E. "Secularization and Social Theory - Swedish Experience in the Context of International Theoretical Debate." ACTA SOCIOLOGICA 26,3-4 (1983): 329-336.

2579. Whetten, N.L., and E.G. Devereux. STUDIES OF SUBURBANIZATION IN CONNECTICUT. Agricultural Experimentation Station Bulletin 212, Storrs, Conn., 1936.

2580. Wilensky, Harold L., and Jack Ladinksy. "From Religious Community to Occupational Group." AMERICAN SOCIOLOGICAL REVIEW 32 (1967): 541-561.

2581. Wilson, Bryan R. RELIGION IN SECULAR SOCIETY. A SOCIOLOGICAL COMMENT. London: C.A. Watts and Co., 1966.

2582. Wilson, Bryan R. CONTEMPORARY TRANSFORMATIONS OF RELIGION. The Riddell Memorial Lectures, Forty-fifth Series Delivered at the University of Newcastle upon Tyne on 2, 3, 4 December 1974. New York: Oxford University Press, 1976.

2583. Wilson, Bryan R. "The Return of the Sacred." JSSR 18,3 (1979): 268-280.

2584. Wuthnow, Robert. "Recent Patterns of Secularization: A Problem of Generations?" AMERICAN SOCIOLOGICAL REVIEW 41 (1976): 850-867.

2585. Xenakis, Janson. "Desupernaturalization." JSSR 3,2 (1964): 181-188.

Disenchantment

This term is used in the literature to refer to a decline of belief in the supernatural and the magical.

* Swatos, William H., Jr. "The Disenchantment of Charisma: A Weberian Assessment of Revolution in a Rationalized World." Cited above as item 84.

2586. Swatos, William H., Jr. "Enchantment and Disenchantment in Modernity: The Significance of 'Religion' as a Sociological Category." SA 44,4 (1983): 321-337.

2587. Wax, Murray L. "Magic, Rationality, and Max Weber." KANSAS JOURNAL OF SOCIOLOGY 3,1 (1967): 12-19.

* Weber, Max. "Religious Rejections of the World and their Directions." Cited above as item 56.

Privatization

Privatization is the retreat of religion from the public forum into the purely personal aspects of life.

2588. Bibby, Reginald W. "Searching for Invisible Thread: Meaning Systems in Contemporary Canada." JSSR 22,2 (1983): 101-119.

* Bourg, Carroll J. "Politics and Religion." Cited above as item 346.

2589. Campiche, Roland, and Jean Kellerhals. "Community Values and Societal Values in Family Exchange: Coexistence or Conflict?" SC 28,4 (1981): 383-403.

2590. Drehsen, Volker. "Dimensions of Religiosity in Modern Society. An Approach to a Systematical Stock-Taking of Structural-Functionalist Analysis." SC 27,1 (1980): 51-62.

2591. Hunter, James Davison. "Subjectivization and the New Evangelical Theodicy." JSSR 20,1 (1982): 39-47.

2592. Luckmann, Thomas. ZUM PROBLEM DER RELIGION IN DER MODERNEN GESELLSCHAFT. Freiburg: Rombach Verlag, 1963.
THE INVISIBLE RELIGION. THE PROBLEM OF RELIGION IN MODERN SOCIETY. New York: Macmillan, 1967.

2593. Machalek, Richard, and Michael Martin. "'Invisible' Religions: Some Preliminary Evidence." JSSR 15,4 (1976): 311-321.

2594. Mason, Michael C. THE PRIVATIZATION OF THE SACRED WORLD. THOMAS LUCKMANN'S PHENOMENOLOGICALLY FOUNDED SOCIOLOGY OF MODERN RELIGION. Unpublished Ph.D. dissertation, Columbia University, 1975.

2595. Milanesi, Giancarlo. "Problemi teorici e metodologici nello studio delle nuovo forme di religiosità extra-istituzionali." ORIENTAMENTI PEDAGOGICI 1 (1974): 121-127.

2596. Nelsen, Hart M., Robert F. Everett, Paul Douglas Mader, and Warren C. Hamby. "A Test of Yinger's Measure of Non-Doctrinal Religion: Implications for Invisible Religion as a Belief System." JSSR 15,3 (1976): 263-267.

* Roof, Wade Clark. COMMUNITY AND COMMITMENT. Cited above as item 2154.

2597. Weigert, Andrew J. "Whose Invisible Religion? Luckmann Revisited." SA 35,3 (1974): 181-188.

SECTION G: PROTESTANT ETHIC

Weber's famous thesis of a causal relationship between the world views of Reformation Protestantism and the industrialization of the West has engendered a vast and often unconnected literature.

2598. Ament, William S. "Religion, Education, and Distinction." SCHOOL AND SOCIETY. September 24, 1927: 399-406.

* Anderson, Grace M. THE RELATIONSHIP BETWEEN RELIGIOUS AFFILIATION AND SECULAR ATTITUDES AND BEHAVIOR. Cited above as item 1517.

2599. Ankerl, Guy G. SOCIOLOGUES ALLEMANDS: ETUDES DE CAS EN SOCIOLOGIE HISTORIQUE ET NON-HISTORIQUE AVEC LE DICTIONNAIRE DE L'ETHIQUE PROTESTANTE ET L'ESPRIT DU CAPITALISME DE MAX WEBER. Neuchatel, Switzerland: A la Baconnière, 1972.

2600. Babbie, Earl R. "The Religious Factor -- Looking Forward." RRR 7 (1965): 42-53.

2601. Ball, Donald W. "Catholics, Calvinists and Rational Control: Further Explorations in the Weberian Thesis." SA 26,4 (1965): 181-188.

2602. Barclay, Harold B. "The Protestant Ethic Versus the Spirit of Capitalism." RRR 10,3 (1969): 151-158.

2603. Bellah, Robert N. "Reflections on the Protestant Ethic Analogy in Asia." JOURNAL OF SOCIAL ISSUES 19,1 (1963): 52-60. Also in R.N. Bellah, BEYOND BELIEF (item 3577), pp. 53-63.

2604. Bendix, Reinhard. MAX WEBER: AN INTELLECTUAL PORTRAIT. Garden City, N.Y.: Anchor-Doubleday, 1962, pp. 71-99.

2605. Bendix, Reinhard. "A Case Study in Cultural and Educational Mobility: Japan and the Protestant Ethic." In N.J. Smelser and S.M. Lipset (eds.), SOCIAL STRUCTURE AND MOBILITY IN ECONOMIC DEVELOPMENT. Chicago: Aldine, 1966, pp. 262-279.

2606. Bendix, Reinhard. "The Protestant Ethic - Revisited." COMPARATIVE STUDIES IN SOCIETY AND HISTORY 9,3 (1967): 266-273.

2607. Berger, Stephen D. "The Sects and the Breakthrough into the Modern World: On the Centrality of the Sects in Weber's Protestant Ethic Thesis." SOCIOLOGICAL QUARTERLY 12 (1971): 486-499.

2608. Besnard, Philippe. PROTESTANTISME ET CAPITALISME. LA CONTROVERSE POSTWEBERIENNE. Paris: Armand Colin, 1970.

2609. Biermann, Benno. "Die Protestantismus-Debatte: Entwicklung, Stand und Bedeutung für eine Soziologie der Unternehmerschaft." In J. Matthes (ed.), BEITRÄGE ZUR RELIGIONSSOZIOLOGISCHEN FORSCHUNG / ESSAYS ON RESEARCH IN THE SOCIOLOGY OF RELIGION. INTERNATIONALES JAHRBUCH FÜR RELIGIONSSOZIOLOGIE 4. Köln and Opladen: Westdeutscher Verlag, 1968, pp. 223-250.

2610. Birnbaum, Norman. "Conflicting Interpretations of the Rise of Capitalism: Marx and Weber." BRITISH JOURNAL OF SOCIOLOGY 6 (1953): 125-141.

2611. Birnbaum, Norman. "The Zwinglian Reformation in Zurich." ARCHIVES DE SOCIOLOGIE DES RELIGIONS 4,8 (1959): 15-30. Also in N. Birnbaum, TOWARD A CRITICAL SOCIOLOGY. New York: Oxford University Press, 1971, pp. 133-161. Also in PAST AND PRESENT 15 (1959): 24-47.

2612. Bouma, Gary D. "Beyond Lenski: A Critical Review of Recent 'Protestant Ethic' Research." JSSR 12,2 (1973): 141-155.

2613. Bressler, Marvin, and Charles F. Westoff. "Catholic Education, Economic Values, and Achievement." AMERICAN JOURNAL OF SOCIOLOGY 69 (1963): 225-233.

2614. Bronson, L., and A. Meadow. "The Need Achievement Orientation of Catholic and Protestant Mexican-Americans." REVISTA INTER-AMERICANA DE PSICHOLOGIA 2 (1968): 159-168.

2615. Buchignani, Norman L. "The Weberian Thesis in India/La thèse wébérienne en Inde." ARCHIVES DE SCIENCES SOCIALES DES RELIGIONS 21,42 (1976): 17-33.

* Campbell, Douglas F. RELIGION AND VALUES AMONG NOVA SCOTIA COLLEGE STUDENTS. Cited above as item 1540.

* Campbell, Douglas F. "Religion and Values among Nova Scotian College Students." Cited above as item 1541.

2616. Carsh, H. "The Protestant Ethic and the Popular Idol in America. A Case Study." SC 15,1 (1968): 45-69.

2617. Clark, S.D. "Religion and Economic Backward Areas." AMERICAN ECONOMIC REVIEW 41 (1951): 258-265.

2618. Crespi, Irving. "Occupational Status and Religion." AMERICAN SOCIOLOGICAL REVIEW 28 (1963): 131.

2619. Crowley, James W., and John A. Ballweg. "Religious Preference and Worldly Success: An Empirical Test in a Midwestern City." SA 32,2 (1971): 71-80.

2620. Datta, Lois-Ellin. "Family Religious Background and Early Scientific Creativity." AMERICAN SOCIOLOGICAL REVIEW 32 (1967): 626-635.

2621. Eisenstadt, Samuel N. (ed.) THE PROTESTANT ETHIC AND MODERNIZATION: A COMPARATIVE VIEW. New York: Basic, 1968.

2622. Eisenstadt, Samuel N. "Die protestantische Ethik und der Geist des Kapitalismus." KÖLNER ZEITSCHRIFT FÜR SOZIOLOGIE UND SOZIALPSYCHOLOGIE 22,1 (1970): 1-23; 22,2 (1970): 265-299.

2623. Fanfani, Amintore. "Riforma e capitalismo moderno nella recente letteratura." REVUE INTERNATIONAL DES SCIENCES SOCIALES 38 (1930): 358-365.

2624. Fanfani, Amintore. CATTOLICISMO E PROTESTANTESIMO NELLA FORMAZIONE ETICA DEL CAPITALISMO. Milano: Vita e Pensiero, 1934. CATHOLICISM, PROTESTANTISM AND CAPITALISM. London: Sheed and Ward, 1935.

2625. Field, Arthur Jordan. "Comment on 'The Protestant Ethic, Level of Aspiration, and Social Mobility.'" AMERICAN SOCIOLOGICAL REVIEW 21 (1956): 621.

2626. Fischer, Karl H. "Kritische Beiträge zur Prof. Max Webers Abhandlung: 'Die protestantisches Ethik und der Geist der Kapitalismus." ARCHIV FÜR SOZIALWISSENSCHAFT UND SOZIALPOLITIK 25 (1907): 232-242.

2627. Fischer, Karl H. "Protestantische Ethik und der 'Geist der Kapitalismus.' Replik auf Herrn Prof. Max Webers Gegenkritik." ARCHIV FÜR SOZIALWISSENSCHAFT UND SOZIALPOLITIK 26 (1908): 270-274.

2628. Fischoff, Ephraim. "The Protestant Ethic and the Spirit of Capitalism: The History of a Controversy." SOCIAL RESEARCH 11 (1944): 53-77.

2629. Forcese, Dennis P. "Calvinism, Capitalism and Confusion: The Weberian Thesis Revisited." SA 29,4 (1968): 193-201.

2630. Freund, Julien. "L'éthique économique et les religions mondiales selon Max Weber." ARCHIVES DE SOCIOLOGIE DES RELIGIONS 26 (1968): 3-26.

2631. Gaede, Stan. "Religious Affiliation, Social Mobility, and the Problem of Causality: A Methodological Critique of Catholic-Protestant Socioeconomic Achievement Studies." RRR 19,1 (1977): 54-62.

2632. Glenn, Norval, and R. Hyland. "Religious Preference and Worldly Success." AMERICAN SOCIOLOGICAL REVIEW 32 (1967): 73-85.

2633. Goitein, Bernard, and Mordechai Rotenberg. "Protestantism and Retrospective Labeling: A Cross-Cultural Study in Person Perception." HUMAN RELATIONS 30 (1977): 487-497.

2634. Goldstein, B., and R.L. Eichhorn. "The Changing Protestant Ethic: Rural Patterns in Health, Work, and Leisure." AMERICAN SOCIOLOGICAL REVIEW 26 (1961): 557-565.

2635. Gray, D.M. "The Protestant Ethic and Equal Opportunity for Working Class Whites: A Research Note." ETHNICITY 2,2 (1975): 225-228.

2636. Greeley, Andrew M. RELIGION AND CAREER. New York: Sheed and Ward, 1963.

2637. Greeley, Andrew M. "Influence of the 'Religious Factor' on Career Plans and Occupational Values of College Graduates." AMERICAN JOURNAL OF SOCIOLOGY 68 (1963): 658-671.

2638. Greeley, Andrew M. "The Protestant Ethic: Time for a Moratorium." SA 25 (1965): 20-33.

* Greeley, Andrew M. THE AMERICAN CATHOLIC. A SOCIAL PORTRAIT. Cited above as item 634.

2639. Green, Robert W. (ed.) PROTESTANTISM AND CAPITALISM: THE WEBER THESIS AND ITS CRITICS. Indianapolis: Heath, 1959.

2640. Gurwitsch, A. "Zur Bedeutung der Prädestinationslehre für die Ausbildung des 'kapitalistischen Geistes.'" ARCHIV FÜR SOZIALWISSENSCHAFT UND SOZIALPOLITIK 68,5 (1932-33): 616-622.

2641. Halbwachs, Maurice. "Une controverse: puritanisme et capitalisme." ANNALES D'HISTOIRE ECONOMIQUE ET SOCIALE 7,1 (1935): 97-99.

2642. Hammond, Phillip E., and Kirk R. Williams. "The Protestant Ethic Thesis: A Social-Psychological Assessment." SOCIAL FORCES 54,3 (1976): 579-589.

2643. Hansen, Niles M. "The Protestant Ethic as a General Precondition for Economic Development." CANADIAN JOURNAL OF ECONOMICS AND POLITICAL SCIENCE 24,4 (1963): 462-474.

2644. Hassan, Riaz. "A Protestant Ethic Scale." SC 18,4 (1971): 575-591.

2645. Hayes, John. "The Protestant Ethic Thesis and its Critics." SOCIAL STUDIES 7,1 (1982-83): 67-91.

2646. Honigsheim, P. "Katholizisimus und kapitalistische Mentalität in der nordfranzösischen Textilindustrie. Ein Beitrag zu Max Webers 'Calvinismus-Kapitalismus Problem.'" KÖLNER ZEITSCHRIFT FÜR SOZIOLOGIE UND SOZIALPSYCHOLOGIE 13 (1961): 685-701.

2647. Hudson, Winthrop S. "Puritanism and the Spirit of Capitalism." CHURCH HISTORY 18 (1949): 3-17.

2648. Hudson, Winthrop S. "The Weber Thesis Reconsidered." CHURCH HISTORY 30 (1961): 88-99.

2649. Hunt, Larry L., and Janet G. Hunt. "Black Catholicism and the Spirit of Weber." THE SOCIOLOGICAL QUARTERLY 17 (1976): 369-377.

2650. Jackson, Elton F., William S. Fox, and Harry J. Crockett, Jr. "Religion and Occupational Achievement." AMERICAN SOCIOLOGICAL REVIEW 35 (1970): 48-63.

2651. Jonassen, C.T. "The Protestant Ethic and the Spirit of Capitalism in Norway." AMERICAN SOCIOLOGICAL REVIEW 12 (1947): 676-686.

2652. Kennedy, Robert E., Jr. "The Protestant Ethic and the Parsis." AMERICAN JOURNAL OF SOCIOLOGY 68 (1962): 11-20.

2653. Kim, Hei C. "The Relationship of Protestant Ethic Beliefs and Values to Achievement." JSSR 16,3 (1977): 255-262.

2654. Kosa, John, and Leo D. Rachiele. "The Spirit of Capitalism, Traditionalism and Religiousness." SOCIOLOGICAL QUARTERLY 4 (1963): 243-260.

* Lenski, Gerhard. THE RELIGIOUS FACTOR. A SOCIOLOGIST'S INQUIRY. Cited above as item 1195.

2655. Lewellen, Ted C. "Deviant Religion and Cultural Evolution: The Aymara Case." JSSR 18,3 (1979): 243-251.

2656. Lovell, Terry. "Weber, Goldmann and the Sociology of Beliefs." ARCHIVES EUROPEENNES DE SOCIOLOGIE 14,2 (1973): 304-323.

2657. Lüthy, Herbert. "Once Again: Calvinism and Capitalism." ENCOUNTER 22 (1964): 26-38.

2658. Lüthy, Herbert. "Calvinisme et capitalisme. Après soixante ans de débat." CAHIERS VILFREDO PARETO 2 (1966): 5-35.

2659. Mack, R.W., R.J. Murphy, and S. Yellin. "The Protestant Ethic, Level of Aspiration, and Social Mobility: An Empirical Test." AMERICAN SOCIOLOGICAL REVIEW 21 (1956): 295-300.

2660. Manglapus, Raul S. "Philippine Culture and Modernization." In R.N. Bellah (ed.), RELIGION AND PROGRESS IN MODERN ASIA (volume cited in item 1872).

2661. Marshall, Gordon. "The Dark Side of the Weber Thesis: The Case of Scotland." BRITISH JOURNAL OF SOCIOLOGY 31,3 (1980): 419-440.

2662. Marshall, Gordon. PRESBYTERIES AND PROFITS: CALVINISM AND THE DEVELOPMENT OF CAPITALISM IN SCOTLAND, 1560-1707. New York: Oxford University Press, 1980.

2663. Marshall, Gordon. IN SEARCH OF THE SPIRIT OF CAPITALISM. Irvington, N.Y.: Columbia University Press, 1982.

2664. Martin, Richard M. THE WEBER THESIS: ITS THEORY, METHOD, AND APPLICATION. Unpublished Ph.D. dissertation, Duke University, 1974.

2665. Maurer, Heinrich H. "The Sociology of Protestantism." AMERICAN JOURNAL OF SOCIOLOGY 30 (1924): 257-286.

2666. Mayer, Albert J., and Harry Sharp. "Religious Preference and Worldly Success." AMERICAN SOCIOLOGICAL REVIEW 27 (1962): 218-227.

2667. McClelland, David C. "Some Social Consequences of Achievement Motivation." In Marshall R. Jones (ed.), NEBRASKA SYMPOSIUM ON MOTIVATION, VOL. 3. Lincoln: University of Nebraska Press, 1955, pp. 41-72.

2668. McClelland, David C. THE ACHIEVING SOCIETY. New York: Van Nostrand Reinhold, 1961.

2669. Means, Richard L. "Weber's Thesis of the Protestant Ethic." JOURNAL OF RELIGION 45 (1965): 1-11.

2670. Means, Richard L. "American Protestantism and Max Weber's Protestant Ethic." RELIGIOUS EDUCATION 60,2 (1965): 90-98.

2671. Means, Richard L. "Protestantism and Economic Institutions: Auxiliary Theories to Weber's Protestant Ethic." SOCIAL FORCES 44 (1966): 372-381.

2672. Merton, Robert K. "Science, Technology and Society in 17th Century England." OSIRIS 4 (1938): 360-362.

2673. Merton, Robert K. SOCIAL THEORY AND SOCIAL STRUCTURE. New York: Free Press, 1949, pp. 574-627.

2674. Michaelsen, Robert S. "Changes in the Puritan Concept of Calling or Vocation." NEW ENGLAND QUARTERLY 26 (1953): 315-336.

2675. Mirels, H.L., and J.B. Garrett. "The Protestant Ethic as a Personality Variable." JOURNAL OF CONSULTING AND CLINICAL PSYCHOLOGY 36 (1971): 40-44.

2676. Mol, Johannes J. (Hans). "Marginality and Commitment as Hidden Variables in the Jellinek/Weber/Merton Theses on the Calvinist Ethic." CURRENT SOCIOLOGY 22,1-3 (1974): 279-297.

2677. Moore, Robert. "History, Economics and Religion: A Review of 'The Max Weber Thesis' Thesis." In A. Sahay (ed.), MAX WEBER AND MODERN SOCIOLOGY. London: Routledge and Kegan Paul, 1971.

2678. Nelson, Benjamin. "Conscience and the Making of Early Cultures: The Protestant Ethic beyond Max Weber." SOCIAL RESEARCH 36,1 (1969): 5-21.

2679. Nelson, Benjamin. "Weber's Protestant Ethic: Its Origins, Wanderings, and Foreseeable Futures." In C.Y. Glock and P.E. Hammond (eds.), BEYOND THE CLASSICS? New York: Harper and Row, 1973, pp. 71-130.

2680. Nelson, Benjamin. "Droit canon, protestantisme et 'Esprit du Capitalisme.'" ARCHIVES DE SOCIOLOGIE DES RELIGIONS 34 (1972): 3-23.

2681. Paquette, Michèle. ETUDE COMPARATIVE DES ORIENTATIONS ACADEMIQUES ET DE LA MOBILITE SOCIALE CHEZ LES DIPLOMES CANADIENS-FRANÇAIS CATHOLIQUES ET CANADIENS-ANGLAIS PROTESTANTS DE DEUX UNIVERSITES MONTREALAISES. Unpublished M.A. thesis, Université de Montréal, 1968.

2682. Parsons, Talcott. "H.M. Robertson on Max Weber and his School." JOURNAL OF POLITICAL ECONOMY 43 (1935): 688-696.

2683. Passerin d'Entreves, Ettore. L'INCIDENZA DEL PROTESTANTESIMO SULLE TRASFORMAZIONI CULTURALI, POLITICHE E SOCIALI IN EUROPA; RIFLESSIONI SULL'IPOTESI DI MAX WEBER. Torino: Giappichelli, 1972.

2684. Peacock, James L. "Religion, Communications and Modernization: A Weberian Critique of some Recent Views." HUMAN ORGANIZATION 28,1 (1969): 35-41.

2685. Peacock, James L. MUSLIM PURITANS: REFORMIST PSYCHOLOGY IN SOUTH-EAST ASIA ISLAM. Berkeley: University of California Press, 1978.

2686. Poggi, Gianfranco. CALVINISM AND THE CAPITALIST SPIRIT: MAX WEBER'S PROTESTANT ETHIC. Amherst: University of Massachusetts Press, 1983.

2687. Ray, John J. "Christianism...the Protestant Ethic among Unbelievers." JOURNAL OF CHRISTIAN EDUCATION 13 (1970): 169-176.

2688. Razzell, P. "The Protestant Ethic and the Spirit of Capitalism: A Natural Scientific Critique." BRITISH JOURNAL OF SOCIOLOGY 28,1 (1977): 17-37.

2689. Rickero, Peter. VALEURS PROFESSIONNELLES ET IDENTIFICATION CULTURELLE DES JEUNES INGENIEURS DE MONTREAL. Unpublished M.A. thesis, Université de Montréal, 1966.

2690. Robert, Nicole. APPARTENANCE RELIGIEUSE ET VALEURS SOCIO-ECONOMIQUES CHEZ LES INGENIEURS CANADIANS-FRANÇAIS ET CANADIENS-ANGLAIS. Unpublished M.A. thesis, Université de Montréal, 1968.

2691. Robertson, Hector Monteith. ASPECTS OF THE RISE OF ECONOMIC INDIVIDUALISM IN THE WEST: A CRITICISM OF MAX WEBER AND HIS SCHOOL. Cambridge: Cambridge University Press, 1933.

2692. Robertson, Hector Monteith. "A Criticism of Max Weber and his School." In R.W. Green (ed.), PROTESTANTISM AND CAPITALISM. Boston: Heath, 1959.

2693. Robinson, Chalfant. "Economic Results of the Protestant Reformation Doctrines." PRINCETON THEOLOGICAL REVIEW 15 (1917): 623-644.

* Rojek, Dean G. "The Protestant Ethic and Political Preference." Cited above as item 1674.

2694. Roof, Wade Clark. "White American Socio-Religious Groups and Work Values." ETHNICITY 7 (1980): 218-224.

2695. Rosen, Bernard. "Race, Ethnicity, and the Achievement Syndrome." AMERICAN SOCIOLOGICAL REVIEW 24,1 (1959): 47-60.

2696. Rotenberg, Mordechai. "The Protestant Ethic against the Spirit of Psychiatry: The Other Side of Weber's Thesis." BRITISH JOURNAL OF SOCIOLOGY 26,1 (1975): 52-65.

2697. Sahay, Arun. "Comparative Conclusions from Hindu Reformist Ethics and the Weber Thesis: An Application of Max Weber's Methodology." SOCIOLOGICAL ANALYSIS AND THEORY (London) 3,2 (1973): 43-59.

2698. Samuelson, Kurt. RELIGION AND ECONOMIC ACTION: A CRITIQUE OF MAX WEBER. New York: Harper, 1961.

* Scheler, Max. "The Thomist Ethic and the Spirit of Capitalism." Cited above as item 518.

2699. Schuman, Howard. "The Religious Factor in Detroit: Review, Replication, and Reanalysis." AMERICAN SOCIOLOGICAL REVIEW 36 (1971): 30-48.

2700. Seyfart, Constans, and Walter M. Sprondel (eds.) SEMINAR: RELIGION UND GESELLSCHAFTLICHE ENTWICKLUNG: STUDIEN ZUR PROTESTANTISMUS-KAPITALISMUS-THESE MAX WEBERS. Frankfurt a.M.: Suhrkamp, 1973.

2701. Smith, J.A. THE PROTESTANT ETHIC CONTROVERSY. Unpublished Ph.D. thesis, University of Cambridge, 1981.

2702. Sombart, Werner. DER BOURGEOIS: ZUR GEISTESGESCHICHTE DES MODERNEN WIRTSCHAFTSSMENCHEN. München/Leipzig: Duncker und Humblot, 1902. THE QUINTESSENCE OF CAPITALISM. London: Unwin, 1915.

2703. Sparhawk, Frank J. "The Protestant Ethic Thesis: An Internal Critique." MID-AMERICAN REVIEW OF SOCIOLOGY 1,1 (1976): 27-40.

2704. Sprondel, Walter M. "Sozialer Wandel, Ideen und Interessen: Systematisierungen zu Max Webers Protestantische Ethik." In C. Seyfarth and W.M. Sprondel (eds.), SEMINAR: RELIGION UND GESELLSCHAFTLICHE ENTWICKLUNG. Frankfurt: Suhrkamp, 1973.

2705. Stark, Werner. "The Protestant Ethic and the Spirit of Sociology." SC 13 (1966): 373-377.

2706. Stark, Werner. "Die Sektenethiken und der Geist des Kapitalismus." REVUE INTERNATIONALE DE SOCIOLOGIE 25,99-100 (1967): 5-16.

2707. Stokes, Randall G. "Afrikaner Calvinism and Economic Action: The Weberian Thesis in South Africa." AMERICAN JOURNAL OF SOCIOLOGY 81 (1975): 62-81.

2708. Suolinna, Kirsti. "Weber's Thesis on the Protestant Ethic. A Micro and Macrosociological Perspective." TEMENOS (Finland) 9 (1973): 80-107.

2709. Tawney, R.H. "Religious Thought on Social and Economic Questions in the Sixteenth and Seventeenth Centuries. I. The Medieval Background (August, 461f). II. The Collision of Standards (October, 673f). III. The Social Ethics of Puritanism (December, 804f)." JOURNAL OF POLITICAL ECONOMY 31 (1923).

2710. Tawney, R.H. RELIGION AND THE RISE OF CAPITALISM. Baltimore: Penguin, 1947.

2711. Thorner, Isidor. "Ascetic Protestantism and the Development of Science and Technology." AMERICAN JOURNAL OF SOCIOLOGY 58 (1952): 25-33.

2712. Tiryakian, Edward A. "Neither Marx nor Durkheim...Perhaps Weber." AMERICAN JOURNAL OF SOCIOLOGY 81 (1975): 1-33.

2713. Veroff, J., S. Feld, and G. Gurin. "Achievement Motivation and Religious Background." AMERICAN SOCIOLOGICAL REVIEW 27 (1962): 205-217.

2714. Viner, Jacob. RELIGIOUS THOUGHT AND ECONOMIC SOCIETY: FOUR CHAPTERS OF AN UNFINISHED WORK, edited by Jacques Melitz and Donald Winch. Durham, N.C.: Duke University Press, 1978.

2715. Wagner, Helmut. "The Protestant Ethic: A Mid Twentieth Century View." SA 25 (1964): 34-40.

2716. Wagner, Helmut R., Katheryn Doyle, and Victor Fisher. "Religious Background and Higher Education." AMERICAN SOCIOLOGICAL REVIEW 24 (1959): 852-856.

* Warren, Bruce L. THE RELATIONSHIPS BETWEEN RELIGIOUS PREFERENCE AND SOCIO-ECONOMIC ACHIEVEMENT OF AMERICAN MEN. Cited above as item 1293.

* Warren, Bruce L. "Socioeconomic Achievement and Religion: The American Case." Cited above as item 1294.

2717. Wax, Murray. "Ancient Judaism and the Protestant Ethic." AMERICAN JOURNAL OF SOCIOLOGY 65,5 (1960): 449-455.

2718. Weber, Max. "Die protestantische Ethik und der 'Geist' des Kapitalismus. I: Das Problem." ARCHIV FÜR SOZIALWISSENSCHAFT UND SOZIALPOLITIK 20 (1904): 1-54.
"II: Die Berufsidee des asketischen Protestantismus." ARCHIV FÜR SOZIALWISSENSCHAFT UND SOZIALPOLITIK 21 (1905): 1-110.
THE PROTESTANT ETHIC AND THE SPIRIT OF CAPITALISM, translated by Talcott Parsons. New York: Scribners, 1958.

2719. Weber, Max. "Anticritical Last Word on The Spirit of Capitalism," translated with an introduction by Wallace M. Davis. AMERICAN JOURNAL OF SOCIOLOGY 83,5 (1978): 1105-1131.

* Weber, Max. "Die protestantischen Sekten und der Geist des Kapitalismus."
"The Protestant Sects and the Spirit of Capitalism." Cited above as item 57.

2720. Winter, J. Alan. "Elective Affinities between Religious Beliefs and Ideologies of Management in Two Eras." AMERICAN JOURNAL OF SOCIOLOGY 79 (1974): 1134-1150.

2721. Winter, J. Alan. "Review Article: Quantitative Studies of the Applicability of the Weber Thesis to Post-World War II U.S.A.: A Call for Redirected Efforts." RRR 16,1 (1974): 47-58.

* Yinger, J. Milton. RELIGION IN THE STRUGGLE FOR POWER: A STUDY IN THE SOCIOLOGY OF RELIGION. Cited above as item 296.

SECTION H: EVOLUTION (SOCIETAL)

Herbert Spencer and his followers conceived of societies evolving from primitive undifferentiated states toward higher greatly-differentiated states. A few writers have applied this model to the study of religion.

2722. Bellah, Robert N. "Religious Evolution." AMERICAN SOCIOLOGICAL REVIEW 29 (1964): 358-374. Also in R.N. Bellah, BEYOND BELIEF (item 3577), pp. 20-50.

2723. Bird, Frederick. "Max Weber's Perspectives on Religious Evolution." SCIENCES RELIGIEUSES/STUDIES IN RELIGION 13,2 (1984): 215-225.

2724. Burney, Pierre. "Implications religieuses de l'évolution sociale." CAHIERS INTERNATIONAUX DE SOCIOLOGIE 44 (1968): 95-118.

2725. Hayes, E.C. "The Evolution of Religion." AMERICAN JOURNAL OF SOCIOLOGY 21,1 (1915): 45-64.

2726. Klingender, F.D. "Palaeolithic Religion and the Principle of Social Evolution." BRITISH JOURNAL OF SOCIOLOGY 5,2 (1954): 138-153.

2727. Leone, Mark P. "The Economic Basis for the Evolution of Mormon Religion." In Irving I. Zaretsky and Mark P. Leone (eds.), RELIGIOUS MOVEMENTS IN CONTEMPORARY AMERICA. Princeton: Princeton University Press, 1974, pp. 722-766.

2728. Luhmann, Niklas. DIE FUNKTION DER RELIGION. Frankfurt: Suhrkamp, 1977.
RELIGIOUS DOGMATICS AND THE EVOLUTION OF SOCIETIES, translated by Peter Beyer. New York: Edwin Mellen, 1984.

2729. Pepper, George. "Religion and Evolution." SA 31,2 (1970): 78-91.

2730. Pruett, Gordon E. "A Note on Robert Bellah's Theory of Religious Evolution: The Early Modern Period." SA 34,1 (1973): 50-55.

2731. Robertson, Roland. "Parsons on the Evolutionary Significance of American Religion." SA 43,4 (1982): 307-326.

2732. Sheils, Dean. "An Evolutionary Explanation of Supportive Monotheism: A Comparative Study." INTERNATIONAL JOURNAL OF COMPARATIVE SOCIOLOGY 15,1-2 (1974): 47-56.

2733. White, O. Kendall, and Daryl White. "A Critique of Leone's and Dogin's Application of Bellah's Evolutionary Model to Mormonism." RRR 23,1 (1981): 39-53.

CHAPTER THREE: DISCIPLINARY CONCEPTUALIZATIONS

While the previous two chapters have focused on the sociology of religion's objects of study, this chapter focuses on the theories and concepts of the subdiscipline.

SECTION A: DEFINITION OF RELIGION

Most people have some idea of what religion is, but it has proven to be a difficult term to define. Most definitions which seem adequate for some religions turn out to be inadequate for others. In addition, the definition one uses in a study may well determine the findings one will be able to make.

2734. Alatas, Syed Hussein. "Les difficultés de définir la religion." REVUE INTERNATIONALE DE SCIENCES SOCIALES 29,2 (1977): 233-256.

2735. Barnhart, J.E. THE STUDY OF RELIGION AND ITS MEANING. The Hague: Mouton, 1977.

* Berger, Peter L. "Sociological Definitions of Religion." In P.L. Berger, THE SACRED CANOPY (item 2152), pp. 175-177.

2736. Berger, Peter L. "Some Second Thoughts on Substantive Versus Functional Definitions of Religion." JSSR 13 (1974): 125-133.

2737. Blasi, Anthony J. "Definition of Religion and Phenomenological Approach towards a Problematic." LES CAHIERS DU CENTRE DE RECHERCHES EN SOCIOLOGIE RELIGIEUSE 3 (1980): 55-70.

2738. Clark, W.H. "How do Social Scientists Define Religion?" JOURNAL OF SOCIAL PSYCHOLOGY 47 (1958): 143-147.

2739. Cohen, Morris R. "Baseball as a National Religion." In M.R. Cohen, THE FAITH OF A LIBERAL. New York: Holt, 1946, pp. 334-336. Also in L. Schneider (ed.), RELIGION, CULTURE AND SOCIETY (volume cited in item 1824), pp. 36-38.

2740. Cohn, Werner. "Is Religion Universal? Problems of Definition." JSSR 2 (1962): 25-33.

2741. Deconchy, J.P. "La définition de la religion chez William James. Dans quelle mesure peut-on l'opérationaliser?" ARCHIVES DE SOCIOLOGIE DES RELIGIONS 27 (1969): 51-70.

2742. Dimock, H.S. "Trends in the Redefinition of Religion." JOURNAL OF RELIGION 8 (1928): 434-452.

* Dobbelaere, Karel, and Jan Lauwers. "Definition of Religion: A Sociological Critique." Cited above as item 2470.

2743. Durkheim, Emile. "De la définition des phénomènes religieux." L'ANNEE SOCIOLOGIQUE 2 (1898): 1-28.

2744. Durkheim, Emile. ELEMENTARY FORMS OF THE RELIGIOUS LIFE, translated by J.W. Swain. New York: Free Press, 1969, pp. 36-47. Relevant passages in J.M. Yinger (ed.), RELIGION, SOCIETY AND THE INDIVIDUAL (volume cited in item 943), pp. 344-350.

2745. Eister, Allan W. "Introduction." In A.W. Eister (ed.), CHANGING PERSPECTIVES IN THE SCIENTIFIC STUDY OF RELIGION (volume cited in item 353), pp. 1-11.

2746. Garrett, William R. "Troublesome Transcendence: The Supernatural in the Scientific Study of Religion." SA 35,3 (1974): 167-180.

2747. Glock, Charles Y., and Rodney Stark. Ch. 1 in RELIGION AND SOCIETY IN TENSION (volume cited in item 141).

2748. Goody, Jack. "Religion and Ritual: The Definitional Problem." BRITISH JOURNAL OF SOCIOLOGY 12 (1961): 142-164.

2749. Grossman, Nathan. "Comment on Peter Berger's Definition of Religion." JSSR 14,3 (1975): 289-292.

2750. Horton, Robin. "A Definition of Religion and its Uses." JOURNAL OF THE ROYAL ANTHROPOLOGICAL INSTITUTE 90 (1960): 201-226.

2751. Kishimoto, Hideo. "An Operational Definition of Religion." NUMEN 8,3 (1961): 236-240.

2752. Lemert, Charles C. "Defining Non-Church Religion." RRR 16,3 (1975): 186-198.

2753. Machalek, Richard. "Definitional Strategies in the Study of Religion." JSSR 16,4 (1977): 395-401.

* Machalek, Richard, and Michael Martin. "'Invisible' Religions: Some Preliminary Evidence." Cited above as item 2593.

2754. Maduro, Otto. CAMPO RELIGIOSO Y CONFLICTOS SOCIALES. MARCO TEORICO PARA EL ANALISIS DE SUS INTERRELACIONES EN LATINOAMERICA. Travail de fin d'études présenté en vue de l'obtention du grade de Licencié en Sociologie, Université Catholique de Louvain, 1978.
RELIGION Y LUCHA DE CLASES. Caracas: Editorial Ateneo de Caracas, 1979.
RELIGION AND SOCIAL CONFLICTS, translated by Robert R. Barr. Maryknoll, N.Y.: Orbis, 1982.

2755. Maier, J. "Sulla definizione sociologica della religione." IL MULINO 4,8-9 (1955): 728-733.

2756. Malinowski, Bronislaw. MAGIC, SCIENCE AND RELIGION AND OTHER ESSAYS. Garden City, N.Y.: Anchor-Doubleday, 1948.

2757. Martinez Scheifler, Mercedes. "Acercamiento sociológico al concepto de religión." REVISTA INTERNACIONAL DE SOCIOLOGIA 30,1-2 (1973): 242-248.

2758. Natanson, Maurice. Ch. 7. "Religion," in M. Natanson, THE JOURNEYING SELF. A STUDY IN PHILOSOPHY AND SOCIAL ROLE. Reading, Massachusetts: Addison-Wesley, 1970, pp. 128-149.

2759. Penner, Hans H. "The Problem of Semantics in the Study of Religion." In Robert D. Baird (ed.), METHODOLOGICAL ISSUES IN RELIGIOUS STUDIES. Chico: New Horizons Press, 1975, pp. 79-94.

2760. Piwowarski, Wladyslaw. "The Sociological Definition of Religion." STUPDIA SOCOLOGICZNE KWARTALNIK 53,2 (1974): 197-218.

2761. Prades, José A. "Sur le concept de religion." STUDIES IN RELIGION/ SCIENCES RELIGIEUSES 3 (1973): 47-62.

2762. Richard, Réginald. "Le concept de religion: specificité ou homologie." CAHIERS DU CENTRE DE RECHERCHES EN SOCIOLOGIE RELIGIEUSE 2 (1978): 3-17.

* Robertson, Roland. "Religion and Sociological Factors in the Analysis of Secularization." Cited above as item 2548.

2763. Sanchez Cano, José. "La sociologia de la religión y el concepto de religión." REVISTA DE ESTUDIOS POLITICOS (Spain): 204 (1975): 207-218.

2764. Schneider, Louis. "The Sociology of Religion: Some Areas of Theoretical Potential." SA 31,3 (1970): 131-144.

2765. Schneider, Louis. "The Scope of 'The Religious Factor' and the Sociology of Religion: Notes on Definition, Idolatry and Magic." SOCIAL RESEARCH 41,2 (1974): 340-361.

2766. Simmel, Georg. "De la religion au point de vue de la théorie de la connaissance." In BIBLIOTHEQUE DU CONGRES INTERNATIONAL DE PHILOSOPHIE, 1st, Paris, Vol. II, "Morale Générale." Paris: Librairie Armand Colin, 1903, pp. 319-337.
Translation by Eleanor M. Miller and Dale J. Jaffe in RELIGION, THE CUTTING EDGE. NEW ENGLAND SOCIOLOGIST 5,1 (1984): 66-77.

2767. Sissons, Peter L. "The Sociological Definition of Religion." EXPOSITORY TIMES 82,5 (1971): 132-137.

2768. Spiro, Melford E. "Religion: Problems of Definition and Explanation." In Michael Banton (ed.), ANTHROPOLOGICAL APPROACHES TO THE STUDY OF RELIGION. London: Tavistock, 1966.

* Stark, Rodney, and William Sims Bainbridge. "Of Churches, Sects, and Cults: Preliminary Concepts for a Theory of Religious Movements." Cited above as item 2272.

2769. Swatos, William H., Jr. "Religion, Secularization, and Social Process." RELIGION, THE CUTTING EDGE. NEW ENGLAND SOCIOLOGIST 5,1 (1984): 95-112.

2770. Thorman, Donald J. "The Sociological Concept of Religion." AMERICAN CATHOLIC SOCIOLOGICAL REVIEW 12,3 (1951): 148-153.

2771. Turner, Robert G., Jr. "Consciousness, Valuation, and Religion: Toward A Paradigm." RRR 18,1 (1976): 25-35.

2772. Wach, Joachim. "Universals in Religion." In J. Wach, TYPES OF RELIGIOUS EXPERIENCE (item 3009), pp. 30-47.

2773. Ward, Lester F. "The Essential Nature of Religion." INTERNATIONAL JOURNAL OF ETHICS 8 (1898): 169-192.

2774. Weigert, Andrew J. "Functional, Substantive, or Political? A Comment on Berger's 'Second Thoughts on Defining Religion.'" JSSR 13,4 (1974): 483-486.

2775. Wells, A.R. "Is Supernatural Belief Essential in a Definition of Religion?" JOURNAL OF PHILOSOPHY 18 (1921): 269-275.

2776. Williams, J. Paul. "The Nature of Religion." JSSR 2 (1962): 3-17.

2777. Yinger, J. Milton. "A Comparative Study of the Substructures of Religion." JSSR 16,1 (1977): 67-86.

SECTION B: RELIGIOSITY

Religiosity (general)

2778. Bibby, Reginald W. "The Nature of Religiosity in Canada." In C. Beattie and S. Crysdale (eds.), SOCIOLOGY CANADA: READINGS, 2nd edition. Toronto: Butterworth 1977.

* Campbell, Colin, and Robert W. Coles. "Religiosity, Religious Affiliation and Religious Belief." Cited above as item 931.

* Clayton, Richard R. "Religiosity and Premarital Sexual Permissiveness: Elaboration of the Relationship and Debate." Cited above as item 316.

* Clayton, Richard R., and W.L. Tolone. "Religiosity and Attitudes toward Induced Abortion: An Elaboration of the Relationship." Cited above as item 210.

* Eckhardt, Kenneth W. "Religiosity and Civil Rights Militancy." Cited above as item 2293.

2779. Erskine, H.G. "The Polls: Personal Religion." PUBLIC OPINION QUARTERLY 29,1 (1965): 145-157.

2780. Estus, Charles W., and Michael A. Overington. "The Meaning and the End of Religiosity." AMERICAN JOURNAL OF SOCIOLOGY 75 (1970): 760-781.

* Faulkner, Joseph E., and Gordon F. DeJong. "A Note on Religiosity and Moral Behavior of a Sample of College Students." Cited above as item 182.

2781. Fichter, Joseph H. "Sociological Measurement of Religiosity." RRR 10 (1969): 169-177.

* Finner, Stephen L., and Jerome D. Gamache. "The Relation between Religious Commitment and Attitudes toward Induced Abortion." Cited above as item 212.

2782. Houtart, François. LA MENTALIDAD RELIGIOSA Y SU EVOLUCION EN LAS CIUDADES. Bogotá: Facultad de Sociologia, Universidad Nacional de Colombia, 1959.

2783. Hunt, Richard A., and Morton B. King. "Religiosity and Marriage." JSSR 17,4 (1978): 399-406.

2784. Kauffman, J. Howard. "Social Correlates of Spiritual Maturity among North American Mennonites." SA 40,1 (1979): 27-42.

2785. Kenkel, William F., et al. "Religious Socialization, Present Devoutness and Willingness to Enter a Mixed Religious Marriage." SA 26,1 (1965): 30-37.

* Lenski, Gerhard. "Social Correlates of Religious Interest." Cited above as item 1107.

2786. Nelsen, Hart M., Raytha Yokley, and Thomas W. Madron. "Rural-Urban Differences in Religiosity." RURAL SOCIOLOGY 36 (1971): 389-396.

* Perkins, H. Wesley. "Organized Religion as Opiate or Prophetic Stimulant: A Study of American and English Assessments of Social Justice in Two Urban Settings." Cited above as item 95.

* Photiadis, John D., and Jeanne Biggar. "Religiosity, Education and Ethnic Distance." Cited above as item 457.

2787. Roberts, Michael K., and James D. Davidson. "The Nature and Sources of Religious Involvement." RRR 25,4 (1984): 334-350.

2788. Roof, W. Clark. "The Local-Cosmopolitan Orientation and Traditional Religious Commitment." SA 33,1 (1972): 1-15.

* Ruppel, Howard J., Jr. "Religiosity and Premarital Sexual Permissiveness: A Methodological Note." Cited above as item 331.

* Thalheimer, Fred. "Continuity and Change in Religiosity." Cited above as item 1882.

* Tygart, Clarence E. "Religiosity and University Student Anti-Vietnam War Attitudes: A Negative or Curvilinear Relationship?" Cited above as item 293.

* Weigert, Andrew J., and Darwin L. Thomas. "Secularization and Religiosity: A Cross-National Study of Catholic Adolescents in Five Societies." Cited above as item 2575.

2789. Yinger, J. Milton. "A Structural Examination of Religion." JSSR 8 (1969): 88-99.

Belief

2790. Alston, John P. "Perceived Strength of Religious Beliefs. Review of the Polls." JSSR 12,1 (1973): 109-112.

2791. Bango, J.F. "Convictions religieuses de la jeunesse hongroise scolaire et étudiante." SC 15 (1968): 403-411.

2792. Becker, Lee B. INFLUENCES OF INTERPERSONAL COMMUNICATION AND OTHER PEER AND FAMILY VARIABLES ON CHANGE IN RELIGIOUS VALUES AND BEHAVIORS DURING COLLEGE. Unpublished Ph.D. dissertation, University of Wisconsin, 1974.

2793. Becker, Lee B. "Predictors of Change in Religious Beliefs and Behaviors during College." SA 38,1 (1977): 65-74.

2794. Bellah, Robert N. "Religion and Belief: The Historical Background of 'Non-Belief.'" In R.N. Bellah, BEYOND BELIEF (item 3577), pp. 216-229.

* Betts, George Herbert. THE BELIEFS OF 700 MINISTERS. Cited above as item 548.

2795. Borhek, James T., and Richard F. Curtis. A SOCIOLOGY OF BELIEF. New York: Wiley, 1975.

* Bourdillon, M.F.C. "Pluralism and Problems of Belief." Cited above as item 345.

2796. Bovy, Lambert. "Sondage sur la 'mentalité chrétienne' de la population canadienne-française de Montréal." ARCHIVES DE SOCIOLOGIE DES RELIGIONS 9,17 (1964): 135-146.

2797. Brennan, John Stephen. "Mayan Belief Systems: A Network Interpretation." MID-AMERICAN REVIEW OF SOCIOLOGY 4,2 (1979): 17-37.

* Campbell, Colin, and Robert W. Coles. "Religiosity, Religious Affiliation and Religious Belief: The Exploration of a Typology." Cited above as item 931.

2798. Crysdale, Stewart. THE CHANGING CHURCH IN CANADA: BELIEFS AND SOCIAL ATTITUDES OF UNITED CHURCH PEOPLE. Toronto: United Church of Canada Publishing House, 1965.

2799. Currie, Raymond. RELIGION AND IMAGES OF MAN AMONG CALGARY YOUTH. Unpublished Ph.D. dissertation, Fordham University, 1973.

* Davidson, James D. "Patterns of Belief at the Denominational and Congregational Levels." Cited above as item 1271.

2800. Davidson, James D. "Religious Belief as a Dependent Variable." SA 33,2 (1972): 81-94.

2801. Davidson, James D., J.A. Schlangen, and William V. D'Antonio. "Some Implications of Interfaith Perception, Patterns of Belief, and Perceptions of Church Structure." SA 28 (1967): 123-141.

2802. Deniel, Raymond. "Croyances religieuses en milieu urbain: Ouagadougou." SC 16,1 (1969): 101-108.

2803. Dixon, Keith. THE SOCIOLOGY OF BELIEF: FALLACY AND FOUNDATION. Boston: Routledge and Kegan Paul, 1980.

2804. Dornbusch, Sanford M. "Two Studies in the Flexibility of Belief." In P.E. Hammond and B. Johnson (eds.), AMERICAN MOSAIC (volume cited above in item 559), pp. 100-110.

2805. Driedger, Leo. "Doctrinal Belief: A Major Factor in the Differential Perception of Social Issues." SOCIOLOGICAL QUARTERLY 15 (1974): 66-80.

2806. Fuse, Toyomasa. SOCIOLOGICAL ANALYSIS OF NEO-ORTHODOXY IN AMERICAN PROTESTANTISM. Unpublished Ph.D. dissertation, University of California at Berkeley, 1961.

2807. Fuse, Toyomasa. "Religion, Society and Accommodation. Some Remarks on Neo-Orthodoxy in American Protestantism." SC 12,4 (1965): 345-358.

2808. Gaede, Stan. "A Causal Model of Belief-Orthodoxy: Proposal and Empirical Test." SA 37,3 (1976): 205-217.

* Gannon, Thomas M. THE INTERNAL SOCIAL ORGANIZATION AND BELIEF SYSTEM OF AMERICAN PRIESTS. Cited above as item 621.

* Glock, Charles Y., and Rodney Stark. CHRISTIAN BELEIFS AND ANTI-SEMITISM. Cited above as item 438.

2809. Gustafson, Paul M. "Exegesis on the Gospel according to St. Max." SA 34,1 (1973): 12-25.

2810. Hertel, Bradley R. "Inconsistency of Beliefs in the Existence of Heaven and Afterlife." RRR 21,2 (1980): 171-183.

* Hertel, Bradley R., and Hart M. Nelsen. "Are We Entering a Post-Christian Era? Religious Belief and Attendance in America, 1957-1968." Cited above as item 2501.

2811. Hoge, Dean R., Everett L. Perry, and Gerald L. Klever. "Theology as a Source of Disagreement about Protestant Church Goals and Priorities." RRR 19,2 (1978): 116-138.

* Hoge, Dean R., and David T. Polk. "A Test of Theories of Protestant Church Participation and Commitment." Cited above as item 146.

* Hoge, Dean R., et al. "Desired Outcomes of Religious Education and Youth Ministry in Six Denominations." Cited above as item 338.

* Hoge, Dean R., and John E. Dyble. "The Influence of Assimilation on American Protestant Ministers' Beliefs, 1928-1978." Cited above as item 651.

* Johnson, Benton. "Theology and the Position of Pastors on Public Issues." Cited above as item 660.

2812. Kim, Hei Chu. THE ROLE OF RELIGIOUS BELIEF AND SOCIAL STRUCTURE IN KOREA'S BREAKTHROUGH INTO MODERNITY. Unpublished Ph.D. dissertation, New School for Social Research, New York, 1973.

2813. Limberto, Sergio. "Tipologie di credenze e di atteggiamenti nei confronti della Chiesa Cattolica." BOLLETTINO DI STATISTICA E SOCIOLOGIA RELIGIOSA (Italy) 2 (1974): 21-38.

* Longino, Charles F., Jr., and Jeffrey K. Hadden. "Dimensionality of Belief among Mainstream Protestant Clergy." Cited above as item 686.

* Lovell, Terry. "Weber, Goldmann and the Sociology of Beliefs." Cited above as item 2656.

2814. Mader, Paul D. COLLEGE STUDENTS AND RELIGION: AN EXAMINATION OF YINGER'S NON-DOCTRINAL RELIGION QUESTIONS AS "RESIDUAL RELIGION." Unpublished M.A. thesis, Western Kentucky University, 1972.

2815. Maier, J., and W. Spinrad. "Comparison of Religious Beliefs and Practices of Jewish, Catholic and Protestant Students." PHYLON 18 (1958): 355-360.

2816. Maier, J., and W. Spinrad. "Religiöse Überzeugungen und religiöse Verhaltungsweisen." KÖLNER ZEITSCHRIFT FÜR SOZIOLOGIE UND SOZIALPSYCHOLOGIE 10 (1958): 439-445.

* McConahay, John B., and Joseph C. Hough, Jr. "Love and Guilt-Oriented Dimensions of Christian Belief." Cited above as item 1737.

2817. Middleton, Russell. "Do Christian Beliefs Cause Anti-Semitism?" AMERICAN SOCIOLOGICAL REVIEW 38,1 (1973): 33-52.

* Neal, Marie Augusta. "The Relation between Religious Belief and Structural Change in Religious Orders: Developing An Effective Measuring Instrument." Cited above as item 1054.

* Neal, Marie Augusta. "The Relation between Religious Belief and Structural Change in Religious Orders: Some Evidence." Cited above as item 1055.

* Nelsen, Hart M. "The Influence of Social and Theological Factors upon the Goals of Religious Education." Cited above as item 1285.

2818. Poythress, Norman G. "Literal, Antiliteral, and Mythological Religious Orientations." JSSR 14 (1975): 271-284.

* Putney, Snell, and Russell Middleton. "Dimensions and Correlates of Religious Ideologies." Cited above as item 495.

2819. Schwartz, David F. RECONSTRUCTION OF A BELIEF INDEX: MODERN VALUES AND PRE-VATICAN BELIEF. Unpublished M.A. thesis, Loyola University of Chicago, 1975.

* Shand, J.A. RELIGIOUS BELIEFS OF CHICAGO CLERGY. Cited above as item 755.

2820. Sigelman, Lee. "Review of the Polls: Multi-Nation Surveys of Religious Beliefs." JSSR 16,3 (1977): 289-294.

* Simmons, J.L. "On Maintaining Deviant Belief Systems. A Case Study." Cited above as item 2155.

* Snow, David A., and Richard Machalek. "On the Presumed Fragility of Unconventional Beliefs." Cited above as item 2156.

* Snow, David A., and Richard Machalek. "Second Thoughts on the Presumed Fragility of Unconventional Beliefs." Cited above as item 2157.

2821. Spaulding, Kent E. "The Theology of the Pew." RRR 13,3 (1972): 206-211.

* Stark, Rodney, and Charles Y. Glock. AMERICAN PIETY: THE NATURE OF RELIGIOUS COMMITMENT. Cited above as item 497.

* Thomas, John L. RELIGION AND THE AMERICAN PEOPLE. Cited above as item 2220.

2822. Turner, Bryan S. "Belief, Ritual and Experience: The Case of Methodism." SC 18,2 (1971): 187-201.

* Tygart, Clarence E. "The Role of Theology among Other 'Belief' Variables for Clergy Civil Rights Activism." Cited above as item 787.

2823. Wenzel, Kristen. "The Religious Belief System: A Further Refinement on the Defined Relationship between Religion and Society." SA 32,1 (1971): 45-60.

2824. Winter, J. Alan. "The Metaphoric Parallelist Approach to the Sociology of Theistic Beliefs: Theme, Variations and Implications." SA 34,3 (1973): 212-229.

* Winter, J. Alan. "Elective Affinities between Religious Beliefs and Ideologies of Management in Two Eras." Cited above as item 2720.

Atheism

2825. Black, Alan W. "Organized Irreligion: The New South Wales Humanist Society." In A. Black and P. Glasner (eds.), PRACTICE AND BELIEF (volume cited in item 824), pp. 154-166.

2826. Budd, Susan. "The Loss of Faith: Reasons for Unbelief among Members of the Secular Movement in England, 1850-1950." PAST AND PRESENT 36 (1967): 106-125.

2827. Budd, Susan. VARIETIES OF UNBELIEF. ATHEISTS AND AGNOSTICS IN ENGLISH SOCIETY, 1850-1950. London: Heineman, 1977.

2828. Campbell, Colin. TOWARD A SOCIOLOGY OF IRRELIGION. London: Macmillan, 1972; New York: Herder and Herder, 1972.

2829. Campbell, Colin. "Analyzing the Rejection of Religion." SC 24,4 (1977): 339-346.

2830. Caporale, Rocco, and Antonio Grumelli (eds.) THE CULTURE OF UNBELIEF. STUDIES AND PROCEEDINGS FROM THE FIRST INTERNATIONAL SYMPOSIUM ON BELIEF HELD AT ROME, MARCH 22-27, 1969. Berkeley: University of California Press, 1971. Contains item 2492.

* Cheal, David J. "Political Radicalism and Religion: Competitors for Commitment." Cited above as item 1548.

2831. Davis, J.H. THE DISBELIEF GRADIENT AND FRAME OF REFERENCE. Unpublished M.A. thesis, Michigan State University, 1958.

2832. Demerath, Nicholas J., III. "Irreligion, A-Religion, and the Rise of the Religionless Church: Two Case Studies in Organizational Convergence." SA 30,4 (1969): 191-203.

2833. Demerath, Nicholas J., III, and Victor Thiessen. "On Spitting against the Wind: Organizational Precariousness and American Irreligion." AMERICAN JOURNAL OF SOCIOLOGY 71 (1966): 674-687.

* Grumelli, Antonio. "Athéisme et sécularization: La dimension sociologique." Cited above as item 2491.

2834. Grumelli, Antonio, and G. Bolino. "Per una tipologie dell'ateismo." STUDI SOCIALI 10,1 (1972): 162-168.

2835. Guyua, M. THE NON-RELIGION OF THE FUTURE: A SOCIOLOGICAL STUDY. New York: Schocken, 1962.

2836. Hadaway, C. Kirk, and Wade Clark Roof. "Those Who Stay Religious 'Nones' and Those Who Don't: A Research Note." JSSR 18,2 (1979): 194-200.

2837. Hogan, Michael. "Australian Secularity: The Disavowal of Denominational Allegiance." JSSR 18,4 (1979): 390-404.

2838. Klohr, Olaf (ed.) RELIGION UND ATHEISM HEUTE. ERGEBNISSE UND AUFGEBEN MARXISTISCHER RELIGIONSSOZIOLOGIE. Berlin: VEB Deutsche Verlag der Wissenschaft, 1966.

2839. Ladrière, Paul. "L'athéisme à Vatican II. De la condamnation du communisme à la négociation avec l'humanisme athée." SC 24,4 (1977): 347-391.

2840. Nesti, Arnaldo. "L'ateismo come fatto sociale." IDOC INTERNAZIONALE 1 (1975): 49-55.

* O'Dea, Thomas F. ALIENATION, ATHEISM AND THE RELIGIOUS CRISIS. Cited above as item 5.

2841. Pivovarov, V.G. "The Methodology of Collection and Processing of Primary Sociological Information in Study of Problems of Religion and Atheism." SC 21,2 (1974): 191-206.

2842. Powell, David E. ANTIRELIGIOUS PROPAGANDA IN THE SOVIET UNION: A STUDY OF MASS PERSUASION. Cambridge, Massachusetts: MIT Press, 1975.

2843. Santy, H. "A propos d'une étude. Entre athée et croyant -- une typologie." SC 14,22 (1967): 133-136.

2844. Steeman, Theodore M. "The Study of Atheism. Sociological Approach." IDOC,dossier 20-22 (1966).
THE STUDY OF ATHEISM. A SOCIOLOGICAL APPROACH. Louvain: FERES, 1966.

2845. Steeman, Theodore M. "Psychological and Sociological Aspects of Modern Atheism." CONCILIUM 23 (1967): 46-59.

2846. Steeman, Theodore M. "Atheism as Religious Crisis Phenomenon. A Reflexion on the Nature of the Problem." SC 24,4 (1977): 311-321.

2847. Swanborn, P.G., and J. Weima. "A Social-Psychological Study of Religious Non-Believers. A Critique and a Replication." SC 13,2 (1966): 158-164.

2848. Tamney, Joseph B., K. Hopkins, and J. Jacovini. "A Social-Psychological Study of Religious Non-Believers." SC 12,3 (1965): 177-186.

2849. Thompson, Andrew D. "Open-Mindedness and Indiscriminate Anti-Religious Orientation." JSSR 13,4 (1974): 471-477.

2850. Tomka, Miklós. "Les rites de passage dans les pays socialistes de l'Europe de l'Est." SC 29,2-3 (1982): 135-152.

2851. Veevers, J.E., and D.F. Cousineau. "The Heathen Canadians: Demographic Correlates of Non-Belief." PACIFIC SOCIOLOGICAL REVIEW 23 (1980): 199-216.

2852. Vernon, Glenn M. "The Religious Nones: A Neglected Category." JSSR 7 (1968): 219-229.

* Watzke, James. "Paganization and Dechristianization, or the Crisis in Institutional Symbols." Cited above as item 2573.

2853. Welch, Michael R. "Religious Non-Affiliates and Worldly Success." JSSR 17,1 (1978): 59-61.

2854. Welch, Michael R. "Review of the Polls. The Unchurched: Black Religious Non-Affiliates." JSSR 17,3 (1978): 289-293.

Death of God

2855. Fenn, Richard K. "The Death of God: An Analysis of Ideological Crisis." RRR 9 (1968): 171-181.

Fundamentalism

2856. Alexander, D. "Le fondamentalisme est-il un intégrisme?" SCHWEIZERISCHE ZEITSCHRIFT FÜR SOZIOLOGIE 9 (1983): 509-536.

2857. Ammerman, Nancy T. "Comment: Operationalizing Evangelicalism: An Amendment." SA 43,2 (1982): 170-171.

* Berg, Phillip L. "Self-Identified Fundamentalism among Protestant Seminarians: A Study of Persistence and Change in Value-Orientations." Cited above as item 992.

* DeJong, Gordon F. "Religious Fundamentalism, Socio-Economic Status, and Fertility Attitudes in the Southern Appalachians." Cited above as item 1778.

* DeJong, Gordon F., and Thomas R. Ford: "Religious Fundamentalism and Denominational Preference in the Southern Appalachian Region." Cited above as item 1272.

* Dudley, Roger Louis. "Alienation from Religion in Adolescents from Fundamentalist Religious Homes." Cited above as item 2051.

* Ethridge, F. Maurice, and Joe R. Feagin. "Varieties of Fundamentalism: A Conceptual and Empirical Analysis of two Protestant Denominations." Cited above as item 1274.

* Feagin, Joe R. "Prejudice and Religious Types: A Focused Study of Southern Fundamentalists." Cited above as item 432.

* Ford, Thomas R. "Status, Residence, and Fundamentalist Beliefs in the Southern Appalachian Region." Cited above as item 1794.

* Greeley, Andrew M., and William C. McCready. ETHNICITY IN THE UNITED STATES. Cited above as item 1576.

* Hendricks, John Stephen. RELIGIOUS AND POLITICAL FUNDAMENTALISM: THE LINK BETWEEN ALIENATION AND IDEOLOGY. Cited above as item 1589.

2858. Hudson, Charles. "The Structure of a Fundamentalist Christian Belief-System." In Samuel S. Hill (ed.), RELIGION AND THE SOLID SOUTH. Nashville: Abingdon, 1972, pp. 122-142.

* Jackson, Audrey R. "A Model for Determining Information Diffusion in a Family Planning Program." Cited above as item 251.

2859. Lamar, Ralph E. FUNDAMENTALISM AND SELECTED SOCIAL FACTORS IN THE SOUTHERN APPALACHIAN REGION. Unpublished M.A. thesis, University of Kentucky, 1962.

2860. Lechner, Frank J. "Forms of Fundamentalism. A Comparative Perspective on Cultural Revitalization in Modern Societies." SOCIALE WETENSCHAPPEN 25,4 (1982): 322-336.

2861. Maranell, Gary M. "Regional Patterns of Fundamentalistic Attitude Configuration." KANSAS JOURNAL OF SOCIOLOGY 4 (1968): 159-174.

* Maranell, Gary M., Richard A. Dodder, and David F. Mitchell. "Social Class and Premarital Sexual Permissiveness: A Subsequent Test." Cited above as item 328.

2862. Moberg, David O. "Fundamentalists and Evangelicals in Society." In David F. Wells and John D Woodbridge (eds.), THE EVANGELICALS. Nashville: Abingdon, 1975, pp. 143-169.

2863. Monoghan, Robert R. "Three Faces of the True Believer: Motivations for Attending a Fundamentalist Church." JSSR 6,2 (1967): 236-245.

* Peek, Charles W. "Deficient Methods or Different Data?" Cited above as item 481.

* Peek, Charles W., and Sharon Brown. "Sex Prejudice among White Protestants: Like or Unlike Ethnic Prejudice?" Cited above as item 482.

* Perry, Everett L. "Socio-Economic Factors and American Fundamentalism." Cited above as item 1856.

* Philibert, Paul J., and Dean R. Hoge. "Teachers, Pedagogy and the Process of Religious Education." Cited above as item 1287.

* Powell, Brian, and Lala Carr Steelman. "Fundamentalism and Sexism: A Reanalysis of Peek and Brown." Cited above as item 483.

* Quinney, Richard. "Political Conservatism, Alienation, and Fatalism: Contingencies of Social Status and Religious Fundamentalism." Cited above as item 8.

* Reinhardt, Robert M. RELIGION AND POLITICS: THE POLITICAL BEHAVIOR OF WEST VIRGINIA PROTESTANT FUNDAMENTALIST SECTARIANS. Cited above as item 1670.

2864. Richardson, James T. "New Forms of Deviancy in a Fundamentalist Church: A Case Study." RRR 16 (1975): 134-141.

* Richardson, James T., Mary White Stewart, and Robert B. Simmonds. "Conversion to Fundamentalism." Cited above as item 2019.

2865. Stones, Christopher R. "The Jesus People: Fundamentalism and Changes in Factors Associated with Conservatism." JSSR 17,2 (1978): 155-158.

* Willems, Emilio. FOLLOWERS OF THE NEW FAITH. Cited above as item 1894.

God, image of

2866. Benson, Peter, and Bernard Spilka. "God Image as a Function of Self-Esteem and Locus of Control." JSSR 12 (1973): 297-309.

* Greeley, Andrew M. THE RELIGIOUS IMAGINATION. Cited above as item 305.

2867. Hutsebaut, Dirk. "The Representation of God: Two Complementary Approaches." SC 19,3 (1972): 389-406.

2868. Lopez de Ceballos, Paloma. "Imágenes de Dios: perspectivas sociológicas." RAZON Y FE 877 (1971): 196-203.

2869. Mocciaro, Rosario. "Sviluppe del pensiere e immagine du Dio nel fanciulle e nel preadolescente." SOCIOLOGIA 17,1 (Nuova Serie, 1983): 297-304.

2870. Piazza, T., and Charles Y. Glock. "Images of God and Their Social Meanings." In R.Wuthnow (ed.), THE RELIGIOUS DIMENSION (volume cited in item 2164), pp. 69-92.

2871. Potvin, Raymond H. "Adolescent God Images." RRR 19,1 (1977): 43-53.

2872. Roof, Wade Clark, and Jennifer L. Roof. "Review of the Polls: Images of God among Americans." JSSR 23,2 (1984): 201-205.

2873. Spilka, Bernard, Phillip Armatas, and June Nussbaum. "The Concept of God. A Factor-Analytic Approach." RRR 6,1 (1964): 28-36.

2874. Van Aerde, Mark. "The Attitude of Adults towards God." SC 19,3 (1972): 407-413.

2875. Vercruysse, Godelieve. "The Meaning of God: A Factoranalytic Study." SC 19,3 (1972): 347-364.

2876. Vergote, Antoine, et al. "Concept of God and Parental Images." JSSR 8,1 (1969): 79-87.

2877. Vergote, Antoine, and Catherine Aubert. "Parental Images and Representations of God." SC 19,3 (1972): 431-444.

Heresy

2878. Adams, Robert L. "Conflict over Charges of Heresy in American Protestant Seminaries." SC 17,2 (1970): 243-260.

2879. Kurtz, Lester R. "The Politics of Heresy." AMERICAN JOURNAL OF SOCIOLOGY 88,6 (1983): 1085-1115.

2880. Zito, George V. "Toward a Sociology of Heresy." SA 44,2 (1983): 123-130.

Literalism

2881. Greeley, Andrew M. "Comment on Hunt's 'Mythological-Symbolic Religious Commitment: The LAM Scales.'" JSSR 11 (1972): 287-289.

2882. Hunt, Richard A. "Mythological-Symobolic Religious Commitment: The LAM Scales." JSSR 10 (1972): 42-52.

2883. Orlowski, Chad D. "Linguistic Dimension of Religious Measurement." JSSR 18,3 (1979): 306-311.

* Poythress, Norman G. "Literal, Antiliteral, and Mythological Religious Orientations." Cited above as item 2818.

Orthodoxy (doctrinal)

* Bahr, Howard M., Lois Franz Bartel, and Bruce A. Chadwick. "Orthodoxy, Activism, and the Salience of Religion." Cited above as item 488.

2884. Balswick, Jack O., and James W. Balkwell. "Religious Orthodoxy and Emotionality." RRR 19,3 (1978): 308-319.

* Clayton, Richard R. "Religious Orthodoxy and Premarital Sex." Cited above as item 315.

2885. Davidson, James D., and Gary J. Quinn. "Theological and Sociological Uses of the Concept 'Orthodoxy.'" RRR 18,1 (1976): 74-80

2886. Deconchy, Jean-Pierre. L'ORTHODOXIE RELIGIEUSE: ESSAI DE LOGIQUE PSYCHOSOCIALE. Paris: Ed. Ouvrières, 1971.

2887. Deconchy, Jean-Pierre. "La structure interne d'une corpus orthodoxe." ARCHIVES DE SOCIOLOGIE DES RELIGIONS 32 (1971): 107-119.

2888. Deconchy, Jean-Pierre. "Corpus orthodoxe et intégration de propositions 'nouvelles.'" ARCHIVES DE SOCIOLOGIE DES RELIGIONS 34 (1972): 101-110.

2889. Deconchy, Jean-Pierre. "L'orthodoxie enseignée par renforcement du règlage de l'appartenance." ARCHIVES DE SCIENCES SOCIALES DES RELIGIONS 38 (1974): 91-108.

2890. Deconchy, Jean-Pierre. ORTHODOXIE RELIGIEUSE ET SCIENCES HUMAINES. The Hague: Mouton, 1980.

2891. Erny, P. "(Re)naissance de l'orthodoxie occidentale. Traditionalisme et novation." SCHWEIZERISCHE ZEITSCHRIFT FÜR SOZIOLOGIE 9 (1983): 601-616.

* Feagin, Joseph R. "Prejudice, Orthodoxy, and the Social Situation." Cited above as item 433.

2892. Fullerton, J. Timothy, and Bruce Hunsberger. "A Unidimensional Measure of Christian Orthodoxy." JSSR 21,4 (1982): 317-326.

* Gaede, Stan. "A Causal Model of Belief-Orthodoxy: Proposal and Empirical Test." Cited above as item 2808.

* Gaede, Stan. "Religious Participation, Socioeconomic Status, and Belief-Orthodoxy." Cited above as item 1797.

* Gibbs, David R., Samuel A. Mueller, and James R. Wood. "Doctrinal Orthodoxy, Salience, and the Consequential Dimension." Cited above as item 491.

* Gregory, W. Edgar. "The Orthodoxy of the Authoritarian Personality." Cited above as item 440.

* Hartley, Shirley F., and Mary G. Taylor. "Religious Beliefs of Clergy Wives." Cited above as item 913.

* Keedy, T.C. "Anomie and Religious Orthodoxy." Cited above as item 28.

* Knudten, Richard D. "The Religion of the Indiana Baptist Prisoner." Cited above as item 2135.

* Lotz, Roy. "Another Look at the Orthodoxy-Anti-Semitism Nexus." Cited above as item 449.

* Maranell, Gary M. Ch. 11 in RESPONSES TO RELIGION. STUDIES IN THE SOCIAL PSYCHOLOGY OF RELIGIOUS BELIEF. Cited above as item 4.

2893. Mol, Johannes J. (Hans). "Towards a Sociology of Religious Orthodoxy." SOCIOLOGIA NEERLANDICA 10,2 (1974): 202-211.

* Nelsen, Hart M., Thomas W. Madron, and Raytha C. Yokley. "Black Religion's Promethean Motif: Orthodoxy and Militancy." Cited above as item 2303.

2894. Photiadis, J.D., and Arthur L. Johnson. "Orthodoxy, Church Participation, and Authoritarianism." AMERICAN JOURNAL OF SOCIOLOGY 71 (1963): 244-248.

* Putney, Snell, and Russell Middleton. "Dimensions and Correlates of Religious Ideologies." Cited above as item 495.

* Roof, W. Clark. "Religious Orthodoxy and Minority Prejudice: Causal Relationship or Reflection of Localistic World View?" Cited above as item 460.

2895. Rousseau, André. ESSAI SUR LA FONCTION SOCIALE DE L'ORTHODOXIE RELIGIEUSE. Paris: Centre Lebret, 1973.

* Stark, Rodney, and Charles Y. Glock. AMERICAN PIETY: THE NATURE OF RELIGIOUS COMMITMENT. Cited above as item 497.

2896. Tapley, Joel L. A STUDY OF RELIGIOUS EXPERIENCES AS RELATED TO CHURCH ORTHODOXY. Unpublished M.S. thesis, Brigham Young University, 1969.

* Thompson, Robert C., Jerry B. Michel, and T. John Alexander. "Christian Orthodoxy, Authoritarianism and Prejudice." Cited above as item 475.

* Van Roy, Ralph F., Frank D. Bean, and James R. Wood. "Social Mobility and Doctrinal Orthodoxy." Cited above as item 1952.

2897. Vernon, Glenn. "An Inquiry into the Scalability of Church Orthodoxy." SOCIOLOGY AND SOCIAL RESEARCH 39 (1955): 324-327.

2898. Vernon, Glenn M. "Background Factors Related to Church Orthodoxy." SOCIAL FORCES 34 (1956): 252-254.

* Wagenaar, Theodore C., and Patricia E. Bartos. "Orthodoxy and Attitudes of Clergymen toward Homosexuality and Abortion." Cited above as item 237.

2899. Welch, Kevin W. "An Interpersonal Influence Model of Traditional Religious Commitment." SOCIOLOGICAL QUARTERLY 22,1 (1981): 81-92.

Commitment

* Cheal, David J. "Political Radicalism and Religion: Competitors for Commitment." Cited above as item 1548.

* Currie, Raymond F. "Belonging, Commitment and Early Socialization in a Western City." Cited above as item 935.

2900. Davidson, James D., and Dean D. Knudsen. "A New Approach to Religious Commitment." SOCIOLOGICAL FOCUS 10 (1977): 151-173.

2901. Denys, Joseph. A COMPARATIVE STUDY OF THE EFFECTS OF ROMAN CATHOLIC HIGH SCHOOLS AND PUBLIC HIGH SCHOOL ON THE ROMAN CATHOLIC COMMITMENT OF ROMAN CATHOLIC STUDENTS IN SOUTHERN ONTARIO. Unpublished Ph.D. dissertation, University of Waterloo, 1972.

* Finner, Stephen L., and J.D. Gamache. "The Relation between Religious Commitment and Attitudes toward Induced Abortion." Cited above as item 212.

* Finney, John M., III. THE RELIGIOUS COMMITMENT OF AMERICAN WOMEN. Cited above as item 1097.

2902. Hardin, Bert L., and Günter Kehrer. "Identity and Commitment." In H. Mol (ed.), IDENTITY AND RELIGION (item 170), pp. 83-96.

2903. Harrison, Michael I. THE ORGANIZATION OF COMMITMENT IN THE CATHOLIC PENTECOSTAL MOVEMENT. Unpublished Ph.D. dissertation, University of Michigan, 1971.

2904. Hine, Virginia H. "Bridge Burners: Commitment and Participation in a Religious Movement." SA 31,2 (1970): 61-66.

* Hoge, Dean R., and David T. Polk. "A Test of Theories of Protestant Church Participation and Commitment." Cited above as item 146.

2905. Hood, Ralph W., Jr. "Forms of Religious Commitment and Intense Religious Experience." RRR 15 (1973): 29-36.

* Hougland, James G., and James R. Wood. "Control in Organizations and the Commitment of Members." Cited above as item 1148.

2906. Johnson, Martin A. "Family Life and Religious Commitment." RRR 14 (1973): 144-150.

* McGaw, Douglas B. CONGREGATION AND RELIGIOUS COMMITMENT. Cited above as item 1446.

* McGaw, Douglas B. "Commitment and Religious Community: A Comparison of a Charismatic and a Mainline Congregation." Cited above as item 1447.

* Nieves, Alvar. CORRELATES OF CLERGY COMMITMENT: THE SALVATION ARMY OFFICERS, AN ILLUSTRATIVE CASE STUDY. Cited above as item 710.

2907. Payne, Barbara P., and Kirk W. Elifson. "Commitment: A Comment on Uses of the Concept." RRR 17,3 (1976): 209-215.

2908. Pittard, Barbara B. THE MEANING AND MEASUREMENT OF COMMITMENT TO THE CHURCH. Unpublished Ph.D. dissertation, Emory University, 1963.

2909. Pittard, Barbara B. THE MEANING AND MEASUREMENT OF COMMITMENT TO THE CHURCH (Research Paper No. 13). Atlanta: Georgia State College School of Arts and Sciences, 1966.

2910. Roof, Wade Clark. "Concepts and Indicators of Religious Commitment: A Critical Review." In R. Wuthnow (ed.), THE RELIGIOUS DIMENSION (volume cited in item 2164), pp. 17-46.

* Roof, Wade Clark, and Richard B. Perkins. "On Conceptualizing Salience in Religious Commitment." Cited above as item 496.

2911. Sasaki, M.S. "Status Inconsistency and Religious Commitment." In R. Wuthnow (ed.), THE RELIGIOUS DIMENSION (volume cited in item 496), pp. 135-156.

2912. Shepherd, Gary, and Gordon Shepherd. "Mormon Commitment Rhetoric." JSSR 23,2 (1984): 129-139.

* Smidt, Corwin, and James M. Penning. "Religious Commitment, Political Conservatism, and Political and Social Tolerance in the United States: A Longitudinal Analysis." Cited above as item 124.

2913. Stark, Rodney. "Psychopathology and Religious Commitment." RRR 12 (1971): 165-176.

2914. Stark, Rodney, and William Sims Bainbridge. "Towards a Theory of Religion: Religious Commitment." JSSR 19,2 (1980): 114-128.

2915. Stuebing, William Kenneth. A PRELIMINARY SKETCH OF METHODOLOGICAL PROBLEMS ASSOCIATED WITH THE MEASUREMENT OF RELIGIOSITY, AND AN ANALYSIS OF SOCIAL AND PERSONALITY CORRELATES OF DIFFERENTIAL RELIGIOUS COMMITMENT. Unpublished M.A. thesis, University of Manitoba, 1969.

2916. Thun, Theophil. DIE RELIGIÖSE ENTSCHEIDUNG DER JUGEND. EINE RELIGIONS-PSYCHOLOGISCHE UNTERSUCHUNG NACH NIEDERSCHRIFTEN VON SCHÜLERN BEIDER BEKENTNISSE IN DER VOLKSSCHULE DER HÖHEREN SCHULE UND DER BERUFSSCHULE. Stuttgart: E. Klett, 1963.

2917. Wimberley, Ronald C. "Toward the Measurement of Commitment Strength." SA 35,3 (1974): 211-215.

2918. Wölber, Hans-Otto. RELIGION OHNE ENTSCHEIDUNG. Göttingen, 1959.

* Wuthnow, Robert. "Religious Commitment and Conservatism: In Search of an Elusive Relationship." Cited above as item 129.

2919. Wuthnow, Robert. "A Longitudinal, Cross-National Indicator of Societal Religious Commitment." JSSR 16,1 (1977): 87-99.

2920. Zahn, Gordon C. "The Commitment Dimension." SA 31,4 (1970): 203-208.

Dimensions of religiosity

2921. Allen, E.E., and R.W. Hites. "Factors in Religious Attitudes of Older Adolescents." JOURNAL OF SOCIAL PSYCHOLOGY 55 (1961): 265-273.

2922. Boos-Nünning, Ursula. DIMENSIONEN DER RELIGIOSITÄT. ZUR OPERATIONALISIERUNG UND MESSUNG RELIGIÖSER EINSTELLUNGEN. München and Mainz: Grünewald-Kaiser, 1972.

2923. Broen, William E., Jr. "A Factor-Analytic Study of Religious Attitudes." JOURNAL OF ABNORMAL PSYCHOLOGY 54 (1957): 176-179.

2924. Campbell, Douglas F., and Dennis W. Magill. "Religious Involvement and Intellectuality among University Students." SA 29,2 (1968): 79-93.

* Cardwell, Jerry D. "The Relationship between Religious Commitment and Premarital Sexual Permissiveness: A Five Dimensional Analysis." Cited above as item 313.

2925. Carlos, Serge. "Religious Participation and the Urban-Suburban Continuum." AMERICAN JOURNAL OF SOCIOLOGY 75,3 (1970): 742-759.

2926. Clayton, Richard R. "Religiosity in 5-D: A Southern Test." SOCIAL FORCES 47 (1968): 80-83.

2927. Clayton, Richard R. "5-D or 1?" JSSR 10 (1971): 37-40.

2928. Clayton, Richard R., and James W. Gladden. "The Five Dimensions of Religiosity: Toward Demythologizing a Sacred Artifact." JSSR 13,2 (1974): 135-143.

2929. Cline, V.B., and J.M. Richards, Jr. "A Factor-Analytic Study of Religious Belief and Behavior." JOURNAL OF PERSONALITY AND SOCIAL PSYCHOLOGY 1 (1965): 569-578.

* Currie, Raymond. RELIGION AND IMAGES OF MAN AMONG CALGARY YOUTH. Cited above as item 2799.

* Cygnar, Thomas E., Cardell K. Jacobson, and Donald L. Noel. "Religiosity and Prejudice: An Interdimensional Analysis." Cited above as item 429.

* Davidson, James D., Jr. SOCIAL CLASS AND TEN DIMENSIONS OF RELIGIOUS INVOLVEMENT. Cited above as item 1773.

2930. Davidson, James D. "Glock's Model of Religious Commitment: Assessing Some Different Approaches and Results." RRR 16 (1975): 83-93.

* Davidson, James D. "Socio-Economic Status and Ten Dimensions of Religious Commitment." Cited above as item 1774.

2931. DeJong, Gordon F., and Joseph E. Faulkner. "Religion and Intellectuals: Findings from a Sample of University Faculty." RRR 14 (1972): 15-24.

2932. DeJong, Gordon F., Joseph E. Faulkner, and Rex H. Warland. "Dimensions of Religiosity Reconsidered: Evidence from a Cross-Cultural Study." SOCIAL FORCES 54,4 (1976): 866-889.

* Demerath, Nicholas J., III. SOCIAL CLASS IN AMERICAN PROTESTANTISM. Cited above as item 1228.

2933. Faulkner, Joseph E., and Gordon F. DeJong. "Religiosity in 5-D: An Empirical Analysis." SOCIAL FORCES 45 (1966): 246-254.

2934. Faulkner, Joseph E., and Gordon F. DeJong. "On Measuring the Religious Variable." SOCIAL FORCES 48 (1969): 263-267.

* Finner, Stephen L. "New Methods for the Sociology of Religion." Cited above as item 532.

2935. Finney, John M. "A Theory of Religious Commitment." SA 39,1 (1978): 19-35.

2936. Finney, John M., and Gary R. Lee. "Age Differences on Five Dimensions of Religious Involvement." RRR 18,2 (1977): 173-179.

* Fukuyama, Yoshio. THE MAJOR DIMENSIONS OF CHURCH MEMBERSHIP. Cited above as item 945.

* Fukuyama, Yoshio. "The Major Dimensions of Church Membership." Cited above as item 946.

* Gibbs, David R., Samuel A. Mueller, and James R. Wood. "Doctrinal Orthodoxy, Salience, and the Consequential Dimension." Cited above as item 491.

2937. Gibbs, James O., and Kelly W. Crader. "A Criticism of Two Recent Attempts to Scale Glock and Stark's Dimensions of Religiosity: A Research Note." SA 31,2 (1970): 107-114.

* Glasner, Peter E. THE SOCIOLOGY OF SECULARISATION. A CRITIQUE OF A CONCEPT. Cited above as item 2485.

2938. Glock, Charles Y. "On the Study of Religious Commitment." RELIGIOUS EDUCATION (Research Supplement) 42 (1962): 98-110. Reprinted as Chapter 2 in C.Y. Glock and R. Stark, RELIGION AND SOCIETY IN TENSION. Chicago: Rand McNally, 1965.

2939. Grönblom, Gunnar. DIMENSIONS OF RELIGIOSITY. THE OPERATIONALIZATION AND MEASUREMENT OF RELIGIOSITY WITH SPECIAL REGARD TO THE PROBLEM OF DIMENSIONALITY. Abo, Finland: Abo Akademi, 1984.

2940. Hassenger, Robert. "Varieties of Religious Orientation." SA 25 (1964): 189-199.

2941. Hastings, Philip K., and Dean R. Hoge. "Religious Change among College Students over Two Decades." SOCIAL FORCES 49 (1970): 16-28.

2942. Hilty, Dale M., Rick L. Morgan, and Joan E. Burns. "King and Hunt Revisited: Dimensions of Religious Involvement." JSSR 23,3 (1984): 252-266.

2943. Himmelfarb, Harold S. "Measuring Religious Involvement." SOCIAL FORCES 53 (1975): 606-618.

2944. Holl, Adolf, and Gerhard H. Fischer. KIRCHE AUF DISTANZ. Wien and Stuttgart: Braumüller, 1968.

* Johnson, Doyle P. "Religious Commitment, Social Distance, and Authoritarianism." Cited above as item 443.

2945. King, Morton. "Measuring the Religious Variable: Nine Proposed Dimensions." JSSR 6 (1967): 173-190.

2946. King, Morton B., and Richard A. Hunt. "Measuring the Religious Variable: Amended Findings." JSSR 8 (1969): 321-323.

2947. King, Morton B., and Richard A. Hunt. "Measuring the Religious Variable: Replication." JSSR 11 (1972): 240-251.

2948. King, Morton B., and Richard A. Hunt. MEASURING RELIGIOUS DIMENSIONS. Dallas: Southern Methodist University, 1972.

2949. King, Morton B., and Richard A. Hunt. "Religious Dimensions: Entities or Constructs?" SOCIOLOGICAL FOCUS 8 (1975): 57-63.

2950. King, Morton B., and Richard A. Hunt. "Measuring the Religious Variable: National Replication." JSSR 14 (1975): 13-22.

* Klemmack, David L., and Jerry D. Cardwell. "Interfaith Comparison of Multidimensional Measures of Religiosity." Cited above as item 1280.

2951. Kuhre, Bruce E. "The Religious Involvement of the College Student from a Multi-Dimensional Perspective." SA 32,1 (1971): 61-69.

* Maranell, Gary M. RESPONSES TO RELIGION. STUDIES IN THE SOCIAL PSYCHOLOGY OF RELIGIOUS BELIEF. Cited above as item 4.

2952. Martins, A. "L'analyse hierarchique des attitudes religieuses." ARCHIVES DE SOCIOLOGIE DES RELIGIONS 11 (1961): 71-92.

2953. Mueller, Gert H. "The Dimensions of Religiosity." SA 41,1 (1980): 1-24.

* Nelson, L.D. "Functions and Dimensions of Religion." Cited above as item 2169.

2954. Nudelman, Arthur E. "Dimensions of Religiosity: A Factor-Analytic View of Protestants, Catholics and Christian Scientists." RRR 13 (1971): 42-56.

* O'Connell, Brian J. "Dimensions of Religiosity among Catholics." Cited above as item 253.

* Roof, Wade Clark. COMMUNITY AND COMMITMENT. Cited above as item 2154.

* Stark, Rodney, and Charles Y. Glock. AMERICAN PIETY: THE NATURE OF RELIGIOUS COMMITMENT. Cited above as item 497.

2955. Tapp, Robert B. "Dimensions of Religiosity in a Post-Traditional Group." JSSR 10 (1971): 41-47.

2956. Tilanus, C.P.G. EMPIRISCHE DIMENSIONEN DER RELIGIOSITÄT. ZUM BEGRIFF UND DEN SOZIALWISSENSCHAFTLICHEN MESSMETHODEN. Augsburg-Steppach: OSA-Verlag, 1972.

2957. Verbit, Mervin F. "The Components and Dimensions of Religious Behavior: Toward a Reconceptualization of Religiosity." In Phillip E. Hammond and Benton Johnson (eds.), AMERICAN MOSAIC. SOCIAL PATTERNS OF RELIGION IN THE UNITED STATES. New York: Random House, 1970, pp. 24-38.

2958. Wearing, Andrew J., and L.B. Brown. "The Dimensionality of Religion." BRITISH JOURNAL OF SOCIAL AND CLINICAL PSYCHOLOGY 11,2 (1972): 143-148.

2959. Weigert, Andrew J., and Darwin L. Thomas. "Religiosity in 5-D: A Critical Note." SOCIAL FORCES 48 (1969): 260-263.

* Weigert, Andrew J., and Darwin L. Thomas. "Secularization: A Cross-National Study of Catholic Male Adolescents." Cited above as item 2574.

2960. Welch, Michael R. MULTIDIMENSIONAL SCALING AS A SECT CLASSIFICATION DEVICE: A PRELIMINARY INVESTIGATION. Unpublished M.A. thesis, University of North Carolina, Chapel Hill, 1974.

2961. Welch, Michael R., and Jerry Barrish. "Bringing Religious Motivation Back In: A Multivariate Analysis of Motivational Predictors of Student Religiosity." RRR 23,4 (1982): 357-369. Followed by a commentary by Dean R. Hoge, pp. 369-371.

* Wimberley, Ronald C. "Dimensions of Commitment: Generalizing from Religion to Politics." Cited above as item 1718.

2962. Wimberley, Ronald C., Donald A. Clelland, Thomas C. Hood, and C.M. Lipsey. "The Civil Religious Dimension: Is It There?" SOCIAL FORCES 54,4 (1976): 890-900.

Cognitive dimension

2963. Bainbridge, William Sims, and Rodney Stark. "The 'Consciousness Reformation' Reconsidered." JSSR 20,1 (1981): 1-16.

2964. DeLissovoy, V. "A Sociological Approach to Religious Literacy." JOURNAL OF EDUCATIONAL SOCIOLOGY 27,9 (1954): 419-424.

* Greil, Arthur L. "Previous Dispositions and Conversion to Perspectives of Social and Religious Movements." Cited above as item 1978.

2965. Kosa, John, and Cyril O. Schommer. "Religious Participation, Religious Knowledge, and Scholastic Aptitude: An Empirical Study." JSSR 1,1 (1961): 88-97.

2966. Stryckman, Paul. "Religious Knowledge and Attitudes in Mexico City." SC 14,5-6 (1967): 469-482.

* Wuthnow, Robert. THE CONSCIOUSNESS REFORMATION. Cited above as item 2436.

* Wuthnow, Robert. EXPERIMENTATION IN AMERICAN RELIGION. Cited above as item 1722.

2967. Wuthnow, Robert. "Two Traditions in the Study of Religion." JSSR 20,1 (1981): 16-32.

Consequential dimension

* Duke, James T., and Barry L. Johnson. "Spiritual Well-Being and the Consequential Dimension of Religiosity." Cited above as item 521.

* Gibbs, David R., Samuel A. Mueller, and James R. Wood. "Doctrinal Orthodoxy, Salience, and the Consequential Dimension." Cited above as item 491.

2968. Lane, Ralph. "The Consequential Dimension of Religiosity among Catholics." SA 27 (1966): 94-100.

* Perkins, Richard. TRADITIONAL RELIGIOSITY AND THE CONSEQUENTIAL DIMENSION: THE INFLUENCE OF SALIENCE AS AN ORIENTATIONAL STYLE. Cited above as item 494.

2969. Stark, Rodney. "Religion and Conformity: Reaffirming a Sociology of Religion." SA 45,4 (1984): 273-282.

Devotionalism

2970. Bahr, Howard M. "Private Devotions." In Theodore Caplow, Howard M. Bahr, Bruce A. Chadwick, et al., ALL FAITHFUL PEOPLE. CHANGE AND CONTINUITY IN MIDDLETOWN'S RELIGION. Minneapolis: University of Minnesota, 1983, pp. 146-162.

* Lenski, Gerhard. THE RELIGIOUS FACTOR. Cited above as item 1195.

* Nelson, L.D., and Russell R. Dynes. "The Impact of Devotionalism and Attendance on Ordinary and Emergency Helping Behavior." Cited above as item 16.

* Stark, Rodney, and Charles Y. Glock. Ch. 5. "Religious Practice - Devotionalism." In Stark and Glock, AMERICAN PIETY: THE NATURE OF RELIGIOUS COMMITMENT (item 497), pp. 108-124.

Experiential dimension

2971. Bastide, Roger. LE REVE, LA TRANSE ET LA FOLIE. Paris: Flammarion, 1972.

* Boisen, Anton T. "Economic Distress and Religious Experience." Cited above as item 133.

2972. Bourque, Linda Brookover. "Social Correlates of Transcendental Experiences." SA 30,3 (1969): 151-163.

2973. Burger, Gary K., and John Allen. "Perceived Dimensions of Religious Experience." SA 34,4 (1973): 255-264.

* Currie, Raymond, Leo F. Klug, and Charles R. McCombs. "Intimacy and Saliency: Dimensions for Ordering Religious Experiences." Cited above as item 490.

2974. de Souza, B. Muniz. A EXPERIENCIA DA SALVAÇAO, PENTECOSTAIS EM SAO PAULO. São Paulo: Livraria Duas Cidades, 1969.

2975. Elkind, David, and Sally Elkind. "Varieties of Religious Experience in Young Adolescents." JSSR 2 (1962): 102-112.

2976. Fuchs, Albert. "Untersuchungen zur emotionalen Bedeutung religiöser Konzepte." In G. Dux and Thomas Luckmann (eds.), BEITRÄGE ZUR WISSENSSOZIOLOGIE. BEITRÄGE ZUR RELIGIONSSOZIOLOGIE/ CONTRIBUTIONS TO THE SOCIOLOGY OF KNOWLEDGE. CONTRIBUTIONS TO THE SOCIOLOGY OF RELIGION. INTERNATIONALES JAHRBUCH FÜR WISSENS- UND RELIGIONSSOZIOLOGIE. Bd. 10. Opladen: Westdeutscher Verlag, 1976, pp. 117-149.

2977. Glock, Charles Y., and Rodney Stark. Ch. 3 and Ch. 8 in RELIGION AND SOCIETY IN TENSION (volume cited in item 141). Ch. 3 is a reprint of R. Stark, "A Taxonomy of Religious Experience." JSSR 5,1 (1965): 97-116.

2978. Goodman, Felicitas, Jeanette H. Henney, and Esther Pressel. TRANCE, HEALING, AND HALLUCINATION: THREE FIELD STUDIES IN RELIGIOUS EXPERIENCE. New York: Wiley-Interscience, 1974.

2979. Gorlow, Leon, and Harold E. Schroeder. "Motives for Participating in the Religious Experience." JSSR 7,2 (1968): 241-254.

2980. Greeley, Andrew M. ECSTASY, A WAY OF KNOWING. Englewood Cliffs: Prentice-Hall, 1974.

2981. Greeley, Andrew M. THE SOCIOLOGY OF THE PARANORMAL: A RECONNAISSANCE. Beverly Hills: Sage, 1975.

* Greeley, Andrew M. THE RELIGIOUS IMAGINATION. Cited above as item 305.

2982. Harms, E. "The Development of Religious Experience in Children." AMERICAN JOURNAL OF SOCIOLOGY 50 (1944): 112-122.

2983. Hay, David. "Religious Experience amongst a Group of Post-Graduate Students - A Qualitative Study." JSSR 18,2 (1979): 164-182.

2984. Hay, David, and Ann Morisy. "Reports of Ecstatic, Paranormal, or Religious Experience in Great Britain and the United States -- a Comparison of Trends." JSSR 17,3 (1978): 255-268.

2985. Hoge, Dean R., and Ella I. Smith. "Normative and Non-Normative Religious Experience among High School Youth." SA 43,1 (1982): 69-82.

* Holt, A.E. "Case Records as Data for Studying the Condition of Religious Experience by Social Factors." Cited above as item 147.

2986. Hood, Ralph W., Jr. "Normative and Motivational Determinants of Reported Religious Experience in Two Baptist Samples." RRR 13,3 (1972): 192-196.

* Hood, Ralph W., Jr. "Forms of Religious Commitment and Intense Religious Experience." Cited above as item 2905.

2987. Hood, Ralph W., Jr. "Religious Orientation and the Experience of Transcendence." JSSR 12 (1973): 441-448.

2988. Hood, Ralph W., Jr. "The Construction and Preliminary Validation of a Measure of Reported Mystical Experience." JSSR 14,1 (1975): 29-41.

2989. Hood, Ralph W., Jr. "Social Legitimacy, Dogmatism, and the Evaluation of Intense Experiences." RRR 21,2 (1980): 184-194.

2990. Hood, Ralph W., Jr., and James R. Hill. "Gender Differences in the Description of Erotic and Mystical Experiences." RRR 21,2 (1980): 195-207.

2991. Hood, Ralph W., Jr., and Ronald J. Morris. "Knowledge and Experience Criteria in the Report of Mystical Experiences." RRR 23,1 (1981): 76-84.

2992. Huth, W. "Religiöse Erfahrungen und Drogen." STIMMEN DER ZEIT 96,11 (1971): 291-310.

2993. James, William. THE VARIETIES OF RELIGIOUS EXPERIENCE. New York: Mentor, 1958.

2994. Jules-Rosette, Bennetta. "Ceremonial Trance Behavior in an African Church: Private Experience and Public Expression." JSSR 19,1 (1980): 1-16.

2995. Margolis, Robert D. AN EMPIRICAL TYPOLOGY OF RELIGIOUS EXPERIENCE: ITS VALIDATION AND RELATIONSHIP TO PSYCHOTIC EXPERIENCE. Unpublished Ph.D. dissertation, Georgia State University, 1977.

2996. Margolis, Robert D., and Kirk W. Elifson. "A Typology of Religious Experience." JSSR 18,1 (1979): 61-67.

2997. McCombs, Charles R. RELIGIOUS EXPERIENCES AMONG CALGARY YOUTH: TAXONOMIC AND SOCIAL CONTEXTUAL CONSIDERATIONS. Unpublished M.A. thesis, University of Manitoba, 1975.

2998. Otto, Rudolph. THE IDEA OF THE HOLY. London: Oxford University Press, 1958.

2999. Searles, Herbert L. "An Empirical Inquiry into the God Experience of One Hundred and Forty College Students." RELIGIOUS EDUCATION 21,4 (1926): 334-342.

3000. Séguy, Jean. "Expérience religieuse et sociologie des religions. Joachim Wach, sociologue des religions." ARCHIVES DE SOCIOLOGIE DES RELIGIONS 14 (1962): 27-34.

3001. Sévigny, R. "La conception de l'expérience religieuse: quelques éléments pour une psycho-sociologie de la jeunesse." SOCIOLOGIE ET SOCIETES 1,1 (1969): 7-21.

3002. Stark, Rodney. "Social Contexts and Religious Experience." RRR 7,1 (1965): 17-28.

3003. Stone, Donald. "New Religious Consciousness and Personal Religious Experience." SA 39,2 (1978): 123-134.

3004. Straus, Roger A. "The Social-Psychology of Religious Experience: A Naturalistic Approach." SA 42,1 (1981): 57-67.

3005. Swanson, Guy E. "Life with God: Some Variations of Religious Experience in a Modern City." JSSR 10 (1971): 169-199.

3006. Swanson, Guy E. "Trance and Possession: Studies of Charismatic Influence." RRR 18,3 (1978): 253-278.

* Tapley, Joel L. A STUDY OF RELIGIOUS EXPERIENCES AS RELATED TO CHURCH ORTHODOXY. Cited above as item 2896.

3007. Thorner, Isidor. "Prophetic and Mystic Experience: Comparison and Consequences." JSSR 5 (1965): 82-96.

* Turner, Bryan S. "Belief, Ritual and Experience: The Case of Methodism." Cited above as item 2822.

3008. Wach, Joachim. "Das religiöse Gefühl." VORTRÄGE DES INSTITUTS FÜR GESCHICHTE DER MEDIEN AN DER UNIVERSITÄT LEIPZIG 4 (1932): 9-33

3009. Wach, Joachim. TYPES OF RELIGIOUS EXPERIENCE. Chicago: University of Chicago Press, 1951.

3010. Wach, Joachim. "Problématique et typologie de l'expérience religieuse." ARCHIVES DE SOCIOLOGIE DES RELIGIONS 14 (1962): 35-76.

* Welch, Kevin W. "An Interpersonal Influence Model of Traditional Religious Commitment." Cited above as item 2899.

Popular religion

Also called Folk Religion, this refers to grass-roots religiosity in distinction from the culture of elites.

3011. Appolis, Emile. "En marge du catholicisme contemporain: millénaristes, cordiphores et naundorffistes autour du 'secret' de la Salette." ARCHIVES DE SOCIOLOGIE DES RELIGIONS 14 (1962): 103-121.

3012. Arellano, E. EL CATOLICISMO POPULAR VISTO POR UN SOCIOLOGO. Bogotá: Estudios de pastoral popular, no. 14, 1972.

3013. Azevedo, Thales de. "Popular Catholicism in Brazil. Typology and Functions." In R.S. Sayers (ed.), PORTUGAL AND BRAZIL IN TRANSITION. Minneapolis: 1968, pp. 175-178.

3014. Babb, Lawrence A. THE DIVINE HIERARCHY: POPULAR HINDUISM IN CENTRAL INDIA. New York: Columbia University Press, 1975.

3015. Bastide, Roger. "Religion and the Church in Brazil." In T.L. Smith and A. Marchant (eds.), BRAZIL: PORTRAIT OF HALF A CONTINENT. New York: Dryden, 1951.

3016. Benko, Antonius. "Aspectos psico-sociais da religiosidade popular no Estado da Guanabara." SINTESE 2,3 (1975): 49-104.

3017. Berger, Monroe. ISLAM IN EGYPT: SOCIAL AND POLITICAL ASPECTS OF POPULAR RELIGION. Cambridge, 1970.

3018. Bock, E. Wilbur. "Symbols in Conflict: Official Versus Folk Religion." JSSR 5,2 (1965-66): 204-212.

3019. Bourdieu, Pierre. "Genèse et structure du champ religieux." REVUE FRANÇAISE DE SOCIOLOGIE 12 (1971): 295-334.

3020. Brandão, C.R. OS DE USES DO POVO, UM ESTUDO SOBRE A RELIGIÃO POPULAR. São Paulo: Livraria Brasiliense Editora, 1980.

3021. Büntig, Aldo J. "Hipótesis para una interpretación del Catolicismo Popular en la Argentina." CIAS 171 (1968): 7-39.

3022. Büntig, Aldo J. EL CATOLICISMO POPULAR EN LA ARGENTINA. Buenos Aires: Bonum, 1969.

3023. Büntig, Aldo J. "Interpretación motivacional del catolicismo popular." VISPERA 10 (1969): 13-20. Also published in pamphlet form - Lima: Centro de Estudios y Publicaciones, 1970.

* Cipriani, Roberto. "La religiosité populaire en Italie: deux recherches sur la magie et la politique dans le sud du pays." Cited above as item 1550.

3024. Clark, David. BETWEEN PULPIT AND PEW. FOLK RELIGION IN A NORTH YORKSHIRE VILLAGE. Cambridge: Cambridge University Press, 1982.

3025. Condominas, G. "Notes sur le Bouddhisme populaire en milieu rural Lao." ARCHIVES DE SOCIOLOGIE DES RELIGIONS 25 (1968): 81-110; 26 (1968): 111-150.

3026. Drehsen, Volker, and Julius Morel. "The Phenomena of Popular Piety. Le phénomène de la piété populaire." SC 29,2-3 (1982): 99-101.

3027. Dumont, Fernand. "A propos du concept de religion populaire." In Benoît Lacroix and Pietro Boglioni (eds.), LES RELIGIONS POPULAIRES. Québec: Presses de l'Université Laval, 1972, pp. 22-31.

3028. Gilsenan, Michael. "L'Islam dans l'Egypte contemporaine: religion d'Etat, religion populaire." ANNALES 35,3-4 (1980): 598-614.

3029. Giuriati, Paolo. "Religiosità popolare." In N.A. de Carlo and P. Scapin, RELIGIONE OGGI. ELEMENTI PER L'INDAGINE EMPIRICA DEL FENOMENO RELIGIOSO. Brescia: Marcelliana, 1982, pp. 111-172.

3030. Glasner, Peter E. "The Study of Australian Folk Religion: Some Theoretical and Practical Problems." In A. Black and P. Glasner (eds.), PRACTICE AND BELIEF (volume cited in item 824), pp. 167-180.

3031. Gonzalez Anleo, Juan. "Un punto de vista sociológico de la religiosidad popular." FOMENTO SOCIAL 127 (1977): 227-235.

3032. Haddox, Benjamin Edward. Chapter 5 of B.E. Haddox, SOCIEDAD Y RELIGION EN COLOMBIA, traducción de Jorge Zalamea. Bogotá: Ediciones Tercer Mundo, and Facultad de Sociologia, Universidad Nacional de Colombia, 1965.

3033. Huotari, Voitto. "Finnish Revivalism as an Expression of Popular Piety." SC 29,2-3 (1982): 113-123.

3034. Isambert, François-A. "Autour du catholicisme populaire -- Réflexions sociologiques sur un debat." SC 22,2 (1975): 193-210.

3035. Isambert, François-A. "Religion populaire, sociologie, histoire et folklore." ARCHIVES DE SCIENCES SOCIALES DES RELIGIONS 43,2 (1977): 161-184.

3036. Isambert, François-A. "Religion populaire. Sociologie, histoire et folklore. II. -- De Saint Besse à Saint Rouin." ARCHIVES DE SCIENCES SOCIALES DES RELIGIONS 46,1 (1978): 111-133.

3037. Isambert, François-A., and R. Courtas. "Ethnologues et sociologues aux prises avec la notion de 'populaire.'" MAISON DIEU 122 (1975): 20-43.

3038. Lanternari, Vittorio. "La religion populaire. Prospective historique et anthropologique." ARCHIVES DE SCIENCES SOCIALES DES RELIGIONS 53,1 (1982): 121-144.

3039. Maitre, Jacques. "Religion populaire et populations religieuses." CAHIERS INTERNATIONAUX DE SOCIOLOGIE 27 (1959): 95-120.

* Manglapus, Raul S. "Philippine Culture and Modernizaton." Cited above as item 2660.

3040. Mensching, Gustav. "The Masses, Folk Belief and Universal Religion." In L. Schneider (ed.), RELIGION, CULTURE AND SOCIETY (volume cited in item 1824), pp. 269-273; translated by Schneider from SOZIOLOGIE DER RELIGION. Bonn: Rohrscheid, 1947, pp. 137-148.

3041. Mensching, Gustav. "Folk and Universal Religion." In L. Schneider (ed.), RELIGION, CULTURE AND SOCIETY. New York: Wiley, 1964, pp. 254-261; translated by Schneider from DIE RELIGION. Stuttgart: Schwab, 1959, pp. 65-77.

3042. Meslin, Michel. "Le phénomène religieux populaire." In B. LaCroix and P. Boglioni (eds.), LES RELIGIONS POPULAIRES (volume cited in item 3027), pp. 3-15.

* Nesti, Arnaldo. "Problemi e tendenze nella religione popolare come fenomeno delle classi subalterne." Cited above as item 1847.

3043. Nesti, Arnaldo. "Gramsci et la religion populaire." SC 22 (1975): 343-354.
"Gramsci e la religione populaire." IDOC INTERNAZIONALE (Italy) 3-4 (1976): 68-76.

* Nesti, Arnaldo. "Religion et classe ouvrière dans les sociétés industrielles. Une hypothèse de recherche." Cited above as item 1848.

3044. Nesti, Arnaldo, and Carlo Prandi. "La religiosità popolare in Italia." IDOC INTERNAZIONALE 3 (1973): 37-43.

3045. Pace, Enzo. "Il dibattito sulla religiosità popolare." SOCIOLOGIA 11,1 (1977): 95-102.

3046. Pierre, Roland. "Caribbean Religion: The Voodoo Case." SA 38,1 (1977); 25-36.

* Piwowarski, Wladyslaw. "Industrialization and Popular Religiosity in Poland." Cited above as item 2541.

3047. Piwowarski, Wladyslaw. "La religiosité populaire polonaise. Continuité et changement." CONCILIUM 151 (French Series, 1980): 69-80.

3048. Piwowarski, Wladyslaw. "Continuity and Change of Ritual in Polish Folk Piety." SC 29,2-3 (1982): 125-134.

* Rama, Carlos M. LA RELIGION EN EL URUGUAY. Cited above as item 1863.

3049. Ribeiro de Oliveira, Pedro A. CATOLICISMO POPULAR NO BRASIL. Rio de Janeiro: CERIS, Estudos Socio-Religiosos 9, 1970.

3050. Ribeiro de Oliveira, Pedro A. CATOLICISMO POPULAR NA AMERICA LATINA. Rio de Janeiro: CERIS, 1971.

3051. Ribeiro de Oliveira, Pedro A. "Le Catholicisme populaire en Amérique Latine." SC 19,4 (1972): 567-584.

3052. Ribeiro de Oliveira, Pedro A. "Catolicismo popular e Romanização do Catolicismo Brasileiro." REVISTA ECLESIASTICA BRASILEIRA 36,141 (1976): 131-141.

3053. Ribeiro de Oliveira, Pedro A. "Catholicisme populaire et hégémonie bourgeoise au Brésil." ARCHIVES DE SCIENCES SOCIALES DES RELIGIONS 47,1 (1979): 53-80.

* Rodrigues, José Honorio. BRAZIL AND AFRICA. Cited above as item 403.

3054. Rolim, Francisco C. "Condicionamentos sociais do Catolicismo popular." REVISTA ECLESIASTICA BRASILEIRA 36,141 (1976): 142-170.

* Sarachandra, Ediriweera R. "Traditional Values and the Modernization of a Buddhist Society: The Case of Ceylon." Cited above as item 1932.

3055. Schaden, Francisco S.F. "Magia e crenças populares numa comunidade teutobrasileira." SOCIOLOGIA 8 (São Paulo, 1946): 77-87.

3056. Schmitt, Jean-Claude. "'Religion populaire' et culture folklorique." ANNALES 31,5 (1976): 941-953.

3057. Schneider, Louis, and Sandford M. Dornbusch. POPULAR RELIGION: INSPIRATIONAL BOOKS IN AMERICA. Chicago: University of Chicago Press, 1958.

3058. Scott, James C. "Protest and Profanation: Agrarian Revolt and the Little Tradition, Part I." THEORY AND SOCIETY 4,1 (1975): 1-38. "Part II." THEORY AND SOCIETY 4,2 (1975): 211-246.

3059. Séguy, Jean. "Images et 'religion populaire' -- réflexions sur un colloque." ARCHIVES DE SCIENCES SOCIALES DES RELIGIONS 44,1 (1977): 25-43.

3060. Souffrant, Claude. "La religion du paysan haïtien. De l'anathème au dialogue." SC 19,4 (1972): 585-597.

3061. Suk-jay, Yim. "Introduction au Mouïsme. La religion populaire coréene." SC 25,2 (1978): 175-189.

3062. Tavares de Andrade, José Maria. "Le champ de la religiosité. Projet d'analyse de la religiosité au Brésil." SC 19,4 (1972): 599-611.

3063. Tortosa, José M. "Ritual and Cultural Lag: The Feast of San Isidoro in Tiraque (Bolivia)." SC 19,4 (1972): 613-616.

3064. Towler, Robert, and Audrey Chamberlain. "Common Religion." SOCIOLOGICAL YEARBOOK OF RELIGION IN BRITAIN 6 (1973): 1-28.

3065. Urbano, Henrique Osvaldo. "Religion populaire et discours théologique." LES CAHIERS DU CENTRE DE RECHERCHES EN SOCIOLOGIE RELIGIEUSE 3 (1980): 71-81.

3066. Valle, Edênio. "Psicologia social e Catolicismo popular." REVISTA ECLESIASTICA BRASILEIRA 36,141 (1976): 171-188.

3067. Vrijhof, Pieter H., and Jacques Waardenburg (eds.) OFFICIAL AND POPULAR RELIGION: ANALYSIS OF A THEME FOR RELIGIOUS STUDIES. The Hague: Mouton, 1979.

3068. Waardenburg, Jacques. "Official and Popular Religions in Islam." SC 25,3-4 (1978): 315-341.

3069. Walters, M. "The Penitents: A Folk Observance." SOCIAL FORCES 6,2 (1927): 253-256.

3070. Williams, Peter W. POPULAR RELIGION IN AMERICA. Englewood Cliffs, N.J.: Prentice-Hall, 1980.

3071. Xidieh, Oswaldo Elias. "Elementos magicos no folk mogiano." SOCIOLOGIA 5 (São Paul, 1943): 116-133.

3072. Xidieh, Oswaldo Elias. "Elementos magicos no folk paulista: o intermediario." SOCIOLOGIA 7 (São Paulo, 1945): 11-29.

3073. Zulehner, Paul M. "La 'religion des gens.' A propos de diverses enquêtes réalisées en Austriche (1970-1980)." SC 29,2-3 (1982): 209-221.

SECTION C: PRACTICES AND RITUAL

Practices

Almsgiving

3074. Heilman, Samuel C. "The Gift of Alms: Face-to-Face Almsgiving among Orthodox Jews." URBAN LIFE AND CULTURE 3 (1975): 371-395.

Baptism

3075. Charpin, Fernand. PRATIQUE RELIGIEUSE ET FORMATION D'UNE GRANDE VILLE. LE GESTE DU BAPTEME ET SA SIGNIFICATION EN SOCIOLOGIE RELIGIEUSE (MARSEILLE, 1806-1958). Paris: Ed. du Centurion, 1964.

3076. Maitre, Jacques. "Les fréquences des prénoms de baptême en France. Rite de dénomination et linguistique statistiques." ANNEE SOCIOLOGIQUE (Série 3, 1964): 31-74.

3077. Maitre, Jacques. "Problèmes épistémologiques posés par une sociologie du baptême." EPISTEMOLOGIE SOCIOLOGIQUE 5 (1967): 35-64.

Confession

3078. Hahn, Alois. "Zur Soziologie der Beichte." KÖLNER ZEITSCHRIFT FÜR SOZIOLOGIE UND SOZIALPSYCHOLOGIE 34 (1982): 407-434.

* Harris, Mary, Sheldon M. Benson, and Carroll L. Hall. "The Effects of Confession on Altruism." Cited above as item 13.

* Hepworth, Mike, and Bryan S. Turner. CONFESSION. STUDIES IN DEVIANCE AND RELIGION. Cited above as item 2134.

3079. Johnson, C. Lincoln, and Andrew J. Weigert. "Frames in Confession: The Social Construction of Sexual Sin." JSSR 19,4 (1980): 368-381.

* Sorokin, Pitirim A. THE WAYS AND POWER OF LOVE: TYPES, FACTORS, AND TECHNIQUES OF MORAL TRANSFORMATION. Cited above as item 17.

Contributions

* Berk, Marc. "Pluralist Theory and Church Policy Positions on Racial and Sexual Equality." Cited above as item 344.

3080. Bhatnagar, S. Rani. "From Charity to Taxes. Observations on the Sociology of Religious and Secular Giving." JSSR 9,3 (1970): 209-218.

3081. Bromley, David G., and Anson D. Shupe, Jr. "Financing the New Religions: A Resource Mobilization Approach." JSSR 19,3 (1980): 227-239.

3082. Cohen, Steven M. "Will Jews Keep Giving? Prospects for the Jewish Charitable Community." JOURNAL OF JEWISH COMMUNAL SERVICE 55 (1978): 59-71.

3083. Evans, Bernard F. "Campaign for Human Development: Church Involvement in Social Change." RRR 20,3 (1979): 264-278.

3084. Hilke, John C. "Voluntary Contributions and Monitoring Efforts: Revealed Preference for the Services of Religious Organizations." JSSR 19,2 (1980): 138-145.

* Hoge, Dean R., and Jackson W. Carroll. "Determinants of Commitment and Participation in Suburban Protestant Churches." Cited above as item 145.

3085. Hougland, James G., and James R. Wood. "Correlates of Participation in Local Churches." SOCIOLOGICAL FOCUS 13,4 (1980): 343-358.

3086. Lutterman, Kenneth J. GIVING TO CHURCHES: A SOCIOLOGICAL STUDY OF THE CONTRIBUTIONS TO EIGHT CATHOLIC AND LUTHERAN CHURCHES. Unpublished Ph.D. dissertation, University of Wisconsin, 1962.

* Nuesse, C. Joseph. "The Relation of Financial Assessments to Status in a Rural Parish." Cited above as item 1455.

* Stark, Rodney, and Charles Y. Glock. AMERICAN PIETY: THE NATURE OF RELIGIOUS COMMITMENT. Cited above as item 497.

* Thiessen, Victor. WHO GIVES A DAMN? A STUDY OF CHARITABLE CONTRIBUTIONS. Cited above as item 20.

Cursillo

3087. Marcoux, Marcene. CURSILLO, ANATOMY OF A MOVEMENT: THE EXPERIENCE OF SPIRITUAL RENEWAL. New York: Lambeth Press, 1982.

Fasting

3088. Tamney, Joseph B. "Muslim and Christian Attitudes toward Fasting in Southeast Asia." RRR 19,1 (1977): 3-15.

* Tamney, Joseph B. "Fasting and Modernization." Cited above as item 52.

Glossolalia

3089. Cohn, Werner. "Personality, Pentecostalism and Glossolalia: A Research Note on Some Unsuccessful Research." CANADIAN REVIEW OF SOCIOLOGY AND ANTHROPOLOGY 5,1 (1968): 36-39.

3090. Couture, André. "Glossolalie et mantra." LES CAHIERS DU CENTRE DE RECHERCHES EN SOCIOLOGIE RELIGIEUSE 3 (1980): 105-116.

3091. Fields, Karen E. "Charismatic Religion as Popular Protest." THEORY AND SOCIETY 11,3 (1982): 321-361.

3092. Goodman, Felicitas D. "Phonetic Analysis of Glossolalia in Four Cultural Settings." JSSR 8,2 (1969): 227-239.

3093. Goodman, Felicitas D. SPEAKING IN TONGUES: A CROSS-CULTURAL STUDY OF GLOSSOLALIA. Chicago: University of Chicago Press, 1972.

3094. Goodman, Felicitas D. "Prognosis: A New Religion?" In Irving I. Zaretsky and Mark P. Leone (eds.), RELIGIOUS MOVEMENTS IN CONTEMPORARY AMERICA. Princeton: Princeton University Press, 1974, pp. 244-254.

3095. Hine, Virginia. "Pentecostal Glossolalia: Toward a Functional Interpretation." JSSR 8 (1969): 211-226.

3096. May, L. Carlyle. "A Survey of Glossolalia and Related Phenomena in Non-Christian Religions." AMERICAN ANTHROPOLOGIST 58,1 (1956): 75-96.

3097. Richardson, James T. "Psychological Interpretations of Glossolalia: A Reexamination of Research." JSSR 12 (1973): 199-207.

3098. Sadler, A.W. "Glossolalia and Possession: An Appeal to the Episcopal Study Commission." JSSR 4,1 (1964-65): 84-90.

3099. Samarin, William J. "Making Sense of Glossolalic Nonsense." SOCIAL RESEARCH 46,1 (1979): 88-105.

3100. Stanley, Gordon, W.K. Bartlett, and Terri Moyle. "Some Characteristics of Charismatic Experience: Glossolalia in Australia." JSSR 17,3 (1978): 269-278.

* Wilson, John, and Harvey K. Clow. "Themes of Power and Control in a Pentecostal Assembly." Cited above as item 1501.

Healing

3101. Allen, Gillian, and Roy Wallis. "Pentecostalists as a Medical Minority." In Roy Wallis and Peter Morley (eds.), MARGINAL MEDICINE. New York: Free Press, 1976, pp. 110-137.

* Elinson, Howard. "The Implications of Pentecostal Religion for Intellectualism, Politics, and Race Relations." Cited above as item 1564.

* Goodman, Felicitas, Jeanette H. Henney, and Esther Pressel. TRANCE, HEALING AND HALLUCINATION: THREE FIELD STUDIES IN RELIGIOUS EXPERIENCE. Cited above as item 2978.

3102. Harwood, Alan. RX: SPIRITIST AS NEEDED. A STUDY OF A PUERTO RICAN COMMUNITY MENTAL HEALTH RESOURCE. New York: Wiley, 1977.

3103. Julliard, André. "Le don de guérisseur. Une position religieuse obligée." ARCHIVES DE SCIENCES SOCIALES DES RELIGIONS 54,1 (1982): 43-62.

3104. Koss, Joan D. "Terapeutica del sistema de una secta en Puerto Rico." REVISTA DE CIENCIAS SOCIALES 14,2 (1970): 259-278.

3105. Laplantine, François. "La maladie, la guérison et le sacré." ARCHIVES DE SCIENCES SOCIALES DES RELIGIONS 54,1 (1982): 63-76.

3106. McGuire, Meredith B. PENTECOSTAL CATHOLICS. POWER, CHARISMA, AND ORDER IN A RELIGIOUS MOVEMENT. Philadelphia: Temple University Press, 1982.

* Pereira de Queiroz, Maria Isaura. "Messies, thaumaturges et 'dualité catholique' au Brésil." Cited above as item 2368.

3107. Wardwell, Walter I. "Christian Science Healing." JSSR 4,2 (1964-65): 175-181. Sleeper, David E. "Christian Science Healing: Comment." JSSR 5,2 (1965-66): 296-297. Wardwell, Walter I. "Reply to D.E. Sleeper." JSRR 5,2 (1965-66): 298.

3108. West, Martin. "Thérapie et changement social dans les Eglises urbaines d'Afrique du Sud." SC 19,1 (1972): 49-62.

* Xidieh, Oswaldo Elias. "Elementos magicos no folk mogiano." Cited above as item 3071.

Meditation

* Preston, David L. "Meditative Ritual Practice and Spiritual Conversion-Commitment: Theoretical Implications Based on the Case of Zen." Cited above as item 2012.

Pilgrimage

3109. Bernard, Henri. LE PELERINAGE: UNE REPONSE A L'ALIENTATION DES MALADES ET INFIRMES. Montréal: Ed. Maison, 1975.

3110. Glazier, Stephen D. "Caribbean Pilgrimages: A Typology." JSSR 22,4 (1983): 316-325.

3111. Turner, Victor. "Pilgrimages as Social Processes." In V. Turner, DRAMAS, FIELDS, AND METAPHORS. SYMBOLIC ACTION IN HUMAN SOCIETY. Ithaca: Cornell University Press, 1974, pp. 166-230. First published as "The Center Out There: Pilgrims' Goal." HISTORY OF RELIGIONS 12,3 (1973): 191-230.

3112. Turner, Victor, and Edith Turner. IMAGE AND PILGRIMAGE IN CHRISTIAN CULTURE. New York: Columbia University Press, 1979.

Possession

3113. Alland, Alexander, Jr. "'Possession' in a Revivalistic Negro Church." JSSR 1 (1962): 204-213.

3114. Bourguignon, Erika. "The Self, the Behavioral Environment, and the Theory of Spirit Possession." In Melford E. Spiro (ed.), CONTEXT AND MEANING IN CULTURAL ANTHROPOLOGY. New York: Free Press, 1965, pp. 39-60.

3115. Echard, Nicole. "Petites lectures sur des phénomènes de possession africains." ARCHIVES DE SCIENCES SOCIALES DES RELIGIONS 20,40 (1975): 145-156.

3116. Ribeiro, René. "Análises socio-psicológico de la posesión en los cultos afrobrasileños." ACTA NEUROPSIQUIATRICA ARGENTINA 5 (1959): 249-262.

3117. Shupe, Anson D., and David G. Bromley. "Witches, Moonies, and Accusations of Evil." In T. Robbins and D. Anthony (eds.), IN GODS WE TRUST (item 367), pp. 247-261.

* Swanson, Guy E. "Trance and Possession: Studies of Charismatic Influence." Cited above as item 3006.

* Wilson, John, and Harvey K. Clow. "Themes of Power and Control in a Pentecostal Assembly." Cited above as item 1501.

Prayer

3118. Moberg, David O., and Jean N. McEnery. "Prayer Habits and Attitudes of Catholic Students, 1961-1971." SOCIAL SCIENCE 51,2 (1976): 76-85.

3119. Swatos, William H. "The Power of Prayer: A Prolegomenon to an Ascetical Sociology." RRR 24,2 (1982): 153-163.

Preaching

3120. Burgalassi, Silvano. "Aspetti psicosociologici della predicazione." RIVISTA DI SOCIOLOGIA 3,7 (1965): 51-112.

3121. Centre Régional d'Etudes Socio-Religieuses. "Sermon ou homélie: la fonction de la prédication." SC 27,4 (1980): 363-373.

3122. Daiber, K.F., et al. PREDIGEN UND HÖREN, BAND II. KOMMUNIKATION SWISCHEN PREDIGERN UND HÖREN - SOZIALWISSENSCHAFTLICHE UNTERSUCHUNGEN. München: Kaiser Verlag, 1983.

3123. Dassetto, Felice. "La production homilétique catholique." SC 27,4 (1980): 375-396.

3124. Fernandez Vargas, Valentina. "El púlpito como medio de communicación de masas." REVISTA INTERNACIONAL DE SOCIOLOGIA 29 (1979): 105-116.

* Koller, Norman B., and Joseph D. Retzer. "The Sounds of Silence Revisted." Cited above as item 673.

3125. Lampinen, Tapio. "The Content of the Parochial Sermons in the Evangelical Lutheran Church of Finland as Indicators of the Openness and Closeness of the Church as System." SC 27,4 (1980): 417-435.

3126. Mickey, Thomas J. "Social Order and Preaching." SC 27,4 (1980): 347-362.

3127. Price, Dennis L., W. Robert Terry, and B. Conrad Johnston. "The Measurement of the Effect of Preaching and Preaching Plus Small Group Dialogue in one Baptist Church." JSSR 19,2 (1980): 186-197.

3128. Van Calster, Stephan. "Bible, société, prédication." SC 27,4 (1980): 397-416.

Proselytizing

* Bibby, Reginald W., and Merlin B. Brinkerhoff. "When Proselytizing Fails: An Organizational Analysis." Cited above as item 1965.

3129. Munters, Quirinus J. "Recruitment as a Vocation: The Case of Jehovah's Witnesses." SOCIOLOGIA NEERLANDICA 7 (1971): 88-100.

Revivalism

3130. Archer, Anthony. "Remaining in the State in Which God Has Called You. An Evangelical Revival/Vivre dans l'état auquel Dieu vous a appelés. Un réveil évangélique." ARCHIVES DE SCIENCES SOCIALES DES RELIGIONS 20,40 (1975): 67-78.

3131. Bruce, Dickson D. AND THEY ALL SANG HALLELUJAH. PLAIN-FOLK CAMP-MEETING RELIGION, 1800-1845. Knoxville: University of Tennessee Press, 1973.

3132. Clelland, Donald A., Thomas C. Hood, C.M. Lipsey, and Ronald Wimberley. "In the Company of the Converted: Characteristics of a Billy Graham Crusade Audience." SA 35,1 (1974): 45-56.

3133. Dike, S.W. "A Study of New England Revivals." AMERICAN JOURNAL OF SOCIOLOGY 15,3 (1909): 361-378.

3134. Gordon-McCutchan, R.C. "Great Awakenings?" SA 44,2 (1983): 83-90.

* Hammond, John L. "Revival Religion and Anti-Slavery Politics." Cited above as item 1583.

* Hammond, John L. THE POLITICS OF BENEVOLENCE. REVIVAL RELIGION AND AMERICAN VOTING BEHAVIOR. Cited above as item 1584.

3135. Hammond, John L. "The Reality of Revivals." SA 44,2 (1983): 111-116.

3136. Hammond, Phillip, and R.C.Gordon-McCutchan. "Cults and the Civil Religion: A Tale of Two Centuries." REVUE FRANÇAISE D'ETUDES AMERICAINES 12 (1981): 173-185.

* Huotari, Voitto. "Finnish Revivalism as an Expression of Popular Piety." Cited above as item 3033.

3137. Johnson, Weldon T. "The Religious Crusade: Revival or Ritual?" AMERICAN JOURNAL OF SOCIOLOGY 76 (1971): 873-890.

3138. McLoughlin, William G. "Timepieces and Butterflies: A Note on the Great-Awakening-Construct and its Critics." SA 44,2 (1983): 103-110.

3139. Smith, Timothy L. REVIVALISM AND SOCIAL REFORM. New York: Harper Torchbooks, 1965.

3140. Smith, Timothy L. "My Rejection of a Cyclical View of 'Great Awakenings.'" SA 44,2 (1983): 97-102.

3141. Ward, David A. "Toward a Normative Explanation of 'Old Fashioned Revivals.'" QUALITATIVE SOCIOLOGY 3,1 (1980): 3-22.

3142. Whitlam, F.L. "Revivalism as Institutionalized Behavior: An Analysis of the Social Base of a Billy Graham Crusade." SOCIAL SCIENCE QUARTERLY 1 (1968): 115-127.

3143. Wilson, John F. "Perspectives on the Historiography of Religious Awakenings." SA 44,2 (1983): 117-120.

* Wimberley, Ronald C., Thomas Hood, et al. "Conversion in a Billy Graham Crusade." Cited above as item 2046.

Testimony

3144. England, R.W. "Some Aspects of Christian Science as Reflected in Letters of Testimony." AMERICAN JOURNAL OF SOCIOLOGY 59,5 (1954): 448-453.

3145. Kroll-Smith, J. Stephen. "The Testimony as Performance: The Relationship of an Expressive Event to the Belief System of a Holiness Sect." JSSR 19,1 (1980): 16-25.

3146. McGuire, Meredith B. "Testimony as a Commitment Mechanism in Catholic Pentecostal Prayer Groups." JSSR 16,2 (1977): 165-168.

3147. Xidieh, O.R. "Religiöse Volkerzählungen und ihre soziale Bedeutung." STADEN-JAHRBUCH 9/10 (1961-62): 77-87.

Ritual

3148. Ahler, J.G., and Joseph B. Tamney. "Some Functions of Religious Ritual in a Catastrophe." SA 25,4 (1964): 212-230.

3149. Alpert, Harry. "Durkheim's Functional Theory of Ritual." SOCIOLOGY AND SOCIAL RESEARCH 23 (1938): 103-108. Reprinted in R.A. Nisbet (ed.), EMILE DURKHEIM. Englewood Cliffs: Prentice-Hall, 1965, pp. 137-141.

* Bird, Frederick. "Charisma and Ritual in New Religious Movements." Cited above as item 64.

3150. Bloch, Maurice. "Symbols, Song, Dance and Features of Articulation, or Is Religion an Extreme Form of Traditional Authority?" ARCHIVES EUROPEENNES DE SOCIOLOGIE 15,1 (1974): 55-81.

3151. Bocock, Robert J. "Ritual: Civic and Religious." BRITISH JOURNAL OF SOCIOLOGY 21,3 (1970): 285-297.

3152. Bocock, Robert J. RITUAL IN INDUSTRIAL SOCIETY. A SOCIOLOGICAL ANALYSIS OF RITUALISM IN MODERN ENGLAND. London: Allen & Unwin, 1974.

3153. Bocock, Robert J. "Towards a Sociology of Ritual Action." JOURNAL OF RELIGION AND RELIGIONS 4,3 (1974): 114-117.

3154. Bourdieu, Pierre. "Le langage autorisé: note sur les conditions sociales de l'efficacité du discours rituel." ACTES DE LA RECHERCHE EN SCIENCES SOCIALES 5,6 (1975): 183-190.

3155. Branford, V. "The Purpose of Liturgy." SOCIOLOGICAL REVIEW 20,1 (1928): 1-17.

3156. Cazeneuve, Jean. "Le principe de répétition dans le rite." CAHIERS INTERNATIONAUX DE SOCIOLOGIE 23 (1957): 23-57.

3157. Cazeneuve, Jean. LES RITES ET LA CONDITION HUMAINE. Paris: Presses Universitaires de France, 1958.

3158. Cazeneuve, Jean. SOCIOLOGIE DU RITE (TABOU, MAGIE, SACRE). Paris: Presses Universitaires de France, 1971.

3159. Delcourt, M. "Valeur sociale d'un rite religieux: la première communion collective." DIOGENES 36 (1961): 76-86.

3160. Ducey, Michael H. SUNDAY MORNING. ASPECTS OF URBAN RITUAL. New York: Free Press (Macmillan), 1977.

3161. Duncan, H.D. "The Development of Durkheim's Concept of Ritual and the Problem of Social Disrelationships." In Kurt H. Wolff (ed.), EMILE DURKHEIM 1858-1917. Columbia: Ohio State University Press, 1960, pp. 97-117.

3162. Fraga de Azevedo, Henrique O. "Sociologia do rito." VOZES 68,7 (1974): 509-514.

3163. Frundt, Henry J. "Rite Involvement and Community Formation." SA 30,2 (1969): 91-109.

3164. Furman, Frida Kerner. "Ritual as Social Mirror and Agent of Cultural Change: A Case Study in Synagogue Life." JSSR 20,3 (1981): 228-241.

3165. George, Gordon. "The Sociology of Ritual." AMERICAN CATHOLIC SOCIOLOGICAL REVIEW 17 (1956): 117-130.

* Goody, Jack. "Religion and Ritual: The Definitional Problem." Cited above as item 2748.

3166. Greeley, Andrew M. "Religious Symbolism, Liturgy and Community." CONCILIUM 62 (1971): 59-69.

3167. Greenwald, David E. "Durkheim on Society, Thought and Ritual." SA 34,3 (1973): 157-168.

3168. Hennig, J. "Zur Grundlegung der Liturgiesoziologie." ZEITSCHRIFT FÜR RELIGIONS UND GEISTESGESCHICHTE 20 (1968): 44-60.

3169. Herrlin, O. "On Liturgy and Society." ACTA SOCIOLOGICA 3,2-3 (1958): 91-97.

3170. Hesser, Garry, and Andrew J. Weigert. "Comparative Dimensions of Liturgy: A Conceptual Framework and Feasibility Application." SA 41,3 (1980): 215-229.

3171. Isambert, François. RITE ET EFFICACITE SYMBOLIQUE. Paris: Cerf, 1979.

3172. Jaspard, Jean-Marie. "Loi rituelle et structuration de l'attitude religieuse chez l'enfant." SC 19 (1972): 459-471.

* Jules-Rosette, Bennetta. AFRICAN APOSTLES: RITUAL AND CONVERSION IN THE CHURCH OF JOHN MARANKE. Cited above as item 1986.

3173. Jules-Rosette, Bennetta. "Song and Spirit: The Use of Song in the Management of Ritual Settings." AFRICA 45,2 (1975): 150-166.

* Jules-Rosette, Bennetta. "Ceremonial Trance Behavior in an African Church: Private Experience and Public Expression." Cited above as item 2994.

3174. Kersevan, Marko. "Le traitement des morts dans la société socialiste." SC 29,2-3 (1982): 153-165.

3175. Klapp, Orin E. RITUAL AND CULT: A SOCIOLOGICAL INTERPRETATION. Washington: Public Affairs Press, 1956.

3176. Le Bras, Gabriel. "Liturgie et sociologie." REVUE DE SCIENCES RELIGIEUSES (1956): 291-304.

* Lüschen, Günther, Zaharj Staikof, Veronica Stolte Heiskanen, and Conor Ward. "Family, Ritual and Secularization. A Cross-National Study Conducted in Bulgaria, Finland, Germany and Ireland." Cited above as item 2518.

3177. Meddin, Jay. "Symbols, Anxiety, and Ritual: A Functional Interpretation." QUALITATIVE SOCIOLOGY 3,4 (1980): 251-271.

3178. Mol, Johannes J. (Hans). "Ritual." In H. Mol, IDENTITY AND THE SACRED. Oxford: Blackwell, 1976, pp. 233-245.

3179. Mori, Tōgo. "La disfunciones de los rituales." REVISTA MEXICANA DE SOCIOLOGIA 27 (1965): 535-540.

3180. Nagendra, S.P. "Max Weber's Theory of Ritual." INDIAN JOURNAL OF SOCIOLOGY 1 (1970): 173-184.

3181. Nagendra, S.P. THE CONCEPT OF RITUAL IN MODERN SOCIOLOGICAL THEORY. New Delhi: The Academic Journals of India, 1971.

3182. Newell, W.H. "The Sociology of Ritual in Early China." SOCIOLOGICAL BULLETIN 6,1 (1957): 1-13.

3183. Newton, Denise (ed.) LITURGY AND CHANGE. Birmingham, England: University of Birmingham, Institute for the Study of Worship and Religious Architecture, 1984.

* Piwowarski, Wladyslaw. "Continuity and Change of Ritual in Polish Folk Piety." Cited above as item 3048.

3184. Power, Joseph P. "The Theatre of the Catholic Church, its Roots and Relationship to Psychodrama." HANDBOOK OF INTERNATIONAL SOCIOMETRY 7 (1973): 55-59.

3185. Rappaport, Roy A. "The Obvious Aspects of Ritual." CAMBRIDGE ANTHROPOLOGY 2,1 (1974): 3-69. Also in R. Rappaport, ECOLOGY, MEANING AND RELIGION. Richmond, California: North Atlantic Books, 1979, pp. 173-221.

3186. Remy, Jean, Jean-Pierre Hiernaux, and Emile Servais. "Formes liturgiques et symboliques sociales." SC 22,2 (1975): 175-192.

3187. Roth, J.A. "Ritual and Magic in the Control of Contagion." AMERICAN SOCIOLOGICAL REVIEW 22 (1957): 310-314.

3188. Segal, Robert A. "Victor Turner's Theory of Ritual." ZYGON 18,3 (1983): 327-335.

3189. Séguy, Jean. "Suggestions pour une sociologie des liturgies chrétiennes." ARCHIVES DE SOCIOLOGIE DES RELIGIONS 22 (1966): 145-151.

3190. Séguy, Jean. "Approches sociologiques de la liturgie. Liturgies et différenciations sociales." LA MAISON DIEU 107 (1971): 62-74.

3191. Servais, E., and J. Bonmariage. "Sunday Mass Attendance as a Cultural Institution." SC 16,3 (1969): 369-386.

* Sharot, Stephen. "Religious Change in Native Orthodoxy in London, 1870-1914: The Synagogue Service." Cited above as item 756.

3192. Shils, Edward. "Ritual and Crisis." In D.R. Cutler (ed.), THE RELIGIOUS SITUATION 1968 (volume cited in item 919), pp. 733-756.

3193. Swatos, William H., Jr. "Liturgy and Lebensform." PERSPECTIVES IN RELIGIOUS STUDIES 8 (1980): 38-49.

3194. Tamney, Joseph B. "Middletown's Rituals, 1924-1980." In Theodore Caplow et al., ALL FAITHFUL PEOPLE (volume cited in item 2970), pp. 128-145.

3195. Tamney, Joseph B. "A Quantitative Analysis of Religious Ritual in Middletown: A Research Note." SA 45,1 (1984): 57-64.

* Tomka, Miklós. "Les rites de passage dans les pays socialistes de l'Europe de l'Est." Cited above as item 2850.

* Tortosa, José M. "Ritual and Cultural Lag: The Feast of San Isidoro in Tiraque (Bolivia)." Cited above as item 3063.

3196. Traulle, Claude. "Problèmes méthodologiques d'une recherche sur la signification de la messe." SC 11,4 (1964): 37-46.

* Turner, Bryan S. "Belief, Ritual and Experience: The Case of Methodism." Cited above as item 2822.

3197. Turner, Victor W. THE RITUAL PROCESS: STRUCTURE AND ANTI-STRUCTURE. Chicago: Aldine, 1969.

3198. Turner, Victor, and Edith Turner. "Religious Celebrations." In Victor Turner (ed.), CELEBRATION. STUDIES IN FESTIVITY AND RITUAL. Washington: Smithsonian Institution Press, 1982, pp. 201-219.

3199. Turner, Victor, et al. "Symposium on 'Ritual in Human Adaptation.'" ZYGON 18,3 (1983): 209-325.

* Vattel, E. Daniel. "Ritual and Stratification in Chicago Negro Churches." Cited above as item 1884.

3200. Vecchi, A. "Appunti sul gesto rituale." SOCIOLOGIA RELIGIOSA 11-12 (1964): 13-30.

3201. Volpe, Rainer. "La liturgie en tant que comportement social -- Réflexions en vue de l'élaboration de méthodes empiriques de recherches." SC 22,2 (1975): 157-174.

3202. Wallace, Anthony, F.C. "Ritual: Sacred and Profane." Zygon 1,1 (1966): 60-81.

3203. Wiepel, W. "Erwägungen zur soziologischen Hermeneutik urchristlicher Gottesdienstformen." KAIROS 14,1 (1972): 36-51.

SECTION D: TYPOLOGY

Sectarianism

Religious partisanship which is often associated with the belief that one's religion has the unique and exclusive means to salvation.

3204. Alston, Jon P., and B.E. Aguirre. "Congregational Size and the Decline of Sectarian Commitment: The Case of the Jehovah's Witnesses in South and North America." SA 40,1 (1970): 63-70.

3205. Bainbridge, William Sims, and Rodney Stark. "Sectarian Tension." RRR 22,2 (1980): 105-124. Also in P.H. McNamara (ed.), RELIGION: NORTH AMERICAN STYLE (volume cited in item 117), pp. 118-121.

3206. Berger, Peter L. "The Sociological Study of Sectarianism." SOCIAL RESEARCH 21 (1954): 485-497.

3207. Berger, Peter L. "Sectarianism and Religious Sociation." AMERICAN JOURNAL OF SOCIOLOGY 64 (1958): 41-44.

* DeJong, Gordon F., and Thomas R. Ford. "Religious Fundamentalism and Denominational Preference in the Southern Appalachian Region." Cited above as item 1272.

3208. Dynes, Russell R. "Rurality, Migration and Sectarianism." RURAL SOCIOLOGY 21 (1956): 25-28.

* Dynes, Russell R. "The Consequences of Sectarianism for Social Participation." Cited above as item 1229.

3209. Eisenstadt, Samuel N. "Hétérodoxie, sectarisme et dynamique des civilisations." DIOGENE 120 (1982): 3-25.

* Garrison, Vivian. "Sectarianism and Psychosocial Adjustment: A Controlled Comparison of Puerto Rican Pentecostals and Catholics." Cited above as item 140.

3210. Hartley, Loyde H. SECTARIANISM AND SOCIAL PARTICIPATION. Unpublished Ph.D. dissertation, Emory University, 1968.

* Nelsen, Hart M. "Sectarianism, World View, and Anomie." Cited above as item 34.

* O'Dea, Thomas F. "Catholic Sectarianism: A Sociological Analysis of the So-Called Boston Heresy Case." Cited above as item 2229.

3211. Wallis, Roy. "The Sectarianism of Scientology." SOCIOLOGICAL YEARBOOK OF RELIGION IN BRITAIN 6 (1973): 136-155.

3212. Wallis, Roy (ed.) SECTARIANISM: ANALYSES OF RELIGIOUS AND NON-RELIGIOUS SECTS. London: Peter Owen, 1975. Contains items 1123, 1265, 1971.

3213. Wilson, Bryan R. (ed.) PATTERNS OF SECTARIANISM. ORGANIZATION AND IDEOLOGY IN SOCIAL AND RELIGIOUS MOVEMENTS. London: Heinemann, 1967. Contains items 798, 3294.

Types

The identification of distinctive organizational patterns, quality of commitment and religious mentality provides a disciplinary stratagem.

* Adams, Robert Lynn, and John Mogey. "Marriage, Membership and Mobility in Church and Sect." Cited above as item 1954.

3214. Becker, Howard. "Sacred and Secular Societies Considered with Reference to Folk, State, and Similar Classifications." SOCIAL FORCES 28,4 (1950): 361-376.

3215. Becker, Howard, and Leopold von Wiese. SYSTEMATIC SOCIOLOGY. New York: John Wiley and Sons, 1932, pp. 624-628.

3216. Beckford, James A. "New Wine in New Bottles: A Departure from Church-Sect Conceptual Tradition." SC 23,1 (1976): 71-85.

3217. Bhatt, Gaurio Shanker. "Brahma Samaj, Arya Samaj, and the Church-Sect Typology." RRR 10 (1968): 23-32.

3218. Blasi, Anthony J. "Dialecticizing the Types." SA 42,2 (1981): 163-172.

3219. Boling, T. Edwin. "Sectarian Protestants, Churchly Protestants and Roman Catholics: A Comparison in a Mid-American City." RRR 14,3 (1973): 159-168.

3220. Burgalassi, S. "Classificazioni e tipologie nella società religiosa." SOCIOLOGIA RELIGIOSA 3-4 (1959): 95-150.

* Campbell, Colin, and Robert W. Coles. "Religiosity, Religious Affiliation and Religious Belief: The Exploration of a Typology." Cited above as item 931.

3221. Coleman, John A. "Church-Sect Typology and Organizational Precariousness." SA 29,2 (1968): 55-66.

* Demerath, Nicholas J. "Social Stratification and Church Involvement: The Church-Sect Distinction Applied to Individual Participation." Cited above as item 1780.

3222. Dempf, Alois. RELIGIONSSOZIOLOGIE DER CHRISTENHEIT. ZUR TYPOLOGIE CHRISTLICHER GEMEINSCHAFTSBILDUNGEN. München, Wien: R. Oldenbourg, 1972.

3223. Dent, O.F. "Church-Sect Typologies in the Description of Religious Groups." THE AUSTRALIAN AND NEW ZEALAND JOURNAL OF SOCIOLOGY 6,1 (1970): 10-27.

3224. Desroche, Henri. "Sociologie et théologie dans la typologie religieuse de Joachim Wach." ARCHIVES DE SOCIOLOGIE DES RELIGIONS 1 (1956): 41-63.

3225. Desroche, Henri. SOCIOLOGIES RELIGIEUSES. Paris: Presses Universitaires de France, 1968.
JACOB AND THE ANGEL. AN ESSAY IN SOCIOLOGIES OF RELIGION, translated by John K. Savacool. Amherst: University of Massachusetts Press, 1973.

3226. Dewitt, Robert Lee. THE LUTHERAN CHURCH IN FREDERICKTON. Unpublished M.A. thesis, University of New Brunswick, 1965.

3227. Dienel, Peter. "Kirche und Sekte I. Einblick in eine empirische Untersuchung in Form begrifflicher Erwägungen." In D. Goldschmidt and J. Matthes (eds.), PROBLEME DER RELIGIONSSOZIOLOGIE. KÖLNER ZEITSCHRIFT FÜR SOZIOLOGIE UND SOZIALPSYCHOLOGIE, SONDERHEFT 6. Köln, Opladen: Westdeutscher Verlag, 1962, 1966, pp. 232-242.

3228. Dittes, James E. "Typing the Typologies: Some Parallels in the Career of Church-Sect and Extrinsic-Intrinsic." JSSR 10,4 (1971): 375-383.

* Driedger, Leo, and William H. Form. "Religious Typology and the Social Ideology of the Clergy." Cited above as item 601.

3229. Dynes, Russell R. CHURCH-SECT TYPOLOGY: AN EMPIRICAL STUDY. Unpublished Ph.D. dissertation, Ohio State University, 1954.

* Dynes, Russell R. "The Church-Sect Typology and Socio-Economic Status." Cited above as item 1787.

3230. Eister, Allan W. "Toward a Radical Critique of Church-Sect Typologizing: Comment on some Critical Observations on the Church-Sect Dimension." JSSR 6 (1967): 85-90.

3231. Filsinger, Erik E. "Differences in Religious Structures between Empirically Derived Types." RRR 22,3 (1981): 255-267.

3232. Filsinger, Erik E., Joseph E. Faulkner, and Rex H. Warland. "Empirical Taxonomy of Religious Individuals: An Investigation among College Students." SA 40,2 (1979): 136-146.

3233. Goddijn, Walter. "Kirche und Sekte II. Soziologische Betrachtungen über Gruppendifferenzierungen innerhalf des Christentums." In D. Goldschmidt and J. Matthes (ed.), PROBLEME DER RELIGIONSSOZIOLOGIE. KÖLNER ZEITSCHRIFT FÜR SOZIOLOGIE UND SOZIALPSYCHOLOGIE. SONDERHEFT 6. Köln, Opladen: Westdeutscher, Verlag, 1962, 1966, pp. 243-253.

3234. Goode, Erich. "Some Critical Observations on the Church-Sect Dimension." JSSR 6 (1967): 69-84.

3235. Goode, Erich. "Further Reflections on the Church-Sect Dimension." JSSR 6 (1967): 270-277.

3236. Gustafson, Paul M. "UO-US-PS-PO: A Restatement of Troeltsch's Church-Sect Typology." JSSR 6 (1967): 64-68.

3237. Gustafson, Paul M. "Church and Sect or Church and Ascetic Protestantism. Ernst Troeltsch's Problem." ENCOUNTER 30,2 (1969): 142-147.

* Gustafson, Paul M. "Exegesis on the Gospel According to St. Max." Cited above as item 2809.

3238. Hertel, Bradley R. "Church, Sect, and Congregation in Hinduism: An Examination of Social Structure and Religious Authority." JSSR 16,1 (1977): 15-26.

3239. Hood, Ralph W., Jr., and Ronald J. Morris. "A Critical Rejoinder to 'Empirical Taxonomy of Religious Individuals: An Investigation among College Students.'" SA 41,3 (1980): 265-267.
Filsinger, Erik E., Joseph E. Faulkner, and Rex H. Warland. "Reply to Hood and Morris." SA 41,3 (1980): 269-271.

3240. Johnson, Benton. "A Critical Appraisal of the Church-Sect Typology." AMERICAN SOCIOLOGICAL REVIEW 22 (1957): 88-92.

3241. Johnson, Benton. "On Church and Sect." AMERICAN SOCIOLOGICAL REVIEW 28 (1963): 539-549.

3242. Johnson, Benton. "Church and Sect Revisited." JSSR 10 (1971): 124-137.

3243. Liebman, Charles S. "Some Theoretical Elaborations of the Church-Sect Typology." RRR 7,3 (1966): 157-160.

* Margolis, Robert D. AN EMPIRICAL TYPOLOGY OF RELIGIOUS EXPERIENCE: ITS VALIDATION AND RELATIONSHIP TO PSYCHOTIC EXPERIENCE. Cited above as item 2995.

* Margolis, Robert D., and Kirk W. Elifson. "A Typology of Religious Experience." Cited above as item 2996.

3244. Mayer, Carl. SEKTE UND KIRCHE. EIN RELIGIONSSOZIOLOGISCHER VERSUCH. Heidelberg, 1933.

* Mayrl, William W. "Marx' Theory of Social Movements and the Church-Sect Typology." Cited above as item 2258.

* Millett, David. "A Typology of Religious Organizations Suggested by the Canadian Census." Cited above as item 1158.

3245. Moberg, David O. "Potential Uses of the Church-Sect Typology in Comparative Religious Research." INTERNATIONAL JOURNAL OF COMPARATIVE SOCIOLOGY 2 (1961): 47-58.

3246. Newell, William H., and Fumiko Dobashi. "Some Problems of Classification in Religious Sociology as Shown in the History of Tenri Kyokay." JOURNAL OF ASIAN AND AFRICAN STUDIES 3,1-2 (1968): 84-100.

* Niebuhr, H. Richard. THE SOCIAL SOURCES OF DENOMINATIONALISM. Cited above as item 1849.

* Pope, Liston. MILLHANDS AND PREACHERS. Cited above as item 1859.

3247. Ralston, Helen. "The Typologies of Weber and Troeltsch. A Case Study of a Catholic Religious Group in Atlantic Canada." ARCHIVES DE SCIENCES SOCIALES DES RELIGIONS 50,1 (1980): 111-127.

3248. Robertson, Roland. "Comment: Church-Sect and Rationality: Reply to Swatos." JSSR 16,2 (1977): 197-200.

3249. Scanzoni, John. "A Note on Method for the Church-Sect Typology." SA 26,4 (1965): 189-202.

3250. Scanzoni, John. "Innovation and Constancy in the Church-Sect Typology." AMERICAN JOURNAL OF SOCIOLOGY 71 (1965): 325-327.

3251. Snook, John B. "An Alternative to Church-Sect." JSSR 13,2 (1974): 191-204.

* Stark, Rodney, and William Sims Bainbridge. "Of Churches, Sects, and Cults: Preliminary Concepts for a Theory of Religious Movements." Cited above as item 2272.

3252. Steeman, Theodore M. "Church, Sect, Mysticism, Denomination. Periodological Aspects of Troeltsch's Types." SA 36,3 (1975): 181-204.

3253. Swatos, William H., Jr. "Monopolism, Pluralism, Acceptance, and Rejection. An Integrated Model for Church-Sect Theory." RRR 16,3 (1975): 174-185.

3254. Swatos, William H., Jr. "Weber or Troeltsch? Methodology, Syndrome, and the Development of Church-Sect Theory." JSSR 15,2 (1976): 129-144.

3255. Swatos, William H., Jr. "Comment: Quo Vadis: Reply to Robertson." JSSR 16,2 (1977): 201-204.

3256. Swatos, William H., Jr. INTO DENOMINATIONALISM: THE ANGLICAN METAMORPHOSIS. Storrs, Connecticut: Society for the Scientific Study of Religion, 1979.

* Swatos, William H., Jr. "Church-Sect and Cult: Bringing Mysticism Back In." Cited above as item 51.

3257. Troeltsch, Ernst. THE SOCIAL TEACHING OF THE CHRISTIAN CHURCHES (2 vols.), translated by Olive Wyon. New York: Macmillan, 1932. Relevant passages from pp. 331-333, 338-341, in J.M. Yinger (ed.), RELIGION, SOCIETY, AND THE INDIVIDUAL (volume cited in item 943), pp. 416-420.

3258. Wach, Joachim. "Church, Denomination and Sect." In J. Wach, TYPES OF RELIGIOUS EXPERIENCE. Chicago: University of Chicago Press, 1951, pp. 187-208.

* Wallis, Roy. THE ELEMENTARY FORMS OF THE NEW RELIGIOUS LIFE. Cited above as item 2430.

3259. Weber, Max, with Ferdinand Toennies. "Max Weber on Church, Sect, and Mysticism." SA 34,2 (1973): 140-149.

3260. Wells, C.D. "Religious Institutional Types." SOCIOLOGY AND SOCIAL RESEARCH 17,6 (1933): 551-555.

3261. Yinger, J. Milton. Ch. 13. "Types of Religious Organizations." In J.M. Yinger, THE SCIENTIFIC STUDY OF RELIGION. New York: Macmillan, 1970, pp. 251-281.

Church

A social order wherein the boundaries of the religion and the society are coextensive.

3262. Stark, Werner. THE SOCIOLOGY OF RELIGION, VOL. III. THE UNIVERSAL CHURCH. New York: Fordham University Press, 1967.

3263. Westhues, Kenneth. "The Established Church as an Agent of Change." SA 34,2 (1973): 106-123.

* Westhues, Kenneth. "The Church in Opposition." Cited above as item 969.

Cult

A religious phenomenon characterized by amorphous social organization and the provision of a spiritual good to a client by a specialist.

3264. Ahern, Geoffrey. "Esoteric 'New Religious Movements' and the Western Esoteric Tradition." In E. Barker (ed.), OF GODS AND MEN (item 2396), pp. 165-176.

3265. Ahern, Geoffrey. SUN AT MIDNIGHT: THE RUDOLPH STEINER MOVEMENT AND THE WESTERN ESOTERIC TRADITION. Wellingborough, U.K.: Aquarian Press, 1984.

3266. Bainbridge, William Sims. SATAN'S POWER: A DEVIANT PSYCHOTHERAPY CULT. Berkeley: University of California Press, 1978.

* Bainbridge, William Sims, and Rodney Stark. "Cult Formation: Three Compatible Models." Cited above as item 2392.

3267. Bainbridge, William Sims, and Rodney Stark. "Client and Audience Cults in America." SA 41,3 (1980): 199-214.

3268. Beynon, E.D. "The Voodoo Cult among Negro Migrants in Detroit." AMERICAN JOURNAL OF SOCIOLOGY 43,6 (1938): 894-907.

3269. Braden, C.H. THESE ALSO BELIEVE: A STUDY OF MODERN AMERICAN CULTS AND MINORITY RELIGIOUS MOVEMENTS. New York: Macmillan, 1949.

3270. Campbell, Bruce. WISDOM OF THE SOUL: A CONTEMPORARY THEOSOPHICAL CULT. Unpublished Ph.D. dissertation, University of California, Santa Barbara, 1977.

3271. Campbell, Bruce. "A Typology of Cults." SA 39,3 (1978): 228-240.

* Campbell, Colin. "The Cult, the Cultic Milieu and Secularization." Cited above as item 2460.

3272. Campbell, Colin. "Clarifying the Cult." BRITISH JOURNAL OF SOCIOLOGY 28,3 (1977): 375-388.

* Campbell, Colin. "The Secret Religion of the Educated Classes." Cited above as item 1765.

3273. Catton, William R., Sr. "What Kind of People Does a Religious Cult Attract?" AMERICAN SOCIOLOGICAL REVIEW 22 (1957): 561-566.

3274. Eister, Allan W. "The Oxford Group Movement: A Typological Analysis." SOCIOLOGY AND SOCIAL RESEARCH 34 (1949): 116-124.

3275. Eister, Allan W. DRAWING-ROOM CONVERSION: A SOCIOLOGICAL ACCOUNT OF THE OXFORD GROUP MOVEMENT. Durham: Duke University Press, 1950.

3276. Eister, Allan W. "An Outline of a Structural Theory of Cults." JSSR 11 (1972): 319-333.

3277. Eister, Allan W. "Culture Crises and New Religious Movements: A Paradigmatic Statement of a Theory of Cults." In I. Zaretsky and M.P. Leone (eds.), RELIGIOUS MOVEMENTS IN CONTEMPORARY AMERICA (volume cited in item 140), pp. 612-627.

3278. Fichter, Joseph H. THE CATHOLIC CULT OF THE PARACLETE. New York: Sheed and Ward, 1975.

3279. Griswold, Alfred W. "New Thought: A Cult of Success." AMERICAN JOURNAL OF SOCIOLOGY 40 (1934): 309-318.

3280. Jackson, J., and R. Jobling. "Towards an Analysis of Contemporary Cults." In D. Martin (ed.), A SOCIOLOGICAL YEARBOOK OF RELIGION IN BRITAIN 1. London: SCM Press, 1968, pp. 94-105.

3281. Koss, Joan D. "El porqué de los cultos religiosos: el caso del Espiritismo en Puerto Rico." REVISTA DE CIENCIAS SOCIALES 16,1 (1972): 61-72.

3282. Lehrburger, E. STRANGE SECTS AND CULTS. A STUDY OF THEIR ORIGINS AND INFLUENCE. London: Barker, 1971.

3283. Locke, Ralph G. "Who am I in the City of Mammon? The Self, Doubt and Certainty in a Spiritualist Cult." In A. Black and P. Glasner (eds.), PRACTICE AND BELIEF (volume cited in item 824), pp. 108-133.

* Mann, William E. SECT, CULT, AND CHURCH IN ALBERTA. Cited above as item 1633.

3284. Martz, M.E. "Sects and Cults." ANNALS OF THE AMERICAN ACADEMY OF POLITICAL AND SOCIAL SCIENCE 332 (1960): 125-134.

3285. Nelson, Geoffrey K. "The Analysis of a Cult: Spiritualism." SC 15,6 (1968): 469-481.

3286. Nelson, Geoffrey K. "The Concept of Cult." SOCIOLOGICAL REVIEW 16,3 (1968): 351-362.

3287. Nelson, Geoffrey K. "The Spiritualist Movement: A Need for the Redefinition of the Concept of the Cult." JSSR 8 (1969): 152-160.

3288. Nelson, Geoffrey K. "The Membership of a Cult: The Spiritualists National Union." RRR 13 (1972): 170-177.

3289. Pavlos, Andrew J. THE CULT EXPERIENCE. Westport, Connecticut: Greenwood, 1982.

3290. Poulat, Emile. "Les cultes dans les statistiques officielles en France au XIXème siècle." ARCHIVES DE SOCIOLOGIE DES RELIGIONS 2 (1956): 22-26.

3291. Richardson, James T. "An Oppositional and General Conceptualization of Cult." ANNUAL REVIEW OF THE SOCIAL SCIENCES OF RELIGION 2,2 (1978): 29-52.

* Richardson, James T. "From Cult to Sect: Creative Eclecticism in New Religious Movements." Cited above as item 2420.

3292. Sharma, U.M. "The Immortal Cowherd and the Saintly Carrier. An Essay in the Study of Cults." SOCIOLOGICAL BULLETIN 19,2 (1970): 137-152.

* Stark, Rodney, and William Sims Bainbridge. "Of Churches, Sects, and Cults: Preliminary Concepts for a Theory of Religious Movements." Cited above as item 2272.

3293. Stark, Rodney, William Sims Bainbridge, and Daniel P. Doyle. "Cults of America: A Reconnaissance in Space and Time." SA 40,4 (1979): 347-359.

* Stark, Rodney, William Sims Bainbridge, and Lori Kent. "Cult Membership in the Roaring Twenties: Assessing Local Receptivity." Cited above as item 965.

* Stark, Rodney, and William Sims Bainbridge. "Secularization, Revival, and Cult Formation." Cited above as item 2564.

* Stark, Rodney, and William Sims Bainbridge. "Secularization and Cult Formation in the Jazz Age." Cited above as item 2565.

* Swatos, William H., Jr. "Church-Sect and Cult: Bringing Mysticism Back In." Cited above as item 51.

* Wallis, Roy. "Ideology, Authority, and the Development of Cultic Movements." Cited above as item 1210.

* Wilson, Bryan R. CONTEMPORARY TRANSFORMATIONS OF RELIGION. Cited above as item 2582.

* Yinger, J. Milton. "Religion and Social Change: Functions and Dysfunctions of Sects and Cults among the Disprivileged." Cited above as item 1896.

Denomination (type)

A non-exclusive religion compatible with religious pluralism.

3294. Isichei, Elizabeth Allo. "From Sect to Denomination in English Quakerism." BRITISH JOURNAL OF SOCIOLOGY 15 (1964): 207-222. Also in B.R. Wilson (ed.), PATTERNS OF SECTARIANISM (item 3213), pp. 161-181.

3295. Martin, David A. "The Denomination." BRITISH JOURNAL OF SOCIOLOGY 13 (1961): 1-14.

3296. Swatos, William H., Jr. "Beyond Denominationalism?: Community and Culture in American Religion." JSSR 20,3 (1981): 217-227.

Mysticism

Union with the divine.

3297. Beylier, C. "Un première enquête de Roger Bastide: Image du Nordeste mystique en noir et blanc." ARCHIVES INTERNATIONALES DE LA SOCIOLOGIE DE LA COOPERATION ET DU DEVELOPPEMENT 40 (1976): 15-34.

3298. Damrell, Joseph. SEEKING SPIRITUAL MEANING. THE WORLD OF VEDANTA. Beverly Hills, Calif.: Sage, 1977.

3299. Drees, W. KATHOLISCHE MYSTIK ALS SOZIOLOGISCHES PHÄNOMEN. Elberfeld, 1929.

3300. Garrett, William R. "Maligned Mysticism: The Maledicted Career of Troeltsch's Third Type." SA 36,3 (1975): 205-223.

* Greeley, Andrew M. ECSTASY: A WAY OF KNOWING. Cited above as item 2980.

3301. Greeley, Andrew M., and William M. McCready. "Are We a Nation of Mystics?" NEW YORK TIMES MAGAZINE, Jan. 26, 1975, pp. 12-24.

3302. Gustafson, Paul M. "The Missing Member of Troeltsch's Trinity: Thoughts Generated by Weber's Comments." SA 36,3 (1975): 224-226.

3303. Honigsheim, Paul. "Soziologie der Mystik." In Max Scheler (ed.), VERSUCHE ZU EINER SOZIOLOGIE DES WISSENS. München and Leipzig: Duncker & Humblot, 1924, pp. 323-346.

* Hood, Ralph W., and Ronald J. Morris. "Knowledge and Experience Criteria in the Report of Mystical Experiences." Cited above as item 2991.

* Mueller, Gert H. "Asceticism and Mysticism. A Contribution towards the Sociology of Faith." Cited above as item 48.

3304. Mukerjee, R. "Sociology and Mysticism." SOCIOLOGY AND SOCIAL RESEARCH 15,4 (1931): 303-310.

3305. Nielson, F. "The Return to Mysticism." AMERICAN JOURNAL OF ECONOMICS AND SOCIOLOGY 2,4 (1943): 503-516.

3306. Robbins, Thomas. "Getting Straight with Meher Baba. A Study of Mysticism, Drug Rehabilitation, and Post-Adolescent Role Conflict." JSSR 11,2 (1972): 122-140.

3307. Robertson, Roland. "On the Analysis of Mysticism: Pre-Weberian, Weberian, and Post-Weberian Perspectives." SA 36,3 (1975): 241-266.

3308. Robertson, Roland. "Inner-Worldly Mysticism: Before and After Weber." In R. Robertson, MEANING AND CHANGE (volume cited in item 2021), pp. 103-147.

3309. Roumeguere-Eberhardt, Jacqueline. "Sociologie de la connaissance et connaissance mystique chez les Bantu." CAHIERS INTERNATIONAUX DE SOCIOLOGIE 35 (1963): 113-126.

* Sharot, Stephen. MESSIANISM, MYSTICISM, AND MAGIC: A SOCIOLOGICAL ANALYSIS OF JEWISH RELIGIOUS MOVEMENTS. Cited above as item 2374.

* Simmons, J.L. "On Maintaining Deviant Belief Systems: A Case Study." Cited above as item 2155.

* Steeman, Theodore M. "Church, Sect, Mysticism, Denomination. Periodological Aspects of Troeltsch's Types." Cited above as item 3252.

* Swatos, William H., Jr. "Church-Sect and Cult: Bringing Mysticism Back In." Cited above as item 51.

3310. Thomas, L. Eugene, and Pamela E. Cooper. "Measurement and Incidence of Mystical Experiences: An Exploratory Study." JSSR 17,4 (1978): 433-437.

* Thorner, Isidor. "Prophetic and Mystic Experience: Comparison and Consequences." Cited above as item 3007.

* Wuthnow, Robert. THE CONSCIOUSNESS REFORMATION. Cited above as item 2436.

* Wuthnow, Robert. EXPERIMENTATION IN AMERICAN RELIGION. Cited above as item 1722.

3311. Yalman, Nur. "Islamic Reform and the Mystic Tradition in Eastern Turkey." ARCHIVES EUROPEENNES DE SOCIOLOGIE 10 (1969): 41-60.

Sect

A religious organization which normally manifests a high degree of tension with the "external world."

* Baer, Hans A. THE LEVITES OF UTAH: THE DEVELOPMENT OF AND CONVERSION TO A SMALL MILLENARIAN SECT. Cited above as item 1237.

* Barthel, Diane L. AMANA: FROM PIETIST SECT TO AMERICAN COMMUNITY. Cited above as item 1238.

3312. Beckford, James A. "The Embryonic Stage of a Religious Sect's Development: The Jehovah's Witnesses." In M. Hill (ed.), A SOCIOLOGICAL YEARBOOK OF RELIGION IN BRITAIN 5. London: SCM Press, 1972.

* Beckford, James A. "Two Contrasting Types of Sectarian Organization." Cited above as item 1123.

3313. Beckford, James A. "Sociological Stereotypes of the Religious Sect." SOCIOLOGICAL REVIEW 26,1 (1978): 109-123.

* Berger, Stephen D. "The Sects and the Breakthrough into the Modern World: On the Centrality of the Sects in Weber's Protestant Ethic Thesis." Cited above as item 2607.

3314. Bernard, G. "The Nature of Sociological Research: Religious Sects in the West of the Congo." CAHIERS ECONOMIQUES ET SOCIAUX 3 (1964): 261-269.

* Boisen, Anton. RELIGION IN CRISIS AND CUSTOM. Cited above as item 1756.

3315. Boling, T. Edwin. "Black and White Religion: A Comparison in the Lower Class." SA 36,1 (1975): 73-80.

3316. Brewer, Earl D.C. METHODISM IN CHANGING AMERICAN SOCIETY. Unpublished Ph.D. dissertation, University of North Carolina, 1950.

3317. Brewer, Earl D.C. "Sect and Church in Methodism." SOCIAL FORCES 30 (1952): 400-408. Also in L. Schneider (ed.), RELIGION, CULTURE AND SOCIETY (volume cited in item 1824), pp. 471-482.

3318. Calley, M.J.C. "Pentecostal Sects among West Indian Migrants." RACE 3 (1962): 55-64.

3319. Calley, M.J.C. GOD'S PEOPLE: WEST INDIAN PENTECOSTAL SECTS IN ENGLAND. New York: Oxford University Press, 1965.

3320. Chaffee, G.E. "The Isolated Religious Sect as an Object for Social Research." AMERICAN JOURNAL OF SOCIOLOGY 35,4 (1930): 618-630.

3321. Chamberlayne, John H. "From Sect to Church in British Methodism." BRITISH JOURNAL OF SOCIOLOGY 15,2 (1964): 139-149.

3322. Chambre, Henri. "Deux études sur des sectes chrétiennes en Union Soviétique." ARCHIVES DE SOCIOLOGIE DES RELIGIONS 20 (1965): 95-96.

3323. Chattopadhyaya, S. THE EVOLUTION OF THE THEISTIC SECTS IN ANCIENT INDIA UP TO THE TIME OF SAMKRARACARYA. Calcutta: Progressive Publishers, 1962.

3324. Clark, Elmer T. THE SMALL SECTS IN AMERICA. Nashville: Abingdon, 1949. A typological passage, pp. 22-24, is reprinted in J.M. Yinger (ed.), RELIGION, SOCIETY AND THE INDIVIDUAL. New York: Macmillan, 1957, pp. 421-423.

3325. Clark, S.D. "Religious Organization and the Rise of the Canadian Nation, 1850-1885." REPORT OF THE ANNUAL MEETING OF THE CANADIAN HISTORICAL ASSOCIATION, 1944, pp. 86-96. Also in S.D. Clark, THE DEVELOPING CANADIAN COMMUNITY (volume cited in item 1552).

* Clark, S.D. "The Religious Sect in Canadian Politics." Cited above as item 1552.

3326. Clark, S.D. "The Religious Sect in Canadian Economic Development." CANADIAN JOURNAL OF ECONOMICS AND POLITICAL SCIENCE 12,4 (1946): 439-453. Also in S.D. Clark, THE DEVELOPING CANADIAN COMMUNITY (volume cited in item 1552).

3327. Clark, S.D. "The Religious Influence in Canadian Society." In THE TASKS OF ECONOMIC HISTORY, a supplement of the JOURNAL OF ECONOMIC HISTORY, 1947, pp. 89-103. Also in S.D. Clark, THE DEVELOPING CANADIAN COMMUNITY (volume cited in item 1552).

* Clark, S.D. CHURCH AND SECT IN CANADA. Cited above as item 1771.

3328. Cohn, Werner. JEHOVAH'S WITNESSES AS A PROLETARIAN SECT. Unpublished thesis, New School for Social Research, 1954.

3329. Coser, Lewis. "Sects and Sectarianism." DISSENT 6 (1954): 360-369.

3330. Dearman, Marion Veurl. DO HOLINESS SECTS SOCIALIZE IN DOMINANT VALUES? AN EMPIRICAL INQUIRY. Unpublished Ph.D. dissertation, University of Oregon, 1972.

* Demerath, Nicholas J., III. SOCIAL CLASS IN AMERICAN PROTESTANTISM. Cited above as item 1228.

3331. Desroche, Henri. "Sociologie des sectes. Dissidences religieuses et socialismes utopiques." ANNEE SOCIOLOGIQUE 1952, 3e série (1955): 393-429.

3332. Desroche, Henri. "Autour de la sociologie dite 'des sectes.'" ANNEE SOCIOLOGIQUE 1955-56, 3e série (1958): 395-421.

3333. Faris, Ellsworth. "The Sect and the Sectarian." AMERICAN JOURNAL OF SOCIOLOGY 60,6 (1955): 75-89.

* Foucart, Eric. "Le phénomène des sectes: essai de synthèse." Cited above as item 2406.

3334. Foucart, Eric. "La vision des sectes au Québec. Mécanismes et résultats." LES CAHIERS DU CENTRE DE RECHERCHES EN SOCIOLOGIE RELIGIEUSE 3 (1980): 117-128.

3335. Gerth, Hans H. "Midwestern Sectarian Community." SOCIAL RESEARCH 11,3 (1944): 354-362.

3336. Giddings, Franklin H. "Cultural Conflicts and the Organization of Sects." In Robert E. Park and Ernest W. Burgess (eds.), INTRODUCTION TO THE SCIENCE OF SOCIOLOGY. Chicago: University of Chicago Press, 1924, pp. 613-619.

3337. Gillen, John. "A Contribution to the Sociology of Sects." AMERICAN JOURNAL OF SOCIOLOGY 16 (1910): 236-252.

3338. Hammond, Phillip E. "The Migrating Sect: An Illustration from Early Norwegian Immigration." SOCIAL FORCES 41,3 (1963): 275-283.

* Hampshire, Annette P., and James A. Beckford. "Religious Sects and the Concept of Deviance." Cited above as item 2133.

3339. Heddendorf, R. "The Sect and Religious Autonomy." SOCIOLOGICAL QUARTERLY 6,1 (1965): 45-58.

* Hill, Clifford. "Immigrant Sect Development in Britain: A Case of Status Deprivation?" Cited above as item 143.

3340. Hill, Clifford. "From Church to Sect: West Indian Religious Sect Development in Britain." JSSR 10,2 (1971): 114-123.

* Holt, John B. "Holiness Religion: Cultural Shock and Social Reorganization." Cited above as item 1811.

* Isichei, Elizabeth Allo. "From Sect to Denomination in English Quakerism." Cited above as item 3294.

* Johnson, Benton. "Do Holiness Sects Socialize in Dominant Values?" Cited above as item 511.

3341. Knudsen, Dean D., John R. Earle, and Donald W. Shriner, Jr. "The Conception of Sectarian Religion: An Effort at Clarification." RRR 20,1 (1978): 44-60.

* Koss, Joan D. "Terapeutica del sistema de una secta en Puerto Rico." Cited above as item 3104.

3342. Kowalewski, David, and Arthur L. Greil. "Religious Sectarianism and the Soviet Stage. The Dynamics of Believer Protest and Regime Response." RRR 24,3 (1983): 245-260.

3343. Lalive d'Epinay, Christian. "Changements sociaux et développement d'une secte. Le pentecôtisme au Chile." ARCHIVES DE SOCIOLOGIE DES RELIGIONS 12 (1967): 65-90.

* Lehrburger, E. STRANGE SECTS AND CULTS. A STUDY OF THEIR ORIGINS AND INFLUENCE. Cited above as item 3282.

* Mat-Hasquin, Michèle. LES SECTES CONTEMPORAINES. Cited above as item 2415.

* Mann, William E. SECT, CULT, AND CHURCH IN ALBERTA. Cited above as item 1633.

* Martz, M.E. "Sects and Cults." Cited above as item 3284.

* Maurer, H.H. "The Consciousness of Kind of a Fundamentalist Group." Cited above as item 168.

* McNall, Scott G. "The Sect Movement." Cited above as item 2259.

* O'Dea, Thomas, and Renato Poblete Barth. "Anomie and the 'Quest for Community': The Formation of Sects among the Puerto Ricans of New York." Cited above as item 35.

3344. O'Toole, Roger. "Underground Traditions in the Study of Sectarianism: Non-Religious Uses of the Concept 'Sect.'" JSSR 15 (1976): 145-156.

3345. Park, Robert E. "Characteristics of the Sect." In Ralph H. Turner (ed.), ON SOCIAL CONTROL AND COLLECTIVE BEHAVIOR. Chicago: University of Chicago Press, 1967, pp. 240-248.

3346. Poblete Barth, Renato. "Sociological Approach to the Sects." SC 7,5-6 (1960): 383-406.

* Redekop, Calvin. "Decision-Making in a Sect." Cited above as item 1499.

3347. Redekop, Calvin. "The Sect from a New Perspective." MENNONITE QUARTERLY REVIEW 39,3 (1965): 204-217.

3348. Redekop, Calvin. "A New Look at Sect Development." JSSR 13 (1974): 345-352.

* Richardson, James T. "From Cult to Sect: Creative Eclecticism in New Religious Movements." Cited above as item 2420.

3349. Robbins, Thomas, Dick Anthony, and Thomas E. Curtis. "The Limits of Symbolic Realism: Problems of Empathy. Field Research in a Sectarian Context." JSSR 12,3 (1973): 259-271.

3350. Roberts, Bryan R. "Protestant Groups and Coping with Urban Life in Guatemala City." AMERICAN JOURNAL OF SOCIOLOGY 73 (1968): 753-767.

3351. Robertson, Roland. "Religious Movements and Modern Societies: Toward a Progressive Problemshift." SA 40,4 (1979): 297-314.

* Ross, Jack C. TRADITIONALISM AND CHARISMA IN A RELIGIOUS GROUP: MEMBERSHIP CAREERS AND ROLE CONTINGENCIES OF QUAKERS. Unpublished Ph.D. dissertation, University of Minnesota, 1964. Cited above as item 75.

3352. Ross, Jack C. "The Establishment Process in a Middle-Class Sect." SC 16,4 (1969): 500-507.

3353. Roucek, Joseph S. "The Role of Sects in American Life." SOCIOLOGIA RELIGIOSA 11-12 (1964): 35-60.

* Schrey, Henry H. "Sectes et mouvements religieux." Cited above as item 2268.

* Schwartz, Gary. SECT IDEOLOGIES AND SOCIAL STATUS. Cited above as item 151.

3354. Séguy, Jean. LES SECTES PROTESTANTES DANS LA FRANCE CONTEMPORAINE. Paris: Beauchesne, 1956.

3355. Séguy, Jean. "Les sectes d'origine protestant et le monde ouvrier français aux XIX siècle." ARCHIVES DE SOCIOLOGIE DES RELIGIONS 6 (1958): 119-126.

3356. Séguy, Jean. "Sectes chrétiennes et développement." ARCHIVES DE SOCIOLOGIE DES RELIGIONS 13 (1962): 5-15.

3357. Séguy, Jean. "Sectes et religions nouvelles." ETUDES (1963): 328-341.

3358. Séguy, Jean. "Les problèmes de la typologie dans l'étude des sectes." SC 12,3 (1965): 165-170.

3359. Séguy, Jean. "Les sectes comme mode d'insertion sociale." In J. Séguy, EGLISES ET GROUPES RELIGIEUX DANS LA SOCIETE FRANÇAISE. Strasbourg: Cerdic Publications, 1977, pp. 293-316.

* Sprague, T.W. "Some Notable Features in the Authority Structure of a Sect." Cited above as item 1205.

3360. Stark, Rodney, and William Sims Bainbridge. "American-Born Sects: Initial Findings." JSSR 20,2 (1981): 130-149.

3361. Stark, Werner. THE SOCIOLOGY OF RELIGION. A STUDY OF CHRISTENDOM. VOLUME II SECTARIAN RELIGION. New York: Fordham University Press, 1967.

3362. Vincente, A.G. L'EVOLUTION DES SECTES. Louvain: Centre de Recherches Socio-Religieuses, 1967.

3363. Wallis, Roy. "Religious Sects and the Fear of Publicity." NEW SOCIETY 24,557 (1973): 545-547.

* Weber, Paul-Günter. RELIGIOSITÄT UND SOZIALE ORGANISATIONS-FORMEN IN SEKTEN. EINE RELIGIONSSOZIOLOGISCHE STUDIE DREIER SEKTENGRUPPEN. Cited above as item 1183.

* Welch, Michael R. MULTIDIMENSIONAL SCALING AS A SECT CLASSIFICATION DEVICE: A PRELIMINARY INVESTIGATION. Cited above as item 2960.

3364. Welch, Michael R. "Analyzing Religious Sects: An Empirical Examination of Wilson's Sect Typology." JSSR 16,2 (1977): 125-141.

* Whitworth, John McKelvie. GOD'S BLUEPRINTS: A SOCIOLOGICAL STUDY OF THREE UTOPIAN SECTS. Cited above as item 1264.

3365. Wilson, Bryan R. SOCIAL ASPECTS OF RELIGIOUS SECTS: A STUDY OF SOME CONTEMPORARY GROUPS IN GREAT BRITAIN. Unpublished Ph.D. thesis, University of London, 1955.

3366. Wilson, Bryan R. "Apparition et persistance des sectes dans un milieu social en évolution." ARCHIVES DE SOCIOLOGIE DES RELIGIONS 5 (1958): 140-150.

3367. Wilson, Bryan R. "An Analysis of Sect Development." AMERICAN SOCIOLOGICAL REVIEW 24 (1959): 3-15.

3368. Wilson, Bryan R. SECTS AND SOCIETY: A SOCIOLOGICAL STUDY OF ELIM TABERNACLE, CHRISTIAN SCIENCE, AND CHRISTADELPHIANS. Berkeley: University of California Press, 1961.

3369. Wilson, Bryan R. "Typologie des sectes dans une perspective dynamique et comparative." ARCHIVES DE SOCIOLOGIE DES RELIGIONS 8,16 (1963): 49-63.

3370. Wilson, Bryan R. "Migrating Sects: Review Article." BRITISH JOURNAL OF SOCIOLOGY 18 (1967): 303-317.

* Wilson, Bryan R. (ed.) PATTERNS OF SECTARIANISM. Cited above as item 3213.

3371. Wilson, Bryan R. "A Typology of Sects." In Roland Robertson (ed.), THE SOCIOLOGY OF RELIGION, SELECTED READINGS. London: Penguin, 1969.

3372. Wilson, Bryan R. RELIGIOUS SECTS. New York: McGraw, 1970.

* Wilson, Bryan R. MAGIC AND THE MILLENNIUM. Cited above as item 2384.

3373. Wilson, Bryan R. "American Religious Sects in Europe." In C.W.E. Bigsby (ed.), SUPERCULTURE: AMERICAN POPULAR CULTURE AND EUROPE. London: Elek, 1975, pp. 107-122.

* Yinger, J. Milton. "Religion and Social Change: Functions and Dysfunctions of Sects and Cults among the Disprivileged." Cited above as item 1896.

3374. Young, Frank W. "Adaptation and Pattern Integration of a California Sect." RRR 1,4 (1960): 137-150. Reprinted in R.D. Knudten (ed.), THE SOCIOLOGY OF RELIGION, AN ANTHOLOGY (volume cited in item 375), pp. 136-146.

SECTION E: THEORIES AND PROBLEMATICS

A social theory is a conceptual framework which is developed as a model of what occurs in the social world. A problematic describes the objective a researcher has in mind when putting a theory to use. Both theories and problematics take on lives of their own as they evolve in a discipline, become modified, serve as centers of discussion, and become identified with traditions of research and research findings.

Theories and problematics (general)

3375. Douglas, Mary. "Passive Voice Theories in Religious Sociology." RRR 21,1 (1979): 51-61.

3376. Lemert, Charles C. "Theorizing, Policy-Making, and the Critique of Europeanism." RRR 21,1 (1979): 3-23.

3377. McNamara, Robert J. "Description and Theory: A Plea for Understanding." SA 31,4 (1970): 216-219.

* Schneider, Louis. "The Sociology of Religion: Some Areas of Theoretical Potential." Cited above as item 2764.

3378. Stark, Werner. "Description and Theory: A Plea for Cooperation." SA 31,4 (1970): 209-215.

Civil religion

The theory that complex societies may symbolize their aspirations and values in religious references which transcend specific religious traditions.

* Anthony, Dick, and Thomas Robbins. "Spiritual Innovation and the Crisis of American Civil Religion." Cited above as item 2390.

3379. Azevedo, Thales de. "La 'religion civile.' Introduction au cas Brésilien." ARCHIVES DE SCIENCES SOCIALES DES RELIGIONS 47,1 (1979): 7-22.
"A 'religião civil': introdução ao caso brasileiro." RELIGIÃO E SOCIEDADE 6 (1980): 69-89.

3380. Bellah, Robert N. "Civil Religion in America." DAEDALUS 96 (1967): 1-21. Reprinted in R.E. Richey and D.G. Jones (eds.), AMERICAN CIVIL RELIGION (item 3412), pp. 21-44. Also in R. Bellah, BEYOND BELIEF (item 3577), pp. 168-189. Also in P.H. McNamara (ed.), RELIGION: NORTH AMERICAN STYLE (volume cited in item 117), pp. 39-52.

3381. Bellah, Robert N. "Christianity and Symbolic Realism." JSSR 9 (1970): 89-96.

3382. Bellah, Robert N. "American Civil Religion in the 1970's." ANGLICAN THEOLOGICAL REVIEW, SUPPLEMENTARY SERIES 1 (1973): 8-20. Also in R.E. Richey and D.G. Jones (eds.), AMERICAN CIVIL RELIGION (item 3412), pp. 255-272.

3383. Bellah, Robert N. "Religion and Polity in America." ANDOVER NEWTON QUARTERLY 15 (1974): 107-123.

3384. Bellah, Robert N. THE BROKEN COVENANT: AMERICAN CIVIL RELIGION IN TIME OF TRIAL. New York: Seabury, 1975.

3385. Bellah, Robert N. "Religion and Legitimation in the American Republic." In T. Robbins and D. Anthony (eds.), IN GODS WE TRUST (item 367), pp. 35-49.

3386. Bellah, Robert N., and Phillip E. Hammond. VARIETIES OF CIVIL RELIGION. New York: Harper and Row, 1980.

3387. Bennett, W. Lance. "Political Sanctification: The Civil Religion and American Politics." SOCIAL SCIENCE INFORMATION 14 (1975): 79-102.

3388. Bennett, W. Lance. "Imitation, Ambiguity, and Drama in Political Life: Civil Religion and the Dilemmas of Public Morality." JOURNAL OF POLITICS 41 (1979): 106-133.

3389. Bourg, Carroll J. "A Symposium on Civil Religion." SA 37,2 (1976): 141-149. Summary of papers by Richard Fenn, William Garrett, Robert Stauffer, and Ronald Wimberley.
Johnson, Benton. "Comments." Pp. 150-152.
Bellah, Robert N. "Response to the Panel on Civil Religion." Pp. 153-159.

3390. Christenson, James A., and Ronald C. Wimberley. "Who is Civil Religious?" SA 39,1 (1978): 77-83. Also in P.H. McNamara (ed.), RELIGION: NORTH AMERICAN STYLE (volume cited in item 117), pp. 52-59.

* Cole, William A., and Phillip E. Hammond. "Religious Pluralism, Legal Development, and Societal Complexity: Rudimentary Forms of Civil Religion." Cited above as item 347.

3391. Coleman, John A. "Civil Religion." SA 31,2 (1970): 67-77.

3392. Cuddihy, John Murray. NO OFFENSE. CIVIL RELIGION AND PROTESTANT TASTE. New York: Seabury, 1978.

3393. Fenn, Richard K. "Bellah and the New Orthodoxy." SA 37,2 (1976): 160-166.
Bellah, Robert N. "Comment on 'Bellah and the New Orthodoxy.'" SA 37,2 (1976): 167-168.

3394. Garrett, J.L. "'Civil Religion.' Clarifying the Semantic Problem." JOURNAL OF CHURCH AND STATE 2 (1974): 187-196.

3395. Gehrig, Gail. AMERICAN CIVIL RELIGION: AN ASSESSMENT. Storrs, Connecticut: Society for the Scientific Study of Religion, 1981.

3396. Gehrig, Gail. "The American Civil Religion Debate: A Source for Theory Construction." JSSR 20,1 (1981): 51-63.

3397. Greeley, Andrew M. "Civil Religion and Ethnic Americans." WORLDVIEW 16,2 (1973): 21-27.

* Hammond, Phillip E. "Religious Pluralism and Durkheim's Integration Thesis." Cited above as item 353.

3398. Hammond, Phillip E. "The Sociology of American Civil Religion: A Bibliographic Essay." SA 37,2 (1976): 169-182.

* Hammond, Phillip, and R.C. Gordon-McCutchan. "Cults and the Civil Religion: A Tale of Two Centuries." Cited above as item 3136.

3399. Herberg, Will. "America's Civil Religion: What It Is and Whence It Comes." In R.E. Richey and D.G. Jones (eds.), AMERICAN CIVIL RELIGION (item 3312), pp. 76-88.

3400. Hughes, Richard T. "Civil Religion, the Theology of the Republic, and the Free Church Tradition." JOURNAL OF CHURCH AND STATE 22,1 (1980): 75-87.

3401. Hughey, Michael W. CIVIL RELIGION AND MORAL ORDER. Westport: Greenwood, 1983.

3402. Jolicoeur, Pamela M., and Louis L. Knowles. "Fraternal Associations and Civil Religion: Scottish Rite Freemasonry." RRR 20,1 (1978): 3-22.

3403. Kearl, Michael C., and Anoel Rinaldi. "The Political Uses of the Dead as Symbols in Contemporary Civil Religions." SOCIAL FORCES 61,3 (1983): 693-708.

3404. Kessler, Sanford. "Tocqueville on Civil Religion and Liberal Democracy." JOURNAL OF POLITICS 39 (1977): 119-146.

3405. Liebman, Charles S., and Eliezer Don-Yehiya. CIVIL RELIGION IN ISRAEL: POLITICAL CULTURE AND TRADITIONAL JUDAISM IN THE JEWISH STATE. Berkeley: University of California Press, 1983.

3406. Luhmann, Niklas. "Grundwerte als Zivilreligion." In N. Luhmann, SOZIOLOGISCHE AUFKLÄRUNG 3: SOZIALES SYSTEM, GESELLSCHAFT, ORGANISATION. Opladen, Westdeutscher Verlag, 1981, pp. 293-308.

3407. Markoff, John, and Daniel Regan. "The Rise and Fall of Civil Religion: Comparative Perspectives." SA 42,4 (1982): 333-352.

* Moodie, T. Dunbar. THE RISE OF AFRIKANERDOM: POWER, APARTHEID, AND THE AFRIKANER CIVIL RELIGION. Cited above as item 1654.

3408. Moodie, T. Dunbar. "The Afrikaner Civil Religion." In H. Mol (ed.), IDENTITY AND RELIGION (item 170), pp. 203-228.

3409. Mount, C. Eric. "Realism, Norm, Story and Character: Issues in the Civil Religion Discussion." JOURNAL OF CHURCH AND STATE 22,1 (1980): 41-52.

3410. Phelan, Michael. "Transcendental Meditation. A Revitalization of the American Civil Religion." ARCHIVES DE SCIENCES SOCIALES DES RELIGIONS 48,1 (1979): 5-20.

3411. Regan, Daniel. "Islam, Intellectuals and Civil Religion in Malaysia." SA 37,2 (1976): 95-110.

3412. Richey, Russell E., and Donald G. Jones (eds.) AMERICAN CIVIL RELIGION. New York: Harper and Row, 1974. Contains items 3380, 3382, 3399, 3423.

3413. Robbins, Thomas, Dick Anthony, Madeline Doucas, and Thomas Curtis. "The Last Civil Religion: Reverend Moon and the Unification Church." SA 37,2 (1976): 111-125.

3414. Robertson, Roland. "Individuation, Societalization and the Civil Religion Problem." In R. Robertson, MEANING AND CHANGE (volume cited in item 2021), pp. 148-185.

3415. Saurma, Adalbert. "Quelques formes de 'piété politique' en Suisse." SC 28,4 (1981): 341-356.

3416. Searle, R.W. "The Church's Responsibility for Good Citizenship." AMERICAN JOURNAL OF ECONOMICS AND SOCIOLOGY 9,1 (1947): 117-124.

3417. Smidt, Corwin. "Civil Religious Orientations among Elementary School Children." SA 41,1 (1980): 25-40.

3418. Stauffer, Robert E. "Civil Religion, Technocracy, and the Private Sphere: Further Comments on Cultural Integration in Advanced Societies." JSSR 12 (1973): 415-425.

3419. Stauffer, Robert E. "Bellah's Civil Religion." JSSR 14 (1976): 390-394.

3420. Thomas, Michael C., and Charles C. Flippen. "American Civil Religion: An Empirical Study." SOCIAL FORCES 51 (1972): 218-225.

3421. Toolin, Cynthia. "American Civil Religion from 1789-1981: A Content Analysis of Presidential Inaugural Addresses." RRR 25,1 (1983): 39-48.

3422. Wallace, Ruth A. "Emile Durkheim and the Civil Religion Concept." RRR 18,3 (1977): 287-290.

3423. Warner, W. Lloyd. "An American Sacred Ceremony." In W.L. Warner, AMERICAN LIFE: DREAM AND REALITY. Chicago: University of Chicago Press, 1953. Also in R.E. Richey and D.G. Jones (eds.), AMERICAN CIVIL RELIGION (item 3412), pp. 89-111.

3424. West, Ellis M. "A Proposed Neutral Definition of Civil Religion." JOURNAL OF CHURCH AND STATE 22,1 (1980): 23-40.

3425. Wilson, John F. "The Status of 'Civil Religion' in America." In Elwyn A. Smith (ed.), THE RELIGION OF THE REPUBLIC. Philadelphia: Fortress, 1971, pp. 1-21.

3426. Wilson, John F. PUBLIC RELIGION IN AMERICAN CULTURE. Philadelphia: Temple University Press, 1979.

3427. Wilson, John F. "Voluntary Associations and Civil Religion: The Case of Freemasonry." RRR 22,2 (1980): 125-136.

3428. Wimberley, Ronald C. "Testing the Civil Religion Hypothesis." SA 37,4 (1976): 341-352.

3429. Wimberley, Ronald C. "Continuity in the Measurement of Civil Religion." SA 40,1 (1979): 59-62.

* Wimberley, Ronald C. "Civil Religion and the Choice for President: Nixon in '72." Cited above as item 1719.

3430. Wimberley, Ronald C., and James A. Christenson. "Civil Religion and Church and State." SOCIOLOGICAL QUARTERLY 21 (1980): 35-40.

* Wimberley, Ronald C., and James A. Christenson. "Civil Religion and Other Religious Identities." Cited above as item 1295.

* Wimberley, Ronald C., Donald A. Clelland, Thomas C. Hood, and C.M. Lipsey. "The Civil Religious Dimension: Is It There?" Cited above as item 2962.

Conflict theory

3431. Neal, Marie Augusta. "The Comparative Implications of Functional and Conflict Theory as Theoretical Frameworks for Religious Research and Religious Decision Making." RRR 21,1 (1979): 24-50.

Critical theory

Critical theory focuses on the distortive aspects of human consciousness. It views the accepted modes of rationality, cognition and artistic production as counterparts in societies to the rationalizations of compulsive activity in individual psychologies. What cannot be faced by the members of a society who believe in the legitimacy of the society's culture would be brought into focus by critical theory.

3432. Mörth, Ingo. "La sociologie de la religion comme théorie critique." SC 27,1 (1980): 27-50.

3433. Nederman, Cary J., and James Wray Goulding. "Popular Occultism and Critical Social Theory: Exploring Some Themes in Adorno's Critique of Astrology and the Occult." SA 42,4 (1982): 325-332.

3434. Siebert, Rudolf J. "Religion in the Perspective of Critical Sociology." CONCILIUM 91 (1974): 56-59.

3435. Siebert, Rudolf J. HORKHEIMER'S CRITICAL SOCIOLOGY OF RELIGION. Washington: University Press of America, 1979.

Functionalism

Early functionalism likened society to an organism, so that every persisting structure had some quasi-purpose which contributed to the survival of the whole. Religion would be assessed as a structure which created a meaningful coherence among the various other institutions of the society. This coherence is usually termed "social integration." In a sense, functionalism may be seen as an early form of systems theory.

* Azevedo, Thales de. "Popular Catholicism in Brazil. Typology and Functions." Cited above as item 3013.

3436. Beckford, James A. "Functionalism and Ethics in Sociology: The Relationship between 'Ought' and 'Function.'" ANNUAL REVIEW OF THE SOCIAL SCIENCES OF RELIGION 5 (1981): 101-131.

3437. Bellah, Robert N. "The Place of Religion in Human Action." REVIEW OF RELIGION 22 (1958): 137-154.

3438. Burhenn, Herbert. "Functionalism and the Explanation of Religion." JSSR 19,4 (1980): 350-360.

* Collins, Randall. SOCIOLOGICAL INSIGHT. AN INTRODUCTION TO NON-OBVIOUS SOCIOLOGY. Cited above as item 163.

3439. Desroche, Henri. "Sociologie religieuse et sociologie fonctionelle." ARCHIVES DE SOCIOLOGIE DES RELIGIONS 23 (1967): 3-17.

3440. Döbert, Rainer. SYSTEMTHEORIE UND DIE ENTWICKLUNG RELIGIÖSER DEUTUNGSSYSTEME: ZUR LOGIK DES SOZIALWISSENSCHAFTLICHEN FUNKTIONALISMUS. Frankfurt/Main: Suhrkamp Verlag, 1973.

* Drehsen, Volker. "Dimensions of Religiosity in Modern Society. An Approach to a Systematical Stock-Taking of Structural-Functionalist Analysis." Cited above as item 2590.

3441. Eister, Allan W. "Religious Institutions in Complex Societies: Difficulties in the Theoretical Specification of Functions." AMERICAN SOCIOLOGICAL REVIEW 22 (1957): 387-391.

3442. Fukuyama, Yoshio. "Functional Analysis of Religious Belief." RELIGIOUS EDUCATION 56 (1961): 446-451.

3443. Grönblom, Gunnar, and Jørgen Thorgaard. "The Notion of Functional Equivalence with Special Regard to its Usage in Empirical Sociology of Religion." ANNUAL REVIEW OF THE SOCIAL SCIENCES OF RELIGION 5 (1981): 133-165.

3444. Hoult, Thomas Ford. "A Functional Theory of Religion." SOCIOLOGY AND SOCIAL RESEARCH 41,4 (1957): 277-280.

3445. Klugl, Johann. "Zur Kritik der strukturell-funktionalistischen Religionssoziologie." RELIGIONSSOZIOLOGIE. PHILOSOPHISCHES INSTITUT DER FRIEDRICH-SCHILLER-UNIVERSITÄT, IENA. INTERNATIONALES FORSCHUNGSBERICHTE 2 (1966): 51-55.

* Kolb, William. "Values, Positivism, and the Functional Theory of Religion: The Growth of a Moral Dilemma." Cited above as item 513.

3446. Lidz, Victor M. THE FUNCTIONING OF SECULAR MORAL CULTURE: STEPS TOWARD A SYSTEMATIC ANALYSIS. Unpublished Ph.D. dissertation, Harvard University, 1976.

3447. Luhmann, Niklas. "Institutionalized Religion in the Perspective of Functional Sociology." CONCILIUM 91 (1974): 45-55.

* Luhmann, Niklas. DIE FUNKTION DER RELIGION. Cited above as item 2728.

* Mol, Johannes J. (Hans). IDENTITY AND THE SACRED. Cited above as item 169.

3448. Mol, Johannes J. (Hans). "Time and Transcendence in a Dialectical Sociology of Religion." SA 42,4 (1982): 317-324.

* Neal, Marie Augusta. "The Comparative Implications of Functional and Conflict Theory as Theoretical Frameworks for Religious Research and Religious Decision Making." Cited above as item 3431.

* Nelson, L.D. "Functions and Dimensions of Religion." Cited above as item 2169.

3449. O'Dea, Thomas F. "Sociology and the Study of Religion." In T. O'Dea, SOCIOLOGY AND THE STUDY OF RELIGION (volume cited in item 2177), pp. 201-220.

3450. Pemberton, Prentiss L. "An Examination of Some Criticisms of Talcott Parsons' Sociology of Religion." JOURNAL OF RELIGION 36 (1956): 241-256.

3451. Schneider, Louis, and Sanford M. Dornbusch. "Inspirational Religious Literature: From Latent to Manifest Functions of Religion." AMERICAN JOURNAL OF SOCIOLOGY 62,5 (1957): 476-481. Also in L. Schneider (ed.), RELIGION, CULTURE AND SOCIETY (volume cited in item 1824), pp. 157-163; and in E. Misruchi (ed.), THE SUBSTANCE OF SOCIOLOGY. New York: Appleton-Century-Crofts, 1967, pp. 302-308.

3452. Schöfthaler, Traugott. "La théorie systémique dans la sociologie de la religion dans les pays de langue allemande." SC 27,1 (1980): 63-74.

3453. Schreuder, Osmund. "Die strukturell-funktionale Theorie und die Religionssoziologie." In J. Matthes (ed.), THEORETISCHE ASPEKTE DER RELIGIONSSOZIOLOGIE I / SOCIOLOGY OF RELIGION: THEORETICAL PERSPECTIVES I. INTERNATIONALES JAHRBUCH FÜR RELIGIONSSOZIOLOGIE 2. Köln: Westdeutscher Verlag, 1966, pp. 99-134.

3454. Siebert, Rudolf J. "Parsons' Analytical Theory of Religion as Ultimate Reality." In G. Baum (ed.), SOCIOLOGY AND HUMAN DESTINY. ESSAYS ON SOCIOLOGY, RELIGION AND SOCIETY. New York: Seabury, 1980, pp. 27-55.

3455. Sykes, Richard E. "An Appraisal of the Theory of Functional-Structural Differentiation of Religious Collectivities." JSSR 8,2 (1969): 289-299.

3456. Thurlings, J.M.G. "Functionalism, Social Change and the Sociology of Religion." SC 8,5 (1961): 407-423.

3457. Tufari, P. "L'analisi funzionale in sociologia religiosa." SOCIOLOGIA RELIGIOSA 5-6 (1960): 5-37.
"Functional Analysis in the Sociology of Religion." SC 7,1 (1960): 9-20.

3458. Winthrop, Henry. "The Rebirth of Academic Interest in the Social Functions of Religion." SOCIOLOGIA RELIGIOSA 17-18 (1968): 121-131.

Integration (social)

3459. Adelman, Kenneth. THE INFLUENCE OF RELIGION ON NATIONAL INTEGRATION IN ZAIRE. Unpublished Ph.D. dissertation, Georgetown University, Washington, 1975.

* Blizzard, Samuel. "The Protestant Parish Minister's Integrating Roles." Cited above as item 828.

* Campiche, Roland. "Religion, source de conflits ou ciment de l'unité suisse?" Cited above as item 2178.

* Desai, A.R. "National Integration and Religion." Cited above as item 1558.

3460. Fichter, Joseph H. "Religion: Integrator of the Culture?" THOUGHT 33 (1958): 361-382.

* Fichter, Joseph H. "The Parish and Social Integration." Cited above as item 1410.

3461. Fürstenberg, F. "Soziale Integrationsformen moderner Religiosität." SCHWEIZERISCHE ZEITSCHRIFT FÜR SOZIOLOGIE 9 (1983): 495-508.

3462. Glock, Charles Y. "Religion and the Integration of Society." RRR 2,2 (1960): 49-61. Reprinted in C.Y. Glock and R. Stark, RELIGION AND SOCIETY IN TENSION (volume cited in item 141), pp. 170-184.

3463. Goddijn, Walter. "Catholic Minorities and Social Integration." SC 7,2 (1960): 161-176.

3464. Hammond, Phillip E. "The Durkheim Integration Thesis Reexamined: A Study of Religious Pluralism and Legal Institutions." In A.W. Eister (ed.), CHANGING PERSPECTIVES IN THE SCIENTIFIC STUDY OF RELIGION (volume cited in item 353), pp. 115-142.

* Harper, Edward B. "Ritual Pollution as an Integrator of Caste and Religion." Cited above as item 1900.

3465. Houtart, François. "Les variables qui affectent le rôle intégrateur de la religion." SC 7,1 (1960): 21-38.

3466. Keyes, Charles F. "Buddhism and National Integration in Thailand." JOURNAL OF ASIAN STUDIES 30,3 (1971): 552-553.

3467. Lalive D'Epinay, Christian. "Religion, culture et dépendance en Amérique Latine. Note sur la place et le programme d'une sociologie de la culture integrée à une sociologie de la dépendance." ARCHIVES DE SOCIOLOGIE DES RELIGIONS 32 (1971): 121-141.

3468. Lee, Raymond L.M., and S.E. Ackerman. "Conflict and Solidarity in a Pentecostal Group in Urban Malaysia." SOCIOLOGICAL REVIEW 28,4 (1980): 809-828.

* Martin, Jack, and Steven Stack. "The Effect of Religiosity on Alienation: A Multivariate Analysis of Normlessness." Cited above as item 32.

* Mol, Johannes, J. (Hans). "Secularization and Cohesion." Cited above as item 2529.

* Murvar, Vatro. "Integrative and Revolutionary Capabilities of Religion." Cited above as item 1299.

3469. Pin, Emile. "Religion et intégration sociale." REVUE DE L'ACTION POPULAIRE 132 (1959): 1006-1014. Also translated as "El análisis funcional de los fenómenos religiosos." In Herve Carrier and Emile Pin, ENSAYOS DE SOCIOLOGIA RELIGIOSA. Bilbao, España: Mensajero.

* Remy, J., and F. Hambye. "L'appartenance religieuse comme expression de structures culturelles latentes: problème de méthode." Cited above as item 960.

3470. Robbins, Thomas, Dick Anthony, and Thomas Curtis. "Youth Culture Religious Movements: Evaluating the Integrative Hypothesis." SOCIOLOGICAL QUARTERLY 16,1 (1975): 48-64.

3471. Rodinson, Maxime. "Un étude sur l'Islam: W. Montgomery Watt, 'Islam and the Integration of Society.'" ARCHIVES DE SOCIOLOGIE DES RELIGIONS 15 (1963): 137-143.

* Stauffer, Robert E. "Civil Religion, Technocracy, and the Private Sphere: Further Comments on Cultural Integration in Advanced Societies." Cited above as item 3418.

* Turner, Bryan S. "Class Solidarity and System Integration." Cited above as item 1925.

3472. Watt, W. Montgomery. ISLAM AND THE INTEGRATION OF SOCIETY. London: Routledge and Kegan Paul, 1961.

Interpretive and hermeneutic sociology

The endeavor to understand religious activity first as the religious actor understands it and second as it appears in its social context.

3473. Blasi, Anthony J., and Andrew J. Weigert. "Towards a Sociology of Religion: An Interpretive Sociology Approach." SA 37,3 (1976): 189-204.

* Chesebro, Scott E. THE MENNONITE URBAN COMMUNE: A HERMENEUTIC-DIALECTICAL UNDERSTANDING OF ITS ANABAPTIST IDEOLOGY AND PRACTICE. Cited above as item 1241.

3474. Slotten, Ralph. "Exoteric and Esoteric Modes of Apprehension." SA 38,3 (1977): 185-208.

3475. Smart, Ninian. THE SCIENCE OF RELIGION AND THE SOCIOLOGY OF KNOWLEDGE. Princeton: Princeton University Press, 1977.

3476. Wood, Charles M. THEORY AND RELIGIOUS UNDERSTANDING: A CRITIQUE OF THE HERMENEUTICS OF JOACHIM WACH. Missoula: Scholars Press, University of Montana, 1975.

Levels of inclusiveness

Social phenomena can be investigated at the social-psychological, institutional, community, national and civilizational levels.

Levels of inclusiveness (general)

* Aidala, Angela A. "Worldviews, Ideologies and Social Experimentation: Clarification and Replication of 'The Consciousness Reformation.'" Cited above as item 1236.

* Blasi, Anthony J. "Dialecticizing the Types." Cited above as item 3218.

* Blasi, Anthony J., and Andrew J. Weigert. "Towards a Sociology of Religion: An Interpretive Sociology Approach." Cited above as item 3473.

* Davidson, James D. "Patterns of Belief at the Denominational and Congregational Levels." Cited above as item 1271.

* Leites, Edmund. "Autonomy and the Rationalization of Moral Discourse." Cited above as item 187.

3477. Lemert, Charles C. "Social Structure and the Absent Center: An Alternative to New Sociologies of Religion." SA 36,2 (1975): 95-107.

* Luckmann, Thomas. "On Religion in Modern Society: Individual Consciousness, World View, Institution." Cited above as item 2515.

* Weber, Max. "Anticritical Last Word on The Spirit of Capitalism," translated with an introduction by Wallace M. Davis. Cited above as item 2719.

* Westhues, Kenneth. "The Church in Opposition." Cited above as item 969.

* Willaime, Jean-Paul. "De la fonction infrapolitique du religieux." Cited above as item 2151.

Localism

The local and cosmopolitan environments help structure distinct interpretations of the social world, with two corresponding religious viewpoints.

* Ammerman, Nancy T. "The Civil Rights Movement and the Clergy in a Southern Community." Cited above as item 543.

3478. Cumings, Scott, Richard Briggs, and James Mercy. "Preachers versus Teachers: Local-Cosmopolitan Conflicts over Textbook Censorship in an Appalachian Community." RURAL SOCIOLOGY 42 (1977): 7-21.

* Hoge, Dean R., and Jackson W. Carroll. "Determinants of Commitment and Participation in Suburban Protestant Churches." Cited above as item 145.

3479. Martinson, Oscar B., E.A. Wilkening, and F.H. Buttel. "Religion and Community-Oriented Attitudes." JSSR 21,1 (1982): 48-58.

* Petersen, Larry R., and K. Peter Takayama. "Local-Cosmopolitan Theory and Religiosity among Catholic Nuns and Brothers." Cited above as item 1358.

* Petersen, Larry R., and K. Peter Takayama. "Religious Commitment and Conservatism: Toward Understanding an Elusive Relationship." Cited above as item 455.

* Roof, W. Clark. "The Local-Cosmopolitan Orientation and Traditional Religious Commitment." Cited above as item 2788.

* Roof, Wade Clark. "Religious Orthodoxy and Minority Prejudice: Causal Relationship or Reflection of Localistic World View?" Cited above as item 460.

3480. Roof, W. Clark. "Explaining Traditional Religion in Contemporary Society." In Allan W. Eister (ed.), CHANGING PERSPECTIVES IN THE SCIENTIFIC STUDY OF RELIGION (volume cited in item 353), pp. 295-314.

3481. Roof, Wade Clark. "Traditional Religion in Contemporary Society: A Theory of Local-Cosmopolitan Plausibility." AMERICAN SOCIOLOGICAL REVIEW 41,2 (1976): 195-208.

* Roof, Wade Clark. COMMUNITY AND COMMITMENT. Cited above as item 2154.

* Swatos, William H., Jr. "Beyond Denominationalism?: Community and Culture in American Religion." Cited above as item 3296.

3482. Tamney, Joseph B. "Established Religiosity in Modern Society: Islam in Indonesia." SA 40,2 (1979): 125-135.

* Wilson, John, and Kenneth Manton. "Localism and Temperance." Cited above as item 2440.

* Winter, J. Alan. "The Attitudes of Societally-Oriented and Parish-Oriented Clergy: An Empirical Comparison." Cited above as item 799.

Marxism

The tradition of Karl Marx in sociology has a pluralism of its own. The economic determinism of Engels and party Marxists represents one interpretation of Marx, and it suggests an economic explanation of religious phenomena. The dialectical approach of the philosophical Marx, wherein people's theories themselves become part of the material causes of social phenomena, suggests a rather different version of "materialism," a version in which religion can become an explanation of some other social phenomena. The principal process in this latter interpretation of Marx - neo-Marxism or "Marxian" theory - is the development of a popular consciousness of the social world.

* Birnbaum, Norman. "Conflicting Interpretations of the Rise of Capitalism: Marx and Weber." Cited above as item 2610.

3483. Birnbaum, Norman. "Beyond Marx in the Sociology of Religion." In C.Y. Glock and P. Hammond (eds.), BEYOND THE CLASSICS? (volume cited in item 2679), pp. 3-70.

3484. Bonte, Pierre. "Cattle for God: An Attempt at a Marxist Analysis of the Religion of East African Herdsmen." SC 22 (1975): 381-396.

* Bourdieu, Pierre. "Genèse et structure du champ religieux." Cited above as item 3019.

3485. Bourdieu, Pierre. "Une interprétation de la théorie de la religion selon Max Weber." ARCHIVES EUROPEENNES DE SOCIOLOGIE 12,1 (1971): 3-21.

3486. Bühler, Antoine. "Production de sens et légitimation sociale. Karl Marx et Max Weber." SC 23,4 (1976): 317-344.

3487. Cottier, Georges M.-M. L'ATHEISME DU JEUNE MARX. SES ORIGINES HEGELIENNES. Paris: Vrin, 1969.

3488. Desroche, Henri. MARXISME ET RELIGIONS. Paris: Presses Universitaires de France, 1962.

3489. Desroche, Henri. SOCIALISMES ET SOCIOLOGIE RELIGIEUSE. Paris: Cujas, 1965.

3490. Fattorini, Emma. "Note sulla 'questione cattolica' in Gramsci." TESTIMONIANZE (ITALY) 182 (1976): 126-134.

3491. Fedele, Marcello. "Ideologia cattolica e società borghese." CRITICA SOCIOLOGICA 17 (1971): 34-57.

3492. Fullat, Octavi. MARX Y LA RELIGION. Barcelona: Ed. Planeta, 1974

3493. Giorgetti, Giorgio. NOTE SULLA RELIGIONE NEL PENSIERO MARXISTA E ALTRI SCRITTI POLITICI. Florence: Guaraldi, 1977.

3494. Godelier, Maurice. "Marxisme, anthropologie et religion." In various authors, EPISTEMOLOGIE ET MARXISME 10,18. Paris: Union Générale d'Editions, 1972, pp. 209-265.

3495. Godelier, Maurice. "Vers une théorie marxiste des faits religieux." LUMIERE ET VIE 23,117-118 (1974): 85-94.

3496. Gramsci, Antonio. IL VATICANO E L'ITALIA. Rome: Editori Riuniti, 1972.

3497. Hannon, James. "Religion as Ideology and Praxis: Current Considerations in Marxist Theory." RELIGION, THE CUTTING EDGE. NEW ENGLAND SOCIOLOGIST 5,1 (1984): 37-57.

3498. Hollitscher, Walter. "Marxist Sociology of Religion." CONCURRENCE 1,3 (1969): 89-94.

3499. Houtart, François. RELIGION ET MODES DE PRODUCTION PRECAPITALISTES. Bruxelles: Editions de l'Université Bruxelles, 1980.

* Houtart, François. "Religion et éthique: une approche marxiste." Cited above as item 183.

3500. Houtart, François, and Geneviève Lemercinier. "Religion et mode de production tributaire." SC 24,2-3 (1977): 157-170.

3501. Kemp, Peter. "Marx et le poème religieux -- Le christianisme dans 'Le Capital.'" RECHERCHES DE SCIENCES RELIGIEUSES 64,1 (1976): 25-38.

3502. Kersevan, Marko. "Religion and the Marxist Concept of Social Formation." SC 22 (1975): 323-342.

* Klohr, Olaf (ed.) RELIGION UND ATHEISM HEUTE. ERGEBNISSE UND AUFGABEN MARXISTISCHER RELIGIONSSOZIOLOGIE. Cited above as item 2838.

3503. Maduro, Otto. "Marxist Analysis and the Sociology of Religion: an Introduction / Analyse marxiste et sociologie des religions: en guise d'introduction." SC 22 (1975): 305-322.

3504. Maduro, Otto. "Analisi marxista e sociologia della religione." IDOC INTERNAZIONALE 3-4 (1976): 21-25.

3505. Maduro, Otto. MARXISMO Y RELIGION. Caracas: Monte Avila Editores, 1977.

3506. Maduro, Otto. "New Marxist Approaches to the Relative Autonomy of Religion." SA 38,4 (1977): 359-367.

* Maduro, Otto. RELIGION Y LUCHA DE CLASES. RELIGION AND SOCIAL CONFLICTS. Cited above as item 2754.

* Maduro, Otto. "Trabajo y religión segun Karl Marx." "Travail et religion selon Karl Marx." Cited above as item 3.

3507. Maduro, Otto. LA CUESTION RELIGIOSA EN EL ENGELS PREMARXISTA. Caracas: Monte Avila Editores, 1981.

3508. Maitre, Jacques. "Recension sur le thème marxisme et religion." ARCHIVES DE SOCIOLOGIE DES RELIGIONS 10 (1960): 195-199.

3509. Mandic, Oleg. "A Marxist Perspective on Contemporary Religious Revivals." SOCIAL RESEARCH 37,2 (1970): 237-258.

* Mayrl, William W. "Marx' Theory of Social Movements and the Church-Sect Typology." Cited above as item 2258.

3510. McKown, Delos B. THE CLASSICAL MARXIST CRITIQUES OF RELIGION: MARX, ENGELS, LENIN, KAUTSKY. The Hague: Nijhoff, 1975.

3511. Miller, Donald E. "Troeltsch's Critique of Karl Marx." JSSR 1,1 (1961-62): 117-121.

* Nesti, Arnaldo. "Gramsci et la religion populaire." "Gramsci e la religione popolare." Cited above as item 3043.

3512. Ngoc Vu, Nguyen. IDEOLOGIE ET RELIGION D'APRES KARL MARX ET F. ENGELS. Paris: Aubrier Montaigne, 1975.

3513. Nowicki, A. "Les catégories centrales de la science marxiste des religions." EUHEMER 1-2 (1969): 3-17.

3514. Nuño, Juan A. EL MARXISMO Y LAS NACIONALIDADES. EL PLANTEAMIENTO DE LA CUESTION JUDIA EN EL MARXISMO CLASICO. Bogotá: Tercer Mundo, 1972.

3515. Orsolic, Marco. "La sociologie de la religion d'inspiration Marxiste en Yougoslavie." SC 20,1 (1973): 73-82.

3516. Portelli, Hughes. GRAMSCI ET LA QUESTION RELIGIEUSE. Paris: Anthropos, 1974.

3517. Portelli, Hugues. "La fonction idéologique de l'Eglise d'après A. Gramsci." PROJET 99 (1975): 1075-1085.

3518. Post, Werner. LA CRITICA DE LA RELIGION EN KARL MARX. Barcelona: Herder, 1972.

3519. Quinney, Richard. PROVIDENCE: THE RECONSTRUCTION OF SOCIAL AND MORAL ORDER. New York: Longman, 1980.

3520. Robbe, Martin. "Marxismus und Religionsforschung." In J. Matthes (ed.), THEORETISCHE ASPEKTE DER RELIGIONSSOZIOLOGIE I / SOCIOLOGY OF RELIGION: THEORETICAL PERSPECTIVES I. INTERNATIONALES JAHRBUCH FÜR RELIGIONSSOZIOLOGIE 2. Köln: Westdeutscher Verlag, 1966, pp. 157-184.

3521. Serrano Villafañe, Emilio. "Christianismo y marxismo. Liberación marxist y liberación cristiana." REVISTA DE ESTUDIOS POLITICOS (Spain) 206-207 (1972): 137-168.

3522. Stark, Werner. "La interpretación marxista de la religión y la interpretación religiosa del marxismo." REVISTA INTERNACIONAL DE SOCIOLOGIA 12:45 (1954): 33-43.

3523. Tovar, Cecilia, and Tokihiro Kudó. "La critica de la religión. Ensayo sobre la conciencia social según Karl Marx." REVISTA DE LA UNIVERSIDAD CATOLICA (nueva seria) 4 (1978): 69-96.

3524. Vidal, Daniel. "Pour une lecture marxist du prophétisme: champ autre et champ outre." SC 22 (1975): 355-380.

3525. Wackenheim, Charles. LA FAILLITE DE LA RELIGION D'APRES KARL MARX. Paris: Presses Universitaires de France, 1963.

3526. Warburton, T. Rennie. "Religion, Sociology and Liberation." RRR 19,1 (1977): 90-94.

* Willaime, Jean-Paul. "La relégation superstructurelle des références culturelles. Essai sur le champ religieux dans les sociétés capitalistes post-industrielles." Cited above as item 498.

3527. Young, T.R. "The Typifications of Christ at Christmas and Easter: Political and Social Uses of the Jesus Symbol." RELIGION, THE CUTTING EDGE. NEW ENGLAND SOCIOLOGIST 5,1 (1984): 1-21.

Phenomenology

The attempt to investigate social phenomena in terms of the manner in which people are aware of them.

* Berger, Peter L. THE SACRED CANOPY. Cited above as item 2152.

* Blasi, Anthony J. "Definition of Religion and Phenomenological Approach towards a Problematic." Cited above as item 2737.

* Garrett, William R. "Troublesome Transcendence: The Supernatural in the Scientific Study of Religion." Cited above as item 2746.

* Mason, Michael C. THE PRIVATIZATION OF THE SACRED WORLD. THOMAS LUCKMANN'S PHENOMENOLOGICALLY FOUNDED SOCIOLOGY OF MODERN RELIGION. Cited above as item 2594.

* Natanson, Maurice. Ch. 7. "Religion." In M. Natanson, THE JOURNEYING SELF. Cited above as item 2758.

3528. Schroeder, W. Widick. "Measuring the Muse: Reflections on the Use of Survey Methods in the Study of Religious Phenomena." RRR 18,2 (1977): 148-162.

* Smart, Ninian. THE SCIENCE OF RELIGION AND THE SOCIOLOGY OF KNOWLEDGE. Cited above as item 3475.

* Turner, Robert G., Jr. "Consciousness, Valuation, and Religion: Toward a Paradigm." Cited above as item 2771.

Positivism

Positivism represents the basic methodological philosophy of those researchers and theoreticians who view "science" in verificationist and/or falsificationist terms. Since religious consciousness is inconsistent with positivist epistemology, there is some question whether a positivist account of religion can be either adequate or non-partisan.

Positivism (general)

* Kolb, William L. "Values, Positivism, and the Functional Theory of Religion: The Growth of a Moral Dilemma." Cited above as item 513.

Reductionism

The explanation of religious phenomena in strictly non-religious, naturalistic terms.

3529. Bainbridge, William Sims, and Rodney Stark. "Formal Explanation of Religion: A Progress Report." SA 45,2 (1984): 145-158.

3530. Fenton, John Y. "Reductionism in the Study of Religion." SOUNDINGS 53 (1970): 61-76.

* Garrett, William R. "Troublesome Transcendence: The Supernatural in the Scientific Study of Religion." Cited above as item 2746.

* Neal, Marie Augusta. "Commitment to Altruism in Sociological Analysis." Cited above as item 15.

3531. Swanson, Guy E. THE BIRTH OF THE GODS. THE ORIGIN OF PRIMITIVE BELIEF. Ann Arbor: University of Michigan Press, 1960.

* Wallis, Roy, and Steve Bruce. "The Stark-Bainbridge Theory of Religion: A Critical Analysis and Counter Proposals." Cited above as item 153.

3532. White, H.W. REDUCTIVE EXPLANATIONS OF RELIGION WITH SPECIAL REFERENCE TO DURKHEIM. Unpublished Ph.D. dissertation, McGill University, 1977.

Science and religion

3533. Bernard, L.L. "Mito, superstición, hipótesis, ciencia." REVISTA MEXICANA DE SOCIOLOGIA 11,3 (1949): 385-408.

* Datta, Lois-Ellin. "Family Religious Background and Early Scientific Creativity." Cited above as item 2620.

3534. Durkheim, Emile. Discussion on "Science et religion," by E. Boutroux. BULLETIN DE LA SOCIETE FRANÇAISE DE PHILOSOPHIE 9 (1908-1909).

3535. Eister, Allan W. "Religion and Science in A.D. 1977: Conflict? Accommodation? Mutual Indifference? Or What?" JSSR 17,4 (1978): 347-358.

3536. Ferrarotti, Franco. IL PARADOSSO DEL SACRO. Bari: Laterza, 1983.

3537. Ferrarotti, Franco. "Le destin de la raison et le paradoxe du sacré." SC 31,2-3 (1984): 133-155.

3538. Grunwald, Constantin de. "Science et religion en Union Soviétique." ARCHIVES DE SOCIOLOGIE DES RELIGIONS 16 (1963): 125-137.

3539. Hooykaas, R. "La riforma protestante e la scienza." COMMUNITA 173 (1974): 115-159.

3540. Johnson, Benton. "Sociological Theory and Religious Truth." SA 38,4 (1977): 368-388.

3541. King, Morton B., and Richard A. Hunt. "Moral Man and Immoral Science?" SA 35,4 (1974): 240-250.

3542. Lemert, Charles. "Science, Religion and Secularization." SOCIOLOGICAL QUARTERLY 20 (1979): 445-461.

3543. Lemieux, Raymond. "Production scientifique et pratique québécoise de la sociologie de la religion." LES CAHIERS DU CENTRE DE RECHERCHES EN SOCIOLOGIE RELIGIEUSE 3 (1980): 13-53.

3544. Leuba, James H. "Religious Beliefs of American Scientists." HARPER'S MONTHLY MAGAZINE 169 (1934): 292-300.

3545. McAulay, Robert. "Velikovsky and the Infrastructure of Science: The Metaphysics of a Close Encounter." THEORY AND SOCIETY 6,3 (1978): 313-342.

3546. Merton, Robert K. "Puritanism, Pietism and Science." SOCIOLOGICAL REVIEW 28,1 (1936): 1-30.

* Merton, Robert K. "Science, Technology and Society in 17th Century England." Cited above as item 2672.

3547. Moberg, David O. "Science and the Spiritual Nature of Man." JOURNAL OF THE AMERICAN SCIENTIFIC AFFILIATION 19 (1967): 12-17.

3548. Moberg, David O. "The Encounter of Scientific and Religious Values Pertinent to Man's Spiritual Nature." SA 28 (1967): 22-33.

3549. Nudelman, Arthur E. "Christian Science and Secular Science: Adaptation on the College Scene." JSSR 11,3 (1972): 271-276.

3550. Ragan, Claude, H. Newton Maloney, and Benjamin Beit-Hallahmi. "Psychologists and Religion: Professional Factors and Personal Belief." RRR 21,2 (1980): 208-217.

3551. Rogers, David Price. "Some Religious Beliefs of Scientists and the Effect of the Scientific Method." RRR 7 (1966): 70-77.

3552. Shils, Edward A. "Faith, Utility, and the Legitimacy of Science." DAEDALUS 103 (1974): 1-15.

3553. Stark, Rodney. "On the Incompatibility of Religion and Science: A Survey of American Graduate Students." JSSR 3,1 (1963): 3-20. Reprinted as Ch. 14 in Charles Y. Glock and Rodney Stark, RELIGION AND SOCIETY IN TENSION (volume cited in item 141).

3554. Stark, Werner. "Capitalism, Calvinism and the Rise of Modern Science." SOCIOLOGICAL REVIEW 43,5 (1951): 95-104.

3555. Stark, Werner. "The Socio-Religious Origins of Modern Science." REVISTA INTERNACIONAL DE SOCIOLOGIA 20,79 (1962): 323-331.

* Thorner, Isidor. "Ascetic Protestantism and the Development of Science and Technology." Cited above as item 2711.

3556. Vaughan, Ted R., Douglas Howard Smith, and Gideon Sjoberg. "The Religious Orientations of American Natural Scientists." SOCIAL FORCES 44,4 (1963): 519-526.

Sociolinguistics

From this perspective, language differences within a social setting may disclose social structures and processes.

3557. Fenn, Richard K. LITURGIES AND TRIALS. THE SECULARIZATION OF RELIGIOUS LANGUAGE. New York: Pilgrim, 1982.

Sociology of knowledge

3558. Berger, Peter L., and Thomas Luckmann. "Sociology of Religion and Sociology of Knowledge." SOCIOLOGY AND SOCIAL RESEARCH 47,4 (1963): 417-427.

Structuralism

Structuralism abstracts a common pattern from several different orders of reality which overlap in a given phenomenon - e.g., the biological, the social interactional, and the symbolic - and attributes some determinative potential to the possibilities which are inherent in the pattern itself.

3559. Anthony, Dick, and Thomas Robbins. "From Symbolic Realism to Structuralism." JSSR 14 (1975): 403-413.

3560. Cipriani, Roberto. "Strutturalismo e religione." LA CRITICA SOCIOLOGICA 32 (1974-75): 85-96.

3561. Strenski, Ivan. "Lévi-Strauss and the Buddhists." COMPARATIVE STUDIES IN SOCIETY AND HISTORY 22,1 (1980): 3-22.

3562. Weiting, Stephen G. "Myth and Symbol Analysis of Claude Lévi-Strauss and V. Turner." SC 19,2 (1972): 139-154.

Surrogates for religion

3563. Coles, R.W. "Football as a 'Surrogate' Religion?" In M. Hill (ed.), A SOCIOLOGICAL YEARBOOK OF RELIGION IN BRITAIN 8 (1975). London: SCM Press, pp. 61-77.

* Grönblom, Gunnar, and Jørgen Thorgaard. "The Notion of Functional Equivalence with Special Regard to its Usage in Empirical Sociology of Religion." Cited above as item 3443.

3564. Gurian, Waldemar. "Totalitarianism as Political Religion." In Carl J. Friedrich (ed.), TOTALITARIANISM. Cambridge: Harvard University Press, 1954, pp. 119-127.

3565. Kallen, Horace M. "Secularism as the Common Religion of a Free Society." JSSR 4,4 (1965): 145-151.

* Krejci, Jaroslav. "Religion and Anti-Religion: Experience of a Transition." Cited above as item 2507.

* Martin, David. THE DILEMMAS OF CONTEMPORARY RELIGION. Cited above as item 2526.

3566. Rivière, Claude. "A quoi servent les rites séculiers." SC 29,4 (1982): 369-387.

* Sironneau, Jean-Pierre. SECULARISATION ET RELIGIONS POLITIQUES. Cited above as item 1696.

3567. Wuthnow, Robert. "Astrology and Marginality." JSSR 15,2 (1976): 157-168.

3568. Zeldin, M.-B. "The Religious Nature of Russian Marxism." JSSR 8 (1969): 100-111.

Symbolic interactionism

The philosophy of George H. Mead serves as a basic philosophical anthropology for many sociologists. Under the name "symbolic interactionism," coined by Herbert Blumer, it has introduced such sensitizing concepts as "the definition of the situation," the "self-concept" and the "generalized other" into sociology.

* Bankston, William B., Craig J. Forsyth, and H. Hugh Floyd, Jr. "Toward a General Model of the Process of Radical Conversion: An Interactionist Perspective on the Transformation of Self-Identity." Cited above as item 1962.

* Brinkerhoff, Merlin B., and Kathryn L. Burke. "Disaffiliation: Some Notes on 'Falling from the Faith.'" Cited above as item 2049.

3569. D'Agostino, Federica. "Il rituale e la festa come punti di intersezione tra rappresentazione collective e interazione simbolica." RASSEGNA ITALIANA DI SOCIOLOGIA 4 (1978): 593-614.

3570. Fischer, Wolfram, and Wolfgang Marhold. "The Concept of Symbolic Interactionism in the German Sociology of Religion." SC 27,1 (1980): 75-84.

3571. Gaede, Stan D. AN INTERACTIONIST APPROACH TO THE SOCIOLOGY OF RELIGION. Unpublished Ph.D. dissertation, Vanderbilt University, 1974.

* Goitein, Bernard, and Mordechai Rotenberg. "Protestantism and Retrospective Labeling: A Cross-Cultural Study in Person Perception." Cited above as item 2633.

3572. Harrison, Paul M. "Toward a Dramaturgical Interpretation of Religion." SA 38,4 (1977): 389-396.

3573. Kuhn, Manford H., and Thomas S. McPartland. "An Empirical Investigation of Self-Attitudes." AMERICAN SOCIOLOGICAL REVIEW 19 (1954): 68-76.

3574. Nye, William P. "George Herbert Mead and the Paradox of Prediction." SA 38,2 (1977):91-105.

* Preston, David L. "Becoming a Zen Practitioner." Cited above as item 2418.

* Sacks, Howard L. "The Effect of Spiritual Exercises on the Integration of Self-System." Cited above as item 1361.

3575. Smith, T.V. "The Religious Bearings of a Secular Mind: George Herbert Mead." JOURNAL OF RELIGION 12 (1932): 200-213.

* Snow, David A. "A Dramaturgical Analysis of Movement Accommodation: Building Idiosyncrasy Credit as a Movement Mobilization Strategy." Cited above as item 377.

3576. Sykes, Richard E. "Toward a Sociology of Religion Based on the Philosophy of George Herbert Mead." In G. Baum (ed.), SOCIOLOGY AND HUMAN DESTINY (volume cited in item 3454), pp. 167-182.

Symbolic realism

Symbolic realism begins with the assumption that religious symbols cannot be confected, that they are not made up. Nevertheless, they are products of what is specifically human about human experience.

* Anthony, Dick, and Thomas Robbins. "From Symbolic Realism to Structuralism." Cited above as item 3559.

* Bellah, Robert N. "Christianity and Symbolic Realism." Cited above as item 3381.

3577. Bellah, Robert N. BEYOND BELIEF. ESSAYS ON RELIGION IN A POST-TRADITIONAL WORLD. New York: Harper and Row, 1970. Contains items 3380, 3581.

* Bellah, Robert N. THE BROKEN COVENANT. Cited above as item 3384.

3578. Bellah, Robert N. "New Religious Consciousness and the Crisis of Modernity." In C.Y. Glock and R.N. Bellah (eds.), THE NEW RELIGIOUS CONSCIOUSNESS (item 2407), pp. 333-352.

* Johnson, Benton. "Sociological Theory and Religious Truth." Cited above as item 3540.

3579. Karcher, Barbara C., Jack O. Balswick, and Ira E. Robinson. "Empiricism, Symbolic Realism, and the Mystique of the Extreme." SOCIOLOGICAL QUARTERLY 22,1 (1981): 93-103.

* Robbins, Thomas, Dick Anthony, and Thomas E. Curtis. "The Limits of Symbolic Realism: Problems of Empathetic Field Observation in a Sectarian Context." Cited above as item 3349.

Systems theory

The various institutions in a society, with their associated symbolic universes, condition and are conditioned by one another, and altogether tend toward or achieve a balance. Moreover, they take their physical environment into this network of adjustive relationships.

* Dahm, Karl, N. Luhmann, and D. Stoodt. RELIGION - SYSTEM UND SOZIALISATION. BAND II, REIHE THEOLOGIE UND POLITIK. Cited above as item 1555.

* Döbert, Rainer. SYSTEMTHEORIE UND DIE ENTWICKLUNG RELIGIÖSER DEUTUNGSSYSTEME: ZUR LOGIK DES SOZIALWISSENSCHAFTLICHEN FUNKTIONALISMUS. Cited above as item 3440.

* Lampinen, Tapio. "The Content of the Parochial Sermons in the Evangelical Lutheran Church of Finland as Indicators of the Openness and Closeness of the Church as System." Cited above as item 3125.

* Scherer, Ross P. (ed.) AMERICAN DENOMINATIONAL ORGANIZATION. A SOCIOLOGICAL VIEW. Cited above as item 1172.

* Schöfthaler, Traugott. "La théorie systémique dans la sociologie de la religion dans les pays de langue allemande." Cited above as item 3452.

3580. Schöfthaler, Traugott. "Religion paradox: Der systemtheoretische Ansatz in der deutschsprachigen Religionssoziologie." In K.-F. Daiber and Thomas Luckmann (eds.), RELIGION IN DEN GEGENWARTSSTRÖMUNGEN DER DEUTSCHEN SOZIOLOGIE. München: Kaiser, 1983, pp. 136-156.

* Schöfthaler, Traugott. "The Social Foundations of Morality: Durkheimian Problems and the Vicissitudes of Niklas Luhmann's Systems Theories of Religion, Morality and Personality." Cited above as item 192.

Transcendence

Transcendence is a theological idea of that which is transempirical and cannot be grasped intellectually with adequacy or conceptual closure.

3581. Bellah, Robert N. "Transcendence in Contemporary Piety." In R. Bellah, BEYOND BELIEF (item 3577), pp. 196-208. Also in H.W. Richardson and D.R. Cutler (eds.), TRANSCENDENCE. Boston: Beacon, 1969.

* Garrett, William R. "Troublesome Transcendence: The Supernatural in the Scientific Study of Religion." Cited above as item 2746.

3582. Stark, Rodney. "Must all Religions be Supernatural?" In Bryan R. Wilson (ed.), THE SOCIAL IMPACT OF NEW RELIGIOUS MOVEMENTS (item 2434), pp. 159-177.

AUTHOR INDEX
(Numbers refer to items.)

A

Abbott, A. 820
Abbott, M. 1375
Abercrombie, C.L. 133
Aberle, D.F. 131
Abernathy, T. See King, K.
Abrams, J., and L.R. Della Fave. 2123
Ackermann, S.E. See Lee, Raymond L.
Acock, A.C., and V.L. Bengston. 301
Acquaviva,S.S. 2387, 2441, 2442, 2443
And G. Guizzardi. 2444, 2445
Adams, R.L. 2878
And J. Mogey. 1954
Adelman, K. 3459
Adler, F. 499
Agodi, M.C. 59
Aguirre, B.E. See Alton, J.P.
Ahern, G. 3264, 3265
Ahler, J.G., and J.B. Tamney. 3148
Aidala, A.A. 1235, 1236
Aiken, M.T. See Demerath, N.J.
Akhavi, S. 1510
Alant, C.J. 1750
Alatas, S.H. 2734
Alba, R.D. 380
Albert, A.A. See Porter, Judith R.
Albrecht, G.L. See Higgins, P.C.
Albrecht, S.L., and H.M. Bahr. 2048
Albrecht, S.L., B.A. Chadwick, and D.S. Alcorn. 2124
Albrecht, S.L., and T.B. Heaton. 2446
Alcorn, D.S. See Albrecht, S.L.
Aleshiere, D. See Gorsuch, R.L.
Alexander, D. 2856
Alexander, K.C. 1897
Alexander, R.J. 1511
Alexander, T.J. See Thompson, R.C.
Alford, R.R. 1512, 1513
Alfred, R.H. 1066
Allan, G. 2310
Alland, A. 3113
Allen, D.E., and H.S. Sandhu. 2125
Allen, E.E., and R.W. Hites. 2921
Allen, G., and R. Wallis. 3101
Allen, James E. 989
Allen, John. See Burger, G.K.
Allen, John L. 2437
Allen, R.O. 412
And B. Spilka. 413
Allen, S. 1751
Allingham, J.D. 1752
See Balakrishnan, T.R.
Allinsmith, B. See Allinsmith, W.
Allinsmith, W., and B. Allinsmith. 1267
Allison, J. 1955
Allport, G.W. 414
And J.A. Gillespie and J. Yount. 415
And J.M. Ross. 416
Alpert, H. 3149
Alston, J.P. 260, 264, 302, 1753, 1754, 1935, 1936, 2790
And B.E. Aguirre. 3204
And R.C. Hollinger. 2447
And W.A. McIntosh. 1755
And C. Peek, and C.R. Wingrove. 1514
And L.A. Platt. 541
See McIntosh, W.A.
Alston, L.T. See McIntosh, W.A.
Ament, W.S. 2598
Amerson, P.A. 417
And J.W. Carroll. 418
Amir Arjomand, S. 1515
Ammentorp, W., and B. Fitch. 1311
Ammerman, N.T. 542, 543, 2857
Anderson, C.H. 1224, 1225, 1226, 1227
Anderson, D.N. 1516
Anderson, G.M. 1517, 1518
Anderson, R. See Toch, H.H.
Anderson, Scott M. See Peterman, Dan J.

Anderson, Susan. 1376
Andezian, S. 1089.
Andrewski, S. 419
Anfossi, A. 1377
Angell, R.C. 177
Ankerl, Guy G. 2599
Ansart, P., J. Cazeneuve, and P.H. Maucorps. 178
Anthony, D., and T. Robbins. 2388, 2389, 2390, 3559
And P. Schwartz. 2391
See Robbins, T.
Anzai, S. 1956
Apostal, R.A., and J.R. Ditzler. 1378
Appolis, E. 3011
Aquina, M. 1032
Archer, A. 3130
Arellano, E. 2448, 3012
Armatas, P.J. 420
See Spilka, B.
Aronis, A.B. 972
Ashby, J. See Covello, V.T.
Aubert, C. See Vergote, A.
Austin, R.L. 1957, 1958
Aver, E., C. Hames, J. Maitre, and G. Michelat. 1519
Avesing, F. See Curtis, J.H.
Aviad, J. 1959
Avila, R. 1520, 1521
Azevedo, T. de. 3013, 3379
Azzi, R. 1197

B

Baan, M.A. 1312
And L. Grond. 1313
Babb, L.A. 3014
Babbie, E.R. 2600
Babchuck, N., H.J. Crockett, and J.A. Bailey. 1960
Babin, P. 803
Bachi, R., and J. Matras, 238
Baer, H.A. 132, 1237
Bahr, H.M. 1268, 2970
And L.F. Barthel, and B.A. Chadwick. 488
See Albrecht, S.L.
Bailey, J.A. See Babchuck, N.
Bainbridge, W.S. 3266
And L.R. Hatch. 1090
And R. Stark. 489, 2392, 2963, 3205, 3267, 3529
See Stark, R.
Baker, R.K., L.K. Epstein, and R.D. Forth. 204
Balakrishnan, T.R., S. Ross, J. Allingham, and J.F. Kanter. 228
Balandier, G. 2311, 2312
Balch, R.W. 1961, 2393
Balkwell, J.W. See Balswick, J.O.
Ball, D.W. 2601
Ballweg, J.A. See Crowley, J.W.
Balswick, J.O. 544
And J.W. Balkwell. 2884
And G.L. Faulkner. 545
And N.R. Layne. 1121
See Karcher, B.C.
See King, K.
See Layne, N.R.
Bango, J.F. 2791
Bankston, W.B., C.J. Forsyth, and H.H. Floyd. 1962
Barabas, A.M. 2313
Barber, B. 2314
Barclay, H.B. 2449, 2602
Bardis, P. 205
Barker, E. 1963, 2394, 2395, 2396
Barkum, M. 2315
Barnes, D.F. 60
Barnhart, J.E. 2735
Barnsley, J.H. 179
Baron, S.W. 267
Barrish, G. (J.), and M.R. Welch. 480. See Welch, M.R.
Bartel, L.F. See Bahr, H.M.
Barthel, D.L. 1238
Bartholomew, J.N. 1198
Bartlett, W.K. See Stanley, G.
Bartos, P.E. See Wagenaar, T.C.
Basaure Avila, L. 546
Bastenier, A. 268
Bastian, J.-P. 1522
Bastide, R. 396, 397, 398, 2316, 2317, 2318, 2319, 2971, 3015
Batson, C.D. 421
And S.J. Naifeh, and S. Pate. 422
Baubérot, J. 61
Bauer, J. 1523
Baxter, S. See Nelsen, H.M.

Bayart, J.-F. 1524
Bayer, A.E. 2320
Baylar, J.C. See King, H.
Beach, S.W. 1525
Bean, F.D. See Van Roy, R.F.
Beasley, J.D. See Harter, C.L.
Becker, H. 500, 2450, 2451, 3214
And L. von Wiese. 3215
Becker, L.B. 2792, 2793
Beckford, J.A. 1122, 1123, 1124, 1494, 1964, 2235, 2236, 2281, 2397, 2398, 2399, 2400, 3216, 3312, 3313, 3436
See Hampshire, A.P.
Bedouelle, G. 1526
Beech, L.A. 821
Beemsterboer, K. 269
Behrman, L.G. 1527
Beit-Hallahmi, B. See Ragan, C.
Belanger, P. 1379
Bell, B.D. 529
Bell, R.R., and J.B. Chaskes. 312
Bell, Robert. See Koval, J.
Bell, W., and M.T. Force. 1269
Bellah, R.N. 2603, 2722, 2794, 3380, 3381, 3382, 3383, 3384, 3385, 3389, 3393, 3437, 3577, 3578, 3581
And P.E. Hammond. 3386
See Glock, C.Y.
Bendix, R. 2604, 2605, 2606
Bengston, V.L. See Acock, A.C.
Benko, A. 3016
Bennett, F.A. 1033
Bennett, W. Lance. 3387, 3388
Bennett, Walter H.
See Harrison, D.E.
Benoit, A. 501
Bensimon, D. 2452
Benson, J.K., and J.H. Dorsett. 1125
And E.W. Hassinger. 1126
See Hassinger, E.W.
Benson, P., and B. Spilka. 2866
Benson, S.M. See Harris, M.B.
Bentz, W.K. 822, 823
Berenson, W., K.W Elifson, and T. Tollerson. 547
Berg, P.L. 990, 991, 992
Berger, A.L. 62
Berger, M. 3017
Berger, P.L. 63, 342, 343, 2152, 2185, 2321, 2453, 2454, 2455, 2736, 3206, 3207
And T. Luckmann. 3558
See Nash, D.J.
Berger, S.D. 2607
Bergeron, C. 1314
Bergesen, A. 1528, 1529, 1530
Bergman, R.D. 1380
Berk, M. 344
Berkes, N. 2456
Bernard, G. 3314
And P. Caprasse. 2237
Bernard, H. 3109
Bernard, L.L. 3533
Berreman, J.V. See Wade, A.L.
Besnard, P. 2608
Betts, G.H. 548, 549
Beylier, C. 3297
Beynon, E.D. 3268
Bhatnagar, S.R. 3080
Bhatt, G.S. 3217
Bibby, R.W. 2588, 2778
And M.B. Brinkerhoff. 96, 97, 1965
Biermann, B. 2609
Biggar, J. See Photidadis, J.D.
Billette, A. 1966, 1967
Billiet, J. 2457
Bird, F. 64, 180, 2723
And W. Reimer. 2401, 2402
Birnbaum, N. 2322, 2458, 2610, 2611, 3483
Birrell, W.D., J.E. Greer, and D.J.D. Roche. 550
Birrell, W.D. See Roche, D.J.D.
Black, A.W. 2186, 2825
Black, C. See Smith, R.
Blacker, C. 1726
Blaikie, N.W.H. 11, 551, 552, 824
Blake, J. 206, 207, 229
Blake, R.H. See Seggar, J.F.
Blanchard, D.A. 553, 554
Blanchard, J.L.
See Pickering, W.S.F.
Blasi, A.J. 2071, 2072, 2290, 2737, 3218
And P. MacNeil, and R. O'Neill. 208
And A.J. Weigert. 3473

Blass, J.H. 825
Blazowich, A. 1300
Blizzard, S.W. 555, 826, 827, 828, 829, 830
Bloch, M. 3150
Bloom, J. 2291
Blum, B.S., and J.H. Mann. 423
Bluth, E.J. 1034
Bock, E.W. 556, 557, 3018
Bocock, R.J. 831, 3151, 3152, 3153
Bode, J.G. 1937
Boecken, C. 1091
Bogan, R.V. 558
Bogen, I. 239
Bohr, R.H. 1315
Bohrnstedt, G.W.
  See Schulz, B.
Boisen, A.T. 133, 134, 925, 1756
Boldon, D.A. 2187
Boldt, E.D. 1239
  See Peter, K.
Boling, T.E. 926, 1968, 3219, 3315
Bolino, G. See Grumelli, A.
Bondolfi, A. 155
Bonham, J.M.
  See Price-Bonham, S.
Bonifield, W.C. 559
  And E.W. Mills. 560
Bonmariage, J. See Servais, E.
Bonn, R.L., and R.T. Doyle. 561
Bonnet, S. 1531
Bonte, P. 3484
Bonte, W. de. 1316
Boos-Nünning, U. 2922
Bopegamage, A. 1938
Borgatta, E.F. See Schulz, B.
Borhek, J.T.,
  and R.F. Curtis. 2795
Bormann, G. 832, 833, 1127
  And S. Bormann-Heischkeil. 1128
Bormann-Heischkeil, S.
  See Bormann, G.
Borowski, K. 1240
Bosk, C.L. 65
Boulard, F. 562, 993, 1381
Bouma, G.D. 98, 99, 927, 928, 2612
Bourdieu, P. 3019, 3154, 3485
  And M. de Saint Martin. 1532
Bourdillon, M.F.C. 345
Bourg, C.J. 346, 1533, 3389
Bourguignon, E. 3114
Bourque, L.B. 2972
Bouvier, L.F. See Rao, S.L.N.
Bovay, C. See Campiche, R.J.
Bovy, L. 2796
Bowdern, T.S. 994, 2073, 2074.
Bowman, J.F. 995
Braden, C.H. 3269
Bradfield, C.D. 135, 136
  And R.A. Myers. 563
Braga, G. 1382
Brandão, C.R. 3020
Branford, V. 3155
Brannon, R.C.L. 1129
Braswell, G.W. 1134
Braude, L. 564
Brechon, P., and B. Denni. 1535
Breines, A.E. 1926
Brekke, M. See Schuller, D.S.
  See Strommen, M.P.
Brennan, J.S. 2798
Bressan, V. 1383
Bressler, M., and C.F. Westoff. 2613
Brewer, E.D.C. 3316, 3317
  Et al. 1384
Briggs, R. See Cumings, S.
Brinkerhoff, M.B. 1079
  And K.L. Burke. 2049
  And M.M. MacKie. 209
  See Bibby, R.W.
  See Burke, K.L.
  See Kunz, P.R.
  See Middendorp, C.P.
Brock, T.C. 1969
Broderick, C. See Heltsley, M.E.
Brodrick, J. 1317
Broen, W.E. 2923
Brogan, D., and N.G. Kutner. 1080
Bromley, D.G., and J.T. Richardson. 2282
Bromley, D.G., and A.D. Shupe. 100, 2238, 2239, 2403, 3081
Bromley, D.G. See Shupe, A.D.
Bronson, L., and A. Meadow. 2614
Brooks, M.L. 485
Brooks, R.M. 996

Brothers, J.B. 834, 835, 1385, 2459
Broughton, W. 1728
And E.W. Mills. 565
Brown, D. 1757
Brown, J.S. 1758
Brown, L.B. See Hunsberger, B.
See Wearing, A.J.
Brown, R.E., and J.H. Fichter. 566
Brown, Sharon. See Peek, C.W.
Brown, Sheila. 502
Browne, J.P. 1318
Brownstein, H.H. 1502
Bruce, D.D. 3131
Bruce, S. 101, 102, 103
See Wallis, R.
Bruneau, T.C. 1215, 1536
Brunetta, G. 1319, 1759
Brusek, P.M. See Moberg, D.O.
Bryman, A. 1927
And C.R.Hinings. 2188
And S. Ranson, and C.R. Hinings. 2189
See Hinings, C.R.
See Ranson, S.
Buchignani, N.L. 2615
Budd, S. 1537, 2826, 2827
Bühler, A. 3486
Bultena, L. 929
Bumpass, L. See Westoff, C.F.
Bunis, W. See Johnson, N.R.
Bunnik, R.J. 567
Büntig, A.-J. 1, 1216, 3021, 3022, 3023
Burch, G.W. 568, 2068
See Jud, G.J.
Burch, H.A. 1130
Burchard, W.W. 973, 974, 1270
Burchinal, L.G. 1760
And L.E. Chancellor. 1761
And W.F. Kenkel. 1762
Burgalassi, S. 569, 570, 1320, 1763, 2075, 2076, 2077, 3120, 3220
Burger, A. 930
Burger, G.K., and J. Allen. 2973
Burhenn, H. 3438
Burke, K.L., and M.B. Brinkerhoff. 66
Burke, K.L. See Brinkerhoff, M.B.
Burkett, S.R., and M. White. 2158
Burkman, T.W. 406
Burney, P. 2724
Burnham, K.E., J.F. Connors, and R.C. Leonard. 242
Burnham, K.E. See Connors, J.F.
Burns, J.E. See Hilty, D.M.
Burns, M.S. 1321
Burridge, K. 2323
Burton, L. 1764
Busch, L. 2324
Busian, C. 804
Bussi, N. 1386
Buttel, F.H. See Martinson, O.B.
Bystryn, M.H. See Greenberg, D.F.

C

Caceres Prendes, J. 1538
Caillat, C. 40
Cain, L.D. 381
Calabro, W.V. 1322
Calkins, S. See Heaton, T.B.
Call, L.R. 2190
Calley, M.J.C. 3318, 3319
Calvo, R. 1539
Campbell, B. 3270, 3271
Campbell, C. 1765, 2460, 2828, 2829, 3272
And R.W. Coles. 931
Campbell, D.F. 1540, 1541
And D.W. Magill. 2924
Campbell, E.Q., and T.F. Pettigrew. 571, 572
Campbell, K.E. 270
And D. Granberg. 271
See Granberg, D.
Campbell, T.C., and Y. Fukuyama. 932
Campbell-Jones, S. 1035
Campiche, R.J. 2178
And C. Bovay. 836
And J. Kellerhals. 2589
And G. de Rham. 1542
Campos, G.G. 573
Cannon, L.W. See Takayama, K.P.
Cantrell, R., J.F. Krile, and G.A. Donohue. 1131, 1132, 1729.
Cantril, H. 1766

Capelo, M. 1543
Caplovitz, D., and F.Sherrow. 2050
Caplow, T. 2461
Caporale, R. 1133, 1134
And A. Grumelli, 2830
Cardwell, J.D. 313
See Klemmack, D.L.
Carey, R.G. 574
Carli, R., F. Crespi, and G. Pavan. 1323
Carlin, J.E., and S.H. Mendlovitz. 575
Carlos, S. 2925
Carlton, E. 2078
Carlton, F.T. 1544
Carns, D.E. 314
Carpenter, N., and M.E. Wagner. 1767
Carr, L.G., and W.J. Hauser. 21
Carrier, H. 486, 933, 2079
Carroll, J.W. 576, 837, 997
And R.L. Wilson. 577, 578
See Amerson, P.A.
See Hoge, D.R.
Carron, J. 579
Carsh, H. 580, 581, 2616
Carstairs, G.M. 1898
Casey, C.E. 1036
Castellani, B.
See Valenzano, P.M.
Catton, W.R. 3273
Cayrac-Blanchard, F. 1545
Cazeneuve, J. 181, 3156, 3157, 3158
See Ansart, P.
Cela, J. 399
Centre Régional d'Etudes Socio-Religieuses. 3121
Centro de Estudios Cristianos. 1768
Chadwick, B.A.
See Albrecht, S.L.
See Bahr, H.M.
Chaffee, G.E. 3320
Chalfant, H.P. 1769
And C.W. Peek. 425
See Chambers, P.P.
See Peek, C.W.
Chamberlain, A. See Towler, R.
Chamberlayne, J.H. 3321
Chambers, P.P., and H.P. Chalfant. 1092
Chambre, H. 3322
Chancellor, L.E.
See Burchinal, L.G.
Chanteloup, R.E. 272
Chapman, S.H. 838, 839
Charpin, F. 3075
Chartain, F. 1546
Chaskes, J.B. See Bell, R.R.
Chattopadhyaya, S. 3323
Cheal, D.J. 1547, 1548
Chesebro, S.E. 1241
Chesneaux, J. 2325
Choate, D.A.
See Johnson, N.R.
Christenson, J.A. 12
And R.C. Wimberley. 3390
See Wimberley, R.C.
Christiano, K. See Wuthnow, R.
Christie, A. 1549
Christopher, S., J. Fearon, J. J. McCoy, and C. Nobbe. 137
Christy, R.D. 1387
Cieslak, M.J. 1388
Ciesluk, J.E. 1389
Cipriani, R. 1550, 1551, 1770, 2462, 2463, 3560
Clark, David. 3024
Clark, David B. 1390
Clark, E.T. 3324
Clark, S.D. 1552, 1771, 2617, 3325, 3326, 3327
Clark, W.H. 2738
Clarke, P.B. 582
Clarke, T 1391, 1392
Clasby, M. See Neal, M.A.
Clavan, S. See Robak, N.
Clayton, R.R. 315, 316, 317, 2926, 2927
And J.W. Gladden. 2928
And W.L. Tolone. 210
And H.L. Voss. 318
Clelland, D.A., T.C. Hood, C.M. Lipsey, and R.C. Wimberley. 3132
Clelland, D.A. See Wimberley, R.C.
Clews, R.A. See Nelson, G.K.

Clow, H.K. See Wilson, John.
Cline, V.B., and J.M. Richards. 2929
Clyde, R.W. See Lee, G.R.
Coakley, J.J. See Lamanna, R.A.
Coates, C.H., and R.C. Kistler. 583, 840
Cobb, J.C. 240
Cody, W. 426
Cohen, M.R. 2739
Cohen, S.M. 3082
And R.E. Kapsis. 1553
Cohn, N. 2326, 2327, 2328
Cohn, W. 2740, 3089, 3328
Coiner, H.G. See Nauss, A.H.
Cole, W.A., and P.E. Hammond. 347
Coleman, John. 2404
Coleman, John A. 3221, 3391
Coles, R.W. 3563
See Campbell, C.
Collins, R. 163
Comfort, R.Q. 584
Compton, P.A., L. Goldstrom, and J.M. Goldstrom. 197
Condominas, G. 3025
Condran, J.G. See Tamney, J.B.
Connors, J.F., R.C. Leonard, and K.E. Burnham. 273
Connors, J.F. See Burnham, K.E.
Contigualia, C. 1393
Converse, P.E. 1554
Coogan, J.E. 2126
Cook, T.C. See Thorson, J.A.
Cooper, C.W. 585
Cooper, P.E. See Thomas L.E.
Corbetta, P.G., and F. Ricardo. 2464
Corbon, J. 2191
Corm, G.G. 348
Coser, L. 1324, 3329
Costa, R. 586, 587, 588
Cote, P. 1093
Cottier, G.M.-M. 3487
Courtas, R. See Isambert, F.A.
Cousineau, D.F.
See Veavers, J.E.
Couture, A. 3090
Covello, V.T., and J.A. Ashby. 1772
Coxon, A.P.M. 2080, 2081
See Towler, R.
Cozin, M. 2329
Crader, K.W. See Gibbs, J.O.
Crane, W.H. 2
Crespi, F. 427
See Carli, R.
See Klineberg, O.
Crespi, I. 2618
Crockett, H. See Babchuck, N.
See Jackson, E.F.
Cross, J.L. 428
Crow, K.E. See Pinto, L.J.
Crowley, J.W., and J.A. Ballweg. 2619
Cryns, A.G. 589
Crysdale, S. 2798
Cuadrench, J. 1296
Cuber, J.F. 934
Cuddihy, J.M. 3392
Culligan, M.J. 1325
Cumings, S., R. Briggs, and J. Mercy. 3478
Cummings, C. See Cummings, E.
Cummings, D. See Dudley, R.L.
Cummings, E., and C. Cummings. 841
Cuneo, M.W. 1242
Curcione, N.R. 2082, 2083
Currie, Raymond. 935, 2799
And L.F. Klug, and C.R. McCombs. 490
Currie, Robert. 2192
Currin, T.E.V. 1970
Curtis, J.H., F. Avesing, and I. Klosek. 1394
Curtis, R.F. 1939
Curtis, T.E. See Robbins, T.
Cusack, A. 590
Cutler, S.J. See Yinger, J.M.
Cygnar, T., C.K. Jacobson, and D.L. Noel. 429

D

D'Agostino, F. 3569
Dahlke, H.D. 274
Dahm, C.W. 1199
Dahm, K.-W. 591
And N. Luhmann, and D. Stoodt. 1555

Daiber, K.F., et al. 3122
Dallaire, M. 1326
Damrell, J. 3298
Daner, F.J. 1971
Daniel, M. 592
Dann, G.M.S. 936
Dann, N.K. 1556
D'Antonio, W.V.,
  and S. Stack. 411
D'Antonio, W.V.
  See Davidson, J.D.
  See Maiolo, J.R.
  See Newman, W.M.
  See Woodrum, E.
Dashefsky, A. 164
Dassetto, F. 3123
Datta, L.-E. 2620
Davidson, J.K.,
  and G.R. Leslie. 319
Davidson, James D. 1271, 1773, 1774, 2800, 2930
  And D.D. Knudsen. 2900
  And G.J. Quinn. 2885
  And J.A. Schlangen,
  and W.V. D'Antonio. 2801
  See Myers, P.G.
  See Rogers, M.K.
Davies, J.K. 1775
Davis, J.H. 2831
Davis, Jerome. 1135, 1730
Davis, K.E. See Lyness, J.L.
Davis, N.J. 198
Davis, R.G. See Travers, J.F.
Davis, W. 937
Day, G., and M. Fitton. 1776
Daynes, B.W.,
  and R. Tatalovich. 199
Dean, D.C. 22
  And J.A. Reeves. 23
Dearman, M.V. 3330
Decker, C.C. 1777
Deconchy, J.-P. 938, 2741, 2886, 2887, 2888, 2889, 2890
De Craemer, W. 2240
Deegan, A.X.
  See O'Donovan, T.R.
Deelen, G. 1217
DeJong, G.F. 1778
  And J.E. Faulkner. 104, 2931
  And J.E. Faulkner,
  and R.H. Warland. 2932
  And T.R. Ford. 1272
  See Faulkner, J.E.
DeKadt, E. 1731
Delacroix, S. 1395
Delcourt, M. 3159
Del Grande, M.V. 503
DeLissovoy, V. 2964
Dellacava, F.A. 2063, 2064
Della Fave, L.R. See Abrams, J.K.
  And G.A. Hillery. 1301
Dellepoort, J. 2084, 2085
  And N. Greinacher,
  and W. Menges. 593, 594
Delooz, P. 982, 983
Demange, J. See Raphaël, F.
Debinsky, L. 1557
Demerath, N.J. 1228, 1779, 1780, 1972, 2832
  And G. Marwell,
  and M.T. Aiken. 1732
  And V. Thiessen. 2833
Dempf, A. 3222
Dempsey, K. 595
Denault, B. 1327
  And B. Lévesque. 1328
De Neuter, P. 303
De Neve, A. 2465
Deniel, R. 2802
Denni, B. See Brechon, P.
Dent, O.F. 3223
Denys, J. 2901
Derks, F. See Lans, J.M.
De Rosa, G. 1329
Desai, A.R. 1558
Deschwanden, L. von. 842
Deshen, S. 2466
De Souza, M. 2974
Desroche, H. 1243, 2330, 2331, 2332, 2333, 3224, 3225, 3331, 3332, 3439, 3488, 3489
  And J. Gutwirth. 2334
  And A. Vauchez,
  and J. Maitre. 984
De Vaus, D.A. 1094
Dever, J.P. 430
Devereux, E.G. See Whetten, N.L.
Dewey, G.J. 596, 843
Dewitt, R.L. 3226
Dhooghe, J. 939
Diaz-Mozaz, J.M. 2086

Dienel, P. 3227
Dijck, C. van. 1559
Dike, S.W. 3133
Dillingham, H.C. 1781, 1782
Dimock, H.S. 2742
Dittes, J.E. 138, 597, 2467, 3228
Ditzler, J.R. See Apostal, R.A.
Di Valenza, A.C. 1396
Dixon, K. 2803
Dobashi, F. See Newell, W.H.
Dobbelaere, K. 940, 2468, 2469
And J. Lauwers. 2470
And J. Lauwers, and M. Ghesquiere-Waelkens. 2471
Döbert, R. 3440
Dodder, R.A. See Maranell, G.M.
Dodson, M. 1560
Doherty, J.F. 805
Doherty, R.W. 2224, 2225
Dominic, R.G.S. 2127
Donahue, G. See Cantrell, R.
Donovan, J.D. 598, 599, 1397
Donovan, P.A. 2087
Donus, R.B. 1398
Don-Yehiya, E.
See Liebman, C.S.
Doratis, D. See Ray, J.J.
Dornbusch, S.M. 2804
And R. Irle. 2193
See Schneider, L.
Dorsett, J.H. See Benson, J.K.
See Hassinger, E.W.
Dougherty, D. 998
Dougherty, J. 999
Douglas, M. 3375
Douglass, H.P. 2194
Dowdall, J.A. 1095
Dowdy, E., and G. Lupton. 600, 1136
Downton, J.V. 1973, 1974
Doyle, D.P. See Stark, R.
Doyle, K. See Wagner, H.R.
Doyle, R.T., and S.M. Kelly. 1273
Doyle, R.T. See Bonn, R.L.
Drees, W. 3299
Drehsen, V. 2590
And J. Morel. 3026
Driedger, L. 2805
And W.H. Form. 601
Driel, B. van.
See Richardson, James T.
Droba, D.D. 275
Dubach, A.T. 602
Dubar, C. 1783
Du Bois, W.E.B. 1784
Ducey, M.H. 3160
Dudley, C.J., and G.A. Hillery. 1302
Dudley, C.J. See Hillery, G.A.
Dudley, R.L. 2051
Dujardin, D., P. Raphaël, and H. Rosenfeld. 1561
Duke, J.T., and B.L. Johnson. 521
Dulong, R. 1915
Dumont, F. 1137, 3027
Dumont-Johnson, M. 1096
Duncan, H.D. 3161
Duncan, H.G. 604
Duocastella Rosell, R. 1399, 1785
Durkheim, E. 2743, 2744, 3534
Durkin, M.G. See Greeley, A.M.
Dutra, E.R. de F. 1786
Dyble, J.E. See Hoge, D.R.
Dykstra, J.W. 349
Dynes, R.R. 1229, 1787, 3208, 3229
See Nelson, L.D.

E

Earle, C.J. 2292
Earle, J.R. See Knudsen, D.D.
Easthope, G. 276
Ebanks, G.E. See Grindstaff, C.F.
Ebaugh, H.R.F. 1037
And C.A. Haney. 105
And P. Ritterband. 1038
And S.L. Vaughn. 1975
Eberhardt, J. 2335
Eberts, P.R. 1562
Eccel, A.C. 1928, 2472
Echard, N. 3115
Eckhardt, K.W. 2293
And G.E. Hendershot. 340
Eckhardt, W. 277
Eckstein, S. 1563
Egberink, L. 1400
Eichhorn, R.L. See Goldstein, B.
Eichler, M. 2336

Eisenstadt, S.N. 605, 2621, 2622, 3209
Eisikovits, R.A. 1039
Eister, A.W. 2745, 3230, 3274, 3275, 3276, 3277, 3441, 3535
Elifson, K.W., and J. Irwin. 247
Elifson, K.W., D.M. Petersen, and C.K. Hadaway. 2128
Elifson, K.W. See Berenson, W.
Elifson, K.W. See Margolis, R.D.
Elifson, K.W. See Payne, B.P.
Elinson, H. 1564
Elkind, D., and S. Elkind. 2975
Elkind, S. See Elkind, D.
Ellwood, R.S. 2139, 2405
Emmons, C.F., and J. Sobal. 139
Engelman, V.Z. 1503
England, C.D. See Obenhaus, V.
England, R.W. 3144
Ennis, J.G. 535
Enroth, R.M. 265
Epstein, L.K. See Baker, R.K.
Ergil, D. 1788
Erickson, M.L. See Jensen, G.F.
Erikson, K.T. 2130
Erny, P. 2891
Erskine, H.G. 431, 1789, 1790, 2779
Estruch, J. 941
See Jiminez, J.
Estus, C.W., and M.A. Overington. 2780
Ethridge, F.M., and J.R. Feagin. 1274
Evans, B.F. 3083
Evans, Robert H. 606
Evans, Robert R.
See Schulz, B.
Evans, T.Q. 844
Everett, R.F. See Nelsen, H.M.
Evers, H.D. 1138
Evjen, R. 607
Ezcurra, A.M. 106

F

Faase, T.P. 504, 505, 506, 507, 1330
Fabian, J. 977
Fahey, F.J., and D.J. Vrga. 24
Fahey, F.J. See Vrga, D.
Faia, M.A. 2473
Falardeau, J.-C. 1401
Falk, G. 2131
Fallding, H. 2474
Fanfani, A. 2623, 2624, 2626
Faouzi, A. 1565
Faris, E. 3333
Farquhar, J.N. 2241
Fasola-Bologna, A. 845
Fathi, A. 1566
Fattorini, E. 3490
Faulkner, G.L. See Balswick, J.O.
And G.F. DeJong. 182, 2933, 2934
See Filsinger, E.E.
Faure, G.-O. 67
Favreau, B. 1402
Fay, L.F. 25
Fay, P.J. See Middleton, W.C.
Feagin, J.R. 432, 433
See Ethridge, F.M.
See Woodrum, E.
Fearon, J. See Christopher, S.
Featherman, D.L. 1791
Fecher, C.J. 1331
Fedele, M. 3491
Fee, J.L. 1567
And A.M. Greeley, W.C. McCready, and T.A. Sullivan. 530
Feige, A. 942
Feld, S. See Veroff, J.
Fenn, R.K. 2148, 2475, 2476, 2477, 2478, 2855, 3393, 3557
Fenton, J.Y. 3530
Ference, T.P., F.H. Goldner, and R.R. Ritti, 608
Ference, T.P. See Goldner, F.H.
See Riti, R.R.
Fernandes, G. 400
Fernandez, J.W. 2242
Fernandez Vargas, V. 3124
Ferrar, A. See Wulf, J.
Ferrarotti, F. 3536, 3537
Ferreira de Camargo, P.C. 1940, 2243
And M. Berezousky Singer. 1792
Fichter, J.H. 531, 609, 610, 611, 612, 613, 614, 615, 616, 617, 618, 619, 943, 1040, 1403, 1404, 1405, 1406, 1407, 1408, 1409, 1410, 1411, 1916, 2088, 2781, 3278, 3460
See Brown, R.E.

Field, A.J. 2625
Fields, K.E. 3091
File, Ed. 2195
Filippone, V. 434, 2196
Filippone-Thaulero, V.
See Klineberg, O.
Filsinger, E.E. 407, 3231
And J.E. Faulkner,
and R.H. Warland. 3232
Finch, J. 911
Fine, G.A. See Kleinman, S.
Finkler, K. 1793
Finn, J. 2244
Finner, S.L. 532, 944
And J.D. Gamache. 212
Finney, J.M. 1097, 2935
And G.R. Lee 2936
Fischer, G.H. See Holl, A.
Fischer, K.M. 2626, 2627
Fischer, W., and W. Marhold. 3570
Fischoff, E. 2628
Fish, J., G. Nelson, W. Stuhr,
and L. Witmer. 2294
Fisher, V. See Wagner, H.R.
Fitch, B. See Ammentorp, W.
Fitch, S.D. See McIntosh, W.A.
Fitzpatrick, J.P. 350, 508
Flatt, B. 1000
Fleming, J.J.,
and G.W. Marks. 107
Flint, J.T. 2479
Flippen, C.C. See Thomas, M.C.
Flora, C.B. 1230
Floyd, H.H. See Bankston, W.B.
Flynn, N.J. 2197
Force, M.T. See Bell, W.
Forcese, D.P. 2629
Ford, C.E.,
and G. Schinert. 435
Ford, C.E. See Shinert, G.
Ford, T.R. 1794, 1795
Form, W.H. See Driedger, L.
Forster, P.G. 2480
Forsyth, C.J. See Bankston, W.B.
Forth, R.D. See Baker, R.K.
Fortin, G. 1412
Fosselman, D.H. 1413
Foster, B.D.
See Hinings, C.R.
Foucart, E. 2406, 3334
Fouilloux, E. 1568
Fox, S.W. See Richardson, James T.
Fox, W.S. See Jackson, E.F.
Fraga de Azevedo, H.O. 3162
Francis, E.K. 1332
Franklyn, J. 1067
Freiberg, J.W. 1796
Freund, J. 68, 278, 2630
Friedrichs, R.W. 436, 437
Friendland, W.H. 69
Frigolé Reinach, J. 1569
Froyen, V. 1414
Frundt, H.J. 3163
Fry, C.L. 1929
Fry, P.F. 2245
Fuchs, A. 2976
Fuchs, S. 2337
Fukuyama, Y. 620, 945, 946, 2295,
3442
See Campbell, T.C.
Fullat, Octavi. 3492
Fullerton, J.T.,
and B. Hunsberger. 2892
Fulton, R.L. 846
Furfey, P.H. 509
Furman, F.K. 3164
Fürstenberg, F. 1415, 3461
Fuse, T. 279, 2806, 2807

G

Gabovitch, B. 1244
Gaede, S. 1797, 2631, 2808, 3571
Galilea, C., K. Gilfeather,
and J. Puga. 1098
Gallagher, C.F. 1798
Gamache, J.D. See Finner, S.L.
Gandhi, R.S. 1899, 1941
Gannon, T.M. 108, 621, 622, 623,
847, 848, 1333, 2132, 2159
Garcia de Cortazar, F. 918
Gargarin, I.V. 2481
Garrett, J.B. See Mirels, H.L.
Garrett, J.L. 3394
Garrett, W.R. 487, 1733, 2198,
2746, 3300
Garrison, V. 140
Gaudet, R. 624
Gedricks, A. See Hammond, P.E.
Gehrig, G. 3395, 3396
Gellner, E. 2149, 2482
George, G. 3165

Gerharz, G.P. 2160
Gerlach, L.P., and V.H. Hine. 2246, 2247
Germain-Brodeur, E. 625
Germani, G. 2483
Gerry, K.M. See Hoge, D.R.
Gershuny, T. See Smythe, H.H.
Gerth, H.H. 3335
Gessner, J.C. 626
Ghurye, G.S. 41
Gibbs, D.R., S.A. Mueller, and J.R. Wood. 491
Gibbs, J.O., and K.W. Crader. 2937
Giddings, F.H. 3336
Gilbert, J.D. 1001
Giles, H.H. 2179
Gilfeather, K.A. 1041, 1042, 1099
  See Galilea, C.
Gillen, J. 3337
Gillespie, J.W. See Allport, G.
Gilsenan, M. 3028
Giorgetti, G. 3493
Girling, P.A.
  See Roscoe, J.T.
Girod, R. 1570
Giuriati, P. 2089, 3029
Gladden, J.W. See Clayton, R.R.
Glantz, O. 1571
Glasner, A.M. 849
Glasner, P.E. 1275, 2484, 2485, 3030
Glass, J.C. 320, 850
Glazer, N. 1504
Glazier, S.D. 3110
Glenn, N., and R. Hyland. 2632
Glick, S. 915
Globetti, G. See Harrison, D.E.
Glock, C.Y. 141, 1139, 2938, 3462
  Et al. 92
  And R.N. Bellah. 2407
  And B. Ringer. 627
  And P. Ross. 806
  And R. Stark. 438, 1416, 1572, 2747, 2977
  See Piazza, T.
  See Ringer, B.B.
  See Stark, R.
  See Wuthnow, R.
Gockel, G.L. 1799
Goddijn, H.P.M. 1303, 1334
Goddijn, W. 351, 851, 852, 3233, 3463
  See Kruijt, J.P.
Godelier, M. 3494, 3495
Goitein, B., and M. Rotenberg. 2633
Gold, D. 1573
Golde, G. 1574
Goldner, F.H., T.P. Ference, and R.R. Ritti. 628, 629
Goldner, F.H. See Ference, T.P.
  See Ritti, R.R.
Goldschmidt, D., F. Greiner, and H. Schelsky. 1417
Goldschmidt, W. 1800
Goldstein, B., and R.L. Eichhorn. 2634
Goldstein, R. 1418
Goldstein, Sidney. 1276
Goldstein, Sidney I. 853
Goldstrom, L., and J.M. Goldstrom.
  See Compton, P.A.
Gollin, G.L. 1245, 1246
Gonzalez, S. 2486
Gonzalez Anleo, J. 3031
Gonzalez-Estefani y Robles, J.M. 2338
Goodall, R.M. 1801
Goode, E. 1802, 1803, 1804, 2487, 3234, 3235
Goodman, F.D. 3092, 3093, 3094
  And J.E. Henney, and E. Pressel. 2978
Goodman, J.D. See Rigney, D.
Goodridge, R.M. 2488
Goody, J. 2748
Gordon, D. 165
Gordon, M. 382
Gordon, S. 1976
Gordon-McCutchan, R.C. 3134
  See Hammond, P.E.
Gorlow, L., and H.E. Schroeder. 2979
Gorsuch, R.L., And D. Aleshiere. 439
Goulding, J.W. See Nederman, C.J.
Goussidis, A. 630
Gramsci, A. 3496

Granberg, D.,
and K.E.Campbell. 280
Granberg, D. See Campbell, K.E.
Grand'Maison, J. 1575
Gray, D.M. 2635
Gray, L. See Libby, R.W.
Greeley, A.M. 304, 305, 631, 632, 633, 634, 1277, 1419, 1420, 1421, 1805, 1977, 2052, 2489, 2490, 2636, 2637, 2638, 2881, 2980, 2981, 3166, 3397
And M.G. Durkin. 1100
And W.C. McCready. 1576, 3301
See Fee, J.L.
See Schoenherr, R.A.
Green, R.W. 2639
Greenberg, D.F.,
and M.H. Bystryn. 266
Greenwald, D.E. 3167
Greer, J.E. See Birrell, W.D.
See Roche, D.J.D.
Greer, S. 1577
Gregory, A. 1218
Gregory, W.E. 440, 1578
Greil, A.L. 1978
And D.R. Rudy. 1979
See Kowalewski, D.
Greilsammer, A. 1579
Greinacher, N. von. 1422
Greiner, F.
See Goldschmidt, D.
Greytag, J. 1423
Grichting, W.L. 1424, 1425
Griffin, J. 635
Grignon, C. 1580
Grim, J.A. 1031
Grimm, J.W. See Hertel, B.R.
Grindstaff, C.F.,
and G.E. Ebanks. 341
Griswold, A.W. 3279
Groat, H.T., A.G. Neal,
and E.C. Knisely. 248
Groenenberg, A.L. 383
Grönblom, G. 2939
And J. Thorgaard. 3443
Grond, L. See Baan, M.A.
Grossman, N. 2749
Grumelli, A. 1426, 2491, 2492
And G. Bolino. 2834
See Caporale, R.
Grunewald, T. See Moles, A.A.
Grunwald, C. de. 3538
Grupp, F.W.,
and W.M. Newman. 1581
Guiart, J. 2339, 2340
And P. Worsley. 2341
Guilbaud, G.T. 2227
Guindon, H. 2493
Guizzardi, G. 2494, 2495, 2496, 2497
See Acquaviva, S.S.
Gundlach, G. 1335, 1427
Gupta, G.R. 2498
Gurian, W. 3564
Gurin, G. See Veroff, J.
Gurwitsch, A. 2640
Gusfield, J.R. 1942, 2438
Gustafson, J.M. 636, 854
Gustafson, P.M. 1140, 2809, 3236, 3237, 3302
Gustafsson, B. 807, 1806
Gustavus, W.T. 1002
Guth, J.L. 637, 638
Gutwirth, J. See Desroche, H.
Guyua, M. 2835

H

Hacker, H. 1101
Hadaway, C.K. 109, 947, 948, 1980
And W.C. Roof. 492, 2836
See Elifson, K.W.
See Roof, W.C.
Hadden, J.K. 110, 111, 639, 640, 855, 1582
And R.C. Rymph, 1734, 1735
See Long, T.E.
See Longino, C.F.
See Rymph, R.C.
Haddox, B.E. 3032
Hadzimichali, N. 2342
Hagstrom, W.O. 856
Hahn, A. 3078
Haimes, P., and M. Hetherington. 641
Halbwachs, M. 2641
Hall, C.L. See Harris, M.B.
Hall, D.T., and B. Schneider. 642
Hall, J.O. 1003

Hall, John R. 1247
Halsey, J.J. 978
Hamby, W.C. See Nelsen, H.M.
Hambye, F., and J. Remy. 352
Hambye, F. See Remy, J.
See Servais, E.
Hamelin, L.-E. 643, 2090
Hames, C. See Aver, E.
Hamilton, R.F. 281
Hammersmith, S.K. 1043
Hammond, J.L. 1583, 1584, 3135
Hammond, P.E. 112, 353, 536, 537, 1585, 2499, 3338, 3398, 3464
And A. Gedricks, E. Lawler, and L. Turner. 857
And R.C. Gordon-McCutchan. 3136
And J.D. Hunter. 2153
And R.E. Mitchell. 538
And Luis Salinas, and D. Sloane. 70
And K.R. Williams. 2642
See Bellah, R.N.
See Cole, W.A.
Hampe, G.D. 306
Hampshire, A.P., and J.A. Beckford. 2133
Haney, C.A. See Ebaugh, H.R.F.
Hanf, T. 1586
Hanna, M.T. 1587
Hannon, J. 3497
Hansen, N.M. 2643
Hansum, D. See Wulf, J.
Harder, M.W. 1081, 1248
See Simmonds, R.B.
Hardin, B.L. 2408, 2409
And G. Kehrer. 2902
And W. Kuner. 2410
See Shupe, A.D.
Hargrove, B. 539, 644
Harms, E. 1981, 2982
Harper, C.L., and K. Leicht. 113
Harper, E.B. 1900
Harris, M.B., S.M. Benson, and C.L. Hall. 13
Harris, R. 441
Harrison, D.E., W.H. Bennett, and G. Globetti. 322
Harrison, M.I. 1982, 2248, 2903
And B. Lazerwitz. 1278
And J.K. Maniha. 2249
See Lazerwitz, B.
Harrison, P. 919, 1141, 3572
Harte, T. See Nuesse, C.J.
Harter, C.L., and J.D. Beasley. 230
Hartley, L.H. 3210
And D.S. Schuller. 1004
Hartley, S.F. 912
And M.G. Taylor. 913
See Taylor, M.G.
Harwood, A. 3102
Hashimoto, H., and W. McPherson. 142
Hassan, R. 2644
Hassenger, R. 2940
Hassinger, E.W., J.K. Benson, J.H. Dorsett, and J.S. Holik. 645
Hassinger, E.W. See Benson, J.K.
Hastings, P.K., and D.R. Hoge. 2941
Hatch, L.R.
See Bainbridge, W.S.
Haubert, M. 2343
Hauser, W.J. See Carr, L.G.
Hay, D. 2983
And A. Morisey. 2984
Hayashida, C.T. 920
Hayes, E.C. 2725
Hayes, J. 2645
Haywood, C.L. 1102
Hazelrigg, L.E. 1588, 1807
Healy, C.C. 2091
Heaton, T.B., and S. Calkins. 249
Heaton, T.B. See Albrecht, S.L.
Heddendorf, R. 3339
Hégy, P. 1200
Heilman, S.C. 3074
Heimer, D.D. 213
Heirich, M. 1983
Heiskanen, V.S. See Lüschen, G.
Heltsley, M.E., and C. Broderick. 323
Hendershot, G.E.
See Eckhardt, K.W.
See Hertel, B.R.
Hendricks, J.S. 1589
Henney, J.H. See Goodman, F.D.

Hennig, J. 3168
Henriot, P.J. 646
Henze, L.F.,
and J.W. Hudson. 324
Hepworth, M.,
and B.S. Turner. 2134
Herberg, W. 354, 355, 384,
2500, 3399
Herman, N.J. 1428
Hermassi, E. 1590
Hermet, G. 1591
Hero, A.O. 1592
Herrlin, O. 3169
Hertel, B.R. 2810, 3238
And G.E. Hendershot,
and J.W. Grimm. 214
And H.M. Nelsen. 2501
Hesselbart, S. See Martin, P.Y.
Hessels, A. 1279
Hesser, G.W. 647
And A.J. Weigert. 3170
See Mills, E.W.
Hetherington, M. See Haimes, P.
Hicks, F. 858
Hicks, T.H. 648
Hiernaux, J.-P. See Remy, J.
Higgins, E. 649
Higgins, P.C.,
and G.L. Albrecht. 2161
Hilhorst, H. 261
Hilke, J.C. 3084
Hill, B. 1044
Hill, C. 143, 3340
Hill, J.R. See Hood, R.W.
Hill, M. 1336, 1337, 1338
See Turner, B.S.
Hill, R. 949
Hill, S.S. 114
Hiller, H.H. 1231
See Nelson, J.J.
Hillery, G.A. 1045, 1249, 1304
And C.J. Dudley,
and P.C. Morrow. 1305
And P.C. Morrow. 1250
See Dudley, C.J.
Hilty, D.M., R.L. Morgan,
and J.E. Burns. 2942
Himmelfarb, H.S. 2943
Hine, V. 144, 2904, 3095
See Gerlach, L.P.
Hinings, C.R.,
and A. Bryman. 1142
Hinings, C.R,
and B.D. Foster. 1143
Hinings, C.R. (B.). See Bryman, A.
See Ranson, S.
Hirikoshi, H. 650
Hirschi, T., and R. Stark. 2162
Hites, R.W. See Allen, E.E.
Hobart, C.W. 93, 325
Hoben, A. 1808
Hoc, J.M.N.-H. 1144
Hoffman, B. See Smith, R.
Hoffman, D. See Schindeler, F.
Hogan, M. 2837
Hoge, D.R. 1984
Et al. 338
And J.W. Carroll. 145, 442
And J.E. Dyble. 651
And J.E. Dyble and D.T. Polk. 652, 859
And E.L. Perry,
and G.L. Klever. 2811
And D.T. Polk. 146
And R.H. Potvin,
and K.M. Gerry. 2092
And D.A. Roozen. 950
And E.I. Smith. 2985
See Hastings, P.K.
See McKinney, W.
See Perry, E.L.
See Philibert, P.J.
Holik, J.S. See Hassinger, E.W.
Holl, A., and G.H. Fischer. 2944
Holl, A. See Lindner, T.
Holland, J.B.,
and C.P. Loomis. 653
Hollinger, R.C. See Alston, J.P.
Hollingshead, A. 1809, 1810
Hollitscher, W. 3498
Holt, A.E. 147
Holt, J.B. 1811
Homan, R. 1812
Homer, D.G. 1145
Hong, L.K. 26
Honigsheim, P. 42, 2646, 3303
Honsberger, H.,
and J. Zisyadis. 1593
Hood, R.W. 2905, 2986, 2987,
2988, 2989
And J.R. Hill. 2990
And R.J. Morris. 2991, 3239

Hood, T.C. See Clelland, D.A.
See Wimberley, R.C.
Hoonaert, E. 654
Hooykaas, R. 3539
Hopkins, K. See Tamney, J.B.
Hopkins, R.F. 1594
Hornick, J.P. 307
Horrigan, J.P. 2093
And K. Westhues. 2094
Horton, R. 2750
Hostie, R. 1339
Hough, R.L. See Summers, G.F.
Hougland, J.G. 1146
And J.M. Shepard,
and J.R. Wood. 1201
And J.R. Wood. 1147, 1148, 1495, 3085
And J.R. Wood,
and S.A. Mueller. 2439
Hoult, T.F. 1917, 3444
Houtart, F. 183, 282, 655, 1202, 1429, 1430, 1431, 1432, 1433, 1506, 1595, 1596, 1597, 1598, 1599, 1813, 2095, 2096, 2250, 2782, 3465, 3499
And G. Lemercinier. 1600, 1814, 1901, 1902, 3500
And A. Rousseau. 2251
Hudson, C. 2858
Hudson, J.W. See Henze, L.F.
Hudson, W.S. 2647, 2648
Hughes, J.E. See Young, B.
Hughes, M. See Wood, M.
Hughes, R.T. 3400
Hughey, M.W. 2502, 3401
Hultgren, D.D. See Webb, S.C.
Humphreys, C. 656
Hunsberger, B. 2053, 2054
And L.B. Brown. 2055
See Fullerton, J.T.
Hunt, C.L. 1601, 2163
Hunt, J.G. See Hunt, L.L.
Hunt, L.L., and J.G. Hunt. 2296, 2649
Hunt, R.A. 2882
And M.B. King. 2783
Hunter, J.D. 115, 1602, 2591.
See Hammond, P.E.
Huotari, V. 3033
Hutcheon, P.D. 510
Hutchinson, H.W. 1815
Huth, W. 2992
Hutjes, J.M. 250
Hutjes, Jan. See Schreuder, O.
Hutsebaut, D. 2867
Hyland, R. See Glenn, N.

I

Iguacen Glaria, F. 2503
Imse, T.P. 921
Ingram, L.C. 860, 861
Iqbal, S.M. 1603
Irle, R. See Dornbusch, S.M.
Irvine, W.P. 1604
Irwin, J. See Elifson, K.W.
Isambert, F.A. 156, 1605, 1606, 1607, 1816, 1918, 1919, 1920, 2504, 3034, 3035, 3046, 3171
And R. Courtas. 3037
Ishwaran, K. 1232
Isichei, E.A. 1149, 3294

J

Jackson, A.R. 251
Jackson, E.F., W.S. Fox,
and H.J. Crockett. 2650
Jackson, J.,
and R. Jobling. 3280
Jackson, J.E.W.
See Pickering, W.S.F.
Jacobs, J. 1103
Jacobson, C.K. See Cygnar, T.E.
See Pilarzyk, T.J.
Jacovini, J. See Tamney, J.B.
Jaeckels, R. 2097
Jaehne, E.M. See Kunz, P.R.
Jain, S.P. 1903
James, William. 2993
James, William R. 2098
Jamison, M. See Lofland, J.
Jamison, W.G. 1005
Jammes, J.-M. 862
Janosik, R.J. 1608
Jarvis, P. 863, 864
Jaspard, J.-M. 3172
Jeffrey, R. 1904
Jeffries, V.,
and C.E. Tygart. 657
Jelen, T.G. 215
Jenkins, R. 2180

Jensen, G.F.,
and M.L. Erickson. 2164
Jiminez, J.,
and J. Estruch. 2505
Jiminez Cadeña, G. 658
Jioultsis, B. 1341
Jobling, R. See Jackson, J.
Johnson, A.L.
See Photiadis, J.D.
See Strommen, M.P.
Johnson, Barry L. See Duke, J.T.
Johnson, Benton. 43, 44, 94,
511, 659, 660, 3240, 3241, 3242,
3389, 3540
Johnson, C.L.,
and A.J. Weigert. 148, 3079
Johnson, D.P. 71, 443
See Summers, G.F.
Johnson, J.G. 865
Johnson, M.A. 2906
Johnson, N.R., D.A. Choates,
and W. Bunis. 2252
Johnson, S.D.,
and J.B. Tamney. 1609
Johnson, W.T. 3137
See Mueller, C.W.
Johnston, B.C. See Price, D.L.
Johnstone, R.L. 661, 808, 809,
2297
Jolicoeur, P.M.,
and L.L. Knowles. 3402
Jolson, Alfred J. 866, 2099
Jonassen, C.T. 2651
Jończyk, Jósef. 1006
Jones, D.G. See Richey, R.E.
Jones, E.F. See Westoff, C.F.
Jones, G., and D. Nortman. 241
Jones, L.A. 184, 185
Jones, R.K. 1985
Juarez Rubens Brandão Lopes. 27
Jud, G.J., E.W. Mills,
and G.W. Burch. 662
Jules-Rosette, B. 1986, 2994,
3173
Julliard, A. 3103

K

Kail, R.C. 2199
Kaiser, M.A. 663
Kallen, H.M. 3565
Kanavy, M.J. See Stack, S.
Kane, J.J. 2181
Kang, W.J. 1610
Kannan, C.T. 1905
Kanter, J.F.
See Balakrishnan, T.R.
Kanter, R.M. 1251, 2344
Kaplan, B. 1817
Kapsis, R.E. See Cohen, S.M.
Karcher, B.C., I.E. Robinson,
and J.O. Balswick. 1434
Karcher, B.C., J.O. Balswick,
and I.E. Robinson. 3579
Kauffman, J.H. 2784
Kauffman, M. 664
Kaufman, H. 1818
Kaufman, H.F. 1151
Kaufmann, F.-X. 1150
Kaufmann, R. 2345
Kayal, J.M. See Kayal, P.M.
Kayal, P.M., and J.M. Kayal. 385
Kearl, M.C., and A. Rinaldi. 3403
Keedy, T.C. 28
Kehrer, Günter. 1921
See Hardin, B.
Keller, H.E. 665
Kellerhals, J. See Campiche, R.
Kelley, D.M. 116, 117
Kelley, J.M. See Schallert, E.J.
Kelly, H.E. 666
Kelly, J.R. 283, 667, 2200, 2201,
2202, 2203
Kelly, S. See Doyle, R.T.
Kemp, P. 3501
Kenkel, W.F., et al. 2785
Kennedy, R.D. 2100
Kennedy, R.E. 2652
Kent, L. See Stark, R.
Kephart, W.M. 1819
Kerkhofs, J. 668, 867
Kersevan, M. 3174, 3502
Kertzer, D.T. 1611
Kessler, C.S. 1612
Kessler, S. 3404
Keyes, C.F. 3466
Kiernan, J. 669
Kilbourne, B.K. 2411
And James T. Richardson. 2412,
2413

Kim, Byong-suh. 1987
Kim, Hei C. 2653, 2812
Kimwra, Y. 284
Kincheloe, S.C. 979, 1435
King, A. 2253
King, H., and
J.C. Baylar. 670, 671
King, K., T. Abernathy,
I. Robinson, and J. Balswick.
308
King, M.O. See Prothro, E.T.
King, Morton B. 2945
And R.A. Hunt. 190, 2946, 2947,
2948, 2949, 2950, 3541
See Hunt, R.A.
Kirk, R.E. See Lindskoog, D.
Kirsten, L.K. 672
Kishimoto, H. 2751
Kistler, R.C. See Coates, C.H.
Kitay, P.M. 118
Kitson, G.C. See Longino, C.F.
Klapp, O.E. 3175
Klein, J. 1152
Kleinman, S. 1007, 1008
And G.A. Fine. 1009
Klemmack, D.L.,
and J.D. Cardwell. 1280
Klever, G.L. See Hoge, D.R.
Klineberg, O., T. Tentori,
F. Crespi, and V. Filippone-
Thaulero. 444
Klingender, F.D. 2726
Klohr, O. 2838
Klosek, I. See Curtis, J.H.
Kluckhohn, C., et al. 512
Kluegel, J.R. 1988
Klug, L.F. See Currie, Raymond.
Klugl, J. 3445
Knisely, E.C. See Groat, H.T.
Knoke, D. 1613, 1614
Knowles, L.L.
See Jolicoeur, P.M.
Knudsen, D.D., J.R. Earle,
and D.W. Shriner. 3341
Knudsen, D.D. See Davidson, J.D.
Knudten, R.D. 2135
And M. Knudten. 2136
Knudten, M. See Knudten, R.D.
Kohn, R. 922
Kolb, W.L. 513
Koller, D.B. 1203
Koller, N.B.,
and J.D. Retzer. 673
Kooman, W. See Middendorp, C.P.
Kosa, J., et al. 1104
Kosa, J., and J. Nash. 1943
Kosa, J., and L.D. Rachiele. 2654
Kosa, J., and C.O. Schommer. 2965
Kosa, J. See Schommer, C.O.
Koss, J.D. 3104, 3281
Köster, R 1436
Koval, J., and R. Bell. 674
Koval, J. See Mills, E.W.
Kovalevsky, P. 2346, 2347
Kowalewski, D. 1615
And A.L. Greil. 3342
Krausy, E. 1944
Krausz, E. 2506
Krejci, J. 2507
Krile, J.F. See Cantrell, R.
Kroef, J.M.A. van der. 1153
Kroll-Smith, J.S. 3145
Krueger, E.T. 1820
Kruijt, J.P. 1281
And W. Goddijn. 356
Kudō, T. See Tovar, C.
Kuhn, M.N.,
and T.S. McPartland. 3573
Kuhre, B.E. 2951
Kuner, W. See Hardin, B.
Kunz, P.R.,
and M.B. Brinkerhoff. 951
Kunz, P.R., and E.M. Jaehne. 186
Kunz, P.R. See Seggar, J.F.
Kurtz, L.R. 2879
Kutner, N.G. See Brogan, D.
Kuzlowski, J. See Wuthnow, R.
Kvaraceus, W.C. 2165

L

La Barre, W. 2348
Labbens, J. 2508
Labelle, Y.,
and G. Perez Ramirez. 1010
Labelle, Y. See Perez Ramirez, G.
Lacelle, E. 1105
Ladinsky, J. See Wilensky, H.L.
Ladrière, P. 200, 2839

Laeyendecker, L. 2509
Lalive d'Epinay, C. 157, 1616, 2204, 3343, 3467
Et al. 158
And J. Zylberberg. 1821
Laloux, J. 1342
Lamanna, R.A., and J.J. Coakley. 2298
Lamanna, R.A., and J.B. Stephenson. 445
Lamar, R.E. 2859
Lampe, P.E. 386, 387
Lampinen, T. 3125
Landa, J.F. 1989
Landis, B.Y. 952
Lane, R. 2968
Langford, B.J., and C.C. Langford. 14
Langford, C.C. See Langford, B.J.
Langrod, G. 1154
Lans, J.M. van der, and F. Derks. 2414
Lanternari, V. 401, 2349, 3038
Laplantine, F. 3105
Lapointe, G. 514
Largement, R. 45
Larkin, G. 2510
Larson, D.E. 1437
Larson, R.F. 675, 676, 677, 868
Latreille, A., and A. Siegfried. 1617
Lauer, R.H. 678, 1945
Laumann, E.O. 1822
And D. Segal. 1618
Lauwers, J. 2511
Lawler, E. See Hammond, P.E.
Layne, N.R., and J.O. Balswick. 1438, 1439
Layne, N.R. See Balswick. J.O.
Lazar, M.M. 1106
Lazerine, N.G. 662
See Nagi, M.
Lazerwitz, B. 166, 167, 953, 1823, 1824, 1990, 1991
And M. Harrison. 954, 1282
See Harrison, M.I.
See Tabory, E.
Leat, D. 679
Lebedev, A.A. 2512
Lebra, T.S. 388, 1992, 1993
Le Bras, G. 46, 810, 955, 1343, 1440, 2513, 3176
Lechner, F.J. 2860
Lee, C. 2299
Lee, G.R., and R.W. Clyde. 29
Lee, G.R. See Finney, J.M.
Lee, J.O. 1825
Lee, Raymond L., and S.E. Ackerman. 3468
Lee, Robert. 2205
Leent, J.A.A. van. 1441
Lefever, H.G. 1826, 1827, 1828
Légaré, J. 1344
Léger, D. 72
Lehman, E.C. 680, 681, 682
Lehrburger, E. 3282
Leicht, K. See Harper, C.L.
Leidy, T.R. See Peyton, F.W.
Leiffer, M.H. 869
Leites, E. 187
Lemercinier, G. 1829, 1906, 1907
See Houtart, F.
Lemert, C.C. 357, 2752, 3376, 3477, 3542
Lemieux, R. 2166, 3543
Lennon, J., et al. 683, 684, 1345, 1346, 1347
Lenski, G.E. 358, 1107, 1195
Lentner, L. See Lindner, T.
Leon, J.J., and P.G. Steinhoff. 242
Leonard, R.C. See Burnham, K.E.
See Connors, J.F.
Leone, M.P. 2727
Leslie, G.R. See Davidson, J.K.
Lessard, M.-A., and J.-P. Montminy. 1348
Leuba, J.H. 1544
Leverrier, R. 2254
Lévesque, B. 1349, 1350
See Denault, B.
Levine, D.H. 1619
Lewellen, T.C. 2655
Lewins, F. 1155
Lewis, G. See Melamed, A.R.
Lewis, H.S. 1830
Lewis, R.A. 285
Lewy, Guenter, 1620, 2350
Libby, R.W., L. Gray, and M. White. 309

Lidz, V.M. 2514, 3446
Liebman, C.S. 1621, 3243
And E.Don-Yehiya. 1622, 3405
Liebman, R.C. 2255
And R.Wuthnow. 119
Liénard, G.,
and A. Rousseau. 1623
Lijphart, A. 1624
Limberto, S. 2813
Linblade, Z.G. 685
Linden, I., and J. Linden. 1625
Linden, J. See Linden, I.
Lindenthal, J.J. 2101, 2102
Lindner, T., L. Lentner,
and A. Holl. 2103
Lindskoog, D.,
and R.E. Kirk. 1011
Linz, J. 1626
Lipetz, M.E. See Lynes, J.L.
Lipman, V.D. 1505
Lipman-Blumen, J. 1082
Lipset, S.M. 446, 1627, 1628
Lipsey, C.M. See Clelland, D.A.
See Wimberley, R.C.
Lipson, G., and D. Wolman. 231
Littlejohn, J. 1442
Liu, W.T. 30, 31, 216, 447
See Maiolo, J.R.
See Murphy, Roseanne.
Lizcano, M. 956
Lizza, G. 1443
Lockard, K. 1629
Locke, R. 3283
Lodato, F. See Loveless, E.
Lofland, J. 987, 1994, 1995
And M. Jamison. 2256
And N. Skonovd. 1996, 1997
And R. Stark. 1998
Long, T.E.,
and J.K. Hadden. 1999
Longino, C.F.,
and J.K. Hadden. 686
Longino, C.F.,
and G.C. Kitson. 687
Lonsway, F.A. 1012, 1013
Loomis, C.P., and J. Samora. 448
Loomis, C.P. See Holland, J.B.
Lopez de Ceballos, P. 2000, 2868
Lorentzen, L.J. 120
Lotz, R. 449
Loubser, J.J. 1831
Lourie, R. 980
Lovelace, A.B. 1630
Loveless, E., and F. Lodato. 2167
Lovell, T. 2656
Luckmann, T. 1444, 2515, 2516, 2592
See Berger, P.L.
Luft, M.C. 2517
Luhmann, N. 188, 2728, 3406, 3447
See Dahm, K.
Luidens, D.A. 1496
Lunt, P.S. See Warner, W.L.
Lupton, G. See Dowdy, E.
Lüschen, G., Z. Staikof,
V.S. Heiskanen, and C. Ward. 2518
Lüthy, H. 2657, 2658
Lutterman, K.J. 3086
Lynch, F.R. 2001
Lynd, H. See Lynd, R.
Lynd, R., and H. Lynd. 1832
Lyness, J.L., M.E. Lipetz,
and K.E. Davis. 326

M

McAulay, R. 3545
McAuley, E.A.N. 1046
McBride, J. See Schwartz, Paul A.
McCallister, I. 1283
McCarrick, T.E. 2106, 2107
McClelland, D.C. 2667, 2668
McClerren, B.F. 1638
McCloskey, D.D. 33
McCombs, C.R. 2997
See Currie, Raymond.
McConahay, J.B.,
and J.C. Hough. 1737
McConnell, J.W. 1836
McCormick, E.P. 218
McCoy, C.S. 2302
McCoy, J. See Christopher, S.
McCready, W.C. See Fee, J.L.
See Greeley, A.M.
MacDonald, A.F. 870
McDonald, L. 1639
McDonough, E.E. See Peñaloza, F.
McEnery, J.N. See Moberg, D.O.
McGaw, D.B. 1446, 1447, 1448
And E.Wright. 1449

McGee, M. 2003
McGovern, E.M. 1640
MacGreil, M. 1014
McGuire, M.B. 1497, 1507, 1508, 3106, 3146
Machalek, R. 2753
And M. Martin. 2593
See Rigney, D.
See Snow, D.A.
McIntosh, W.A., and J.P. Alston. 232
McIntosh, W.A., L.T. Alston, and J.P. Alston. 219
McIntosh, W.A., S.D. Fitch, J.B. Wilson, and K.L. Nyberg. 2168
McIntosh, W.A. See Alston, J.P.
MacIntyre, A. 189
Mack, R.W., R.J. Murphy, and S. Yellin. 2659
McKeefery, W.J. 2004
Mackie, M.M.
See Brinkerhoff, M.B.
McKinley, D.G. 1837
McKinney, M.M. 1641
McKinney, R.I. 1838
McKinney, W., and D.R. Hoge. 958
McKown, D.B. 3510
MacLaren, A.A. 1833
McLeod, H. 1839, 1840, 1841
McLoughlin, W.G. 3138
McMurry, M.J. 1108, 1109
McNall, S.G. 2259
McNamara, P.H. 389, 690, 1738
And A. St. George. 149
See St. George, A.
McNamara, R.J. 1017, 3377
MacNeil, P. See Blasi, A.J.
McPartland, T.S. See Kuhn, M.H.
McRae, J.A. 1233
MacRae, P.H. 2206
McSweeney, B. 873
Madden, J. 688
Mader, P.D. 2814
See Nelsen, H.M.
Madigan, F.C. 871, 1351
Madron, T.W., H.M. Nelsen, and R.L.Yokley. 1631
Madron, T.W. See Nelsen, H.M.
Maduro, O. 3, 2754, 3503, 3504, 3505, 3506, 3507,
Maertens, J.-T. 2519
Magill, D.W. See Campbell, D.F.
Magni, K.G. 1015
Magrauer, B. 872
Maguire, M.A. See Nelsen, H.M.
Mahoney, E.R. 327
See Tedrow, L.M.
Maier, J. 2755
And W. Spinrad. 2815, 2816
Maiolo, J.R., W.V. D'Antonio, and W.T. Liu. 2257
Mair, L. 1068
Maitre, J. 1632, 3039, 3076, 3077, 3508
See Aver, E.
See Desroche, H.
Makler, H.M. 1156
Malak, S.J. 217
Malina, B.J. 73
Malinowski, B. 2756
Maloney, D.J. 1016
Maloney, H.N. See Ragan, C.
Mamiya, L.H. 1834
Mammer, C. See Moore, E.H.
Mandelbaum, D.G. 1930
Mandelker, I.L. 1252
Mandic, O. 3509
Manglapus, R.S. 2660
Maniha, J.K. See Harrison, M.I.
Mann, J.H. See Blum, B.S.
Mann, W.E. 1633, 2207
Manton, K. See Wilson, John.
Mantzaridis, G. 1306, 2208
Maranell, G.M. 4, 450, 2861
And R.A. Doder, and D.F. Mitchell. 328
Marcoux, M. 3087
Margolis, R.D. 2995
And K.W. Elifson. 2996
Marhold, W. See Fischer, W.
Mariante, B.R. 359
Markert, D.D. 811
Markhoff, J., and D. Regan. 3407
Marks, G.W. See Fleming, J.J.
Marliere, M. 1307
Marshall, G. 2661, 2662, 2663
Martin, D.A. 286, 689, 2520, 2521, 2522, 2523, 2524, 2525, 2526, 3295

Martin, J.G.,
  and F.W. Westie. 451
Martin, Jack, and S. Stack. 32
Martin, P.Y., M.W. Osmond,
  S. Hesselbart, and M. Wood.
  1083
Martin, R.M. 2664
Martin, W. 1736
Martindale, D. 981
Martinez Scheifler, M. 2757
Martins, A. 2952
Martinson, O.B., E.A. Wilkening,
  and F.H. Buttel. 3479
Martz, M.E. 3284
Marwell, G. See Demerath, N.J.
Marx, G.T. 2300, 2301
Maryo, J.S. 957
Marzal, A. 1634
Mason, M.C. 2594
Masson, J. 2104
Mat-Hasquin, M. 2415
Matras, J. See Bachi, R.
Mattez, M.T. 2105
Matthes, J. 360, 1445, 2527
Matthews, A.T.J.
  See Morrow, W.R.
Matthijssen, A.J.M. 361
Maucorps, P.H. See Ansart, P.
Maurer, H.H. 168, 1635, 2665
Mauss, A.L. 452, 453, 2056
  See Petersen, L.R.
Maves, P.B. 2002
May, L.C. 3096
Mayer, A.J., and H. Sharp. 2666
Mayer, C. 3244
Mayeur, J.M. 1636, 1637
Maynard, J. 1835
Mayrl, W.W. 2258
Means, R.L. 2669, 2670, 2671
Meddin, J. 3177
Mehl, R. 2209
Mehok, W.J. 1352, 1353
Meisel, J. 1642
Melamed, A.R., M.S. Silverman,
  and G. Lewis. 1047
Mendelson, E.M. 1308, 1643
Mendlovitz, S.H.
  See Carlin, J.E.
Menendez, A.J. 1644
Menges, W. 1354, 1842
Mensching, G. 408, 409, 1157,
  3040, 3041
Mercy, J. See Cumings, S.
Merton, R.K. 2672, 2673, 3546
Meslin, M. 3042
Metraux, A. 2351, 2352
Michaelsen, R.S. 2674
Michel, J.B. See Thompson, R.C.
Michelat, G., and M. Simon.
  1645, 1646, 1647
Michelat, G. See Aver, E.
Mickey, T.J. 3126
Middendorp, C.P., W. Brinkman,
  and W. Kooman. 329
Middleton, R. 2817
  And S. Putney. 2137
  See Putney, S.
Middleton, W.C.,
  and P.J. Fay. 2138
Mikkelsen, M.A. 1253
Milanesi, G. 1648, 2595
Miller, D.E. 3511
Miller, M. 2139
Miller, M.J. See Scalf, J.H.
Miller, W.E.,
  and P.C. Stouthard. 1649
Miller, William L. 1650
Millett, D. 1158
Mills, B.E. 1018
Mills, E.W. 691, 874
  And G. Hesser. 692
  And J.P. Koval. 693
  See Broughton, W.
  See Jud, G.J.
Milner, S.B. See Smith, R.
Miner, H. 1450
Mirels, H.L.,
  and J.B. Garrett. 2675
Mitchell, D.F. See Maranell, G.M.
Mitchell, J.C. 1843
Mitchell, R.C. 2228
Mitchell, R.E. 694, 695, 696, 817
  See Hammond, P.E.
Moberg, D.O. 47, 493, 522, 523,
  1159, 1739, 1844, 2528, 2862,
  3245, 3547, 3548
  And P.M. Brusek. 524
  And J.N. McEnery. 3118
Mobley, G.M. 1651
Mocciaro, R. 2869

Mogey, J. See Adams, R.L.
Mol, J.J. (H.) 169, 170, 1652, 2110, 2529, 2676, 2893, 3178, 3448
Moles, A.A., and T. Grunewald. 171
Molitor, M.M.A. 1048
Molm, L.D. 1084
Monoghan, R.R. 2863
Montezemolo, M.E. 697
Montminy, J.P. See Lessard, M.-A.
Monzel, N. 1451
Moodie, T.D. 1653, 1654, 3408
Moore, E.H., and C. Mammer. 698
Moore, J. 699, 875
Moore, M. 876
Moore, Maurice J. 252
Moore, R. 1655, 2677
Moran, R.E. 700, 1049
Morelli, A. 1254, 2416, 2417
Moreux, C. 362, 1452, 1498
Morgan, D.H.J. 701
Morgan, J.G. 2260
Morgan, R.L. See Hilty, D.M.
Morgan, S.P. 190
Mori, T. 3179
Morisy, A. See Hay, D.
Morland, J.K. 172
Mormont, M., C. Mougenot, and D. Ruquoy. 201
Morris, R.J. See Hood, R.W.
Morrow, P.C. See Hillery, G.A.
Morrow, W.R., and A.T.J. Matthews, 877
Mörth, I. 363, 3432
Mosca, G. 1656
Mougenot, C. See Mormont, M.
Moulin, L. 1160, 1161, 1162, 1163, 1355
Mount, C.E. 3409
Moyle, T. See Stanley, G.
Muelder, W.G. 2108
Mueller, C.W., and W.T. Johnson. 1845
Mueller, G.H. 48, 2953
Mueller, S.A. 1164, 1946, 2005
  See Gibbs, D.R.
  See Hougland, J.G.
Mühlmann, W.E. 2353, 2354
Mukerjee, R. 3304
Munick, J. 1356
Munters, Q.J. 3129
Murphy, R.J. See Mack, R.W.
Murphy, Roseanne. 1050, 1051, 1052
  And W.T. Liu. 1053
Murvar, V. 1298, 1299, 1657, 2261, 2355
Musgrove, F. 2109
Myers, P.G., and J.D. Davidson. 2211
Myers, R.A. See Bradfield, C.D.

N

Naegele, K.D. 702
Nagendra, S.P. 3180, 3181
Nagi, M., M.D Pugh, and N.G. Lazerine. 263
Naifeh, S.J. See Batson, C.D.
Nash, D.J., and P.L. Berger. 2006
Nash, J. See Kosa, J.
Natanson, M. 2758
Nauss, A.H. 818, 878, 1019
  And H.G. Coiner. 703
Neal, A.G. See Groat, H.T.
Neal, M.A. 15, 310, 339, 704, 1054, 1055, 1056, 1110, 1111, 1112, 3431
  And M. Clasby. 705
Nebreda, J. 2110, 2111
Nederman, C.J., and J.W. Goulding. 3433
Negrão, L.N. 2356
Neitz, M.J. 220
Nelsen, H.M. 34, 706, 1284, 1285
  Et al. 1740
  And S. Baxter. 1658
  And R.F. Everett. 707
  And R.F. Everett, P.D. Mader, and W.C. Hamby. 2596
  And T.W. Madron, and R. Yokley. 2303
  And M.A. Maguire. 708
  And R.H. Potvin. 1846
  And W.E. Snizek. 1947
  And R. Yokley. 2304, 2305
  And R. Yokley, and T.W. Madron. 2786
  See Hertel, B.R.
  See Madron, T.W.
  See Whitt, H.P.

Nelson, B. 2678, 2679, 2680
Nelson, C.H. 2262
Nelson, E. 533
Nelson, G.K. 150, 1196, 3285, 3286, 3287, 3288
And R.A. Clews. 1948
Nelson, Gordon, See Fish, J.
Nelson, J.J., and H.H. Hiller. 1453
Nelson, L.D. 2169
And R.R. Dynes. 16
Nesti, A. 1454, 1847, 1848, 2840, 3043
And C. Prandi. 3044
Newell, W.H. 3182
Newell, William H., and F. Dobashi. 3246
Newman, J. 709
And L. Ryan, and C.K. Ward. 2112
Newman, W.M. 1020, 2212
And W.V. D'Antonio. 2263
See Grupp, F.W.
Newport, F. 2007
See Rothenberg, S.
Newson, J.A. 2065
Newton, D. 3183
Ngoc Vu, N. 3512
Nguyen van Phone, J. 2008
Nicholls, D. 1659
Niebuhr, H.R. 1849
Nielson, F. 3305
Nieves, A. 710
Nobbe, C. See Christopher, S.
Noel, D.L. See Cygnar, T.E.
Nordquist, T. 1255
Norr, J.L., and J. Schweickert. 1057
Nortman, D. See Jones, G.
Nosanchuk, T.A. 1286
Nowicki, A. 3513
Nudelman, A.E. 2954, 3549
Nuesse, C.J. 1455, 1456, 1457
And T. Harte. 1458
Nunn, C.Z. 1850
Nuño, J.A. 3514
Nussbaum, J. See Spilka, B.
Nyberg, K.L. See McIntosh, W.A.
Nye, W.P. 3574

O

Obenhaus, V., W.W. Schroeder, and C.D. England. 1851
O'Connell, B.J. 253
O'Connell, J.J. 1357
O'Connor, M. 2357
O'Dea, T.F. 5, 1204, 2176, 2177, 2229, 2530, 3449
And R. Poblete. 35
See Poblete, R.
O'Donovan, T.R., and A.X. Deegan. 711, 712
Ofshe, R. 1165
O'Kane, J. 1949
Olaechea Labeyan, J.B. 1660
Oliss, P.A. 1058
Omark, R. 1661
O'Neill, R. See Blasi, A.J.
Opazo, A., and D. Smith. 1219
Opazo Bernales, A. 1852, 1853, 1854
Oppen, D. von. 1459, 2531
O'Reilly, C.T., and E.J. O'Reilly. 454
O'Reilly, E.J. See O'Reilly, C.T.
Organic, H. 1950
Orlowski, C.D. 2883
Orsini, G. di. 2113
Orsolic, M. 3515
Ortiz, R. 402
Orum, A.M. 1662
Osmond, M.W. See Martin, P.Y.
O'Toole, M.G. 1059
O'Toole, R. 1663, 1664, 1665, 3344
Otto, R. 2998
Overington, M.A. See Estus, C.W.

P

Pace, E. 1666, 3045
Page, C.H. 1222
Pangborn, C.R. 1741
Paquette, M. 2681
Parenti, M. 515
Parisi, A. 2532
Park, R.E. 3345

Parrucci, D.J. 2009
Parsons, T. 364, 516, 1166, 2533, 2682
Pasamanick, B. See Rettig, S.
Passerin d'Entreves, E. 2683
Pate, S. See Batson, C.D.
Paulson, S.K. 2534
Pavan, G. See Carli, R.
Pavlos, A.J. 3289
Payne, B.P., and K.W. Elifson. 2907
Peachy, P. 713
Peacock, J.L. 2684, 2685
Pearson, D.G. 1742
Peek, C.W. 481
And S. Brown. 482
And H.P. Chalfant, and E.V. Wilton. 2170
See Alston, J.P.
See Chalfant, H.P.
Pemberton, P.L. 3450
Peñaloza, F., and E.E. McDonough. 1951
Penner, H.H. 2759
Penning, J.M. See Smidt, C.
Pepper, G. 2729
Pereira de Queiroz, M.I. 2358, 2359, 2360, 2361, 2362, 2363, 2364, 2365, 2366, 2367, 2368
Perez Ramirez, G. 254
And Y. Labelle. 714
And I. Wust. 715
See Labelle, Y.
Perkins, H.W. 95, 2535
Perkins, R.B. 494
See Roof, W.C.
Perlman, M.L. 1855
Perry, E.L. 1460, 1856
And D.R. Hoge. 959
See Hoge, D.R.
Peter, K., E.D. Boldt, I. Whitaker, and L.W. Roberts. 2057
Peterman, D.J., C.A. Ridley, and S.M. Anderson. 330
Petersen, D.M. See Elifson, K.W.
Petersen, J.C. 1167
Petersen, L.R. 221
And A.L. Mauss. 222
And K.P. Takayama. 455, 1358
Peterson, R.W. 716
And R.A. Schoenherr. 717
See Szafran, R.F.
Petropoulos, N.P. 456
Pett, M.E. 202
Pettigrew, T.F.
See Campbell, E.Q.
Petursson, P. 2536
Peyton, F.W., A.R. Starry, and T.R. Leidy. 233
Pfautz, H.W. 2264, 2537, 2538
Phadnis, U. 1667
Phelan, M. 3410
Philibert, P.J. 191
And D.R. Hoge. 1287
Phillips, C. See Snow, D.A.
Photiadis, J.D. 2171
And J. Biggar. 457
And A.L. Johnson. 2894
And J.F. Schnabel. 6
And W. Schweiker. 2010
Piazza, T., and C.Y. Glock. 2870
Pickering, W.S.F. 879, 1461, 2172, 2265, 2539
And J.E.W. Jackson. 1462
Piepe, A. 74
Pierre, R. 3046
Pilarzyk, T.J. 2011
And C.K. Jacobson. 1256
Pillai, M. 1857
Pin, E.J. 7, 719, 880, 881, 1359, 1463, 1464, 1465, 1466, 1467, 1858, 3469
Pinder, R. 2540
Pinto, L.J., and K.E. Crow. 1468
Pion, R.J., et al. 243
Pittard, B.B. 2908, 2909
Pivovarov, V.G. 2841
Piwowarski, W. 812, 2541, 2760, 3047, 3048
Platt, L.A. See Alston, J.P.
Pletsch, D.J. 2213
Plotnicov, L. 1931
Plyler, H.E. 882
Poblete Barth, R. 365, 720, 721, 2114, 2542, 3346
And T.F. O'Dea. 35
See O'Dea, T.F.
Poeisz, J.J. 722, 2115

Poggi, G. 2686
Poisson, B. 1168
Poit, C.H. 1288
Polk, D.T. See Hoge, D.R.
Pomian-Srzednicki, M. 1668
Ponce Garcia, J.,
 and O. Uzin Fernandes. 723
Pope, L. 1859, 1922
Portelli, H. 3516, 3517
Porter, John. 1860
Porter, Judith R. 2543
 And A.A. Albert. 390
Porterfield, E.A. 1113
Post, W. 3518
Potel, J. 724
Potter, S. 976
Potvin, R.H. 36, 2871
 And A. Suziedelis. 1021
 And C.F. Westoff,
 and N.B. Ryder. 255
 See Hoge, D.R.
 See Nelsen, H.M.
 See Suziedelis, A.
Poulat, E. 1075, 1076, 1077,
 1078, 2266, 3290
Powell, B.,
 and L.C. Steelman. 483
Powell, D.E. 2842
Power, J.P. 3184
Powers, G.E. 2140
Poythress, N.G. 2818
Prades, J.A. 2761
Prandi, C. 1861
 See Nesti, A.
Pratt, H.J. 1169
Prentice, D. See Wulf, J.
Pressel, E. See Goodman, F.D.
Preston, D.L. 2012, 2418
Preston, H. 1862
Price, D.L., W.R. Terry,
 and B.C. Johnston. 3127
Price-Bonham, S., B. Santes,
 and J.M. Bonham. 223
Prothro, E.T.,
 and M.O. King. 458
Pruett, G.E. 2730
Prus, R.C. 2013
Puga, J. See Galilea, C.
Pugh, M.D. See Nagi, M.
Putney, S.,
 and R. Middleton. 37, 495

Q

Queiroz, V.M. de. 2369
Quinley, H.E. 287, 288, 289, 1743
 See Stark, R.
Quinney, R. 8, 3519

R

Rachiele, L.D. See Kosa, J.
 See Schommer, C.O.
Ragan, C., H.N. Maloney,
 and B. Beit-Hallahmi. 3550
Rajana, E.W. 2419
Ralston, H. 3247
Rama, C.M. 1863
Rambo, L.R. 2014
Ramold, M.R. 1060
Ramu, G.N.,
 and P.D. Wiebe. 1908
Rankin, R.P. 1170
Ranson, S., A. Bryman,
 and B. (C.R.) Hinings. 725
Ranson, S. See Bryman, A.
Rao, S.L.N.,
 and L.F. Bouvier. 234
Raphaël, F. 2544
 And J. Demange,
 and H. Rosenfeld. 1669
 See Dujardin, D.
Rappaport, R.A. 3185
Ray, J.J. 2687
 And D. Doratis. 459
Razzell, P. 2688
Redekop, C. 1499, 3347, 3348
Redman, B.J. 1864
Reeves, J.A. See Dean, D.C.
Regan, D. 3411
 See Markoff, J.
Reidy, M.T.V.,
 and L.C. White. 726
Reilly, M.E. 883, 884
Reimer, W. See Bird, F.
Reinhardt, R.M. 1670
Reinheimer, G.E. 2066
Remond, R. 727
Remy, J. 159, 160, 366
 And F. Hambye. 960
Rendtorff, T. 728, 1470, 1471,
 2545
Reny, P.,
 and J.-P. Rouleau. 813, 1671

Renzi, M. 224
Requena, M. 244
Rettig, S.,
and B. Pasamanick. 517
Retzer, J.D. See Koller, N.B.
Reyna, J.L. See Soares, G.A.D.
Reynolds, J.F. See Spilka, B.
Rham, G. de. See Campiche, R.
Rhodes, A., and A. Reiss. 2141
Rhodes, C. See Woodrun, E.
Ribeiro, R. 3116
Ribeiro de Oliveira, P.A. 1865, 3049, 3050, 3051, 3052, 3053
Ricardo, F. See Corbetta, P.G.
Riccamboni, G. 1672
Rice, M. 1060
Rich, M. 1472
Richard, R. 2762
Richard, Y. 885
Richards, J.M. See Cline, V.B.
Richardson, James T. 1114, 2015, 2016, 2017, 2420, 2421, 2422, 2864, 3097, 3291
And B. van Driel. 2283
And S.W. Fox. 225, 235
And M.W. Stewart. 2018
And M.W. Stewart, and R.B. Simmonds. 1257, 2019
See Bromley, D.G.
See Kilbourne, B.
See Simmonds, R.B.
Richardson, John G., and G.A. Weatherby. 2173
Richey, R.E. 1289
And D.G. Jones. 3412
Rickero, P. 2689
Ridley, C.A.
See Peterman, D.J.
Rigali, L.J. 1473
Rigby, A.,
and B.S. Turner. 1258
Rigney, D., R. Machalek, and J.D. Goodman. 2546
Ringer, B.B.,
and C.Y. Glock. 1673
Ringer, B.B. See Glock, C.Y.
Ritterband, P.
See Ebaugh, H.R.F.
Ritti, R.R., T.P. Ference, and F.H. Goldner. 729
Ritti, R.R. See Ference, T.P.
Ritti, R.R. See Goldner, F.H.
Rivière, C. 3566
Robak, N., and S. Clavan. 1085
Robbe, M. 3520
Robbins, J.M. 49
Robbins, T. 2020, 2284, 2423, 3306
And D. Anthony. 367, 2285, 2424
And D. Anthony, and T.E. Curtis. 3349, 3413, 3470
See Anthony, D.
Robert, N. 2690
Roberts, B.R. 3350
Roberts, H.W. 730, 731
Roberts, L.W. See Peter, K.
Roberts, Lynne. See Stark, R.
Roberts, M.K.,
and J.D. Davidson. 2787
Robertson, H.M. 2691, 2692
Robertson, R. 2021, 2547, 2548, 2549, 2731, 3248, 3307, 3308, 3351, 3414
Robinson, C. 2693
Robinson, I.E. See Karcher, B.C.
See King, K.
Roche, D.J.D., W.D. Birrell, and J.E. Greer. 732
Roche, D.J.D. See Birrell, W.D.
Roche de Coppens, P. 733
Rochte, F.C. 734
Rodd, L.S. 961
Rodehaver, M.W. 735
And L.M. Smith. 736
Rodinson, M. 2267, 3471
Rodrigues, J.H. 403
Rodriguez, J.F. 2550, 2551
Rogers, D.P. 3551
Rogerson, A. 2230
Roggero, E. 2552
Rojek, D.G. 1674
Rokkan, S. 1866
Rolim, F.C. 1220, 1867, 3054
Roof, J.L. See Roof, W.C.
Roof, W.C. 460, 1868, 1869, 2058, 2154, 2694, 2788, 2910, 3480, 3481
And C.K. Hadaway. 2022, 2023
And R.B. Perkins. 496
And J.L. Roof. 2872
See Hadaway, C.K.

Roozen, D.A. See Hoge, D.R.
Rosanna, E. 2553
Rosato, N. 814
Roscoe, J.T.,
and P.A. Girling. 1022
Rose, A.M. 1675
Rosen, B. 2695
Rosenblum, A.L. 461
Rosenfeld, H.
See Dujardin, D.
See Raphaël, F.
Rosenthal, E.I.J. 1676
Ross, E.A. 2174
Ross, J.M. See Allport, G.W.
Ross, Jack C. 75, 3352
Ross, P. See Glock, C.Y.
Ross, S. See Balakrishnan, T.R.
Rotenberg, M. 2696
See Goitein, B.
Roth, G. 2554
Roth, J.A. 3187
Rothenberg, S.,
and F. Newport. 1677
Roucek, J.S. 76, 1678, 3353
Rouleau, J.-P. 815, 1360
See Reny, P.
Roumeguere-Eberhardt, J. 3309
Rousseau, A. 737, 1679, 1870, 1871, 2895
See Houtart, F.
Routhier, F.,
and P. Stryckman. 1023
Routhier, F.,
and G. Tremblay. 1024
Roux, R.R. de. 886
Rovan, J. 1680
Roy, A. 1909
Roy, R.L. 462, 1681, 2306
Royle, M.H. 738
Ruark, K. 739
Rudy, D.R. See Greil, A.L.
Ruesink, D.C. 887
Rueth, T.W. 740
Ruiz Olabuenaga, J.I. 741, 2067
Rulland, W.B. 1682
Ruppel, H.J. 331, 332
Ruquoy, D. See Mormont, M.
Rusconi, G.E. 2555
Russel, M. 2024
Ryan, B. 1910
Ryan, C. 2556
Ryan, E.J. 2116
Ryan, L. See Newman, J.
Ryan, M.D. 742
Ryder, N.B.,
and C.F. Westoff. 236
Ryder, N.B. See Potvin, R.H.
Rye, G.C. 743
Rymph, R.C.,
and J.K. Hadden. 463
Rymph, R.C. See Hadden, J.K.

S

Sachchidananda. 1911
Sacks, D.G. See Takayama, K.P.
Sacks, H.L. 1361
Sadler, A.W. 3098
Sahay, A. 2697
St. George, A.,
and P.H. McNamara. 525
St. George, A. See McNamara, P.H.
Saint Martin, M. de.
See Bourdieu, P.
Salazar, R.C. 1062
Salinas, L. See Hammond, P.E.
Salisbury, W.S. 173, 2182, 2557
Saloutos, T. 391
Samarin, W.J. 3099
Samora, J. See Loomis, C.P.
Sampson, S.F. 1362, 1363
Samuelson, K. 2698
Sanchez Cano, J. 2763
Sandhu, H.S. See Allen, D.E.
SanGiovanni, L.F. 1063
Saniel, J.M. 1872
Sans Vila, J. 1025
Santopolo, F.A. See Scheuer, J.F.
Santos, B. See Price-Bonham, S.
Santy, H. 1364, 2843
Sarachandra, E.R. 1932
Sargent, L. 1873
Särlvik, B. 1683
Sartain, J.A. 464
Sasaki, M.S. 2911
Saunders, J.V.D. 1234
Saunders, L.E. 2214
Saurma, A. 3415
Savramis, D. 744, 1309, 2558

Sayari, B. 1684
Scalf, J.H., M. Miller,
and C.W. Thomas. 1171
Scanzoni, J. 888, 889, 3249,
3250
Scarpati, R. 962
Scarvagliere, G. 1365
Schaden, F. 3055
Schallert, E.J.,
and J.M. Kelley. 745
Schasching, J. 1474
Scheler, M. 518
Schelsky, H.
See Goldschmidt, D.
Scherer, R.P. 1172
Scheuer, J.F. 1475
And J.B. Schuyler,
and F.A. Santopolo. 1476
Schiff, G.S. 1685
Schindeler, F.,
and D. Hoffman. 121
Schinert, G. See Ford, C.E.
Schlangen, J.A.
See Davidson, J.D.
Schmidtchen, G. 1290
Schmitt, J.-C. 3056
Schnabel, J.F. 746
See Photiadis, J.D.
Schneider, B. See Hall, D.T.
Schneider, L. 2764, 2765
And S.M. Dornbusch. 3057, 3451
And L.A. Zurcher. 747
Schnepp, G. 1477
Schoenfeld, E. 122, 1686
Schoenherr, R.,
and A.M. Greeley. 748
Schoenherr, R.A.,
and Annemette Sorensen. 749
Schoenherr, R.A.
See Petersen, R.W.
See Szafran, R.F.
Schöfthaler, T. 192, 3452, 3580
Schommer, C.O., L.D Rachiele,
and J. Kosa. 1874
Schommer, C.O. See Kosa, J.
Schreuder, O. 816, 890, 1478,
1479, 3453
And J. Hutjes. 256
Schrey, H.H. 2268
Schroeder, H.E. See Gorlow, L.
Schroeder, W.W. 534, 891, 3528
See Obenhaus, V.
Schuller, D.S., M.P. Strommen,
and M. Brekke. 892
Schuller, D.S. See Hartley, L.H.
Schulz, B., G.W. Bohrnstedt,
E.F. Borgatta,
and R.R. Evans. 333
Schuman, H. 2699
Schuyler, J.B. 1480, 1481, 1482
See Scheuer, J.F.
Schwartz, D.F. 750, 2819
Schwartz, G. 151
Schwartz, M. 1687
Schwartz, N.B. 1875
Schwartz, P. See Anthony, D.
Schwartz, Paul A.,
and J. McBride. 123
Schweickert, J. See Norr, J.L.
Schweiker, W. See Photiadis, J.D.
Scotford-Archer, M.,
and M. Vaughan. 2559
Scott, G.G. 1069, 1500
Scott, J.C. 3058
Scoville, W.C. 1876
Searle, R.W. 3416
Searles, H.L. 2999
Segal, D. See Laumann, E.O.
Segal, R.A. 3188
Seggar, J.F.,
and R.H. Blake. 2025
Seggar, J.F., and P.R. Kunz. 2026
Séguy, Jean. 50, 77, 1173, 1310,
2215, 2216, 2217, 2370, 2371,
2372, 3000, 3059, 3189, 3190,
3354, 3355, 3356, 3357, 3358,
3359
Seidler, J. 751, 752, 753, 754
Serrano Villafañe, E. 3521
Servais, E.,
and J. Bonmariage. 3191
Servais, E., and F. Hambye. 1366
Servais, E. See Remy, J.
Settle, L.M. 1483
Sevigny, R. 3001
Seyfart, C.,
and W.M. Sprondel. 2700
Shakir, M. 1115
Shanabruch, C. 392
Shand, J.A. 755

Sharma, A. 1367
Sharma, U.M. 3292
Sharot, S. 78, 393, 394, 756, 893, 1933, 2373, 2374, 2560
Sheils, D. 2732
Shepard, J.M.
  See Hougland, J.G.
Shepherd, Gary,
  and Gordon Shepherd. 2912
Shepherd, Gordon.
  See Shepherd, Gary.
Shepherd, W.C. 2027
Sherrow, F. See Caplovitz, D.
Shils, E. 79, 3192, 3552
Shimada, K. 894
Shiner, L. 2561, 2562
Shinert, G., and C. Ford. 465
Shokeid, M. 80
Shriner, D.W. See Knudsen, D.D.
Shupe, A.D. 1688, 2269, 2425
  And D.G. Bromley. 2270, 2286, 2287, 3117
  And B.L. Hardin, and D.G. Bromley. 2288
  And R. Spielmann, and S. Stigall. 2289
  And W.A. Stacey. 757, 1689
  And J.R. Wood. 758
  See Stacey, W.A.
Siebel, W. 1174
Siebert, R.J. 3434, 3435, 3454
Siefer, G. 759
Siegfried, A.
  See Latreille, A.
Siffredi, A. 2271
Sigelman, L. 2820
Silva, R.C. 1690
Silverman, D. 760
Silverman, M.S.
  See Melamed, A.R.
Silverstein, S. 1691
Simey, L. 519
Simmel, G. 1923, 2766
Simmonds, R.B. 1259, 2028
  And James T. Richardson, and M.W. Harder. 152, 1260
  See Richardson, James T.
Simmons, J.L. 2155
Simmons, J.R. 290
Simon, M. See Michelat, G.
Simpson, G.E. 1692
Simpson, J.H. 1693
  And J. Hagan. 1877
Simson, U. 1694
Sinda, M. 1695
Singer, M. 2029
Sironneau, J.-P. 1696
Sissons, P.L. 963, 2767
Sixel, F.W. 193
Sjoberg, G. See Smith, James O.
  See Vaughan, T.R.
Skocpol, T. 1697
Skonovd, N. 2059
  See Lofland, J.
Sleeper, D.E. 3107
Sloane, D. See Hammond, P.E.
Slotten, R. 3474
Small, A.W. 1924
Smart, N. 3475
Smidt, C. 3417
  And J.M. Penning. 124
Smith, B.H. 1698
Smith, David. See Opazo, A.
Smith, Donald E. 1699
Smith, Donald P. 895
Smith, Douglas H. See
  See Vaughan, T.R.
Smith, E.I. See Hoge, D.R.
Smith, H.W. 914
Smith, J.A. 2701
Smith, James A. 923
Smith, James O.,
  and G. Sjoberg. 761
Smith, L.M. 819
  See Rodehaver, M.W.
Smith, P.M. 2218
Smith, Philip M. 2142
Smith, R., C. Black, B. Hoffman, and S.B. Milner. 896
Smith, R.W. 1700
Smith, T. Lynn. 404
Smith, T.V. 3575
Smith, Timothy L. 3139, 3140
Smith, Thomas R. 762
Smythe, H.H.,
  and T. Gershuny. 1912
Snizek, W.E. See Nelsen, H.M.
Snook, J.B. 174, 763, 3251
Snow, D.A. 377
  And R. Machalek. 2156, 2157
  And C. Phillips. 2030

Soares, G.A.D.,
and J.L. Reyna. 1878
Sobal, J. See Emmons, C.F.
Sockell-Richarté, P.F.-P. 1701
Sokolski, A. 1484
Sombart, W. 2702
Sommerfeld, R.E. 897, 1175
Sorensen, Andrew A. 764, 765, 766
Sorensen, Annemette.
See Schoenherr, R.A.
Sorokin, P.A. 17
Souffrant, C. 162, 3060
Sparhawk, F.J. 2703
Spaulding, K.E. 2821
Spenner, K. 9
Spiegel, Y. 1879
Spielmann, R. See Shupe, A.D.
Spilka, B. 18
And P. Armatas,
and J. Nussbaum. 2873
And J.F. Reynolds. 466
See Allen, R.O.
See Benson, P.
See Wulf, J.
Spinrad, W. See Maier, J.
Spiro, M.E. 2768
Spoerl, D.T. 467
Sprague, T.W. 1205
Sprondel, W.M. 2704
See Seyfart, C.
Srivinas, M.N. 1913
Stacey, W.A.,
and A.D. Shupe. 125
Stacey, W.A. See Shupe, A.D.
Stack, S., and M.J. Kanavy. 334
Stack, S. See Martin, Jack.
Staikof, Z. See Lüschen, G.
Stange, D.C. 1702
Stanley, G. 2031
And W.K. Bartlett,
and T. Moyle. 3100
Stark, R. 468, 469, 964, 1703,
1880, 2426, 2563, 2913, 2969,
3002, 3553, 3582
And W.S. Bainbridge. 2032,
2272, 2564, 2565, 2914, 3360
And W.S. Bainbridge,
and D.P. Doyle. 3293
And W.S. Bainbridge,
and L. Kent. 965
And D.P. Doyle, and L. Kent.
2143, 2144, 2145
And C.Y. Glock. 470, 497, 1291
And C.Y. Glock, and H.E. Quinley.
471
And Lynne Roberts. 81
See Bainbridge, W.S.
See Glock, C.Y.
See Hirschi, T.
See Lofland, J.
Stark, W. 82, 83, 194, 2375,
2705, 2706, 3262, 3361, 3378,
3522, 3554, 3555
Starr, J.M. 291
Starry, A.R. See Peyton, F.W.
Stauffer, R.E. 368, 3418, 3419
Steelman, L.C. See Powell, B.
Steeman, T.M. 369, 1509, 2844,
2845, 2846, 3252
Steiber, S.R. 410
Steiner, J.F. 2183
Steinhoff, P.G. 245
See Leon, J.J.
Steinitz, L.Y. 526
Stellway, R.J. 1704
Stenger, H. 1026
Stephan, K.H. 1261
Stephenson, J.B.
See Lamanna, R.A.
Stewart, C.S. See Verner, A.M.
Stewart, J.H. 767, 768, 769,
770, 898
Stewart, M.W.
See Richardson, James T.
Stigall, S. See Shupe, A.D.
Stokes, R.G. 2707
Stone, David R. 771
Stone, Donald. 3003
Stones, C.R. 2865
Stoodt, D. See Dahm, K.
Stoop, W. 1368
Stouthard, P.C. See Miller, W.E.
Straelen, H. van. 2376
Straus, R.A. 988, 2033, 3004
Strenski, I. 3561
Strickland, B.R.,
and S.C. Weddell. 472
Strizower, S. 1914
Strommen, M.P. 473
And M.L. Brekke, R.C. Underwager,
and A.L. Johnson. 772
See Schuller, D.S.

Strong, L.D. 335
Struening, E.L. 474
Struzzo, J.A. 773
Stryckman, P. 774, 775, 776, 899, 900, 901, 2966
And R. Gaudet. 777, 778
See Routhier, F.
Stuebing, W.K. 2915
Stuhr, W.M. 902
See Fish, J.
Suaud, C. 2034, 2117, 2118
Subramaniam, K. 779
Suk-jay, Yim. 3061
Sullivan, T. 1485
Sullivan, Theresa A. See Fee, J.L.
Summers, G.F., D.P. Johnson, R.L. Hough, and K. Veatch. 1705
Sundbach, S. 292
Suolinna, K. 2708
Suziedelis, A., and R.H. Potvin. 1086
Suziedelis, A. See Potvin, R.H.
Svenson, E. 38
Swanborn, P.G., and J. Weima. 2947
Swanson, G.E. 1706, 3005, 3006, 3531
Swatos, W.H. 51, 84, 85, 2566, 2586, 2769, 3119, 3193, 3253, 3254, 3255, 3256, 3296
Sweetser, T. 1486
Sykes, R.E. 1881, 3455, 3576
Symington, T.A. 126
Szafran, R.F. 780, 1176
And R.W. Peterson, and R.A. Schoenherr. 781

T

Tabory, E., and B. Lazerwitz. 1292
Taggart, M. 2219
Takayama, K.P. 1177, 1178, 1179, 2231
And L.W. Cannon. 1180
And D.G. Sachs. 1181
See Petersen, L.R.
Talmon, Y. 2377, 2378, 2379
Tamney, J.B. 52, 1707, 2035, 2036, 2567, 3088, 3194, 3195, 3482
And J.G. Condran. 370
And K. Hopkins, and J. Jacovini. 2848
See Ahler, J.G.
See Johnson, S.D.
Tapley, J.L. 2896
Tapp, R.B. 2955
Taras, P. 2119
Tarleton, M.R.B. 2120
Tatalovich, R. See Daynes, B.W.
Tavares de Andrade, J.M. 3062
Tawney, R.H. 2709, 2710
Taylor, B. 2037
Taylor, D. 2038
Taylor, M.G. 1206
And S.F. Hartley. 903
See Hartley, S.F.
Tedlin, K. 1116
Tedrow, L.M., and E.R. Mahoney. 226
Tennekes, J. 1708
Tentori, T. See Klineberg, O.
Terian, S.M.K. 19
Terry, W.R. See Price D.L.
Thalheimer, F. 1882, 2568
Theobald, R. 86
Thiessen, V. 20
See Demerath, N.J.
Thomas, C.W. See Scalf, J.H.
Thomas, D.L. See Weigert, A.J.
Thomas, J.L. 371, 2220
Thomas, L.E., and P.E Cooper. 3310
Thomas, M.C. 540
And C.C. Flippen. 3420
Thomlinson, R. 257
Thompson, A.D. 2849
Thompson, K.A. 1223
Thompson, M. 1064
Thompson, R.C. 782
And J.B. Michel, and T.J. Alexander. 475
Thorgaard, J. See Grönblom, G.
Thorman, D.J. 2770
Thorner, I. 53, 54, 2711, 3007
Thorson, J.A., and T.C. Cook. 527
Thun, T. 2916
Thung, M.A. 372

Thurlings, J.M.G. 373, 374, 3456
Tibi, B. 1709
Tilanus, C.P.G. 2956
Tipton, S. 195, 196, 2427, 2428
Tiryakian, E.A. 1071, 2712
Tittle, C.R., and M.R. Welch. 2146
Toch, H.H., and R. Anderson. 2569
Toennies, F. See Weber, M.
Tollerson, T.
See Berenson, W.
Tomeh, A.K. 1087
Tomka, M. 2570, 2850
Tonna, B. 904
Toolin, C. 3421
Tortosa, J.M. 3063
Toth, M.A. 87
Tovar, C., and Tokihiro Kudō. 3523
Towler, R. 783, 905, 2121
And A. Chamberlain. 3064
And A.P.M. Coxon. 784
Traina, F.J. 227
Traulle, C. 3196
Travers, J.F., and R.G. Davis. 2175
Travisano, R.V. 2039, 2040
Treece, J.W. 1262
Treffers, P.E. 246
Tremblay, G. See Routhier, F.
Tremmel, W.C. 2041
Troeltsch, E. 3257
Trotter, D.F. 1207
Truzzi, M. 1071, 1072
Tuberville, G. 2232
Tufari, P. 3457
Turcotte, P.A. 1883
Turner, B.S. 1925, 2221, 2222, 2822
And M. Hill. 1710
See Hepworth, M.
See Rigby, A.
Turner, D.E. 1182
Turner, E. See Turner, V.
Turner, L. See Hammond, P.E.
Turner, P.R. 2042
Turner, R.G. 2771
Turner, V. 3111, 3197
Et al. 3199
And E. Turner. 3112, 3198
Tygart, C.E. 10, 293, 294, 785, 786, 787
See Jeffries, V.

U

Ulbrich, H., and M. Wallace. 1117
Underwager, R.C.
See Strommen, M.P.
Underwood, K.W. 2184
Urbano, H.O. 2380, 3065
Utrecht, E. 1711, 1712
Uzin Fernandes, O.
See Ponce Garcia, J.

V

Vaillancourt, J.-G. 966, 1713
See Vallier, I.
Vajda, G. 55
Valente, W. 405
Valenzano, P.M., and B. Castellani. 788
Valle, E. 3066
Vallier, I. 1297, 1934
And J.-G. Vaillancourt. 967
Van Aerde, M. 2874
Van Billoen, E. 1208
Van Calster, S. 3128
Vanecko, J.J. 476, 477
Vanfossen, B.E. 1088
Van Hemert, M. 1487
Van Leeuwen, B. 2223
Van Nostrand, M.E. 1027
Van Roy, R.F., F.D. Bean, and J.R. Wood. 1952
Varacalli, J.A. 1744, 1745, 2571
Varga, I. 1714, 2572
Vassallo, M. 789
Vattel, E.D. 1884
Vauchez, A. See Desroche, H.
Vaughan, M.
See Scotford-Archer, M.
Vaughan, T.R., D.H. Smith, and G. Sjoberg. 3556
Vaughn, S.L. See Ebaugh, H.R.F.
Vazquez, J.M. 1369, 1370
Veatch, K. See Summers, G.F.
Vecchi, A. 3200
Veevers, J.E., and D.F. Cousineau. 2851

Ventimiglia, J.C. 1028, 1029
Vera, H. 790
Verbit, M.F. 2957
Vercruysse, G. 2875
Verdonk, A.L.T. 1371
Vergote, A., et al. 2876
Vergote, A.,
and C. Aubert. 2877
Verner, A.M.,
and C.S. Stewart. 336
Vernon, G.M. 2852, 2897, 2898
Veroff, J., S. Feld,
and G. Gurin. 2713
Verryn, T.D. 791, 906
Verscheure, J. 792
Vidal, D. 3524
Vincent, G. 1209
Vincente, A.G. 3362
Viner, J. 2714
Voisin, M. 1263
Volinn, E. 1194
Vollmer, H.M. 1372
Volpe, R. 3201
Von Martin, A. 1885
Voyé, L. 161
Vrcan, S. 1886
Vrga, D.,
and F.J. Fahey. 2233
Vrga, D. See Fahey, F.J.
Vrijhof, P.H. 1488
And J. Waardenburg. 3067

W

Waardenburg, J. 3068
See Vrijhof, P.H.
Wach, J. 916, 917, 2772, 3008, 3009, 3010, 3258
Wachenheim, C. 3525
Wade, A.L.,
and J.V. Berreman. 793
Wagenaar, T.C.,
and P.E. Bartos. 237
Wagner, A. 794
Wagner, H.R. 2715
And K. Doyle,
and V. Fisher. 2716
Walker, P.R. 295
Wall, D.F. 1489
Wallace, A.F.C. 2273, 3202
Wallace, M. See Ulbrich, H.
Wallace, R.A. 484, 2043, 2044, 3422
Wallis, R. 88, 89, 90, 1210, 2274, 2429, 2430, 3211, 3212, 3363
And S. Bruce. 153
See Allen, G.
Wallis, W.D. 2381, 2382
Walter, E.V. 970
Walters, M. 3069
Waltz, A.K., and R.L. Wilson. 795
Warburton, T.R. 1887, 3526
Ward, C.K. 796, 1490
See Lüschen, G.
See Newman, J.
Ward, D.A. 3141
Ward, L.F. 2773
Wardwell, W.I. 3107
Warenski, M. 1118
Warland, R.H. See Filsinger, E.E.
Warner, R.S. 968
Warner, W.L. 3423
Et al. 1888
And P.S. Lunt. 1889
Warren, B.L. 1293, 1294
Warwick, D 1211
Wassef, W.Y. 39
Watson, G.L. 2275
Watt, W.M. 3472
Wattenberg, W. 2147
Watzke, J. 2573
Wax, M.L. 2587, 2717
Wearing, A.J.,
and L.B. Brown. 2958
Weatherby, G.A.
See Richardson, James T.
Webb, S.C.,
and D.D. Hultgren. 797
Weber, M. 56, 57, 58, 2718, 2719
And F. Toennies. 3259
Weber, P.-G. 1183
Weddell, S.C.
See Strickland, B.R.
Wedge, R.B. (A.M.) 1065
Weigert, A.J. 1373, 2597, 2774
And D.L. Thomas. 2574, 2575, 2959
See Blasi, A.J.
See Hesser, G.W.
See Johnson, C.L.

Weima, J. 127, 520
See Swanborn, P.G.
Weisman, R. 1073
Weissbrod, L. 1715, 2150, 2576
Weiting, S.G. 3562
Welch, K.W. 2899
Welch, M.R. 1119, 2853, 2854, 2960, 3364
And G. (J.) Barrish. 2961
See Barrish, G. (J.)
See Tittle, C.R.
Welch, S. 1120
Weller, N.J. 1953
Wells, A.R. 2775
Wells, C.D. 3260
Welz Scroeter, C. 1221
Wenzel, K. 2823
Werner, E. 2383
Wertheim, W.F. 2276
West, E.M. 3424
West, J. 1890
West, M. 3108
Westhues, K. 969, 1184, 2577, 3263
See Horrigan, J.P.
Westie, F.W. See Martin, J.G.
Westley, F. 2431, 2432, 2433
Westoff, C.F., and L. Bumpass. 258
Westoff, C.F., and E.F. Jones. 259
Westoff, C.F. See Bressler, M.
See Potvin, R.H.
See Ryder, N.B.
Weston, D.E. 2578
Whetten, N.L., and E.G. Devereux. 2579
Whipple, C. 907
Whitaker, I. See Peter, K.
White, D. See White, O.K.
White, H.W. 3532
White, L.C. See Reidy, M.T.V.
White, M. See Burkett, S.R.
See Libby, R.W.
White, O.K. 378, 379, 1185
And D. White. 2733
Whitlam, F.L. 3142
Whitley, C.M. 1374
Whitman, F.L. 478
Whitt, H.P., and H.M. Nelsen. 411
Whitworth, J.M. 1264, 1265
Whyte, J. 1716
Wichmann, A.A. 1717
Wick, J.A. 175
Wickham, E.R. 1891
Wiepel, W. 3203
Wiese, L. von. See H. Becker.
Wilensky, H.L., and J. Ladinsky. 2580
Wiley, N. 128
Wilkening, E.A.
See Martinson, O.B.
Willaime, J.-P. 498, 2069, 2151
Willems, E. 1212, 1892, 1893, 1894, 2277
Williams, C.R. 1895
Williams, D.G. 203
Williams, J.P. 2776
Williams, K.R.
See Hammond, P.E.
Williams, P.W. 3070
Wilson, B.R. 91, 798, 908, 2384, 2434, 2581, 2582, 2583, 3213, 3365, 3366, 3367, 3368, 3369, 3370, 3371, 3372, 3373
Wilson, C.L. 1491
Wilson, J. Branton.
See McIntosh, W.A.
Wilson, John. 1186, 2234
And H.K. Clow. 1501
And K. Manton. 2440
Wilson, John F. 3143, 3425, 3426, 3427
Wilson, M.H. 1074
Wilson, R.L. See Waltz, A.K.
Wilson, Robert L.
See Carroll, J.W.
Wilson, Robert W. 2070
Wilson, Stephen. 985, 986
Wilson, Stephen R. 2045
Wilson, W.C. 479
Wilton, E.V. See Peek, C.W.
Wimberley, R.C. 909, 1718, 1719, 2917, 3428, 3429, 3430
And J.A. Christenson. 1295
And D.A. Clelland, T.C. Hood, and C.M. Lipsey. 2962
And T.C. Hood et al. 2046
See Clelland, D.A.
Wingrove, C.R. See Alston, J.P.
Winter, G. 1187, 1188

Winter, J.A. 799, 1720, 1746,
1747, 2720, 2721, 2824
Winthrop, H. 3458
Witmer, L. See Fish, J.
Wölber, H.-O. 2918
Wolcott, R.T. 1748
Wolfe, J. 1492
Wolman, D. See Lipson, G.
Wood, C.M. 3476
Wood, J.R. 924, 1189, 1190, 1191,
1213, 2307, 2308
And M.N. Zald. 2309
See Gibbs, D.R.
See Hougland, J.G.
See Shupe, A.D.
See Van Roy, R.F.
Wood, Meredith.
See Martin, P.Y.
Wood, Michael,
and M. Hughes. 299
Woodrum, E., C. Rhodes,
and J.R. Feagin. 395
Worsley, P. 2385
See Guiart, J.
Wright, E. See McGaw, D.B.
Wright, F. 1721
Wright, S.A. 2060, 2435
And W.V. D'Antonio. 154
Wrobel, P. 1493
Wulf, J., D. Prentice,
D. Hansum, A. Ferrar,
and B. Spilka. 311
Wurzbacher, G., et al. 800
Wust, I. See Perez Ramirez, G.
Wuthnow, R. 129, 1030, 1722,
1723, 2278, 2436, 2584, 2919,
2967, 3567
And K. Christiano,
and J. Kuzlowski. 528
And C.Y. Glock. 337
See Liebman, R.C.

X

Xenakis, J. 2585
Xidieh, O.R. 3147
Xidieh, Oswaldo E. 3071, 3072

Y

Yalman, N. 3311
Yeandel, F.A. 1214
Yellin, S. See Mack, R.W.
Yeo, S.A. 1192
Yinger, J.M. 296, 375, 376, 1896,
2777, 2789, 3261
And S.J. Cutler. 1724
Yokley, R. See Madron, T.W.
See Nelsen, H.M.
Young, B.,
and J.E. Hughes. 1193
Young, F.W. 3374
Young, T.R. 3527
Yount, J. See Allport, G.

Z

Zablocki, B.D. 1266
Zahn, G.C. 297, 298, 975, 1749,
2920
Zald, M.N. 2279
See Wood, J.R.
Zdaniewicz, W. 2122
Zeegers, G.H.L. 801
Zelan, J. 2061, 2062
Zeldin, M.-B. 3568
Zerubavel, E. 176
Zetterberg, H.L. 2047
Zimmerman, F.K. 130
Zishka, R.L. 910
Zisyadis, J. See Honsberger, H.
Zito, G.V. 2880
Zulehner, P.M. 3073
And S.R. Graupe. 802
Zurcher, L.A., et al. 300
Zurcher, L.A. See Schneider, L.
Zygmunt, J.F. 2386
Zylberberg, J. 1725, 2280
See Lalive d'Epinay, C.

SUBJECT INDEX

(Numbers refer to items.)

A

Abortion. 197-227
  Abortion attitudes and denomination. 228-236
  Abortion attitudes and orthodoxy. 237
  Abortion practice. 238-246
Accommodation. 377-379
Activism. 1726-1749
Alienation. 1-10
Almsgiving. 3074
Altruism. 11-20
Anomie. 21-39
Anti-cult movement. 2281-2289
Apostasy. 2048-2062
Apprentice. 534ff.
Asceticism. 40-58
Ashram. 1194
Assimilation and related phenomena. 380-395
Associational. 1195-1196
Atheism. 2825-2854
Authority. 1197-1214

B

Baptism. 3075-3077
Base communities. 1215-1221
Belief. 2790-2824
Birth control. 247-259
Bureaucracy. 1222-1223

C

Campus ministry. 535-540
Capital punishment. 259ff.
Caste. 1897-1914
Charisma. 59-91
Church. 3262-3263
Civil religion. 3379-3430
Civil rights. 2290-2309
Class. 1915-1925
Clergy (general). 541-802
  Clergy image. 803-816
  Clergy mobility. 817-819
  Clergy role: content and role conflict. 820-910
Clergy wives. 911-914
Cognitive dimension. 2963-2967
Comfort. 92-95
Commitment. 2900-2920
Communality. 1224-1234
Commune. 1235-1266
Confession. 3078-3079
Conflict. See Inter-religious conflict.
Conflict theory. 3431
Congregation (local). See Parish/local congregation.
Consequential dimension. 2968-2969
Conservative. 96-130
Contributions. 3080-3086
Conversion. 1954-2047
Critical theory. 3432-3435
Cult. 3264-3293
Cursillo. 3087-3088

D

Death of God. 2855
Definition of religion. 2734-2777
Denomination. 1267-1295, 3294-3296
Deprivation. 131-154
Deviance. 2123-2147
Devotionalism. 2970
Dimensions of religiosity. 2921-2962
Diocese. 1296-1297
Discipleship. 915-917
Disenchantment. 2586-2587

E

Ecumenism. See Merger and ecumenism.
Elite. 1926-1934
Euthanasia. 260-263
Everyday life. 155-161
Evolution (societal). 2722-2733
Ex-clergy. 2063-2070
Ex-nuns. 2070ff.
Experiential dimension. 2971-3010

F

Fatalism. 162
Founder. 917ff
Functionalism. 3436-3458
Fundamentalism. 2856-2865

G

Glossolalia. 3089-3100.
God, image of. 2866-2877.

H

Healing. 3101-3108
Heresy. 2878-2880
Hermeneutic. See Interpretive and hermeneutic sociology.
Hierocracy. 1298-1299
Homosexuality. 264-266

I

Identity. 163-176
Institutionalization. 2176-2177
Integration (social). 3459-3472
Interpretive and hermeneutic sociology. 3473-3476
Inter-religious conflict. 2178-2184

L

Leadership. 918-924
Legitimation. 2148-2151
Levels of inclusiveness. 3477
Life cycle. 529-534
Literalism. 2881-2883
Localism. 3478-3482

M

Marxism. 3483-3527
Meditation. 3108ff.
Membership. 925-969
Mendicancy. 970
Merger and ecumenism. 2185-2223
Messianism and millenarianism 2310-2386
Military chaplain. 971-975
Missionary. 976
Mobility (vertical). 1935-1953
Monasticism. 1300-1310
Morality (general). 177-196
Mysticism. 3297-3311

N

New religions. 2387-2436
Nun. See Sister.

O

Orders/congregations. 1311-1374
Organization (general). 1121-1193
Orthodoxy (doctrinal). 2884-2899

P

Papacy. 1374ff.
Parish/local congregation. 1375-1493
Peace and war. 267-298
Phenomenology. 3528
Pilgrimage. 3109-3112
Plausibility structures. 2152-2157
Pluralism (general). 342-376
Politics (general). 1510-1725
Popular religion. 3011-3073
Pornography. 299-300.
Positivism (general). 3528ff.
Possession. 3113-3117
Power. 1494-1501.
Practices. See Ch. III, Section C.
Prayer. 3118-3119
Preaching. 3120-3128
Prejudice (general). 412-479
Privatization. 2588-2597
Prophet. 977-981.
Proselytizing. 3129
Protestant ethic. 2598-2721

R

Reductionism. 3529-3532
Reference group. 485-487
Religiosity (general). 2778-2789
Revivalism. 3130-3143
Ritual. 3148-3203
Role. See Ch. I., Section B.

S

Saint. 982-986
Salience. 488-498
Science and reigion. 3533-3556
Schism. 2224-2234
Sect. 3312-3374
Sectarianism. 3204-3213
Seeker. 987-988
Seminarian. 989-1030
Sexism. 480-484
Sex roles (general). 1079-1088
Sexual attitudes. 301-311
Sexual conduct. 312-337
Shaman. 1031
Sister. 1032-1065
Situation ethics. 337ff.
Social control. 2158-2175
Social justice. 338-339
Social movements (general). 2235-2280
Sociolinguistics. 3557
Sociology of knowledge. 3558
Sterilization and vasectomy. 340-341
Stratification (general). 1750-1896
Structuralism. 3559-3562
Surrogates for religion. 3563-3568
Symbolic interactionism. 3569-3576
Symbolic realism. 3577-3579
Synagogue. 1502-1505
Syncretism. 396-405
Systems theory. 3580

T

Temperance movement. 2437-2440
Testimony. 3144-3147
Theories and problematics (general). 3375-3378
Tolerance. 406-411
Transcendence. 3581-3592
Types. 3214-3261

U

Underground church. 1506-1509

V

Value. 499-520
Vocations. 2071-2122

W

Well-being. 521-528
Witch. 1066-1074
Women. 1089-1120
Worker priests. 1075-1078

Y

Youth ministry. 1078ff.